MAZDA | TRUCKS
1972-86 REPAIR MANUAL

CHILTON'S

Senior Vice President	Ronald A. Hoxter
Publisher & Editor-In-Chief	Kerry A. Freeman, S.A.E.
Executive Editors	Dean F. Morgantini, S.A.E., W. Calvin Settle, Jr., S.A.E.
Managing Editor	Nick D'Andrea
Senior Editors	Jacques Gordon, Michael L. Grady, Ben Greisler, S.A.E., Debra McCall, Kevin M. G. Maher, Richard J. Rivele, S.A.E., Richard T. Smith, Jim Taylor, Ron Webb
Project Managers	Martin J. Gunther, Will Kessler, A.S.E., Richard Schwartz
Production Manager	Andrea Steiger
Product Systems Manager	Robert Maxey
Director of Manufacturing	Mike D'Imperio
Editor	Todd Stidham

CHILTON BOOK COMPANY

ONE OF THE **DIVERSIFIED PUBLISHING COMPANIES**,
A PART OF **CAPITAL CITIES/ABC, INC.**

Manufactured in USA
© 1997 Chilton Book Company
Chilton Way, Radnor, PA 19089
ISBN 0-8019-9057-2
Library of Congress Catalog Card No. 97-65887
1234567890 6543210987

Contents

Contents

DRIVE TRAIN   **7**

SUSPENSION AND STEERING   **8**

BRAKES   **9**

BODY   **10**

GLOSSARY

MASTER INDEX

SAFETY NOTICE

Proper service and repair procedures are vital to the safe, reliable operation of all motor vehicles, as well as the personal safety of those performing repairs. This manual outlines procedures for servicing and repairing vehicles using safe, effective methods. The procedures contain many NOTES, CAUTIONS and WARNINGS which should be followed along with standard procedures to eliminate the possibility of personal injury or improper service which could damage the vehicle or compromise its safety.

It is important to note that the repair procedures and techniques, tools and parts for servicing motor vehicles, as well as the skill and experience of the individual performing the work vary widely. It is not possible to anticipate all of the conceivable ways or conditions under which vehicles may be serviced, or to provide cautions as to all of the possible hazards that may result. Standard and accepted safety precautions and equipment should be used when handling toxic or flammable fluids, and safety goggles or other protection should be used during cutting, grinding, chiseling, prying, or any other process that can cause material removal or projectiles.

Some procedures require the use of tools specially designed for a specific purpose. Before substituting another tool or procedure, you must be completely satisfied that neither your personal safety, nor the performance of the vehicle will be endangered.

Although information in this manual is based on industry sources and is complete as possible at the time of publication, the possibility exists that some car manufacturers made later changes which could not be included here. While striving for total accuracy, Chilton Book Company cannot assume responsibility for any errors, changes or omissions that may occur in the compilation of this data.

PART NUMBERS

Part numbers listed in this reference are not recommendation by Chilton for any product by brand name. They are references that can be used with interchange manuals and aftermarket supplier catalogs to locate each brand supplier's discrete part number.

SPECIAL TOOLS

Special tools are recommended by the vehicle manufacturer to perform their specific job. Use has been kept to a minimum, but where absolutely necessary, they are referred to in the text by the part number of the tool manufacturer. These tools can be purchased, under the appropriate part number, from your local dealer or regional distributor, or an equivalent tool can be purchased locally from a tool supplier or parts outlet. Before substituting any tool for the one recommended, read the SAFETY NOTICE at the top of this page.

ACKNOWLEDGMENTS

The Chilton Book Company expresses appreciation to Mazda Motor Corporation for their generous assistance.

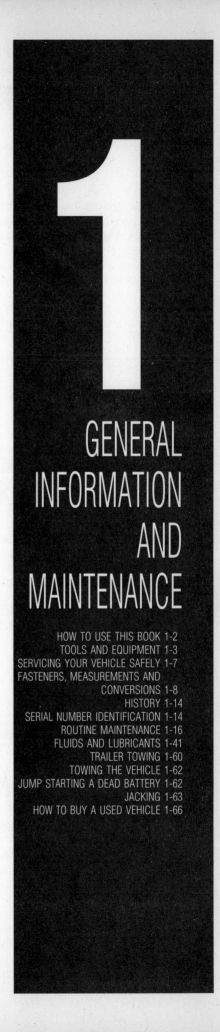

1

GENERAL INFORMATION AND MAINTENANCE

HOW TO USE THIS BOOK

Chilton's Total Car Care manual is intended to help you learn more about the inner workings of your vehicle while saving you money on its upkeep and operation.

The beginning of the book will likely be referred to the most, since that is where you will find information for maintenance and tune-up. The other sections deal with the more complex systems of your vehicle. Operating systems from engine through brakes are covered to the extent that the average do-it-yourselfer becomes mechanically involved. This book will not explain such things as rebuilding a differential for the simple reason that the expertise required and the investment in special tools make this task uneconomical. It will, however, give you detailed instructions to help you change your own brake pads and shoes, replace spark plugs, and perform many more jobs that can save you money, give you personal satisfaction and help you avoid expensive problems.

A secondary purpose of this book is a reference for owners who want to understand their vehicle and/or their mechanics better. In this case, no tools at all are required.

Where to Begin

Before removing any bolts, read through the entire procedure. This will give you the overall view of what tools and supplies will be required. There is nothing more frustrating than having to walk to the bus stop on Monday morning because you were short one bolt on Sunday afternoon. So read ahead and plan ahead. Each operation should be approached logically and all procedures thoroughly understood before attempting any work.

All sections contain adjustments, maintenance, removal and installation procedures, and in some cases, repair or overhaul procedures. When repair is not considered practical, we tell you how to remove the part and then how to install the new or rebuilt replacement. In this way, you at least save the labor costs. Backyard repair of some components is just not practical.

Avoiding Trouble

Many procedures in this book require you to "label and disconnect . . ." a group of lines, hoses or wires. Don't be lulled into thinking you can remember where everything goes—you won't. If you hook up vacuum or fuel lines incorrectly, the vehicle will run poorly, if at all. If you hook up electrical wiring incorrectly, you may instantly learn a very expensive lesson.

You don't need to know the official or engineering name for each hose or line. A piece of masking tape on the hose and a piece on its fitting will allow you to assign your own label such as the letter A or a short name. As long as you remember your own code, the lines can be reconnected by matching similar letters or names. Do remember that tape will dissolve in gasoline or other fluids; if a component is to be washed or cleaned, use another method of identification. A permanent felt-tipped marker can be very handy for marking metal parts. Remove any tape or paper labels after assembly.

Maintenance or Repair?

It's necessary to mention the difference between maintenance and repair. Maintenance includes routine inspections, adjustments, and replacement of parts which show signs of normal wear. Maintenance compensates for wear or deterioration. Repair implies that something has broken or is not working. A need for repair is often caused by lack of maintenance. Example: draining and refilling the automatic transmission fluid is maintenance recommended by the manufacturer at specific mileage intervals. Failure to do this can ruin the transmission/transaxle, requiring very expensive repairs. While no maintenance program can prevent items from breaking or wearing out, a general rule can be stated: MAINTENANCE IS CHEAPER THAN REPAIR.

Two basic mechanic's rules should be mentioned here. First, whenever the left side of the vehicle or engine is referred to, it is meant to specify the driver's side. Conversely, the right side of the vehicle means the passenger's side. Second, most screws and bolts are removed by turning counterclockwise, and tightened by turning clockwise.

Safety is always the most important rule. Constantly be aware of the dangers involved in working on an automobile and take the proper precautions. See the information in this section regarding SERVICING YOUR VEHICLE SAFELY and the SAFETY NOTICE on the acknowledgment page.

Avoiding the Most Common Mistakes

Pay attention to the instructions provided. There are 3 common mistakes in mechanical work:

1. **Incorrect order of assembly, disassembly or adjustment.** When taking something apart or putting it together, performing steps in the wrong order usually just costs you extra time; however, it CAN break something. Read the entire procedure before beginning disassembly. Perform everything in the order in which the instructions say you should, even if you can't immediately see a reason for it. When you're taking apart something that is very intricate, you might want to draw a picture of how it looks when assembled at one point in order to make sure you get everything back in its proper position. We will supply exploded views whenever possible. When making adjustments, perform them in the proper order; often, one adjustment affects another, and you cannot expect even satisfactory results unless each adjustment is made only when it cannot be changed by any other.

2. **Overtorquing (or undertorquing).** While it is more common for overtorquing to cause damage, undertorquing may allow a fastener to vibrate loose causing serious damage. Especially when dealing with aluminum parts, pay attention to torque specifications and utilize a torque wrench in assembly. If a torque figure is not available, remember that if you are using the right tool to perform the job, you will probably not have to strain yourself to get a fastener tight enough. The pitch of most threads is so slight that the tension you put on the wrench will be multiplied many times in actual force on what you are tightening. A good example of how critical torque is can be seen in the case of spark plug in-

stallation, especially where you are putting the plug into an aluminum cylinder head. Too little torque can fail to crush the gasket, causing leakage of combustion gases and consequent overheating of the plug and engine parts. Too much torque can damage the threads or distort the plug, changing the spark gap.

There are many commercial products available for ensuring that fasteners won't come loose, even if they are not torqued just right (a very common brand is Loctite®). If you're worried about getting something together tight enough to hold, but loose enough to avoid mechanical damage during assembly, one of these products might offer substantial insurance. Before choosing a threadlocking compound, read the label on the package and make sure the product is compatible with the materials, fluids, etc. involved.

3. **Crossthreading.** This occurs when a part such as a bolt is screwed into a nut or casting at the wrong angle and forced. Crossthreading is more likely to occur if access is difficult. It helps to clean and lubricate fasteners, then to start threading with the part to be installed positioned straight in. Then, start the bolt, spark plug, etc. with your fingers. If you encounter resistance, unscrew the part and start over again at a different angle until it can be inserted and turned several times without much effort. Keep in mind that many parts, especially spark plugs, have tapered threads, so that gentle turning will automatically bring the part you're threading to the proper angle, but only if you don't force it or resist a change in angle. Don't put a wrench on the part until it's been tightened a couple of turns by hand. If you suddenly encounter resistance, and the part has not seated fully, don't force it. Pull it back out to make sure it's clean and threading properly.

Always take your time and be patient; once you have some experience, working on your vehicle may well become an enjoyable hobby.

TOOLS AND EQUIPMENT

Naturally, without the proper tools and equipment it is impossible to properly service your vehicle. It would also be virtually impossible to catalog every tool that you would need to perform all of the operations in this book. Of course, It would be unwise for the amateur to rush out and buy an expensive set of tools on the theory that he/she may need one or more of them at some time.

The best approach is to proceed slowly, gathering a good quality set of those tools that are used most frequently. Don't be misled by the low cost of bargain tools. It is far better to spend a little more for better quality. Forged wrenches, 6 or 12-point sockets and fine tooth ratchets are by far preferable to their less expensive counterparts. As any good mechanic can tell you, there are few worse experiences than trying to work on a vehicle with bad tools. Your monetary savings will be far outweighed by frustration and mangled knuckles.

Begin accumulating those tools that are used most frequently: those associated with routine maintenance and tune-up. In addition to the normal assortment of screwdrivers and pliers, you should have the following tools:

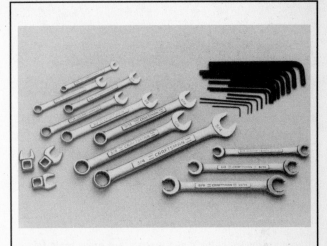

In addition to ratchets, a good set of wrenches and hex keys will be necessary

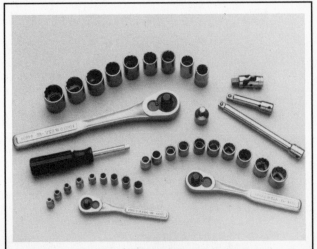

All but the most basic procedures will require an assortment of ratchets and sockets

A hydraulic floor jack and a set of jackstands are essential for lifting and supporting the vehicle

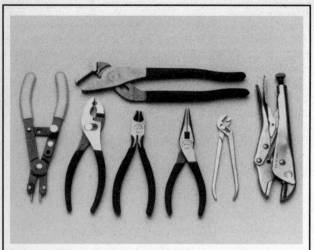

An assortment of pliers, grippers and cutters will be handy for old rusted parts and stripped bolt heads

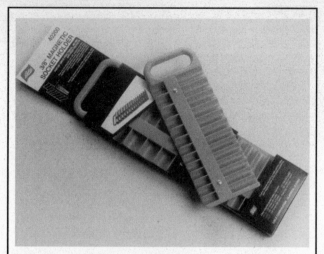

Tools from specialty manufacturers such as Lisle® are designed to make your job easier . . .

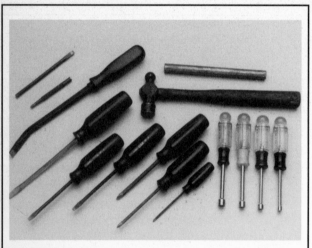

Various drivers, chisels and prybars are great tools to have in your toolbox

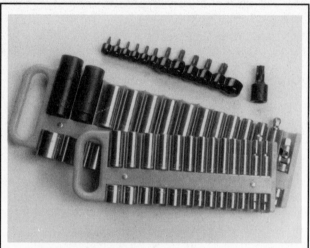

. . . these Torx® drivers and magnetic socket holders are just 2 examples of their handy products

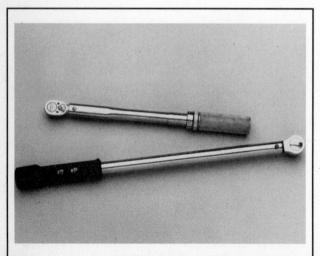

Many repairs will require the use of a torque wrench to assure the components are properly fastened

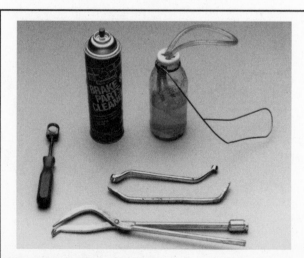

Although not always necessary, using specialized brake tools will save time

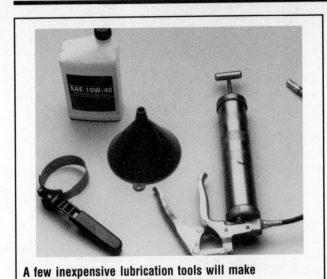

A few inexpensive lubrication tools will make maintenance easier

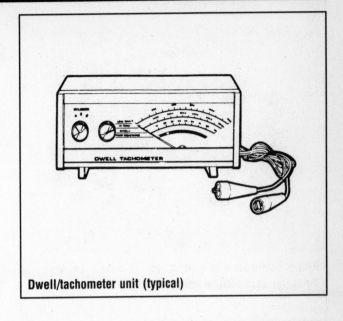

Dwell/tachometer unit (typical)

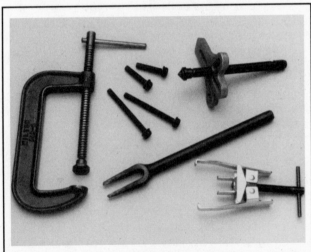

Various pullers, clamps and separator tools are needed for many larger, more complicated repairs

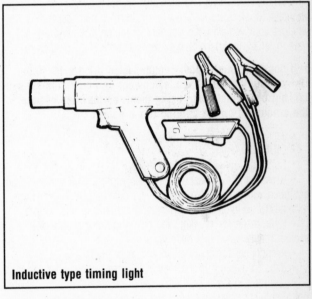

Inductive type timing light

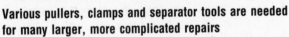

A variety of tools and gauges should be used for spark plug gapping and installation

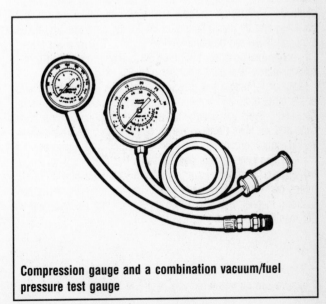

Compression gauge and a combination vacuum/fuel pressure test gauge

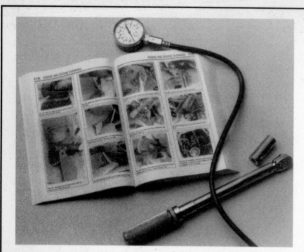

Proper information is vital, so always have a Chilton Total Car Care manual handy

• Wrenches/sockets and combination open end/box end wrenches in sizes from ⅛–¾ in. or 3mm–19mm (depending on whether your vehicle uses standard or metric fasteners) and a ¹³⁄₁₆ in. or ⅝ in. spark plug socket (depending on plug type).

➡**If possible, buy various length socket drive extensions. Universal-joint and wobble extensions can be extremely useful, but be careful when using them, as they can change the amount of torque applied to the socket.**

• Jackstands for support.
• Oil filter wrench.
• Spout or funnel for pouring fluids.
• Grease gun for chassis lubrication (unless your vehicle is not equipped with any grease fittings—for details, please refer to information on Fluids and Lubricants found later in this section).
• Hydrometer for checking the battery (unless equipped with a sealed, maintenance-free battery).
• A container for draining oil and other fluids.
• Rags for wiping up the inevitable mess.

In addition to the above items there are several others that are not absolutely necessary, but handy to have around. These include Oil Dry® (or an equivalent oil absorbent gravel—such as cat litter) and the usual supply of lubricants, antifreeze and fluids, although these can be purchased as needed. This is a basic list for routine maintenance, but only your personal needs and desire can accurately determine your list of tools.

After performing a few projects on the vehicle, you'll be amazed at the other tools and non-tools on your workbench. Some useful household items are: a large turkey baster or siphon, empty coffee cans and ice trays (to store parts), ball of twine, electrical tape for wiring, small rolls of colored tape for tagging lines or hoses, markers and pens, a note pad, golf tees (for plugging vacuum lines), metal coat hangers or a roll of mechanics's wire (to hold things out of the way), dental pick or similar long, pointed probe, a strong magnet, and a small mirror (to see into recesses and under manifolds).

A more advanced set of tools, suitable for tune-up work, can be drawn up easily. While the tools are slightly more sophisticated, they need not be outrageously expensive. There are several inexpensive tach/dwell meters on the market that are every bit as good for the average mechanic as a professional model. Just be sure that it goes to a least 1200–1500 rpm on the tach scale and that it works on 4, 6 and 8-cylinder engines. (If you own one or more vehicles with a diesel engine, a special tachometer is required since diesels don't use spark plug ignition systems). The key to these purchases is to make them with an eye towards adaptability and wide range. A basic list of tune-up tools could include:

• Tach/dwell meter.
• Spark plug wrench and gapping tool.
• Feeler gauges for valve or point adjustment. (Even if your vehicle does not use points or require valve adjustments, a feeler gauge is helpful for many repair/overhaul procedures).

A tachometer/dwell meter will ensure accurate tune-up work on vehicles without electronic ignition. The choice of a timing light should be made carefully. A light which works on the DC current supplied by the vehicle's battery is the best choice; it should have a xenon tube for brightness. On any vehicle with an electronic ignition system, a timing light with an inductive pickup that clamps around the No. 1 spark plug cable is preferred.

In addition to these basic tools, there are several other tools and gauges you may find useful. These include:

• Compression gauge. The screw-in type is slower to use, but eliminates the possibility of a faulty reading due to escaping pressure.
• Manifold vacuum gauge.
• 12V test light.
• A combination volt/ohmmeter
• Induction Ammeter. This is used for determining whether or not there is current in a wire. These are handy for use if a wire is broken somewhere in a wiring harness.

As a final note, you will probably find a torque wrench necessary for all but the most basic work. The beam type models are perfectly adequate, although the newer click types (breakaway) are easier to use. The click type torque wrenches tend to be more expensive. Also keep in mind that all types of torque wrenches should be periodically checked and/or recalibrated. You will have to decide for yourself which better fits your purpose.

Special Tools

Normally, the use of special factory tools is avoided for repair procedures, since these are not readily available for the do-it-yourself mechanic. When it is possible to perform the job with more commonly available tools, it will be pointed out, but occasionally, a special tool was designed to perform a specific function and should be used. Before substituting another tool, you should be convinced that neither your safety nor the performance of the vehicle will be compromised.

Special tools can usually be purchased from an automotive parts store or from your dealer. In some cases special tools may be available directly from the tool manufacturer.

SERVICING YOUR VEHICLE SAFELY

It is virtually impossible to anticipate all of the hazards involved with automotive maintenance and service, but care and common sense will prevent most accidents.

The rules of safety for mechanics range from "don't smoke around gasoline," to "use the proper tool(s) for the job." The trick to avoiding injuries is to develop safe work habits and to take every possible precaution.

Do's

- Do keep a fire extinguisher and first aid kit handy.
- Do wear safety glasses or goggles when cutting, drilling, grinding or prying, even if you have 20–20 vision. If you wear glasses for the sake of vision, wear safety goggles over your regular glasses.
- Do shield your eyes whenever you work around the battery. Batteries contain sulfuric acid. In case of contact with the eyes or

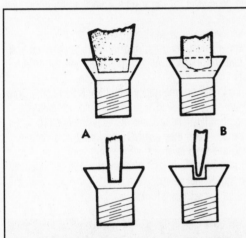

Screwdrivers should be kept in good condition to prevent injury or damage which could result if the blade slips from the screw

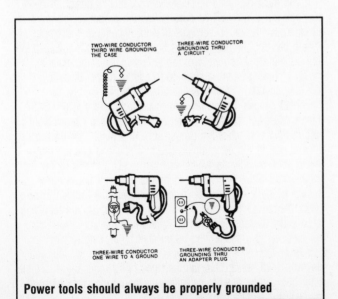

Power tools should always be properly grounded

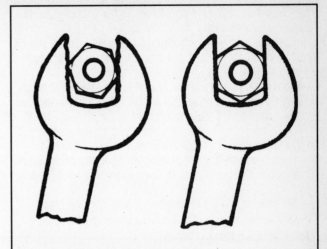

Using the correct size wrench will help prevent the possibility of rounding off a nut

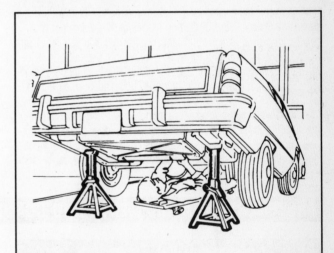

NEVER work under a vehicle unless it is supported using safety stands (jackstands)

skin, flush the area with water or a mixture of water and baking soda, then seek immediate medical attention.

- Do use safety stands (jackstands) for any undervehicle service. Jacks are for raising vehicles; jackstands are for making sure the vehicle stays raised until you want it to come down. Whenever the vehicle is raised, block the wheels remaining on the ground and set the parking brake.
- Do use adequate ventilation when working with any chemicals or hazardous materials. Like carbon monoxide, the asbestos dust resulting from some brake lining wear can be hazardous in sufficient quantities.
- Do disconnect the negative battery cable when working on the electrical system. The secondary ignition system contains EXTREMELY HIGH VOLTAGE. In some cases it can even exceed 50,000 volts.
- Do follow manufacturer's directions whenever working with potentially hazardous materials. Most chemicals and fluids are poisonous if taken internally.

• Do properly maintain your tools. Loose hammerheads, mushroomed punches and chisels, frayed or poorly grounded electrical cords, excessively worn screwdrivers, spread wrenches (open end), cracked sockets, slipping ratchets, or faulty droplight sockets can cause accidents.

• Likewise, keep your tools clean; a greasy wrench can slip off a bolt head, ruining the bolt and often harming your knuckles in the process.

• Do use the proper size and type of tool for the job at hand. Do select a wrench or socket that fits the nut or bolt. The wrench or socket should sit straight, not cocked.

• Do, when possible, pull on a wrench handle rather than push on it, and adjust your stance to prevent a fall.

• Do be sure that adjustable wrenches are tightly closed on the nut or bolt and pulled so that the force is on the side of the fixed jaw.

• Do strike squarely with a hammer; avoid glancing blows.

• Do set the parking brake and block the drive wheels if the work requires a running engine.

Don'ts

• Don't run the engine in a garage or anywhere else without proper ventilation—EVER! Carbon monoxide is poisonous; it takes a long time to leave the human body and you can build up a deadly supply of it in your system by simply breathing in a little every day. You may not realize you are slowly poisoning yourself. Always use power vents, windows, fans and/or open the garage door.

• Don't work around moving parts while wearing loose clothing. Short sleeves are much safer than long, loose sleeves. Hard-toed shoes with neoprene soles protect your toes and give a better grip on slippery surfaces. Jewelry such as watches, fancy belt buckles, beads or body adornment of any kind is not safe working around a vehicle. Long hair should be tied back under a hat or cap.

• Don't use pockets for toolboxes. A fall or bump can drive a screwdriver deep into your body. Even a rag hanging from your back pocket can wrap around a spinning shaft or fan.

• Don't smoke when working around gasoline, cleaning solvent or other flammable material.

• Don't smoke when working around the battery. When the battery is being charged, it gives off explosive hydrogen gas.

• Don't use gasoline to wash your hands; there are excellent soaps available. Gasoline contains dangerous additives which can enter the body through a cut or through your pores. Gasoline also removes all the natural oils from the skin so that bone dry hands will suck up oil and grease.

• Don't service the air conditioning system unless you are equipped with the necessary tools and training. When liquid or compressed gas refrigerant is released to atmospheric pressure it will absorb heat from whatever it contacts. This will chill or freeze anything it touches. Although refrigerant is normally non-toxic, R-12 becomes a deadly poisonous gas in the presence of an open flame. One good whiff of the vapors from burning refrigerant can be fatal.

• Don't use screwdrivers for anything other than driving screws! A screwdriver used as an prying tool can snap when you least expect it, causing injuries. At the very least, you'll ruin a good screwdriver.

• Don't use a bumper or emergency jack (that little ratchet, scissors, or pantograph jack supplied with the vehicle) for anything other than changing a flat! These jacks are only intended for emergency use out on the road; they are NOT designed as a maintenance tool. If you are serious about maintaining your vehicle yourself, invest in a hydraulic floor jack of at least a 1½ ton capacity, and at least two sturdy jackstands.

FASTENERS, MEASUREMENTS AND CONVERSIONS

Bolts, Nuts and Other Threaded Retainers

Although there are a great variety of fasteners found in the modern car or truck, the most commonly used retainer is the threaded fastener (nuts, bolts, screws, studs, etc). Most threaded retainers may be reused, provided that they are not damaged in use or during the repair. Some retainers (such as stretch bolts or torque prevailing nuts) are designed to deform when tightened or in use and should not be reinstalled.

Whenever possible, we will note any special retainers which should be replaced during a procedure. But you should always inspect the condition of a retainer when it is removed and replace any that show signs of damage. Check all threads for rust or corrosion which can increase the torque necessary to achieve the desired clamp load for which that fastener was originally selected. Additionally, be sure that the driver surface of the fastener has not been compromised by rounding or other damage. In some cases a driver surface may become only partially rounded, allowing the driver to catch in only one direction. In many of these occurrences, a fastener may be installed and tightened, but the driver would not be able to grip and loosen the fastener again. (This could lead to frustration down the line should that component ever need to be disassembled again).

If you must replace a fastener, whether due to design or damage, you must ALWAYS be sure to use the proper replacement. In all cases, a retainer of the same design, material and strength should be used. Markings on the heads of most bolts will help determine the proper strength of the fastener. The same material, thread and pitch must be selected to assure proper installation and safe operation of the vehicle afterwards.

Thread gauges are available to help measure a bolt or stud's thread. Most automotive and hardware stores keep gauges available to help you select the proper size. In a pinch, you can use another nut or bolt for a thread gauge. If the bolt you are replacing is not too badly damaged, you can select a match by finding another bolt which will thread in its place. If you find a nut which threads properly onto the damaged bolt, then use that nut to help select the replacement bolt. If however, the bolt you are replacing is so badly damaged (broken or drilled out) that its threads cannot be used as a gauge, you might start by looking for another bolt (from the same assembly or a similar location on your vehicle) which will thread into the damaged bolt's mounting. If so, the other bolt can be used to select a nut; the nut can then be used to select the replacement bolt.

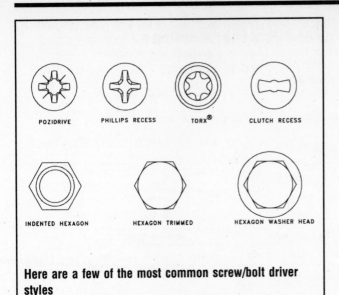

Here are a few of the most common screw/bolt driver styles

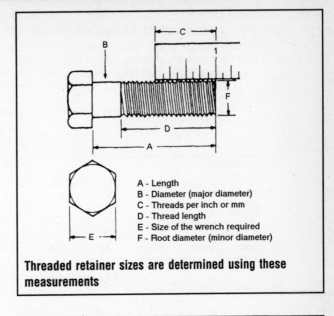

A - Length
B - Diameter (major diameter)
C - Threads per inch or mm
D - Thread length
E - Size of the wrench required
F - Root diameter (minor diameter)

Threaded retainer sizes are determined using these measurements

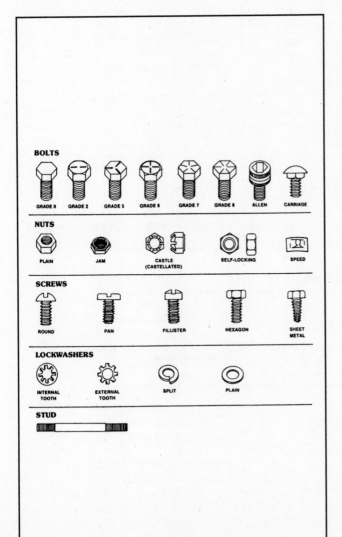

There are many different types of threaded retainers found on vehicles

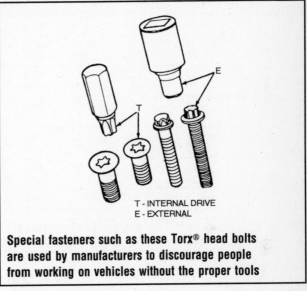

T - INTERNAL DRIVE
E - EXTERNAL

Special fasteners such as these Torx® head bolts are used by manufacturers to discourage people from working on vehicles without the proper tools

In all cases, be absolutely sure you have selected the proper replacement. Don't be shy, you can always ask the store clerk for help.

❊❊ WARNING

Be aware that when you find a bolt with damaged threads, you may also find the nut or drilled hole it was threaded into has also been damaged. If this is the case, you may have to drill and tap the hole, replace the nut or otherwise repair the threads. NEVER try to force a replacement bolt to fit into the damaged threads.

Torque

Torque is defined as the measurement of resistance to turning or rotating. It tends to twist a body about an axis of rotation. A common example of this would be tightening a threaded retainer such as a nut, bolt or screw. Measuring torque is one of the most

Standard Torque Specifications and Fastener Markings

In the absence of specific torques, the following chart can be used as a guide to the maximum safe torque of a particular size/grade of fastener.

- There is no torque difference for fine or coarse threads.
- Torque values are based on clean, dry threads. Reduce the value by 10% if threads are oiled prior to assembly.
- The torque required for aluminum components or fasteners is considerably less.

U.S. Bolts

SAE Grade Number	1 or 2			5			6 or 7		
Number of lines always 2 less than the grade number.									
Bolt Size (Inches)—(Thread)	Maximum Torque			Maximum Torque			Maximum Torque		
	Ft./Lbs.	Kgm	Nm	Ft./Lbs.	Kgm	Nm	Ft./Lbs.	Kgm	Nm
¼ — 20	5	0.7	6.8	8	1.1	10.8	10	1.4	13.5
— 28	6	0.8	8.1	10	1.4	13.6			
⁵⁄₁₆ — 18	11	1.5	14.9	17	2.3	23.0	19	2.6	25.8
— 24	13	1.8	17.6	19	2.6	25.7			
⅜ — 16	18	2.5	24.4	31	4.3	42.0	34	4.7	46.0
— 24	20	2.75	27.1	35	4.8	47.5			
⁷⁄₁₆ — 14	28	3.8	37.0	49	6.8	66.4	55	7.6	74.5
— 20	30	4.2	40.7	55	7.6	74.5			
½ — 13	39	5.4	52.8	75	10.4	101.7	85	11.75	115.2
— 20	41	5.7	55.6	85	11.7	115.2			
⁹⁄₁₆ — 12	51	7.0	69.2	110	15.2	149.1	120	16.6	162.7
— 18	55	7.6	74.5	120	16.6	162.7			
⅝ — 11	83	11.5	112.5	150	20.7	203.3	167	23.0	226.5
— 18	95	13.1	128.8	170	23.5	230.5			
¾ — 10	105	14.5	142.3	270	37.3	366.0	280	38.7	379.6
— 16	115	15.9	155.9	295	40.8	400.0			
⅞ — 9	160	22.1	216.9	395	54.6	535.5	440	60.9	596.5
— 14	175	24.2	237.2	435	60.1	589.7			
1 — 8	236	32.5	318.6	590	81.6	799.9	660	91.3	894.8
— 14	250	34.6	338.9	660	91.3	849.8			

Metric Bolts

Relative Strength Marking	4.6, 4.8			8.8		
Bolt Markings						
Bolt Size Thread Size x Pitch (mm)	Maximum Torque			Maximum Torque		
	Ft./Lbs.	Kgm	Nm	Ft./Lbs.	Kgm	Nm
6 x 1.0	2–3	.2–.4	3–4	3–6	4–.8	5–8
8 x 1.25	6–8	.8–1	8–12	9–14	1.2–1.9	13–19
10 x 1.25	12–17	1.5–2.3	16–23	20–29	2.7–4.0	27–39
12 x 1.25	21–32	2.9–4.4	29–43	35–53	4.8–7.3	47–72
14 x 1.5	35–52	4.8–7.1	48–70	57–85	7.8–11.7	77–110
16 x 1.5	51–77	7.0–10.6	67–100	90–120	12.4–16.5	130–160
18 x 1.5	74–110	10.2–15.1	100–150	130–170	17.9–23.4	180–230
20 x 1.5	110–140	15.1–19.3	150–190	190–240	26.2–46.9	160–320
22 x 1.5	150–190	22.0–26.2	200–260	250–320	34.5–44.1	340–430
24 x 1.5	190–240	26.2–46.9	260–320	310–410	42.7–56.5	420–550

Standard and metric bolt torque specifications based on bolt strengths—WARNING: use only as a guide

common ways to help assure that a threaded retainer has been properly fastened.

When tightening a threaded fastener, torque is applied in three distinct areas, the head, the bearing surface and the clamp load. About 50 percent of the measured torque is used in overcoming bearing friction. This is the friction between the bearing surface of the bolt head, screw head or nut face and the base material or washer (the surface on which the fastener is rotating). Approximately 40 percent of the applied torque is used in overcoming thread friction. This leaves only about 10 percent of the applied torque to develop a useful clamp load (the force which holds a joint together). This means that friction can account for as much as 90 percent of the applied torque on a fastener.

TORQUE WRENCHES

In most applications, a torque wrench can be used to assure proper installation of a fastener. Torque wrenches come in various designs and most automotive supply stores will carry a variety to suit your needs. A torque wrench should be used any time we supply a specific torque value for a fastener. A torque wrench can also be used if you are following the general guidelines in the accompanying charts. Keep in mind that because there is no worldwide standardization of fasteners, the charts are a general guideline and should be used with caution. Again, the general rule of "if you are using the right tool for the job, you should not have to strain to tighten a fastener" applies here.

Beam Type

The beam type torque wrench is one of the most popular types. It consists of a pointer attached to the head that runs the length of the flexible beam (shaft) to a scale located near the handle. As the wrench is pulled, the beam bends and the pointer indicates the torque using the scale.

Click (Breakaway) Type

Another popular design of torque wrench is the click type. To use the click type wrench you pre-adjust it to a torque setting. Once the torque is reached, the wrench has a reflex signalling fea-

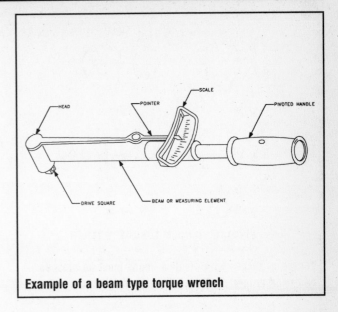

Example of a beam type torque wrench

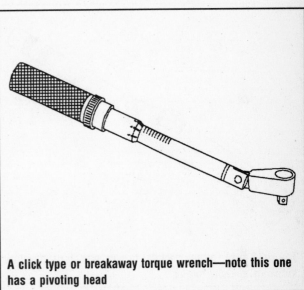

A click type or breakaway torque wrench—note this one has a pivoting head

ture that causes a momentary breakaway of the torque wrench body, sending an impulse to the operator's hand.

Pivot Head Type

Some torque wrenches (usually of the click type) may be equipped with a pivot head which can allow it to be used in areas of limited access. BUT, it must be used properly. To hold a pivot head wrench, grasp the handle lightly, and as you pull on the handle, it should be floated on the pivot point. If the handle comes in contact with the yoke extension during the process of pulling, there is a very good chance the torque readings will be inaccurate because this could alter the wrench loading point. The design of the handle is usually such as to make it inconvenient to deliberately misuse the wrench.

➡️**It should be mentioned that the use of any U-joint, wobble or extension will have an effect on the torque readings, no matter what type of wrench you are using. For the most accurate readings, install the socket directly on the wrench driver. If necessary, straight extensions (which hold a**

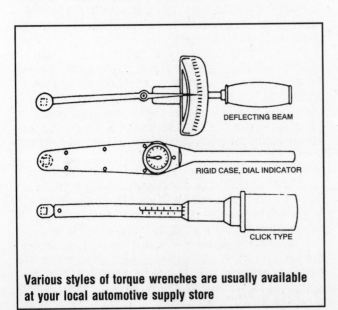

Various styles of torque wrenches are usually available at your local automotive supply store

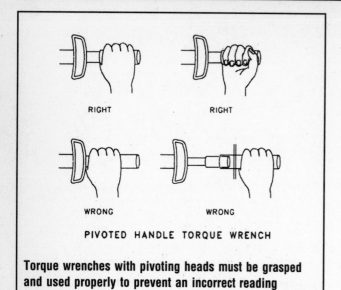

RIGHT   RIGHT

WRONG   WRONG

PIVOTED HANDLE TORQUE WRENCH

Torque wrenches with pivoting heads must be grasped and used properly to prevent an incorrect reading

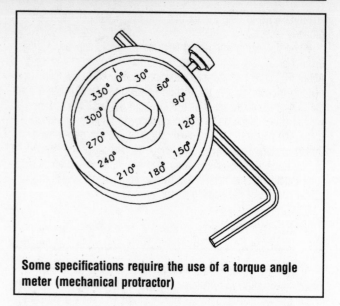

Some specifications require the use of a torque angle meter (mechanical protractor)

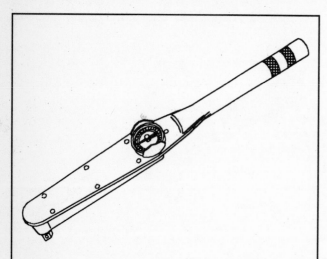

The rigid case (direct reading) torque wrench uses a dial indicator to show torque

socket directly under the wrench driver) will have the least effect on the torque reading. Avoid any extension that alters the length of the wrench from the handle to the head/driving point (such as a crow's foot). U-joint or Wobble extensions can greatly affect the readings; avoid their use at all times.

Rigid Case (Direct Reading)

A rigid case or direct reading torque wrench is equipped with a dial indicator to show torque values. One advantage of these wrenches is that they can be held at any position on the wrench without affecting accuracy. These wrenches are often preferred because they tend to be compact, easy to read and have a great degree of accuracy.

TORQUE ANGLE METERS

Because the frictional characteristics of each fastener or threaded hole will vary, clamp loads which are based strictly on

torque will vary as well. In most applications, this variance is not significant enough to cause worry. But, in certain applications, a manufacturer's engineers may determine that more precise clamp loads are necessary (such is the case with many aluminum cylinder heads). In these cases, a torque angle method of installation would be specified. When installing fasteners which are torque angle tightened, a predetermined seating torque and standard torque wrench are usually used first to remove any compliance from the joint. The fastener is then tightened the specified additional portion of a turn measured in degrees. A torque angle gauge (mechanical protractor) is used for these applications.

Standard and Metric Measurements

Throughout this manual, specifications are given to help you determine the condition of various components on your vehicle, or to assist you in their installation. Some of the most common measurements include length (in. or cm/mm), torque (ft. lbs., inch lbs. or Nm) and pressure (psi, in. Hg, kPa or mm Hg). In most cases, we strive to provide the proper measurement as determined by the manufacturer's engineers.

Though, in some cases, that value may not be conveniently measured with what is available in your toolbox. Luckily, many of the measuring devices which are available today will have two scales so the Standard or Metric measurements may easily be taken. If any of the various measuring tools which are available to you do not contain the same scale as listed in the specifications, use the accompanying conversion factors to determine the proper value.

The conversion factor chart is used by taking the given specification and multiplying it by the necessary conversion factor. For instance, looking at the first line, if you have a measurement in inches such as "free-play should be 2 in." but your ruler reads only in millimeters, multiply 2 in. by the conversion factor of 25.4 to get the metric equivalent of 50.8mm. Likewise, if the specification was given only in a Metric measurement, for example in Newton Meters (Nm), then look at the center column first. If the measurement is 100 Nm, multiply it by the conversion factor of 0.738 to get 73.8 ft. lbs.

CONVERSION FACTORS

LENGTH–DISTANCE

Inches (in.)	x 25.4	= Millimeters (mm)	x .0394	= Inches
Feet (ft.)	x .305	= Meters (m)	x 3.281	= Feet
Miles	x 1.609	= Kilometers (km)	x .0621	= Miles

VOLUME

Cubic Inches (in3)	x 16.387	= Cubic Centimeters	x .061	= in3
IMP Pints (IMP pt.)	x .568	= Liters (L)	x 1.76	= IMP pt.
IMP Quarts (IMP qt.)	x 1.137	= Liters (L)	x .88	= IMP qt.
IMP Gallons (IMP gal.)	x 4.546	= Liters (L)	x .22	= IMP gal.
IMP Quarts (IMP qt.)	x 1.201	= US Quarts (US qt.)	x .833	= IMP qt.
IMP Gallons (IMP gal.)	x 1.201	= US Gallons (US gal.)	x .833	= IMP gal.
Fl. Ounces	x 29.573	= Milliliters	x .034	= Ounces
US Pints (US pt.)	x .473	= Liters (L)	x 2.113	= Pints
US Quarts (US qt.)	x .946	= Liters (L)	x 1.057	= Quarts
US Gallons (US gal.)	x 3.785	= Liters (L)	x .264	= Gallons

MASS–WEIGHT

Ounces (oz.)	x 28.35	= Grams (g)	x .035	= Ounces
Pounds (lb.)	x .454	= Kilograms (kg)	x 2.205	= Pounds

PRESSURE

Pounds Per Sq. In. (psi)	x 6.895	= Kilopascals (kPa)	x .145	= psi
Inches of Mercury (Hg)	x .4912	= psi	x 2.036	= Hg
Inches of Mercury (Hg)	x 3.377	= Kilopascals (kPa)	x .2961	= Hg
Inches of Water (H_2O)	x .07355	= Inches of Mercury	x 13.783	= H_2O
Inches of Water (H_2O)	x .03613	= psi	x 27.684	= H_2O
Inches of Water (H_2O)	x .248	= Kilopascals (kPa)	x 4.026	= H_2O

TORQUE

Pounds–Force Inches (in–lb)	x .113	= Newton Meters (N·m)	x 8.85	= in–lb
Pounds–Force Feet (ft–lb)	x 1.356	= Newton Meters (N·m)	x .738	= ft–lb

VELOCITY

Miles Per Hour (MPH)	x 1.609	= Kilometers Per Hour (KPH)	x .621	= MPH

POWER

Horsepower (Hp)	x .745	= Kilowatts	x 1.34	= Horsepower

FUEL CONSUMPTION*

Miles Per Gallon IMP (MPG)	x .354	= Kilometers Per Liter (Km/L)
Kilometers Per Liter (Km/L)	x 2.352	= IMP MPG
Miles Per Gallon US (MPG)	x .425	= Kilometers Per Liter (Km/L)
Kilometers Per Liter (Km/L)	x 2.352	= US MPG

*It is common to covert from miles per gallon (mpg) to liters/100 kilometers (1/100 km), where mpg (IMP) x 1/100 km = 282 and mpg (US) x 1/100 km = 235.

TEMPERATURE

Degree Fahrenheit (°F)	= (°C x 1.8) + 32
Degree Celsius (°C)	= (°F – 32) x .56

Standard and metric conversion factors chart

HISTORY

The first Mazda pickups arrived in the United States in December of 1972. These were titled as 1972 vehicles and approximately 4,800 were sold. The following year, which was the first full model year for the truck, approximately 14,000 B1600 piston engined trucks were sold.

In 1976 Mazda upgraded the truck with the use of a new engine, calling it the B1800. This was followed by a styling change, with the truck becoming more sophisticated in 1979. In that year, the engine was enlarged to 1,970cc and the model renamed the B2000.

In 1982 a 2,209cc diesel was offered for the first time. This engine was optional equipment through the 1984 model year.

It is important to note, at this time, that there is no 1985 model year truck. Mazda totally redesigned their truck after the 1984 model year and introduced the new truck as a 1986 model. While still called the B2000, the engine, at 1,998cc was totally different, and was, in fact, the same one used in the 626 car.

SERIAL NUMBER IDENTIFICATION

Chassis Number

▶ **See Figures 1 and 2**

The chassis number is stamped on the front of the left frame member on 1972–84 trucks, and, the front of the right frame member, on 1986 trucks, visible from the engine compartment.

Engine Number

▶ **See Figures 3, 4, 5 and 6**

The engine number of the 1,586cc, 1,796cc and 1979–84 1,970cc is stamped on a machined pad on the right, front side of the engine block. On the diesel, it is stamped on a machined pad located on the front left side of the block, just above the injection pump. On the 1986 models, it is located on a machined pad on the left front of the block, just behind the distributor. On the Rotary Pick-up Truck, the engine number is located on a pad at the front of the engine housing, behind the distributor.

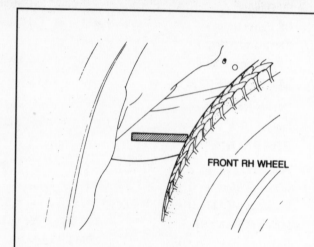

Fig. 2 Chassis identification number location on 1986 trucks

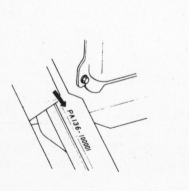

Fig. 1 Chassis identification number location on 1972–84 trucks

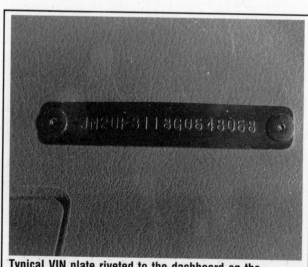

Typical VIN plate riveted to the dashboard on the driver's side

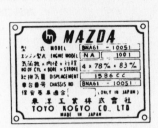

Fig. 3 Engine number location on 1,586cc, 1,796cc and 1,970cc engines

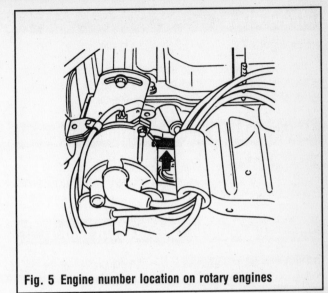

Fig. 5 Engine number location on rotary engines

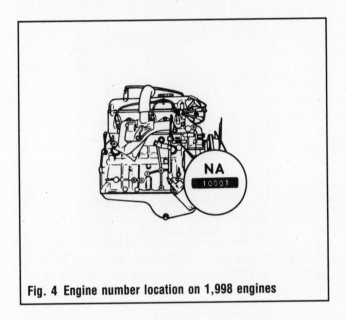

Fig. 4 Engine number location on 1,998 engines

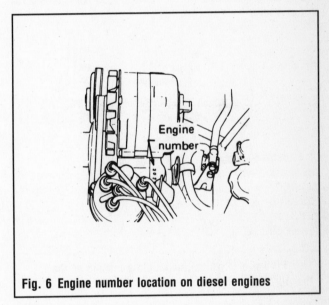

Fig. 6 Engine number location on diesel engines

Engine Identification Chart

No. of Cylinders	Actual Displacement			Fuel System	Type	Manufacturer	Years
	Cu. In.	CC	Liters				
2-rotors	79.8	1308	1.3	4-bbl	Rotary	Mazda	1972-77
4	96.8	1586	1.6	2-bbl	OHC	Mazda	1972-75
4	109.6	1796	1.8	2-bbl	OHC	Mazda	1976-78
4	120.2	1970	2.0	2-bbl	OHC	Mazda	1979-84
4	134.8	2209	2.2	Diesel	OHV	Mitsubishi	1982-84
4	121.9	1998	2.0	2-bbl	OHC	Mitsubishi	1986

2-bbl: Two barrel carburetor
4-bbl: Four barrel carburetor
OHC: Overhead Camshaft
OHV: Overhead Valve

Model Plate

♦ **See Figure 7**

The model plate, containing the truck model, engine model, engine displacement and chassis number is riveted to the right rear corner of the engine compartment on the firewall.

Motor Vehicle Safety Certification Label

This label is attached to the left door lock pillar and proclaims the fact that the truck conforms to all necessary safety regulations in effect at the time of manufacture.

Emission Control Certification Label

This label is found attached to the right-hand panel of the engine compartment, and states that the truck conforms to the emission regulations for the country of destination.

Typical model plate found in the engine compartment to the right on the firewall

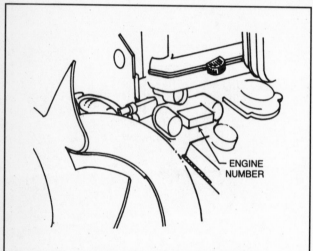

Fig. 7 View of a typical model plate located on the firewall

Typical emission control certification label found in the engine compartment—this label also contains tune-up information

ROUTINE MAINTENANCE

Routine, or preventive maintenance is exactly as it implies; maintenance that is performed at suggested intervals that keeps small problems from becoming large ones. For example, it is much easier (and cheaper in the long run) to check the engine oil regularly than to have the engine run low on oil and damage the bearings (a major overhaul job). Read this section carefully and follow its recommendations closely for as close to optimum performance as possible.

Air Cleaner

♦ **See Figures 8, 9, 10, 11 and 12**

The air cleaner uses a disposable paper element on carbureted, diesel and fuel injected engines. The air filter should be replaced at least every two years or 24,000–30,000 miles. If the car is driven in a dry and dusty climate, clean or replace the air filter twice as often. Inspect the air cleaner element for accumulations of dirt and oil and wipe the air cleaner housing with a cleaner. Replace the element as necessary.

➡**In severe service, such as off-road use or in extremely dusty areas, the maintenance interval should be cut in half.**

REMOVAL & INSTALLATION

Replacing the air cleaner element is a simple, routine maintenance operation. You should be careful, however, to keep dust and dirt out of the air cleaner housing, as they accelerate engine wear. If the outside of the air cleaner housing is dusty, wipe it with a clean rag before beginning work.

MAINTENANCE COMPONENT LOCATIONS - 1986 B2000 SHOWN

1. Radiator cap
2. Upper radiator hose
3. Battery positive terminal
4. Battery negative terminal
5. Evaporative canister
6. Fuel filter
7. Air cleaner assembly
8. Model plate
9. PCV valve
10. Oil fill cap
11. Spark plug wires
12. Brake master cylinder
13. Clutch master cylinder
14. Fresh air hose
15. Windshield washer tank
16. Coolant overflow tank
17. Power steering oil fill/dipstick
18. Distributor
19. Radiator
20. Wiper motor

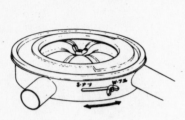

Fig. 8 View of the 1,586cc engine air cleaner housing—to help prevent icing, move the lever to W when temperatures drop below 50°F; above 50°F, move the lever to S

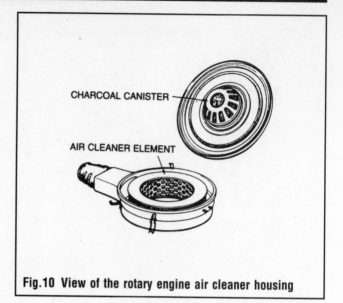

Fig.10 View of the rotary engine air cleaner housing

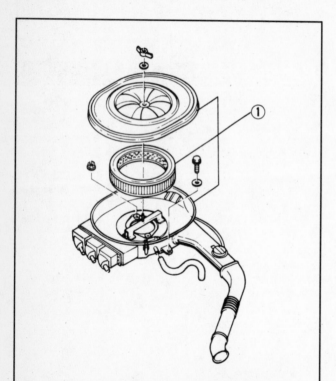

Fig. 9 View of the 1,998cc air cleaner housing—the filter element (1) should be replaced every 24,000 miles or 2 years

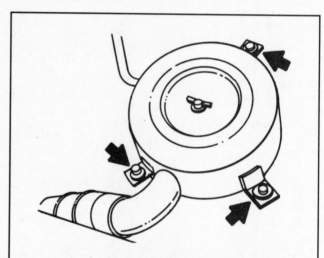

Fig. 11 View of the diesel engine air cleaner housing—the arrows show the mounting points

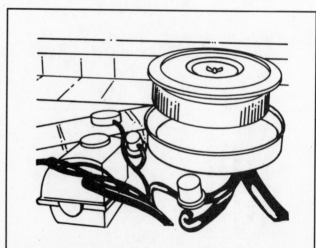

Fig. 12 View of the 1,796cc and 1,970cc engine air cleaner housing

On carburetor equipped engines, you typically have to remove only the top cover of the air cleaner. Remove the wingnut at the center of the housing and then unclip the three clips situated around the sides. Then, pull the top cover off and remove the air cleaner element. When installing the new element, make sure it seats squarely around the bulge in the center of the lower air cleaner housing. Install the housing top, turning it until the wingnut mounting stud lines up with the hole in the top (it's usually off center). Note that the top cover should seat tightly all around. Install the wingnut and reclip the clips.

To change the air filter, remove the wingnut at the center of the air cleaner assembly . . .

While you have the lid off the air cleaner, check the breather filter and replace as necessary

Air Pump Filter

REPLACEMENT

1972–73 California Models Only
▶ See Figure 13

Mazdas built to be sold in California in 1972 and 1973 have an air filter for the air pump. The air pump is used for purposes of emission control; more information on the air pump system can be found in Section 4. The filter must be replaced at 24,000 mile intervals.

1. Remove the wing nut holding the filter housing cover in place.
2. Remove the cover. Remove the old filter and discard it.
3. Install the new filter and install the cover. Replace the wing nut and tighten it securely.

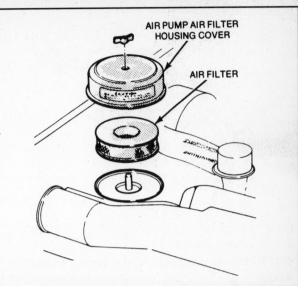

Fig. 13 View of the air pump air filter assembly used on 1972–73 California models—replace the filter element at 24,000 mile intervals

Fuel Filter

LOCATION

▶ See Figures 14, 15 and 16

The fuel filter is located on the center of the left frame member near the fuel tank on 1,586cc, 1,796cc and 1979–81 1,970cc engines.

On 1982–84 1,970cc engines, it is located in a bracket on the front center of the fuel tank, immediately below the cargo bed.

On the 1,998cc engine, the filter is located in the engine compartment, secured by a bracket, to the firewall.

On the B2200 diesel, it is a spin-on type filter, much like an oil filter, located between the water separator and the injection pump. On Rotary Pick-Ups, it's under the left side of the cargo

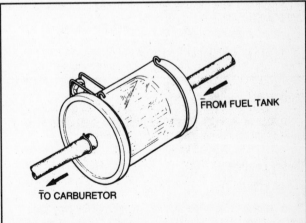

Fig. 14 Fuel filter used on 1972–81 trucks—including rotary engine models

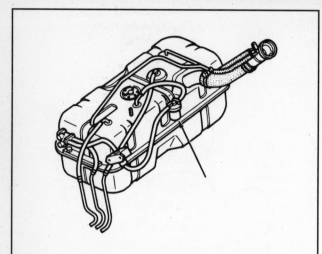

Fig. 15 Gasoline fuel filter location (arrow) on 1982–84 trucks

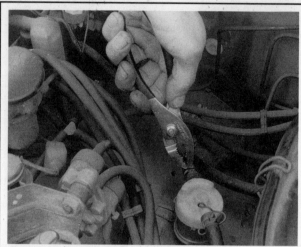

To remove the fuel filter, use pliers to loosen the spring clamps and slide them away from the filter . . .

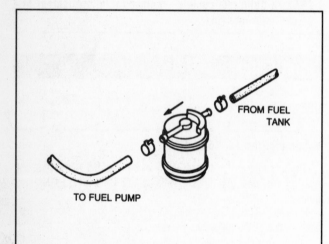

Fig. 16 Fuel filter used on 1986 carbureted trucks (1982–84 trucks similar)

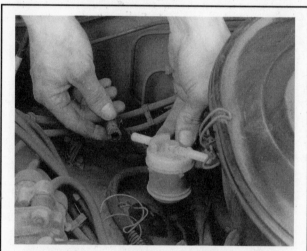

. . . then remove the fuel lines and pull the filter free from its bracket

bed, just forward of the rear wheel. All trucks use a fuel filter that is replaceable.

REMOVAL & INSTALLATION

Carbureted Engines

To replace the filter, loosen the clamps at both ends of the filter and pull off the hoses. Pop the filter from its clamp.

Diesel Engines
▶ See Figure 17

To replace the filter on diesels, use an oil filter type strap wrench to loosen the filter, then unscrew it. To install the new filter, coat the O-ring with clean diesel fuel and spin the new filter into place until it contacts the mounting base, then turn it ½ additional turn. Loosen the vent screw and bleed any air using the priming pump.

Diesel Fuel Sedimenter

SERVICE

Water should be drained from the diesel fuel sedimenter whenever the light on the instrument panel comes on or every 5,000 miles. More frequent drain intervals may be required depending on the quality of the fuel used.

✳✳ CAUTION

The truck must be stopped with the engine off when draining the sedimenter. Fuel may ignite if sedimenter is drained while the engine is running or the truck is moving.

The instrument panel warning light **(WATER IN FUEL)** will glow when approximately ½ liter of water has accumulated in the sedimenter. When the warning light glows, shut off the engine as

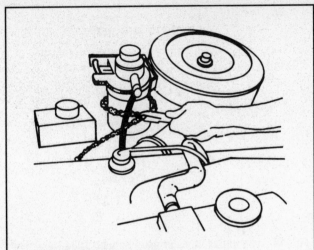

Fig. 17 Removing the diesel fuel filter with an oil filter type wrench

soon as safely possible. A suitable drain pan or container should be placed under the sedimenter, which is mounted inside the frame rail, underneath the driver's side of the cab. To drain the fuel sedimenter, pull up on the T-handle (located on the cab floor behind the driver's seat) until resistance is felt. Turn the ignition switch to the **ON** position so the warning light glows and hold T-handle up for approximately 45 seconds after light goes out.

To stop draining fuel, release T-handle and inspect sedimenter to verify that draining has stopped. Discard drained fluid suitably.

PCV Valve

♦ **See Figure 18**

The Positive Crankcase Ventilation (PCV) valve should be inspected for blockage periodically. On trucks through 1984, it is located in a special fitting in the intake manifold, just below the car-

buretor. On 1986 trucks, it is located in the valve cover, connected to the intake manifold by a vacuum hose.

TESTING

The simplest test for the PCV valve is to remove it from its fitting and shake it. A distinct rattle should be heard; if not, replace the valve.

REMOVAL & INSTALLATION

Through 1984

1. Remove the air cleaner.
2. Disconnect the hose from the PCV valve.

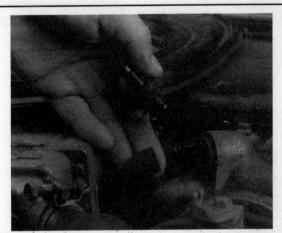

To remove the PCV valve, simply pull it free of the grommet and then remove the hose attached to the other end

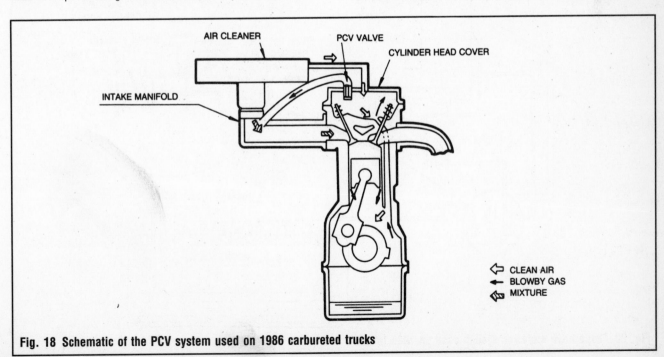

Fig. 18 Schematic of the PCV system used on 1986 carbureted trucks

AIR CLEANER

PCV VALVE

CYLINDER HEAD COVER

INTAKE MANIFOLD

⇦ CLEAN AIR
◄ BLOWBY GAS
⇦ MIXTURE

3. Remove the valve from the special fitting in the intake manifold.

4. Install the valve in the intake manifold fitting and connect the hose to the valve.

5. Connect the hose to the air cleaner and install the air filter.

6. Check for loose clamps or cracks in the PCV lines and replace the hoses if cracked.

1986 Vehicles

Simply pull the PCV valve from the grommet in the valve cover and remove the hose clamp. Then, pull it from the hose. Install the new valve and install the clamp.

➡If your engine exhibits lower than normal gas mileage and poor idle characteristics for no apparent reason, suspect the PCV valve. It is probably blocked and should be replaced.

Evaporator Canister

▸ See Figures 19 and 20

REMOVAL & INSTALLATION

Rotary Pick-Up

The charcoal filter for the evaporative emission control (EEC) system is located in the top of the air cleaner housing. It should be checked as indicated.

1. Unfasten the clips and remove the top of the air cleaner case.

2. Inspect the air cleaner element and clean it as necessary.

3. Check the condition of the PCV valve as outlined above.

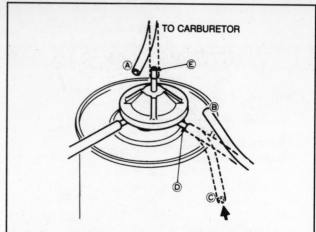

Fig. 19 Evaporative canister used through 1984 models—the canister should be replaced every 50,000 miles

Piston Engine

The evaporative canister is located under the hood in the engine compartment and is designed to store fuel vapors and prevent their escaping into the atmosphere. On early models, when the engine is not running, fuel that has evaporated into the condenser tank is returned to the fuel tank as the ambient temperatures rise and the vapors are condensed. Later models do not have a condenser tank. During periods when the engine is running, fuel vapor that has not condensed in the condenser tank moves to the carbon canister. The stored vapors are removed by fresh air through the bottom of the inlet hole and passed through the air cleaner to the combustion chamber. Because of the design of the sys-

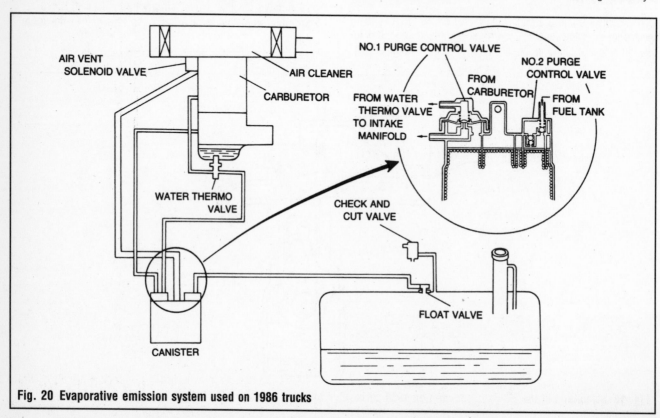

Fig. 20 Evaporative emission system used on 1986 trucks

tem, the only maintenance associated with the canister is to replace it periodically as indicated in the Maintenance Interval charts.

Battery

GENERAL MAINTENANCE

All batteries, regardless of type, should be carefully secured by a battery hold-down device. If this is not done, the battery terminals or casing may crack from stress applied to the battery during vehicle operation. A battery which is not secured may allow acid to leak out, making it discharge faster; such leaking corrosive acid can also eat away components under the hood. A battery that is not sealed must be checked periodically for electrolyte level. You cannot add water to a sealed maintenance-free battery (though not all maintenance-free batteries are sealed), but a sealed battery must also be checked for proper electrolyte level as indicated by the color of the built-in hydrometer "eye."

Keep the top of the battery clean, as a film of dirt can help completely discharge a battery that is not used for long periods. A solution of baking soda and water may be used for cleaning, but be careful to flush this off with clear water. DO NOT let any of the solution into the filler holes. Baking soda neutralizes battery acid and will de-activate a battery cell.

✳✳ CAUTION

Always use caution when working on or near the battery. Never allow a tool to bridge the gap between the negative and positive battery terminals. Also, be careful not to allow a tool to provide a ground between the positive cable/terminal and any metal component on the vehicle. Either of these conditions will cause a short circuit leading to sparks and possible personal injury.

Batteries in vehicles which are not operated on a regular basis can fall victim to parasitic loads (small current drains which are constantly drawing current from the battery). Normal parasitic loads may drain a battery on a vehicle that is in storage and not used for 6–8 weeks. Vehicles that have additional accessories such as a cellular phone, an alarm system or other devices that increase parasitic load may discharge a battery sooner. If the vehicle is to be stored for 6–8 weeks in a secure area and the alarm system, if present, is not necessary, the negative battery cable should be disconnected at the onset of storage to protect the battery charge.

Remember that constantly discharging and recharging will shorten battery life. Take care not to allow a battery to be needlessly discharged.

BATTERY FLUID

✳✳ CAUTION

Battery electrolyte contains sulfuric acid. If you should splash any on your skin or in your eyes, flush the affected area with plenty of clear water. If it lands in your eyes, get medical help immediately.

The fluid (sulfuric acid solution) contained in the battery cells will tell you many things about the condition of the battery. Because the cell plates must be kept submerged below the fluid level in order to operate, maintaining the fluid level is extremely important. And, because the specific gravity of the acid is an indication of electrical charge, testing the fluid can be an aid in determining if the battery must be replaced. A battery in a vehicle with a properly operating charging system should require little maintenance, but careful, periodic inspection should reveal problems before they leave you stranded.

Fluid Level

Check the battery electrolyte level at least once a month, or more often in hot weather or during periods of extended vehicle operation. On non-sealed batteries, the level can be checked either through the case on translucent batteries or by removing the cell caps on opaque-cased types. The electrolyte level in each cell should be kept filled to the split ring inside each cell, or the line marked on the outside of the case.

If the level is low, add only distilled water through the opening

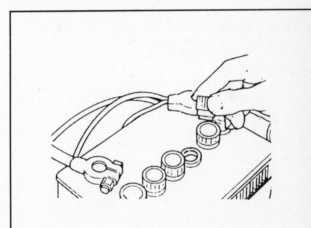

On non-maintenance free batteries, the level can be checked through the case on translucent batteries; the cell caps must be removed on other models

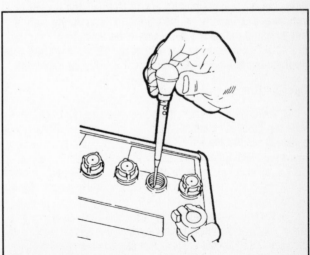

Check the specific gravity of the battery's electrolyte with a hydrometer

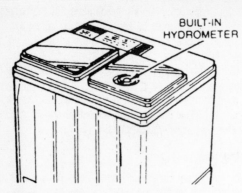

BUILT-IN HYDROMETER

Location of Indicator on sealed battery

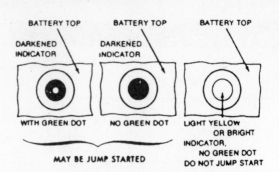

BATTERY TOP	BATTERY TOP	BATTERY TOP
DARKENED INDICATOR	DARKENED INDICATOR	LIGHT YELLOW OR BRIGHT INDICATOR. NO GREEN DOT DO NOT JUMP START
WITH GREEN DOT	NO GREEN DOT	

MAY BE JUMP STARTED

Check the appearance of the charge indicator on top of the battery before attempting a jump start; if it's not green or dark, do not jump start the car

A typical sealed (maintenance-free) battery with a built-in hydrometer—NOTE that the hydrometer eye may vary between battery manufacturers; always refer to the battery's label

until the level is correct. Each cell is separate from the others, so each must be checked and filled individually. Distilled water should be used, because the chemicals and minerals found in most drinking water are harmful to the battery and could significantly shorten its life.

If water is added in freezing weather, the vehicle should be driven several miles to allow the water to mix with the electrolyte. Otherwise, the battery could freeze.

Although some maintenance-free batteries have removable cell caps for access to the electrolyte, the electrolyte condition and level on all sealed maintenance-free batteries must be checked using the built-in hydrometer "eye." The exact type of eye varies between battery manufacturers, but most apply a sticker to the battery itself explaining the possible readings. When in doubt, refer to the battery manufacturer's instructions to interpret battery condition using the built-in hydrometer.

➡**Although the readings from built-in hydrometers found in sealed batteries may vary, a green eye usually indicates a properly charged battery with sufficient fluid level. A dark eye is normally an indicator of a battery with sufficient fluid, but one which may be low in charge. And a light or yellow eye is usually an indication that electrolyte supply has dropped below the necessary level for battery (and hydrometer) operation. In this last case, sealed batteries with an insufficient electrolyte level must usually be discarded.**

Specific Gravity

As stated earlier, the specific gravity of a battery's electrolyte level can be used as an indication of battery charge. At least once a year, check the specific gravity of the battery. It should be between 1.20 and 1.26 on the gravity scale. Most auto supply stores carry a variety of inexpensive battery testing hydrometers. These can be used on any non-sealed battery to test the specific gravity in each cell.

The battery testing hydrometer has a squeeze bulb at one end and a nozzle at the other. Battery electrolyte is sucked into the hydrometer until the float is lifted from its seat. The specific gravity is then read by noting the position of the float. If gravity is low in one or more cells, the battery should be slowly charged and checked again to see if the gravity has come up. Generally, if after

charging, the specific gravity between any two cells varies more than 50 points (0.50), the battery should be replaced as it can no longer produce sufficient voltage to guarantee proper operation.

On sealed batteries, the built-in hydrometer is the only way of checking specific gravity. Again, check with your battery's manufacturer for proper interpretation of its built-in hydrometer readings.

CABLES

Once a year (or as necessary), the battery terminals and the cable clamps should be cleaned. Loosen the clamps and remove the cables, negative cable first. On batteries with posts on top, the use of a puller specially made for this purpose is recommended. These are inexpensive and available in most auto parts stores. Side terminal battery cables are secured with a small bolt.

Clean the cable clamps and the battery terminal with a wire brush, until all corrosion, grease, etc., is removed and the metal is shiny. It is especially important to clean the inside of the clamp (an old knife is useful here) thoroughly, since a small deposit of

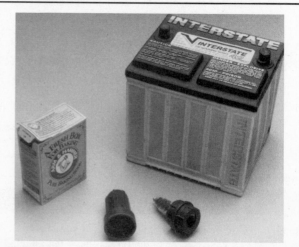

Maintenance is performed with household items and with special tools like this post cleaner

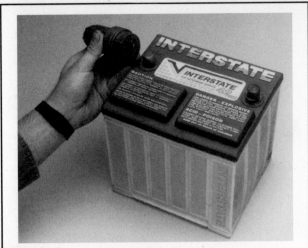

The underside of this special battery tool has a wire brush to clean post terminals

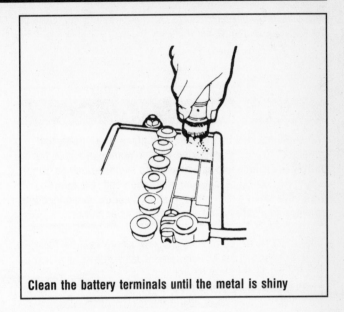

Clean the battery terminals until the metal is shiny

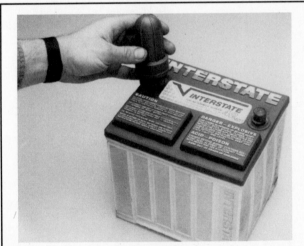

Place the tool over the terminals and twist to clean the post

The cable ends should be cleaned as well

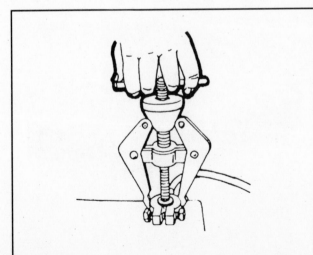

A special tool is available to pull the clamp from the post

foreign material or oxidation there will prevent a sound electrical connection and inhibit either starting or charging. Special tools are available for cleaning these parts, one type for conventional top post batteries and another type for side terminal batteries.

Before installing the cables, loosen the battery hold-down clamp or strap, remove the battery and check the battery tray. Clear it of any debris, and check it for soundness (the battery tray can be cleaned with a baking soda and water solution). Rust should be wire brushed away, and the metal given a couple coats of anti-rust paint. Install the battery and tighten the hold-down clamp or strap securely. Do not overtighten, as this can crack the battery case.

After the clamps and terminals are clean, reinstall the cables, negative cable last; DO NOT hammer the clamps onto post batteries. Tighten the clamps securely, but do not distort them. Give the clamps and terminals a thin external coating of grease after installation, to retard corrosion.

Check the cables at the same time that the terminals are cleaned. If the cable insulation is cracked or broken, or if the ends are frayed, the cable should be replaced with a new cable of the same length and gauge.

CHARGING

A battery should be charged at a slow rate to keep the plates inside from getting too hot. However, if some maintenance-free batteries are allowed to discharge until they are almost "dead," they may have to be charged at a high rate to bring them back to "life." Always follow the charger manufacturer's instructions on charging the battery.

REPLACEMENT

When it becomes necessary to replace the battery, select one with a rating equal to or greater than the battery originally installed. Deterioration and just plain aging of the battery cables, starter motor, and associated wires makes the battery's job harder in successive years. The slow increase in electrical resistance over time makes it prudent to install a new battery with a greater capacity than the old.

Belts

INSPECTION

Inspect the belts for signs of glazing or cracking. A glazed belt will be perfectly smooth from slippage, while a good belt will

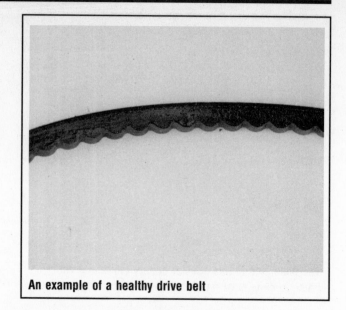

An example of a healthy drive belt

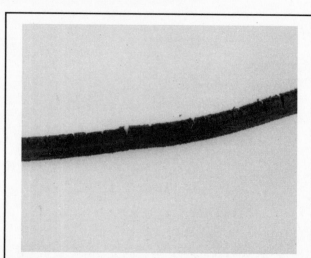

Deep cracks in this belt will cause flex, building up heat that will eventually lead to belt failure

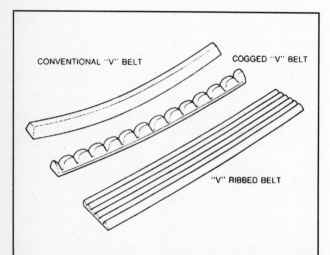

There are typically 3 types of accessory drive belts found on vehicles today

The cover of this belt is worn, exposing the critical reinforcing cords to excessive wear

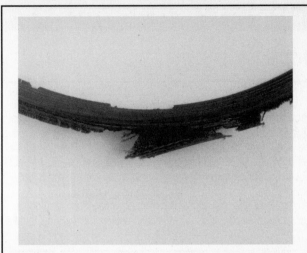

Installing too wide a belt can result in serious belt wear and/or breakage

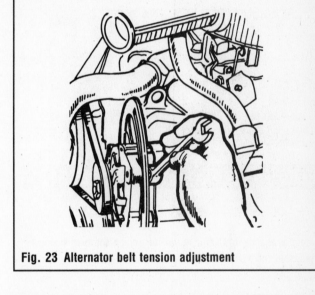

Fig. 22 Various belt tension adjustments on the diesel engine

have a slight texture of fabric visible. Cracks will usually start at the inner edge of the belt and run outward. All worn or damaged drive belts should be replaced immediately. It is best to replace all drive belts at one time, as a preventive maintenance measure, during this service operation.

TENSION CHECKING & ADJUSTING

♦ **See Figures 21, 22, 23 and 24**

Fan Belt

1. Apply thumb pressure (about 22 lbs.) to the fan belt midway between the pulleys and check the deflection. It should be approximately ⅜ in. for new belts and ½ in. for used belts.

2. To adjust the tension, loosen the alternator mounting bolt and adjusting bolt.

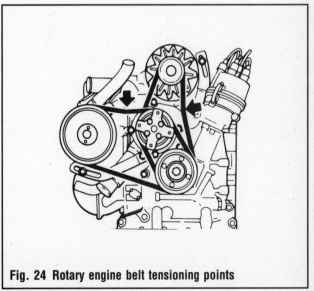

Fig. 23 Alternator belt tension adjustment

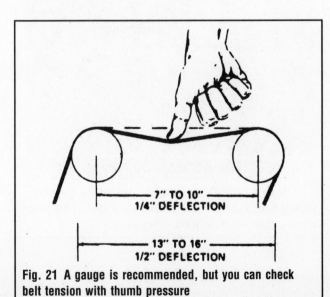

Fig. 21 A gauge is recommended, but you can check belt tension with thumb pressure

Fig. 24 Rotary engine belt tensioning points

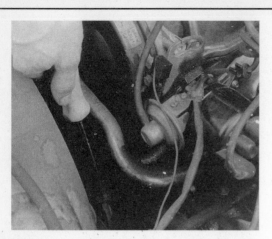

Some belts have adjuster pulleys that allow you to tighten and loosen tension simply by turning a screw . . .

. . . while others require you to pry on them to tighten tension and push on them to loosen

3. Move the alternator in the direction necessary to loosen or tighten the tension.

4. Tighten the mounting and adjusting bolts and recheck the tension.

Thermactor Air Pump Belt

1. Check the air pump drive belt tension by applying thumb pressure at a point midway between the air pump pulley and the crankshaft pulley. The deflection should be $\frac{1}{2}$–$\frac{5}{8}$ in.

2. If the tension is not correct, loosen the mounting and adjusting bolts slightly.

3. Pry the air pump outward (or inward) until the proper deflection is obtained.

4. Tighten the adjusting and lower bolts to 22 ft. lbs.

Hoses

INSPECTION

Upper and lower radiator hoses along with the heater hoses should be checked for deterioration, leaks and loose hose clamps at least every 15,000 miles (24,000 km). It is also wise to check the hoses periodically in early spring and at the beginning of the fall or winter when you are performing other maintenance. A quick visual inspection could discover a weakened hose which might have left you stranded if it had remained unrepaired.

Whenever you are checking the hoses, make sure the engine and cooling system are cold. Visually inspect for cracking, rotting

Hoses are fastened either by a screw clamp, which uses a screw to draw a metal band tighter around the hose . . .

. . . or by a spring clamp made of spring steel—pliers usually work best although sometimes tight quarters may require needlenose or some other variation

or collapsed hoses, and replace as necessary. Run your hand along the length of the hose. If a weak or swollen spot is noted when squeezing the hose wall, the hose should be replaced.

REMOVAL & INSTALLATION

1. Remove the radiator pressure cap.

✳✳ CAUTION

Never remove the pressure cap while the engine is running, or personal injury from scalding hot coolant or steam may result. If possible, wait until the engine has cooled to remove the pressure cap. If this is not possible, wrap a thick cloth around the pressure cap and turn it slowly to the stop. Step back while the pressure is released from the cooling system. When you are sure all the pressure has been released, use the cloth to turn and remove the cap.

2. Position a clean container under the radiator and/or engine draincock or plug, then open the drain and allow the cooling system to drain to an appropriate level. For some upper hoses, only a little coolant must be drained. To remove hoses positioned lower on the engine, such as a lower radiator hose, the entire cooling system must be emptied.

✳✳ CAUTION

When draining coolant, keep in mind that cats and dogs are attracted by ethylene glycol antifreeze, and are quite likely to drink any that is left in an uncovered container or in puddles on the ground. This will prove fatal in sufficient quantity. Always drain coolant into a sealable container. Coolant may be reused unless it is contaminated or several years old.

3. Loosen the hose clamps at each end of the hose requiring replacement. Clamps are usually either of the spring tension type (which require pliers to squeeze the tabs and loosen) or of the

A hose clamp that is too tight can cause older hoses to separate and tear on either side of the clamp

A soft spongy hose (identifiable by the swollen section) will eventually burst and should be replaced

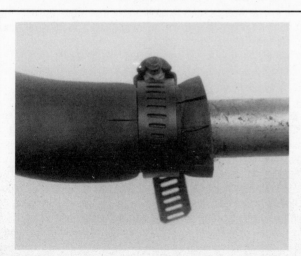

The cracks developing along this hose are a result of age-related hardening

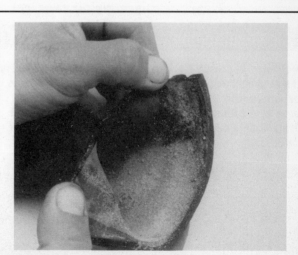

Hoses are likely to deteriorate from the inside if the cooling system is not periodically flushed

screw tension type (which require screw or hex drivers to loosen). Pull the clamps back on the hose away from the connection.

4. Twist, pull and slide the hose off the fitting, taking care not to damage the neck of the component from which the hose is being removed.

➡ **If the hose is stuck at the connection, do not try to insert a screwdriver or other sharp tool under the hose end in an effort to free it, as the connection and/or hose may become damaged. Heater connections especially may be easily damaged by such a procedure. If the hose is to be replaced, use a single-edged razor blade to make a slice along the portion of the hose which is stuck on the connection, perpendicular to the end of the hose. Do not cut deep so as to prevent damaging the connection. The hose can then be peeled from the connection and discarded.**

5. Clean both hose mounting connections. Inspect the condition of the hose clamps and replace them, if necessary.

To install:

6. Dip the ends of the new hose into clean engine coolant to ease installation.

7. Slide the clamps over the replacement hose, then slide the hose ends over the connections into position.

8. Position and secure the clamps at least ¼ in. (6.35mm) from the ends of the hose. Make sure they are located beyond the raised bead of the connector.

9. Close the radiator or engine drains and properly refill the cooling system with the clean drained engine coolant or a suitable mixture of ethylene glycol coolant and water.

10. If available, install a pressure tester and check for leaks. If a pressure tester is not available, run the engine until normal operating temperature is reached (allowing the system to naturally pressurize), then check for leaks.

✳✳ CAUTION

If you are checking for leaks with the system at normal operating temperature, BE EXTREMELY CAREFUL not to touch any moving or hot engine parts. Once temperature has been reached, shut the engine OFF, and check for leaks around the hose fittings and connections which were removed earlier.

Air Conditioning

➡ **Be sure to consult the laws in your area before servicing the air conditioning system. In most areas, it is illegal to perform repairs involving refrigerant unless the work is done by a certified technician. Also, it is quite likely that you will not be able to purchase refrigerant without proof of certification.**

SAFETY PRECAUTIONS

There are two major hazards associated with air conditioning systems and they both relate to the refrigerant gas. First, the refrigerant gas (R-12) is an extremely cold substance. When exposed to air, it will instantly freeze any surface it comes in contact with, including your eyes. The other hazard relates to fire. Although normally non-toxic, the R-12 gas becomes highly poisonous in the presence of an open flame. One good whiff of the vapor formed by burning R-12 can be fatal. Keep all forms of fire (including cigarettes) well clear of the air conditioning system.

Because of the inherent dangers involved with working on air conditioning systems and R-12 refrigerant, these safety precautions must be strictly followed.

• Avoid contact with a charged refrigeration system, even when working on another part of the air conditioning system or vehicle. If a heavy tool comes into contact with a section of tubing or a heat exchanger, it can easily cause the relatively soft material to rupture.

• When it is necessary to apply force to a fitting which contains refrigerant, as when checking that all system couplings are securely tightened, use a wrench on both parts of the fitting involved, if possible. This will avoid putting torque on refrigerant tubing. (It is also advisable to use tube or line wrenches when tightening these flare nut fittings.)

➡ **R-12 refrigerant is a chlorofluorocarbon which, when released into the atmosphere, can contribute to the depletion of the ozone layer in the upper atmosphere. Ozone filters out harmful radiation from the sun.**

• Do not attempt to discharge the system without the proper tools. Precise control is possible only when using the service gauges and a proper A/C refrigerant recovery station. Wear protective gloves when connecting or disconnecting service gauge hoses.

• Discharge the system only in a well ventilated area, as high concentrations of the gas which might accidentally escape can exclude oxygen and act as an anesthetic. When leak testing or soldering, this is particularly important, as toxic gas is formed when R-12 contacts any flame.

• Never start a system without first verifying that both service valves are properly installed, and that all fittings throughout the system are snugly connected.

• Avoid applying heat to any refrigerant line or storage vessel. Charging may be aided by using water heated to less than 125°F (50°C) to warm the refrigerant container. Never allow a refrigerant storage container to sit out in the sun, or near any other source of heat, such as a radiator or heater.

• Always wear goggles to protect your eyes when working on a system. If refrigerant contacts the eyes, it is advisable in all cases to consult a physician immediately.

• Frostbite from liquid refrigerant should be treated by first gradually warming the area with cool water, and then gently applying petroleum jelly. A physician should be consulted.

• Always keep refrigerant drum fittings capped when not in use. If the container is equipped with a safety cap to protect the valve, make sure the cap is in place when the can is not being used. Avoid sudden shock to the drum, which might occur from dropping it, or from banging a heavy tool against it. Never carry a drum in the passenger compartment of a vehicle.

• Always completely discharge the system into a suitable recovery unit before painting the vehicle (if the paint is to be baked on), or before welding anywhere near refrigerant lines.

• When servicing the system, minimize the time that any refrigerant line or fitting is open to the air in order to prevent moisture or dirt from entering the system. Contaminants such as moisture or dirt can damage internal system components. Always replace O-rings on lines or fittings which are disconnected. Prior to installation coat, but do not soak, replacement O-rings with suitable compressor oil.

GENERAL SERVICING PROCEDURES

➡**It is recommended, and possibly required by law, that a qualified technician perform the following services.**

The most important aspect of air conditioning service is the maintenance of a pure and adequate charge of refrigerant in the system. A refrigeration system cannot function properly if a significant percentage of the charge is lost. Leaks are common because the severe vibration encountered underhood in an automobile can easily cause a sufficient cracking or loosening of the air conditioning fittings; allowing, the extreme operating pressures of the system to force refrigerant out.

The problem can be understood by considering what happens to the system as it is operated with a continuous leak. Because the expansion valve regulates the flow of refrigerant to the evaporator, the level of refrigerant there is fairly constant. The receiver/drier stores any excess refrigerant, and so a loss will first appear there as a reduction in the level of liquid. As this level nears the bottom of the vessel, some refrigerant vapor bubbles will begin to appear in the stream of liquid supplied to the expansion valve. This vapor decreases the capacity of the expansion valve very little as the valve opens to compensate for its presence. As the quantity of liquid in the condenser decreases, the operating pressure will drop there and throughout the high side of the system. As the R-12 continues to be expelled, the pressure available to force the liquid through the expansion valve will continue to decrease, and, eventually, the valve's orifice will prove to be too much of a restriction for adequate flow even with the needle fully withdrawn.

At this point, low side pressure will start to drop, and a severe reduction in cooling capacity, marked by freeze-up of the evaporator coil, will result. Eventually, the operating pressure of the evaporator will be lower than the pressure of the atmosphere surrounding it, and air will be drawn into the system wherever there are leaks in the low side.

Because all atmospheric air contains at least some moisture, water will enter the system and mix with the R-12 and the oil. Trace amounts of moisture will cause sludging of the oil, and corrosion of the system. Saturation and clogging of the filter/drier, and freezing of the expansion valve orifice will eventually result. As air fills the system to a greater and greater extent, it will interfere more and more with the normal flows of refrigerant and heat.

From this description, it should be obvious that much of the repairman's focus in on detecting leaks, repairing them, and then restoring the purity and quantity of the refrigerant charge. A list of general rules should be followed in addition to all safety precautions:

• Keep all tools as clean and dry as possible.

• Thoroughly purge the service gauges/hoses of air and moisture before connecting them to the system. Keep them capped when not in use.

• Thoroughly clean any refrigerant fitting before disconnecting it, in order to minimize the entrance of dirt into the system.

• Plan any operation that requires opening the system beforehand, in order to minimize the length of time it will be exposed to open air. Cap or seal the open ends to minimize the entrance of foreign material.

• When adding oil, pour it through an extremely clean and dry tube or funnel. Keep the oil capped whenever possible. Do not use oil that has not been kept tightly sealed.

• Use only R-12 refrigerant. Purchase refrigerant intended for use only in automatic air conditioning systems.

• Completely evacuate any system that has been opened for service, or that has leaked sufficiently to draw in moisture and air. This requires evacuating air and moisture with a good vacuum pump for at least one hour. If a system has been open for a considerable length of time it may be advisable to evacuate the system for up to 12 hours (overnight).

• Use a wrench on both halves of a fitting that is to be disconnected, so as to avoid placing torque on any of the refrigerant lines.

• When overhauling a compressor, pour some of the oil into a clean glass and inspect it. If there is evidence of dirt, metal particles, or both, flush all refrigerant components with clean refrigerant before evacuating and recharging the system. In addition, if metal particles are present, the compressor should be replaced.

• Schrader valves may leak only when under full operating pressure. Therefore, if leakage is suspected but cannot be located, operate the system with a full charge of refrigerant and look for leaks from all Schrader valves. Replace any faulty valves.

Additional Preventive Maintenance

USING THE SYSTEM

The easiest and most important preventive maintenance for your A/C system is to be sure that it is used on a regular basis. Running the system for five minutes each month (no matter what the season) will help assure that the seals and all internal components remain lubricated.

ANTIFREEZE

In order to prevent heater core freeze-up during A/C operation, it is necessary to maintain a proper antifreeze protection. Use a hand-held antifreeze tester (hydrometer) to periodically check the condition of the antifreeze in your engine's cooling system.

➡**Antifreeze should not be used longer than the manufacturer specifies.**

RADIATOR CAP

For efficient operation of an air conditioned vehicle's cooling system, the radiator cap should have a holding pressure which meets manufacturer's specifications. A cap which fails to hold these pressures should be replaced.

CONDENSER

Any obstruction of or damage to the condenser configuration will restrict the air flow which is essential to its efficient operation. It is therefore a good rule to keep this unit clean and in proper physical shape.

➡**Bug screens which are mounted in front of the condenser, (unless they are original equipment), are regarded as obstructions.**

CONDENSATION DRAIN TUBE

This single molded drain tube expels the condensation, which accumulates on the bottom of the evaporator housing, into the engine compartment. If this tube is obstructed, the air conditioning performance can be restricted and condensation buildup can spill over onto the vehicle's floor.

SYSTEM INSPECTION

➡**R-12 refrigerant is a chlorofluorocarbon which, when released into the atmosphere, can contribute to the depletion of the ozone layer in the upper atmosphere. Ozone filters out harmful radiation from the sun.**

The easiest and often most important check for the air conditioning system consists of a visual inspection of the system components. Visually inspect the air conditioning system for refrigerant leaks, damaged compressor clutch, compressor drive belt tension and condition, plugged evaporator drain tube, blocked condenser fins, disconnected or broken wires, blown fuses, corroded connections and poor insulation.

A refrigerant leak will usually appear as an oily residue at the leakage point in the system. The oily residue soon picks up dust or dirt particles from the surrounding air and appears greasy. Through time, this will build up and appear to be a heavy dirt impregnated grease. Most leaks are caused by damaged or missing O-ring seals at the component connections, damaged charging valve cores or missing service gauge port caps.

For a thorough visual and operational inspection, check the following:

1. Check the surface of the radiator and condenser for dirt, leaves or other material which might block air flow.

2. Check for kinks in hoses and lines. Check the system for leaks.

3. Make sure the drive belt is under the proper tension. When the air conditioning is operating, make sure the drive belt is free of noise or slippage.

4. Make sure the blower motor operates at all appropriate positions, then check for distribution of the air from all outlets with the blower on **HIGH**.

➡**Keep in mind that under conditions of high humidity, air discharged from the A/C vents may not feel as cold as expected, even if the system is working properly. This is because the vaporized moisture in humid air retains heat more effectively than does dry air, making the humid air more difficult to cool.**

Make sure the air passage selection lever is operating correctly. Start the engine and warm it to normal operating temperature, then make sure the hot/cold selection lever is operating correctly.

DISCHARGING, EVACUATING AND CHARGING

Discharging, evacuating and charging the air conditioning system must be performed by a properly trained and certified mechanic in a facility equipped with refrigerant recovery/recycling equipment that meets SAE standards for the type of system to be serviced.

An antifreeze tester can be used to determine the freezing and boiling levels of the coolant

If you don't have access to the necessary equipment, we recommend that you take your vehicle to a reputable service station to have the work done. If you still wish to perform repairs on the vehicle, have them discharge the system, then take your vehicle home and perform the necessary work. When you are finished, return the vehicle to the station for evacuation and charging. Just be sure to cap ALL A/C system fittings immediately after opening them and keep them protected until the system is recharged.

Windshield Wipers

ELEMENT (REFILL) CARE AND REPLACEMENT

For maximum effectiveness and longest element life, the windshield and wiper blades should be kept clean. Dirt, tree sap, road tar and so on will cause streaking, smearing and blade deterioration if left on the glass. It is advisable to wash the windshield

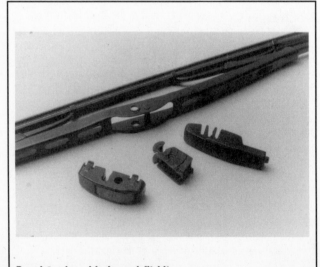

Bosch® wiper blade and fit kit

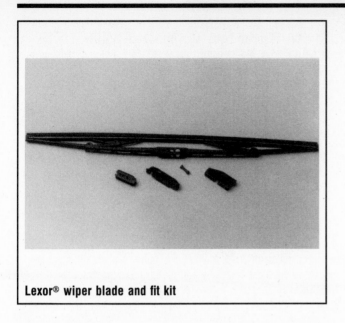

Lexor® wiper blade and fit kit

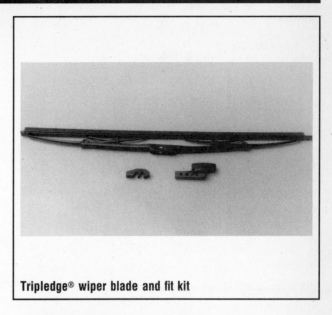

Tripledge® wiper blade and fit kit

Pylon® wiper blade and adaptor

To remove and install a Lexor® wiper blade refill, slip out the old insert and slide in a new one

Trico® wiper blade and fit kit

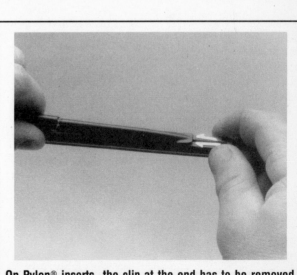

On Pylon® inserts, the clip at the end has to be removed prior to sliding the insert off

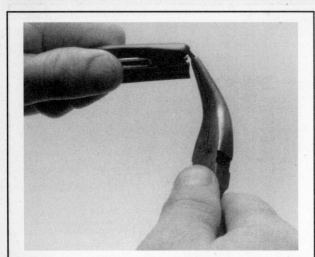

On Trico® wiper blades, the tab at the end of the blade must be turned up . . .

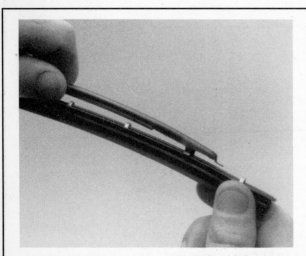

. . . then the insert can be removed. After installing the replacement insert, bend the tab back

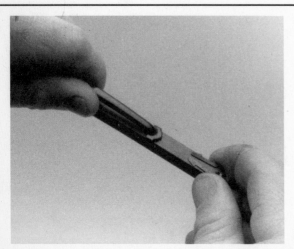

The Tripledge® wiper blade insert is removed and installed using a securing clip

carefully with a commercial glass cleaner at least once a month. Wipe off the rubber blades with the wet rag afterwards. Do not attempt to move wipers across the windshield by hand; damage to the motor and drive mechanism will result.

To inspect and/or replace the wiper blade elements, place the wiper switch in the **LOW** speed position and the ignition switch in the **ACC** position. When the wiper blades are approximately vertical on the windshield, turn the ignition switch to **OFF**.

Examine the wiper blade elements. If they are found to be cracked, broken or torn, they should be replaced immediately. Replacement intervals will vary with usage, although ozone deterioration usually limits element life to about one year. If the wiper pattern is smeared or streaked, or if the blade chatters across the glass, the elements should be replaced. It is easiest and most sensible to replace the elements in pairs.

If your vehicle is equipped with aftermarket blades, there are several different types of refills and your vehicle might have any kind. Aftermarket blades and arms rarely use the exact same type blade or refill as the original equipment. Here are some typical aftermarket blades; not all may be available for your vehicle:

The Anco® type uses a release button that is pushed down to allow the refill to slide out of the yoke jaws. The new refill slides back into the frame and locks in place.

Some Trico® refills are removed by locating where the metal backing strip or the refill is wider. Insert a small screwdriver blade between the frame and metal backing strip. Press down to release the refill from the retaining tab.

Other types of Trico® refills have two metal tabs which are unlocked by squeezing them together. The rubber filler can then be withdrawn from the frame jaws. A new refill is installed by inserting the refill into the front frame jaws and sliding it rearward to engage the remaining frame jaws. There are usually four jaws; be certain when installing that the refill is engaged in all of them. At the end of its travel, the tabs will lock into place on the front jaws of the wiper blade frame.

Another type of refill is made from polycarbonate. The refill has a simple locking device at one end which flexes downward out of the groove into which the jaws of the holder fit, allowing easy release. By sliding the new refill through all the jaws and pushing through the slight resistance when it reaches the end of its travel, the refill will lock into position.

To replace the Tridon® refill, it is necessary to remove the wiper blade. This refill has a plastic backing strip with a notch about 1 in. (25mm) from the end. Hold the blade (frame) on a hard surface so that the frame is tightly bowed. Grip the tip of the backing strip and pull up while twisting counterclockwise. The backing strip will snap out of the retaining tab. Do this for the remaining tabs until the refill is free of the blade. The length of these refills is molded into the end and they should be replaced with identical types.

Regardless of the type of refill used, be sure to follow the part manufacturer's instructions closely. Make sure that all of the frame jaws are engaged as the refill is pushed into place and locked. If the metal blade holder and frame are allowed to touch the glass during wiper operation, the glass will be scratched.

Tires and Wheels

Common sense and good driving habits will afford maximum tire life. Fast starts, sudden stops and hard cornering are hard on tires and will shorten their useful life span. Make sure that you

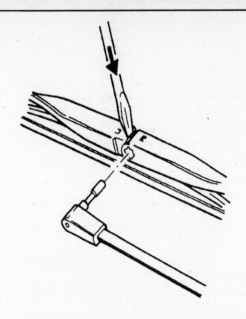

BLADE REPLACEMENT

1. CYCLE ARM AND BLADE ASSEMBLY TO UP POSITION-ON THE WINDSHIELD WHERE REMOVAL OF BLADE ASSEMBLY CAN BE PERFORMED WITHOUT DIFFICULTY. TURN IGNITION KEY OFF AT DESIRED POSITION.

2. TO REMOVE BLADE ASSEMBLY, INSERT SCREWDRIVER IN SLOT, PUSH DOWN ON SPRING LOCK AND PULL BLADE ASSEMBLY FROM PIN (VIEW A)

3. TO INSTALL, PUSH THE BLADE ASSEMBLY ON THE PIN SO THAT THE SPRING LOCK ENGAGES THE PIN (VIEW A). BE SURE THE BLADE ASSEMBLY IS SECURELY ATTACHED TO PIN

VIEW A

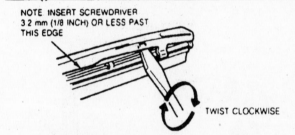

NOTE INSERT SCREWDRIVER 3.2 mm (1/8 INCH) OR LESS PAST THIS EDGE

TWIST CLOCKWISE

ELEMENT REPLACEMENT

1. INSERT SCREWDRIVER BETWEEN THE EDGE OF THE SUPER STRUCTURE AND THE BLADE BACKING DRIP (VIEW B) TWIST SCREWDRIVER SLOWLY UNTIL ELEMENT CLEARS ONE SIDE OF THE SUPER STRUC-TURE CLAW

2. SLIDE THE ELEMENT INTO THE SUPER STRUCTURE CLAWS

VIEW B

4. INSERT ELEMENT INTO ONE SIDE OF THE END CLAWS (VIEW D) AND WITH A ROCKING MOTION PUSH ELEMENT UPWARD UNTIL IT SNAPS IN (VIEW E)

VIEW D

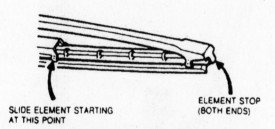

SLIDE ELEMENT STARTING AT THIS POINT

ELEMENT STOP (BOTH ENDS)

3. SLIDE THE ELEMENT INTO THE SUPER STRUCTURE CLAWS, STARTING WITH SECOND SET FROM EITHER END (VIEW C) AND CONTINUE TO SLIDE THE BLADE ELEMENT INTO ALL THE SUPER STRUCTURE CLAWS TO THE ELEMENT STOP (VIEW C)

VIEW C

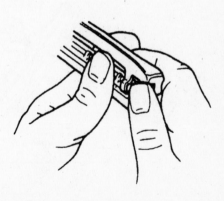

VIEW E

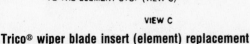
Trico® wiper blade insert (element) replacement

BLADE REPLACEMENT

1. Cycle arm and blade assembly to a position on the windshield where removal of blade assembly can be performed without difficulty. Turn ignition key off at desired position.
2. To remove blade assembly from wiper arm, pull up on spring lock and pull blade assembly from pin (View A). Be sure spring lock is not pulled excessively or it will become distorted.
3. To install, push the blade assembly onto the pin so that the spring lock engages the pin (View A). Be sure the blade assembly is securely attached to pin.

ELEMENT REPLACEMENT

1. In the plastic backing strip which is part of the rubber blade assembly, there is an 11.11mm (7/16 inch) long notch located approximately one inch from either end. Locate either notch.
2. Place the frame of the wiper blade assembly on a firm surface with either notched end of the backing strip visible.
3. Grasp the frame portion of the wiper blade assembly and push down until the blade assembly is tightly bowed.
4. With the blade assembly in the bowed position, grasp the tip of the backing strip firmly, pulling up and twisting C.C.W. at the same time. The backing strip will then snap out of the retaining tab on the end of the frame.
5. Lift the wiper blade assembly from the surface and slide the backing strip down the frame until the notch lines up with the next retaining tab, twist slightly, and the backing strip will snap out. Continue this operation with the remaining tabs until the blade element is completely detached from the frame.
6. To install blade element, reverse the above procedure, making sure all six (6) tabs are locked to the backing strip before installing blade to wiper arm.

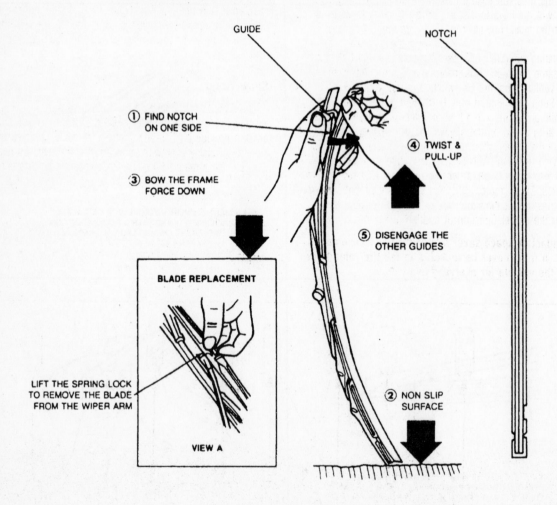

GUIDE

NOTCH

① FIND NOTCH ON ONE SIDE

③ BOW THE FRAME FORCE DOWN

④ TWIST & PULL-UP

⑤ DISENGAGE THE OTHER GUIDES

BLADE REPLACEMENT

LIFT THE SPRING LOCK TO REMOVE THE BLADE FROM THE WIPER ARM

VIEW A

② NON SLIP SURFACE

Tridon® wiper blade insert (element) replacement

don't overload the vehicle or run with incorrect pressure in the tires. Both of these practices will increase tread wear.

➡️For optimum tire life, keep the tires properly inflated, rotate them often and have the wheel alignment checked periodically.

Inspect your tires frequently. Be especially careful to watch for bubbles in the tread or sidewall, deep cuts or underinflation. Replace any tires with bubbles in the sidewall. If cuts are so deep that they penetrate to the cords, discard the tire. Any cut in the sidewall of a radial tire renders it unsafe. Also look for uneven tread wear patterns that may indicate the front end is out of alignment or that the tires are out of balance.

TIRE ROTATION

Tires must be rotated periodically to equalize wear patterns that vary with a tire's position on the vehicle. Tires will also wear in an uneven way as the front steering/suspension system wears to the point where the alignment should be reset.

Rotating the tires will ensure maximum life for the tires as a set, so you will not have to discard a tire early due to wear on only part of the tread. Regular rotation is required to equalize wear.

When rotating "unidirectional tires," make sure that they always roll in the same direction. This means that a tire used on the left side of the vehicle must not be switched to the right side and vice-versa. Such tires should only be rotated front-to-rear or rear-to-front, while always remaining on the same side of the vehicle. These tires are marked on the sidewall as to the direction of rotation; observe the marks when reinstalling the tire(s).

Some styled or "mag" wheels may have different offsets front to rear. In these cases, the rear wheels must not be used up front and vice-versa. Furthermore, if these wheels are equipped with unidirectional tires, they cannot be rotated unless the tire is remounted for the proper direction of rotation.

➡️The compact or space-saver spare is strictly for emergency use. It must never be included in the tire rotation or placed on the vehicle for everyday use.

TIRE DESIGN

For maximum satisfaction, tires should be used in sets of four. Mixing of different types (radial, bias-belted, fiberglass belted) must be avoided. In most cases, the vehicle manufacturer has designated a type of tire on which the vehicle will perform best. Your first choice when replacing tires should be to use the same type of tire that the manufacturer recommends.

When radial tires are used, tire sizes and wheel diameters should be selected to maintain ground clearance and tire load capacity equivalent to the original specified tire. Radial tires should always be used in sets of four.

✳️✳️ CAUTION

Radial tires should never be used on only the front axle.

When selecting tires, pay attention to the original size as marked on the tire. Most tires are described using an industry size code sometimes referred to as P-Metric. This allows the exact identification of the tire specifications, regardless of the manufacturer. If selecting a different tire size or brand, remember to check the installed tire for any sign of interference with the body or suspension while the vehicle is stopping, turning sharply or heavily loaded.

Snow Tires

Good radial tires can produce a big advantage in slippery weather, but in snow, a street radial tire does not have sufficient tread to provide traction and control. The small grooves of a street tire quickly pack with snow and the tire behaves like a billiard ball on a marble floor. The more open, chunky tread of a snow tire will self-clean as the tire turns, providing much better grip on snowy surfaces.

To satisfy municipalities requiring snow tires during weather emergencies, most snow tires carry either an M + S designation after the tire size stamped on the sidewall, or the designation "all-season." In general, no change in tire size is necessary when buying snow tires.

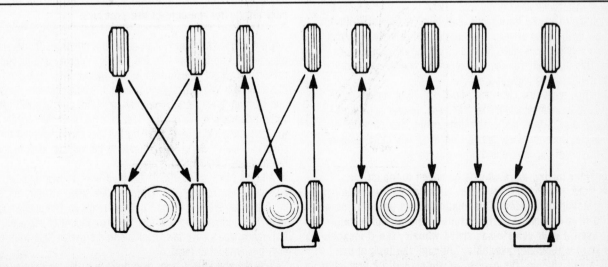

Common tire rotation patterns for 4 and 5-wheel rotations

Unidirectional tires are identifiable by sidewall arrows and/or the word "rotation"

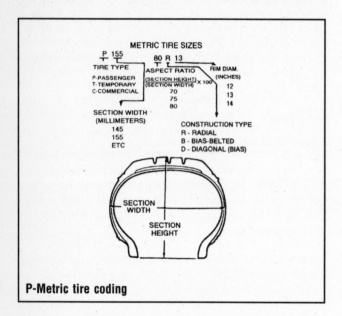

P-Metric tire coding

Most manufacturers strongly recommend the use of 4 snow tires on their vehicles for reasons of stability. If snow tires are fitted only to the drive wheels, the opposite end of the vehicle may become very unstable when braking or turning on slippery surfaces. This instability can lead to unpleasant endings if the driver can't counteract the slide in time.

Note that snow tires, whether 2 or 4, will affect vehicle handling in all non-snow situations. The stiffer, heavier snow tires will noticeably change the turning and braking characteristics of the vehicle. Once the snow tires are installed, you must re-learn the behavior of the vehicle and drive accordingly.

➡**Consider buying extra wheels on which to mount the snow tires. Once done, the "snow wheels" can be installed and removed as needed. This eliminates the potential damage to tires or wheels from seasonal removal and installation. Even if your vehicle has styled wheels, see if inexpensive steel wheels are available. Although the look of the vehicle will change, the expensive wheels will be protected from salt, curb hits and pothole damage.**

TIRE STORAGE

If they are mounted on wheels, store the tires at proper inflation pressure. All tires should be kept in a cool, dry place. If they are stored in the garage or basement, do not let them stand on a concrete floor; set them on strips of wood, a mat or a large stack of newspaper. Keeping them away from direct moisture is of paramount importance. Tires should not be stored upright, but in a flat position.

INFLATION & INSPECTION

The importance of proper tire inflation cannot be overemphasized. A tire employs air as part of its structure. It is designed around the supporting strength of the air at a specified pressure. For this reason, improper inflation drastically reduces the tires's ability to perform as intended. A tire will lose some air in day-to-day use; having to add a few pounds of air periodically is not necessarily a sign of a leaking tire.

Two items should be a permanent fixture in every glove compartment: an accurate tire pressure gauge and a tread depth gauge. Check the tire pressure (including the spare) regularly with a pocket type gauge. Too often, the gauge on the end of the air hose at your corner garage is not accurate because it suffers too much abuse. Always check tire pressure when the tires are cold, as pressure increases with temperature. If you must move the vehicle to check the tire inflation, do not drive more than a mile before checking. A cold tire is generally one that has not been driven for more than three hours.

A plate or sticker is normally provided somewhere in the vehicle (door post, hood, tailgate or trunk lid) which shows the proper pressure for the tires. Never counteract excessive pressure build-up by bleeding off air pressure (letting some air out). This will cause the tire to run hotter and wear quicker.

✳✳ CAUTION

Never exceed the maximum tire pressure embossed on the tire! This is the pressure to be used when the tire is at maximum loading, but it is rarely the correct pressure for everyday driving. Consult the owner's manual or the tire pressure sticker for the correct tire pressure.

Once you've maintained the correct tire pressures for several weeks, you'll be familiar with the vehicle's braking and handling personality. Slight adjustments in tire pressures can fine-tune these characteristics, but never change the cold pressure specification by more than 2 psi. A slightly softer tire pressure will give a softer ride but also yield lower fuel mileage. A slightly harder tire will give crisper dry road handling but can cause skidding on wet surfaces. Unless you're fully attuned to the vehicle, stick to the recommended inflation pressures.

All tires made since 1968 have built-in tread wear indicator bars that show up as ½ in. (13mm) wide smooth bands across the tire when ¹⁄₁₆ in. (1.5mm) of tread remains. The appearance of tread wear indicators means that the tires should be replaced. In fact, many states have laws prohibiting the use of tires with less than this amount of tread.

You can check your own tread depth with an inexpensive gauge or by using a Lincoln head penny. Slip the Lincoln penny

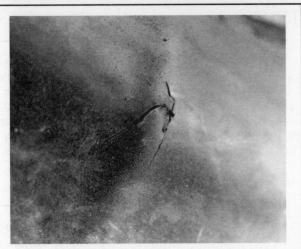

Tires should be checked frequently for any sign of puncture or damage

Tires with deep cuts, or cuts which show bulging should be replaced immediately

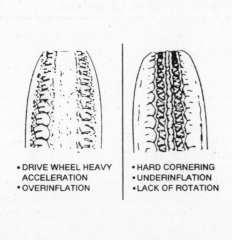

Examples of inflation-related tire wear patterns

• DRIVE WHEEL HEAVY
  ACCELERATION
• OVERINFLATION

• HARD CORNERING
• UNDERINFLATION
• LACK OF ROTATION

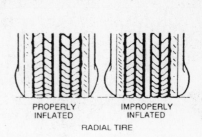

PROPERLY INFLATED   IMPROPERLY INFLATED

RADIAL TIRE

Radial tires have a characteristic sidewall bulge; don't try to measure pressure by looking at the tire. Use a quality air pressure gauge

(with Lincoln's head upside-down) into several tread grooves. If you can see the top of Lincoln's head in 2 adjacent grooves, the tire has less than 1/16 in. (1.5mm) tread left and should be replaced. You can measure snow tires in the same manner by using the "tails" side of the Lincoln penny. If you can see the top of the Lincoln memorial, it's time to replace the snow tire(s).

CARE OF SPECIAL WHEELS

If you have invested money in magnesium, aluminum alloy or sport wheels, special precautions should be taken to make sure your investment is not wasted and that your special wheels look good for the life of the vehicle.

Special wheels are easily damaged and/or scratched. Occasionally check the rims for cracking, impact damage or air leaks. If any of these are found, replace the wheel. But in order to prevent this type of damage and the costly replacement of a special wheel, observe the following precautions:

• Use extra care not to damage the wheels during removal, installation, balancing, etc. After removal of the wheels from the vehicle, place them on a mat or other protective surface. If they are to be stored for any length of time, support them on strips of wood. Never store tires and wheels upright; the tread may develop flat spots.

• When driving, watch for hazards; it doesn't take much to crack a wheel.

• When washing, use a mild soap or non-abrasive dish detergent (keeping in mind that detergent tends to remove wax). Avoid cleansers with abrasives or the use of hard brushes. There are many cleaners and polishes for special wheels.

• If possible, remove the wheels during the winter. Salt and sand used for snow removal can severely damage the finish of a wheel.

• Make certain the recommended lug nut torque is never exceeded or the wheel may crack. Never use snow chains on special wheels; severe scratching will occur.

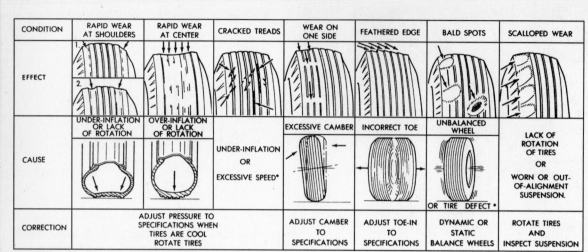

CONDITION	RAPID WEAR AT SHOULDERS	RAPID WEAR AT CENTER	CRACKED TREADS	WEAR ON ONE SIDE	FEATHERED EDGE	BALD SPOTS	SCALLOPED WEAR
EFFECT	1. 2.						
CAUSE	UNDER-INFLATION OR LACK OF ROTATION	OVER-INFLATION OR LACK OF ROTATION	UNDER-INFLATION OR EXCESSIVE SPEED*	EXCESSIVE CAMBER	INCORRECT TOE	UNBALANCED WHEEL	LACK OF ROTATION OF TIRES OR WORN OR OUT-OF-ALIGNMENT SUSPENSION.
						OR TIRE DEFECT *	
CORRECTION	ADJUST PRESSURE TO SPECIFICATIONS WHEN TIRES ARE COOL ROTATE TIRES			ADJUST CAMBER TO SPECIFICATIONS	ADJUST TOE-IN TO SPECIFICATIONS	DYNAMIC OR STATIC BALANCE WHEELS	ROTATE TIRES AND INSPECT SUSPENSION

*HAVE TIRE INSPECTED FOR FURTHER USE.

Common tire wear patterns and causes

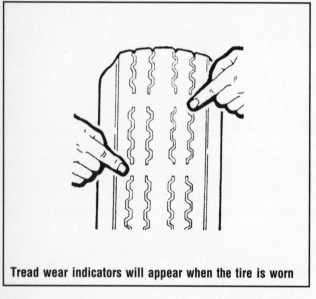

Tread wear indicators will appear when the tire is worn

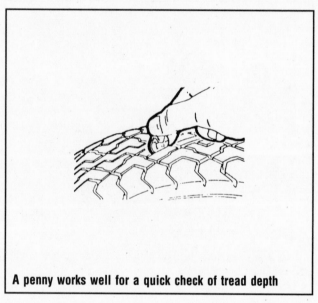

A penny works well for a quick check of tread depth

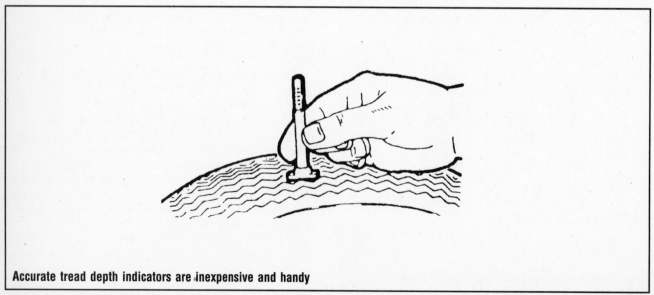

Accurate tread depth indicators are inexpensive and handy

FLUIDS AND LUBRICANTS

Fluid Disposal

Used fluids such as engine oil, transmission fluid, antifreeze and brake fluid are hazardous wastes and must be disposed of properly. Before draining any fluids, consult with the local authorities; in many areas, waste oil, etc. is being accepted as a part of recycling programs. A number of service stations and auto parts stores are also accepting waste fluids for recycling.

Be sure of the recycling center's policies before draining any fluids, as many will not accept different fluids that have been mixed together, such as oil and antifreeze.

Oil and Fuel Recommendations

FUEL

All gasoline engines through 1976 are designed to operate on leaded fuel of 91 research octane or higher, sold as Regular gas. All 1977 and later Mazdas sold in the U.S. use unleaded fuel of 91 research octane or higher. Regular leaded fuel may not be used in these models, because they are equipped with a catalytic converter for emission control purposes. Leaded fuel will render the converter useless, raising the emission content of the exhaust to illegal and environmentally unacceptable levels. It will also block the converter passages, increasing exhaust back pressure; in extreme cases, exhaust blockage will be raised to the point where the engine will not run. Most 1977 and later Mazdas sold in Canada are able to use regular fuel; however, converter equipped models must use unleaded fuel. In either case, fuel used in Canadian models must also have an octane rating of 91 or higher (research method).

Fuels of the same octane rating have varying anti-knock qualities. Thus if your engine knocks or pings, try switching brands of gasoline before trying a more expensive higher octane fuel. If you must use unleaded fuel, this may be your only alternative.

Your engine's fuel requirements can change with time, due to carbon buildup which changes the compression ratio. If switching brands or grades of gas doesn't work, check the ignition timing. If it is necessary to retard timing from specifications, don't change it more than about four degrees. Retard timing will reduce power output and fuel mileage and increase engine temperature.

The diesel engine in your Mazda is designed to run on No. 2 diesel fuel with a cetane rating of 40. For operation when the outdoor air temperature is consistently below freezing, the use of No. 1 diesel fuel or the addition of a cold weather additive, is recommended.

ENGINE OIL

▶ **See Figures 25, 26 and 27**

The SAE grade number indicates the viscosity of the engine oil, or its ability to lubricate under a given temperature. The lower the SAE grade number, the lighter the oil; the lower the viscosity, the easier it is to crank the engine in cold weather.

Look for the API oil identification label when choosing your engine oil

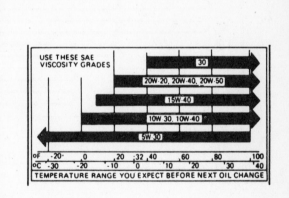

Fig. 25 Oil viscosity chart for gasoline engines—except rotary engines

The API (American Petroleum Institute) designation indicates the classification of engine oil for use under given operating conditions. For gasoline engines, only oils designated for Service SE/SF, or just SF, should be used. For diesel engines, use only those oils designated Service CC. These oils provide maximum engine protection. Both the SAE grade number and the API designation can be found on the top of a can of oil.

➥ **Non-detergent or straight mineral oils should not be used.**

Oil viscosities should be chosen from those oils recommended for the lowest anticipated temperatures during the oil change interval.

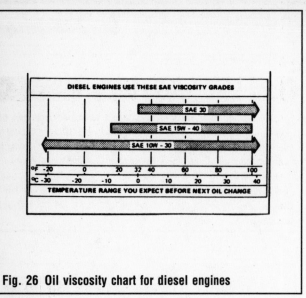

Fig. 26 Oil viscosity chart for diesel engines

Engine

OIL LEVEL CHECK

♦ **See Figures 28 and 29**

Under normal operating conditions, the Mazda rotary engine burns about one quart of oil every 1,000–1,400 miles as part of its combustion process. Therefore, the oil level should be checked frequently. The engine oil should be checked on a regular basis, ideally at each fuel stop. If the truck is used for trailer towing, or for heavy-duty use, it would be wise to check it more often.

When checking the oil level, it is best that the oil be at operating temperature, although checking the level immediately after stopping will give a false reading because all of the oil will not have drained back into the crankcase. Be sure that the truck is on a level surface, allowing time for all of the oil to drain back into the crankcase.

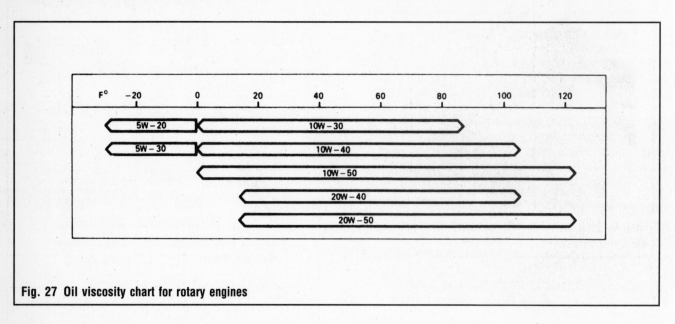

Fig. 27 Oil viscosity chart for rotary engines

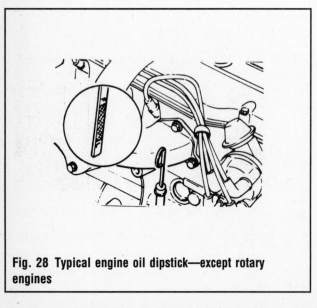

Fig. 28 Typical engine oil dipstick—except rotary engines

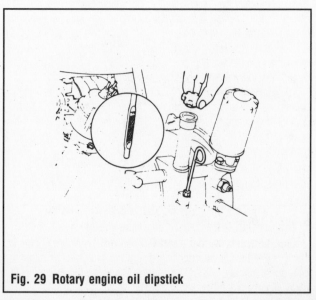

Fig. 29 Rotary engine oil dipstick

1. Open the hood and locate the dipstick. It is located on the right-hand (passenger's side) of the engine just behind the alternator.

2. Remove the dipstick and wipe it clean with a rag.

3. Insert the dipstick fully into the tube and remove it again. Hold the dipstick horizontal and read the level on the dipstick. The level should be between the **F** (Full) and **L** (Low) marks. If the oil level is at or below the **L** mark, sufficient oil level is at or below the **L** mark, sufficient oil should be added to restore the level to the proper place. Oil is added through the capped opening in the top of the valve cover. See the section on "Oil and Fuel Recommendations" for the proper viscosity and oil to use.

4. Replace the dipstick and check the level after adding oil. Be careful not to overfill the crankcase.

OIL AND FILTER CHANGE

See Figures 30, 31 and 32

✳✳ CAUTION

The EPA warns that prolonged contact with used engine oil may cause a number of skin disorders, including cancer! You should make every effort to minimize your exposure to used engine oil. Protective gloves should be worn when changing the oil. Wash your hands and any other exposed skin areas as soon as possible after exposure to used engine oil. Soap and water, or waterless hand cleaner should be used.

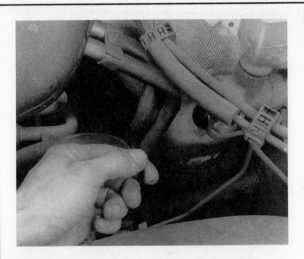

After locating the engine oil dipstick (1986 model shown), pull it free . . .

If it reads at the L mark or lower, add oil to bring the level up to full by removing the oil fill cap . . .

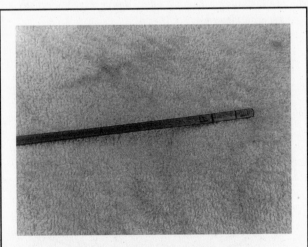

. . . wipe off the dipstick and re-insert it into the engine. Pull it free again and read the level—it should read between the two marks (F = full L = low)

. . . and, using a funnel, pour oil of the proper grade into the oil fill—check the level often while filling and be sure not to overfill

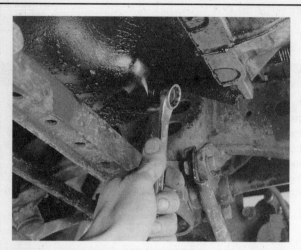

Position a drain pan or bucket, then loosen and remove the engine oil drain plug to drain the oil

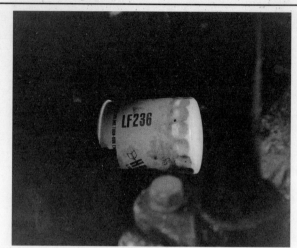

When removing the oil filter, there is usually only room for your arm and filter wrench

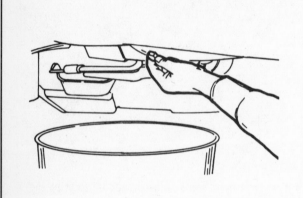

Fig. 30 Keep an inward pressure on the plug as you unscrew it, so the oil won't escape until you pull the plug away

Before installing a new oil filter, lightly coat the rubber gasket with clean oil

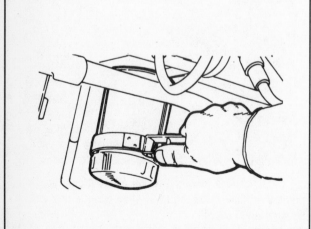

Fig. 31 Use a strap wrench to remove the oil filter

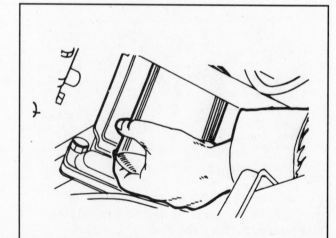

Fig. 32 Install the new filter by hand only; DO NOT use a filter wrench

The engine oil and filter should always be changed together. To skip an oil filter change is to leave a quart of contaminated oil in the engine. Engine oil and filter should be changed according to the schedule in the Maintenance Intervals chart. Under conditions such as:

• Driving in dusty conditions
• Continuous trailer pulling or RV use
• Extensive or prolonged idling
• Extensive short trip operation in freezing temperatures (when the engine is not thoroughly warmed up)
• Frequent long runs at high speeds and high ambient temperatures
• Stop-and-go service, such as delivery trucks

The oil change interval and filter replacement interval should be cut in half. Operation of the engine in severe conditions, such as a dust storm, may require an immediate oil and filter change.

To change the engine oil and filter, the truck should be parked on a level surface and the engine should be at operating temperature. This is to ensure that foreign matter will be drained away with the oil and not left behind in the engine to form sludge, which will happen if the engine is drained cold. Oil that is slightly brownish when drained is a good sign that the contaminants are being drained away. You should have available a container that will hold at least five quarts, a wrench to fit the oil drain plug, a spout for pouring in new oil and some rags to clean up the inevitable mess. If the filter is being replaced, you will also need a band wrench to fit the filter.

1. Position the truck on a level surface and set the parking brake or block the wheels. Slide a drain pan under the oil drain plug.

2. From under the truck, loosen, but do not remove the oil drain plug. Cover your hand with a heavy rag or glove and slowly unscrew the drain plug. Push the plug against the threads to prevent oil from leaking past the threads.

✳✳ CAUTION

The engine oil will be hot. Keep your arms, face and hands away from the oil as it drains out.

3. As the plug comes to the end of the threads, whisk it away from the hole, letting the oil drain into the pan, which hopefully is still under the drain plug. This method usually avoids the messy task of reaching into a tub full of hot, dirty oil to retrieve a usually elusive drain plug. Crawl out from under the truck and wait for the oil to drain.

4. When the oil is drained, install the drain plug. If you are replacing the filter on a Rotary Pick-Up, leave the plug out.

5. Change the engine oil filter as necessary or desired. On the 1,586cc, the filter is located at the right front of the engine, down below and behind the alternator. Loosen the filter with a band wrench and spin the filter off by hand. Be careful of the one quart of hot, dirty oil that inevitably overflows the filter. On Rotary Pick-Ups, the engine oil filter is on top of the engine, next to the dipstick. To remove it, punch a hole in the top of the filter to allow the oil in the filter to drain out through the engine. After the oil is drained from the filter, loosen it with a band wrench and remove it. When oil ceases to flow from the engine, replace the drain plug.

6. Coat the rubber gasket on a new filter with engine oil and install the filter. Screw the filter onto the mounting stud and tighten according to the directions on the filter.

7. Refill the engine with the specified amount of clean engine oil. Be sure to use the proper viscosity. Pour the oil in through the capped opening.

8. Run the engine for several minutes, checking for oil pressure and leaks. Check the level of the oil and add if necessary.

Manual Transmission

◆ **See Figures 33, 34 and 35**

LEVEL CHECK

1. Clean the dirt away from the area of the filler plug.
2. Jack the truck if necessary and support it on jackstands.
3. Remove the filler plug from the case. The filler plug is the one on the side of the case. Do not remove the plug from the bottom of the case unless you wish to drain the transmission.
4. If lubricant flows from the area of the filler plug as it is re-

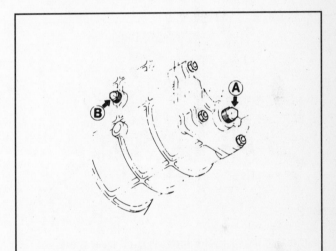

Fig. 33 Oil drain plug (A) and fill plug (B) locations for 1972–84 manual transmissions(except rotary engines)

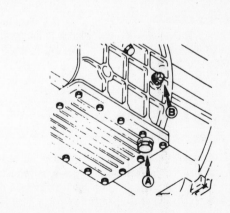

Fig. 34 Oil drain plug (A) and fill plug (B) locations for rotary engine manual transmission

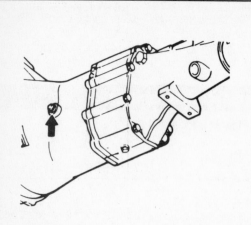

Fig. 35 1986 manual transmission fill plug location—the drain plug can be seen on the bottom of the case

To drain the manual transmission, leave the oil level check plug out and remove the lower drain plug

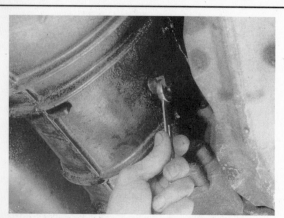

Loosening the manual transmission oil level check plug—if some oil trickles out when this plug is removed, the transmission is full; otherwise, it should be at the level of the hole

moved, the level is satisfactory. If lubricant does not flow from the filler hole when the plug is removed, add enough of the specified lubricant to bring the level to the bottom of the filler hole with the truck in a level position.

DRAIN AND REFILL

The same procedure is used for both 4-speed and 5-speed transmission, but note that 5-speed transmission have two filler plugs and two drain plugs. Thus, to drain the 5-speed, both drain plugs must be removed, and to fill it, both filler plugs must be removed. The truck should be parked on a level surface, and the transmission should be at normal operating temperature (oil hot).

1. With the truck parked on a level surface (parking brake applied), place a pan of at least four quarts capacity under the transmission drain plug(s).

2. Remove the filler plug(s) to provide a vent; this will speed the draining process.

3. Remove the drain plug(s) and allow the old oil to drain into the pan.

4. Clean the drain plug(s) thoroughly and replace. Tighten to 15–20 ft. lbs. if you have a torque wrench handy; otherwise, just snug the plug or plugs in. Overtightening will strip the aluminum threads in the case.

5. Add lubricant through the filler plug(s) until it comes right up to the edge of the filler hole. Use SAE 90 EP gear oil. It usually comes in a squeeze bottle with a nozzle attached to the cap, but you can use a squeeze bulb or suction gun for additions.

6. Install the filler plug(s). Tightening torque is 15–20 ft. lbs. Check for leaks after the truck has been driven for a few miles.

Automatic Transmission

An automatic transmission was first used on the Rotary Pick-Up in 1974. This unit was the 3-speed JATCO R3A.

The first automatic in a piston engined truck was the JATCO 3N71B, 3-speed unit used in the 1984 B2000. No automatics were offered for 1986.

LEVEL CHECK

▶ **See Figures 36 and 37**

1. Drive the vehicle for several miles to bring the fluid level to operating temperature.

2. Park the truck on a level surface.

3. Put the automatic transmission in PARK. Leave the engine running.

4. Remove the dipstick from the tube and wipe it clean.

5. Reinsert the dipstick so that it is fully seated.

6. Remove the dipstick and note the reading. If the fluid is at or below the **Add** mark, add sufficient fluid to bring the level to the **Full** mark. Do not overfill the transmission. Overfilling will lead to fluid aeration.

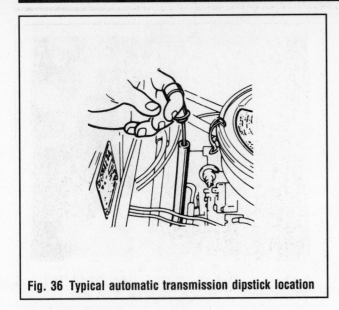

Fig. 36 Typical automatic transmission dipstick location

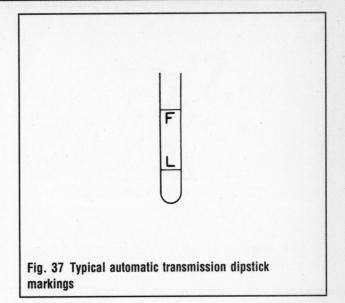

Fig. 37 Typical automatic transmission dipstick markings

FLUID RECOMMENDATIONS

- R3A: Type F
- 1984 3N71B: Type F

DRAIN AND REFILL

▶ **See Figures 38, 39 and 40**

The automatic transmission fluid is a long lasting type, and Mazda does not specify that it need ever be changed. However, if you have brought the truck used, driven it in water deep enough to reach the transmission, or used the truck for trailer pulling or delivery service, you may want to change the fluid and filter. It is a good idea to measure the amount of fluid drained from the transmission, and to use this as a guide when refilling. Some parts of the transmission, such as the torque converter, will not drain completely, and using the dry refill capacity listed in the Capacities chart may lead to overfilling.

1. Drive the truck until it is at normal operating temperature.

2. If a hoist is not being used, park the truck on a level surface, block the wheels, and set the parking brake. If you raise the truck on jackstands, check to see that it is reasonably level before draining the transmission.

3. There is no drain plug, so the transmission pan must be removed to drain the fluid. Carefully remove the screws from the pan and lower the pan at the corner. Allow the fluid to drain into a suitable container. After the fluid has drained, remove the pan.

4. The filter consists of a screen bolted to the lower valve body. Remove the screen attaching bolts and remove the screen. Clean it thoroughly in solvent, allow it to air dry completely, and replace it. Tightening torque for the attaching bolts is only 2.2–2.9 ft. lbs., so be careful not to overtighten them.

5. Remove the old gasket and install a new one. The pan may be cleaned with solvent, if desired. After cleaning, allow the pan to air dry thoroughly. Do not use a rag to dry it, or you risk leaving bits of lint in the pan that will clog the transmission fluid passages. When the pan is completely dry, replace it, and tighten the

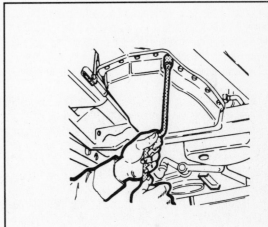

Fig. 38 The pan must be removed to drain the automatic transmission

Fig. 39 Install the new gasket to the pan, not the transmission flange

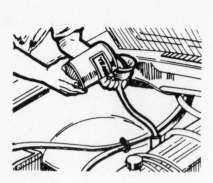

Fig. 40 Transmission fluid is added through the dipstick tube—a funnel that fits the dipstick tube prevents messy spills

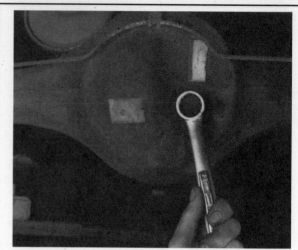

To check the drive axle oil level, remove the oil level check plug . . .

bolts in a circular pattern, working from the center outward. Tighten gently to 3.5–5.0 ft. lbs.

6. Refill the transmission. Fluid is added through the dipstick tube. This process is considerably easier if you have a funnel and a long tube to pour through. Add three quarts (2.8 liters) of fluid initially.

7. After adding fluid, start the engine and allow it to idle. Shift through all gear positions slowly to allow the fluid to fill all the hydraulic passages, and return the shift lever to Park. Do not race the engine.

8. Run the engine at fast idle to allow the fluid to reach operating temperature. Place the selector lever at **N** or **P** and check the fluid level. It should be above the **L** mark on the hot side of the dipstick. If necessary, add enough fluid to bring the level between the **L** and **F** marks. Do not overfill the transmission. Overfilling will cause foaming, fluid loss, and plate slippage.

Drive Axle

LEVEL CHECK

♦ See Figure 41

The drive axle fluid level is checked from underneath the truck.
1. Clean the dirt and grease away from the area of the filler (top) plug.
2. Remove the filler plug. The lubricant level should be even with the bottom of the filler plug hole.
3. If lubricant is required, use only the specified type. It will probably have to be pumped in through the filler hole. Hypoid SAE 90 lubricant usually does not pour very well.

DRAIN AND REFILL

The Mazda uses a removable carrier axle which has a drain and fill plug.
1. Jack the rear of the vehicle and support it with jackstands.

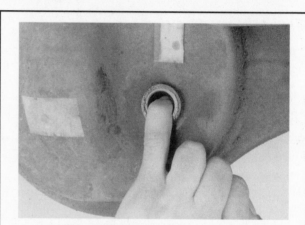

. . . if no oil trickles out of the hole, use your finger to feel for the fluid—it should be at or just below hole level; if no oil is felt, add oil until it trickles out of the hole

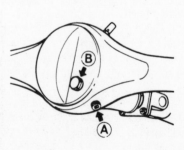

Fig. 41 Rear axle fill plug (B) and drain plug (A) locations

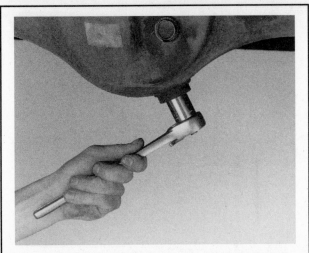

To change drive axle fluid, loosen the lower drain bolt . . .

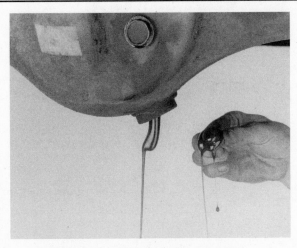

. . . remove the drain bolt and allow to drain completely . . .

. . . which will take several minutes, due to the thick nature of the drive axle fluid

2. Position a suitable container under the axle drain plug. Remove the fill plug to provide a vent.

3. Remove the drain plug and allow the lubricant to drain out.

➡Do not confuse the drain and fill plugs. The drain lug is magnetic to attract fine particles of metal which are inevitably present.

4. Clean the magnetic drain plug.

5. Install the drain plug.

6. Fill the rear axle with the specified amount and type of fluid. Install the filler plug.

7. Lower the truck to the ground and drive the truck, checking for leaks after the fluid is warm.

Cooling System

♦ See Figure 42

✳✳ CAUTION

Never remove the radiator cap under any conditions while the engine is running! Failure to follow these instructions could result in damage to the cooling system or engine and/or personal injury. To avoid having scalding hot coolant or steam blow out of the radiator, use extreme care when removing the radiator cap from a hot radiator. Wait until the engine has cooled, then wrap a thick cloth around the radiator cap and turn it slowly to the first stop. Step back while the pressure is released from the cooling system. When you are sure the pressure has been released, press down on the radiator cap (still have the cloth in position) turn and remove the radiator cap.

At least once every 2 years, the engine cooling system should be inspected, flushed, and refilled with fresh coolant. If the cool-

Fig. 42 Check antifreeze protection level with an inexpensive tester

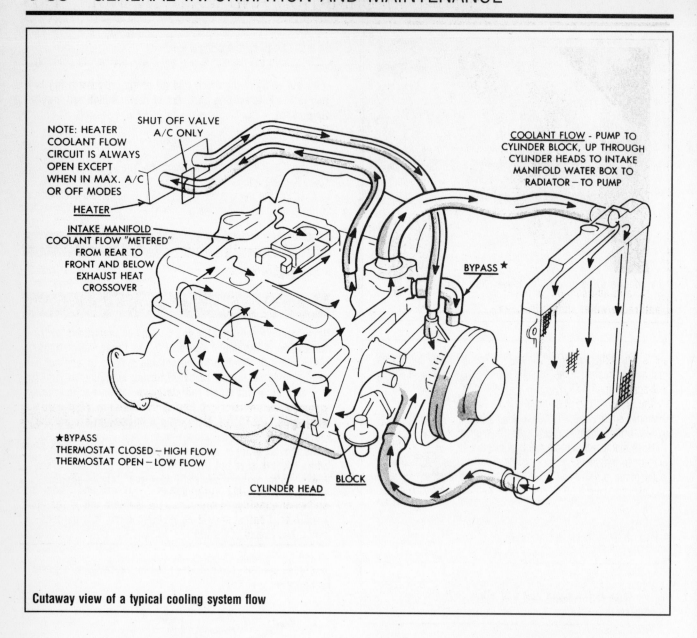

NOTE: HEATER COOLANT FLOW CIRCUIT IS ALWAYS OPEN EXCEPT WHEN IN MAX. A/C OR OFF MODES

SHUT OFF VALVE A/C ONLY

HEATER

INTAKE MANIFOLD COOLANT FLOW "METERED" FROM REAR TO FRONT AND BELOW EXHAUST HEAT CROSSOVER

COOLANT FLOW - PUMP TO CYLINDER BLOCK, UP THROUGH CYLINDER HEADS TO INTAKE MANIFOLD WATER BOX TO RADIATOR – TO PUMP

BYPASS ★

★BYPASS THERMOSTAT CLOSED – HIGH FLOW THERMOSTAT OPEN – LOW FLOW

CYLINDER HEAD   BLOCK

Cutaway view of a typical cooling system flow

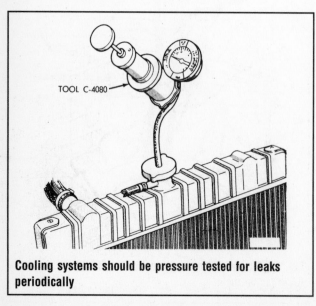

TOOL C-4080

Cooling systems should be pressure tested for leaks periodically

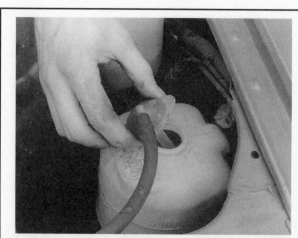

Check coolant level at the coolant reservoir—it should be at or above the FULL mark with the engine at normal operating temperature—if low, remove the cap . . .

. . . and add coolant as necessary—a 50/50 mix of antifreeze/water should be used

ant is left in the system too long, it loses its ability to prevent rust and corrosion. If the coolant has too much water, it won't protect against freezing.

The pressure cap should be looked at for signs of age or deterioration. Fan belt and other drive belts should be inspected and adjusted to the proper tension. (See checking belt tension).

Hose clamps should be tightened, and soft or cracked hoses replaced. Damp spots, or accumulations of rust or dye near hoses, water pump or other areas, indicate possible leakage, which must be corrected before filling the system with fresh coolant.

CHECK THE RADIATOR CAP

While you are checking the coolant level, check the radiator cap for a worn or cracked gasket. If the cap doesn't seal properly, fluid will be lost and the engine will overheat.

Worn caps should be replaced with a new one.

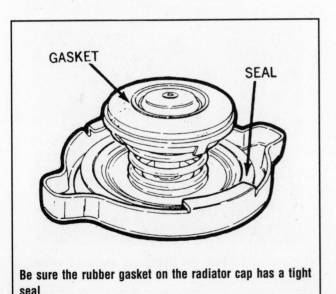

Be sure the rubber gasket on the radiator cap has a tight seal

CLEAN RADIATOR OF DEBRIS

Periodically clean any debris—leaves, paper, insects, etc.—from the radiator fins. Pick the large pieces off by hand. The smaller pieces can be washed away with water pressure from a hose.

Carefully straighten any bent radiator fins with a pair of needle nose pliers. Be careful—the fins are very soft. Don't wiggle the fins back and forth too much. Straighten them once and try not to move them again.

DRAIN AND REFILL

Completely draining and refilling the cooling system at least every two years will remove accumulated rust, scale and other deposits. Coolant in late model trucks is a 50/50 mixture of ethylene glycol and water for year round use. Use a good quality antifreeze with water pump lubricants, rust inhibitors and other corrosion inhibitors along with acid neutralizers.

1. Drain the existing antifreeze and coolant. Open the radiator and engine drain petcocks, or disconnect the bottom radiator hose, at the radiator outlet.

✳✳ CAUTION

When draining the coolant, keep in mind that cats and dogs are attracted by the ethylene glycol antifreeze, and are quite likely to drink any that is left in an uncovered container or in puddles on the ground. This will prove fatal in sufficient quantity. Always drain the coolant into a sealable container. Coolant should be reused unless it is contaminated or several years old.

➡**Before opening the radiator petcock, spray it with some penetrating lubricant.**

2. Close the petcock or reconnect the lower hose and fill the system with water.

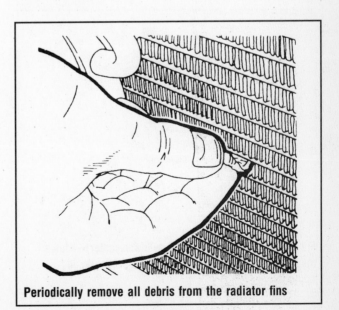

Periodically remove all debris from the radiator fins

3. Add a can of quality radiator flush.

4. Idle the engine until the upper radiator hose gets hot.

5. Drain the system again.

6. Repeat this process until the drained water is clear and free of scale.

7. Close all petcocks and connect all the hoses.

8. If equipped with a coolant recovery system, flush the reservoir with water and leave empty.

9. Determine the capacity of your coolant system (see capacities specifications). Add a 50/50 mix of quality antifreeze (ethylene glycol) and water to provide the desired protection.

10. Run the engine to operating temperature.

11. Stop the engine and check the coolant level.

12. Check the level of protection with an antifreeze tester, replace the cap and check for leaks.

Brake Master Cylinder

◆ See Figure 43

LEVEL CHECK

Check the level of the fluid in the brake master cylinder at the specified interval or more often. The brake master cylinder is located at the left rear corner of the engine compartment.

1. Park the truck on a level surface.

2. Clean all dirt from the area of the master cylinder reservoir cover.

3. Remove the top from the master cylinder reservoir. Be careful when doing this. Brake fluid that is dripped on painted surfaces will quickly destroy the paint.

4. The level should be maintained approximately ½ in. below the top of the reservoir.

5. If brake fluid is needed, use only a good quality brake fluid meeting specifications DOT-3 or DOT-4.

6. If necessary, add fluid to maintain the proper level and replace the top on the master cylinder securely.

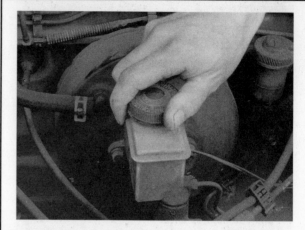

Clean the area around the brake master cylinder reservoir before removing the cap—loosen the cap by turning counterclockwise . . .

. . . lift off the cap . . .

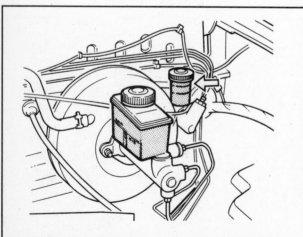

Fig. 43 Typical brake master cylinder(center)—clutch master cylinder (arrow) is smaller, but similar in appearance

. . . pull off the dust seal (this piece may stick inside the cap) . . .

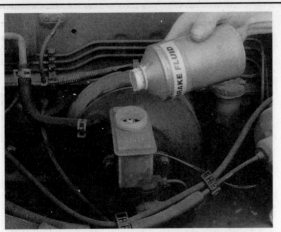

. . . and add fluid as necessary—be careful not to overfill the reservoir, as spilled fluid can damage painted surfaces

➡If the fluid level is constantly low, it would be a good idea to look into the matter. This is a good indication of problems elsewhere in the system.

Clutch Master Cylinder

LEVEL CHECK

The clutch master cylinder is located at the left rear corner of the engine compartment. Check the level in the clutch master cylinder in the same manner as the brake master cylinder. The level should be kept approximately ½ in. from the top of the cylinder. Use brake fluid in the clutch system. Be sure that the truck is on a level surface.

Manual Steering Gear

LEVEL CHECK

♦ See Figure 44

1. Clean the area around the plug and remove the plug from the top of the gear housing.
2. The oil level should just reach the plug hole.
3. If necessary, add 80W-90 gear oil until the fluid is at the proper level.
4. Reinstall the plug.

Power Steering Pump

LEVEL CHECK

♦ See Figure 45

The power steering reservoir is located on the left side of the engine. A dipstick is part of the cap. With the fluid hot—10 min-

Much like the brake master cylinder reservoir, the clutch master cylinder reservoir should be cleaned around the cap opening—remove the cap . . .

. . . and add fluid to the FULL level—indicated by two lines on the housing of the reservoir (upper line = FULL / lower line = LOW)

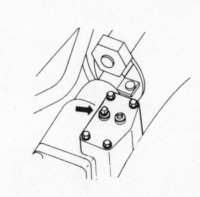

Fig. 44 Manual steering gear fill plug location

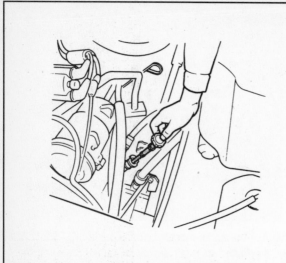

Fig. 45 Checking the power steering fluid level

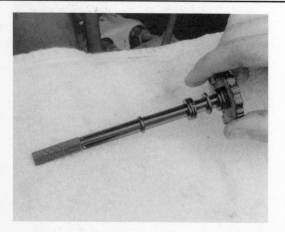

Remove the cap for the power steering unit, which also houses the power steering dipstick, and . . .

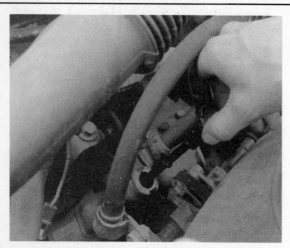

. . . read the level—with the fluid at normal operating temperature (after a minimum 10 minute drive), it should read between the two marks . . .

. . . if the level is low, add fluid—Type F automatic transmission fluid is recommended, however, commercially available power steering fluid is acceptable

utes of driving—the level should be between the F and L marks. Use Type F automatic transmission fluid.

Body Lubrication and Maintenance

LOCK CYLINDERS

Apply graphite lubricant sparingly through the key slot. Insert the key and operate the lock several times to be sure that the lubricant is worked into the lock cylinder.

DOOR HINGES AND HINGE CHECKS

Spray a silicone lubricant on the hinge pivot points to eliminate any binding conditions. Open and close the door several times to be sure that the lubricant is evenly and thoroughly distributed.

TAILGATE

Spray a silicone lubricant on all of the pivot and friction surfaces to eliminate any squeaks or binds. Work the tailgate to distribute the lubricant.

BODY DRAIN HOLES

Be sure that the drain holes in the doors and rocker panels are cleared of obstruction. A small screwdriver can be used to clear them of any debris.

Wheel Bearings

✳✳ CAUTION

Brake shoes contain asbestos, which has been determined to be a cancer causing agent. Never clean the brake surfaces with compressed air! Avoid inhaling any dust from any brake surface! When cleaning brake surfaces, use a commercially available brake cleaning fluid.

ADJUSTMENT

◆ **See Figures 46, 47, 48 and 49**

1. Raise and support the front end on jackstands. Check both the bearing axial play and the ease and smoothness of rotation.

Axial play should be 0; the wheel should rotate smoothly, with no perceptible bearing noise.

2. Remove the wheel. Remove the brake drum or disc brake caliper. Suspend the caliper out of the way. Don't disconnect the brake line.

3. Attach a spring scale to a wheel lug.

4. Pull the scale horizontally and check the force needed to start the wheel turning. The force should be 1.3–2.4 lbs. If the reading is not correct, proceed.

5. Remove the grease cap and cotter pin.

6. Tighten or loosen the hub nut until the correct pull rating is obtained.

7. Align the cotter pin holes and insert a new cotter pin. Replace the grease cap and wheel.

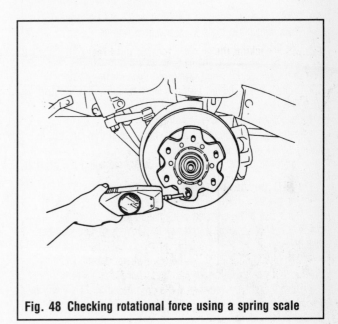

Fig. 48 Checking rotational force using a spring scale

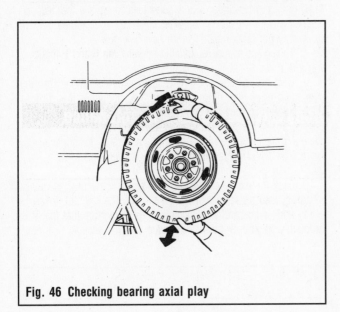

Fig. 46 Checking bearing axial play

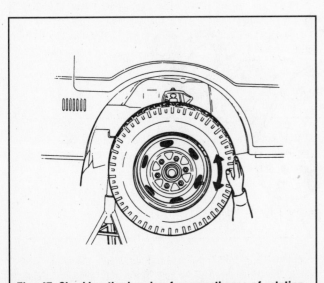

Fig. 47 Checking the bearing for smoothness of rotation

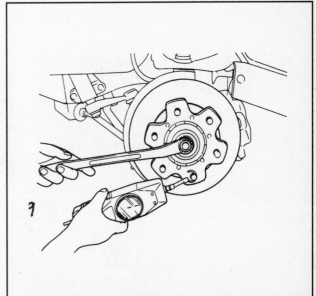

Fig. 49 Adjusting rotational force—tighten or loosen the hub nut until a reading of 1.3–2.4 lbs. is attained

REMOVAL, REPACKING AND INSTALLATION

▶ **See Figures 50 thru 55**

➡**Sodium-based grease is not compatible with lithium-based grease. Read the package labels and be careful not to mix the two types. If there is any doubt as to the type of grease used, completely clean the old grease from the bearing and hub before replacing.**

Before handling the bearings, there are a few things that you should remember to do and not to do.

Remember to DO the following:
• Remove all outside dirt from the housing before exposing the bearing.
• Treat a used bearing as gently as you would a new one.
• Work with clean tools in clean surroundings.
• Use clean, dry canvas gloves, or at least clean, dry hands.
• Clean solvents and flushing fluids are a must.
• Use clean paper when laying out the bearings to dry.
• Protect disassembled bearings from rust and dirt. Cover them up.
• Use clean rags to wipe bearings.
• Keep the bearings in oil-proof paper when they are to be stored or are not in use.
• Clean the inside of the housing before replacing the bearing.

Do NOT do the following:
• Don't work in dirty surroundings.
• Don't use dirty, chipped or damaged tools.
• Try not to work on wooden work benches or use wooden mallets.
• Don't handle bearings with dirty or moist hands.
• Do not use gasoline for cleaning; use a safe solvent.
• Do not spin-dry bearings with compressed air. They will be damaged.

• Do not spin dirty bearings.
• Avoid using cotton waste or dirty cloths to wipe bearings.
• Try not to scratch or nick bearing surfaces.
• Do not allow the bearing to come in contact with dirt or rust at any time.

1. Raise and support the front end on jackstands.
2. Remove the wheel.
3. Remove the grease cap, cotter pin, hub nut and flat washer.
4. On trucks with disc brakes, remove the caliper and suspend it out of the way without disconnecting the brake line. Slowly pull the hub from the spindle, positioning your hand to catch the outer bearing.
5. Remove the spacer, inner seal and inner bearing. Discard the seal.
6. Thoroughly clean the bearings and inside of the hub with a nonflammable solvent. Allow them to air dry.
7. Inspect the bearings for wear, damage, heat discoloration or other signs of fatigue. If they are at all suspect, replace them. When replacing bearings, it is a good idea to replace the bearing races as a set, as bearings do wear the races in a definite pattern which may not be compatible with new bearings.
8. To replace the races, carefully drive them out of the hub with a drift.
9. Coat the outside of the new races with clean wheel bearing grease and drive them into place until they bottom in their bore. Make certain that they are completely bottomed! A drift can be used as a driver, if you hammer evenly around the rim of the race and are very careful not to slip and scratch the surface of the race. A driver made for the purpose is much easier to use.
10. Pack the inside of the hub with clean wheel bearing grease until it is flush packed.
11. Pack each bearing with clean grease, making sure that it is thoroughly packed. Special devices are sold for packing bearings.

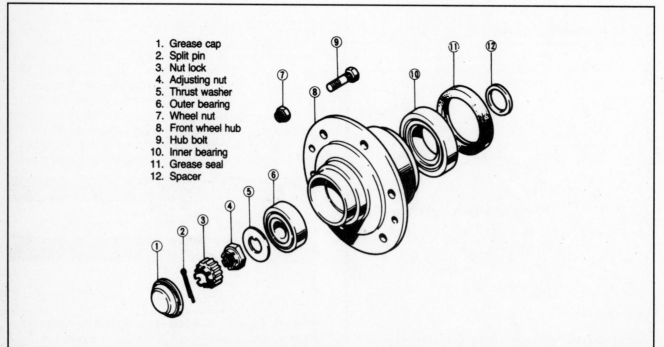

1. Grease cap
2. Split pin
3. Nut lock
4. Adjusting nut
5. Thrust washer
6. Outer bearing
7. Wheel nut
8. Front wheel hub
9. Hub bolt
10. Inner bearing
11. Grease seal
12. Spacer

Fig. 50 Exploded view of front hub components with drum brakes

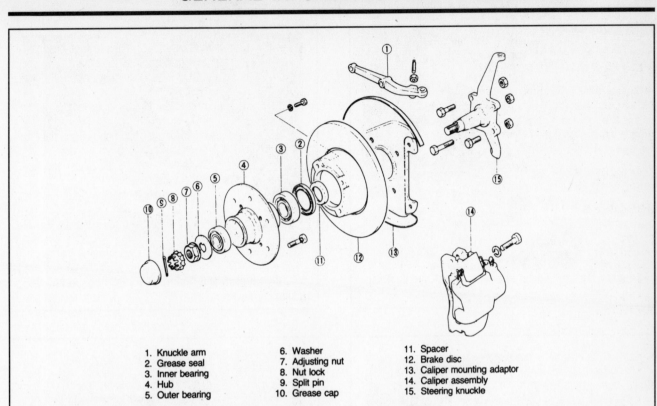

1. Knuckle arm
2. Grease seal
3. Inner bearing
4. Hub
5. Outer bearing
6. Washer
7. Adjusting nut
8. Nut lock
9. Split pin
10. Grease cap
11. Spacer
12. Brake disc
13. Caliper mounting adaptor
14. Caliper assembly
15. Steering knuckle

Fig. 51 Exploded view of front hub components with disc brakes, through 1984

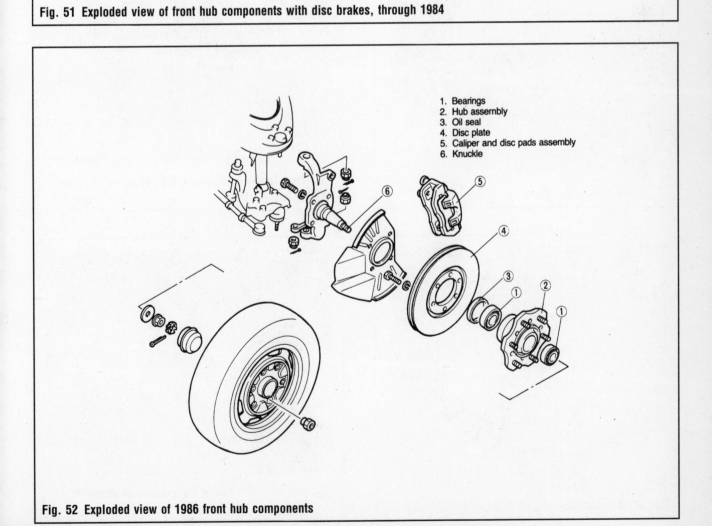

1. Bearings
2. Hub assembly
3. Oil seal
4. Disc plate
5. Caliper and disc pads assembly
6. Knuckle

Fig. 52 Exploded view of 1986 front hub components

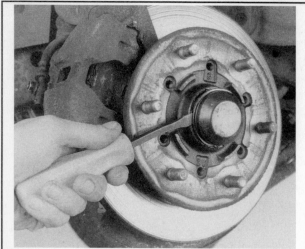

To repack the front wheel bearings, pry off the dust cap . . .

. . . then loosen and remove the adjusting nut and flat washer . . .

. . . remove the cotter pin . . .

. . . next, loosen and remove the caliper bracket-to-steering knuckle bolts . . .

. . . and the nut lock . . .

. . . pull off the complete caliper/bracket assembly . . .

. . . and suspend out of the way with a piece of wire or rope

With the seal removed, the inner bearing may be withdrawn from the hub

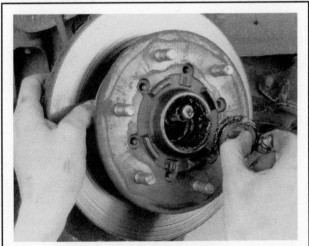

Now grab hold of the rotor and carefully pull it—be sure to catch the outer wheel bearing as you pull the rotor off

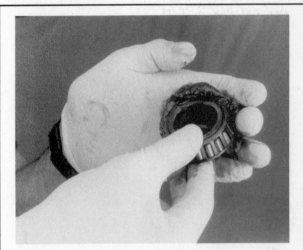

Thoroughly pack the bearing with fresh, high temperature wheel-bearing grease before installation

Pry off the rear grease seal to get to the inner wheel bearing

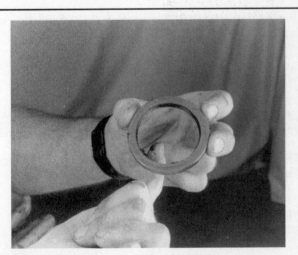

Apply a thin coat of fresh grease to the new inner bearing seal lip

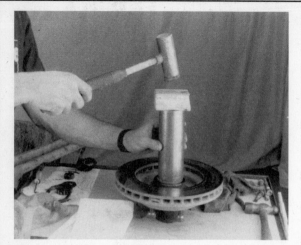

Use a suitably sized driver to install the inner bearing seal to the hub

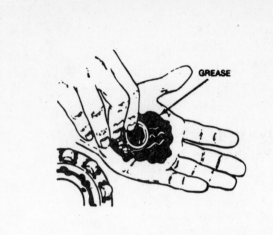

Fig. 54 Thoroughly pack the bearings with grease

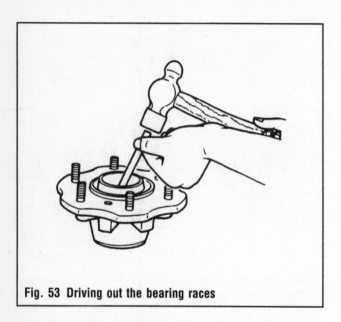

Fig. 53 Driving out the bearing races

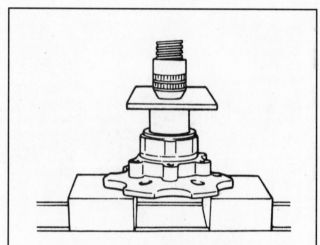

Fig. 55 Pressing the seal into place—a block of wood and a hammer can also be used

They are inexpensive and readily available. If you don't have one, just make certain that the bearing is as full of grease as possible by working it in with your fingers.

12. Install the inner bearing and seal. Drive the seal into place carefully until it is seated.

13. Install the spacer and the hub on the spindle.
14. Install the outer bearing, flat washer and hub nut.
15. Adjust the bearing as explained above.
16. Install the nut cap, cotter pin and grease cap. Install the wheel.

TRAILER TOWING

General Recommendations

Your vehicle was primarily designed to carry passengers and cargo. It is important to remember that towing a trailer will place additional loads on your vehicles engine, drivetrain, steering, braking and other systems. However, if you decide to tow a trailer, using the prior equipment is a must.

Local laws may require specific equipment such as trailer brakes or fender mounted mirrors. Check your local laws.

Trailer Weight

The weight of the trailer is the most important factor. A good weight-to-horsepower ratio is about 35:1, 35 lbs. of Gross Combined Weight (GCW) for every horsepower your engine develops.

Multiply the engine's rated horsepower by 35 and subtract the weight of the vehicle passengers and luggage. The number remaining is the approximate ideal maximum weight you should tow, although a numerically higher axle ratio can help compensate for heavier weight.

Hitch (Tongue) Weight

Calculate the hitch weight in order to select a proper hitch. The weight of the hitch is usually 9–11% of the trailer gross weight and should be measured with the trailer loaded. Hitches fall into various categories: those that mount on the frame and rear bumper, the bolt-on type, or the weld-on distribution type used for larger trailers. Axle mounted or clamp-on bumper hitches should never be used.

Check the gross weight rating of your trailer. Tongue weight is usually figured as 10% of gross trailer weight. Therefore, a trailer with a maximum gross weight of 2000 lbs. will have a maximum tongue weight of 200 lbs. Class I trailers fall into this category. Class II trailers are those with a gross weight rating of 2000–3000 lbs., while Class III trailers fall into the 3500–6000 lbs. category. Class IV trailers are those over 6000 lbs. and are for use with fifth wheel trucks, only.

When you've determined the hitch that you'll need, follow the manufacturer's installation instructions, exactly, especially when it comes to fastener torques. The hitch will subjected to a lot of stress and good hitches come with hardened bolts. Never substitute an inferior bolt for a hardened bolt.

Cooling

ENGINE

Overflow Tank

One of the most common, if not THE most common, problems associated with trailer towing is engine overheating. If you have a cooling system without an expansion tank, you'll definitely need to get an aftermarket expansion tank kit, preferably one with at least a 2 quart capacity. These kits are easily installed on the radiator's overflow hose, and come with a pressure cap designed for expansion tanks.

Flex Fan

Another helpful accessory for vehicles using a belt-driven radiator fan is a flex fan. These fans are large diameter units designed to provide more airflow at low speeds, by using fan blades that have deeply cupped surfaces. The blades then flex, or flatten out, at high speed, when less cooling air is needed. These fans are far lighter in weight than stock fans, requiring less horsepower to drive them. Also, they are far quieter than stock fans. If you do decide to replace your stock fan with a flex fan, note that if your vehicle has a fan clutch, a spacer will be needed between the flex fan and water pump hub.

Oil Cooler

Aftermarket engine oil coolers are helpful for prolonging engine oil life and reducing overall engine temperatures. Both of these

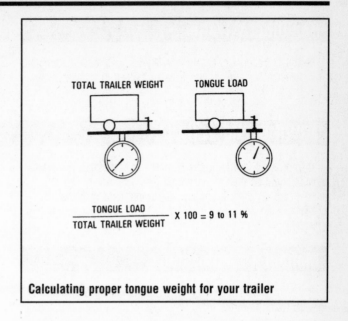

Calculating proper tongue weight for your trailer

factors increase engine life. While not absolutely necessary in towing Class I and some Class II trailers, they are recommended for heavier Class II and all Class III towing. Engine oil cooler systems usually consist of an adapter, screwed on in place of the oil filter, a remote filter mounting and a multi-tube, finned heat exchanger, which is mounted in front of the radiator or air conditioning condenser.

TRANSMISSION

An automatic transmission is usually recommended for trailer towing. Modern automatics have proven reliable and, of course, easy to operate, in trailer towing. The increased load of a trailer, however, causes an increase in the temperature of the automatic transmission fluid. Heat is the worst enemy of an automatic transmission. As the temperature of the fluid increases, the life of the fluid decreases.

It is essential, therefore, that you install an automatic transmission cooler. The cooler, which consists of a multi-tube, finned heat exchanger, is usually installed in front of the radiator or air conditioning compressor, and hooked in-line with the transmission cooler tank inlet line. Follow the cooler manufacturer's installation instructions.

Select a cooler of at least adequate capacity, based upon the combined gross weights of the vehicle and trailer.

Cooler manufacturers recommend that you use an aftermarket cooler in addition to, and not instead of, the present cooling tank in your radiator. If you do want to use it in place of the radiator cooling tank, get a cooler at least two sizes larger than normally necessary.

➡**A transmission cooler can, sometimes, cause slow or harsh shifting in the transmission during cold weather, until the fluid has a chance to come up to normal operating temperature. Some coolers can be purchased with or retrofitted with a temperature bypass valve which will allow fluid flow through the cooler only when the fluid has reached above a certain operating temperature.**

Handling A Trailer

Towing a trailer with ease and safety requires a certain amount of experience. It's a good idea to learn the feel of a trailer by practicing turning, stopping and backing in an open area such as an empty parking lot.

TOWING THE VEHICLE

Do not attach chains to the bumpers or bracketing. All attachments should be made to structural members. Safety chains should also be used. If you are flat towing, remember that the power steering and power brake assists will not work with the engine **OFF.**

Manual Transmission

If the transmission and rear axle are not damaged, the vehicle may be towed from the front. Otherwise it should be lifted and towed from the rear. Be sure that the parking brake is **OFF** and the transmission is in **NEUTRAL.**

Automatic Transmission

With the automatic transmission, the rear wheels must be lifted off the ground or the driveshaft must be disconnected. If this is not done, the transmission may be damaged.

JUMP STARTING A DEAD BATTERY

Whenever a vehicle is jump started, precautions must be followed in order to prevent the possibility of personal injury. Remember that batteries contain a small amount of explosive hydrogen gas which is a by-product of battery charging. Sparks should always be avoided when working around batteries, especially when attaching jumper cables. To minimize the possibility of accidental sparks, follow the procedure carefully.

✳✳ CAUTION

NEVER hook the batteries up in a series circuit or the entire electrical system will go up in smoke, including the starter!

Vehicles equipped with a diesel engine may utilize two 12 volt batteries. If so, the batteries are connected in a parallel circuit (positive terminal to positive terminal, negative terminal to negative terminal). Hooking the batteries up in parallel circuit increases battery cranking power without increasing total battery voltage output. Output remains at 12 volts. On the other hand, hooking two 12 volt batteries up in a series circuit (positive terminal to negative terminal, positive terminal to negative terminal) increases total battery output to 24 volts (12 volts plus 12 volts).

Jump Starting Precautions

• Be sure that both batteries are of the same voltage. Vehicles covered by this manual and most vehicles on the road today utilize a 12 volt charging system.
• Be sure that both batteries are of the same polarity (have the same terminal, in most cases NEGATIVE grounded).
• Be sure that the vehicles are not touching or a short could occur.
• On serviceable batteries, be sure the vent cap holes are not obstructed.

• Do not smoke or allow sparks anywhere near the batteries.
• In cold weather, make sure the battery electrolyte is not frozen. This can occur more readily in a battery that has been in a state of discharge.
• Do not allow electrolyte to contact your skin or clothing.

Jump Starting Procedure

1. Make sure that the voltages of the 2 batteries are the same. Most batteries and charging systems are of the 12 volt variety.
2. Pull the jumping vehicle (with the good battery) into a position so the jumper cables can reach the dead battery and that vehicle's engine. Make sure that the vehicles do NOT touch.

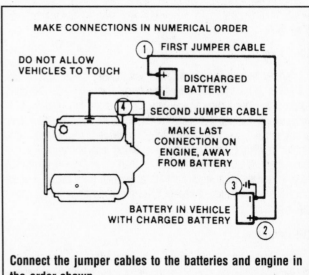

MAKE CONNECTIONS IN NUMERICAL ORDER

DO NOT ALLOW VEHICLES TO TOUCH

1 FIRST JUMPER CABLE

DISCHARGED BATTERY

4 SECOND JUMPER CABLE

MAKE LAST CONNECTION ON ENGINE, AWAY FROM BATTERY

3

BATTERY IN VEHICLE WITH CHARGED BATTERY

2

Connect the jumper cables to the batteries and engine in the order shown

3. Place the transmissions/transaxles of both vehicles in **Neutral** (MT) or **P** (AT), as applicable, then firmly set their parking brakes.

➡**If necessary for safety reasons, the hazard lights on both vehicles may be operated throughout the entire procedure without significantly increasing the difficulty of jumping the dead battery.**

4. Turn all lights and accessories OFF on both vehicles. Make sure the ignition switches on both vehicles are turned to the **OFF** position.

5. Cover the battery cell caps with a rag, but do not cover the terminals.

6. Make sure the terminals on both batteries are clean and free of corrosion or proper electrical connection will be impeded. If necessary, clean the battery terminals before proceeding.

7. Identify the positive (+) and negative (−) terminals on both batteries.

8. Connect the first jumper cable to the positive (+) terminal of the dead battery, then connect the other end of that cable to the positive (+) terminal of the booster (good) battery.

9. Connect one end of the other jumper cable to the negative (−) terminal on the booster battery and the final cable clamp to an engine bolt head, alternator bracket or other solid, metallic point on the engine with the dead battery. Try to pick a ground on the engine that is positioned away from the battery in order to minimize the possibility of the 2 clamps touching should one loosen during the procedure. DO NOT connect this clamp to the negative (−) terminal of the bad battery.

✳✳ CAUTION

Be very careful to keep the jumper cables away from moving parts (cooling fan, belts, etc.) on both engines.

10. Check to make sure that the cables are routed away from any moving parts, then start the donor vehicle's engine. Run the engine at moderate speed for several minutes to allow the dead battery a chance to receive some initial charge.

11. With the donor vehicle's engine still running slightly above idle, try to start the vehicle with the dead battery. Crank the engine for no more than 10 seconds at a time and let the starter cool for at least 20 seconds between tries. If the vehicle does not start in 3 tries, it is likely that something else is also wrong or that the battery needs additional time to charge.

12. Once the vehicle is started, allow it to run at idle for a few seconds to make sure that it is operating properly.

13. Turn ON the headlights, heater blower and, if equipped, the rear defroster of both vehicles in order to reduce the severity of voltage spikes and subsequent risk of damage to the vehicles' electrical systems when the cables are disconnected. This step is especially important to any vehicle equipped with computer control modules.

14. Carefully disconnect the cables in the reverse order of connection. Start with the negative cable that is attached to the engine ground, then the negative cable on the donor battery. Disconnect the positive cable from the donor battery and finally, disconnect the positive cable from the formerly dead battery. Be careful when disconnecting the cables from the positive terminals not to allow the alligator clips to touch any metal on either vehicle or a short and sparks will occur.

JACKING

▶ **See Figures 56, 57 and 58**

Your vehicle was supplied with a jack for emergency road repairs. This jack is fine for changing a flat tire or other short term procedures not requiring you to go beneath the vehicle. If it is used in an emergency situation, carefully follow the instructions provided either with the jack or in your owner's manual. Do not attempt to use the jack on any portions of the vehicle other than specified by the vehicle manufacturer. Always block the diagonally opposite wheel when using a jack.

A more convenient way of jacking is the use of a garage or floor jack.

Never place the jack under the radiator, engine or transmission components. Severe and expensive damage will result when the jack is raised. Additionally, never jack under the floorpan or bodywork; the metal will deform.

Whenever you plan to work under the vehicle, you must support it on jackstands or ramps. Never use cinder blocks or stacks of wood to support the vehicle, even if you're only going to be under it for a few minutes. Never crawl under the vehicle

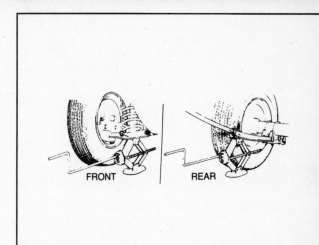

Fig. 56 Jacking points for a scissors type jack on 1972–84 models

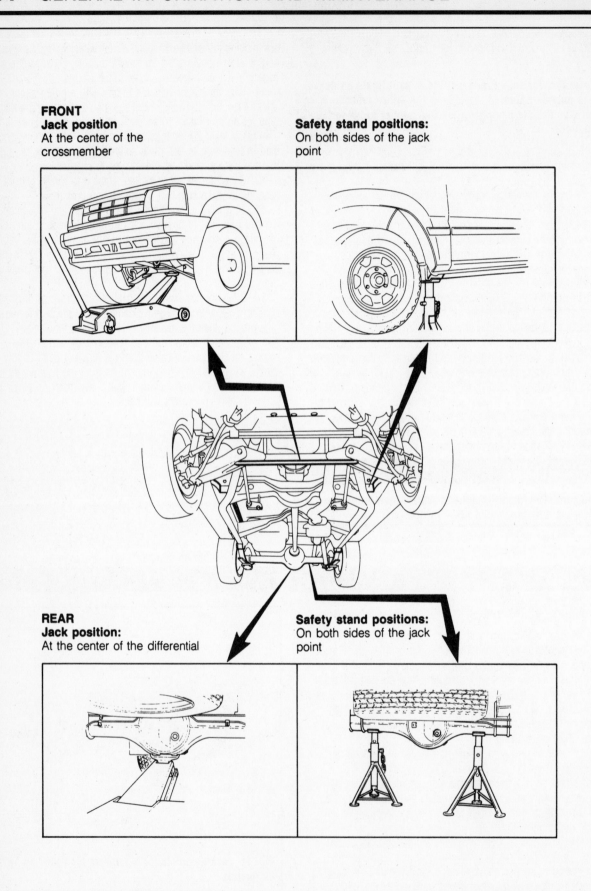

FRONT
Jack position
At the center of the
crossmember

Safety stand positions:
On both sides of the jack
point

REAR
Jack position:
At the center of the differential

Safety stand positions:
On both sides of the jack
point

Fig. 57 Jacking points for 1986 models

Fig. 58 Jacking points for a hydraulic type jack on 1972–84 models

Jack the rear end using the rear differential and place the jackstand under the axle tube as close to the leaf spring as possible or, . . .

Jack the front end using the center crossmember . . .

. . . if working on the rear suspension, place the jackstand under the rear frame rail

. . . and place a sturdy jackstand under the front frame rail

when it is supported only by the tire-changing jack or other floor jack.

➡**Always position a block of wood or small rubber pad on top of the jack or jackstand to protect the lifting point's finish when lifting or supporting the vehicle.**

Small hydraulic, screw, or scissors jacks are satisfactory for raising the vehicle. Drive-on trestles or ramps are also a handy and safe way to both raise and support the vehicle. Be careful though, some ramps may be too steep to drive your vehicle onto without scraping the front bottom panels. Never support the vehicle on any suspension member (unless specifically instructed to do so by a repair manual) or by an underbody panel.

Jacking Precautions

The following safety points cannot be overemphasized:
• Always block the opposite wheel or wheels to keep the vehicle from rolling off the jack.
• When raising the front of the vehicle, firmly apply the parking brake.

• When the drive wheels are to remain on the ground, leave the vehicle in gear to help prevent it from rolling.
• Always use jackstands to support the vehicle when you are working underneath. Place the stands beneath the vehicle's jacking brackets. Before climbing underneath, rock the vehicle a bit to make sure it is firmly supported.

HOW TO BUY A USED VEHICLE

Many people believe that a two or three year old used car or truck is a better buy than a new vehicle. This may be true as most new vehicles suffer the heaviest depreciation in the first two years and, at three years old, a vehicle is usually not old enough to present a lot of costly repair problems. But keep in mind, when buying a non-warranted automobile, there are no guarantees. Whatever the age of the used vehicle you might want to purchase, this section and a little patience should increase your chances of selecting one that is safe and dependable.

Tips

1. First decide what model you want, and how much you want to spend.
2. Check the used car lots and your local newspaper ads. Privately owned vehicles are usually less expensive, however, you may not get a warranty that, in many cases, comes with a used vehicle purchased from a lot. Of course, some aftermarket warranties may not be worth the extra money, so this is a point you will have to debate and consider based on your priorities.
3. Never shop at night. The glare of the lights make it easy to miss faults on the body caused by accident or rust repair.
4. Try to get the name and phone number of the previous owner. Contact him/her and ask about the vehicle. If the owner of a lot refuses this information, look for a vehicle somewhere else.
A private seller can tell you about the vehicle and maintenance. But remember, there's no law requiring honesty from private citizens selling used vehicles. There is a law that forbids tampering with or turning back the odometer mileage. This includes both the private citizen and the lot owner. The law also requires that the seller or anyone transferring ownership of the vehicle must provide the buyer with a signed statement indicating the mileage on the odometer at the time of transfer.
5. You may wish to contact the National Highway Traffic Safety Administration (NHTSA) to find out if the vehicle has ever been included in a manufacturer's recall. Write down the year, model and serial number before you buy the vehicle, then contact NHTSA (there should be a 1-800 number that your phone company's information line can supply). If the vehicle was listed for a recall, make sure the needed repairs were made.
6. Refer to the Used Vehicle Checklist in this section and check all the items on the vehicle you are considering. Some items are more important than others. Only you know how much

money you can afford for repairs, and depending on the price of the vehicle, may consider performing any needed work yourself. Beware, however, of trouble in areas that will affect operation, safety or emission. Problems in the Used Vehicle Checklist break down as follows:
• Numbers 1–8: Two or more problems in these areas indicate a lack of maintenance. You should beware.
• Numbers 9–13: Problems here tend to indicate a lack of proper care, however, these can usually be corrected with a tune-up or relatively simple parts replacement.
• Numbers 14–17: Problems in the engine or transmission can be very expensive. Unless you are looking for a project, walk away from any vehicle with problems in 2 or more of these areas.
7. If you are satisfied with the apparent condition of the vehicle, take it to an independent diagnostic center or mechanic for a complete check. If you have a state inspection program, have it inspected immediately before purchase, or specify on the bill of sale that the sale is conditional on passing state inspection.
8. Road test the vehicle—refer to the Road Test Checklist in this section. If your original evaluation and the road test agree—the rest is up to you.

USED VEHICLE CHECKLIST

➡**The numbers on the illustrations refer to the numbers on this checklist.**

1. Mileage: Average mileage is about 12,000–15,000 miles per year. More than average mileage may indicate hard usage or could indicate many highway miles (which could be less detrimental than half as many tough around town miles).
2. Paint: Check around the tailpipe, molding and windows for overspray indicating that the vehicle has been repainted.
3. Rust: Check fenders, doors, rocker panels, window moldings, wheelwells, floorboards, under floormats, and in the trunk for signs of rust. Any rust at all will be a problem. There is no way to permanently stop the spread of rust, except to replace the part or panel.

➡**If rust repair is suspected, try using a magnet to check for body filler. A magnet should stick to the sheet metal parts of the body, but will not adhere to areas with large amounts of filler.**

4. Body appearance: Check the moldings, bumpers, grille, vinyl roof, glass, doors, trunk lid and body panels for general overall condition. Check for misalignment, loose hold-down clips, ripples, scratches in glass, welding in the trunk, severe misalignment of body panels or ripples, any of which may indicate crash work.

5. Leaks: Get down and look under the vehicle. There are no normal leaks, other than water from the air conditioner evaporator.

6. Tires: Check the tire air pressure. One old trick is to pump the tire pressure up to make the vehicle roll easier. Check the tread wear, then open the trunk and check the spare too. Uneven wear is a clue that the front end may need an alignment.

7. Shock absorbers: Check the shock absorbers by forcing downward sharply on each corner of the vehicle. Good shocks will not allow the vehicle to bounce more than once after you let go.

8. Interior: Check the entire interior. You're looking for an interior condition that agrees with the overall condition of the vehicle. Reasonable wear is expected, but be suspicious of new seat covers on sagging seats, new pedal pads, and worn armrests. These indicate an attempt to cover up hard use. Pull back the carpets and look for evidence of water leaks or flooding. Look for missing hardware, door handles, control knobs, etc. Check lights and signal operations. Make sure all accessories (air conditioner, heater, radio, etc.) work. Check windshield wiper operation.

9. Belts and Hoses: Open the hood, then check all belts and hoses for wear, cracks or weak spots.

10. Battery: Low electrolyte level, corroded terminals and/or cracked case indicate a lack of maintenance.

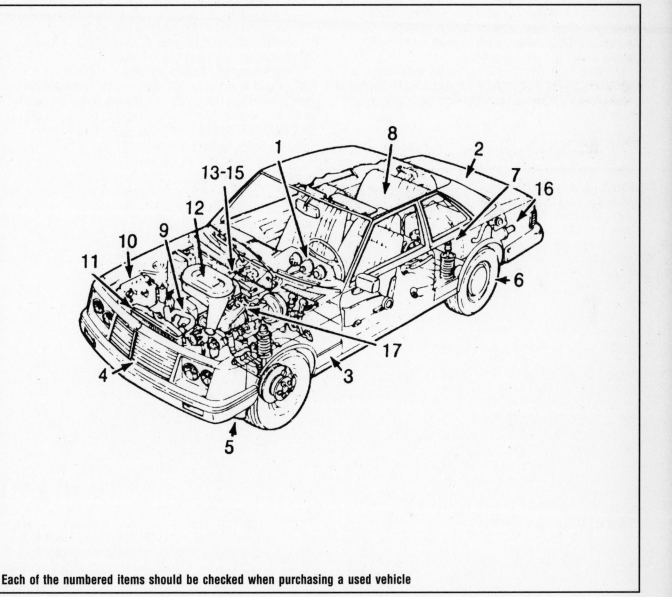

Each of the numbered items should be checked when purchasing a used vehicle

11. Radiator: Look for corrosion or rust in the coolant indicating a lack of maintenance.

12. Air filter: A severely dirty air filter would indicate a lack of maintenance.

13. Ignition wires: Check the ignition wires for cracks, burned spots, or wear. Worn wires will have to be replaced.

14. Oil level: If the oil level is low, chances are the engine uses oil or leaks. Beware of water in the oil (there is probably a cracked block or bad head gasket), excessively thick oil (which is often used to quiet a noisy engine), or thin, dirty oil with a distinct gasoline smell (this may indicate internal engine problems).

15. Automatic Transmission: Pull the transmission dipstick out when the engine is running. The level should read FULL, and the fluid should be clear or bright red. Dark brown or black fluid that has distinct burnt odor, indicates a transmission in need of repair or overhaul.

16. Exhaust: Check the color of the exhaust smoke. Blue smoke indicates, among other problems, worn rings. Black smoke can indicate burnt valves or carburetor problems. Check the exhaust system for leaks; it can be expensive to replace.

17. Spark Plugs: Remove one or all of the spark plugs (the most accessible will do, though all are preferable). An engine in good condition will show plugs with a light tan or gray deposit on the firing tip.

ROAD TEST CHECKLIST

1. Engine Performance: The vehicle should be peppy whether cold or warm, with adequate power and good pickup. It should respond smoothly through the gears.

2. Brakes: They should provide quick, firm stops with no noise, pulling or brake fade.

3. Steering: Sure control with no binding harshness, or looseness and no shimmy in the wheel should be expected. Noise or vibration from the steering wheel when turning the vehicle means trouble.

4. Clutch (Manual Transmission/Transaxle): Clutch action should give quick, smooth response with easy shifting. The clutch pedal should have free-play before it disengages the clutch. Start the engine, set the parking brake, put the transmission in first gear and slowly release the clutch pedal. The engine should begin to stall when the pedal is $\frac{1}{2}-\frac{3}{4}$ of the way up.

5. Automatic Transmission/Transaxle: The transmission should shift rapidly and smoothly, with no noise, hesitation, or slipping.

6. Differential: No noise or thumps should be present. Differentials have no normal leaks.

7. Driveshaft/Universal Joints: Vibration and noise could mean driveshaft problems. Clicking at low speed or coast conditions means worn U-joints.

8. Suspension: Try hitting bumps at different speeds. A vehicle that bounces excessively has weak shock absorbers or struts. Clunks mean worn bushings or ball joints.

9. Frame/Body: Wet the tires and drive in a straight line. Tracks should show two straight lines, not four. Four tire tracks indicate a frame/body bent by collision damage. If the tires can't be wet for this purpose, have a friend drive along behind you and see if the vehicle appears to be traveling in a straight line.

Piston Engine Maintenance Intervals Chart
Intervals are miles or miles/months

Change engine oil and oil filter	7,500/12*
Check drive belts	15,000/12
Replace drive belts	30,000/24
Check & adjust valve clearance	15,000/12
Check and, if necessary, replace ignition points and condenser	4,000/4
Check and, if necessary, replace distributor cap and rotor	12,000/12
Check & adjust ignition timing, 1972–78	6,000/6
Check & adjust ignition timing, 1979–86	50,000/60
Check & adjust idle speed on B1600 & 1800	4,000/4
Check & adjust idle speed on B2000	15,000/12
Check & adjust throttle position system	15,000, then every 50,000
Replace fuel filter	12,000/12
Inspect fuel system for leaks	6,000/6
Replace air cleaner element	24,000/24*
Replace spark plugs, 1972–78	6,000/6
Replace spark plugs, 1979–86	30,000/24*
Replace ignition wires	24,000/24
Tighten intake and exhaust manifold bolts	8,000/12
Tighten the B1600 & 1800 cylinder head bolts	8,000/12
Check engine compression pressure	24,000/24
Replace PCV valve	24,000/24
Replace vacuum, PCV, and secondary air hoses	50,000/60
Replace fuel system hoses, fuel vapor hoses, cooling system hoses, and fuel filler cap	50,000/60
Clean PCV system	50,000/60*
Inspect evaporative system for leaks and replace canister	50,000/60
Replace oxygen sensor	50,000/60
Replace engine timing belt	60,000/60
Check coolant condition and check cooling system for leaks	15,000/12*
Change engine coolant	30,000/24*
Check A/C system and drive belt	15,000/12

*Under severe service conditions (short trips at very cold temperatures, driving in heavy dust, or towing a trailer), change the engine oil and filter every 3 months or 3,000 miles, whichever occurs first. Service the air cleaner filter, PCV system, and spark plugs at more frequent intervals. If the truck is operated in deep water, the manual transmission and rear axle fluids should be changed immediately, and the front wheel bearings should be repacked.

Rotary Engine Maintenance Intervals Chart

Intervals are miles or miles/months

Change engine oil and filter	4,000/4*
Inspect accessory drive belts	4,000/4*
Inspect metering oil pump	4,000/4
Check engine compression pressure	10,000/12
Inspect starting assist system	once each winter
Check idle speed	4,000/4
Check idle mixture	12,000/12
Replace fuel filter	10,000/12*
Replace air cleaner element	10,000/12*
Check carburetor float level	14,000/12
Inspect and lubricate carburetor linkage	10,000/12*
Inspect fuel line connections	4,000/4
Inspect and replace, if needed, evap canister	12,000/12
Check ignition timing	4,000/4
Check and, if needed, replace points	4,000/4
Check and, if needed, replace distributor cap	10,000/12
Check and, if needed, replace rotor and condensers	10,000/12
Replace spark plugs	4,000/4*
Inspect spark plug wires	12,000/12
Replace spark plugs wires	24,000/24
Inspect distributor cam	10,000/10
Inspect and, if needed, replace PCV valve	24,000/24*
Inspect and, if needed, replace PCV hoses	12,000/12*
Inspect air pump	12,000/12
Inspect thermal reactor	12,000/12
Tighten exhaust pipe flange bolts	12,000/12
Inspect and, if needed, replace coolant hoses	12,000/12

*Under severe service conditions (short trips at very cold temperatures, driving in heavy dust, or towing a trailer), change the engine oil and filter every 3 months or 3,000 miles, whichever occurs first. Service the air cleaner filter, PCV system, and spark plugs at more frequent intervals. If the truck is operated in deep water, the manual transmission and rear axle fluids should be changed immediately, and the front wheel bearings should be repacked.

Chassis Maintenance Intervals Chart

Intervals are miles or miles/months

Check brake and hydraulic clutch fluid level and check for leaks in system	15,000/12
Replace brake and hydraulic clutch fluid	60,000/48
Inspect brake front and rear brake linings and hoses	15,000/12*
Inspect ball joint, steering linkage seals	30,000/24
Lubricate front wheel bearings	30,000
Inspect power steering fluid level, hoses, and belt	15,000/12
Change automatic transmission fluid	30,000*
Check manual transmission level	12 months*
Check drive axle fluid	12 months*
Change drive axle fluid	50,000/60
Check all exhaust system connections and inspect for excessive corrosion	15,000/12

*Under severe service conditions (short trips at very cold temperatures, driving in heavy dust, or towing a trailer), change the engine oil and filter every 3 months or 3,000 miles, whichever occurs first. Service the air cleaner filter, PCV system, and spark plugs at more frequent intervals. If the truck is operated in deep water, the manual transmission and rear axle fluids should be changed immediately, and the front wheel bearings should be repacked.

Capacities Chart

Engine Displacement (cc)	Engine Oil with Filter (qts.)	Transmission (pts.)			Drive Axle	Fuel Tank (gal.)	Cooling System (qts.)	
		4-Spd	5-Spd	Auto.			w/AC	wo/AC
1308	6.8	3.6	—	13.2	2.7	21.1	10.2	10.2
1586	4.8	3.2	—	—	2.7	11.7	6.8	6.8
1796	4.8	2.9	3.6	—	2.7	①	7.6	7.6
1970	5.0	3.2	3.6	13.2	2.8	①	7.5	7.5
1998	4.5	3.0	2.6	—	2.8	②	7.9	7.9
2209	5.3	—	3.6	—	2.8	①	14.3	14.3

① Long bed: 15.0
   Short bed: 17.5
② Long bed: 14.6
   Short bed: 15.6

ENGLISH TO METRIC CONVERSION: MASS (WEIGHT)

Current **mass** measurement is expressed in pounds and ounces (lbs. & ozs.). The metric unit of mass (or weight) is the kilogram (kg). Even although this table does not show conversion of masses (weights) larger than 15 lbs, it is easy to calculate larger units by following the data immediately below.

To convert ounces (oz.) to grams (g): multiply th number of ozs. by 28
To convert grams (g) to ounces (oz.): multiply the number of grams by .035

To convert pounds (lbs.) to kilograms (kg): multiply the number of lbs. by .45
To convert kilograms (kg) to pounds (lbs.): multiply the number of kilograms by 2.2

lbs	kg	lbs	kg	oz	kg	oz	kg
0.1	0.04	0.9	0.41	0.1	0.003	0.9	0.024
0.2	0.09	1	0.4	0.2	0.005	1	0.03
0.3	0.14	2	0.9	0.3	0.008	2	0.06
0.4	0.18	3	1.4	0.4	0.011	3	0.08
0.5	0.23	4	1.8	0.5	0.014	4	0.11
0.6	0.27	5	2.3	0.6	0.017	5	0.14
0.7	0.32	10	4.5	0.7	0.020	10	0.28
0.8	0.36	15	6.8	0.8	0.023	15	0.42

ENGLISH TO METRIC CONVERSION: TEMPERATURE

To convert Fahrenheit (°F) to Celsius (°C): take number of °F and subtract 32; multiply result by 5; divide result by 9

To convert Celsius (°C) to Fahrenheit (°F): take number of °C and multiply by 9; divide result by 5; add 32 to total

Fahrenheit (F)	Celsius (C)			Fahrenheit (F)	Celsius (C)			Fahrenheit (F)	Celsius (C)		
°F	°C	°C	°F	°F	°C	°C	°F	°F	°C	°C	°F
−40	−40	−38	−36.4	80	26.7	18	64.4	215	101.7	80	176
−35	−37.2	−36	−32.8	85	29.4	20	68	220	104.4	85	185
−30	−34.4	−34	−29.2	90	32.2	22	71.6	225	107.2	90	194
−25	−31.7	−32	−25.6	95	35.0	24	75.2	230	110.0	95	202
−20	−28.9	−30	−22	100	37.8	26	78.8	235	112.8	100	212
−15	−26.1	−28	−18.4	105	40.6	28	82.4	240	115.6	105	221
−10	−23.3	−26	−14.8	110	43.3	30	86	245	118.3	110	230
−5	−20.6	−24	−11.2	115	46.1	32	89.6	250	121.1	115	239
0	−17.8	−22	−7.6	120	48.9	34	93.2	255	123.9	120	248
1	−17.2	−20	−4	125	51.7	36	96.8	260	126.6	125	257
2	−16.7	−18	−0.4	130	54.4	38	100.4	265	129.4	130	266
3	−16.1	−16	3.2	135	57.2	40	104	270	132.2	135	275
4	−15.6	−14	6.8	140	60.0	42	107.6	275	135.0	140	284
5	−15.0	−12	10.4	145	62.8	44	112.2	280	137.8	145	293
10	−12.2	−10	14	150	65.6	46	114.8	285	140.6	150	302
15	−9.4	−8	17.6	155	68.3	48	118.4	290	143.3	155	311
20	−6.7	−6	21.2	160	71.1	50	122	295	146.1	160	320
25	−3.9	−4	24.8	165	73.9	52	125.6	300	148.9	165	329
30	−1.1	−2	28.4	170	76.7	54	129.2	305	151.7	170	338
35	1.7	0	32	175	79.4	56	132.8	310	154.4	175	347
40	4.4	2	35.6	180	82.2	58	136.4	315	157.2	180	356
45	7.2	4	39.2	185	85.0	60	140	320	160.0	185	365
50	10.0	6	42.8	190	87.8	62	143.6	325	162.8	190	374
55	12.8	8	46.4	195	90.6	64	147.2	330	165.6	195	383
60	15.6	10	50	200	93.3	66	150.8	335	168.3	200	392
65	18.3	12	53.6	205	96.1	68	154.4	340	171.1	205	401
70	21.1	14	57.2	210	98.9	70	158	345	173.9	210	410
75	23.9	16	60.8	212	100.0	75	167	350	176.7	215	414

ENGLISH TO METRIC CONVERSION: LENGTH

To convert inches (ins.) to millimeters (mm): multiply number of inches by 25.4

To convert millimeters (mm) to inches (ins.): multiply number of millimeters by .04

Inches		Decimals	Milli-meters	Inches to millimeters inches	mm	Inches		Decimals	Milli-meters	Inches to millimeters inches	mm
	1/64	0.051625	0.3969	0.0001	0.00254		33/64	0.515625	13.0969	0.6	15.24
1/32		0.03125	0.7937	0.0002	0.00508	17/32		0.53125	13.4937	0.7	17.78
	3/64	0.046875	1.1906	0.0003	0.00762		35/64	0.546875	13.8906	0.8	20.32
1/16		0.0625	1.5875	0.0004	0.01016	9/16		0.5625	14.2875	0.9	22.86
	5/64	0.078125	1.9844	0.0005	0.01270		37/64	0.578125	14.6844	1	25.4
3/32		0.09375	2.3812	0.0006	0.01524	19/32		0.59375	15.0812	2	50.8
	7/64	0.109375	2.7781	0.0007	0.01778		39/64	0.609375	15.4781	3	76.2
1/8		0.125	3.1750	0.0008	0.02032	5/8		0.625	15.8750	4	101.6
	9/64	0.140625	3.5719	0.0009	0.02286		41/64	0.640625	16.2719	5	127.0
5/32		0.15625	3.9687	0.001	0.0254	21/32		0.65625	16.6687	6	152.4
	11/64	0.171875	4.3656	0.002	0.0508		43/64	0.671875	17.0656	7	177.8
3/16		0.1875	4.7625	0.003	0.0762	11/16		0.6875	17.4625	8	203.2
	13/64	0.203125	5.1594	0.004	0.1016		45/64	0.703125	17.8594	9	228.6
7/32		0.21875	5.5562	0.005	0.1270	23/32		0.71875	18.2562	10	254.0
	15/64	0.234375	5.9531	0.006	0.1524		47/64	0.734375	18.6531	11	279.4
1/4		0.25	6.3500	0.007	0.1778	3/4		0.75	19.0500	12	304.8
	17/64	0.265625	6.7469	0.008	0.2032		49/64	0.765625	19.4469	13	330.2
9/32		0.28125	7.1437	0.009	0.2286	25/32		0.78125	19.8437	14	355.6
	19/64	0.296875	7.5406	0.01	0.254		51/64	0.796875	20.2406	15	381.0
5/16		0.3125	7.9375	0.02	0.508	13/16		0.8125	20.6375	16	406.4
	21/64	0.328125	8.3344	0.03	0.762		53/64	0.828125	21.0344	17	431.8
11/32		0.34375	8.7312	0.04	1.016	27/32		0.84375	21.4312	18	457.2
	23/64	0.359375	9.1281	0.05	1.270		55/64	0.859375	21.8281	19	482.6
3/8		0.375	9.5250	0.06	1.524	7/8		0.875	22.2250	20	508.0
	25/64	0.390625	9.9219	0.07	1.778		57/64	0.890625	22.6219	21	533.4
13/32		0.40625	10.3187	0.08	2.032	29/32		0.90625	23.0187	22	558.8
	27/64	0.421875	10.7156	0.09	2.286		59/64	0.921875	23.4156	23	584.2
7/16		0.4375	11.1125	0.1	2.54	15/16		0.9375	23.8125	24	609.6
	29/64	0.453125	11.5094	0.2	5.08		61/64	0.953125	24.2094	25	635.0
15/32		0.46875	11.9062	0.3	7.62	31/32		0.96875	24.6062	26	660.4
	31/64	0.484375	12.3031	0.4	10.16		63/64	0.984375	25.0031	27	690.6
1/2		0.5	12.7000	0.5	12.70						

ENGLISH TO METRIC CONVERSION: TORQUE

To convert foot-pounds (ft. lbs.) to Newton-meters: multiply the number of ft. lbs. by 1.3

To convert inch-pounds (in. lbs.) to Newton-meters: multiply the number of in. lbs. by .11

in lbs	N-m	in lbs	N-m	in lbs	N-m	in lbs	N-m	in lbs	N-m
0.1	0.01	1	0.11	10	1.13	19	2.15	28	3.16
0.2	0.02	2	0.23	11	1.24	20	2.26	29	3.28
0.3	0.03	3	0.34	12	1.36	21	2.37	30	3.39
0.4	0.04	4	0.45	13	1.47	22	2.49	31	3.50
0.5	0.06	5	0.56	14	1.58	23	2.60	32	3.62
0.6	0.07	6	0.68	15	1.70	24	2.71	33	3.73
0.7	0.08	7	0.78	16	1.81	25	2.82	34	3.84
0.8	0.09	8	0.90	17	1.92	26	2.94	35	3.95
0.9	0.10	9	1.02	18	2.03	27	3.05	36	4.0

ENGLISH TO METRIC CONVERSION: TORQUE

Torque is now expressed as either foot-pounds (ft./lbs.) or inch-pounds (in./lbs.). The metric measurement unit for torque is the Newton-meter (Nm). This unit—the Nm—will be used for all SI metric torque references, both the present ft./lbs. and in./lbs.

ft lbs	N-m	ft lbs	N-m	ft lbs	N-m	ft lbs	N-m
0.1	0.1	33	44.7	74	100.3	115	155.9
0.2	0.3	34	46.1	75	101.7	116	157.3
0.3	0.4	35	47.4	76	103.0	117	158.6
0.4	0.5	36	48.8	77	104.4	118	160.0
0.5	0.7	37	50.7	78	105.8	119	161.3
0.6	0.8	38	51.5	79	107.1	120	162.7
0.7	1.0	39	52.9	80	108.5	121	164.0
0.8	1.1	40	54.2	81	109.8	122	165.4
0.9	1.2	41	55.6	82	111.2	123	166.8
1	1.3	42	56.9	83	112.5	124	168.1
2	2.7	43	58.3	84	113.9	125	169.5
3	4.1	44	59.7	85	115.2	126	170.8
4	5.4	45	61.0	86	116.6	127	172.2
5	6.8	46	62.4	87	118.0	128	173.5
6	8.1	47	63.7	88	119.3	129	174.9
7	9.5	48	65.1	89	120.7	130	176.2
8	10.8	49	66.4	90	122.0	131	177.6
9	12.2	50	67.8	91	123.4	132	179.0
10	13.6	51	69.2	92	124.7	133	180.3
11	14.9	52	70.5	93	126.1	134	181.7
12	16.3	53	71.9	94	127.4	135	183.0
13	17.6	54	73.2	95	128.8	136	184.4
14	18.9	55	74.6	96	130.2	137	185.7
15	20.3	56	75.9	97	131.5	138	187.1
16	21.7	57	77.3	98	132.9	139	188.5
17	23.0	58	78.6	99	134.2	140	189.8
18	24.4	59	80.0	100	135.6	141	191.2
19	25.8	60	81.4	101	136.9	142	192.5
20	27.1	61	82.7	102	138.3	143	193.9
21	28.5	62	84.1	103	139.6	144	195.2
22	29.8	63	85.4	104	141.0	145	196.6
23	31.2	64	86.8	105	142.4	146	198.0
24	32.5	65	88.1	106	143.7	147	199.3
25	33.9	66	89.5	107	145.1	148	200.7
26	35.2	67	90.8	108	146.4	149	202.0
27	36.6	68	92.2	109	147.8	150	203.4
28	38.0	69	93.6	110	149.1	151	204.7
29	39.3	70	94.9	111	150.5	152	206.1
30	40.7	71	96.3	112	151.8	153	207.4
31	42.0	72	97.6	113	153.2	154	208.8
32	43.4	73	99.0	114	154.6	155	210.2

ENGLISH TO METRIC CONVERSION: FORCE

Force is presently measured in pounds (lbs.). This type of measurement is used to measure spring pressure, specifically how many pounds it takes to compress a spring. Our present force unit (the pound) will be replaced in SI metric measurements by the Newton (N). This term will eventually see use in specifications for electric motor brush spring pressures, valve spring pressures, etc.

To convert pounds (lbs.) to Newton (N): multiply the number of lbs. by 4.45

lbs	N	lbs	N	lbs	N	oz	N
0.01	0.04	21	93.4	59	262.4	1	0.3
0.02	0.09	22	97.9	60	266.9	2	0.6
0.03	0.13	23	102.3	61	271.3	3	0.8
0.04	0.18	24	106.8	62	275.8	4	1.1
0.05	0.22	25	111.2	63	280.2	5	1.4
0.06	0.27	26	115.6	64	284.6	6	1.7
0.07	0.31	27	120.1	65	289.1	7	2.0
0.08	0.36	28	124.6	66	293.6	8	2.2
0.09	0.40	29	129.0	67	298.0	9	2.5
0.1	0.4	30	133.4	68	302.5	10	2.8
0.2	0.9	31	137.9	69	306.9	11	3.1
0.3	1.3	32	142.3	70	311.4	12	3.3
0.4	1.8	33	146.8	71	315.8	13	3.6
0.5	2.2	34	151.2	72	320.3	14	3.9
0.6	2.7	35	155.7	73	324.7	15	4.2
0.7	3.1	36	160.1	74	329.2	16	4.4
0.8	3.6	37	164.6	75	333.6	17	4.7
0.9	4.0	38	169.0	76	338.1	18	5.0
1	4.4	39	173.5	77	342.5	19	5.3
2	8.9	40	177.9	78	347.0	20	5.6
3	13.4	41	182.4	79	351.4	21	5.8
4	17.8	42	186.8	80	355.9	22	6.1
5	22.2	43	191.3	81	360.3	23	6.4
6	26.7	44	195.7	82	364.8	24	6.7
7	31.1	45	200.2	83	369.2	25	7.0
8	35.6	46	204.6	84	373.6	26	7.2
9	40.0	47	209.1	85	378.1	27	7.5
10	44.5	48	213.5	86	382.6	28	7.8
11	48.9	49	218.0	87	387.0	29	8.1
12	53.4	50	224.4	88	391.4	30	8.3
13	57.8	51	226.9	89	395.9	31	8.6
14	62.3	52	231.3	90	400.3	32	8.9
15	66.7	53	235.8	91	404.8	33	9.2
16	71.2	54	240.2	92	409.2	34	9.4
17	75.6	55	244.6	93	413.7	35	9.7
18	80.1	56	249.1	94	418.1	36	10.0
19	84.5	57	253.6	95	422.6	37	10.3
20	89.0	58	258.0	96	427.0	38	10.6

ENGLISH TO METRIC CONVERSION: LIQUID CAPACITY

Liquid or fluid capacity is presently expressed as pints, quarts or gallons, or a combination of all of these. In the metric system the liter (l) will become the basic unit. Fractions of a liter would be expressed as deciliters, centiliters, or most frequently (and commonly) as milliliters.

To convert pints (pts.) to liters (l): multiply the number of pints by .47
To convert liters (l) to pints (pts.): multiply the number of liters by 2.1
To convert quarts (qts.) to liters (l): multiply the number of quarts by .95

To convert liters (l) to quarts (qts.): multiply the number of liters by 1.06
To convert gallons (gals.) to liters (l): multiply the number of gallons by 3.8
To convert liters (l) to gallons (gals.): multiply the number of liters by .26

gals	liters	qts	liters	pts	liters
0.1	0.38	0.1	0.10	0.1	0.05
0.2	0.76	0.2	0.19	0.2	0.10
0.3	1.1	0.3	0.28	0.3	0.14
0.4	1.5	0.4	0.38	0.4	0.19
0.5	1.9	0.5	0.47	0.5	0.24
0.6	2.3	0.6	0.57	0.6	0.28
0.7	2.6	0.7	0.66	0.7	0.33
0.8	3.0	0.8	0.76	0.8	0.38
0.9	3.4	0.9	0.85	0.9	0.43
1	3.8	1	1.0	1	0.5
2	7.6	2	1.9	2	1.0
3	11.4	3	2.8	3	1.4
4	15.1	4	3.8	4	1.9
5	18.9	5	4.7	5	2.4
6	22.7	6	5.7	6	2.8
7	26.5	7	6.6	7	3.3
8	30.3	8	7.6	8	3.8
9	34.1	9	8.5	9	4.3
10	37.8	10	9.5	10	4.7
11	41.6	11	10.4	11	5.2
12	45.4	12	11.4	12	5.7
13	49.2	13	12.3	13	6.2
14	53.0	14	13.2	14	6.6
15	56.8	15	14.2	15	7.1
16	60.6	16	15.1	16	7.6
17	64.3	17	16.1	17	8.0
18	68.1	18	17.0	18	8.5
19	71.9	19	18.0	19	9.0
20	75.7	20	18.9	20	9.5
21	79.5	21	19.9	21	9.9
22	83.2	22	20.8	22	10.4
23	87.0	23	21.8	23	10.9
24	90.8	24	22.7	24	11.4
25	94.6	25	23.6	25	11.8
26	98.4	26	24.6	26	12.3
27	102.2	27	25.5	27	12.8
28	106.0	28	26.5	28	13.2
29	110.0	29	27.4	29	13.7
30	113.5	30	28.4	30	14.2

ENGLISH TO METRIC CONVERSION: PRESSURE

The basic unit of pressure measurement used today is expressed as pounds per square inch (psi). The metric unit for psi will be the kilopascal (kPa). This will apply to either fluid pressure or air pressure, and will be frequently seen in tire pressure readings, oil pressure specifications, fuel pump pressure, etc.

To convert pounds per square inch (psi) to kilopascals (kPa): multiply the number of psi by 6.89

Psi	kPa	Psi	kPa	Psi	kPa	Psi	kPa
0.1	0.7	37	255.1	82	565.4	127	875.6
0.2	1.4	38	262.0	83	572.3	128	882.5
0.3	2.1	39	268.9	84	579.2	129	889.4
0.4	2.8	40	275.8	85	586.0	130	896.3
0.5	3.4	41	282.7	86	592.9	131	903.2
0.6	4.1	42	289.6	87	599.8	132	910.1
0.7	4.8	43	296.5	88	606.7	133	917.0
0.8	5.5	44	303.4	89	613.6	134	923.9
0.9	6.2	45	310.3	90	620.5	135	930.8
1	6.9	46	317.2	91	627.4	136	937.7
2	13.8	47	324.0	92	634.3	137	944.6
3	20.7	48	331.0	93	641.2	138	951.5
4	27.6	49	337.8	94	648.1	139	958.4
5	34.5	50	344.7	95	655.0	140	965.2
6	41.4	51	351.6	96	661.9	141	972.2
7	48.3	52	358.5	97	668.8	142	979.0
8	55.2	53	365.4	98	675.7	143	985.9
9	62.1	54	372.3	99	682.6	144	992.8
10	69.0	55	379.2	100	689.5	145	999.7
11	75.8	56	386.1	101	696.4	146	1006.6
12	82.7	57	393.0	102	703.3	147	1013.5
13	89.6	58	399.9	103	710.2	148	1020.4
14	96.5	59	406.8	104	717.0	149	1027.3
15	103.4	60	413.7	105	723.9	150	1034.2
16	110.3	61	420.6	106	730.8	151	1041.1
17	117.2	62	427.5	107	737.7	152	1048.0
18	124.1	63	434.4	108	744.6	153	1054.9
19	131.0	64	441.3	109	751.5	154	1061.8
20	137.9	65	448.2	110	758.4	155	1068.7
21	144.8	66	455.0	111	765.3	156	1075.6
22	151.7	67	461.9	112	772.2	157	1082.5
23	158.6	68	468.8	113	779.1	158	1089.4
24	165.5	69	475.7	114	786.0	159	1096.3
25	172.4	70	482.6	115	792.9	160	1103.2
26	179.3	71	489.5	116	799.8	161	1110.0
27	186.2	72	496.4	117	806.7	162	1116.9
28	193.0	73	503.3	118	813.6	163	1123.8
29	200.0	74	510.2	119	820.5	164	1130.7
30	206.8	75	517.1	120	827.4	165	1137.6
31	213.7	76	524.0	121	834.3	166	1144.5
32	220.6	77	530.9	122	841.2	167	1151.4
33	227.5	78	537.8	123	848.0	168	1158.3
34	234.4	79	544.7	124	854.9	169	1165.2
35	241.3	80	551.6	125	861.8	170	1172.1
36	248.2	81	558.5	126	868.7	171	1179.0

ENGLISH TO METRIC CONVERSION: PRESSURE

The basic unit of pressure measurement used today is expressed as pounds per square inch (psi). The metric unit for psi will be the kilopascal (kPa). This will apply to either fluid pressure or air pressure, and will be frequently seen in tire pressure readings, oil pressure specifications, fuel pump pressure, etc.

To convert pounds per square inch (psi) to kilopascals (kPa): multiply the number of psi by 6.89

Psi	kPa	Psi	kPa	Psi	kPa	Psi	kPa
172	1185.9	216	1489.3	260	1792.6	304	2096.0
173	1192.8	217	1496.2	261	1799.5	305	2102.9
174	1199.7	218	1503.1	262	1806.4	306	2109.8
175	1206.6	219	1510.0	263	1813.3	307	2116.7
176	1213.5	220	1516.8	264	1820.2	308	2123.6
177	1220.4	221	1523.7	265	1827.1	309	2130.5
178	1227.3	222	1530.6	266	1834.0	310	2137.4
179	1234.2	223	1537.5	267	1840.9	311	2144.3
180	1241.0	224	1544.4	268	1847.8	312	2151.2
181	1247.9	225	1551.3	269	1854.7	313	2158.1
182	1254.8	226	1558.2	270	1861.6	314	2164.9
183	1261.7	227	1565.1	271	1868.5	315	2171.8
184	1268.6	228	1572.0	272	1875.4	316	2178.7
185	1275.5	229	1578.9	273	1882.3	317	2185.6
186	1282.4	230	1585.8	274	1889.2	318	2192.5
187	1289.3	231	1592.7	275	1896.1	319	2199.4
188	1296.2	232	1599.6	276	1903.0	320	2206.3
189	1303.1	233	1606.5	277	1909.8	321	2213.2
190	1310.0	234	1613.4	278	1916.7	322	2220.1
191	1316.9	235	1620.3	279	1923.6	323	2227.0
192	1323.8	236	1627.2	280	1930.5	324	2233.9
193	1330.7	237	1634.1	281	1937.4	325	2240.8
194	1337.6	238	1641.0	282	1944.3	326	2247.7
195	1344.5	239	1647.8	283	1951.2	327	2254.6
196	1351.4	240	1654.7	284	1958.1	328	2261.5
197	1358.3	241	1661.6	285	1965.0	329	2268.4
198	1365.2	242	1668.5	286	1971.9	330	2275.3
199	1372.0	243	1675.4	287	1978.8	331	2282.2
200	1378.9	244	1682.3	288	1985.7	332	2289.1
201	1385.8	245	1689.2	289	1992.6	333	2295.9
202	1392.7	246	1696.1	290	1999.5	334	2302.8
203	1399.6	247	1703.0	291	2006.4	335	2309.7
204	1406.5	248	1709.9	292	2013.3	336	2316.6
205	1413.4	249	1716.8	293	2020.2	337	2323.5
206	1420.3	250	1723.7	294	2027.1	338	2330.4
207	1427.2	251	1730.6	295	2034.0	339	2337.3
208	1434.1	252	1737.5	296	2040.8	240	2344.2
209	1441.0	253	1744.4	297	2047.7	341	2351.1
210	1447.9	254	1751.3	298	2054.6	342	2358.0
211	1454.8	255	1758.2	299	2061.5	343	2364.9
212	1461.7	256	1765.1	300	2068.4	344	2371.8
213	1468.7	257	1772.0	301	2075.3	345	2378.7
214	1475.5	258	1778.8	302	2082.2	346	2385.6
215	1482.4	259	1785.7	303	2089.1	347	2392.5

2

ENGINE PERFORMANCE AND TUNE-UP

GASOLINE ENGINE TUNE-UP PROCEDURES

Neither tune-up nor troubleshooting can be considered independently since each has direct bearing on the other.

An engine tune-up is a service designed to restore the maximum capability of power, performance, economy and reliability in an engine, and, at the same time, assure the owner of a complete check and more lasting results in efficiency and trouble-free performance. Engine tune-up becomes increasingly important each year, to ensure that pollutant levels are in compliance with federal emissions standards.

A complete tune-up should be performed every 12,000 miles or twelve months, whichever comes first. This interval should be halved if the vehicle is operated under severe conditions, such as trailer towing, prolonged idling, continual stop and start driving, or if starting or running problems are noticed. It is assumed that the routine maintenance described in Section 1 has been kept up, as this will have a decided effect on the results of a tune-up. All of the applicable steps of a tune-up should be followed in order, as the result is a cumulative one.

If the specifications on the tune-up sticker in the engine compartment disagree with the Tune-Up Specifications chart in this section, the figures on the sticker must be used. The sticker often reflects changes made during the production run.

It is advisable to follow a definite and thorough tune-up procedure. Tune-up consists of three separate steps: Analysis, the process of determining whether normal wear is responsible for performance loss, and whether parts require replacement or service; Parts Replacement or Service; and Adjustment, where engine adjustments are returned to the original factory specifications.

The extent of an engine tune-up is usually determined by the length of time since the previous service, although the type of driving and the general mechanical condition of the engine must be considered. Specific maintenance should also be performed at regular intervals, depending on operating conditions.

It is advisable to read the entire section before beginning a tune-up, although those who are more familiar with tune-up procedures may wish to go directly to the instructions.

Tune up time is also a good time to look around the engine compartment for potential problems, such as fuel and oil leaks, cracking or hard radiator or heater hoses, loose or frayed belts, loose wire connections, etc.

✻✻ CAUTION

When working around a running engine, always be certain there is plenty of ventilation. Make sure the transmission is in Neutral (unless otherwise specified) and the parking brake is fully applied. Always keep hands, hair, and clothing away from the fan, hot manifolds and radiator. Remove any jewelry or neckties. When the engine is running, do not grasp the spark plug wires, distributor cap or coil wire, as a shock in excess of 20,000 volts may result. Whenever working around the distributor, even if the engine is not running, make sure that the ignition is switched off. Removing or disturbing the distributor cap on an electronic ignition system with the ignition switch "on" can often cause the system to fire.

Spark Plugs

A typical spark plug consists of a metal shell surrounding a ceramic insulator. A metal electrode extends downward through the center of the insulator and protrudes a small distance. Located at the end of the plug and attached to the side of the outer metal shell is the side electrode. The side electrode bends in at a 90° angle so that its tip is even with, and parallel to, the tip of the center electrode. The distance between these two electrodes (measured in thousandths of an inch) is called the spark plug gap. The spark plug in no way produces a spark but merely provides a gap across which the current can arc. The coil produces anywhere from 20,000 to 40,000 volts which travels to the distributor where it is distributed through the spark plug wires to the spark plugs. The current passes along the center electrode and jumps the gap to the side electrode, and, in so doing, ignites the air/fuel mixture in the combustion chamber.

Tune-Up Specifications Chart
Gasoline Engines
All Measurements are given in inches, unless otherwise noted

| Engines | Spark Plugs | | Distributor | | Ignition Timing (deg.) | | Valve Clearance | | Idle Speed | |
	Type	Gap	Point Gap	Dwell (deg.)	Manual Trans.	Auto Trans.	Intake	Exhaust	Manual Trans.	Auto Trans.
1308	B-7EM	0.028	0.026	58	①	①	—	—	800	750
1586	BP-6ES	0.031	0.020	52	5 BTDC	—	0.012	0.012	825	—
1796	BP-6ES	0.031	0.020	52	8 BTDC	—	0.012	0.012	700	—
1970	BPR-6ES	0.031	Electronic		8 BTDC	8 BTDC	0.012	0.012	650	650
1998	BPR-5ES	0.031	Electronic		6 BTDC		0.012	0.012	850	

BTDC: Before Top Dead Center
ATDC: After Top Dead Center
TDC: Top Dead Center
① Leading: TDC
   Trailing: 15A

Spark plugs ignite the air and fuel mixture in the cylinder as the piston reaches the top of the compression stroke. The controlled explosion that results forces the piston down, turning the crankshaft and the rest of the drive train.

The average life of a spark plug is dependent on a number of factors: the mechanical condition of the engine; the type of engine; the type of fuel; driving conditions; and the driver.

Spark plugs should be checked frequently (approximately 5,000 miles) depending on use. All the recommendations are based on the ambient conditions as well as driving conditions. If you drive at high speeds constantly, the plugs will probably not need as much attention to those used for constant stop-and-start driving.

The electrode end of the plug (the end with the threads) is a good indicator of the internal condition of your engine. If a spark plug has fouled and caused the engine to misfire, the problem will have to be found and corrected. Often, reading the spark plugs will lead you to the cause of the problem. Spark plug conditions and probable causes are shown in the accompanying photos. It is a good idea to pull the plugs once in a while just to get an idea of the internal condition of your engine.

➡**A small amount of light tan colored deposits on the electrode end of the spark plug is quite normal. These plugs need not be replaced unless they are severely worn.**

The gap between the center electrode and the side or ground electrode can be expected to increase not more than 0.001 in. every 1,000 miles under normal conditions.

When a spark plug is functioning normally or, more accurately, when the plug is installed in an engine that is functioning properly, the plugs can be taken out, cleaned, regapped, and reinstalled in the engine without doing the engine any harm.

❋❋ CAUTION

The spark plugs used on the rotary engine are not adjustable. Attempting to adjust the air gap will damage the porcelain!

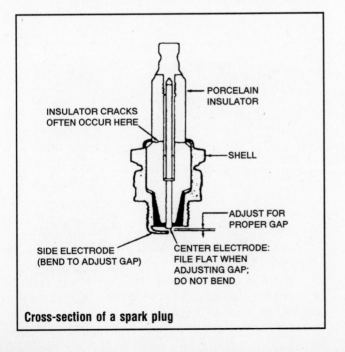

Cross-section of a spark plug

When, and if, a plug fouls and begins to misfire, you will have to investigate, correct the cause of the fouling, and either clean or replace the plug.

SPARK PLUG HEAT RANGE

Spark plug heat range is the ability of the plug to dissipate heat. The longer the insulator (or the farther it extends into the en-

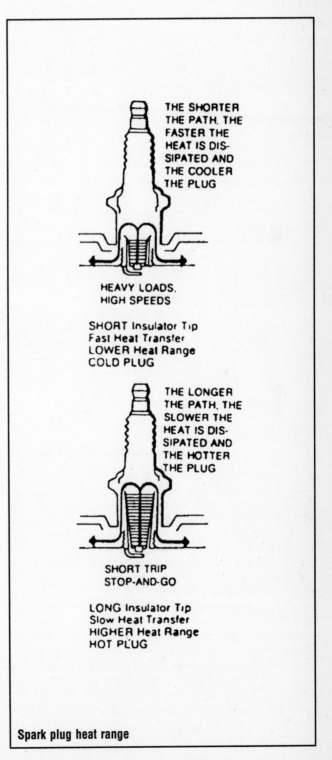

Spark plug heat range

gine), the hotter the plug will operate; the shorter the insulator the cooler it will operate. A plug that absorbs little heat and remains too cool will quickly accumulate deposits of oil and carbon since it is not hot enough to burn them off. This leads to plug fouling and consequently to misfiring. A plug that absorbs too much heat will have no deposits, but, due to the excessive heat, the electrodes will burn away quickly and in some instances, preignition may result. Preignition takes place when plug tips get so hot that they glow sufficiently to ignite the fuel/air mixture before the actual spark occurs. This early ignition will usually cause a pinging during low speeds and heavy loads.

The general rule of thumb for choosing the correct heat range when picking a spark plug is: if most of your driving is long distance, high speed travel, use a colder plug; if most of your driving is stop and go, use a hotter plug. Original equipment plugs are compromise plugs, but most people never have occasion to change their plugs from the factory-recommended heat range.

REMOVAL

1. Raise the hood and locate all the spark plugs.
2. If the spark plug wires are not numbered, mark each one with a small piece of masking tape. Print the number of the cylinder on the piece of tape.
3. Disconnect the wire from the plug by grasping, twisting and pulling the molded cap from the plug. Do not simply yank the wire from the plug as the connection inside the cap can become damaged.
4. Using a spark plug socket, loosen the plug a few turns.
5. If compressed air is available, blow out the area around the base of the spark plug to remove foreign matter.
6. Remove the plug the rest of the way and inspect them. It is a good idea to inspect the plugs whether or not they are going to be reused.

INSPECTION

1. Compare the condition of the spark plugs to the plugs shown in the accompanying photos. It should be remembered that any type of deposit will decrease the efficiency of the plug. If the plugs are not to be replaced, they should be thoroughly cleaned before installation. If the electrode ends of the plugs are worn or damaged and if they are to be reused, wipe off the porcelain insulator on each plug and check for cracks or breaks. If either condition exists, the plug must be replaced.
2. If the plugs are judged reusable, have them cleaned on a plug cleaning machine (found in most service stations) or remove the deposits with a stiff wire brush.
3. Check the plug gap on both new and used plugs before installing them in the engine. The ground electrode must be parallel to the center electrode and the specified size wire gauge should pass through the opening with a slight drag. If the center or ground electrode has worn unevenly, level them off with a file. If the air gap between the two electrodes is not correct, open or close the ground electrode, with the proper tool, to bring it to specifications. Such a tool is usually provided with a gap gauge.

Remove spark plug wires one at a time by gently twisting and pulling—make sure to label all plug wires so that they do not get mixed up

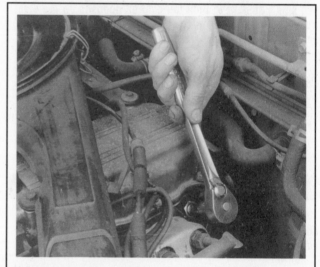

Using a spark plug socket, loosen the spark plug . . .

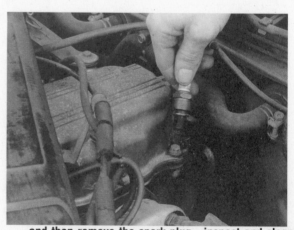

. . . and then remove the spark plug—inspect and clean if reusing the old plug and, when installing (whether old or new), apply anti-seize compound to the threads

A normally worn spark plug should have light tan or gray deposits on the firing tip

A carbon fouled plug, identified by soft, sooty, black deposits, may indicate an improperly tuned vehicle. Check the air cleaner, ignition components and engine control system

A variety of tools and gauges are needed for spark plug service

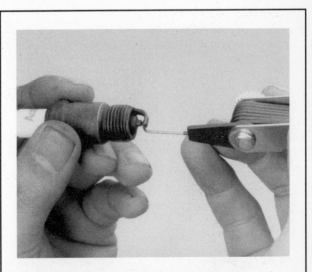

Checking the spark plug gap with a feeler gauge

A physically damaged spark plug may be evidence of severe detonation in that cylinder. Watch that cylinder carefully between services, as a continued detonation will not only damage the plug, but could also damage the engine

An oil fouled spark plug indicates an engine with worn piston rings and/or bad valve seals allowing excessive oil to enter the chamber

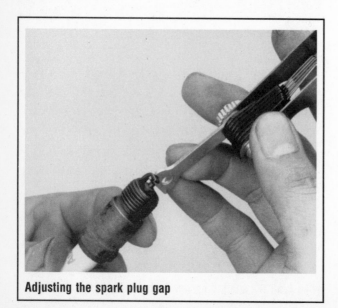

Adjusting the spark plug gap

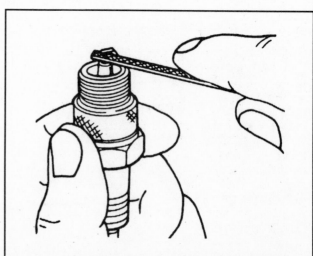

If the standard plug is in good condition, the electrode may be filed flat—CAUTION: do not file platinum plugs

This spark plug has been left in the engine too long, as evidenced by the extreme gap—Plugs with such an extreme gap can cause misfiring and stumbling accompanied by a noticeable lack of power

A bridged or almost bridged spark plug, identified by a build-up between the electrodes caused by excessive carbon or oil build-up on the plug

INSTALLATION

1. Coat the threads of new plugs with an anti-seize compound. Insert the plugs into the engine and tighten them finger-tightly.

2. Be sure that the plugs are not crossthreaded. If the plugs use metal gaskets, new gaskets should be installed each time the plugs are removed and installed.

3. Tighten the spark plugs to 9–13 ft. lbs. (Rotary Pick-Up) or 11–15 ft. lbs. (piston engine).

4. Install the spark plug wires on their respective plugs. Be sure that each wire is firmly connected.

5. While you are checking the spark plugs, the spark plug wires should also be checked. Any wires that are cracked or brittle should be replaced.

Spark Plug Wires

TESTING

Spark plug wires are those which carry electricity between the center tower of the distributor cap and the center tower of the coil, and those that carry electricity between the distributor cap and the spark plugs.

These may be tested visually by gently bending them and inspecting the bends for signs of cracking. If cracks are found, replace the wires. It's a good idea to replace the wires in sets, rather than individually.

The wires should also be tested for resistance with an ohmmeter. Resistance should be 16KΩ per meter (1000mm).

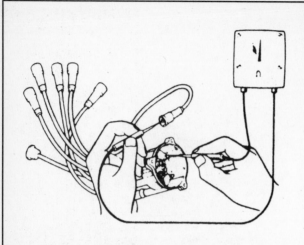

Checking plug wire resistance through the distributor cap with an ohmmeter

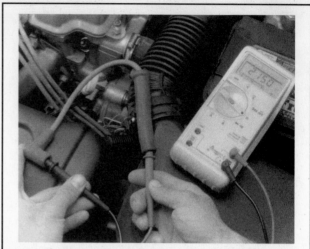

Checking individual plug wire resistance with a digital ohmmeter

FIRING ORDERS

◆ See Figures 1, 2 and 3

➡ To avoid confusion, remove and tag the spark plug wires one at a time, for replacement.

If a distributor is not keyed for installation with only one orientation, it could have been removed previously and rewired. The resultant wiring would hold the correct firing order, but could change the relative placement of the plug towers in relation to the engine. For this reason it is imperative that you label all wires before disconnecting any of them. Also, before removal, compare the current wiring with the accompanying illustrations. If the current wiring does not match, make notes in your book to reflect how your engine is wired.

The firing order of the Rotary Pick-Up engine is alternate (1–2). The distributor cap terminals should be identified by T_1, L_1, T_2 and L_2 (Trailing No. 1 cylinder, Leading No. 1 cylinder, etc.). The top plug of each cylinder is the trailing plug and the bottom is the leading. The rotors are numbered from front to rear.

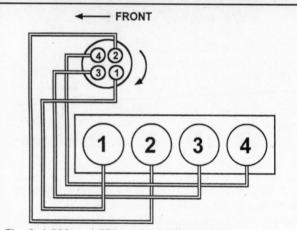

Fig. 2 1,586cc, 1,796cc and 1,970cc engines
Firing order: 1–3–4–2
Distributor rotation: Clockwise

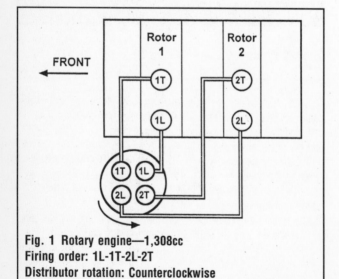

Fig. 1 Rotary engine—1,308cc
Firing order: 1L-1T-2L-2T
Distributor rotation: Counterclockwise

Fig. 3 1,998cc engine
Firing order: 1–3–4–2
Distributor rotation: Clockwise

POINT TYPE IGNITION SYSTEM

Breaker Points and Condenser

OPERATION

➡**Point type ignition was used through the 1978 model year. The following information applies only to these model years. Beginning in 1979, electronic ignition became standard equipment. Testing and adjustments on 1979 and later models is given a little later in this chapter.**

The points function as a circuit breaker for the primary circuit of the ignition system. The ignition coil must boost the 12 volts of electrical pressure supplied by the battery to as much as 25,000 volts in order to fire the plugs. To do this, the coil depends on the points and the condenser to make a clean break in the primary circuit.

The coil has both primary and secondary circuits. When the ignition is turned on, the battery supplies voltage through the coil and onto the points. The points are connected to ground, completing the primary circuit. As the current passes through the coil, a magnetic field is created in the iron center core of the coil. As the cam in the distributor turns, the points open and the primary circuit collapses. The magnetic field in the primary circuit of the coil also collapses and cuts through the secondary circuit windings around the iron core. Because of the scientific phenomenon called electromagnetic induction, the battery voltage is increased to a level sufficient to fire the spark plugs.

When the points open, the electrical charge in the primary circuit jumps the gap created between the two open contacts of the points. If this electrical charge were not transferred elsewhere, the metal contacts of the points would melt and the gap between the points would start to change rapidly. If this gap is not maintained, the points will not break the primary circuit. If the primary circuit is not broken, the secondary circuit will not have enough voltage to fire the spark plugs.

The function of the condenser is to absorb excessive voltage from the points when they open and thus prevent the points from becoming pitted or burned.

It is interesting to note that the above cycle must be completed by the ignition system every time a spark plug fires.

There are two ways to check the breaker point gap. It can be done with a feeler gauge or a dwell meter. Either way you set the points, you are basically adjusting the amount of time that the points remain open. The time is measured in degrees of distributor rotation. When you measure the gap between the breaker points with a feeler gauge, you are setting the maximum amount the points will open when the rubbing block on the points is on a high point of the distributor cam. When you adjust the points with a dwell meter, you are adjusting the number of degrees that the points will remain closed before they start to open as a high point of the distributor cam approaches the rubbing block of the points.

When you replace a set of points, always replace the condenser at the same time.

When you change the point gap or dwell, you will also have changed the ignition timing. So, if the point gap or dwell is changed, the ignition timing must be adjusted also.

INSPECTION OF THE POINTS

1. Disconnect the high tension wire from the top of the distributor and the coil.
2. Remove the distributor cap by prying off the spring clips on the sides of the cap or by turning the screwheaded fasteners.
3. Remove the rotor from the distributor shaft by pulling it straight up. Examine the condition of the rotor. If it is cracked or the metal tip is excessively worn or burned, it should be replaced.
4. Pry open the contacts of the points with a screwdriver and check the condition of the contacts. If they are excessively worn, burned or pitted, they should be replaced.
5. If the points are in good condition, adjust them and replace the rotor and the distributor cap. If the points need to be replaced, follow the replacement procedure given below.

REMOVAL & INSTALLATION

All Models

➡**Because of engine design, the rotary engine uses 2 sets of points in the distributor. Removal and installation is basically the same as for a single set of points.**

1. Raise the hood and locate the distributor. It is on the front of the engine.
2. Scribe an alignment mark on the distributor cap and the distributor body.
3. Remove the distributor cap and rotor. The rotor goes on the shaft only one way.
4. Disconnect the primary and condenser wires from the breaker point terminal. Note the position of the wires before removing them from the terminal.
5. Remove the screws attaching the breaker points to the base plate. If possible, it is best to use a magnetic screwdriver to do this. The screws are very small and can be dropped easily.
6. Lift the breaker point(s) assemblies from the distributor. Remove the condenser.
7. Place the breaker point(s) assemblies on the base plate. Install the attaching screws, again using a magnetic screwdriver, if you have one.
8. Install the condenser. It is always best to install a new condenser each time you replace the points. It is just cheap insurance against condenser failure.
9. Connect the primary and condenser wires to the point(s) terminal and tighten the connection.
10. Be sure that the points are aligned.
11. Set the point gap or dwell angle and install the rotor and distributor cap. Use the alignment marks made previously and install the cap correctly.

DWELL ADJUSTMENT

◗ **See Figures 4, 5, 6, 7 and 8**

The dwell angle or cam angle is the number of degrees that the distributor cam rotates while the points are closed. There is an inverse relationship between dwell angle and point gap. Increasing the point gap will decrease the dwell angle and vice versa. Checking the dwell angle with a meter is a far more accurate method of measuring point opening than the feeler gauge method.

When setting ignition contact points, it is advisable to observe the following general rules:

1. If the points are used, they should not be adjusted using a feeler gauge. The gauge will not give an accurate reading on a pitted surface.

2. Never file the points. This removes their protective coating and results in rapid pitting.

3. When using a feeler gauge to set new points, be certain that

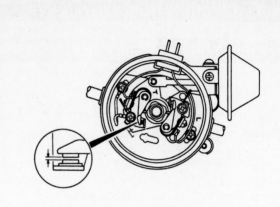

Fig. 6 Adjusting the point gap on the rotary engine. The arrows indicate the setscrews to be loosened

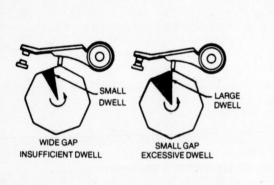

Fig. 4 Dwell is a function of point gap. The dark area is the number of degrees the points will be closed (illustration shows 8 cylinder set up, 4 cylinder is similar)

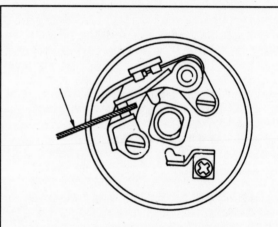

Fig. 7 View of a feeler blade (arrow) inserted between the contact points. Note the rubbing block (in line with feeler blade) resting on distributor cam lobe (center)

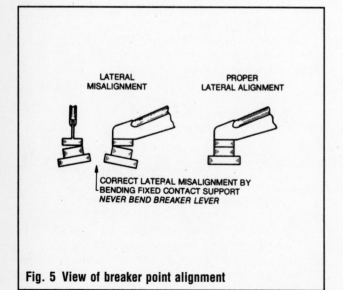

Fig. 5 View of breaker point alignment

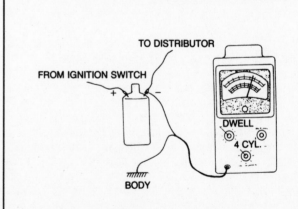
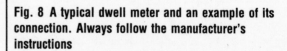

Fig. 8 A typical dwell meter and an example of its connection. Always follow the manufacturer's instructions

the points are fully open. The fiber rubbing block must rest on the highest point of the cam lobe.

4. Always make sure that a feeler gauge is free of oil or grease before setting the points.

5. Make sure that the points are properly aligned and that the feeler gauge is not tilted. If points are misaligned, bend the fixed contact support only, never the movable breakable arm.

A dwell meter virtually eliminates errors in point gap caused by the distributor cam lobes being unequally worn, or human error. In any case, point dwell should be checked as soon as possible after setting with a feeler gauge because it is a far more accurate check of point operation under normal operating conditions. The dwell meter is also capable of detecting high point resistance (oxidation) or poor connections within the distributor.

The dwell meter, actually a modified voltmeter, depends on the nature of contact point operation for its usefulness. In this electromechanical system, a fiber block slides under tension, over a cam. The angle that the block traverses on the cam, during which time current is made available to the coil primary winding, is an inverse function of point gap. In other words, the wider the gap, the smaller the dwell (expressed in degrees); the closer the gap, the greater the dwell.

Because the fiber block wears down gradually in service, it is a good practice to set the dwell on the low side of any dwell range (smaller number of degrees) given in specifications. As the block wears, the dwell becomes greater (toward the center of the range) and point life is increased between adjustments.

To connect the dwell meter, switch the meter to the appropriate cylinder range, as the case may be, and connect one lead to ground. The other lead should be connected to the coil distributor terminal (the one having the wire going to contact points). Follow the manufacturer's instructions if they differ from those listed. Zero the meter, start the engine and gradually allow it to assume normal idle speed. See the Tune-Up Specifications earlier in this section. The meter should agree with the specifications. Any excessive variation in dwell indicates a worn distributor shaft or bushings, or perhaps a worn distributor cam or breaker plate.

It is obvious from the above procedure that some means of measuring engine rpm must also be employed when checking dwell. An external tachometer should be employed. Hook-up is the same as for the dwell meter and both can be used in conjunction. Most commercial dwell meters have a tachometer scale built in and switching between them is possible.

Single and Dual Point Distributors

There are two methods to adjust the breaker point gap, the feeler blade method and the dwell meter method, of which, the latter is preferred.

FEELER BLADE METHOD

1. Remove the distributor high tension lead and ground it. Remove the distributor cap and rotor.

2. Check the breaker point alignment (refer to the accompanying illustrations). If necessary, align the contact points by bending the stationary contact. Never bend the moveable arm(s).

3. Crank the engine in short bursts, until the rubbing block on the breaker arm rests on a high point of one of the distributor cam lobes. In this position, the gap between the contact points is largest.

4. Insert a feeler blade of the specified thickness between the breaker points. The feeler blade will slide through the contact points with a slight drag when the gap is correct. If your truck is equipped with a dual point distributor, this step and the following steps should be repeated for each set of points.

5. If adjustment is required, loosen the breaker point attaching screws and move the stationary contact and base until the correct gap is obtained.

6. Tighten the attaching screws and recheck the gap.

7. Install the rotor and distributor cap. Reconnect the high tension lead.

DWELL METER METHOD

1. Disconnect the vacuum line from the distributor and plug it.

2. Connect the dwell meter in accordance with the manufacturer's instructions.

3. Start the engine, and run at idle until normal operating temperature is reached.

4. Observe the dwell meter reading. If the reading is within specifications, turn the engine **OFF** and skip to Step 5. If it is not within specifications, adjust the dwell as follows:

➡**If dwell angle is above the specified amount, the point gap is too small; if it is below the specified amount, the gap is too large.**

 a. Turn the engine **OFF.** Remove the high tension lead and ground it. Remove the distributor cap and rotor.

 b. Loosen the breaker point attaching screws and, while observing the dwell meter, crank the engine. Move the stationary contact(s) and base(s) until the correct dwell reading is obtained.

 c. Tighten the attaching screws. Install the rotor and distributor cap. Reconnect the high tension leads.

5. When the dwell angle check is completed, disconnect the dwell meter and reconnect the vacuum hose to the distributor.

ELECTRONIC IGNITION SYSTEMS

◆ **See Figures 9, 10, 11 and 12**

➡**This book contains simple testing procedures for the electronic ignition. More comprehensive testing on this system and other electronic control systems on your truck can be found in** *CHILTON'S GUIDE TO ELECTRONIC ENGINE CONTROLS,* **book part number 7535, available at your local retailer.**

Used for the first time on the 1979 models, this system replaces the points and condenser in the distributor. It is almost maintenance free. The most commonly replaced parts are the rotor and cap, which are still routine maintenance items. Other items, such as the pick-up coil and signal rotor, are replaced when they fail. An air gap adjustment is possible only on the 1979 models. Adjustments are not possible on later models.

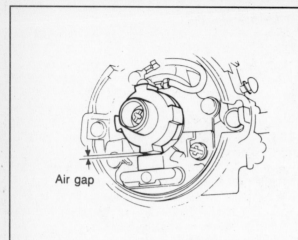

Fig. 9 View of the air gap measurement on electronic distributors

Inspection

1. The distributor cap on all engines is held on by two screws. Remove the screws and lift the cap straight up with the wires still attached. Inspect the cap for cracks, carbon tracking and worn contacts. Replace it, if necessary, transferring the wires one at a time to avoid miswiring.

2. On 1979 models, pull the rotor straight up to remove it. On 1980–86 models, the rotor is held in place by two screws. Use a magnetic screwdriver to remove them and lift off the rotor. Replace the rotor if it appears worn, burned or pitted.

3. Inspect the wires for cracks or brittleness. Replace them, one at a time, if they appear at all suspect. Avoid bending the wires sharply, or kinking them, as the carbon cores are subject to such damage.

Air Gap Adjustment

1979 MODELS

1. Using a wrench on the crankshaft pulley nut, turn the distributor shaft until one of the high points on the pick-up coil is aligned with the signal rotor face.

2. Loosen the setscrews and move the pickup coil until the gap between it and the signal rotor is 0.2–0.6mm, measured with a brass or plastic feeler gauge.

3. Tighten the setscrews and recheck the gap.

Troubleshooting

You will need an accurate ohmmeter, a jumper wire and a 3.4 watt test light. Before proceeding with troubleshooting, make sure that all connections are tight and all wiring is intact.

1. Check for spark at the coil high tension lead by removing the lead from the distributor cap and holding it about ¼ in. from the engine block or other good ground. Use a heavy rubber glove or non-conductive clamp, such as a fuse puller or clothes pin, to

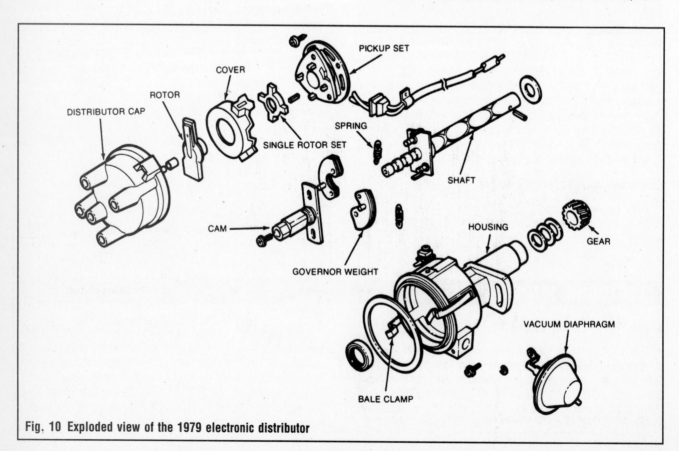

Fig. 10 Exploded view of the 1979 electronic distributor

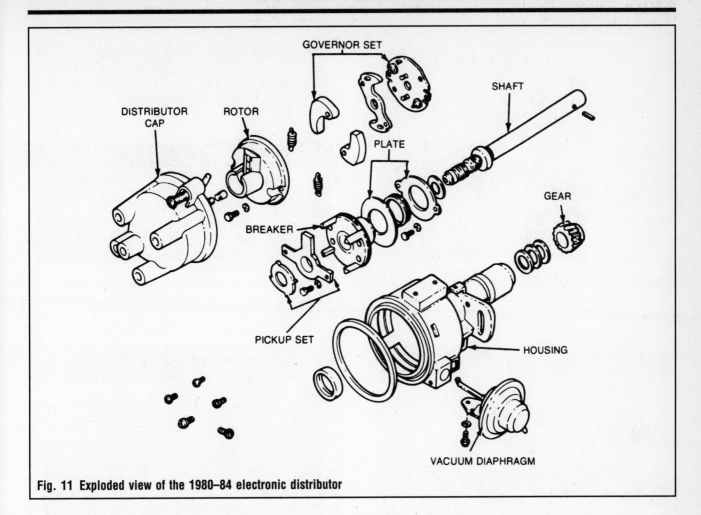

Fig. 11 Exploded view of the 1980–84 electronic distributor

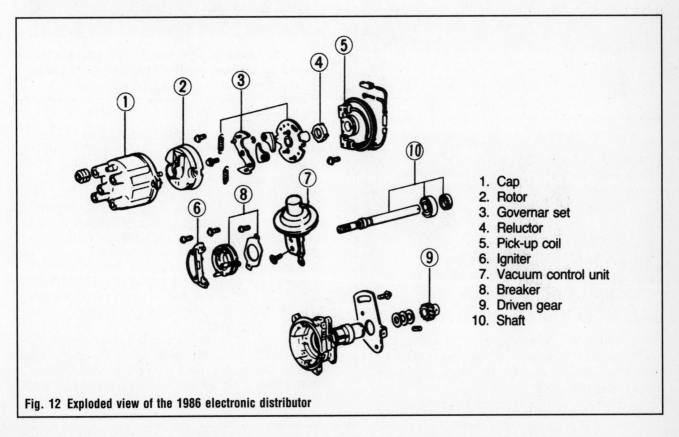

1. Cap
2. Rotor
3. Governar set
4. Reluctor
5. Pick-up coil
6. Igniter
7. Vacuum control unit
8. Breaker
9. Driven gear
10. Shaft

Fig. 12 Exploded view of the 1986 electronic distributor

Before removing the distributor cap, label the spark plug wires in relation to their position and cylinder number

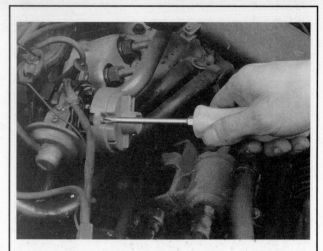

Once the cap is removed, loosen the rotor retaining screws . . .

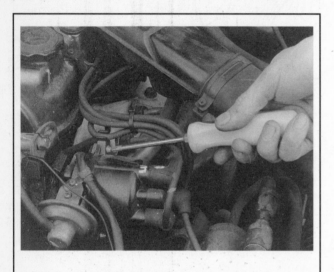

Loosen the distributor cap hold-down screws . . .

. . . and remove the rotor from the distributor shaft—inspect the rotor and distributor cap contacts for pitting, burning & wear; replace as necessary

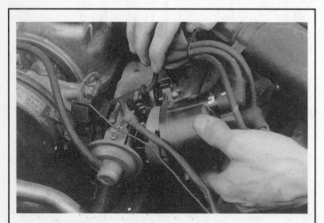

. . . and then pull the distributor cap off, taking care not to upset the firing order—if a new cap is being installed, remove and replace the ignition wires one at a time to avoid confusion

hold the wire. Crank the engine and check for spark. If a good spark is noted, check the cap and rotor; if the spark is weak or nonexistent, replace the high tension lead, clean and tighten the connections and retest. If a weak spark is still noted, proceed to step 2.

2. Check the coil primary resistance. Connect an ohmmeter across the coil primary terminals and check resistance on the low scale. Resistance should be $0.81-0.98\Omega$ @ 70°F (21°C). If not, replace the coil.

3. Check the coil secondary resistance. Connect an ohmmeter across the distributor side of the coil and the coil center tower. Read resistance on the high scale. Resistance should be $6,800-9,200\Omega$ @ 70°F (21°C). If resistance is much higher ($30,000-40,000\Omega$), replace the coil.

4. Next, remove the distributor cap and rotor. Crank the engine until a spoke on the rotor is aligned with the pick-up coil contact. Use a flat feeler gauge to check the gap. Gap should be 0.20–0.60mm. If not, gently bend the pick-up coil contact to correct the adjustment on 1979 models. On 1980 and later models, the gap

is not adjustable. On these models, gap is corrected by parts replacement.

5. Using an ohmmeter, check the pick-up coil resistance. Disconnect the 2-wire (red and green) connector at the distributor. The ignition switch should be in the **OFF** position. Insert the probes of the ohmmeter in the pick-up coil side of the connector. Resistance should be 760–840Ω for 1979 models, or 1,050Ω ± 10% for 1980 and later models. If not, replace the pick-up coil.

6. Finally, test the ignition module. On 1979 models, connect the test light between the positive and negative terminal of the ignition coil. Connect a jumper wire between the positive coil terminal and the red wire of the pick-up coil, at the connector that you unplugged in the previous test. Be sure that you are attaching the wire to the pick-up coil side of the connector. Turn the ignition

switch **ON.** The test light should light. Disconnect the jumper wire from the connector. The light should go out. If not, replace the module.

On 1980 and later models, the only way to test the module is to substitute a known good module in its place.

PICK-UP COIL RESISTANCE

Unplug the primary ignition wire connector and connect an ohmmeter across the two prongs of the pick-up coil connector. Resistance, at 68°F (20°C), should be 800Ω ± 80Ω for 1979 models, 1,050Ω ± 105Ω for 1980 and later models.

IGNITION TIMING

▶ **See Figures 13, 14, 15 and 16**

Ignition timing is an important part of the tune-up. It is always adjusted after the points are gapped (dwell angle changed), since altering the dwell affects the timing. It should also be checked to compensate for timing belt or gear wear on engines with electronic ignition at the interval specified in the Maintenance Chart. Three basic types of timing lights are available, the neon, the DC, and the AC powered. Of the three, the inductive DC light is the most frequently used by professional tuners. The bright flash put out by the DC light makes the timing marks stand out on even the brightest of days. Another advantage of the DC light is that you don't need to be near an electrical outlet. Neon lights are available for a few dollars, but their weak flash makes it necessary to use them in a fairly dark work area. One neon light lead is attached to the spark plug and the other to the plug wire. The DC light attaches to the spark plug and the wire with an adapter and two clips attached to the battery posts for power. The AC unit is similar, except that the power cable is plugged into a house outlet.

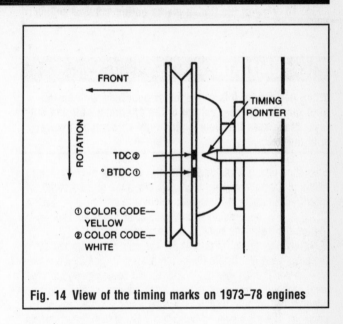

Fig. 14 View of the timing marks on 1973–78 engines

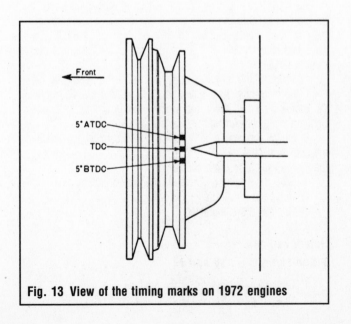

Fig. 13 View of the timing marks on 1972 engines

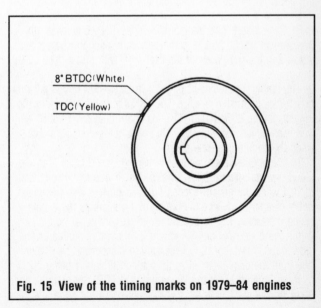

Fig. 15 View of the timing marks on 1979–84 engines

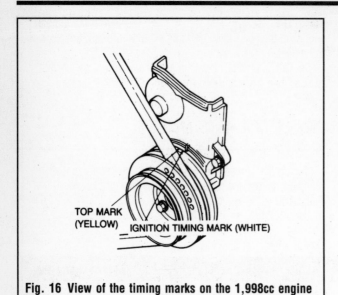

Fig. 16 View of the timing marks on the 1,998cc engine

✸✸ CAUTION

When performing this or any other operation with the engine running, be very careful of the alternator belt and pulleys. Make sure that your timing light wires don't interfere with the belt.

Ignition timing is the measurement, in degrees of crankshaft rotation, of the point at which the spark plugs fire in each of the cylinders. It is measured in degrees before or after Top Dead Center (TDC) of the compression stroke. Ignition timing is adjusted by turning the distributor body in the engine.

Ideally, the air/fuel mixture in the cylinder will be ignited by the spark plug just before the piston passes TDC of the compression stroke. If this happens, the piston will be beginning its downward motion of the power stroke just as the compressed and ignited air/fuel mixture begins to develop a considerable amount of pressure. The expansion of the air/fuel mixture then forces the piston down on the power stroke and turns the crankshaft.

Because it takes time for the mixture to burn, the spark plug must fire a little before the piston reaches TDC. Otherwise, the mixture will not be burned completely early enough in the downstroke and the full power of the explosion will not be used by the engine.

The timing measurement is given in degrees of crankshaft rotation before the piston reaches TDC (BTDC). If the setting for the ignition timing is 5° BTDC (5B), the spark plug must fire 5° before each piston reaches TDC. This only holds true, however, when the engine is at idle speed.

As the engine speed increases, the pistons go faster. The spark plugs have to ignite the fuel even sooner if it is to be completely ignited when the piston reaches TDC. To do this, the distributor has a means to advance the timing of the spark as the engine speed increases. This is accomplished by centrifugal weights within the distributor and a vacuum diaphragm, mounted on the side of the distributor. It is necessary to disconnect the vacuum line from the diaphragm when the ignition timing is being set.

If the ignition is set too far advanced (BTDC), the ignition and expansion of the fuel in the cylinder will occur too soon and there

will be excessive temperature and pressure. This causes engine ping. If the ignition spark is set too far retarded, after TDC (ATDC), the piston will have already passed TDC and started on its way down when the fuel is ignited. This will cause the piston to be forced down for only a portion of its travel and creates less pressure in the cylinder, resulting in poor engine performance and lack of power.

The timing is best checked with a timing light. This device is connected in series (or through induction) with the No. 1 spark plug. The current which fires the spark plug also causes the timing light to flash.

The timing marks are located at the front crankshaft pulley and consist of a notch on the crankshaft pulley and a scale of degrees of crankshaft rotation attached to the front cover.

When the engine is running, the timing light is aimed at the marks on the flywheel pulley and the pointer.

Timing

INSPECTION AND ADJUSTMENT

Piston Engines

1. Raise the hood and clean and mark the timing marks. Chalk or fluorescent paint makes a good, visible mark.

2. Disconnect the vacuum line to the distributor and plug the disconnected line. Disconnect the line at the vacuum source, not at the distributor.

3. Connect a timing light to the front (No. 1) cylinder, a power source and ground. Follow the manufacturer's instructions.

4. Connect a tachometer to the engine.

5. Start the engine and reduce the idle to 700–750 rpm to be sure that the centrifugal advance mechanism is not working.

6. With the engine running, shine the timing light at the timing pointer and observe the position of the pointer in relation to the timing mark on the crankshaft pulley. 1972 49 states/Canada models have three notches on the pulley; all others have two. Looking straight down on the marks, the one on the left is ATDC, the one in the center is TDC, the one on the right is BTDC. On 1973 and later models, the one on the left is TDC, the one on the right is BTDC.

7. If the timing is not as specified, adjust the timing by loosening the distributor hold-down bolt and rotating the distributor in the proper direction. When the proper ignition timing is obtained, tighten the hold-down bolt on the distributor.

8. Check the centrifugal advance mechanism by accelerating the engine to about 2,000 rpm. If the ignition timing advances, the mechanism is working properly.

9. Stop the engine and remove the timing light.

10. Reset the idle to specifications.

11. Remove the tachometer.

Rotary Engines
▶ **See Figures 17, 18 and 19**

1. Connect a tachometer to the engine.
2. Disconnect and plug the vacuum tube on the distributor.

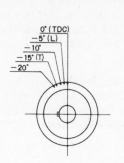

Fig. 17 Timing marks on the rotary engine. Numbers preceded by a minus sign (-) are ATDC

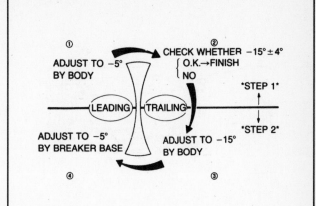

Fig. 18 Schematic diagram of timing procedures for the rotary engine

3. Connect a timing light to the wire from the leading (lower) plug of the front rotor housing.

4. Start the engine and run it idle speed.

5. Shine the timing light on the indicator pin located on the front cover.

6. If the leading timing mark is not correctly aligned with the pointer, stop the engine.

7. Loosen the distributor locknut and rotate the distributor housing (with the engine running) until the timing marks align. Stop the engine and tighten the distributor locknut.

8. Recheck the timing.

9. Change the connection of the timing light to the wire from the trailing (top) plug in the front rotor housing.

10. Start the engine and shine the timing light at the indicator pin. If the trailing timing falls within the specifications, no further adjustments are necessary.

11. If the trailing timing is not within specifications, proceed with the rest of the procedure.

12. If the trailing timing is not within specifications, adjust the trailing and leading timing as follows:

13. Adjust the trailing timing to specification by rotating the distributor body, as in Step 7.

14. Check the leading timing again and record how much it differs from specification.

15. Remove the distributor cap and rotor.

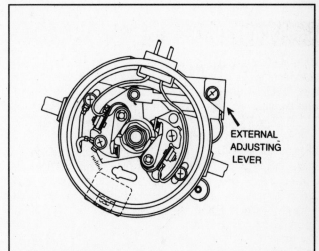

Fig. 19 The external adjusting lever (arrow) on rotary engine distributors

16. Loosen the breaker base setscrews (the ones directly opposite each other near the outside of the distributor base plate until the correct leading plug timing is obtained again.

17. Recheck the timing. If the leading and trailing plug timing marks should both be aligned (or within specifications). If not, repeat the procedure until they are.

VALVE LASH

♦ **See Figures 20, 21 and 22**

Valve adjustment determines how far the valves enter the cylinder and how long they stay open and closed.

If the valve clearance is too large, part of the lift of the camshaft will be used in removing the excessive clearance. Consequently, the valve will not be opening as far as it should, it will start to open too late and will close too early. This condition has two effects: the valve train components will emit a tapping sound as they take up the excessive clearance and as the valves slam shut, and the engine will perform poorly because the valves don't open fully and allow the proper amount of gases to flow into and out of the engine.

If the valve clearance is too small, the intake valves and the exhaust valves will open too far and they will not fully seat on the cylinder head when they close. When a valve seats itself on the cylinder head, it does two things: it seals the combustion chamber so that none of the gasses in the cylinder escape and it cools

Fig. 20 Checking valve clearance at the valve

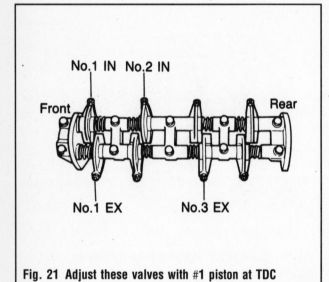

Fig. 21 Adjust these valves with #1 piston at TDC

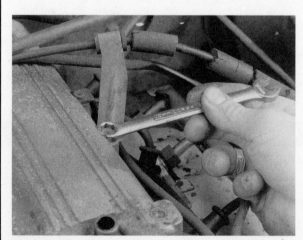

After removing the air cleaner assembly, unbolt any brackets from the valve cover which will inhibit removal

itself by transferring some of the heat it absorbs from the combustion in the cylinder to the cylinder head and to the engine's cooling system. If the valve clearance is too small, the engine will run poorly because of the gases escaping from the combustion chamber. The valves will also become overheated and will warp, since they cannot transfer heat unless they are touching the valve seat in the cylinder head.

➡**While all valve adjustments must be made as accurately as possible, it is better to have the valve adjustment slightly loose than slightly tight, as a burned valve may result from overly tight adjustments.**

This holds true for valve adjustments on most engines.

Adjustment

GASOLINE PISTON ENGINES

1. Run the engine until normal operating temperature is reached.
2. Shut off the engine and remove the rocker cover.
3. Torque the cylinder head bolts to their specified torque, in the proper sequence.
4. Rotate the crankshaft so that the No. 1 cylinder (front) is in the firing position. This can be determined, on gasoline engines, by removing the spark plug from the No. 1 cylinder and putting your thumb over the spark plug port. When compression is felt, the No. 1 cylinder is on the compression stroke. Rotate the engine with a wrench on the crankshaft pulley and stop it at TDC of the compression stroke on the No. 1 cylinder, as confirmed by the alignment of the TDC mark in the crankshaft pulley and the timing pointer.
5. Check the valve clearances by inserting a flat feeler gauge between the end of the valve stem and the rocker arm. The clearance can be checked for No. 1 and No. 2 intake valves and No. 1 and No. 3 exhaust valves.

Remove the valve cover-to-cylinder head mounting bolts . . .

Insert a feeler blade between the rocker arm and valve tip, and check the clearance—this particular vehicle's lash was too tight (0.009 in.); the proper lash clearance is 0.012 in.

. . . and lift off the valve cover

To adjust lash, loosen the locknut and turn the center adjuster in or out to change the clearance—hold the center adjuster from turning when you tighten the locknut and double check clearance afterwards

Inspect the rubber O-ring gasket for cracks or tears that may leak oil—replace as necessary

6. If the valve clearance is incorrect, loosen the adjusting screw locknut and adjust the clearance by turning the adjusting screw with the feeler blade inserted. Hold the adjusting screw in the correct position and tighten the locknut.

7. Rotate the crankshaft (in the normal direction of rotation), until No. 4 piston is at TDC compression. Adjust No. 3 and No. 4 intake valves and No. 2 and No. 4 exhaust valves.

8. Install the rocker arm cover and torque the nuts to 18 inch lbs.

ROTARY ENGINES

Because of its unique design, there are no valves to adjust on the rotary engine.

IDLE SPEED AND MIXTURE ADJUSTMENTS

♦ See Figures 23 and 24

Idle Speed

GASOLINE PISTON ENGINES

1. Thoroughly warm the engine to normal operating temperature. The water temperature gauge will tell you when normal operating temperature is reached.
2. Make sure that the choke valve is fully open. On 1978 and later models, run the engine at 2,000 rpm for 3 minutes. Disconnect the canister purge hose at the canister.
3. Connect a tachometer according to the manufacturer's instructions.
4. Adjust the idle speed screw to specifications.
5. Disconnect the tachometer. Connect the purge hose on 1978 and later models.

ROTARY ENGINES

1. Warm the engine to normal operating temperature.
2. Be sure that the secondary throttle valve is fully returned.
3. Set the parking brake and block the front wheel.
4. Connect a tachometer according to the manufacturer's instructions.
5. Adjust the idle speed to specifications. The idle speed

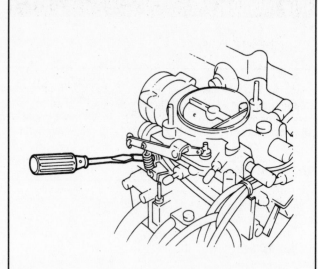

Fig. 24 View of the idle speed adjustment screw location for the 1986 model. Idle mixture should not have to be adjusted, therefore, no provisions are given for such adjustment

1. Throttle adjust screw   2. Mixture adjust screw

Fig. 23 View of the idle speed adjustment screw location for the 1,796cc and 1,970cc engines. Some carburetors have a cap covering the idle mixture adjusting screw, which must be removed with a hacksaw to adjust idle mixture

Idle speed adjuster screw (arrow) on 1986 B2000 models

should ONLY be adjusted with the idle air screw. Never use the idle fuel jet screw to adjust the idle. This screw is preset at the factory and should not be moved.

6. After idle speed adjustment, you should also have the mixture checked with a CO analyzer.

Idle Mixture

GASOLINE ENGINES

If for some reason (tampering or carburetor overhaul) the mixture needs adjustment, use the following procedures. Two procedures are given; one for a HC/CO analyzer and one for a fuel flow meter.

FUEL FLOW METER

It is best to use this procedure to set the idle and throttle screws after they have been disturbed. After you are finished, check the adjustment with a HC/CO analyzer.

1. Adjust the throttle angle opening to specifications with the throttle adjustment screw. The adjustment should be made from the fully closed position. Tighten the locknut after the adjustment is complete.

2. Connect a fuel flow meter.

3. Start the engine and set the approximate idle speed with the idle air screw.

4. Adjust the idle fuel flow to specifications with the idle fuel screw.

5. Use the idle air screw to set the idle speed again.

6. Repeat this procedure (Steps 4 and 5) until both the idle fuel flow and the idle speed are within specifications.

7. Disconnect the fuel flow meter.

HC/CO ANALYZER

1. If you have not already done so, adjust the throttle angle opening to specifications. Make the adjustment from the fully closed position.

2. Lock the nut after adjustment.

3. Start the engine and adjust the idle speed with the idle air screw.

4. Using the gas analyzer, check the HC (hydrocarbon) and CO (carbon monoxide) readings. If the HC is less than 200 ppm (parts per million) and the CO is between 0.1–2.0%, no further adjustment is needed.

5. If the HC and CO are not within specifications, adjust the CO reading to as close to 0.1% as possible, keeping the HC reading below 200 ppm. Use the idle fuel screw to make this adjustment.

6. Recheck the idle speed and adjust if necessary, using the idle air screw.

7. Recheck the HC and CO readings to be sure that they are within limits. Repeat Steps 5 and 6 until the CH, CO and idle speed are all within specifications.

DIESEL ENGINE TUNE-UP PROCEDURES

Because of the simplicity of the diesel engine, tune-up is limited to valve lash adjustment and idle speed adjustment.

Valve Lash

ADJUSTMENT

1. Run the engine until normal operating temperature is reached.

2. Shut off the engine and remove the rocker cover.

3. Torque the cylinder head bolts to their specified torque, in the proper sequence.

4. Rotate the crankshaft so that the No. 1 cylinder (front) is in the firing position. This can be determined by loosening the No. 1 injection pipe at the injection pump. When the engine is slowly cranked, fuel will squirt from the loosened fitting as No. 1 piston approaches TDC. Confirm TDC by the timing mark alignment.

5. Check the valve clearances by inserting a flat feeler gauge between the end of the valve stem and the rocker arm. The clearance can be checked for No. 1 and No. 2 intake valves and No. 1 and No. 3 exhaust valves.

Tune-Up Specifications Chart
Diesel Engines
All measurements are given in inches, unless otherwise noted

Engine	Injection Timing (deg.)	Lift	Nozzle Opening Pressure (psi)	Idle Speed (rpm)	Valve Clearance (cold) Intake	Exhaust	Oil Pressure (psi @ 2000 rpm)
2209	2 ATDC	0.087	1458	700	0.012	0.012	57

ATDC: After Top Dead Center

6. If the valve clearance is incorrect, loosen the adjusting screw locknut and adjust the clearance by turning the adjusting screw with the feeler blade inserted. Hold the adjusting screw in the correct position and tighten the locknut.

7. Rotate the crankshaft (in the normal direction of rotation), until No. 4 piston is at TDC compression. Adjust No. 3 and No. 4 intake valves and No. 2 and No. 4 exhaust valves.

8. Install the rocker arm cover and torque the nuts to 18 inch lbs.

Idle Speed

▶ See Figure 25

ADJUSTMENT

➡ **You'll need a tachometer that works with diesel engines.**

1. Make sure that the throttle cable deflection, at the pump, is 1.0mm–3.0mm. Adjust it with the adjusting nut, if it is not.

2. Loosen the locknut on the idle speed adjusting bolt. Turn the bolt to the right to increase the idle; to the left to decrease it.

3. Race the engine two or three times and let it return to idle. Check the idle speed and readjust if necessary. Idle speed should be 700 rpm.

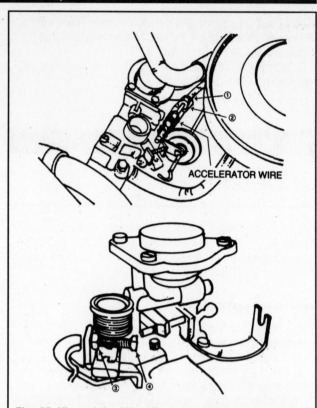

Fig. 25 View of the idle adjustment points on the diesel engine: accelerator cable locknut (1), accelerator cable adjusting nut (2), idle adjusting bolt locknut (3), idle adjusting bolt (4)

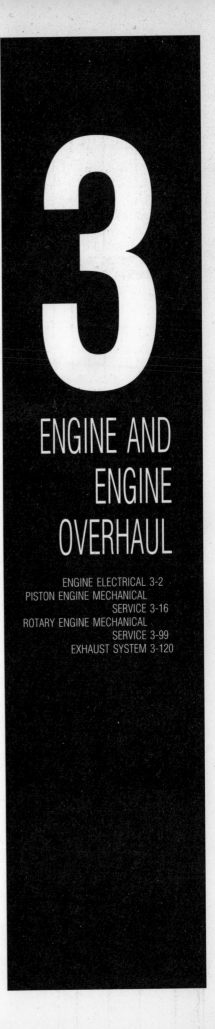

3

ENGINE AND ENGINE OVERHAUL

ENGINE ELECTRICAL

Understanding Electricity

For any electrical system to operate, there must be a complete circuit. This simply means that the power flow from the battery must make a full circle. When an electrical component is operating, power flows from the battery to the components, passes through the component (load) causing it to function, and returns to the battery through the ground path of the circuit. This ground may be either another wire or a metal part of the vehicle (depending upon how the component is designed).

BASIC CIRCUITS

Perhaps the easiest way to visualize a circuit is to think of connecting a light bulb (with two wires attached to it) to the battery. If one of the two wires was attached to the negative post (−) of the battery and the other wire to the positive post (+), the circuit would be complete and the light bulb would illuminate. Electricity could follow a path from the battery to the bulb and back to the battery. It's not hard to see that with longer wires on our light bulb, it could be mounted anywhere on the vehicle. Further, one wire could be fitted with a switch so that the light could be turned on and off. Various other items could be added to our primitive circuit to make the light flash, become brighter or dimmer under certain conditions, or advise the user that it's burned out.

Ground

Some automotive components are grounded through their mounting points. The electrical current runs through the chassis of the vehicle and returns to the battery through the ground (−) cable; if you look, you'll see that the battery ground cable connects between the battery and the body of the vehicle.

Load

Every complete circuit must include a "load" (something to use the electricity coming from the source). If you were to connect a wire between the two terminals of the battery (DON'T do this, but take our word for it) without the light bulb, the battery would attempt to deliver its entire power supply from one pole to another almost instantly. This is a short circuit. The electricity is taking a short cut to get to ground and is not being used by any load in the circuit. This sudden and uncontrolled electrical flow can cause great damage to other components in the circuit and can develop a tremendous amount of heat. A short in an automotive wiring harness can develop sufficient heat to melt the insulation on all the surrounding wires and reduce a multiple wire cable to one sad lump of plastic and copper. Two common causes of shorts are broken insulation (thereby exposing the wire to contact with surrounding metal surfaces or other wires) or a failed switch (the pins inside the switch come out of place and touch each other).

Switches and Relays

Some electrical components which require a large amount of current to operate also have a relay in their circuit. Since these circuits carry a large amount of current (amperage or amps), the thickness of the wire in the circuit (wire gauge) is also greater. If this large wire were connected from the load to the control switch on the dash, the switch would have to carry the high amperage load and the dash would be twice as large to accommodate wiring harnesses as thick as your wrist. To prevent these problems, a relay is used. The large wires in the circuit are connected from the battery to one side of the relay and from the opposite side of the relay to the load. The relay is normally open, preventing current from passing through the circuit. An additional, smaller wire is connected from the relay to the control switch for the circuit. When the control switch is turned on, it grounds the smaller wire to the relay and completes its circuit. The main switch inside the relay closes, sending power to the component without routing the main power through the inside of the vehicle. Some common circuits which may use relays are the horn, headlights, starter and rear window defogger systems.

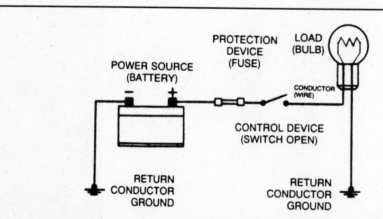

Here is an example of a simple automotive circuit. When the switch is closed, power from the positive battery terminal flows through the fuse, the switch and then the load (light bulb). The light illuminates and the circuit is completed through the return conductor and the vehicle ground. If the light did not work, the tests could be made with a voltmeter or test light at the battery, fuse, switch or bulb socket

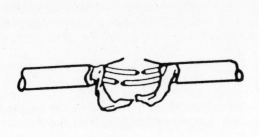

Damaged insulation can allow wires to break (causing an open circuit) or touch (causing a short circuit)

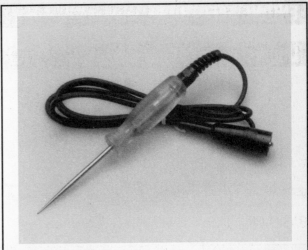

A 12 volt test light is useful when checking parts of a circuit for power

Protective Devices

It is possible for larger surges of current to pass through the electrical system of your vehicle. If this surge of current were to reach the load in the circuit, it could burn it out or severely damage it. To prevent this, fuses, circuit breakers and/or fusible links are connected into the supply wires of the electrical system. These items are nothing more than a built-in weak spot in the system. It's much easier to go to a known location (the fusebox) to see why a circuit is inoperative than to dissect 15 feet of wiring under the dashboard, looking for what happened.

When an electrical current of excessive power passes through the fuse, the fuse blows (the conductor melts) and breaks the circuit, preventing the passage of current and protecting the components.

A circuit breaker is basically a self repairing fuse. It will open the circuit in the same fashion as a fuse, but when either the short is removed or the surge subsides, the circuit breaker resets itself and does not need replacement.

A fuse link (fusible link or main link) is a wire that acts as a fuse. One of these is normally connected between the starter relay and the main wiring harness under the hood. Since the starter is usually the highest electrical draw on the vehicle, an internal short during starting could direct about 130 amps into the wrong places. Consider the damage potential of introducing this current into a system whose wiring is rated at 15 amps and you'll understand the need for protection. Since this link is very early in the electrical path, it's the first place to look if nothing on the vehicle works, but the battery seems to be charged and is properly connected.

TROUBLESHOOTING

Electrical problems generally fall into one of three areas:
• The component that is not functioning is not receiving current.
• The component is receiving power but is not using it or is using it incorrectly (component failure).
• The component is improperly grounded.

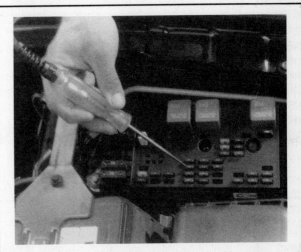

Here, someone is checking a circuit by making sure there is power to the component's fuse

The circuit can be can be checked with a test light and a jumper wire. The test light is a device that looks like a pointed screwdriver with a wire on one end and a bulb in its handle. A jumper wire is simply a piece of wire with alligator clips or special terminals on each end. If a component is not working, you must follow a systematic plan to determine which of the three causes is the villain.

1. Turn ON the switch that controls the item not working.

➡ Some items only work when the ignition switch is turned ON.

2. Disconnect the power supply wire from the component.
3. Attach the ground wire of a test light or a voltmeter to a good metal ground.
4. Touch the end probe of the test light (or the positive lead of the voltmeter) to the power wire; if there is current in the wire, the light in the test light will come on (or the voltmeter will indicate the amount of voltage). You have now established that current is getting to the component.

5. Turn the ignition or dash switch **OFF** and reconnect the wire to the component.

If there was no power, then the problem is between the battery and the component. This includes all the switches, fuses, relays and the battery itself. The next place to look is the fusebox; check carefully either by eye or by using the test light across the fuse clips. The easiest way to check is to simply replace the fuse. If the fuse is blown, and upon replacement, immediately blows again, there is a short between the fuse and the component. This is generally (not always) a sign of an internal short in the component. Disconnect the power wire at the component again and replace the fuse; if the fuse holds, the component is the problem.

✳✳ WARNING

DO NOT test a component by running a jumper wire from the battery UNLESS you are certain that it operates on 12 volts. Many electronic components are designed to operate with less voltage and connecting them to 12 volts could destroy them. Jumper wires are best used to bypass a portion of the circuit (such as a stretch of wire or a switch) that DOES NOT contain a resistor and is suspected to be bad.

If all the fuses are good and the component is not receiving power, find the switch for the circuit. Bypass the switch with the jumper wire. This is done by connecting one end of the jumper to the power wire coming into the switch and the other end to the wire leaving the switch. If the component comes to life, the switch has failed.

✳✳ WARNING

Never substitute the jumper for the component. The circuit needs the electrical load of the component. If you bypass it, you will cause a short circuit.

Checking the ground for any circuit can mean tracing wires to the body, cleaning connections or tightening mounting bolts for the component itself. If the jumper wire can be connected to the case of the component or the ground connector, you can ground the other end to a piece of clean, solid metal on the vehicle. Again, if the component starts working, you've found the problem.

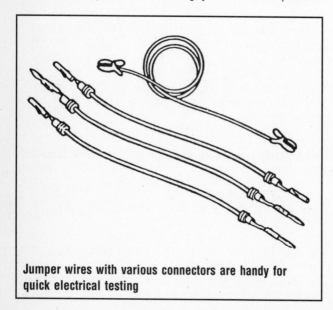

Jumper wires with various connectors are handy for quick electrical testing

A systematic search through the fuse, connectors, switches and the component itself will almost always yield an answer. Loose and/or corroded connectors, particularly in ground circuits, are becoming a larger problem in modern vehicles. The computers and on-board electronic (solid state) systems are highly sensitive to improper grounds and will change their function drastically if one occurs.

Remember that for any electrical circuit to work, ALL the connections must be clean and tight.

➡**For more information on Understanding and Troubleshooting Electrical Systems, please refer to Section 6 of this manual.**

Battery, Starting and Charging Systems

BASIC OPERATING PRINCIPLES

Battery

The battery is the first link in the chain of mechanisms which work together to provide cranking of the automobile engine. In most modern vehicles, the battery is a lead/acid electrochemical device consisting of six 2v subsections (cells) connected in series so the unit is capable of producing approximately 12v of electrical pressure. Each subsection consists of a series of positive and negative plates held a short distance apart in a solution of sulfuric acid and water.

The two types of plates are of dissimilar metals. This sets-up a chemical reaction, and it is this reaction which produces current flow from the battery when its positive and negative terminals are connected to an electrical accessory such as a lamp or motor. The continued transfer of electrons would eventually convert the sulfuric acid to water, and make the two plates identical in chemical composition. As electrical energy is removed from the battery, its voltage output tends to drop. Thus, measuring battery voltage and battery electrolyte composition are two ways of checking the ability of the unit to supply power. During engine cranking, electrical energy is removed from the battery. However, if the charging circuit is in good condition and the operating conditions are normal, the power removed from the battery will be replaced by the alternator which will force electrons back through the battery, reversing the normal flow, and restoring the battery to its original chemical state.

Starting System

The battery and starting motor are linked by very heavy electrical cables designed to minimize resistance to the flow of current. Generally, the major power supply cable that leaves the battery goes directly to the starter, while other electrical system needs are supplied by a smaller cable. During starter operation, power flows from the battery to the starter and is grounded through the vehicle's frame/body or engine and the battery's negative ground strap.

The starter is a specially designed, direct current electric motor capable of producing a great amount of power for its size. One thing that allows the motor to produce a great deal of power is its tremendous rotating speed. It drives the engine through a tiny pinion gear (attached to the starter's armature), which drives the very large flywheel ring gear at a greatly reduced speed. Another factor allowing it to produce so much power is that only intermittent operation is required of it. Thus, little allowance for air circulation is necessary, and the windings can be built into a very small space.

The starter solenoid is a magnetic device which employs the small current supplied by the start circuit of the ignition switch. This magnetic action moves a plunger which mechanically engages the starter and closes the heavy switch connecting it to the battery. The starting switch circuit usually consists of the starting switch contained within the ignition switch, a neutral safety switch or clutch pedal switch, and the wiring necessary to connect these in series with the starter solenoid or relay.

The pinion, a small gear, is mounted to a one way drive clutch. This clutch is splined to the starter armature shaft. When the ignition switch is moved to the **START** position, the solenoid plunger slides the pinion toward the flywheel ring gear via a collar and spring. If the teeth on the pinion and flywheel match properly, the pinion will engage the flywheel immediately. If the gear teeth butt one another, the spring will be compressed and will force the gears to mesh as soon as the starter turns far enough to allow them to do so. As the solenoid plunger reaches the end of its travel, it closes the contacts that connect the battery and starter, then the engine is cranked.

As soon as the engine starts, the flywheel ring gear begins turning fast enough to drive the pinion at an extremely high rate of speed. At this point, the one-way clutch begins allowing the pinion to spin faster than the starter shaft so that the starter will not operate at excessive speed. When the ignition switch is released from the starter position, the solenoid is de-energized, and a spring pulls the gear out of mesh interrupting the current flow to the starter.

Some starters employ a separate relay, mounted away from the starter, to switch the motor and solenoid current on and off. The relay replaces the solenoid electrical switch, but does not eliminate the need for a solenoid mounted on the starter used to mechanically engage the starter drive gears. The relay is used to reduce the amount of current the starting switch must carry.

Charging System

The automobile charging system provides electrical power for operation of the vehicle's ignition system, starting system and all electrical accessories. The battery serves as an electrical surge or storage tank, storing (in chemical form) the energy originally produced by the engine driven generator. The system also provides a means of regulating output to protect the battery from being overcharged and to avoid excessive voltage to the accessories.

The storage battery is a chemical device incorporating parallel lead plates in a tank containing a sulfuric acid/water solution. Adjacent plates are slightly dissimilar, and the chemical reaction of the two dissimilar plates produces electrical energy when the battery is connected to a load such as the starter motor. The chemical reaction is reversible, so that when the generator is producing a voltage (electrical pressure) greater than that produced by the battery, electricity is forced into the battery, and the battery is returned to its fully charged state.

Newer automobiles use alternating current generators or alternators, because they are more efficient, can be rotated at higher speeds, and have fewer brush problems. In an alternator, the field usually rotates while all the current produced passes only through the stator winding. The brushes bear against continuous slip rings. This causes the current produced to periodically reverse the direction of its flow. Diodes (electrical one way valves) block the

flow of current from traveling in the wrong direction. A series of diodes is wired together to permit the alternating flow of the stator to be rectified back to 12 volts DC for use by the vehicle's electrical system.

The voltage regulating function is performed by a regulator. The regulator is often built in to the alternator; this system is termed an integrated or internal regulator.

Ignition Coil

TESTING

Piston Engines Through 1981

Measure the primary resistance by connecting an ohmmeter across the positive (+) and negative (−) terminals of the coil. Primary resistance, at 68°F (20°C), should be $0.9\Omega \pm 0.09\Omega$.

Measure the secondary resistance by connecting an ohmmeter across the center tower connector and the positive (+) terminal. Resistance, at 68°F (20°C), should be 6–30KΩ.

If a megaohm tester is available, connect it between the negative (−) terminal and the outside of the coil casing. This will test the coil insulation and show if there is an internal short. Resistance, at 68°F (20°C), should be >10MΩ.

1982–86 Piston Engines

1. Connect an ohmmeter set to the X1 scale to the plug and minus primary connectors of the coil, as shown. The coil should have good continuity. That is, resistance should be approximately 1–1.3Ω except on the 2,654cc, on which the resistance should be approximately 0.72–0.88Ω.

2. Disconnect the high tension wire and move the connector leading to the minus terminal over to the metallic connector inside the coil tower. Set the ohmmeter to the X1000 scale. Resistance must be 10,000–30,000Ω.

3. You can also check for bad coil insulation by measuring the resistance between the coil (−) primary connection and the metal body (case) of the coil. If resistance is less than 10mΩ, replace the coil. This test may not be entirely satisfactory unless you have a megaohm tester that records 500 volts. If the tests below do not reveal the problem and, especially, if operating the engine at night may produce some bluish sparks around the coil, you may want to remove the coil and have it tested at a diagnostic center.

4. If the coil resistances are not as specified, replace the coil.

If the coil tests out ok, replace the igniter and pickup coil. However, you should make sure before doing this work that there are no basic maintenance problems in the secondary circuit of the system, since it is often impossible to return electrical parts. We suggest that before you replace the igniter and pickup coil, you carefully inspect the cap and rotor for carbon tracks or cracks and disconnect the wires and measure their resistance with an ohmmeter. Resistance should be 16,000Ω per length of 100cm. Also, check for cracks in the insulation. Replace secondary parts as inspection/testing deems necessary before replacing the igniter and pickup coil.

Rotary Engine

Two coils, leading and trailing, are used. The leading coil is type HP5-13J; the trailing, type HP5-13E.

1. Measure the primary resistance by connecting an ohmmeter across the positive ($+$) and negative ($-$) terminals of the coil. Primary resistance, at 68°F (20°C), should be 1.35Ω on the leading coil; 1.46Ω on the trailing coil.

2. Measure the secondary resistance by connecting an ohmmeter across the center tower connector and the positive ($+$) terminal. Resistance, at 68°F (20°C), should be 8.7KΩ on the leading coil; 9.5KΩ on the trailing coil.

3. Check across the external resistor on each coil. Resistance, at 68°F (20°C), should be 1.4Ω on the leading coil; 1.6Ω on the trailing coil.

REMOVAL & INSTALLATION

1. Disconnect the negative battery cable and make sure the ignition switch is off. Remove any protective boots from the top of the coil, if necessary by sliding them back the coil-to-distributor wire.

2. Carefully pull the high tension wire out of the coil, twisting it gently as near as possible to the tower to get it started.

3. Note the routing and colors of the primary wires, and then remove nuts and lockwashers, retaining all parts for installation. Clean the primary terminals with sandpaper, if necessary, to ensure a clean connection. Then, loosen the through bolt or bolts which clamp the coil in place and slide the coil out of its mount.

4. Install the new coil in exact reverse order, making sure the primary connections are tight. Ensure also that the coil-to-distributor wire is fully seated in the tower and that the protective boot is fully installed on the outside of the tower.

Ignition Module

REMOVAL & INSTALLATION

1. Disconnect the harness connector from the top of the igniter.

2. Remove the two attaching screws and remove the igniter.

3. Install the new igniter and secure it with the two attaching screws.

4. Connect the harness connector.

Distributor

REMOVAL & INSTALLATION

▶ **See Figure 1**

Rotary Engine

The distributor is located on the right front side of the engine. In contrast to earlier rotary engines from Mazda, this uses only one distributor, not two.
1. Open the hood and locate the distributor.
2. Remove the distributor cap.
3. Disconnect the vacuum tube from the advance unit.
4. Disconnect the primary wires from the distributor.

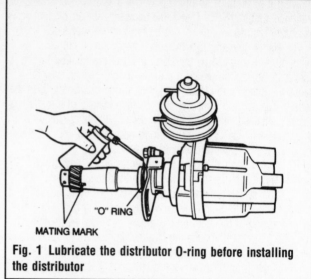

Fig. 1 Lubricate the distributor O-ring before installing the distributor

5. Matchmark the distributor body in relation to the engine front housing.
6. Remove the distributor hold-down bolt.
7. Pull the distributor from the front cover.
8. Turn the eccentric shaft until the TDC mark on the drive pulley aligns with the indicator pin on the front cover.
9. Align the matchmarks on the distributor housing and drive gear.
10. Install the distributor so that the distributor lockbolt is located in the center of the slot. Engage the gears.
11. Rotate the distributor clockwise until the leading contact point set starts to separate, and tighten the distributor lockbolt.
12. Install the distributor cap and connect the primary wires.
13. Set the ignition timing.
14. Connect the vacuum tube to the vacuum unit on the distributor.

Piston Engine

1972–84 VEHICLES

1. Matchmark the distributor cap and the body of the distributor. Remove the distributor cap.
2. Disconnect the vacuum hose from the diaphragm.
3. Scribe matchmarks on the distributor body and the cylinder block to indicate the relative positions.
4. Scribe another mark on the distributor body indicating the position of the rotor.
5. Disconnect the primary wires from the distributor.
6. Remove the distributor hold-down nut, lockwasher and flat washer.
7. Remove the distributor from the engine.

➡**Do not crank the engine while the distributor is removed.**

8. Align the matchmarks on the distributor gear and body.
9. If the engine was cranked while the distributor was removed, turn the crankshaft until the No. 1 cylinder is at the top of the compression stroke. This can be determined by feeling compression with your thumb over the spark plug port. The painted mark (5° BTDC or 8° BTDC) mark on the crankshaft pulley should also be aligned with the timing pointer. Slide the distribu-

tor into the engine with the rotor pointing to the No. 1 cylinder firing position. See the Firing Orders in Section 2.

10. Lubricate the O-ring with clean engine oil. If the engine has not been cranked while the distributor was removed, slide the distributor (with the O-ring) into the engine, aligning the match-marks made during removal.

11. Install the flat washer, lockwasher and hold-down nut.

12. Install the distributor cap and connect the primary wires.

13. Set the ignition timing, and tighten the hold-down nut.

14. Connect the vacuum line.

1986 VEHICLES

1. Disconnect the spark plug wires from the distributor cap and route them off to the side and out of the way.

2. Disconnect the vacuum hoses and wiring.

3. Rotate the engine with a socket wrench on the pulley until the number one piston is at top dead center.

4. Loosen the lockbolts and remove the distributor.

5. Remove the O-ring from the coupling shaft and purchase a new one.

After removing the distributor cap and disconnecting any wires to the distributor, loosen and remove the distributor hold-down bolt . . .

. . . then pull the distributor free from the cylinder head

→**Make sure that the number one piston is at top dead center before installing the distributor.**

6. Install a new O-ring onto the coupling shaft and apply a coat of clean engine oil to the O-ring to the driven gear.

7. Align the dimple on the distributor drive gear with the mark cast into the base of the distributor body by rotating the shaft.

8. Install the distributor and reconnect the wiring connector, vacuum hose(s) and spark plug wires.

9. Set the ignition timing.

Alternator

The alternator charging system is a negative (−) ground system which consists of an alternator, a regulator, a charge indicator, a storage battery and wiring connecting the components, and fuse link wire.

The alternator is belt-driven from the engine. Energy is supplied from the alternator/regulator system to the rotating field through two brushes to two slip-rings. The slip-rings are mounted on the rotor shaft and are connected to the field coil. This energy supplied to the rotating field from the battery is called excitation current and is used to initially energize the field to begin the generation of electricity. Once the alternator starts to generate electricity, the excitation current comes from its own output rather than the battery.

The alternator produces power in the form of alternating current. The alternating current is rectified by 6 diodes into direct current. The direct current is used to charge the battery and power the rest of the electrical system.

When the ignition key is turned on, current flows from the battery, through the charging system indicator light on the instrument panel, to the voltage regulator, and to the alternator. Since the alternator is not producing any current, the alternator warning light comes on. When the engine is started, the alternator begins to produce current and turns the alternator light off. As the alternator turns and produces current, the current is divided in two ways: part to the battery to charge the battery and power the electrical components of the vehicle, and part is returned to the alternator to enable it to increase its output. In this situation, the alternator is receiving current from the battery and from itself. A voltage regulator is wired into the current supply to the alternator to prevent it from receiving too much current which would cause it to put out too much current. Conversely, if the voltage regulator does not allow the alternator to receive enough current, the battery will not be fully charged and will eventually go dead.

The battery is connected to the alternator at all times, whether the ignition key is turned on or not. If the battery were shorted to ground, the alternator would also be shorted. This would damage the alternator. To prevent this, a fuse link is installed in the wiring between the battery and the alternator. If the battery is shorted, the fuse link is melted, protecting the alternator.

ALTERNATOR PRECAUTIONS

Some precautions should be taken when working on this, or any other, AC charging system.

1. Never switch battery polarity.

2. When installing a battery, always connect the grounded terminal first.

3. Never disconnect the battery while the engine is running.

4. If the molded connector is disconnected from the alternator, never ground the hot wire.

5. Never run the alternator with the main output cable disconnected.

6. Never electric weld around the truck without disconnecting the alternator.

7. Never apply any voltage in excess of battery voltage while testing.

8. Never jump a battery for starting purposes with more than 12v.

CHARGING SYSTEM TROUBLESHOOTING

There are many possible ways in which the charging system can malfunction. Often the source of a problem is difficult to diagnose, requiring special equipment and a good deal of experience. This is usually not the case, however, where the charging system fails completely and causes the dash board warning light to come on or the battery to become dead. To troubleshoot a complete system failure only two pieces of equipment are needed: a test light, to determine that current is reaching a certain point; and a current indicator (ammeter), to determine the direction of the current flow and its measurement in amps.

This test works under three assumptions:

1. The battery is known to be good and fully charged.

2. The alternator belt is in good condition and adjusted to the proper tension.

3. All connections in the system are clean and tight.

➡**In order for the current indicator to give a valid reading, the truck must be equipped with battery cables which are of the same gauge size and quality as original equipment battery cables.**

1. Turn off all electrical components on the car. Make sure the doors of the truck are closed. If the truck is equipped with a clock, disconnect the clock by removing the lead wire from the rear of the clock. Disconnect the positive battery cable from the battery and connect the ground wire on a test light to the disconnected positive battery cable. Touch the probe end of the test light to the positive battery post. The test light should not light. If the test light does light, there is a short or open circuit on the car.

2. Disconnect the voltage regulator wiring harness connector at the voltage regulator. Turn on the ignition key. Connect the wire on a test light to a good ground (engine bolt). Touch the probe end of a test light to the ignition wire connector into the voltage regulator wiring connector. This wire corresponds to the **I** terminal on the regulator. If the test light goes on, the charging system warning light circuit is complete. If the test light does not come on and the warning light on the instrument panel is on, either the resistor wire, which is parallel with the warning light, or the wiring to the voltage regulator, is defective. If the test light does not come on and the warning light is not on, either the bulb is defective or the power supply wire from the battery through the ignition switch to the bulb has an open circuit. Connect the wiring harness to the regulator.

3. Examine the fuse link wire in the wiring harness from the starter relay to the alternator. If the insulation on the wire is cracked or split, the fuse link may be melted. Connect a test light to the fuse link by attaching the ground wire on the test light to

an engine bolt and touching the probe end of the light to the bottom of the fuse link wire where it splices into the alternator output wire. If the bulb in the test light does not light, the fuse link is melted.

4. Start the engine and place a current indicator on the positive battery cable. Turn off all electrical accessories and make sure the doors are closed. If the charging system is working properly, the gauge will show a draw of less than 5 amps. If the system is not working properly, the gauge will show a draw of more than 5 amps. A charge moves the needle toward the battery, a draw moves the needle away from the battery. Turn the engine off.

5. Disconnect the wiring harness from the voltage regulator at the regulator at the regulator connector. Connect a male spade terminal (solderless connector) to each end of a jumper wire. Insert one end of the wire into the wiring harness connector which corresponds to the **A** terminal on the regulator. Insert the other end of the wire into the wiring harness connector which corresponds to the **F** terminal on the regulator. Position the connector with the jumper wire installed so that it cannot contact any metal surface under the hood. Position a current indicator gauge on the positive battery cable. Have an assistant start the engine. Observe the reading on the current indicator. Have your assistant slowly raise the speed of the engine to about 2,000 rpm or until the current indicator needle stops moving, whichever comes first. Do not run the engine for more than a short period of time in this condition. If the wiring harness connector or jumper wire becomes excessively hot during this test, turn off the engine and check for a grounded wire in the regulator wiring harness. If the current indicator shows a charge of about three amps less than the output of the alternator, the alternator is working properly. If the previous tests showed a draw, the voltage regulator is defective. If the gauge does not show the proper charging rate, the alternator is defective.

REMOVAL & INSTALLATION

1,586cc, 1,796cc, 1,970cc, 1,998cc and 2,209cc Engines

1. Disconnect the negative (ground) cable. On some models, it may be necessary to remove the battery.

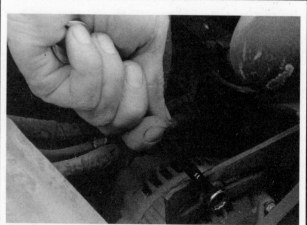

After removing all electrical connections to the alternator, loosen and remove the adjusting arm bolt and drive belt

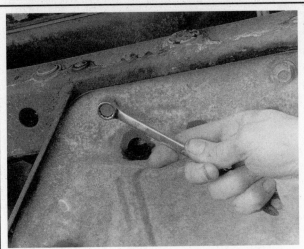

On some models, you must loosen the splash shield bolts . . .

. . . and remove the shield to gain access to the lower alternator bolts

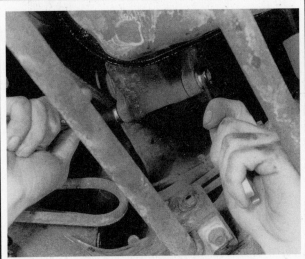

Loosen and remove the lower pivot bolt . . .

. . . and remove the alternator from the vehicle

2. Remove the nut holding the alternator wire to the terminal at the rear of the alternator.

3. Pull the multiple connector from the rear of the alternator.

4. Remove the alternator adjusting arm bolt. Swing the alternator in and disengage the fan belt.

5. On the 1,586cc and 1,796cc, remove the distributor cap and rotor from the distributor.

6. Remove the alternator pivot bolt and remove the alternator from the truck.

7. Installation is the reverse of the removal. Be sure to adjust the drive belt tension and to connect the battery properly.

Rotary Engine

1. Disconnect the battery ground cable at the negative ($-$) terminal.

2. Disconnect all of the leads from the alternator.

3. Remove the alternator adjusting link bolt. Do not remove the adjusting link.

4. Remove the alternator securing nuts and bolts. Withdraw the drive belt and remove the alternator.

5. Installation is performed in the reverse order of removal. Adjust the drive belt tension as detailed below.

BELT TENSION ADJUSTMENT

➡Refer to Section 1 for adjustment procedures.

Regulator

➡1982 and later trucks use an integral regulator, built into the alternator. No adjustments are possible.

REMOVAL & INSTALLATION

Piston Engine

1. Raise the hood and disconnect the negative battery cable.

2. Disconnect the regulator wires at the multiple connector.

3. Remove the two regulator attaching screws and remove the regulator from the splash shield.

4. Position the regulator on the fender splash shield and install the two attaching screws.

5. Connect the regulator wires at the multiple connector.

6. Connect the negative battery cable.

7. Start the engine and be sure that the charging system indicator light goes out.

Rotary Engine

1. Disconnect the battery ground cable at the negative (−) battery terminal.

2. Disconnect the wiring from the regulator.

3. Remove the regulator mounting screws.

4. Remove the regulator.

5. Installation is performed in the reverse order of removal.

TESTING

▶ **See Figures 2 and 3**

The alternator regulator is composed of two control units: a constant voltage relay and a pilot lamp relay.

Checking The Constant Voltage Relay

1. Use an almost fully charged battery and connect a voltmeter between the **A** and **E** terminals of the regulator.

2. Run the engine at 2,000 rpm and read the voltmeter. It should read from 14–15v.

3. If not, adjust the voltage relay.

Checking The Pilot Lamp Relay

1. Using a voltmeter and variable resistor, construct a circuit as shown.

2. Light the pilot lamp.

3. Slide the knob of the variable resistor so that the voltage gradually increases.

4. Read the voltage between the **N** and **E** terminals of the regulator. If the voltage is 3.7–5.7v, it is operating properly.

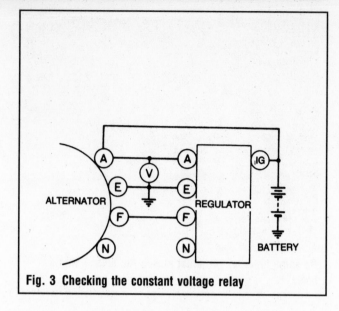

Fig. 3 Checking the constant voltage relay

5. Slide the knob of the variable resistor to decrease the voltage. Note the point on the voltmeter where the light will light again. If the reading is less than 3.5v, the unit is working properly.

6. Disconnect the test instruments.

ADJUSTING

▶ **See Figure 4**

Piston Engine

1. Check the air gap, back gap and point gap with a wire gauge. If they are not within specifications, adjust the gap by bending the stationary bracket.

2. After the gaps are correctly set, adjust the voltage setting. Bend the upper plate down to increase the voltage setting, or bend it up to increase the voltage setting.

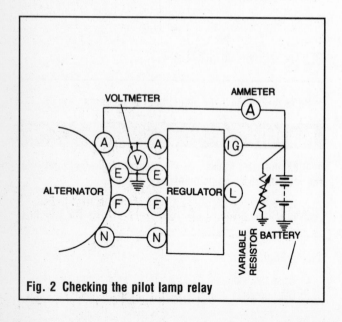

Fig. 2 Checking the pilot lamp relay

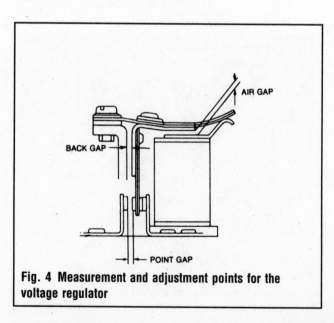

Fig. 4 Measurement and adjustment points for the voltage regulator

Rotary Engine

1. Remove the cover from the regulator.
2. Check the air gap, the point gap, and the back gap with a feeler gauge (see illustration).
3. If they do not fall within the specifications given in the Alternator and Regulator chart above, adjust the gaps by bending the stationary contact bracket.
4. Connect a voltmeter between the **A** and **E** terminals of the regulator.

➡**Be sure that the car's battery is fully charged before proceeding with this test.**

5. Start the engine and run it at 2,000 rpm (4,000 alternator rpm). The voltmeter reading should be 13.5–14.5v.
6. Stop the engine.
7. Bend the upper plate down to decrease the voltage setting, or up to increase the setting as required.
8. If the regulator cannot be brought within specifications, replace it.
9. When the test is completed, disconnect the voltmeter and replace the regulator cover.

Starter

The Mazda starter is a 4-brush, 4-field, 4-pole wound unit. Engine cranking occurs when the starter solenoid (mounted on the starter) in energized through the ignition switch. The solenoid shifts the starter pinion into mesh with the flywheel ring gear. At the same time, the main contacts of the solenoid are closed and the battery current is directed to the starter causing the armature to rotate. After the engine starts, the starter is disengaged when the ignition switch is returned to the RUN position. This opens the circuit to the starter solenoid and the solenoid return spring causes the shift lever to disengage the starter drive from the flywheel ring gear.

The diesel and the Mistubishi-built engines use gear reduction starters. They are similarly constructed, but feature a gearing function which allows them greater cranking torque.

DIAGNOSIS

Starter Won't Crank The Engine

1. Dead battery.
2. Open starter circuit, such as:
   a. Broken or loose battery cables.
   b. Inoperative starter motor solenoid.
   c. Broken or loose wire from ignition switch to solenoid.
   d. Poor solenoid or starter ground.
   e. Bad ignition switch.
3. Defective starter internal circuit, such as:
   a. Dirty or burnt commutator.
   b. Stuck, worn or broken brushes.
   c. Open or shorted armature.
   d. Open or grounded fields.
4. Starter motor mechanical faults, such as:
   a. Jammed armature end bearings.
   b. Bad bearings, allowing armature to rub fields.
   c. Bent shaft.

d. Broken starter housing.
e. Bad starter drive mechanism.
f. Bad starter drive or flywheel-driven gear.
5. Engine hard or impossible to crank, such as:
   a. Hydrostatic lock, water in combustion chamber.
   b. Crankshaft seizing in bearings.
   c. Piston or ring seizing.
   d. Bent or broken connecting rod.
   e. Seizing of connecting rod bearings.
   f. Flywheel jammed or broken.

Starter Spins Freely, Won't Engage

1. Sticking or broken drive mechanism.
2. Damaged ring gear.

REMOVAL & INSTALLATION

1,586cc, 1,796cc, 1,970cc and 1,998cc Engines

1. Raise the hood and disconnect the battery ground cable.
2. Remove the carburetor air cleaner and air intake tube.
3. Disconnect the battery cable from the starter solenoid battery terminal.
4. Pull the ignition switch wire from the solenoid terminal.
5. Raise and support the truck on jackstands.
6. Working under the truck, remove the two starter attaching bolts, washers and nuts.
7. Tilt the drive end of the starter and remove the starter by working it out below the emission system hoses.
   To install:
8. Install the starter and two bolts, washers and nuts.
9. Connect the ignition switch wire to the solenoid terminal.
10. Connect the battery cable to the solenoid battery terminal.
11. Install the carburetor air cleaner and air intake tube.
12. Connect the ground cable to the battery.
13. Lower the truck to the ground and check the operation of the starter.

2,209cc Engine

1. Disconnect the battery ground (negative) cable from the battery.
2. Raise and support the front end on jackstands.
3. Tag and remove the wires connected to the starter motor. Tagging the wires helps when reinstalling the starter motor.
4. Loosen and remove the two mounting bolts, make sure to support the weight of the starter motor.
5. Before installation of the motor, be sure to clean the mating surfaces of both the starter and the engine block.
6. Place the starter motor into position. Secure it with the mounting bolts. Connect the cables and wiring harness.

Rotary Engine

➡**There are two possible locations for the starter motor; one is the lower right-hand side of the engine and the other is on the upper right-hand side.**

1. Remove the ground cable from the negative (−) battery terminal.
2. If the truck is equipped with the lower mounted starter, remove the gravel shield from underneath the engine.

✱✱ CAUTION

Be extremely careful not to contact the hot exhaust pipe, while working underneath the car.

3. Remove the battery cable from the starter terminal.

4. Disconnect the solenoid leads from the solenoid terminals.

5. Remove the starter securing bolts and withdraw the starter assembly.

6. Installation is the reverse of the above steps.

BRUSH REPLACEMENT

1. Remove the starter. Remove the two screws attaching the brush end bearing cover and remove the bearing cover.

2. Remove the through-bolts.

3. Remove the C-washer, washer and spring from the brush end of the armature shaft.

4. Pull the brush end cover from the starter frame.

5. Unsolder the two brushes from the field terminals and slide the brush holder from the armature shaft.

6. Cut the two brush wires at the brush holder and solder two new brushes to the brush holder.

7. Install the brush holder on the armature shaft and install the brushes in the brush holder.

8. Install the brush end cover on the starter frame and be sure that the ear tabs of the brush holder are aligned with the through-bolt holes.

9. Install the through-bolts.

10. Install the rubber gasket, spring, washer and C-washer on the armature shaft.

11. Install the brush end bearing cover on the brush end cover and install the two screws. If the brush holder tabs are not aligned with the through-bolts, the bearing cover screws cannot be installed.

SOLENOID REPLACEMENT

1. Remove the starter from the truck.

2. Disconnect the field strap from the solenoid terminal.

3. Remove the two solenoid attaching screws.

4. Disengage the solenoid plunger from the shift fork and remove the solenoid.

5. Install the solenoid on the drive end housing, making sure that the solenoid plunger hook is engaged with the shift fork.

6. Apply 12v to the solenoid **S** terminal and measure the clearance between the starter drive and the stop-ring retainer. It should be 2.0–5.0mm (0.0787–0.1969 in.). If not, remove the solenoid and adjust the clearance by inserting an adjusting shim between the solenoid body and drive end housing.

7. Check the solenoid for proper operation and install the starter.

8. Check the operation of the starter.

OVERHAUL

◆ **See Figures 5, 6, 7, 8 and 9**

1,586cc, 1,796cc, 1,970cc and 1,998cc Engines

1. Remove the starter from the truck.

2. Disconnect the field strap from the solenoid.

3. Remove the screws attaching the solenoid to the drive end housing. Disengage the solenoid plunger hook from the shift fork and remove the solenoid.

4. Remove the shift fork pivot bolt, nut and lockwasher.

5. Remove the through-bolts and separate the drive end housing from the starter frame. At the same time, disengage the shift fork from the drive assembly.

6. Remove the two screws attaching the brush end bearing cover to the brush end cover.

7. Remove the C-washer, washer and spring from the brush end of the armature shaft.

8. Pull the brush end cover from the starter frame.

9. Slide the armature from the starter frame and brushes.

10. Slide the drive stop-ring retainer toward the armature and remove the stop-ring. Slide the retainer and drive assembly off the armature shaft.

11. Remove the field brushes from the brush holder and separate the brush holder from the starter frame.

12. Position the drive assembly on the armature shaft.

13. Position the drive stop-ring retainer on the armature shaft and install the drive stop-ring. Slide the stop-ring retainer over the stop-ring to secure the stop-ring on the shaft.

14. Position the armature in the starter frame. Install the brush holder on the armature and starter frame. Install the brushes in the brush holder.

15. Install the drive end housing on the armature shaft and starter housing. Engage the shift fork with the starter drive assembly as you move the drive end housing toward the starter frame.

16. Install the brush end cover on the starter frame making sure that the rear tabs of the brush holder are aligned with the through-bolt holes.

17. Install the through-bolts.

18. Install the rubber washer, spring, washer and C-washer on the armature shaft at the brush end. Install the brush end bearing cover on the brush end cover and install the attaching screws. If the brush end cover is not properly positioned, the bearing cover screws cannot be installed.

19. Align the shift fork with the pivot bolt hole and install the pivot bolt, lockwasher and nut. Tighten the nut securely.

20. Position the solenoid on the drive end housing. Be sure that the solenoid plunger hook is engaged with the shift fork.

21. Install the two solenoid retaining screws and washers.

22. Apply 12v to the solenoid S terminal (ground the M terminal) and check the clearance between the starter drive and the stop-ring retainer. The clearance should be 2.0–5.0mm (0.0787–0.1969 in.). If not, the solenoid plunger is not properly adjusted. The clearance can be adjusted by inserting an adjusting shim between the solenoid body and drive end housing.

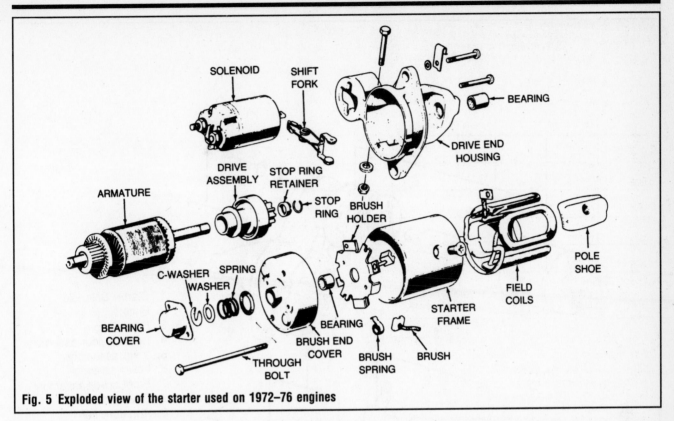

Fig. 5 Exploded view of the starter used on 1972–76 engines

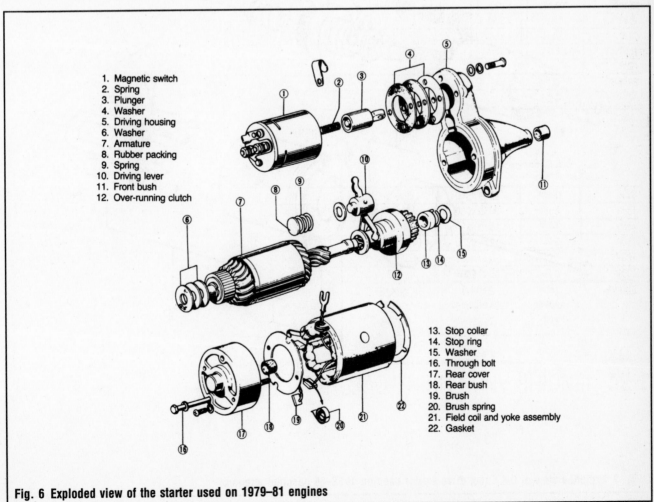

1. Magnetic switch
2. Spring
3. Plunger
4. Washer
5. Driving housing
6. Washer
7. Armature
8. Rubber packing
9. Spring
10. Driving lever
11. Front bush
12. Over-running clutch

13. Stop collar
14. Stop ring
15. Washer
16. Through bolt
17. Rear cover
18. Rear bush
19. Brush
20. Brush spring
21. Field coil and yoke assembly
22. Gasket

Fig. 6 Exploded view of the starter used on 1979–81 engines

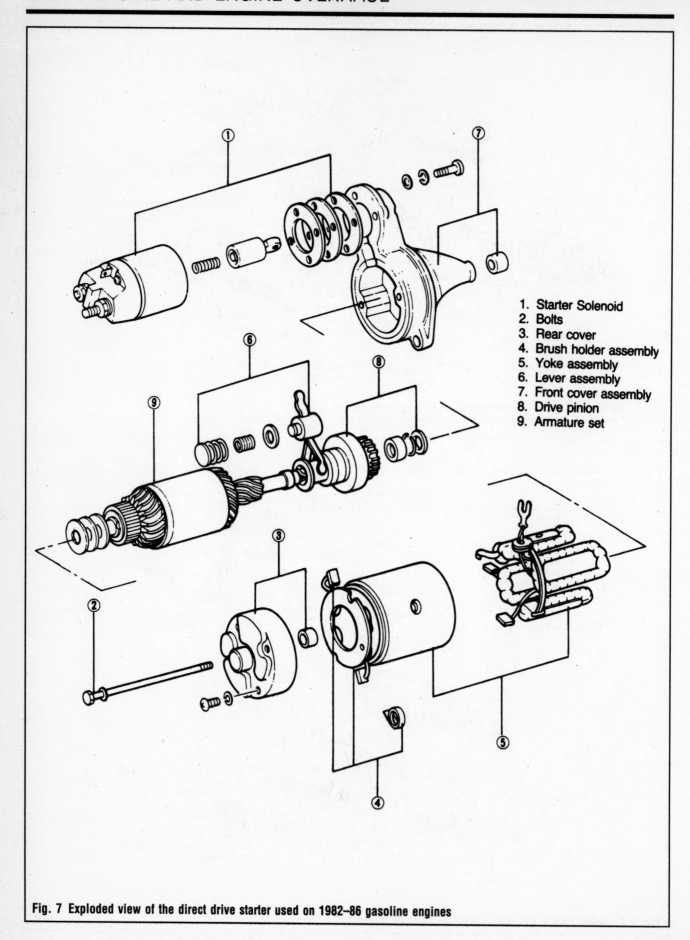

1. Starter Solenoid
2. Bolts
3. Rear cover
4. Brush holder assembly
5. Yoke assembly
6. Lever assembly
7. Front cover assembly
8. Drive pinion
9. Armature set

Fig. 7 Exploded view of the direct drive starter used on 1982–86 gasoline engines

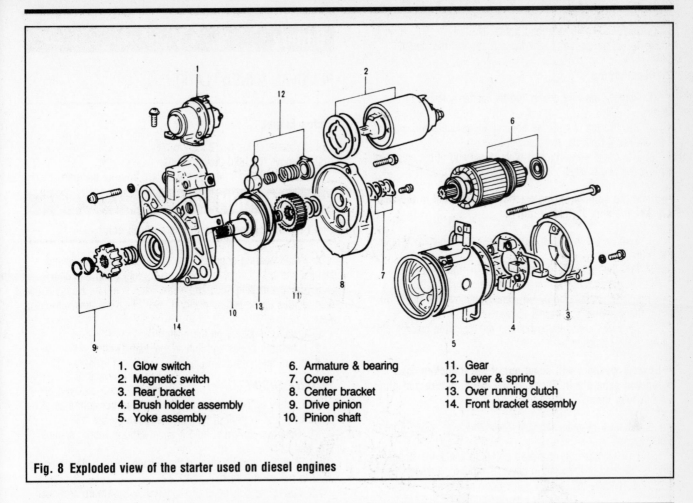

1. Glow switch
2. Magnetic switch
3. Rear bracket
4. Brush holder assembly
5. Yoke assembly
6. Armature & bearing
7. Cover
8. Center bracket
9. Drive pinion
10. Pinion shaft
11. Gear
12. Lever & spring
13. Over running clutch
14. Front bracket assembly

Fig. 8 Exploded view of the starter used on diesel engines

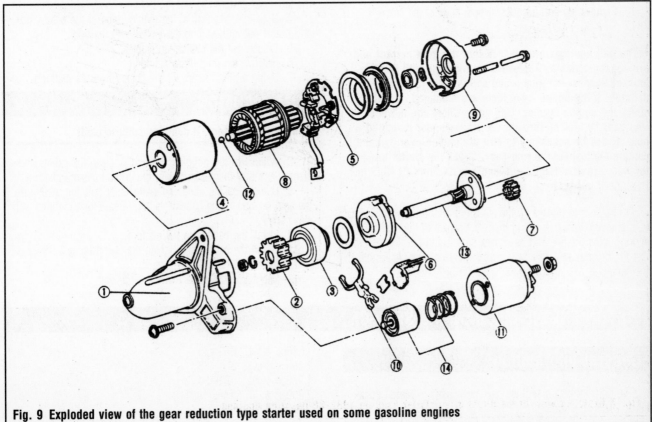

Fig. 9 Exploded view of the gear reduction type starter used on some gasoline engines

23. Install the field strap and tighten the nut.
24. Install the starter. Check the operation of the starter.

2,209cc Engine

1. Remove the wire connecting the starter solenoid to the starter.
2. Remove the two screws holding the solenoid and, pulling out, unhook it from the engagement lever.
3. Remove the two through bolts in the end of the starter and remove the two bracket screws. Pull off the rear bracket.

➡**Since the conical spring washer is contained in the rear bracket, be sure to take it out.**

4. Remove the yoke and brush holder assembly while pulling the brush upward.
5. Pull the armature assembly out of the mounting bracket.
6. On the side of the armature mounting bracket there is a small dust shield held on by two screws, remove the shield. Remove the snapring and washer located under the shield.
7. Remove the remaining bolts in the mounting bracket and separate the reduction case.

➡**Several washers will come out of the reduction case when you separate it. These adjust the armature end-play: do not lose them.**

8. Remove the reduction gear, lever and lever spring from the front bracket.
9. Use a brass drift or a deep socket to knock the stopper ring on the end of the shaft in toward the pinion. Remove the snapring. Remove the stopper, pinion and pinion shaft assembly.
10. Remove the ball bearings at both ends of the armature.

➡**The ball bearings are pressed into the front bracket and are not replaceable. Replace them together with the bracket. Inspect the pinion and spline teeth for wear or damage. If the pinion drive teeth are damaged, visually check the engine flywheel ring gear. Check the flywheel ring gear by looking through the starter motor mounting hole. It will be necessary to turn the engine over by hand to completely inspect the ring gear. Check the starter brushes for wear. Their service limit length is 11.5mm (0.4528 in.). Replace if necessary.**

11. Be sure to replace all the adjusting and thrust washers that you removed. When replacing the rear bracket, fit the conical spring pinion washer with its convex side facing out. Make sure that the brushes seat themselves on the commutator. Assemble the starter.

Battery

REMOVAL & INSTALLATION

Piston Engine

1. Disconnect the two battery cables.
2. Remove the hold-down clamps.
3. Using a lifting strap, lift the battery from its platform.

✳✳ CAUTION

Don't tilt the battery. It contains sulfuric acid!

4. While wearing goggles, thoroughly clean the cables and clamps and buff them with a wire brush until clean and shiny.
5. Using a baking soda and warm water solution, neutralize the acid residue in the battery platform area. Flush the area with clean water.
6. Install the battery on the platform.
7. Install the cables and tighten the clamp bolts.
8. Install the hold-down clamps.

ROTARY ENGINE

The battery is located in a compartment on the right side of the cargo bed, just in front of the rear wheel.

1. Open the door and hold it open with the rubber snubber provided.
2. Pull the latch handle (on the outside of the battery box) upward to release the latch.
3. Swing the outside of the battery box downward and push the top strap upward.
4. Grab the metal tab at the bottom edge of the battery box and pull it outward, sliding the battery into the open.
5. Disconnect the two battery cables.
6. Remove the hold-down clamps.
7. Using a lifting strap, lift the battery from its platform.

✳✳ CAUTION

Don't tilt the battery. It contains sulfuric acid!

8. While wearing goggles, thoroughly clean the cables and clamps and buff them with a wire brush until clean and shiny.
9. Using a baking soda and warm water solution, neutralize the acid residue in the battery platform area. Flush the area with clean water.
10. Install the battery on the platform.
11. Install the cables and tighten the clamp bolts.
12. Install the hold-down clamps.
13. Reposition the battery in the cargo bed.

PISTON ENGINE MECHANICAL SERVICE

General Information

Five different piston engines have been used in Mazda trucks since 1972. They are:

1,586cc 4-cyl., 1972–75
1,796cc 4-cyl., 1976–78
1,970cc 4-cyl., 1979–84
2,209cc 4-cyl. diesel, 1981–84
1,998cc 4-cyl., 1986

Engine Overhaul Tips

Most engine overhaul procedures are fairly standard. In addition to specific parts replacement procedures and specifications for your individual engine, this section is also a guide to acceptable rebuilding procedures. Examples of standard rebuilding practice are given and should be used along with specific details concerning your particular engine.

Competent and accurate machine shop services will ensure maximum performance, reliability and engine life. In most instances it is more profitable for the do-it-yourself mechanic to remove, clean and inspect the component, buy the necessary parts and deliver these to a shop for actual machine work.

On the other hand, much of the rebuilding work (crankshaft, block, bearings, piston rods, and other components) is well within the scope of the do-it-yourself mechanic's tools and abilities. You will have to decide for yourself the depth of involvement you desire in an engine repair or rebuild.

TOOLS

The tools required for an engine overhaul or parts replacement will depend on the depth of your involvement. With a few exceptions, they will be the tools found in a mechanic's tool kit (see Section 1 of this manual). More in-depth work will require some or all of the following:
• A dial indicator (reading in thousandths) mounted on a universal base
• Micrometers and telescope gauges
• Jaw and screw-type pullers
• Scraper
• Valve spring compressor
• Ring groove cleaner
• Piston ring expander and compressor
• Ridge reamer
• Cylinder hone or glaze breaker
• Plastigage®
• Engine stand
The use of most of these tools is illustrated in this chapter. Many can be rented for a one-time use from a local parts jobber or tool supply house specializing in automotive work.

Occasionally, the use of special tools is called for. See the information on Special Tools and the Safety Notice in the front of this book before substituting another tool.

INSPECTION TECHNIQUES

Procedures and specifications are given in this chapter for inspecting, cleaning and assessing the wear limits of most major components. Other procedures such as Magnaflux® and Zyglo® can be used to locate material flaws and stress cracks. Magnaflux® is a magnetic process applicable only to ferrous materials. The Zyglo® process coats the material with a fluorescent dye penetrant and can be used on any material.

Checking for suspected surface cracks can be more readily made using spot check dye. The dye is sprayed onto the suspected area, wiped off and the area sprayed with a developer. Cracks will show up brightly.

OVERHAUL TIPS

Aluminum has become extremely popular for use in engines, due to its low weight. Observe the following precautions when handling aluminum parts:
• Never hot tank aluminum parts (the caustic hot tank solution will eat the aluminum.
• Remove all aluminum parts (identification tag, etc.) from engine parts prior to the tanking.
• Always coat threads lightly with engine oil or anti-seize compounds before installation, to prevent seizure.
• Never overtorque bolts or spark plugs especially in aluminum threads.
Stripped threads in any component can be repaired using any of several commercial repair kits (Heli-Coil®, Microdot®, Keenserts®, etc.).

When assembling the engine, any parts that will be exposed to frictional contact must be prelubed to provide lubrication at initial start-up. Any product specifically formulated for this purpose can be used, but engine oil is not recommended as a prelube in most cases.

When semi-permanent (locked, but removable) installation of bolts or nuts is desired, threads should be cleaned and coated with Loctite® or another similar, commercial non-hardening sealant.

REPAIRING DAMAGED THREADS

Several methods of repairing damaged threads are available. Heli-Coil® (shown here), Keenserts® and Microdot® are among the most widely used. All involve basically the same principle—drilling out stripped threads, tapping the hole and installing a prewound insert—making welding, plugging and oversize fasteners unnecessary.

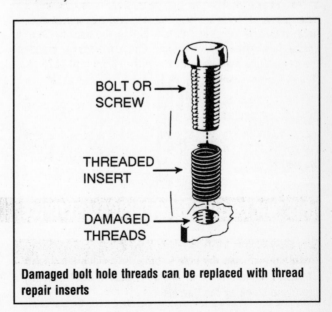

BOLT OR SCREW

THREADED INSERT

DAMAGED THREADS

Damaged bolt hole threads can be replaced with thread repair inserts

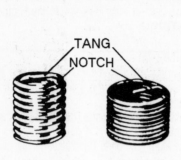

Standard thread repair insert (left), and spark plug thread insert

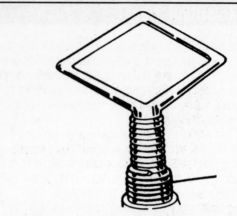

Screw the insert onto the installer tool until the tang engages the slot. Thread the insert into the hole until it is ¼–½ turn below the top surface, then remove the tool and break off the tang using a punch

Drill out the damaged threads with the specified size bit. Be sure to drill completely through the hole or to the bottom of a blind hole

Two types of thread repair inserts are usually supplied: a standard type for most inch coarse, inch fine, metric course and metric fine thread sizes and a spark lug type to fit most spark plug port sizes. Consult the individual tool manufacturer's catalog to determine exact applications. Typical thread repair kits will contain a selection of prewound threaded inserts, a tap (corresponding to the outside diameter threads of the insert) and an installation tool. Spark plug inserts usually differ because they require a tap equipped with pilot threads and a combined reamer/tap section. Most manufacturers also supply blister-packed thread repair inserts separately in addition to a master kit containing a variety of taps and inserts plus installation tools.

Before attempting to repair a threaded hole, remove any snapped, broken or damaged bolts or studs. Penetrating oil can be used to free frozen threads. The offending item can usually be removed with locking pliers or using a screw/stud extractor. After the hole is clear, the thread can be repaired, as shown in the series of accompanying illustrations and in the kit manufacturer's instructions.

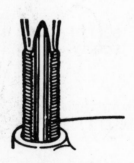

Using the kit, tap the hole in order to receive the thread insert. Keep the tap well oiled and back it out frequently to avoid clogging the threads

Checking Engine Compression

A noticeable lack of engine power, excessive oil consumption and/or poor fuel mileage measured over an extended period are all indicators of internal engine wear. Worn piston rings, scored or worn cylinder bores, blown head gaskets, sticking or burnt valves and worn valve seats are all possible culprits here. A check of each cylinder's compression will help you locate the problems.

As mentioned in the Tools and Equipment section of Chapter 1, a screw-in type compression gauge is more accurate than the type you simply hold against the spark plug hole, although it takes slightly longer to use. It's worth it to obtain a more accurate reading. Follow the procedures below for gasoline and diesel engined trucks.

A screw-in type compression gauge is more accurate and easier to use without an assistant

GASOLINE ENGINES

1. Warm up the engine to normal operating temperature.
2. Remove all spark plugs.
3. Disconnect the high tension lead from the ignition coil.
4. On fully open the throttle either by operating the carburetor throttle linkage by hand or by having an assistant floor the accelerator pedal.
5. Screw the compression gauge into the no. 1 spark plug hole until the fitting is snug.

➡**Be careful not to crossthread the plug hole. On aluminum cylinder heads use extra care, as the threads in these heads are easily ruined.**

6. Ask an assistant to depress the accelerator pedal fully on both carbureted and fuel injected trucks. Then, while you read the compression gauge, ask the assistant to crank the engine two or three times in short bursts using the ignition switch.
7. Read the compression gauge at the end of each series of cranks, and record the highest of these readings. Repeat this procedure for each of the engine's cylinders. Compare the highest reading of each cylinder to the compression pressure specification in the Tune-Up Specifications chart in Chapter 2. The specs in this chart are maximum values.

A cylinder's compression pressure is usually acceptable if it is not less than 80% of maximum. The difference between each cylinder should be no more than 12–14 pounds.

8. If a cylinder is unusually low, pour a tablespoon of clean engine oil into the cylinder through the spark plug hole and repeat the compression test. If the compression comes up after adding the oil, it appears that the cylinder's piston rings or bore are damaged or worn. If the pressure remains low, the valves may not be seating properly (a valve job is needed), or the head gasket may be blown near that cylinder. If compression in any two adjacent cylinders is low, and if the addition of oil doesn't help the com-

pression, there is leakage past the head gasket. Oil and coolant water in the combustion chamber can result from this problem. There may be evidence of water droplets on the engine dipstick when a head gasket has blown.

DIESEL ENGINES

◗ **See Figure 10**

Checking cylinder compression on diesel engines is basically the same procedure as on gasoline engines except for the following:

1. A special compression gauge adaptor suitable for diesel engines (because these engines have much greater compression pressures) must be used.
2. Remove the injector tubes and remove the injectors from each cylinder.

➡**Don't forget to remove the washer underneath each injector; otherwise, it may get lost when the engine is cranked.**

3. When fitting the compression gauge adaptor to the cylinder head, make sure the bleeder of the gauge (if equipped) is closed.
4. When reinstalling the injector assemblies, install new washers underneath each injector.

ROTARY ENGINES

The conventional compression gauges that are used for gasoline and diesel engines are not suitable for use on a rotary engine as they only measure the highest pressure of the three combustion chambers in the rotor housing. To accurately determine compression pressure on rotary engines, a special electronic compression tester (49-F018-9A0) is required. This piece of test equipment reads the compression of all three combustion chambers.

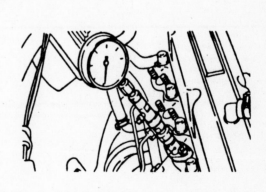

Fig. 10 Diesel engines require a special compression gauge adaptor due to its higher compression ratio

General Engine Specifications

Engine	Fuel System Type	SAE Net Horsepower (@rpm)	SAE Net Torque (ft. lb. @rpm)	Bore X Stroke (in.)	Comp. Ratio	Oil Pressure (psi@ 2000 rpm)
1308	4-bbl	90 @ 6000	96 @ 4000	—	9.2:1	70
1586	2-bbl	70 @ 5000	82 @ 3400	3.071 X 3.267	8.6:1	60
1796	2-bbl	75 @ 4800	93 @ 3000	3.071 X 3.700	8.6:1	60
1970	2-bbl	77 @ 4300	109 @ 2400	3.150 X 3.860	8.6:1	60
1998	2-bbl	80 @ 4500	110 @ 2500	3.386 X 3.386	8.6:1	57
2209	Diesel	58 @ 4000	88 @ 2500	3.500 X 3.500	21.0:1	57

4-bbl: Four barrel carburetor
2-bbl: Two barrel carburetor

Camshaft Specifications

All specifications in inches

Engine	Journal Diameter					Bearing Clearance	Cam Lift		End Play
	1	2	3	4	5		Intake	Exhaust	
1586	1.7717	1.7717	1.7717	—	—	①	1.75	1.75	0.004
1796	1.7717	1.7717	1.7717	—	—	①	1.77	1.78	0.004
1970	1.7717	1.7717	1.7717	—	—	①	1.77	1.77	0.004
1998	1.2578	1.2567	1.2567	1.2567	1.2578	②	1.50	1.50	0.004
2209	2.0472	2.0374	2.0177	—	—	0.0035	1.68	1.68	0.004

① Nos. 1 & 3: 0.0017
  No. 2: 0.0020
② Nos. 1 & 5: 0.0014-0.0031
  Nos. 2, 3, 4: 0.0026-0.0045

Valve Specifications

All measurements in inches unless otherwise noted

Engine	Seat Angle (deg.)	Face Angle (deg.)	Spring Test Pressure (lbs. @ in.)	Spring Free Length	Stem to Guide Clearance		Stem Diameter	
					Intake	Exhaust	Intake	Exhaust
1586	45	45	①	②	0.0007-0.0021	0.0007-0.0023	0.3105-0.3125	0.3105-0.3120
1796	45	45	①	②	0.0007-0.0021	0.0007-0.0023	0.3105-0.3125	0.3105-0.3120
1970	45	45	③	④	0.0007-0.0021	0.0007-0.0023	0.3105-0.3125	0.3105-0.3120
1998	45	45	⑤	⑥	0.0007-0.0021	0.0007-0.0023	0.3105-0.3125	0.3105-0.3120
2209	⑦	⑦	⑧	⑨	0.005 ⑩	0.005 ⑩	0.3115-0.3135	0.3115-0.3130

① Inner: 21 @ 1.260
  Outer: 31.5 @ 1.339
② Inner: 1.449
  Outer: 1.468
③ 1979-81 Inner: 21 @ 1.260
  Outer: 31.5 @ 1.339
  1982-84: Measure valve seat sink. Sink is the distance from the spring seat to the top of the valve. Intake should be
  1.610; exhaust should be 1.492. If sink is greater than +0.0196, the spring can be shimmed. If sink exceeds
  0.060, replace the valve
④ 1979-81 Inner: 1.449
  Outer: 1.469
  1982-83: 1.551
  1984 Inner: 1.449
  Outer: 1.587
⑤ Inner & Outer: No spec. given. Use Spring Free Length. If spring is shorter than spec. replace spring
⑥ Inner: 1.732
  Outer: 2.047
⑦ Intake: 45
  Exhaust: 30
⑧ Inner: 28 @1.488
  Outer: 40 @ 1.587
⑨ Inner: 1.654
  Outer: 1.717
⑩ Maximum allowable limit. If over 0.005 in. valve guide and or valve must be replaced

Crankshaft and Connecting Rod Specifications

All specifications are in inches

Engines	Crankshaft			Thrust on No.	Connecting Rod		
	Main Bearing Journal Diameter	Main Bearing Oil Clearance	Shaft End Play		Journal Diameter	Oil Clearance	Side Clearance
1586	2.4783	0.0012-0.0024	0.0031-0.0094	3	2.0846	0.0011-0.0030	0.0043-0.0083
1796	2.4783	0.0012-0.0024	0.0031-0.0094	3	2.0846	0.0011-0.0030	0.0043-0.0083
1970	2.4783	0.0012-0.0024	0.0031-0.0094	3	2.0846	0.0011-0.0030	0.0043-0.0083
1998	2.3618	0.0012-0.0019	0.0031-0.0071	3	2.0079	0.0010-0.0026	0.0039-0.0098
2209	2.5591	0.0016-0.0035	0.0055-0.0154	3	2.0866	0.0014-0.0031	0.0094-0.0134

Piston and Ring Specifications

All specifications are in inches

Engines	Ring Gap			Ring Side Clearance			Piston-to-Bore Clearance
	#1 Compr.	#2 Compr.	Oil Control	#1 Compr.	#2 Compr.	Oil Control	
1586	0.0079-0.0157	0.0079-0.0157	0.0118-0.0354	0.0014-0.0028	0.0012-0.0025	0.0012-0.0025	0.0022-0.0028
1796	0.0079-0.0157	0.0079-0.0157	0.0118-0.0354	0.0014-0.0028	0.0012-0.0025	snug	0.0022-0.0028
1970	0.0079-0.0157	0.0079-0.0157	0.0118-0.0354	0.0014-0.0028	0.0012-0.0025	snug	①
1998	0.0079-0.0118	0.0059-0.0118	0.0118-0.0354	0.0014-0.0028	0.0014-0.0028	snug	0.0014-0.0030
2209	0.0157-0.0217	0.0118-0.0157	0.0140-0.0217	0.0020-0.0035	0.0016-0.0031	0.0012-0.0031	0.0021-0.0031

① 1979-81: 0.0014-0.0030
1982-84: 0.0019-0.0025

Eccentric Shaft Specifications
Rotary Engine

All Specifications are in inches

Journal Diameter		Oil Clearences		Shaft End Play	Maximum Shaft Run Out
Main Bearing	Rotor Bearing	Main Bearing	Rotor Bearing		
1.6929	2.9134	0.0016-0.0039	0.0016-0.0039	0.0016-0.0035	0.0024

Rotor and Housing Specifications
Rotary Engine
All Specifications are in inches

Rotor		Housings						
Clearance to Side Housing	Standard Protrusion of Land	Front & Rear		Rotor		Intermediate	
		Distortion Limit	Wear Limit	Width	Distortion Limit	Distortion Limit	Wear Limit
0.0039-0.0083	0.0039-0.0059	0.0016	0.0039	3.1496	0.0024	0.0016	0.0039

Seal Clearance Specifications
Rotary Engine
All measurements given in inches

Apex Seals		Corner Seal	Side Seal	
To Side Housing	To Rotor Groove	To Rotor Groove	To Rotor Groove	To Corner Seal
0.0051-0.0118	0.0020-0.0059	0.0018-0.0019	0.0016-0.0039	0.0020-0.0059

Seal Specifications
Rotary Engine
All measurements given in inches

Apex Seal		Corner Seal O.D.	Side Seal		Oil Seal Lip Contact Width	Oil Seal Height
Height	Width		Thickness	Height		
0.2756+	0.1181	0.4331	0.03937	0.1378	<0.0315	0.2205

Torque Specifications
Piston Engines
All Specifications in ft. lbs. (Nm)

Engines	Cyl. Head	Conn. Rod	Main Bearing	Crankshaft Damper	Camshaft Sprocket	Flywheel	Manifolds	
							Intake	Exhaust
1586	①	36–40 (49–54)	61–65 (83–88)	101–108 (137–147)	51–58 (69–79)	112–118 (152–160)	14–19 (19–26)	②
1796	①	36–40 (49–54)	61–65 (83–88)	101–108 (137–147)	51–58 (69–79)	112–118 (152–160)	14–19 (19–26)	16–21 (22–29)
1970	③	④	61–65 (83–88)	⑤	51–58 (69–79)	⑥	14–19 (19–26)	16–21 (22–29)
1998	59–64 (80–87)	37–41 (50–56)	61–65 (83–88)	9–12 (12–16)	35–48 (48–65)	71–76 (97–103)	14–19 (19–26)	16–21 (22–29)
2209	80–85 (109–116)	51–55 (69–75)	81–86 (110–117)	145–181 (197–246)	45–51 (61–69)	95–137 (129–186)	11–17 (15–23)	11–17 (15–23)

① Cold: 56–60 (76–82)
　Normal Operating Temperature: 69–72 (94–98)
② 1972: 12–17 (16–23)
　1973-75: 16–21 (22–29)
③ 1979-81: 59–64 (80–87) Cold
　　　69–72 (94–98) Normal Operating Temperature
　1982-84: 65–69 (88–94) Cold
　　　69–72 (94–98) Normal Operating Temperature
④ 1979-81: 30–33 (41–45)
　1982-84: 36–40 (49–54)
⑤ 1979-82: 101–108 (137–147)
　1983-84: 116–123 (158–167)
⑥ 1979-82: 112–118 (152–161)
　1983-84: 108–118 (147–161)

Torque Specifications
Rotary Engine
All Specifications in ft. lbs. (Nm)

Tension Bolts	Eccentric Shaft Pulley	Flywheel	Manifolds		Oil Pump Sprocket	Oil Pan	Spark Plugs	Oil Filter Cartridge
			Intake	Exhaust				
23–27 (31–37)	72–87 (98–118)	289–362 (393–492)	12–17 (16–23)	32–43 (44–58)	22–25 (30–34)	5–7 (7–10)	9–13 (12–18)	5–7 (7–10)

Engine

REMOVAL & INSTALLATION

1,586cc Engine

1. Scribe the locations of the hood hinges and remove the hood.
2. Remove the engine splash shield.
3. Drain the coolant.

✳✳ CAUTION

When draining engine coolant, keep in mind that cats and dogs are attracted to ethylene glycol antifreeze and could drink any that is left in an uncovered container or in puddles on the ground. This will prove fatal in sufficient quantity. Always drain coolant into a sealable container. Coolant should be reused unless it is contaminated or is several years old.

4. Drain the engine oil.

✳✳ CAUTION

The EPA warns that prolonged contact with used engine oil may cause a number of skin disorders, including cancer! You should make every effort to minimize you exposure to used engine oil. Protective gloves should be worn when changing the oil. Wash your hands and any other exposed skin areas as soon as possible after exposure to used engine oil. Soap and water, or waterless hand cleaner should be used.

5. Disconnect the battery cables and remove the battery.
6. Disconnect the primary wire and coil wire from the distributor.
7. Disconnect the wire at the **B** terminal of the alternator and disconnect the plug from the rear of the alternator.

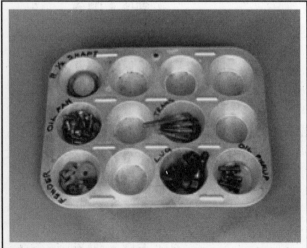

When removing nuts, bolts and other parts, place them in a tray or other container

8. Disconnect the wire from the oil pressure switch.
9. Disconnect the engine ground wire.
10. Remove the air cleaner and heat insulator.
11. Disconnect the breather hose from the rocker cover.
12. Disconnect the water temperature gauge wire and solenoid valve wire.
13. Disconnect the starter wires.
14. Remove the upper and lower radiator hoses.
15. Remove the bolts attaching the radiator cowling. The cowling can only be removed after the radiator has been removed.
16. Unbolt and remove the radiator and cowling.
17. Disconnect the heater hoses from the intake manifold.
18. Disconnect the throttle cable from the carburetor and remove the throttle linkage from the rocker cover attaching point.
19. Disconnect the choke cable from the carburetor.
20. Disconnect the fuel ventilation hose from the oil separator.
21. Disconnect the fuel line at the carburetor and plug the fuel line.

✳✳ CAUTION

Never smoke when working around gasoline! Avoid all sources of sparks or ignition. Gasoline vapors are EXTREMELY volatile!

22. Remove the starter.
23. Disconnect the exhaust pipe from the manifold.
24. Remove the clutch cover plate.
25. Support the transmission with a jack and remove the bolts attaching the engine to the transmission.
26. Unbolt the right and left engine mounts.
27. Attach a lifting sling to the engine and pull the engine forward until it clears the clutch shaft.
28. Lift the engine from the truck.

To install:

29. Lower the engine into the truck.
30. Push the engine rearward until it engages the clutch shaft.
31. Install the bolts attaching the engine to the transmission. Torque the bolts to 40 ft. lbs.
32. Connect the right and left engine mounts. Torque the bolts to 45 ft. lbs.
33. Install the clutch cover plate.
34. Connect the exhaust pipe to the manifold.
35. Install the starter.
36. Connect the fuel line at the carburetor.
37. Connect the fuel ventilation hose at the oil separator.
38. Connect the choke cable at the carburetor.
39. Connect the throttle cable at the carburetor and install the throttle linkage at the rocker cover attaching point.
40. Connect the heater hoses.
41. Install the radiator and cowling.
42. Install the upper and lower radiator hoses.
43. Connect the starter wires.
44. Connect the water temperature gauge wire and solenoid valve wire.
45. Connect the breather at from the rocker cover.
46. Install the air cleaner and heat insulator.
47. Connect the engine ground wire.
48. Connect the wire at the oil pressure switch.
49. Connect the wire at the alternator.

50. Connect the primary wire and coil wire at the distributor.
51. Install the battery.
52. Connect the battery cables.
53. Fill the engine with the proper amount of oil.
54. Fill the cooling system.
55. Install the engine splash shield.
56. Install the hood.

1,796cc and 1,970cc Engines

1. Scribe the locations of the hood hinges and remove the hood.
2. Remove the engine splash shield.
3. Drain the coolant.

✳✳ CAUTION

When draining engine coolant, keep in mind that cats and dogs are attracted to ethylene glycol antifreeze and could drink any that is left in an uncovered container or in puddles on the ground. This will prove fatal in sufficient quantity. Always drain coolant into a sealable container. Coolant should be reused unless it is contaminated or is several years old.

4. Drain the engine oil.

✳✳ CAUTION

The EPA warns that prolonged contact with used engine oil may cause a number of skin disorders, including cancer! You should make every effort to minimize you exposure to used engine oil. Protective gloves should be worn when changing the oil. Wash your hands and any other exposed skin areas as soon as possible after exposure to used engine oil. Soap and water, or waterless hand cleaner should be used.

5. Disconnect the battery cables and remove the battery.
6. Disconnect the primary wire and coil wire from the distributor.
7. Disconnect the wires at the alternator and disconnect the plug from the rear of the alternator. Remove the drive belts from the alternator, thermactor and air conditioning compressor. Remove each of these items from their mounting brackets and position them out of the way. It is not necessary to disconnect any refrigerant lines.
8. Disconnect the wire from the oil pressure switch.
9. Disconnect the engine ground wire.
10. Remove the air cleaner and heat insulator.
11. Disconnect the breather hose from the rocker cover.
12. Disconnect the water temperature gauge wire and solenoid valve wire.
13. Disconnect the starter wires.
14. Remove the upper and lower radiator hoses. On models with automatic transmission, disconnect the cooling lines at the radiator tank.
15. Remove the bolts attaching the radiator cowling. The cowling can only be removed after the radiator has been removed.
16. Unbolt and remove the radiator and cowling.
17. Disconnect the heater hoses from the intake manifold.
18. Disconnect the throttle cable from the carburetor and remove the throttle linkage from the rocker cover attaching point or the intake manifold clamps, on later models.
19. Disconnect the choke cable from the carburetor.
20. Disconnect the fuel ventilation hose from the oil separator.
21. Disconnect the fuel line at the carburetor and plug the fuel line.

✳✳ CAUTION

Never smoke when working around gasoline! Avoid all sources of sparks or ignition. Gasoline vapors are EXTREMELY volatile!

22. Raise and support the truck on jackstands. Remove the starter.
23. Disconnect the exhaust pipe from the manifold.
24. Remove the engine skid plate. Remove the clutch cover plate. On trucks with automatic transmission, disconnect the vacuum line at the modulator. Remove the torque converter access cover, matchmark the converter and drive plate and remove the four converter-to-drive plate bolts.
25. Support the transmission with a jack and remove the bolts attaching the engine to the transmission.
26. Unbolt the right and left engine mounts.
27. Attach a lifting sling to the engine and pull the engine forward until it clears the clutch shaft.
28. Lift the engine from the truck.
To install:
29. Lower the engine into the truck.
30. Pull the engine rearward until it engages the clutch shaft.
31. Install the bolts attaching the engine to the transmission. Torque them to 35 ft. lbs.
32. Connect the right and left engine mounts. Torque the bolts to 35 ft. lbs. Remove the shop crane.
33. Install the four converter-to-drive plate bolts. Torque them to 35 ft. lbs.
34. Install the torque converter access cover.
35. On trucks with automatic transmission, connect the vacuum line at the modulator.
36. Install the clutch cover plate.
37. Install the engine skid plate.
38. Connect the exhaust pipe at the manifold.
39. Install the starter.
40. Connect the fuel line at the carburetor.
41. Connect the fuel ventilation hose at the oil separator.
42. Connect the choke cable at the carburetor.
43. Connect the throttle cable at the carburetor.
44. Install the throttle linkage at the rocker cover attaching point or the intake manifold clamps, on later models.
45. Connect the heater hoses.
46. Install the radiator and cowling.
47. Install the upper and lower radiator hoses.
48. On models with automatic transmission, connect the cooling lines at the radiator tank.
49. Connect the starter wires.
50. Connect the water temperature gauge wire and solenoid valve wire.
51. Connect the breather hose at the rocker cover.
52. Install the air cleaner and heat insulator.
53. Connect the engine ground wire.
54. Connect the wire at the oil pressure switch.

55. Install the alternator.
56. Install the air pump.
57. Install the air conditioning compressor.
58. Connect the wires at the alternator.
59. Install the accessory drive belts.
60. Connect the primary wire and coil wire at the distributor.
61. Install the battery.
62. Connect the battery cables.
63. Fill the engine with the proper amount of oil.
64. Fill the cooling system.
65. Install the engine splash shield.
66. Install the hood.

1,998cc Engine

1. Scribe the locations of the hood hinges and remove the hood.
2. Remove the engine splash shield.
3. Drain the coolant.

✷✷ CAUTION

When draining engine coolant, keep in mind that cats and dogs are attracted to ethylene glycol antifreeze and could drink any that is left in an uncovered container or in puddles on the ground. This will prove fatal in sufficient quantity. Always drain coolant into a sealable container. Coolant should be reused unless it is contaminated or is several years old.

4. Drain the engine oil.

✷✷ CAUTION

The EPA warns that prolonged contact with used engine oil may cause a number of skin disorders, including cancer! You should make every effort to minimize you exposure to used engine oil. Protective gloves should be worn when changing the oil. Wash your hands and any other exposed skin areas as soon as possible after exposure to used engine oil. Soap and water, or waterless hand cleaner should be used.

5. Disconnect the battery cables and remove the battery.
6. Remove the air cleaner and the oil dipstick.
7. Remove the radiator shroud and the engine fan. Place the fan in an upright position to avoid fluid loss from the fan clutch.
8. Disconnect and tag all wires, hoses, cables, pipes and linkage from the engine.

✷✷ CAUTION

Never smoke when working around gasoline! Avoid all sources of sparks or ignition. Gasoline vapors are EXTREMELY volatile!

9. Remove the 3-way solenoid valves, but don't disconnect the vacuum tubes.
10. Remove the duty solenoid valves, but don't disconnect the vacuum tubes.
11. Remove the emissions canister.
12. Remove the radiator.

13. Disconnect the exhaust pipe at the manifold and remove the exhaust manifold.
14. Dismount the air conditioning compressor and position it out of the way. Don't disconnect any refrigerant lines.
15. Dismount the power steering pump and position it out of the way without disconnecting any hoses.
16. Raise and support the truck on jackstands.
17. Remove the starter.
18. Attach a lifting sling and shop crane to the engine lifting eyes and take up the weight of the engine.
19. Support the transmission with a floor jack and remove the transmission-to-engine bolts.
20. Remove the engine support plates and mounting nuts, push the engine forward to clear the transmission and lift it out of the truck.

To install:
21. Lower the engine into the truck.
22. Push the engine rearward to engage the transmission.
23. Install the engine support plates and mounting nuts. Torque the nuts to 35 ft. lbs.
24. Install the transmission-to-engine bolts. Torque the bolts to 35 ft. lbs.
25. On trucks with automatic transmission, install the converter bolts. Torque them to 35 ft. lbs.
26. Remove the shop crane.
27. Install the starter.
28. Install the power steering pump.
29. Install the exhaust manifold. Torque the exhaust manifold-to-engine nuts to 16–21 ft. lbs.
31. Connect the exhaust pipe at the manifold.
32. Install the radiator.
33. Install the emissions canister.
34. Install the duty solenoid valves.
35. Install the 3-way solenoid valves.
36. Connect all wires, hoses, cables, pipes and linkage at the engine.
37. Install the radiator shroud and the engine fan.
38. Install the air cleaner and the oil dipstick.
39. Install the battery.
40. Connect the battery cables.
41. Fill the engine with the proper amount of oil.
42. Fill the cooling system.
43. Install the engine splash shield.
44. Install the hood.

2,209cc Diesel Engine

1. Scribe the locations of the hood hinges and remove the hood.
2. Remove the engine splash shield.
3. Drain the coolant.

✷✷ CAUTION

When draining engine coolant, keep in mind that cats and dogs are attracted to ethylene glycol antifreeze and could drink any that is left in an uncovered container or in puddles on the ground. This will prove fatal in sufficient quantity. Always drain coolant into a sealable container. Coolant should be reused unless it is contaminated or is several years old.

4. Drain the engine oil.

> ## ✳✳ CAUTION
>
> **The EPA warns that prolonged contact with used engine oil may cause a number of skin disorders, including cancer! You should make every effort to minimize you exposure to used engine oil. Protective gloves should be worn when changing the oil. Wash your hands and any other exposed skin areas as soon as possible after exposure to used engine oil. Soap and water, or waterless hand cleaner should be used.**

5. Disconnect the battery cables and remove the battery.
6. Remove the air cleaner and the oil dipstick.
7. Remove the radiator shroud and the engine fan. Place the fan in an upright position to avoid fluid loss from the fan clutch.
8. Disconnect and tag all wires, hoses, cables, pipes and linkage from the engine.

> ## ✳✳ CAUTION
>
> **Never smoke when working around diesel fuel! Avoid all sources of sparks or ignition. Diesel fuel vapors are EXTREMELY volatile!**

9. Remove the clutch release cylinder.
10. Remove the oil cooler.
11. Remove the radiator.
12. Disconnect the exhaust pipe at the manifold and remove the exhaust manifold.
13. Dismount the air conditioning compressor and position it out of the way. Don't disconnect any refrigerant lines.
14. Dismount the power steering pump and position it out of the way without disconnecting any hoses.
15. Raise and support the truck on jackstands.
16. Attach a lifting sling and shop crane to the engine lifting eyes and take up the weight of the engine.
17. Support the transmission with a floor jack and remove the transmission-to-engine bolts.
18. Remove the engine support plates and mounting nuts.
19. Push the engine forward to clear the transmission and lift it out of the truck.

To install:

20. Lower the engine into the truck.
21. Push the engine rearward to engage the transmission.
22. Install the engine support plates and mounting nuts. Torque the nuts to 35 ft. lbs.
23. Install the transmission-to-engine bolts. Torque the bolts to 35 ft. lbs.
24. Remove the shop crane.
25. Install the power steering pump.
26. Install the air conditioning compressor.
27. Install the exhaust manifold.
28. Connect the exhaust pipe at the manifold.
29. Install the radiator.
30. Install the oil cooler.
31. Install the clutch release cylinder.
32. Connect all wires, hoses, cables, pipes and linkage at the engine.
33. Install the radiator shroud and the engine fan.
34. Install the air cleaner and the oil dipstick.
35. Install the battery.
36. Connect the battery cables.
37. Fill the engine with the proper amount of oil.
38. Fill the cooling system.
39. Install the engine splash shield.
40. Install the hood.

Rocker Arm Cover

REMOVAL & INSTALLATION

1,586cc, 1,796cc, 1,970cc, 1,998cc and 2,209cc Engines

1. If so equipped, disconnect the choke cable and the air by-pass valve cable.
2. On carbureted models, remove the air cleaner. On fuel injected models, loosen the clamps and remove the air intake crossover.
3. Disconnect the PCV valve at the cover or PCV line (diesels).
4. Remove the retaining bolts and remove the cam cover.
5. To install the cover, first supply new gaskets and, on the 1,998 engines, seal washers for the bolts.
6. Tighten the bolts in several stages, going back and forth across the cover. You can use the torque figures given for late model engines if you want, but the important point is to tighten the bolts evenly and just until they are slightly snug.
7. Once all the associated components are installed, start the engine and allow it to reach normal operating temperature. Retighten the bolts. Check for leaks.

Rocker Shafts

REMOVAL & INSTALLATION

1,586cc, 1,796cc and 1,970cc Engines
▶ **See Figures 11, 12 and 13**

➡**This operation should only be performed on a cold engine; the bolts which hold the rocker shafts in place also hold the cylinder head to the block.**

1. Raise the hood and cover the fenders.
2. Disconnect the choke cable, if so equipped.
3. If equipped, disconnect the air by-pass valve cable.
4. Disconnect the spark plug wires. Remove the wires from the spark plug wire clips on the rocker covers and position them out of the way.
5. Remove the rocker cover and discard the gasket.
6. Remove the rocker arm shaft attaching bolts evenly and remove the rocker arm shafts.

To install:

7. Install the rocker arm assemblies on the cylinder head. Install the balls on each rocker arm as shown. Temporarily tighten the cylinder head bolts to specifications and offset each rocker arm support 1mm (0.04 in.) from the valve stem center. Torque the bolts to specifications.
8. Adjust the valves cold.

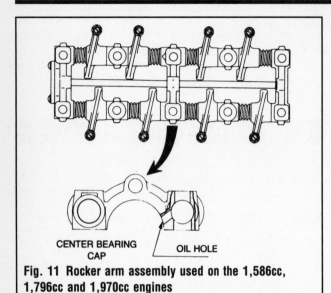

Fig. 11 Rocker arm assembly used on the 1,586cc, 1,796cc and 1,970cc engines

9. Clean the mating surfaces of the cylinder head and rocker cover.

10. Install the rocker cover with a new gasket. Torque the bolts to 24–36 in. lbs.

11. Install the spark plug wire on the plugs. Place the wires in the clips on the rocker cover. Connect the choke and air by-pass valve cable.

12. Start the engine and check for leaks.

13. Allow the engine to reach operating temperature, torque the head bolts to specifications and adjust the valves hot.

1,998cc Engine

♦ **See Figures 14 and 15**

1. Raise the hood and cover the fenders.
2. Disconnect the accelerator cable, if necessary.
3. If equipped, disconnect the air by-pass valve cable.
4. Disconnect the spark plug wires. Remove the wires from the spark plug wire clips on the rocker covers and position them out of the way.

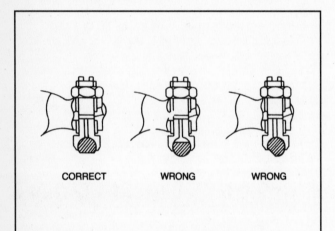

Fig. 12 Proper positioning of the rocker arm adjusting screw ball—make sure the flat portion of the ball contacts the valve tip

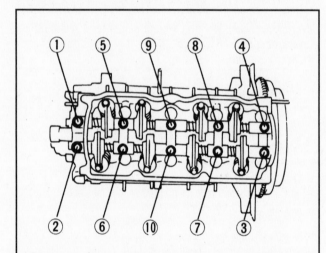

Fig. 14 Rocker arm torque sequence for the 1,998cc engine

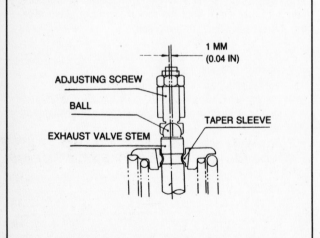

Fig. 13 Exhaust rockers may have a slight offset depending on engine model

Fig. 15 Removing the rocker arm and shaft assembly— some engines use the cylinder head bolts to retain the assembly, while others have separate rocker arm bolts

5. Remove the rocker cover and discard the gasket.

6. Remove the rocker arm shaft attaching bolts evenly, in the order shown, and remove the rocker arm shafts.

To install:

7. Install the rocker arm assemblies on the cylinder head. Torque the bolts, in the order shown, to 13–20 ft. lbs.

8. Check the valve adjustment and reset, if necessary.

9. Clean the mating surfaces of the cylinder head and rocker cover.

10. Install the rocker cover with a new gasket. Torque the bolts to 24–36 in. lbs.

11. Install the spark plug wire on the plugs. Place the wires in the clips on the rocker cover. Connect the choke and air by-pass valve cable.

12. Start the engine and check for leaks.

13. Allow the engine to reach operating temperature, torque the head bolts to specifications and adjust the valves hot.

2,209cc Diesel Engine

♦ **See Figure 16**

➡**This operation should only be performed on a cold engine; the bolts which hold the rocker shafts in place also hold the cylinder head to the block.**

1. Raise the hood and cover the fenders.

2. Disconnect the accelerator cable, if necessary.

3. Remove the rocker cover and discard the gasket.

4. Remove the rocker arm shaft attaching bolts evenly and remove the rocker arm shafts.

5. Lift out the pushrods, keeping them in order for proper installation. When installing the pushrods, make sure they are seated in the depressed bottom section of the tappets.

To install:

6. Install the rocker arm assemblies on the cylinder head. Torque the bolts to specifications.

7. Adjust the valves cold.

8. Clean the mating surfaces of the cylinder head and rocker cover.

9. Install the rocker cover with a new gasket. Torque the bolts to 24–36 in. lbs.

10. Install the spark plug wire on the plugs. Place the wires in

the clips on the rocker cover. Connect the choke and air by-pass valve cable.

11. Start the engine and check for leaks.

12. Allow the engine to reach operating temperature, torque the head bolts to specifications and adjust the valves hot.

DISASSEMBLY

Except Diesel Engine

➡**Don't mix up the parts! Keep them identified!**

1. Lay out a clean piece of heavy paper marked with a location for each component.

2. Remove the end caps and slide each piece from the shafts, placing it on its identifying mark on the paper.

➡**Don't hammer off any piece. If any piece is difficult to remove, soak it in Liquid Wrench®, WD-40® or similar solution. Hammering on any part will distort it!**

3. Check each component for wear, damage, heat scoring or cracks. Replace any suspect part. Clean all parts in a safe solvent. Make sure that all oil holes are clear.

4. Assembly is the reverse of disassembly.

Diesel Engine

➡**Don't mix up the parts! Keep them identified!**

1. Lay out a clean piece of heavy paper marked with a location for each component.

2. Remove the snaprings and washers from the ends of the shaft. Slide each piece from the shaft, placing it on its identifying mark on the paper.

➡**Don't hammer off any piece. If any piece is difficult to remove, soak it in Liquid Wrench®, WD-40® or similar solution. Hammering on any part will distort it!**

3. Check each component for wear, damage, heat scoring or cracks. Replace any suspect part. Clean all parts in a safe solvent. Make sure that all oil holes are clear.

4. Assembly is the reverse of disassembly.

Thermostat

REMOVAL & INSTALLATION

♦ **See Figures 17, 18 and 19**

1. Drain enough coolant to bring the coolant level down below the thermostat housing. The thermostat housing is located on the left front side of the cylinder block.

❋❋ CAUTION

When draining engine coolant, keep in mind that cats and dogs are attracted to ethylene glycol antifreeze and could drink any that is left in an uncovered container or in puddles on the ground. This will prove fatal in sufficient quantity. Always drain coolant into a sealable container. Coolant should be reused unless it is contaminated or is several years old.

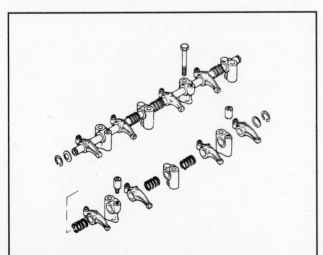

Fig. 16 Exploded view of the diesel rocker arm components

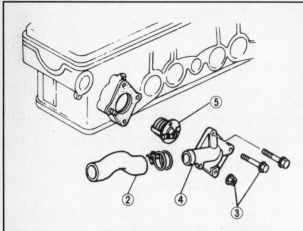

Fig. 17 Thermostat used on the 1,586cc, 1,796cc and 1,970cc engines—remove the parts in the order shown with Step 1 being to drain the engine coolant

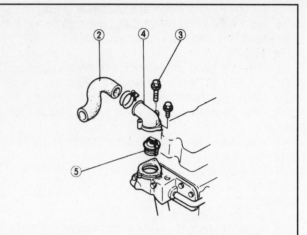

Fig. 18 Thermostat used on the diesel engine—remove the parts in the order shown with Step 1 being to drain the engine coolant

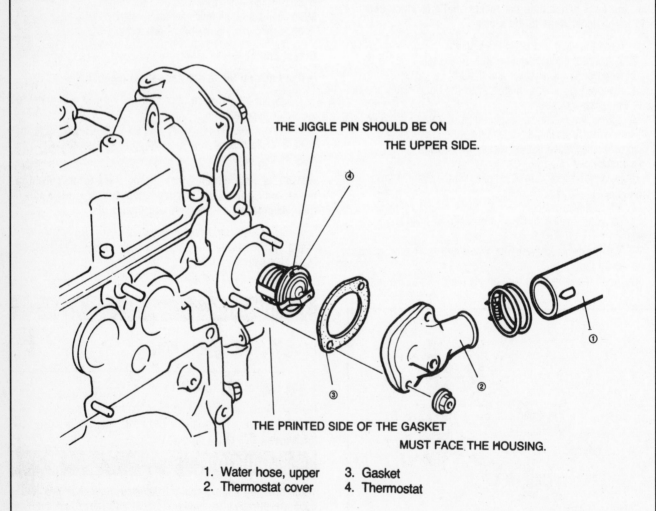

THE JIGGLE PIN SHOULD BE ON THE UPPER SIDE.

THE PRINTED SIDE OF THE GASKET MUST FACE THE HOUSING.

1. Water hose, upper
2. Thermostat cover
3. Gasket
4. Thermostat

Fig. 19 Thermostat used on the 1,998cc engine—drain the engine coolant, then remove the parts in the order shown

To remove the thermostat, first loosen the upper radiator hose-to-thermostat housing hose clamp . . .

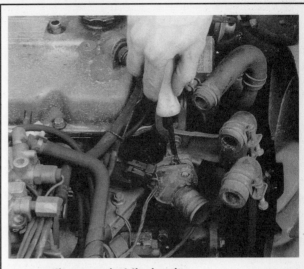

. . . gently pry against the housing . . .

. . . and loosen the thermostat housing nuts, . . .

. . . and remove the housing . . .

. . . then pull the hose off the thermostat housing and remove the housing nuts, . . .

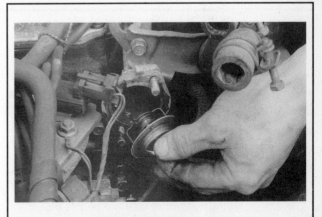

. . . finally, grasp the thermostat and pull it out to remove—note the jiggle pin in the top flange of the thermostat; this must face up to aid in air removal system during refill

2. Disconnect the temperature sending unit wire.

3. Remove the coolant outlet elbow.

4. If so equipped, position the vacuum control valve out of the way. The vacuum control valve is not used on California trucks.

5. Disconnect the coolant by-pass hose from the thermostat housing.

6. Remove the thermostat and housing from the engine.

7. Note the position of the jiggle pin and remove the thermostat from the housing.

8. Remove all gasket material from the parts.

To install:

9. Position the thermostat in the housing with the jiggle pin up. Coat a new gasket with sealer and install it on the thermostat housing.

10. Install the thermostat housing using a new gasket with water resistant sealer. Torque the bolts to 20 ft. lbs.

11. Install the coolant outlet elbow and vacuum control valve (if equipped).

12. Connect the by-pass and radiator hoses.

13. Connect the temperature sending unit wire.

14. Fill the cooling system with the proper coolant. Operate the engine and check the coolant lever. Check for leaks.

Intake Manifold

REMOVAL & INSTALLATION

1,586cc, 1,796cc, 1,970cc and 1,998cc Engines

1. Drain the cooling system.

❉❉ CAUTION

When draining engine coolant, keep in mind that cats and dogs are attracted to ethylene glycol antifreeze and could drink any that is left in an uncovered container or in puddles on the ground. This will prove fatal in sufficient quantity. Always drain coolant into a sealable container. Coolant should be reused unless it is contaminated or is several years old.

2. Remove the air cleaner.

3. Remove the accelerator linkage.

4. Disconnect the choke cable and fuel line. Plug the fuel line.

❉❉ CAUTION

Never smoke when working around gasoline! Avoid all sources of sparks or ignition. Gasoline vapors are EXTREMELY volatile!

5. Disconnect the PCV valve hose.

6. Disconnect the heater return hose and by-pass hose.

7. Remove the intake manifold-to-cylinder head attaching nuts.

8. Remove the manifold and carburetor as an assembly.

9. Clean the gasket mating surfaces.

To install:

10. Install a new gasket and the manifold on the studs. Torque the attaching nuts to specification, working from the center outward.

11. Connect the PCV valve hose to the manifold.

12. Connect the by-pass and heater return hoses.

13. Install the accelerator linkage.

14. Connect the fuel line and choke cable.

15. Replace the air cleaner.

16. Fill the cooling system. Run the engine and check for leaks.

2,209cc Diesel Engine

1. Remove the air inlet tube.

2. Remove the vacuum sensing line.

3. Bleed the fuel system and remove the injection lines. Cap the lines to prevent the entrance of dirt.

❉❉ CAUTION

Never smoke when working around diesel fuel! Avoid all sources of sparks or ignition. Diesel fuel vapors are EXTREMELY volatile!

4. Disconnect the accelerator linkage and any other hose or wire connected to the manifold.

5. Remove the fuel return line.

6. Unbolt and remove the manifold.

7. Discard the gasket and thoroughly clean the gasket surfaces of the head and manifold.

8. Installation is the reverse of removal. Always use a new gasket. Torque the manifold bolts to 11–17 ft. lbs.

Exhaust Manifold

REMOVAL & INSTALLATION

1,586cc, 1,796cc, 1,970cc, 1,998cc and 2,209cc Engines

1. Raise and support the truck.

2. Remove the two attaching nuts from the exhaust pipe at the manifold. On the 1,998cc, remove the exhaust manifold heat shield.

3. Remove the manifold attaching nuts.

4. Remove the manifold.

5. Apply a light film of graphite grease to the exhaust manifold mating surfaces before installation.

6. Install the manifold on the studs and install the attaching nuts. Torque the attaching nuts to specifications.

7. Install a new exhaust pipe gasket. Connect the exhaust pipe gasket. Connect the exhaust pipe and torque the nuts to specifications.

Radiator

REMOVAL & INSTALLATION

1. Drain the cooling system.

2. If necessary, remove the fan shroud.

To remove the radiator, drain the coolant by opening the petcock valve and unplug any electrical connections, . . .

. . . then unbolt the fan shroud from the radiator . . .

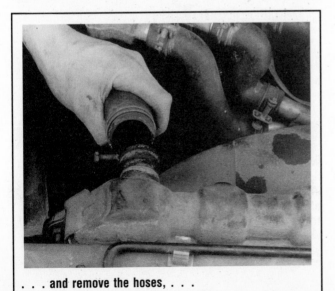

. . . loosen both upper and lower radiator hose clamps . . .

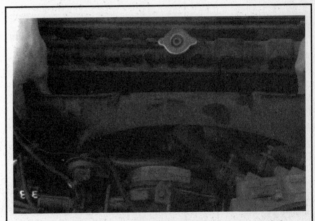

. . . and push back against the engine (some models may require you to remove the fan shroud). Also disconnect the coolant overflow hose (next to the radiator cap) . . .

. . . and remove the hoses, . . .

. . . unbolt the radiator from the radiator support . . .

. . . and lift the radiator out of the vehicle

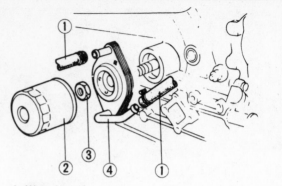

1. Water hoses
2. Oil filter
3. Nut
4. Oil cooler

Fig. 20 View of the engine oil cooler used on the 1,998cc engine

✳✳ CAUTION

When draining engine coolant, keep in mind that cats and dogs are attracted to ethylene glycol antifreeze and could drink any that is left in an uncovered container or in puddles on the ground. This will prove fatal in sufficient quantity. Always drain coolant into a sealable container. Coolant should be reused unless it is contaminated or is several years old.

3. If necessary, remove the fan. Don't lay the fan, if equipped with a fan clutch, on its side. Fluid will be lost and the fan clutch will have to be replaced.
4. Disconnect the upper and lower radiator hoses.
5. Disconnect the coolant reservoir hose.
6. On trucks with automatic transmission, disconnect the cooler lines.
7. Unbolt and remove the radiator.
To install:
8. Install the radiator against the supports and tighten the mounting bolts.
9. Install the hoses on the radiator. Tighten the clamps.
10. Install the fan.
11. If equipped, install the fan shroud.
12. Refill the cooling system with the specified amount and type of coolant. Run the engine and check for leaks.

Oil Cooler

REMOVAL & INSTALLATION

♦ **See Figure 20**

1,998cc Engine

1. Drain the cooling system.
2. Disconnect the coolant hoses at the oil cooler.

✳✳ CAUTION

When draining engine coolant, keep in mind that cats and dogs are attracted to ethylene glycol antifreeze and could drink any that is left in an uncovered container or in puddles on the ground. This will prove fatal in sufficient quantity. Always drain coolant into a sealable container. Coolant should be reused unless it is contaminated or is several years old.

3. Remove the oil filter.
4. Remove the nut securing the cooler to the oil filter mounting stud.
5. Remove the cooler.
6. Installation is the reverse of removal. Coat the O-rings on the filter and cooler with clean engine oil prior to installation.

Water Pump

REMOVAL & INSTALLATION

1,586cc, 1,796cc and 1,970cc Engines

♦ **See Figure 21**

1. Drain the cooling system.

✳✳ CAUTION

When draining engine coolant, keep in mind that cats and dogs are attracted to ethylene glycol antifreeze and could drink any that is left in an uncovered container or in puddles on the ground. This will prove fatal in sufficient quantity. Always drain coolant into a sealable container. Coolant should be reused unless it is contaminated or is several years old.

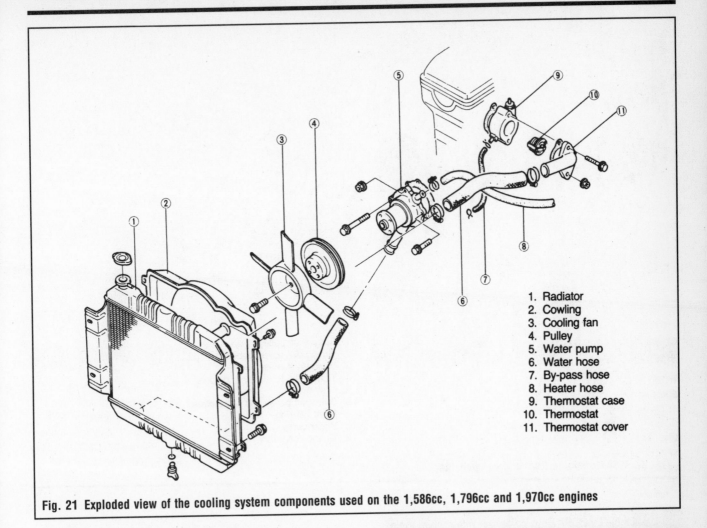

Fig. 21 Exploded view of the cooling system components used on the 1,586cc, 1,796cc and 1,970cc engines

1. Radiator
2. Cowling
3. Cooling fan
4. Pulley
5. Water pump
6. Water hose
7. By-pass hose
8. Heater hose
9. Thermostat case
10. Thermostat
11. Thermostat cover

2. Remove the lower hose from the water pump.

3. Disconnect the upper radiator hose from the engine and the lower radiator hose at the radiator.

4. Remove the radiator.

5. Remove the drive belts.

6. Remove the fan and pulley.

7. Remove the two small hoses from the water pump.

8. Unbolt and remove the water pump.

9. Clean the gasket surfaces of the water pump and cylinder block.

To install:

10. Install the water pump and new gasket on the block.

11. Install the lower hose on the water pump.

12. Install the fan and pulley. Install the crankshaft pulley.

13. Install the drive belts and adjust the tension.

14. Install the radiator.

15. Refill the cooling system with the specified amount and type of coolant. Install the radiator cap and start the engine. Check for leaks.

15. Install the hood.

1,998cc Engine

➡**See Figures 22 and 23**

1. Disconnect the battery ground.

2. Drain the cooling system.

✴✴ CAUTION

When draining engine coolant, keep in mind that cats and dogs are attracted to ethylene glycol antifreeze and could drink any that is left in an uncovered container or in puddles on the ground. This will prove fatal in sufficient quantity. Always drain coolant into a sealable container. Coolant should be reused unless it is contaminated or is several years old.

3. Remove the distributor.

4. Remove the fan shroud and fan.

5. Remove the alternator.

6. Disconnect the air injection pipes.

7. Remove the fan pulley, hub and bracket.

8. If so equipped, remove the air conditioning compressor drive belt.

9. If so equipped, remove the power steering pump drive belt.

10. Remove the crankshaft pulley and baffle plate.

11. Remove the upper, then the lower, belt covers.

12. Turn the crankshaft so that the **A** mark on the camshaft pulley is at the top, aligned with the notch in the front housing.

13. Loosen the tensioner lockbolt and remove the tensioner spring.

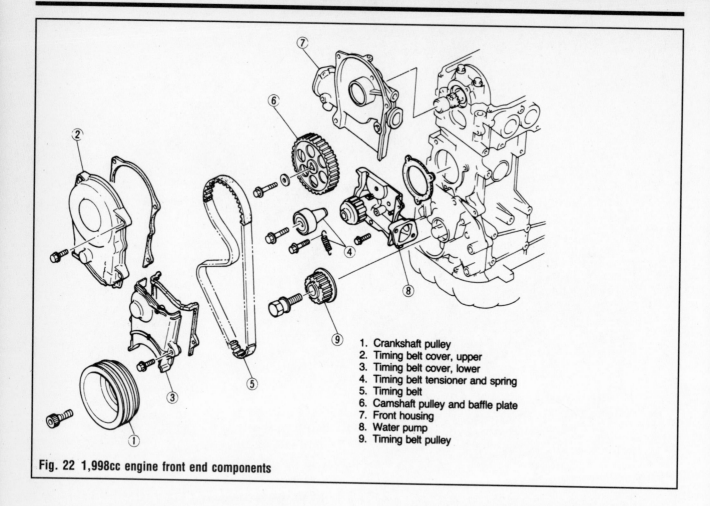

1. Crankshaft pulley
2. Timing belt cover, upper
3. Timing belt cover, lower
4. Timing belt tensioner and spring
5. Timing belt
6. Camshaft pulley and baffle plate
7. Front housing
8. Water pump
9. Timing belt pulley

Fig. 22 1,998cc engine front end components

14. Mark the forward rotation of the belt with paint to avoid confusion upon installation. Remove the belt.

15. Remove the coolant inlet pipe and gasket from the pump.

16. Unbolt and remove the pump. Discard the gasket and O-ring.

17. Install the pump, using a new O-ring coated with clean coolant and a new gasket coated with sealer. Torque the bolts to 14–19 ft. lbs.

18. Install the coolant inlet pipe, using a new gasket coated with sealer.

19. Replace the timing belt if it has been contaminated by oil or grease, or shows any sign of damage, wear, cracks or peeling.

To install:

20. To ease installation of the belt, remove all the spark plugs.

21. Make sure that the timing mark on the camshaft is aligned as described above, and that the timing mark (notch) on the crankshaft sprocket is aligned with the triangular shaped mark on the front housing.

22. Install the tensioner and spring, positioning the tensioner all the way to the intake manifold side and temporarily secure it there with the lockbolt.

23. Install the belt onto the sprockets from YOUR right side. If you are reusing the original belt, make sure you follow the directional mark previously made.

24. Loosen the lockbolt so that the tensioner applies tension to the belt.

25. Turn the crankshaft two full revolutions in the direction of normal rotation. This will apply equal tension to all points of the belt.

26. Make sure that the timing marks are still aligned. If not, repeat the belt installation procedure.

27. Tighten the tensioner lockbolt to 30–35 ft. lbs.

28. Measure the timing belt tension by pressing on the belt at the midpoint of the longest straight run. Belt deflection should be 11–13mm (0.433–0.510 in.). If not, repeat the belt adjustment procedure, above.

29. Install the upper, then the lower, belt covers. Torque the belt cover bolts to 80 in. lbs.

30. Install the crankshaft pulley and baffle plate.

31. If so equipped, install the power steering pump drive belt.

32. If so equipped, install the air conditioning compressor drive belt.

33. Install the fan pulley, hub and bracket.

34. Connect the air injection pipes.

35. Install the alternator.

36. Install the fan shroud and fan.

37. Install the distributor.

38. Fill the cooling system.

39. Connect the battery ground.

When installing the drive belts on the various accessories, check the belt deflection as follows:

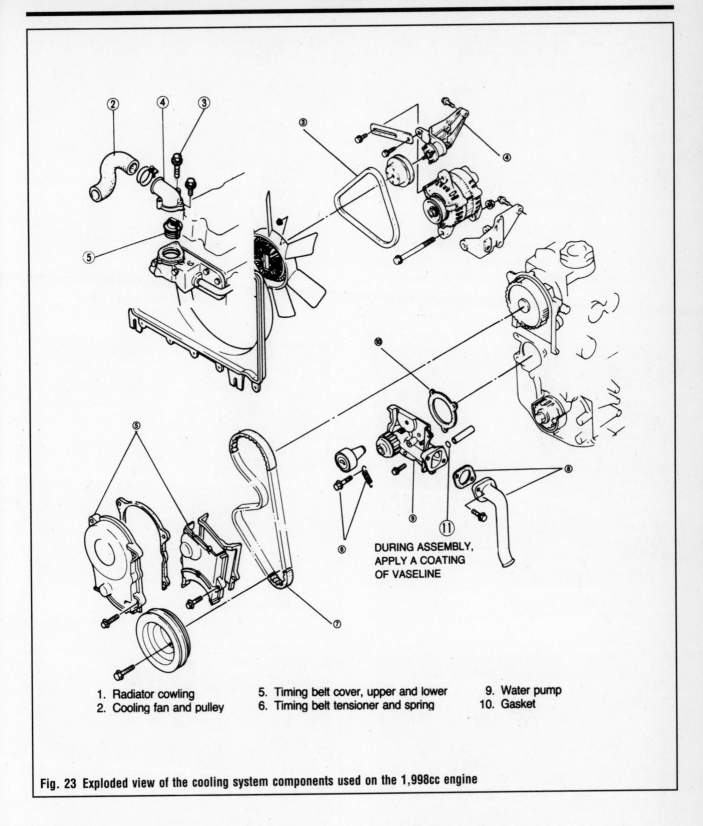

1. Radiator cowling
2. Cooling fan and pulley
5. Timing belt cover, upper and lower
6. Timing belt tensioner and spring
9. Water pump
10. Gasket

DURING ASSEMBLY,
APPLY A COATING
OF VASELINE

Fig. 23 Exploded view of the cooling system components used on the 1,998cc engine

- Alternator
  New: 7–8mm (0.276–0.315 in.)
  Used: 8–9mm (0.315–0.354 in.)
- Power steering pump
  New: 9–11mm (0.354–0.433 in.)

Used: 11–13mm (0.433–0.510 in.)
- Air conditioning compressor
  New: 10–12mm (0.394–0.476 in.)
  Used: 12–14mm (0.476–0.552 in.)

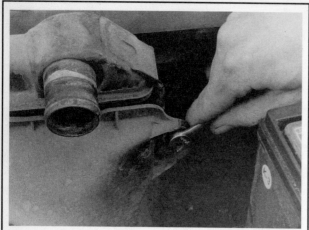

Drain the coolant and disconnect the radiator hoses from the radiator, then loosen and remove the fan shroud attaching bolts . . .

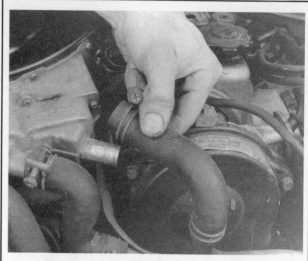

. . . and pull the hoses free from the air cleaner

. . . and remove the fan shroud

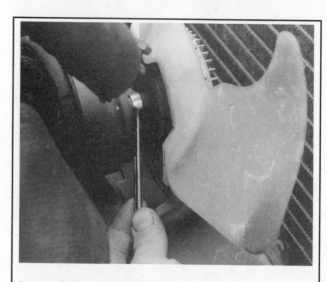

Loosen the fan attaching nuts . . .

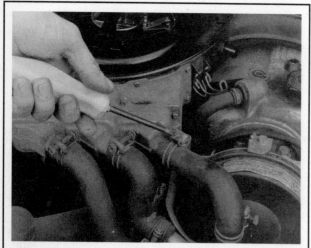

After removing the air cleaner lid and filter, loosen the air injection hose clamps . . .

. . . and remove the fan

After the alternator drive belt has been removed, take off the fan pulley . . .

. . . as well as from the bottom of the exhaust manifold, . . .

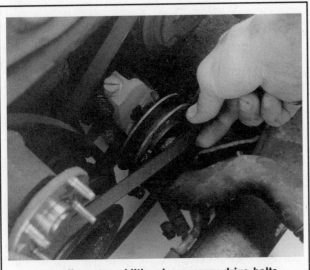

. . . as well as any additional accessory drive belts

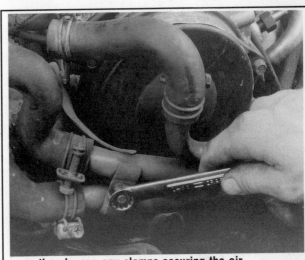

. . . then loosen any clamps securing the air pipes . . .

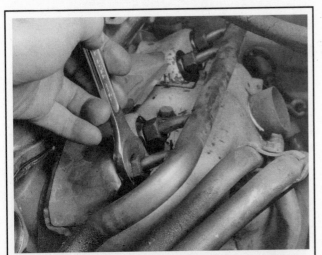

After removing the distributor, loosen the air injection manifold nuts at the top . . .

. . . and remove the air pipes

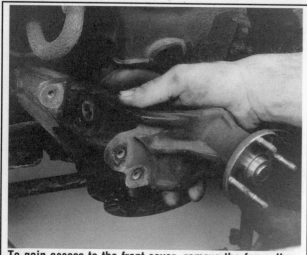

To gain access to the front cover, remove the fan pulley bracket . . .

. . . and then remove the crankshaft pulley (notice the perimeter bolt holes in the center of the pulley)—install the center bolt back into the end of the crankshaft

. . . then loosen the center crankshaft bolt and the six smaller perimeter bolts

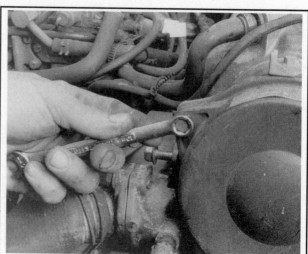

Unfasten the bolts retaining the upper and lower timing belt covers . . .

Remove the bolts . . .

. . . remove the upper cover . . .

. . . followed by the lower cover

Mark the timing belt and camshaft gear . . .

Turn the engine in the direction of normal rotation until the letter A on the camshaft gear aligns with the timing mark cast into the timing belt cover mounting flange (top center)

. . . and remove the belt

Loosen the timing belt tensioner pulley bolt (arrow), then move the pulley away from the belt and tighten the bolt again to lock the pulley in position—there should be little or no tension left on the timing belt

Remove the bolts securing the lower radiator hose housing to the water pump . . .

. . . then remove the water pump retaining bolts . . .

Scrape the old gasket off the sealing surfaces of the water pump and block

. . . and pull the water pump free

Pay attention to this hot water pipe (arrow); it uses an O-ring to seal the pipe to the water pump. Inspect the O-ring for tears or rough edges and replace, if necessary. Lubricate the O-ring with clean antifreeze or grease before installation

2,209cc Diesel Engine

▶ See Figure 24

1. Drain the cooling system.

❋❋ CAUTION

When draining engine coolant, keep in mind that cats and dogs are attracted to ethylene glycol antifreeze and could drink any that is left in an uncovered container or in puddles on the ground. This will prove fatal in sufficient quantity. Always drain coolant into a sealable container. Coolant should be reused unless it is contaminated or is several years old.

2. Remove the fan shroud.
3. Remove the fan, fan belt and pulley.
4. Disconnect the lower hose from the pump.

5. Remove the pump and discard the gasket.
6. Installation is the reverse of removal. Use a new water pump gasket coated with sealer.

Cylinder Head

REMOVAL & INSTALLATION

1,586cc, 1,796cc and 1,970cc Engines

▶ See Figures 25 and 26

➡The engine must be cold before proceeding.

1. Drain the cooling system.
2. Scribe alignment marks around the hood hinges and remove the hood.

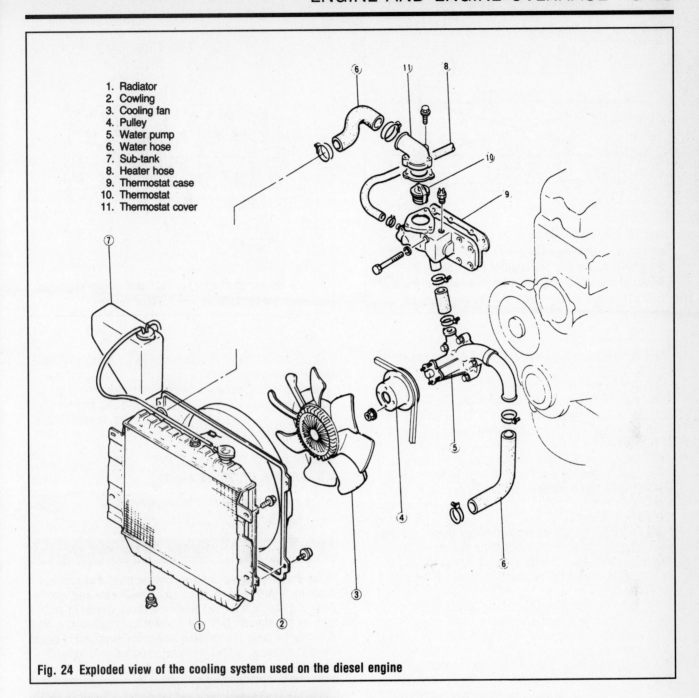

1. Radiator
2. Cowling
3. Cooling fan
4. Pulley
5. Water pump
6. Water hose
7. Sub-tank
8. Heater hose
9. Thermostat case
10. Thermostat
11. Thermostat cover

Fig. 24 Exploded view of the cooling system used on the diesel engine

✳✳ CAUTION

When draining engine coolant, keep in mind that cats and dogs are attracted to ethylene glycol antifreeze and could drink any that is left in an uncovered container or in puddles on the ground. This will prove fatal in sufficient quantity. Always drain coolant into a sealable container. Coolant should be reused unless it is contaminated or is several years old.

3. Remove the air cleaner.
4. Disconnect the coil wire and vacuum line from the distributor.
5. Rotate the crankshaft to put the no. 1 cylinder at TDC on the compression stroke.

6. Remove the plug wires and distributor cap as a unit.
7. Remove the distributor.
8. Remove the rocker arm cover.
9. Raise and support the truck.
10. Disconnect the exhaust pipe from the manifold.
11. Remove the accelerator linkage.
12. Disconnect and tag all wiring, cable and hoses from the engine.
13. Remove the water pump.
14. Remove the nut, washer and the distributor gear from the camshaft.
15. Remove the nut, washer and camshaft gear. Support the timing chain from falling into the timing chain case. Do not remove the cam gear from the timing chain. The relationship between the chain and gear teeth should not be disturbed.

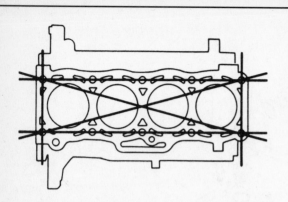

Fig. 25 Check the cylinder block deck for warpage by running a straightedge along both sides, both ends and diagonally as shown. Use a feeler gauge along the length of the straightedge. Maximum allowable warpage is 0.003 inches within 6 inches of the deck surface

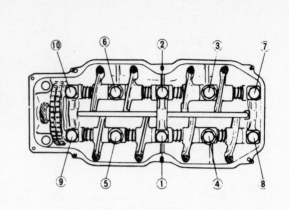

Fig. 26 Rocker shaft/cylinder head bolt torque sequence for the 1,586cc, 1,796cc and 1,970cc engines

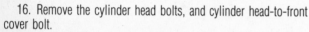

16. Remove the cylinder head bolts, and cylinder head-to-front cover bolt.

17. Remove the rocker arm assembly.

18. Remove the camshaft and camshaft gear.

19. Lift off the cylinder head.

20. Remove all tension from the timing chain.

To install:

21. Clean the rocker cover gasket surface at the head and the cover. Clean the head gasket surface at the head and the block. Clean the water pump gasket surface at the head and the block. Clean the water pump gasket surface at the head gasket surface and the front cover.

22. Check the cylinder head flatness with a straightedge and feeler blades. It should not exceed 0.08mm (0.0031 in.) in any 152mm (5.98 in.) span or 0.15mm (0.038 in.) overall. If necessary, the cylinder head can be milled, not to exceed 0.20mm (0.00787 in.).

23. Clean the cylinder head bolt holes of oil and dirt.

24. Position a new head gasket on the cylinder block.

25. Install the cylinder head on the block using the guides at either end of the block.

26. Install the camshaft on the head and camshaft gear.

27. Install the rocker arm assembly.

28. Install the head bolts. Torque the bolts to specification, in the order shown.

29. Install the camshaft gear washer and nut.

30. Install the distributor gear, washer and nut.

31. Time the engine. Follow the instructions under Timing Chain Tensioner Adjustment.

32. Adjust the timing chain tension. See Timing Chain Tensioner Adjustment.

33. Connect the exhaust pipe to the exhaust manifold. Lower the truck.

34. Install the distributor, distributor cap and plug wires.

35. Install the lower intake bracket bolt.

36. Install the accelerator linkage.

37. Connect the vacuum line and coil wire.

38. Adjust the valve clearance cold.

39. Install the rocker arm cover. Torque the bolts to 24–36 in. lbs. Fill the cooling system.

40. Run the engine until normal operating temperature is reached, and check for leaks. Adjust the valve clearance hot.

41. Adjust the carburetor and ignition timing. Install the air cleaner and install the hood.

1,998cc Engine

♦ **See Figures 27, 28, 29 and 30**

➡**The engine must be cold before proceeding.**

1. Drain the cooling system.

✳✳ CAUTION

When draining engine coolant, keep in mind that cats and dogs are attracted to ethylene glycol antifreeze and could drink any that is left in an uncovered container or in puddles on the ground. This will prove fatal in sufficient quantity. Always drain coolant into a sealable container. Coolant should be reused unless it is contaminated or is several years old.

2. Scribe alignment marks around the hood hinges and remove the hood.

3. Remove the air cleaner.

4. Disconnect, and tag, all wires, hoses, cables, pipes and linkage from the cylinder head.

5. Remove the 3-way solenoid valves, but don't disconnect the vacuum tubes.

6. Remove the duty solenoid valves, but don't disconnect the vacuum tubes.

7. Remove the emissions canister.

8. Remove the distributor cap. Matchmark the rotor position and distributor body, and the body-to-head position. Remove the distributor. Remove the spark plugs.

9. Remove the intake manifold and carburetor as an assembly.

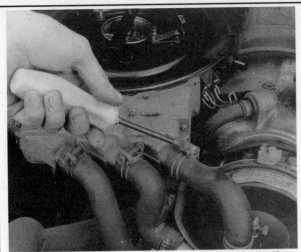

After removing the air cleaner lid and filter, loosen the air injection hose clamps . . .

. . . then loosen and remove the air cleaner-to-valve cover bolts

. . . and pull the hoses free from the air cleaner

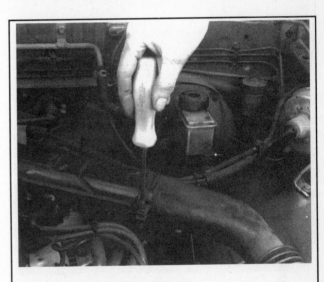

Loosen the fresh air hose clamp . . .

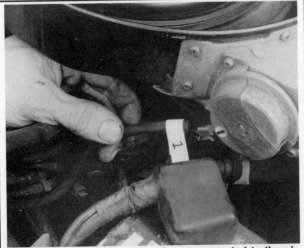

Label and remove all vacuum hoses connected to the air cleaner . . .

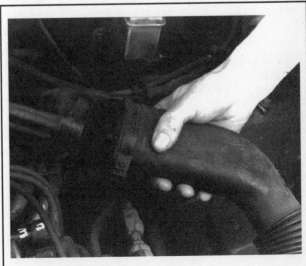

. . . and remove the fresh air hose

Loosen and remove the air cleaner housing-to-carburetor nuts . . .

. . . and remove the fan shroud and radiator

. . . then lift off the air cleaner

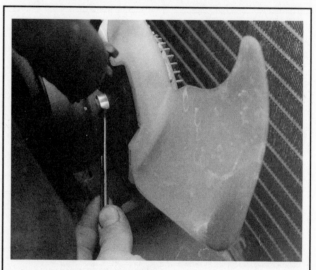

Loosen the fan attaching nuts . . .

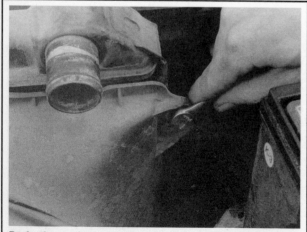

Drain the coolant and disconnect the radiator hoses from the radiator, then loosen and remove the fan shroud attaching bolts and radiator bolts . . .

. . . and remove the fan

After the alternator drive belt has been removed, take off the fan pulley . . .

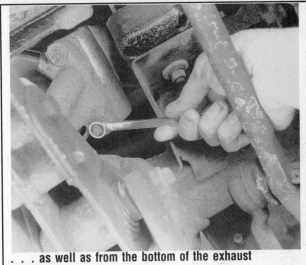

. . . as well as from the bottom of the exhaust manifold, . . .

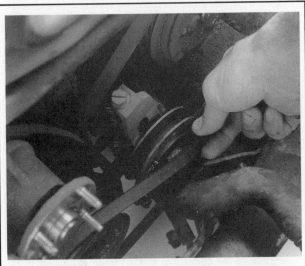

. . . and remove any additional accessory drive belts

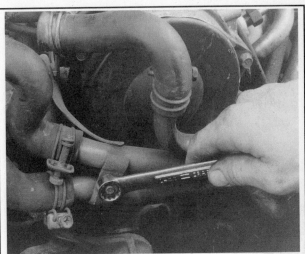

. . . then loosen any clamps securing the air pipes . . .

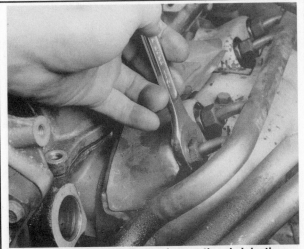

After removing the distributor, loosen the air injection manifold nuts at the top . . .

. . . and remove the air pipes

To gain access to the front cover, remove the fan pulley bracket, . . .

. . . and then remove the crankshaft pulley (notice the perimeter bolt holes in the center of the pulley)—install the center bolt back into the end of the crankshaft

. . . then loosen the center crankshaft bolt and the six smaller perimeter bolts . . .

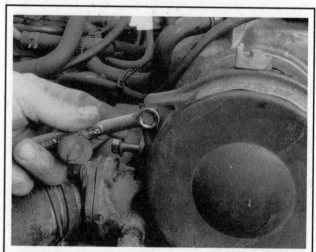

Now remove the upper and lower timing belt cover bolts and . . .

. . . remove the bolts . . .

. . . remove the upper cover . . .

. . . then the lower cover

Mark the timing belt and camshaft gear . . .

Turn the engine in the direction of normal rotation until the letter A on the cam gear aligns with the timing mark cast into timing belt cover mounting flange (top center)

. . . then remove the belt

Loosen the timing belt tensioner pulley bolt (arrow), then move the pulley away from the belt and tighten the bolt again to lock the pulley in position—there should be little or no tension left on the timing belt

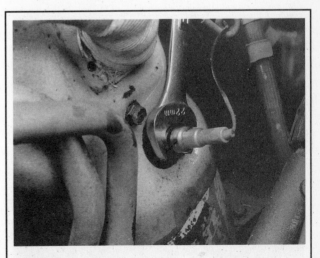

To remove the exhaust manifold, unscrew the oxygen sensor . . .

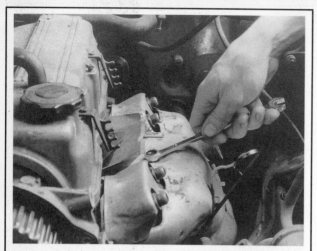

. . . then remove all the heat shield retaining bolts . . .

. . . as well as the exhaust manifold-to-catalytic converter bolts, . . .

. . . and remove the heat shield . . .

. . . then pull off the exhaust manifold . . .

Remove the exhaust manifold-to-cylinder head nuts . . .

. . . and the old exhaust manifold gasket

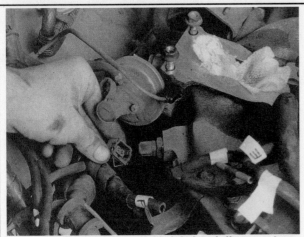

To remove the intake manifold, label and disconnect any vacuum and electrical connections (carburetor removed for clarity) . . .

. . . then lift off the cylinder head—some prying may be necessary, however, never hammer any object between the cylinder head and block, as this could damage the sealing surfaces

. . . then remove the intake manifold-to-cylinder head nuts . . .

Scrape the old gasket off the block and cylinder head surfaces, and wipe them free of any grease or oil

. . . and pull the intake manifold away from the cylinder head. Remove the valve cover, then loosen and remove the cylinder head bolts using the proper loosening sequence . . .

When installing the cylinder head, use an accurate torque wrench and follow the tightening sequence and torque specifications given

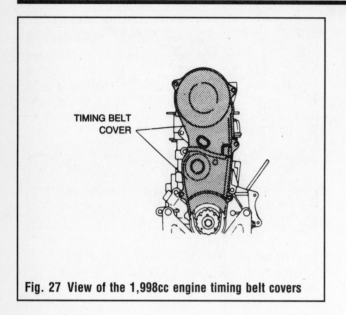

Fig. 27 View of the 1,998cc engine timing belt covers

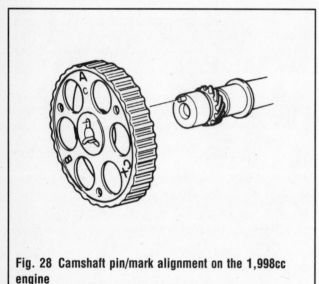

Fig. 28 Camshaft pin/mark alignment on the 1,998cc engine

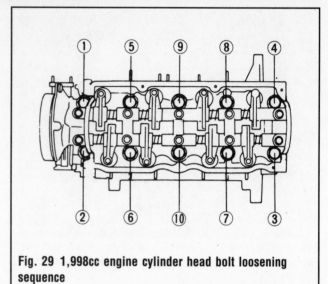

Fig. 29 1,998cc engine cylinder head bolt loosening sequence

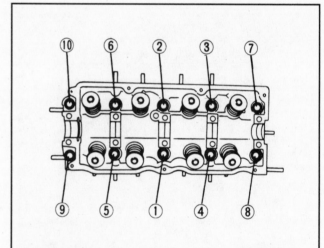

Fig. 30 1,998cc engine cylinder head bolt tightening (torque) sequence

10. Remove the exhaust manifold.

11. Remove the alternator.

12. Disconnect the air injection pipes.

13. Remove the fan pulley, hub and bracket.

14. If so equipped, remove the air conditioning compressor drive belt.

15. If so equipped, remove the power steering pump drive belt.

16. Remove the crankshaft pulley and baffle plate.

17. Remove the upper, then the lower, belt covers.

18. Turn the crankshaft so that the **A** mark on the camshaft pulley is at the top, aligned with the notch in the front housing.

19. Loosen the tensioner lockbolt and remove the tensioner spring.

20. Mark the forward rotation of the belt with paint to avoid confusion upon installation. Remove the belt.

21. Insert a bar through the hole in the camshaft sprocket to hold it in position and remove the sprocket bolt.

22. Remove the rocker arm cover.

23. Remove the head bolts in the sequence shown, and, with the aid of an assistant or a lifting device, lift off the head.

To install:

24. Clean the head and block mating surfaces thoroughly and install a new head gasket on the block.

25. Install the head and tighten the head bolts, in the order shown, to 60–64 ft. lbs. If new head bolts are being used, make sure you use the new, surface treated plain washers.

26. Install the camshaft pulley with the dowel pin on the camshaft engaging the pulley slot just below the **A** mark on the pulley. Tighten the bolt to 40–48 ft. lbs. The timing mark on the front housing and the **A** mark must be aligned.

27. Lubricate the distributor O-ring with clean engine oil, align all the matchmarks and install the distributor.

28. Replace the belt if it has been contaminated by oil or grease, or shows any sign of damage, wear, cracks or peeling.

29. Make sure that the timing mark on the camshaft is aligned as described above, and that the timing mark (notch) on the crankshaft sprocket is aligned with the triangular shaped mark on the front housing.

30. Install the tensioner and spring, positioning the tensioner

all the way to the intake manifold side and temporarily secure it there with the lockbolt.

31. Install the belt onto the sprockets from YOUR right side. If you are reusing the original belt, make sure you follow the directional mark previously made.

32. Loosen the lockbolt so that the tensioner applies tension to the belt.

33. Turn the crankshaft two full revolutions in the direction of normal rotation. This will apply equal tension to all points of the belt.

34. Make sure that the timing marks are still aligned. If not, repeat the belt installation procedure.

35. Tighten the tensioner lockbolt to 30–35 ft. lbs.

36. Measure the timing belt tension by pressing on the belt at the midpoint of the longest straight run. Belt deflection should be 11–13mm (0.433–0.510 in.). If not, repeat the belt adjustment procedure, above.

37. Install the upper, then the lower, belt covers. Torque to 80 in. lbs.

38. Install the crankshaft pulley and baffle plate.

39. If so equipped, install the power steering pump drive belt.

40. If so equipped, install the air conditioning compressor drive belt.

41. Install the fan pulley, hub and bracket. Torque the fan bracket to 40 ft. lbs.

42. Connect the air injection pipes.

43. Install the alternator.

44. Install the exhaust manifold. Torque to 16–21 ft. lbs.

45. Install the intake manifold and carburetor as an assembly. Torque the intake manifold to 14–19 ft. lbs.

46. Install the spark plugs. Torque to 11–17 ft. lbs.

47. Install the distributor.

48. Install the distributor cap.

49. Install the emissions canister.

50. Install the duty solenoid valves.

51. Install the 3-way solenoid valves.

52. Connect, all wires, hoses, cables, pipes and linkage at the cylinder head.

53. Install the air cleaner.

54. Install the hood.

55. Fill the cooling system.

When installing the drive belts on the various accessories, check the belt deflection as follows:

- Alternator
  New: 7–8mm (0.276–0.315 in.)
  Used: 8–9mm (0.315–0.354 in.)
- Power steering pump
  New: 8–12mm (0.315–0.476 in.)
  Used: 11–13mm (0.433–0.510 in.)
- Air conditioning compressor
  New: 10–12mm (0.394–0.476 in.)
  Used: 12–14mm (0.476–0.552 in.)

2,209cc Diesel Engine

➡ **The engine must be cold before proceeding.**

♦ **See Figure 31**

1. Drain the cooling system.
2. Scribe alignment marks around the hood hinges and remove the hood.

✳✳ CAUTION

When draining engine coolant, keep in mind that cats and dogs are attracted to ethylene glycol antifreeze and could drink any that is left in an uncovered container or in puddles on the ground. This will prove fatal in sufficient quantity. Always drain coolant into a sealable container. Coolant should be reused unless it is contaminated or is several years old.

---

3. Remove the air cleaner.

4. Disconnect, and tag, all wires, hoses, cables, pipes and linkage from the cylinder head.

5. Remove the injection lines and injectors. See Section 5.

6. Remove the intake and exhaust manifolds.

7. Dismount the alternator and move it out of the way.

8. Remove the rocker arm cover. Remove the rocker arm assembly and lift out the pushrods, keeping them in order for proper installation.

9. Remove the cylinder head bolts and, with the aid of an assistant, lift off the head.

10. Make sure that the mating surfaces of the head and block are absolutely clean. Use a new head gasket.

To install:

11. Install the cylinder head.

12. Install the cylinder head bolts. Tighten the head bolts, in the order shown, to 80–85 ft. lbs., in three equal steps.

13. Install the pushrods. When inserting the pushrods, make certain that they bottom in the depressed part of the tappet.

14. Install the rocker arm assembly.

15. Install the rocker arm cover. Torque the rocker cover bolts to 24–36 inch lbs.

16. Install the alternator.

17. Install the intake and exhaust manifolds.

18. Install the injection lines and injectors. See Section 5.

19. Connect all wires, hoses, cables, pipes and linkage at the cylinder head.

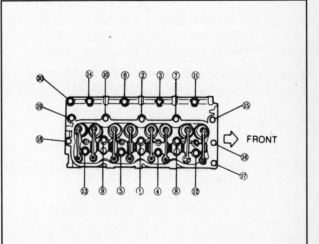

Fig. 31 Diesel engine cylinder head bolt tightening (torque) sequence

20. Install the air cleaner.
21. Install the hood.
22. Fill the cooling system.

CLEANING AND INSPECTION

1. With the valves installed to protect the valve seats, remove deposits from the combustion chambers and valve heads with a scraper and a wire brush. Be careful not to damage the cylinder head gasket surface. After the valves are removed, clean the valve guide bores with a valve guide cleaning tool. Using cleaning solvent to remove dirt, grease and other deposits, clean all bolts holes; be sure the oil passage is clean (V6 engines).
2. Remove all deposits from the valves with a fine wire brush or buffing wheel.
3. Inspect the cylinder heads for cracks or excessively burned areas in the exhaust outlet ports.
4. Check the cylinder head for cracks and inspect the gasket surface for burrs and nicks. Replace the head if it is cracked.
5. On cylinder heads that incorporate valve seat inserts, check the inserts for excessive wear, cracks, or looseness.

RESURFACING

Cylinder Head Flatness

When the cylinder head is removed, check the flatness of the cylinder head gasket surfaces.
1. Place a straightedge across the gasket surface of the cylinder head. Using feeler gauges, determine the clearance at the center of the straightedge.
2. If warpage exceeds 0.08mm (0.0031 in.) in a 152mm (5.98 in.) span, or 0.15mm (0.0059 in.) (0.20mm [0.00787 in.] for the diesel) over the total length, the cylinder head must be resurfaced.
3. If necessary to refinish the cylinder head gasket surface, do not plane or grind off more than 0.25mm (0.0098 in.) (0.05mm [0.00197 in.] for the diesel) from the original gasket surface.

➡ **When milling the cylinder heads of V6 engines, the intake manifold mounting position is altered, and must be corrected by milling the manifold flange a proportionate amount. Consult an experienced machinist about this.**

Valves and Valve Springs

REMOVAL & INSTALLATION

1,586cc, 1,796cc, 1,970cc, 1,998cc and 2,209cc Engines
♦ See Figures 32 thru 43

1. Remove the cylinder head. On the diesel and the 1,998cc, remove the rocker shaft assembly. On the 1,998cc, lift out the camshaft.
2. Remove the deposits from the combustion chambers with a stiff wire brush and scraper before removing the valves. Do not scratch the cylinder head surface.
3. Compress the valve springs with a valve spring compressor. Remove the valve spring retainer locks and release the springs.

Use a valve spring compressor tool to relieve spring tension from the valve caps

A magnet may be helpful in removing the valve keepers

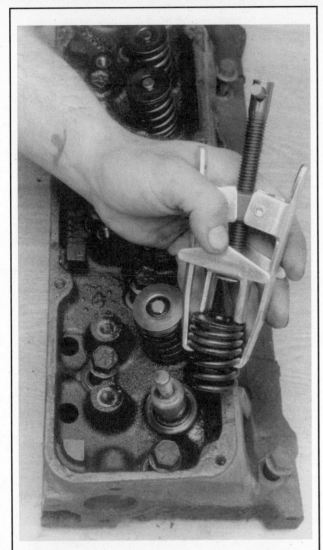

Remove the spring from the valve stem in order to access the seal

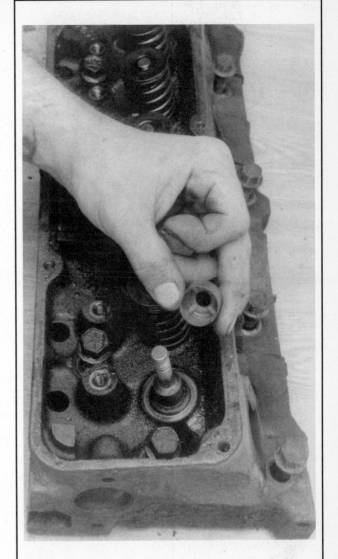

Remove the valve stem seal from the cylinder head

Invert the cylinder head and withdraw the valve from the cylinder head bore

A wire wheel may be used to clean the combustion chambers of carbon deposits

A dial gauge may be used to check valve stem-to-guide clearance

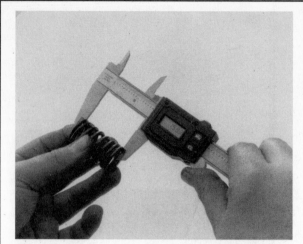

Use a caliper gauge to check the valve spring free-length

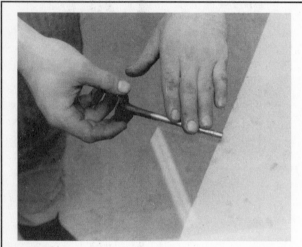

Valve stems may be rolled on a flat surface to check for bends

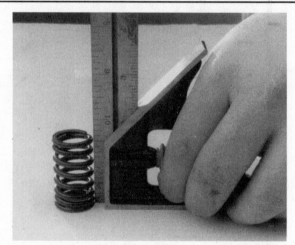

Check the valve spring for squareness on a flat service; a carpenter's square can be used

With the valve spring out of the way, the valve stem seals may now be replaced

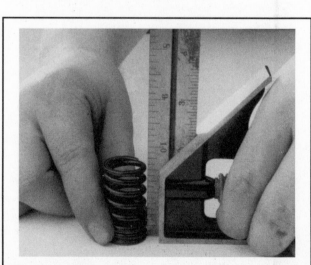

The valve spring should be straight up and down when placed like this

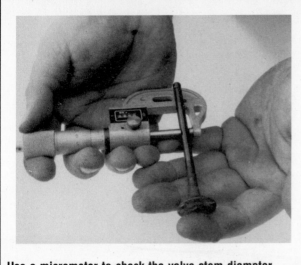

Use a micrometer to check the valve stem diameter

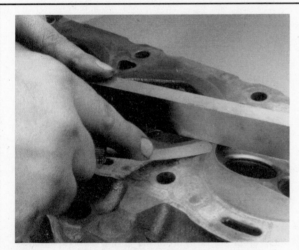

Check the cylinder head for flatness across the head surface

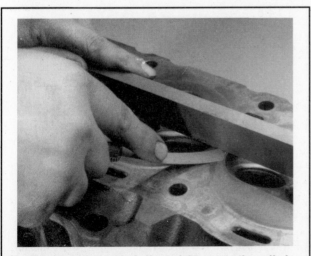

Checks should be made both straight across the cylinder head and at both diagonals

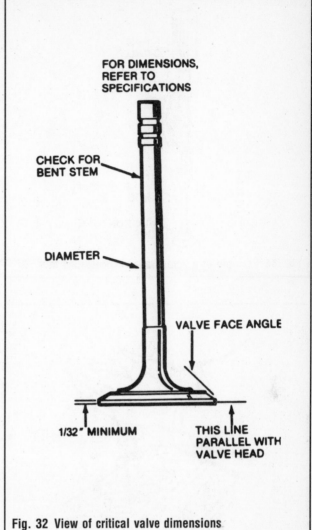

FOR DIMENSIONS, REFER TO SPECIFICATIONS

CHECK FOR BENT STEM

DIAMETER

VALVE FACE ANGLE

1/32" MINIMUM

THIS LINE PARALLEL WITH VALVE HEAD

Fig. 32 View of critical valve dimensions

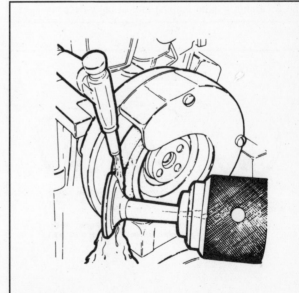

Fig. 33 Using a valve grinding machine to re-face an engine valve

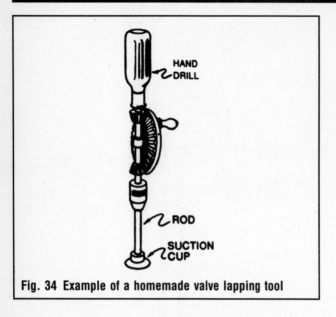

Fig. 34 Example of a homemade valve lapping tool

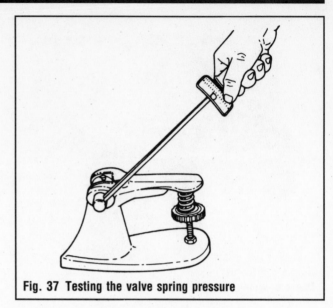

Fig. 37 Testing the valve spring pressure

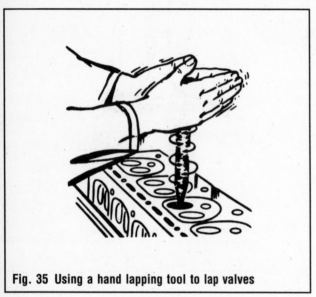

Fig. 35 Using a hand lapping tool to lap valves

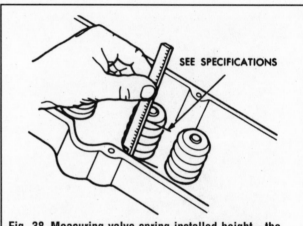

Fig. 38 Measuring valve spring installed height—the measurement is taken from the spring seat (cylinder head), to the top of the spring (bottom edge of the spring retainer)

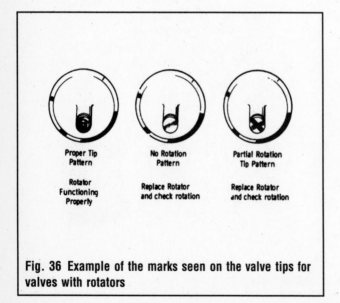

Fig. 36 Example of the marks seen on the valve tips for valves with rotators

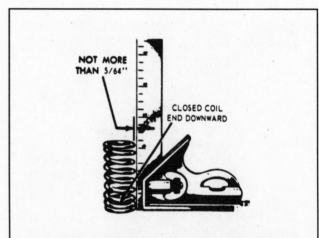

Fig. 39 Measure the springs' free length—there should be no more than 5/64 inch (0.078 inches) variation between springs

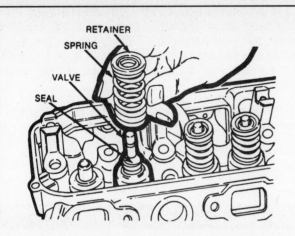

Fig. 40 View of the valve and spring components—not shown are the valve keepers, which sit in the center of the retainer and lock around the valve

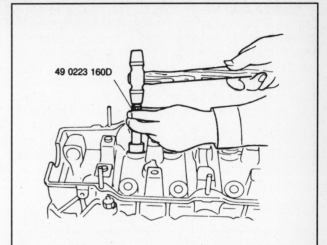

Fig. 42 Using a valve guide driver to install a new valve guide into the head

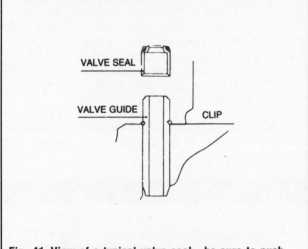

Fig. 41 View of a typical valve seal—be sure to push the new seal firmly over the valve guide

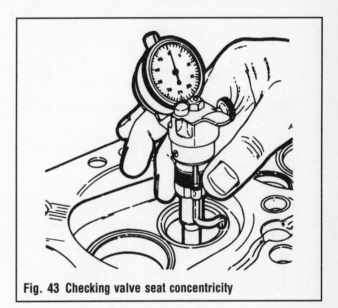

Fig. 43 Checking valve seat concentricity

4. Fabricate a valve arrangement board to use when you remove the valves, which will indicate the port in which each valve was originally installed. Also note that the valve keys, caps, etc. should be arranged in a manner which will allow you to install them on the valve on which they were originally used.

5. Remove and discard the valve seals. On models using the umbrella type seals, note the location of the large and small seals for assembly purposes.

6. Thoroughly clean the valves on the wire wheel of a bench grinder, then clean the cylinder head mating surface with a soft wire wheel, a soft wire brush, or a wooden scraper. Avoid using a metallic scraper, since this can cause damage to the cylinder head mating surface, especially on models with aluminum heads.

7. Using a valve guide cleaner chucked into a drill, clean all of the valve guides.

8. Install each valve into its respective port (guide) of the cylinder head.

9. Mount a dial indicator so that the stem is at 90° to the valve stem, as close to the valve guide as possible.

10. Move the valve off its seat, and measure the valve guide-to-stem clearance by rocking the stem back and forth to actuate the dial indicator.

11. Measure the valve stems using a micrometer, and compare to specifications, to determine whether stem or guide wear is responsible for excessive clearance.

➡**Consult the Specifications tables earlier in this chapter.**

12. Check the cylinder head flatness as described under Cylinder Head Removal and Installation.

REFACING

Using a valve grinder, resurface the valves according to specifications in this chapter.

➡**All machine work should be performed by a competent, professional machine shop. Valve face angle is not always identical to valve seat angle.**

Reface the valves with a refacing tool, following the instructions of the tool manufacturer. See illustrations for dimensions and angles. Remove just enough metal to clean up faces and seats. If, during the refacing process, valve margin becomes less than 1mm (0.04 in.) the valve must be replaced. On the 1,998cc and 2,184cc engines, exhaust valve margin is 1mm (0.04 in.) but intake valve margin need be only 0.5mm (0.00197 in.) or more.

On the diesel, there is no margin limit, provided contact width can be brought to specification, which is 1.7–2.3mm (0.0669–0.0906 in.). To check margin width, apply a thin coating of red lead to the valve seat and then press the valve firmly against the seat without rotating it. Then, measure the width of the mark.

LAPPING

This procedure should be performed after the valves and seats have been machined, to insure that each valve mates to each seat precisely.

1. Invert the cylinder head, lightly lubricate the valve stems, and install the valves in the head as numbered.
2. Coat valve seats with fine grinding compound, and attach the lapping tool suction cup to a valve head.

➡**Moisten the suction cup.**

3. Rotate the tool between your palms, changing position and lifting the tool often to prevent grooving.
4. Lap the valve until a smooth, polished seat is evident.
5. Remove the valve and tool, and rinse away all traces of grinding compound.

VALVE SPRING TESTING

Place the spring on a flat surface next to a square. Measure the height of the spring, and rotate it against the edge of the square to measure distortion. If spring height varies (by comparison) by more than 1.5mm (0.059 in.) or if distortion exceeds 1.5mm (0.059 in.), replace the spring.

In addition to evaluating the spring as above, test the spring pressure at the installed and compressed (installed height minus valve lift) height using a valve spring tester. Spring pressure should be within 1 lb. of all other springs in either position.

VALVE AND SPRING INSTALLATION

➡**Be sure that all traces of lapping compound have been cleaned off before the valves are installed.**

1. Lubricate all of the valve stems with a light coating of engine oil, then install the valves into the proper ports/guides.
2. If umbrella-type valve seals are used, install them at this time. Be sure to use a seal protector to prevent damage to the seals as they are pushed over the valve keeper grooves. If O-ring seals are used, don't install them yet.
3. Install the enlve springs and the spring retainers, and using the valve compressing tool, compress the springs.

4. If umbrella-type seals are used, just install the valve keepers (white grease may be used to hold them in place) and release the pressure on the compressing tool. If O-ring type seals are used, carefully work the seals into the second groove of the valve (closest to the head), install the valve keepers and release the pressure on the tool.

➡**If the O-ring seals are installed BEFORE the springs and retainers are compressed, the seal will be destroyed.**

5. After all of the valves are installed and retained, tap each valve spring retainer with a rubber mallet to seat the keepers in the retainer.

Valve Guides

REMOVAL & INSTALLATION

Valve guides are driven out of the head from the combustion chamber side. Use a driver meant for this purpose. New guides are driven into place from the top of the head, using the proper driver. On the 1,586cc, 1,796cc, and 1,970cc, press the guide in until the ring on the guide just touches the head. On the diesel and the 1,998cc, check the protrusion of the valve guide above the head surface, measuring from the spring seat upward. Protrusion on the diesel should be 16.5mm (0.6496 in.); on the 1998cc, 19.1–19.6mm (0.752–0.772 in.)

➡**On the diesel, the longer type guide goes on the intake side, and the shorter on the exhaust side. Do not mix them up!**

Valve Stem Oil Seals

REMOVAL & INSTALLATION

Positive valves seals are used. The seal fits over to top of the valve guide. Always install new valve stem seals when reassembling the cylinder head.

Valve Seats

REMOVAL & INSTALLATION

1. With the valve removed, check the seat for wear, cracks, damage or uneven contact with the valve. If the damage or contact problem is slight, the valve may be refaced with a lapping compound and lapping tool. The compound is spread on the seat face and the valve inserted. The valve is then ground against the seat with the lapping tool, removing a small amount of metal and creating a polished surface.
2. If the damage or contact problem cannot be rectified by lapping, the insert can be cut with a special seat cutter which will remove the damaged material and cut the correct angle.
3. If the seat insert is cracked, too thin, or burnt, it must be replaced. An automotive machine shop can handle the job for you.

Combustion Chamber Inserts

REMOVAL & INSTALLATION

Diesel Engine

1. Remove the cylinder head from the engine.
2. Remove the rocker arm assembly.
3. Remove the glow plugs.
4. From the top of the head, insert a driver through the glow plug hole and drive out the insert. Discard the welch washer.
5. Position a new insert, aligning it with the welch washer hole. Drive the new welch washer into position, with the projected side out. Mark the washer by lightly striking its center with a punch.

Crankshaft Pulley (Vibration Damper)

REMOVAL & INSTALLATION

1. Remove the fan shroud, as required.
2. On those engines with a separate pulley, remove the retaining bolts and separate the pulley from the vibration damper.
3. Remove the vibration damper/pulley retaining bolt from the crankshaft end.
4. Using a puller, remove the damper/pulley from the crankshaft.
5. Upon installation, align the key slot of the pulley hub to the crankshaft key. Complete the assembly in the reverse order of removal. Torque the retaining bolts to specifications.

Oil Pan

REMOVAL & INSTALLATION

1,586cc, 1,796cc and 1,970cc Engines
▶ See Figure 44

1. Raise and support the truck.
2. Remove the engine skid plate.
3. Drain the engine oil.

✳✳ CAUTION

The EPA warns that prolonged contact with used engine oil may cause a number of skin disorders, including cancer! You should make every effort to minimize you exposure to used engine oil. Protective gloves should be worn when changing the oil. Wash your hands and any other exposed skin areas as soon as possible after exposure to used engine oil. Soap and water, or waterless hand cleaner should be used.

4. Remove the clutch release cylinder attaching nuts. Let the cylinder hang.
5. Remove the clutch cover plate.

6. Remove the oil pan nuts and bolts and let the oil pan rest on the crossmember.
7. Remove the oil pump pickup tube from the pump.
8. Remove the oil pan.
9. Clean all the gasket surfaces.
10. Clean the oil pan, oil pump pickup tube and oil pump screen.
11. Install a new oil pan gasket with oil resistant sealer.
12. Install the oil pump pickup tube and screen.
13. Install the oil pan on the block. Torque the nuts and bolts to specifications.
14. Connect the emission line to the oil pan.
15. Attach the rear engine bracket. Torque the bolts to specifications.
16. Reinstall the clutch release cylinder. Torque the nuts to 5–7 (60–72 in. lbs.).
17. Replace the engine skid plate.
18. Lower the truck. Fill the crankcase, and run the engine. Check for leaks and oil pressure.

1998cc Engine
▶ See Figures 45 and 46

1. Disconnect the battery ground cable.
2. Raise and support the truck on jackstands. Drain the oil.

✳✳ CAUTION

The EPA warns that prolonged contact with used engine oil may cause a number of skin disorders, including cancer! You should make every effort to minimize you exposure to used engine oil. Protective gloves should be worn when changing the oil. Wash your hands and any other exposed skin areas as soon as possible after exposure to used engine oil. Soap and water, or waterless hand cleaner should be used.

3. Remove the skid plate.
4. Place a floor jack under the front of the engine at the crankshaft pulley and take up the weight of the engine. Or use a shop crane to support the engine.
5. Remove the crossmember.
6. Remove the cotter pin and nut and, with a puller, disconnect the idler arm from the center link.
7. Remove the engine mount gusset plates from the sides of the engine.
8. Remove the bell housing front cover.
9. Unbolt and remove the oil pan. A flat tipped screwdriver may be used to break the seal between the pan and block.
10. Clean all the gasket surfaces. Straighten and portion of the pan rim that is bent.
11. Clean the oil pan, oil pump pickup tube and oil pump screen.

To install:
12. If you are using a gasket, install a new oil pan gasket coated with oil resistant sealer. Place RTV silicone sealer at the points shown in the accompanying illustration. If you are using RTV silicone gasket material in place of a conventional gasket, run a 1/8 in. bead around the rim of the pan, going inboard of each bolt hole. Tighten the pan bolts within 30 minutes of application. Tighten the pan bolts to 5–9 ft. lbs.

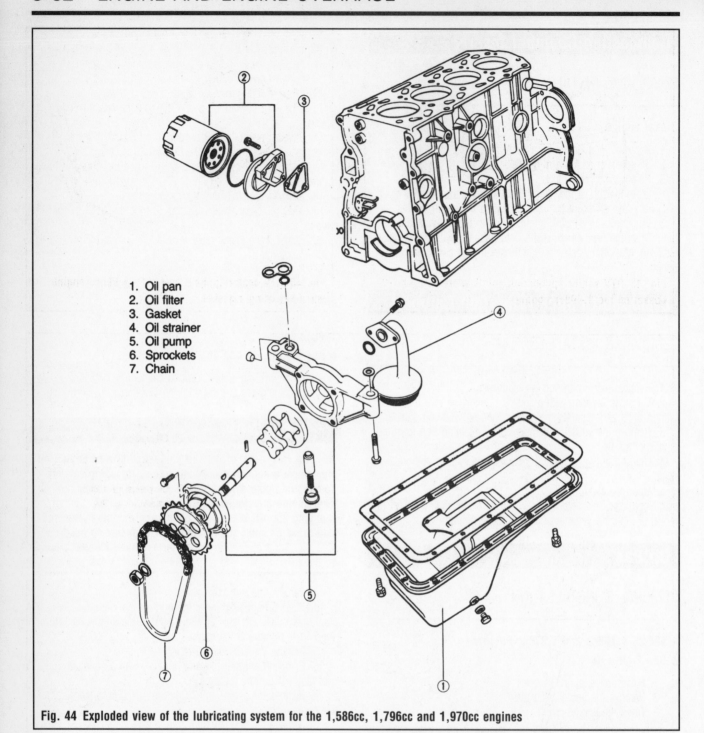

1. Oil pan
2. Oil filter
3. Gasket
4. Oil strainer
5. Oil pump
6. Sprockets
7. Chain

Fig. 44 Exploded view of the lubricating system for the 1,586cc, 1,796cc and 1,970cc engines

13. Install the bell housing front cover. Torque the bell housing cover to 15–20 ft. lbs.

14. Install the engine mount gusset plates from the sides of the engine.

15. Install the idler arm on the center link.

16. Install the cotter pin and nut. Torque the idler arm nut to 25–30 ft. lbs.

17. Install the crossmember.

18. Remove the shop crane.

19. Install the skid plate.

20. Fill the engine with the proper amount of oil.

21. Install the battery ground cable.

2,209cc Diesel Engine

▶ **See Figure 47**

1. Raise and support the truck on jackstands.

2. Remove the skid plate.

3. Drain the oil.

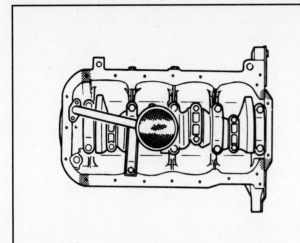

Fig. 45 RTV sealer application points when using a gasket on the 1,998cc engine

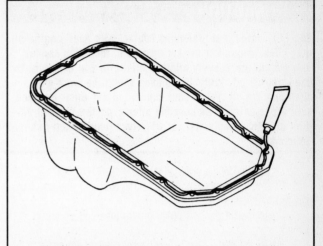

Fig. 46 RTV sealer application on the 1,998cc engine when not using a gasket

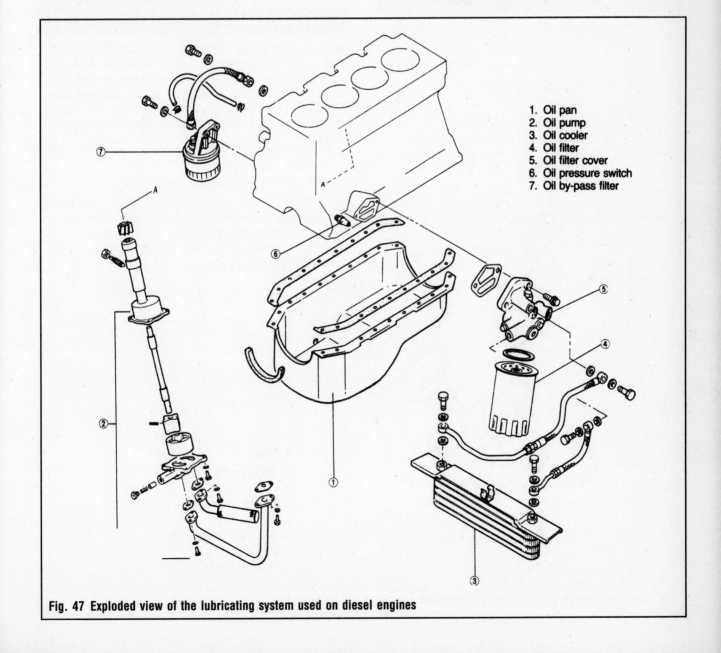

1. Oil pan
2. Oil pump
3. Oil cooler
4. Oil filter
5. Oil filter cover
6. Oil pressure switch
7. Oil by-pass filter

Fig. 47 Exploded view of the lubricating system used on diesel engines

4. Unbolt and remove the oil pan.

5. Clean all the gasket surfaces. Straighten and portion of the pan rim that is bent.

6. Clean the oil pan, oil pump pickup tube and oil pump screen.

7. Install the pan, using a new gasket coated with sealer. Torque the bolts to 5–9 ft. lbs.

Oil Pump

REMOVAL & INSTALLATION

1,586cc, 1,796cc and 1,970cc Engines

1. Remove the oil pan.

2. Remove the oil pump gear attaching nut.

3. Remove the bolts attaching the oil pump to the block. Loosen the gear on the pump.

4. Remove the oil pump and gear.

5. Install the oil pump gear in the chain.

6. Prime the oil pump and install it on the cylinder block. Install the bolts and tighten them securely.

7. Install the washer, gear and nut. Bend the locktab on the washer.

8. Install the oil pan. Fill the engine with oil. Start the engine and check for oil pressure. Check for leaks.

2,209cc Diesel Engine

1. Remove the oil pan.

2. Remove the oil pump set screw.

3. Remove the oil pipe attaching bolts.

4. Remove the oil pump.

5. Installation is the reverse of removal. Torque the pump and pipe bolts to 8 ft. lbs.

1,998cc Engine

♦ See Figure 48

1. Disconnect the battery ground.

2. Drain the cooling system.

3. Remove the distributor.

4. Remove the fan shroud and fan.

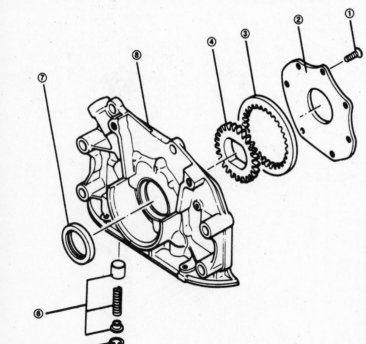

DURING ASSEMBLY, COAT THE THREADS OF THE BOLTS WITH A LOCKING AGENT

1. Bolt
2. Pump cover
3. Outer gear
4. Inner gear
5. Snap ring
6. Plunger assembly
7. Oil seal
8. Pump body

Fig. 48 Exploded view of the oil pump components used on the 1,998cc engine

5. Remove the alternator.

6. Disconnect the air injection pipes.

7. Remove the fan pulley, hub and bracket.

8. If so equipped, remove the air conditioning compressor drive belt.

9. If so equipped, remove the power steering pump drive belt.

10. Remove the crankshaft pulley and baffle plate.

11. Remove the upper, then the lower, belt covers.

12. Turn the crankshaft so that the **A** mark on the camshaft pulley is at the top, aligned with the notch in the front housing.

13. Loosen the tensioner lockbolt and remove the tensioner spring.

14. Mark the forward rotation of the belt with paint to avoid confusion upon installation. Remove the belt.

15. Unbolt and remove the crankshaft sprocket.

16. Drain the oil.

✳✳ CAUTION

The EPA warns that prolonged contact with used engine oil may cause a number of skin disorders, including cancer! You should make every effort to minimize you exposure to used engine oil. Protective gloves should be worn when changing the oil. Wash your hands and any other exposed skin areas as soon as possible after exposure to used engine oil. Soap and water, or waterless hand cleaner should be used.

17. Remove the skid plate.

18. Place a floor jack under the front of the engine at the crankshaft pulley and take up the weight of the engine. Or use a shop crane to support the engine.

19. Remove the crossmember.

20. Remove the cotter pin and nut and, with a puller, disconnect the idler arm from the center link.

21. Remove the engine mount gusset plates from the sides of the engine.

22. Remove the bell housing front cover.

23. Unbolt and remove the oil pan. A flat tipped screwdriver may be used to break the seal between the pan and block.

24. Remove the oil pick-up tube.

25. Unbolt and remove the oil pump.

To install:

26. Apply a thin coating of grease to the O-ring and install it in its recess in the pump body.

27. Apply a thin bead of RTV silicone sealer to the pump mounting surface.

28. Coat the oil seal lip with clean engine oil and install the pump. Torque the bolts to 14–19 ft. lbs.

29. Clean all the gasket surfaces. Straighten and portion of the pan rim that is bent.

30. Clean the oil pan, oil pump pickup tube and oil pump screen.

31. If you are using a gasket, install a new oil pan gasket coated with oil resistant sealer. Place RTV silicone sealer at the points shown in the accompanying illustration. If you are using RTV silicone gasket material in place of a conventional gasket, run a 1/8 in. bead around the rim of the pan, going inboard of each bolt hole. Tighten the pan bolts within 30 minutes of application. Tighten the pan bolts to 5–9 ft. lbs.

32. Install the bell housing front cover. Torque the bolts to 20 ft. lbs.

33. Install the engine mount gusset plates on the sides of the engine. Torque the bolts to 35 ft. lbs.

34. Install the idler arm on the center link. Torque the nut to 30 ft. lbs. Install a new cotter pin.

35. Install the crossmember.

36. Remove the floor jack or shop crane used to support the engine.

37. Install the skid plate.

38. Install the crankshaft sprocket.

39. Replace timing the belt if it has been contaminated by oil or grease, or shows any sign of damage, wear, cracks or peeling.

40. To ease installation of the belt, remove all the spark plugs.

41. Make sure that the timing mark on the camshaft is aligned as described above, and that the timing mark (notch) on the crankshaft sprocket is aligned with the triangular shaped mark on the front housing.

42. Install the tensioner and spring, positioning the tensioner all the way to the intake manifold side and temporarily secure it there with the lockbolt.

43. Install the belt onto the sprockets from **YOUR** right side. If you are reusing the original belt, make sure you follow the directional mark previously made.

44. Loosen the lockbolt so that the tensioner applies tension to the belt.

45. Turn the crankshaft two full revolutions in the direction of normal rotation. This will apply equal tension to all points of the belt.

46. Make sure that the timing marks are still aligned. If not, repeat the belt installation procedure.

47. Tighten the tensioner lockbolt to 30–35 ft. lbs.

48. Measure the timing belt tension by pressing on the belt at the midpoint of the longest straight run. Belt deflection should be 11–13mm (0.43–0.51 in.). If not, repeat the belt adjustment procedure, above.

49. Install the upper, then the lower, belt covers. Torque the belt cover bolts to 80 in. lbs.; the fan bracket bolts to 40 ft. lbs.

50. Install the crankshaft pulley and baffle plate.

51. Install the power steering pump drive belt.

52. Install the air conditioning compressor drive belt.

53. Install the fan pulley, hub and bracket.

54. Install the air injection pipes.

55. Install the alternator.

56. Install the fan shroud and fan.

57. Install the distributor.

58. Fill the engine with the proper amount of oil.

59. Fill the cooling system.

60. Install the battery ground cable.

When installing the drive belts on the various accessories, check the belt deflection as follows:

- Alternator
  New: 7–8mm (0.275–0.315 in.)
  Used: 8–9mm (0.315–0.354 in.)
- Power steering pump
  New: 9–11mm (0.354–0.433 in.)
  Used: 11–13mm (0.433–0.510 in.)
- Air conditioning compressor
  New: 10–12mm (0.394–0.472 in.)
  Used: 12–14mm (0.472–0.552 in.)

INSPECTION

1,586cc, 1,796cc, 2,209cc and 1,970cc Engines
♦ See Figures 49 and 50

PUMP BODY-TO-SHAFT CLEARANCE

Make this check using a dial indicator mounted on a magnet base. Bear the indicator on the drive gear. Clearance should not exceed 0.10mm (0.003937 in.). If it does, replace the pump.

INNER-TO-OUTER ROTOR CLEARANCE

Using a feeler gauge, check between the lobes of the rotors. Standard clearance should be 0.05–0.15mm (0.00196–0.00591 in.). If the clearance is greater than 0.25mm (0.00984 in.), replace both rotors.

OUTER ROTOR-TO-PUMP BODY CLEARANCE

Insert a feeler gauge between the outer rotor and the pump body. Standard clearance is 0.15–0.25mm (0.00591–0.00984 in.).

If clearance exceeds 0.30mm (0.0118 in.), replace the rotor or body.

ROTOR END FLOAT

Place a straightedge across the pump body and measure the clearance between the rotor and the straightedge with a feeler gauge. Then, place the straightedge across the pump cover and, with a feeler gauge, measure between the straightedge and the cover center. If the total of these two measurements exceeds 0.15mm (0.0059 in.), the condition may be corrected by grinding the cover or replacing the cover or pump body.

1,998cc Engine
♦ See Figures 51, 52 and 53

➡The crescent referred to in these procedures is the crescent-shaped slinger between the inner and outer pump gears.

OUTER GEAR TOOTH TIP TO CRESCENT CLEARANCE

Check this clearance with a feeler gauge. If the clearance exceeds 0.33mm (0.01299 in.), replace the gear.

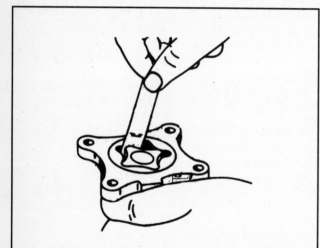

Fig. 49 Checking the inner rotor-to-outer rotor clearance for the 1,586cc, 1,796cc, 1,970cc and 2,209cc engines

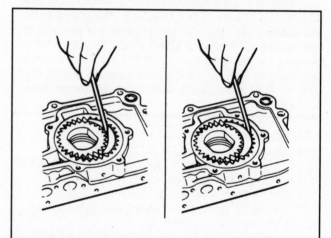

Fig. 51 Inner (left) and outer (right) gear tooth tip-to-crescent clearance measurements on the 1,998cc engine oil pump

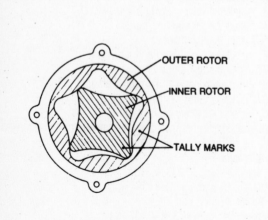

Fig. 50 Inner rotor-to-outer rotor tally marks used for alignment when assembling the oil pump

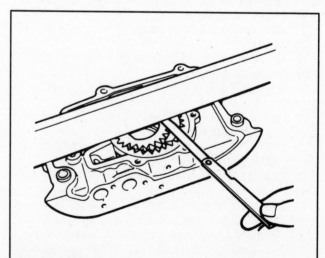

Fig. 52 1,998cc engine oil pump side clearance measurement

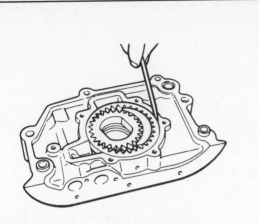

Fig. 53 Outer gear-to-pump body clearance measurement

INNER GEAR TOOTH TIP-TO-CRESCENT CLEARANCE

Check this clearance with a feeler gauge. If the clearance exceeds 0.40mm (0.01575 in.), replace the gear.

SIDE CLEARANCE

Lay a straightedge across the pump body and, using a feeler gauge, measure between the gear faces and straightedge. If the clearance exceeds 0.10mm (0.003937 in.), replace the pump.

OUTER GEAR-TO-PUMP BODY CLEARANCE

Insert a feeler gauge between the outer gear and the pump body. If the clearance exceeds 0.20mm (0.00787 in.), replace the gear or pump body.

Timing Chain Cover

REMOVAL & INSTALLATION

1,586cc, 1,796cc and 1,970cc Engines
▶ See Figure 54

1. Scribe alignment marks on the hood hinges and remove the hood.
2. Drain the cooling system.

✳✳ CAUTION

When draining engine coolant, keep in mind that cats and dogs are attracted to ethylene glycol antifreeze and could drink any that is left in an uncovered container or in puddles on the ground. This will prove fatal in sufficient quantity. Always drain coolant into a sealable container. Coolant should be reused unless it is contaminated or is several years old.

3. Disconnect the upper and lower radiator hose. Remove the radiator.
4. Remove the accessory drive belts.
5. Remove the crankshaft pulley and the water pump.
6. Remove the cylinder head-to-front cover bolt.
7. Raise and support the truck.
8. Remove the engine skid plate.
9. Disconnect the emission line from the oil pan. Drain the oil from the engine.

✳✳ CAUTION

The EPA warns that prolonged contact with used engine oil may cause a number of skin disorders, including cancer! You should make every effort to minimize you exposure to used engine oil. Protective gloves should be worn when changing the oil. Wash your hands and any other exposed skin areas as soon as possible after exposure to used engine oil. Soap and water, or waterless hand cleaner should be used.

10. Remove the oil pan.
11. Remove the alternator and bracket and lay the alternator aside.
12. Remove the steel tube from the front of the engine.
13. Unbolt and remove the front cover.
14. Clean all the gasket mating surfaces.
15. Clean the crankshaft pulley.

To install:

16. Use contact cement to cement a new front cover gasket on the block.
17. Install the front cover and torque the attaching bolts to specifications.
18. Install the air pump (if equipped).
19. Install the alternator and bracket.
20. Install the water pump and a new gasket. Torque the bolts to specifications.
21. Connect the by-pass hose and heater hose to the water pump.
22. Install the crankshaft pulley and attaching bolt. Torque the bolt to specifications.
23. Install the alternator belts, and the water pump pulley.
24. Install the fan. Adjust the tension of the belt(s).
25. Install the radiator and the upper and lower hoses.
26. Install the air cleaner.
27. Install the oil pan and the emission line.
28. Install the engine skid plate.
29. Lower the truck to the ground.
30. Fill the engine with oil and fill the cooling system. Run the engine and check for leaks.
31. Install the hood.

2,209cc Diesel Engine
▶ See Figure 55

1. Disconnect the battery ground.
2. Drain the cooling system.

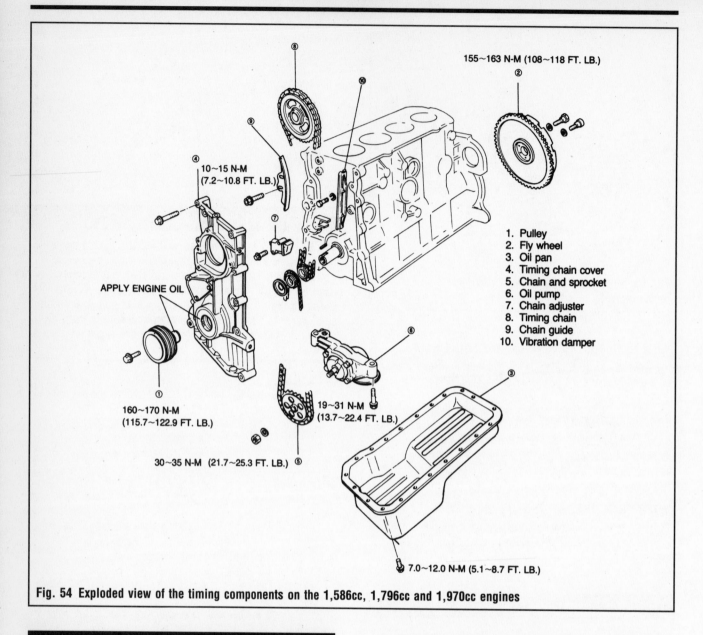

155~163 N-M (108~118 FT. LB.)

10~15 N-M (7.2~10.8 FT. LB.)

APPLY ENGINE OIL

160~170 N-M (115.7~122.9 FT. LB.)

19~31 N-M (13.7~22.4 FT. LB.)

30~35 N-M (21.7~25.3 FT. LB.)

7.0~12.0 N-M (5.1~8.7 FT. LB.)

1. Pulley
2. Fly wheel
3. Oil pan
4. Timing chain cover
5. Chain and sprocket
6. Oil pump
7. Chain adjuster
8. Timing chain
9. Chain guide
10. Vibration damper

Fig. 54 Exploded view of the timing components on the 1,586cc, 1,796cc and 1,970cc engines

✴✴ CAUTION

When draining engine coolant, keep in mind that cats and dogs are attracted to ethylene glycol antifreeze and could drink any that is left in an uncovered container or in puddles on the ground. This will prove fatal in sufficient quantity. Always drain coolant into a sealable container. Coolant should be reused unless it is contaminated or is several years old.

3. Remove the fan and fan shroud.
4. Remove all drive belts from the engine.
5. Remove the power steering pump and its bracket, and position it out of the way, without disconnecting the hoses.
6. Remove the water pump.
7. Remove the crankshaft pulley bolt and, using a puller, remove the pulley.

Unbolt and remove the timing gear cover. Discard the gasket.

8. Installation is the reverse of removal. Make sure that the gasket mating surfaces are clean. Use a new gasket coated with sealer. Tighten the timing gear cover bolts to 12–17 ft. lbs.; the crankshaft pulley bolts to 150–180 ft. lbs.

Timing Belt Covers

REMOVAL & INSTALLATION

1,998cc Engine

◆ **See Figure 55a**

1. Disconnect the battery ground.
2. Remove the distributor.
3. Remove the fan and radiator shroud.
4. Remove the alternator.
5. Disconnect the air injection pipes.
6. Remove the fan pulley, hub and bracket.
7. If so equipped, remove the air conditioning compressor drive belt.

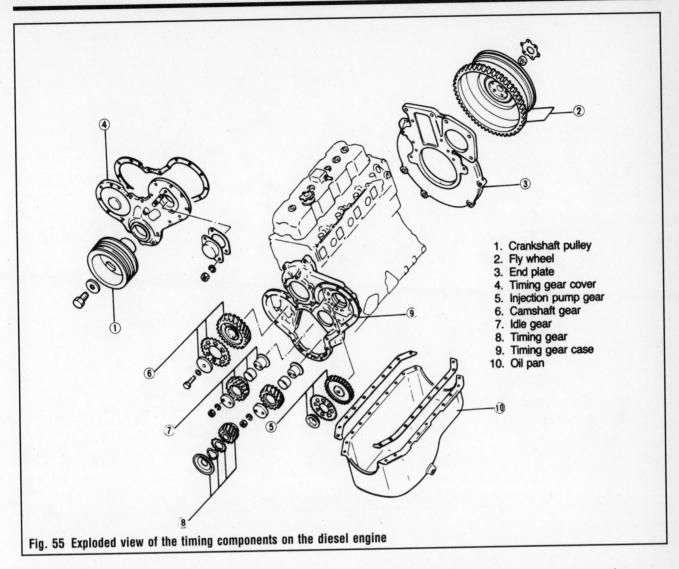

Fig. 55 Exploded view of the timing components on the diesel engine

1. Crankshaft pulley
2. Fly wheel
3. End plate
4. Timing gear cover
5. Injection pump gear
6. Camshaft gear
7. Idle gear
8. Timing gear
9. Timing gear case
10. Oil pan

8. If so equipped, remove the power steering pump drive belt.
9. Remove the crankshaft pulley and baffle plate.
10. Remove the upper, then the lower, belt covers.

To install:

11. Install the upper, then the lower, belt covers.
12. Install the crankshaft pulley and baffle plate.
13. Install the power steering pump drive belt.
14. Install the air conditioning compressor drive belt.
15. Install the fan pulley, hub and bracket.
16. Connect the air injection pipes.
17. Install the alternator.
18. Install the fan and radiator shroud.
19. Install the distributor.
20. Connect the battery ground.

Front Cover Oil Seal

REMOVAL & INSTALLATION

Except Diesel and 1,998cc Engines

The front cover oil seal can be removed and a new one installed without removing the front cover.

1. Scribe alignment marks on the hood hinges and remove the hood.
2. Drain the cooling system.

❋❋ CAUTION

When draining engine coolant, keep in mind that cats and dogs are attracted to ethylene glycol antifreeze and could drink any that is left in an uncovered container or in puddles on the ground. This will prove fatal in sufficient quantity. Always drain coolant into a sealable container. Coolant should be reused unless it is contaminated or is several years old.

3. Disconnect the upper and lower radiator hoses and remove the radiator.
4. Remove the drive belt(s).
5. Remove the crankshaft pulley.
6. Pry the front oil seal from the front cover.
7. Clean the pulley and seal area.

To install:

8. Press a new front seal into position (flush).
9. Install the crankshaft pulley and torque the bolt to specifications.

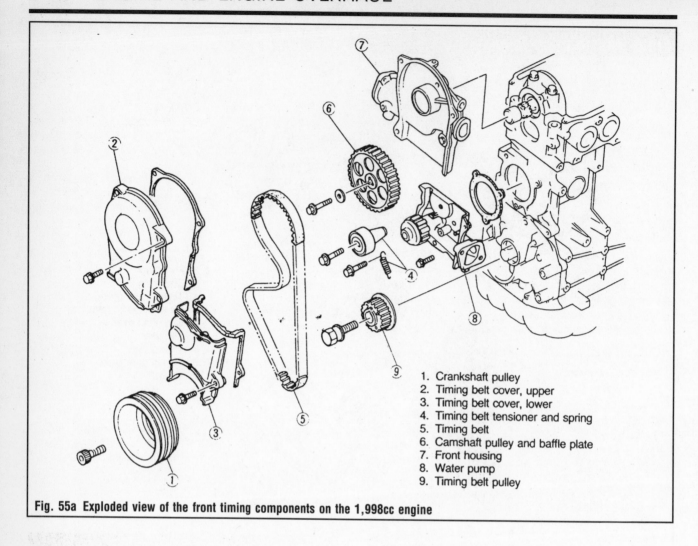

1. Crankshaft pulley
2. Timing belt cover, upper
3. Timing belt cover, lower
4. Timing belt tensioner and spring
5. Timing belt
6. Camshaft pulley and baffle plate
7. Front housing
8. Water pump
9. Timing belt pulley

Fig. 55a Exploded view of the front timing components on the 1,998cc engine

10. Install the drive belt(s) and adjust the tension.
11. Install the radiator and connect the upper and lower hoses. Fill the cooling system.
12. Start the engine and check for leaks.
13. Install the hood.

2,209cc Diesel Engine

1. Disconnect the battery ground.
2. Drain the cooling system.

✳✳ CAUTION

When draining engine coolant, keep in mind that cats and dogs are attracted to ethylene glycol antifreeze and could drink any that is left in an uncovered container or in puddles on the ground. This will prove fatal in sufficient quantity. Always drain coolant into a sealable container. Coolant should be reused unless it is contaminated or is several years old.

3. Remove the fan and fan shroud.
4. Remove all drive belts from the engine.
5. Remove the power steering pump and its bracket, and posi-

tion it out of the way, without disconnecting the hoses.
6. Remove the water pump.
7. Remove the crankshaft pulley bolt and, using a puller, remove the pulley.
Unbolt and remove the timing gear cover. Discard the gasket.
8. Drive out the old seal.
9. Coat the outer circumference of the new seal with sealer, and the sealing surface with clean engine oil.
To install:
10. Coat the outer circumference of the new seal with sealer, and the sealing surface with clean engine oil.
11. Drive in the new seal.
12. Install the timing gear cover. Torque the bolts to 12–17 ft. lbs.
13. Install the pulley. Torque the crankshaft pulley bolt to 150–180 ft. lbs.
14. Install the water pump.
15. Install the power steering pump.
16. Install the accessory drive belts.
17. Install the fan and fan shroud.
18. Fill the cooling system.
19. Connect the battery ground.

Front Housing and Camshaft Oil Seal

REMOVAL & INSTALLATION

1,998cc Engine

1. Disconnect the battery ground.
2. Drain the cooling system.

✳✳ CAUTION

When draining engine coolant, keep in mind that cats and dogs are attracted to ethylene glycol antifreeze and could drink any that is left in an uncovered container or in puddles on the ground. This will prove fatal in sufficient quantity. Always drain coolant into a sealable container. Coolant should be reused unless it is contaminated or is several years old.

3. Remove the distributor.
4. Remove the fan shroud and fan.
5. Remove the alternator.
6. Disconnect the air injection pipes.
7. Remove the fan pulley, hub and bracket.
8. If so equipped, remove the air conditioning compressor drive belt.
9. If so equipped, remove the power steering pump drive belt.
10. Remove the crankshaft pulley and baffle plate.
11. Remove the upper, then the lower, belt covers.
12. Turn the crankshaft so that the **A** mark on the camshaft pulley is at the top, aligned with the notch in the front housing.
13. Loosen the tensioner lockbolt and remove the tensioner spring.
14. Mark the forward rotation of the belt with paint to avoid confusion upon installation. Remove the belt.
15. Unbolt and remove the front housing.
16. Carefully, drive the camshaft seal from the housing.
To install:
17. Coat the outside of a new seal with clean engine oil and press it into place in the front housing.
18. Coat the seal lip with clean engine oil. Install the front housing, using a new gasket. Torque the bolts to 14–19 ft. lbs.
19. Replace the timing belt if it has been contaminated by oil or grease, or shows any sign of damage, wear, cracks or peeling.
20. To ease installation of the belt, remove all the spark plugs.
21. Make sure that the timing mark on the camshaft is aligned as described above, and that the timing mark (notch) on the crankshaft sprocket is aligned with the triangular shaped mark on the front housing.
22. Install the tensioner and spring, positioning the tensioner all the way to the intake manifold side and temporarily secure it there with the lockbolt.
23. Install the belt onto the sprockets from YOUR right side. If you are reusing the original belt, make sure you follow the directional mark previously made.
24. Loosen the lockbolt so that the tensioner applies tension to the belt.

25. Turn the crankshaft two full revolutions in the direction of normal rotation. This will apply equal tension to all points of the belt.
26. Make sure that the timing marks are still aligned. If not, repeat the belt installation procedure.
27. Tighten the tensioner lockbolt to 30–35 ft. lbs.
28. Measure the timing belt tension by pressing on the belt at the midpoint of the longest straight run. Belt deflection should be 11–13mm (0.433–0.510 in.). If not, repeat the belt adjustment procedure, above.
29. Install the lower, then the upper, belt covers. Torque the belt cover bolts to 80 inch lbs.; the fan bracket bolts to 40 ft. lbs.
30. Install the baffle plate and crankshaft pulley.
31. Install the power steering pump drive belt.
32. Install the air conditioning compressor drive belt.
33. Install the fan pulley, hub and bracket.
34. Connect the air injection pipes.
35. Install the alternator.
36. Install the fan shroud and fan.
37. Install the distributor.
38. Fill the cooling system.
39. Connect the battery ground.
    When installing the drive belts on the various accessories, check the belt deflection as follows:
- Alternator
  New: 7–8mm (0.276–0.315 in.)
  Used: 8–9mm (0.315–0.354 in.)
- Power steering pump
  New: 8–12mm (0.315–0.472 in.)
  Used: 11–13mm (0.433–0.510 in.)
- Air conditioning compressor
  New: 10–12mm (0.394–0.472 in.)
  Used: 12–14mm (0.472–0.552 in.)

Timing Chain and Tensioner

The correct installation and adjustment of the camshaft drive chain is mandatory if the engine is to run properly. The camshaft controls the opening of the engine valves through coordination of the movement of the crankshaft and camshaft. When any given piston is on the intake stroke the corresponding intake valve must open to admit air/fuel mixture into the cylinder. When the same piston is on the compression and power strokes, both valves in that cylinder must be closed. When the piston is on the exhaust stroke, the exhaust valve for that cylinder must be open. If the opening and closing of the valves is not coordinated with the movements of the pistons, the engine will run very poorly, if at all.

REMOVAL & INSTALLATION

1,586cc and 1,796cc Engines
♦ **See Figure 56**

1. Remove the cylinder head and front cover. It is not necessary that the intake and exhaust manifolds be removed from the head.
2. Remove the oil pump and chain.

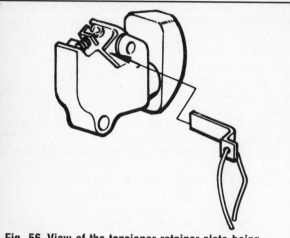

Fig. 56 View of the tensioner retainer plate being inserted into a fully compressed timing chain tensioner, to ease installation on the 1,586cc and 1,796cc engines

3. Remove the timing chain tensioner.
4. Loosen the timing chain guide strip screws.
5. Remove the oil slinger.
6. Remove the oil pump gear and chain as an assembly.
7. Remove the timing chain, crankshaft gear and camshaft gears from the engine.

To install:

8. Position the crankshaft gear in the timing chain.
9. Position the oil pump chain and gear on the crankshaft and oil pump. Check the oil pump drive chain slack. It should be 4mm (0.1575 in.). Adjusting the shims (between the oil pump body and cylinder block) are available in thickness of 0.15mm (0.0059 in.).
10. Install the oil slinger.
11. Install the oil pump washer and nut. Bend the washer over the nut.
12. Install the timing chain tensioner. Fully compress the snubber spring and wedge a screwdriver into the tensioner release mechanism. Without removing the screwdriver, install the tensioner.
13. Install the cylinder head and camshaft. Be sure that the valve timing is as illustrated. It must be exact. You may have to move the cam gear one or two teeth to obtain the correct alignment.
14. Install the rocker arm shafts and cam bearing caps.
15. Install and torque the cylinder head bolts.
16. Adjust the timing chain tension. Press in on the chain guide strip. Tighten the guide strip attaching screws. Remove the screwdriver from the tensioner, allowing the snubber to take up the chain slack.
17. Replace the front cover.
18. Adjust the valve clearance cold.

1,970cc Engine

♦ **See Figures 57, 58 and 59**

➡**Chain adjuster guide, 49 3953 260, is necessary for this procedure.**

1. Remove the cylinder head and front cover. It is not necessary that the intake and exhaust manifolds be removed from the head.
2. Remove the oil pan, oil pump and pump drive chain.
3. Install the chain adjuster guide mentioned above.

4. Loosen the chain guide strip adjusting screws. Slightly rotate the timing chain in the direction of normal engine rotation. Press the top of the chain guide strip with a prybar and tighten the guide strip adjusting screws. Check the protrusion of the chain adjuster head, as shown. If protrusion exceeds 17mm (0.66929 in.), replace the chain.
5. Remove the timing chain tensioner.
6. Remove the timing chain from the gears.
7. When installing the chain, make sure that the gears and chains are aligned as shown. The alignment marks on the gears must appear on the left, and fall between the nickel plated links.
8. Check the slack in the oil pump drive chain, after installation. Press on the chain, midway between the gears. If slack exceeds 4.0mm (0.1575 in.), install adjusting shims between the block and oil pump body. Shims are available in thicknesses of 0.15mm (0.0059 in.). Tighten the oil pump sprocket bolt to 25 ft. lbs.
9. Follow step 4, above, and adjust the timing chain. Remove the guide tool.
10. Install the oil pan, using a new gasket and sealer.
11. Install all other parts in reverse order of removal.

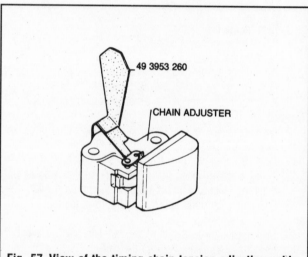

Fig. 57 View of the timing chain tension adjusting guide for the 1,970cc engine

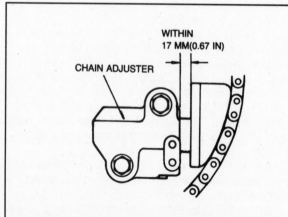

Fig. 58 Checking timing chain stretch on the 1,970cc engine—on 1,586cc and 1,796cc engines, the measurement between the arrows should be less than 0.315 inches (8mm)

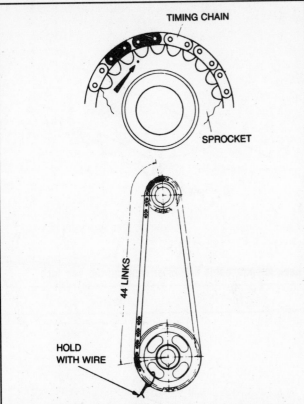

Fig. 59 Timing chain installation on the 1,970cc engine (note that the illustration shows a view of the engine with the cylinder head down)

Timing Belt

The correct installation and adjustment of the camshaft drive belt is mandatory if the engine is to run properly. The camshaft controls the opening of the engine valves through coordination of the movement of the crankshaft and camshaft. When any given piston is on the intake stroke the corresponding intake valve must open to admit air/fuel mixture into the cylinder. When the same piston is on the compression and power strokes, both valves in that cylinder must be closed. When the piston is on the exhaust stroke, the exhaust valve for that cylinder must be open. If the opening and closing of the valves is not coordinated with the movements of the pistons, the engine will run very poorly, if at all.

INSPECTION

Inspect the belt for any visible signs of damage such as missing teeth, deep cracks or scores, or loose threads along the edges of the belt. Check that there is no oil or antifreeze leaking onto the belt, as this will soften the rubber compound and cause premature failure. As as average rule of thumb, the timing belt should be replaced every 60,000 miles (96,000 km). If the belt breaks while the engine is running, or the crankshaft and/or camshaft has been turned separately after the timing belt has been removed from the engine, the valves may strike the piston heads,

and cause engine damage. If replacement is necessary, follow the precedures very closely.

REMOVAL & INSTALLATION

1,998cc Engine

▶ **See Figures 60 thru 71**

➡**Photos of the timing belt removal can be found in the Water Pump and Cylinder Head procedures, earlier in this section.**

1. Disconnect the battery ground.
2. Drain the cooling system.

✱✱ CAUTION

When draining engine coolant, keep in mind that cats and dogs are attracted to ethylene glycol antifreeze and could drink any that is left in an uncovered container or in puddles on the ground. This will prove fatal in sufficient quantity. Always drain coolant into a sealable container. Coolant should be reused unless it is contaminated or is several years old.

3. Remove the distributor.
4. Remove the fan shroud and fan.
5. Remove the alternator.
6. Disconnect the air injection pipes.
7. Remove the fan pulley, hub and bracket.
8. If so equipped, remove the air conditioning compressor drive belt.
9. If so equipped, remove the power steering pump drive belt.
10. Remove the crankshaft pulley and baffle plate.
11. Remove the upper, then the lower, belt covers.
12. Turn the crankshaft so that the **A** mark on the camshaft pulley is at the top, aligned with the notch in the front housing.
13. Loosen the tensioner lockbolt and remove the tensioner spring.
14. Mark the forward rotation of the belt with paint to avoid confusion upon installation. Remove the belt.

Do not bend, twist or turn the timing belt inside out. Never allow oil, water or steam to contact the belt

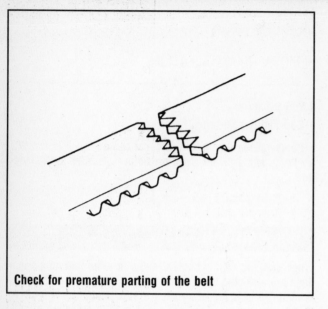

Check for premature parting of the belt

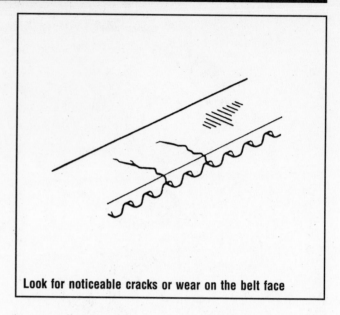

Look for noticeable cracks or wear on the belt face

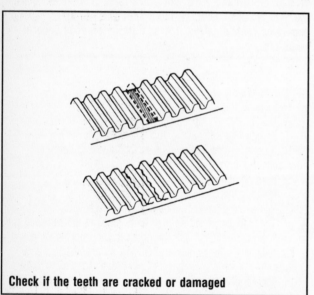

Check if the teeth are cracked or damaged

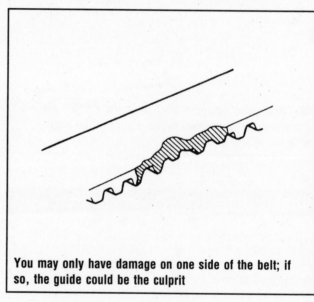

You may only have damage on one side of the belt; if so, the guide could be the culprit

Inspect the timing belt for cracks, fraying, glazing or damage of any kind

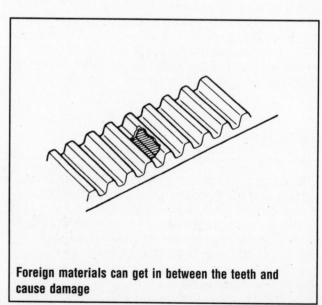

Foreign materials can get in between the teeth and cause damage

Damage on only one side of the timing belt may indicate a faulty guide

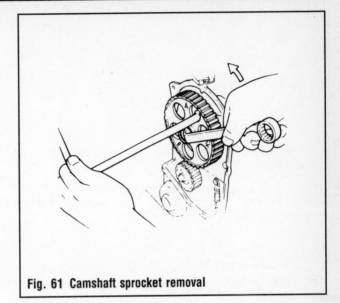

Fig. 61 Camshaft sprocket removal

ALWAYS replace the timing belt at the interval specified by the manufacturer

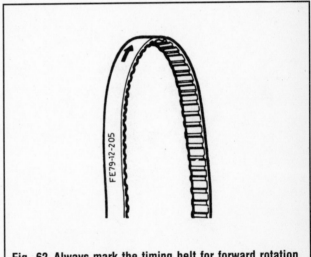

Fig. 62 Always mark the timing belt for forward rotation if reinstalling an old belt

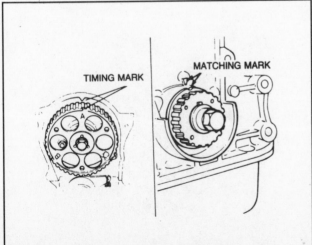

Fig. 60 Camshaft (left) and crankshaft (right) timing marks on the 1,998cc engine

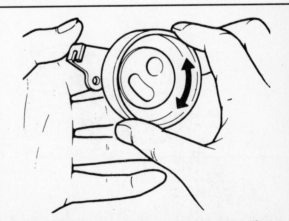

Fig. 63 Check the timing belt tensioner for smoothness of rotation—it's a good idea to replace the tensioner pulley while replacing the timing belt, as it is cheap insurance against a future failure

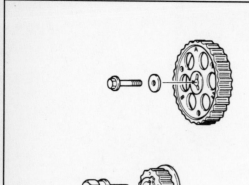

Fig. 64 View of the attaching bolts for the camshaft and crankshaft sprockets on the 1,998cc engine

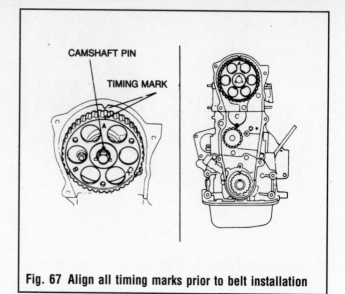

Fig. 67 Align all timing marks prior to belt installation

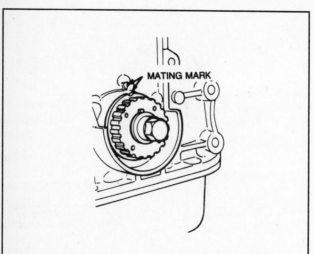

Fig. 65 Closeup view of aligning the crankshaft sprocket notch with the mating mark on the 1,998cc engine

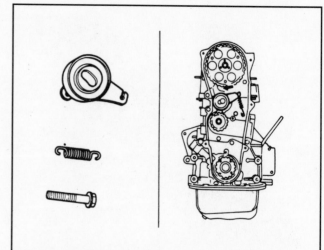

Fig. 68 Timing belt tensioner pulley installation on the 1,998cc engine

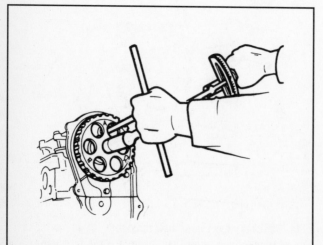

Fig. 66 Camshaft sprocket installation on the 1,998cc engine

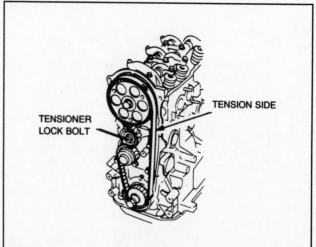

Fig. 69 Location of the timing belt tensioner lockbolt on the 1,998cc engine

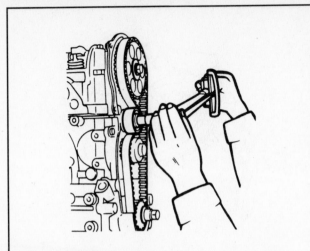

Fig. 70 Tightening the tensioner lockbolt with a torque wrench

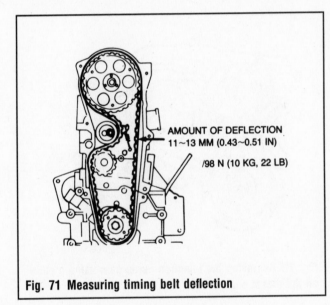

AMOUNT OF DEFLECTION
11~13 MM (0.43~0.51 IN)

/98 N (10 KG, 22 LB)

Fig. 71 Measuring timing belt deflection

15. Replace the belt if it has been contaminated by oil or grease, or shows any sign of damage, wear, cracks or peeling.

To install:

16. To ease installation of the belt, remove all the spark plugs.

17. Make sure that the timing mark on the camshaft is aligned as described above, and that the timing mark (notch) on the crankshaft sprocket is aligned with the triangular shaped mark on the front housing.

18. Install the tensioner and spring, positioning the tensioner all the way to the intake manifold side and temporarily secure it there with the lockbolt.

19. Install the belt onto the sprockets from YOUR right side. If you are reusing the original belt, make sure you follow the directional mark previously made.

20. Loosen the lockbolt so that the tensioner applies tension to the belt.

21. Turn the crankshaft two full revolutions in the direction of normal rotation. This will apply equal tension to all points of the belt.

22. Make sure that the timing marks are still aligned. If not, repeat the belt installation procedure.

23. Tighten the tensioner lockbolt to 30–35 ft. lbs.

24. Measure the timing belt tension by pressing on the belt at the midpoint of the longest straight run. Belt deflection should be 11–13mm (0.433–0.510 in.). If not, repeat the belt adjustment procedure, above.

25. Install the lower, then the upper, belt covers. Torque the belt cover bolts to 80 in. lbs.

26. Install the baffle plate and crankshaft pulley.

27. Install the power steering pump drive belt.

28. Install the air conditioning compressor drive belt.

29. Install the hub and bracket, and fan pulley. Torque the fan bracket bolts to 40 ft. lbs.

30. Connect the air injection pipes.

31. Install the alternator.

32. Install the fan shroud and fan.

33. Install the distributor.

34. Fill the cooling system.

35. Connect the battery ground.

When installing the drive belts on the various accessories, check the belt deflection as follows:

- Alternator
  New: 7–8mm (0.276–0.315 in.)
  Used: 8–9mm (0.315–0.354 in.)
- Power steering pump
  New: 9–11mm (0.354–0.433 in.)
  Used: 12–14mm (0.472–0.552 in.)
- Air conditioning compressor
  New: 10–12mm (0.394–0.472 in.)
  Used: 12–14mm (0.472–0.552 in.)

Timing Gears and Gear Case

The correct installation and adjustment of the camshaft drive gears is mandatory if the engine is to run properly. The camshaft controls the opening of the engine valves through coordination of the movement of the crankshaft and camshaft. When any given piston is on the intake stroke the corresponding intake valve must open to admit air/fuel mixture into the cylinder. When the same piston is on the compression and power strokes, both valves in that cylinder must be closed. When the piston is on the exhaust stroke, the exhaust valve for that cylinder must be open. If the opening and closing of the valves is not coordinated with the movements of the pistons, the engine will run very poorly, if at all.

REMOVAL & INSTALLATION

Diesel Engine
◆ **See Figures 72, 73, 74, 75 and 76**

1. Rotate the engine so that no. 1 piston is on TDC of its firing stroke.

2. Disconnect the battery ground.

3. Drain the cooling system.

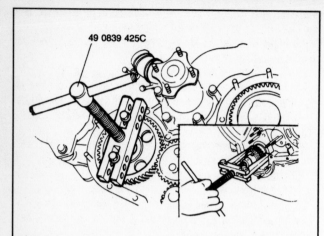

Fig. 72 To remove the timing gears on the diesel engine requires a bolt-on and claw type puller—inset shows a claw type puller removing the crankshaft gear

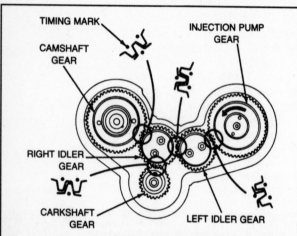

Fig. 73 View of the timing gear alignment on the diesel engine. To avoid confusion, note that the left idler gear has one set of double marks and one single mark, while the right idler gear has two sets of single marks and one set of double marks—all gears are installed with the marks facing outward

✳✳ CAUTION

When draining engine coolant, keep in mind that cats and dogs are attracted to ethylene glycol antifreeze and could drink any that is left in an uncovered container or in puddles on the ground. This will prove fatal in sufficient quantity. Always drain coolant into a sealable container. Coolant should be reused unless it is contaminated or is several years old.

4. Remove the fan and fan shroud.
5. Remove all drive belts from the engine.
6. Remove the power steering pump and its bracket, and position it out of the way, without disconnecting the hoses.
7. Remove the water pump.
8. Remove the crankshaft pulley bolt and, using a puller, remove the pulley.

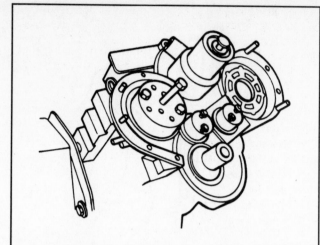

Fig. 74 Removing the camshaft gear using a puller on the diesel engine

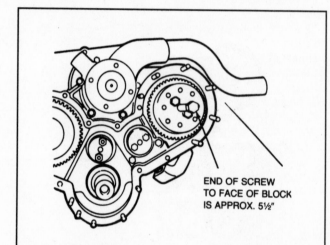

Fig. 75 Removing the injection pump gear using a puller on the diesel engine

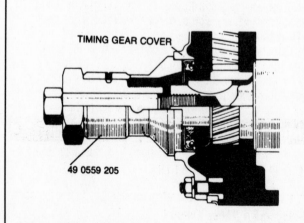

Fig. 76 Using a special tool to install a new timing gear cover seal on the diesel engine

Unbolt and remove the timing gear cover. Discard the gasket. The front cover seal may be replaced at this time. Coat the outer circumference of the new seal with sealer, and the sealing surface with clean engine oil.

9. Remove the oil pan.

10. Make sure that all timing marks are aligned as illustrated. If not, rotate the engine to align them.

11. Remove the bolts from the camshaft gear, and remove the washer and friction gear.

12. Remove the bolts from the injection pump gear, and remove the washer and friction gear.

13. Using a puller, remove the camshaft, crankshaft and injection pump gears.

14. Matchmark the idler gears for installation reference and remove the nuts and gears.

15. Support the injection pump and remove the nuts attaching it to the timing gear case. Support the pump in this position for the rest of the procedure.

16. Remove the bolts attaching the gear case to the block and remove the case.

17. Discard all old gaskets and thoroughly clean the gasket mating surfaces.

18. Check all gears for wear and chipping. Replace any suspect parts.

To install:

19. Replace the front cover seal at this time.

20. Using a new gasket, coated with sealer, install the gear case. Torque the bolts to 12–17 ft. lbs.

21. Aligning all timing marks, as shown in the accompanying illustration, install the gears in the following order:

　a. crankshaft and right idler

　b. camshaft

　c. left idler

　d. injection pump

　e. all friction gears and washers

22. Install all the nuts and bolts on the gears. Observe the following torques:

• Camshaft gear, 45–50 ft. lbs.

• Idler gears, 17–23 ft. lbs.

• Injection pump gear, 40–50 ft. lbs.

23. Using a new gasket coated with sealer, install the timing gear cover. Torque the bolts to 12–17 ft. lbs.

24. Install the oil pan.

25. Install the crankshaft pulley.

26. Install the water pump.

27. Install the power steering pump.

28. Install the accessorydrive belts.

29. Install the fan and fan shroud.

30. Fill the cooling system.

31. Connect the battery ground.

Timing Chain Tensioner

REMOVAL & INSTALLATION

1,586cc and 1,796cc Engines

FRONT COVER INSTALLED

1. Remove the water pump.

2. Remove the tensioner cover.

3. Remove the attaching bolts from the tensioner. Remove the tensioner.

4. Fully compress the snubber spring. Insert a screwdriver into the tensioner release mechanism.

5. Without removing the screwdriver, insert the tensioner and align the bolt holes. Install the torque and bolts.

6. Adjust the chain tension as follows:

　a. Remove the two blind plugs and aluminum washers from the front cover.

　b. Loosen the guide strip attaching screws.

　c. Press the top of the chain guide strip through the adjusting hole in the cylinder head.

　d. Tighten the guide strip attaching screws.

　e. Remove the screwdriver from the tensioner and let the snubber take up the slack in the chain.

　f. Install the blind plugs and aluminum washers.

　g. Install the tensioner cover and gasket.

　h. Install a new gasket and water pump. Install the crankshaft pulley and drive belt and adjust the tension. Check the cooling system level.

ADJUSTMENT

1,586cc and 1,796cc Engines

1. Remove the water pump.

2. Remove the tensioner cover.

3. Fully compress the snubber spring. Insert a screwdriver into the tensioner release mechanism.

4. Without removing the screwdriver, insert the tensioner and align the bolt holes. Install the torque and bolts.

5. Adjust the chain tension as follows:

　a. Remove the two blind plugs and aluminum washers from the front cover.

　b. Loosen the guide strip attaching screws.

　c. Press the top of the chain guide strip through the adjusting hole in the cylinder head.

　d. Tighten the guide strip attaching screws.

　e. Remove the screwdriver from the tensioner and let the snubber take up the slack in the chain.

　f. Install the blind plugs and aluminum washers.

　g. Install the tensioner cover and gasket.

　h. Install a new gasket and water pump. Install the crankshaft pulley and drive belt and adjust the tension. Check the cooling system level.

Timing Belt Tensioner

REMOVAL & INSTALLATION

1,998cc Engine

1. Loosen the alternator mounting bolts, release the belt tension and remove the alternator belt.

2. Remove the attaching bolts and remove the upper front cover and gasket. Rotate the engine in the normal direction of rotation until the camshaft pulley mark aligns with the V-notch at the top of the front housing. The notch in the crankshaft pulley will

now be aligned with the arrow on the front housing, unless the belt has jumped time.

3. With brake pliers or another suitable tool, remove the tensioning spring. Now, remove the bolt from the tensioner and remove the tensioner.

4. Inspect the tensioner for bearing wear. It should rotate freely and smoothly. If not, replace it.

5. Make sure the belt remains engaged at all three sprockets and that crankshaft and camshaft sprockets are properly in time. Locate the tensioner on its swivel pin with the slot through which the mounting bolt passes centered over the bolt hole. Install the bolt, but do not tighten it.

6. Install the tensioner spring. With a wrench on the crankshaft pulley, turn the engine in the normal direction of rotation (clockwise) exactly two full turns until the timing marks are again aligned. Torque the lockbolt to 28–38 ft. lbs.

7. Install the upper cover and alternator belt in reverse of removal. Replace the cover gasket and torque the bolts to 57 ft. lbs.

Camshaft and Bearings

REMOVAL & INSTALLATION

1,586cc, 1,796cc and 1,970cc Engines
▶ See Figures 77, 78 and 79

➡Perform this operation on a cold engine only.

1. Scribe alignment marks on the hood hinges and remove the hood.

2. Remove the water pump.

3. Disconnect the coil wire and vacuum line from the distributor.

4. Rotate the crankshaft to place the No. 1 cylinder on TDC of the compression stroke. This can be determined by removing the spark plug and feeling compression with your thumb. When compression is felt, rotate the crankshaft until the pointer aligns with the **TDC** mark on the pulley.

5. Remove the plug wires and distributor cap. Remove the distributor.

6. Remove the valve cover.

7. Release the tension on the timing chain.

8. Remove the cylinder head bolts. Only do this on a cold engine.

9. Remove the rocker arm assembly.

10. Remove the nut, washer and distributor gear from the camshaft.

11. Remove the nut and washer holding the camshaft gear.

12. Remove the camshaft. Do not remove the camshaft gear from the timing chain. Be sure that the hear teeth and chain relationship is not disturbed. Wire the chain and cam gear to a place so that they will not fall into the front cover.

To install:
13. Clean all the gasket surfaces.

14. Clean the cylinder head bolt holes.

15. Install the camshaft on the head and install the camshaft gear.

16. Check the valve timing.

17. Install the rocker arm assembly.

18. Install and torque the head bolts.

19. Install the cam gear washer and nut.

20. Install the distributor gear, washer and nut.

21. Adjust the timing chain tension.

22. Check the camshaft end-play. It should be 0.025–0.180mm (0.00098–0.00708 in.). If it exceeds 0.20mm (0.00787 in.), replace the thrust plate with a new one.

23. Install the distributor, distributor cap and plug wires.

24. Connect the vacuum line and coil wire.

25. Adjust the valve clearance cold. Install the valve cover and fill the cooling system.

26. Run the engine and check for leaks. When normal operating temperature is reached, adjust the hot valve clearance.

27. Adjust the carburetor and ignition.

28. Install the air cleaner and hood.

1,998cc Engine
▶ See Figures 80 and 81

1. Disconnect the battery ground.
2. Drain the cooling system.

✳✳ CAUTION

When draining engine coolant, keep in mind that cats and dogs are attracted to ethylene glycol antifreeze and could drink any that is left in an uncovered container or in puddles on the ground. This will prove fatal in sufficient quantity. Always drain coolant into a sealable container. Coolant should be reused unless it is contaminated or is several years old.

3. Remove the distributor.

4. Remove the fan shroud and fan.

5. Remove the alternator.

6. Disconnect the air injection pipes.

7. Remove the fan pulley, hub and bracket.

8. If so equipped, remove the air conditioning compressor drive belt.

9. If so equipped, remove the power steering pump drive belt.

10. Remove the crankshaft pulley and baffle plate.

11. Remove the upper, then the lower, belt covers.

12. Turn the crankshaft so that the **A** mark on the camshaft pulley is at the top, aligned with the notch in the front housing.

13. Loosen the tensioner lockbolt and remove the tensioner spring.

14. Mark the forward rotation of the belt with paint to avoid confusion upon installation. Remove the belt.

15. Insert a bar through the hole in the camshaft sprocket to hold it in position and remove the sprocket bolt.

16. Disconnect the accelerator cable, if necessary.

17. If equipped, disconnect the air bypass valve cable.

18. Disconnect the spark plug wires. Remove the wires from the spark plug wire clips on the rocker covers and position them out of the way.

19. Remove the rocker cover and discard the gasket.

20. Remove the rocker arm shaft attaching bolts evenly in the order shown, and remove the rocker arm shafts.

21. Remove the camshaft rear seal cap.

22. Lift out the camshaft.

23. Inspect the camshaft for wear, heat scoring or obvious damage. Replace it if necessary. Check the lobes and journals for wear according to the specifications in the Camshaft Specification Chart.

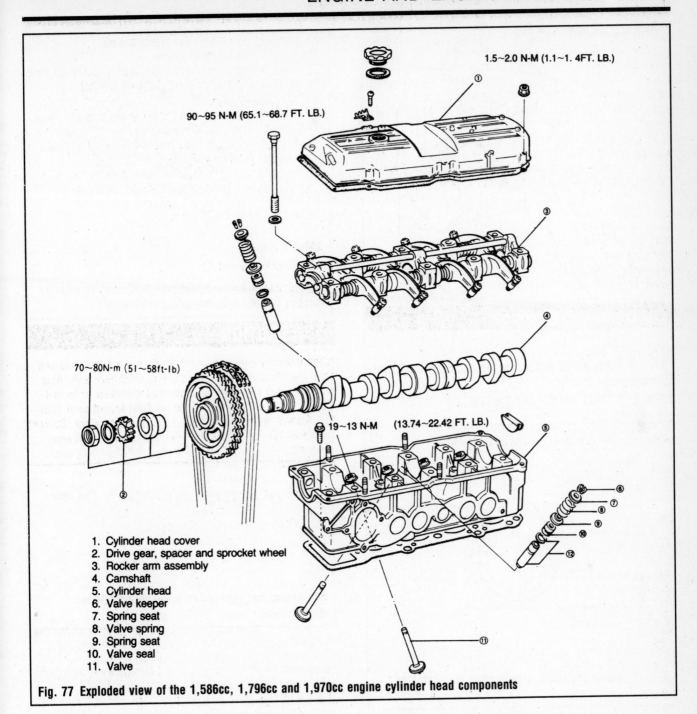

1. Cylinder head cover
2. Drive gear, spacer and sprocket wheel
3. Rocker arm assembly
4. Camshaft
5. Cylinder head
6. Valve keeper
7. Spring seat
8. Valve spring
9. Spring seat
10. Valve seal
11. Valve

Fig. 77 Exploded view of the 1,586cc, 1,796cc and 1,970cc engine cylinder head components

To install:

24. Coat the camshaft with clean engine oil and install it in position, making sure that the lug on the nose of the shaft is at the 12 o'clock position.

25. Apply a thin coat of sealant to the areas shown, and install the rocker shaft assembly. Torque the bolts evenly, and in the order shown, to 15–20 ft. lbs. Install the camshaft sprocket. Torque the camshaft sprocket bolt to 40–45 ft. lbs.

26. Replace the belt if it has been contaminated by oil or grease, or shows any sign of damage, wear, cracks or peeling.

27. To ease installation of the belt, remove all the spark plugs.

28. Make sure that the timing mark on the camshaft is aligned as described above, and that the timing mark (notch) on the crank-shaft sprocket is aligned with the triangular shaped mark on the front housing.

29. Install the tensioner and spring, positioning the tensioner all the way to the intake manifold side and temporarily secure it there with the lockbolt.

30. Install the belt onto the sprockets from YOUR right side. If you are reusing the original belt, make sure you follow the directional mark previously made.

31. Loosen the lockbolt so that the tensioner applies tension to the belt.

32. Turn the crankshaft two full revolutions in the direction of normal rotation. This will apply equal tension to all points of the belt.

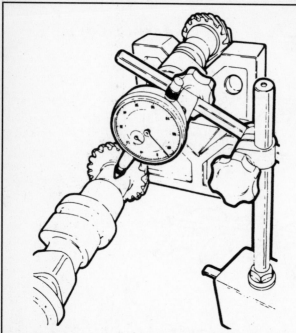

Fig. 78 Using a dial indicator to check the camshaft for straightness

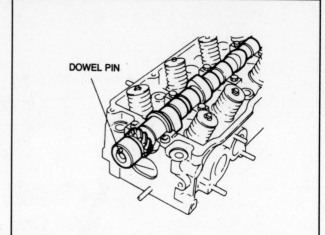

Fig. 80 Installing the 1,998cc engine camshaft with the locating dowel/pin in the 12 o'clock position

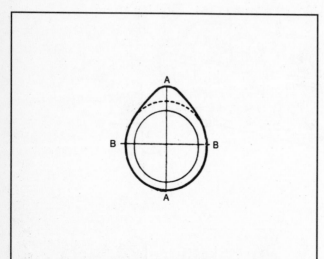

Fig. 79 Measuring points to determine camshaft lobe wear

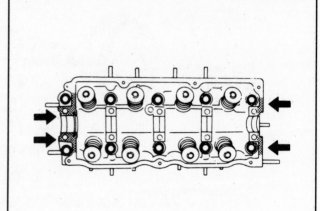

Fig. 81 Sealant application areas on the 1,998cc cylinder head

33. Make sure that the timing marks are still aligned. If not, repeat the belt installation procedure.

34. Tighten the tensioner lockbolt to 30–35 ft. lbs.

35. Measure the timing belt tension by pressing on the belt at the midpoint of the longest straight run. Belt deflection should be 11–13mm (0.433–0.510 in.). If not, repeat the belt adjustment procedure, above.

36. Check the valve adjustment and reset, if necessary.

37. Clean the mating surfaces of the cylinder head and rocker cover.

38. Install the rocker cover with a new gasket.

39. Torque the bolts to 24–36 inch lbs.

40. Install the spark plug wire on the plugs. Place the wires in the clips on the rocker cover. Connect the choke and air by-pass valve cable.

41. Install the lower, then the upper, belt covers. Torque the belt cover bolts to 80 in. lbs.

42. Install the power steering pump drive belt.

43. Install the air conditioning compressor drive belt.

44. Install the fan pulley, hub and bracket. Torque the fan bracket bolts to 40 ft. lbs.

45. Connect the air injection pipes.

46. Install the alternator.

47. Install the fan shroud and fan.

48. Install the distributor.

49. Fill the cooling system.

50. Connect the battery ground.

When installing the drive belts on the various accessories, check the belt deflection as follows:

- Alternator
  New: 7–8mm (0.276–0.315 in.)
  Used: 8–9mm (0.315–0.354 in.)

- Power steering pump
  New: 9–11mm (0.354–0.433 in.)
  Used: 11–13mm (0.433–0.510 in.)
- Air conditioning compressor
  New: 10–12mm (0.394–0.472 in.)
  Used: 12–14mm (0.472–0.552 in.)

2,209cc Diesel Engine

1. Scribe the locations of the hood hinges and remove the hood.
2. Remove the engine splash shield.
3. Drain the coolant.

✳✳ CAUTION

When draining engine coolant, keep in mind that cats and dogs are attracted to ethylene glycol antifreeze and could drink any that is left in an uncovered container or in puddles on the ground. This will prove fatal in sufficient quantity. Always drain coolant into a sealable container. Coolant should be reused unless it is contaminated or is several years old.

4. Drain the engine oil.

✳✳ CAUTION

The EPA warns that prolonged contact with used engine oil may cause a number of skin disorders, including cancer! You should make every effort to minimize you exposure to used engine oil. Protective gloves should be worn when changing the oil. Wash your hands and any other exposed skin areas as soon as possible after exposure to used engine oil. Soap and water, or waterless hand cleaner should be used.

5. Disconnect the battery cables and remove the battery.
6. Remove the air cleaner and the oil dipstick.
7. Remove the radiator shroud and the engine fan. Place the fan in an upright position to avoid fluid loss from the fan clutch.
8. Disconnect and tag all wires, hoses, cables, pipes and linkage from the engine.
9. Remove the clutch release cylinder.
10. Remove the oil cooler.
11. Remove the radiator.
12. Disconnect the exhaust pipe at the manifold and remove the exhaust manifold.
13. Dismount the air conditioning compressor and position it out of the way. Don't disconnect any refrigerant lines.
14. Dismount the power steering pump and position it out of the way without disconnecting any hoses.
15. Raise and support the truck on jackstands.
16. Attach a lifting sling and shop crane to the engine lifting eyes and take up the weight of the engine.
17. Support the transmission with a floor jack and remove the transmission-to-engine bolts.
18. Remove the engine support plates and mounting nuts, push the engine forward to clear the transmission and lift it out of the truck.
19. Remove the rocker arm cover, rocker arm assemblies and pushrods, making sure you keep the pushrods in order of their removal. Remove the lifters, marking them also, for installation.

20. Remove the timing gear case cover.
21. Remove the camshaft gear.
22. Remove the oil pan and oil pump.
23. Remove the camshaft thrust plate.
24. Carefully slide the camshaft from the block.
25. Inspect the camshaft for wear, damage or heat scoring. Check the dimensions of the shaft according to the specifications given in the Camshaft Specifications Chart.

To install:

26. Coat the camshaft journal and bearings with clean engine oil, and the lobes with polyethylene grease, prior to installation.
27. Carefully slide the camshaft into the block.
28. Install the camshaft thrust plate and new gasket. Torque the thrust plate bolts to 95 inch lbs.
29. Install the oil pump.
30. Install the oil pan.
31. Install the camshaft gear.
32. Install the timing gear case cover and new gasket.
33. Install the lifters.
34. Install the pushrods.
35. Install the rocker assemblies.
36. Install the rocker arm cover.
37. Lower the engine into the truck and push it rearward to engage the transmission.
38. Install the support plates and mounting nuts. Torque the fasteners to 35 ft. lbs.
39. Install the transmission-to-engine bolts. Torque them to 35 ft. lbs.
40. Remove the shop crane.
41. Install the power steering pump.
42. Install the air conditioning compressor.
43. Install the exhaust manifold.
44. Connect the exhaust pipe at the manifold.
45. Install the radiator.
46. Install the oil cooler.
47. Install the clutch release cylinder.
48. Connect all wires, hoses, cables, pipes and linkage at the engine.
49. Install the engine fan.
50. Install the radiator shroud.
51. Install the air cleaner.
52. Install the oil dipstick.
53. Install the battery.
54. Connect the battery cables.
55. Fill the engine with the proper amount of oil.
56. Fill the cooling system.
57. Install the engine splash shield.
58. Install the hood.

INSPECTION

Camshaft Lobe Lift

Check the lift of each lobe in consecutive order and make a note of the reading.

1. Remove the fresh air inlet tube and the air cleaner. Remove the heater hose and crankcase ventilation hoses. Remove valve rocker arm cover(s).
2. Remove the rocker arm stud nut or fulcrum bolts, fulcrum seat and rocker arm.
3. Make sure the pushrod is in the valve tappet socket. Install

a dial indicator so that the actuating point of the indicator is in the pushrod socket (or the indicator ball socket adaptor is on the end of the pushrod) and in the same plane as the pushrod movement.

4. Install an auxiliary starter switch. Crank the engine with the ignition switch off. Turn the crankshaft over until the tappet is on the base circle of the camshaft lobe. At this position, the pushrod will be in its lowest position.

5. Zero the dial indicator. Continue to rotate the crankshaft slowly until the pushrod is in the fully raised position.

6. Compare the total lift recorded on the dial indicator with the specification shown on the Camshaft Specification chart.

To check the accuracy of the original indicator reading, continue to rotate the crankshaft until the indicator reads zero. If the left on any lobe is below specified wear limits listed, the camshaft and the valve tappet operating on the worn lobe(s) must be replaced.

7. Install the dial indicator and auxiliary starter switch.

8. Install the rocker arm, fulcrum seat and stud nut or fulcrum bolts. Check the valve clearance. Adjust if required (refer to procedure in this chapter).

9. Install the valve rocker arm cover(s) and the air cleaner.

Camshaft End-Play

→On engines with an aluminum or nylon camshaft sprocket, prying against the sprocket, with the valve train load on the camshaft, can break or damage the sprocket. Therefore, the rocker arm adjusting nuts must be backed off, or the rocker arm and shaft assembly must be loosened sufficiently to free the camshaft. After checking the camshaft end-play, check the valve clearance. Adjust if required (refer to procedure in this chapter).

1. Push the camshaft toward the rear of the engine. Install a dial indicator so that the indicator point is on the camshaft sprocket attaching screw.

2. Zero the dial indicator. Position a prybar between the camshaft gear and the block. Pull the camshaft forward and release it. Compare the dial indicator reading with the specifications.

3. If the end-play is excessive, check the spacer for correct installation before it is removed. If the spacer is correctly installed, replace the thrust plate.

4. Remove the dial indicator.

Pistons and Connecting Rods

REMOVAL

♦ **See Figures 82, 83, 84, 85, 86 and 87**

1. Remove the engine assembly from the truck, see Engine Removal and Installation.

2. Remove the intake manifold and cylinder head.

3. Remove the oil pan.

4. Remove the oil pump assembly.

5. Stamp the cylinder number on the machine surfaces of the bolt bosses of the connecting rod and cap for identification when reinstalling. If the pistons are to be removed from the connecting rod, mark the cylinder number on the piston with a silver pencil

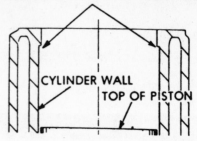

Fig. 82 **Example of the cylinder bore ridge**

Fig. 83 **Using a ridge reamer to remove the cylinder bore ridge will ease removal and installation of the piston and rod assemblies**

Place rubber hose over the connecting rod studs to protect the crank and bores from damage

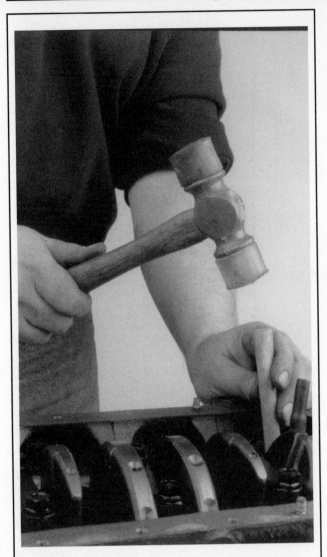

Carefully tap the piston out of the bore using a wooden dowel

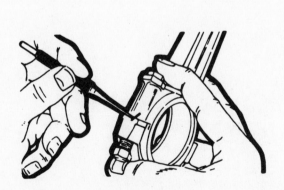

Fig. 84 Matchmarking the connecting rods to their caps using a scribe

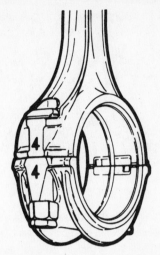

Fig. 85 Matchmarking the connecting rods to their caps using a number stamp—you can also use a center punch and mark the appropriate number of dots on each rod and rod cap

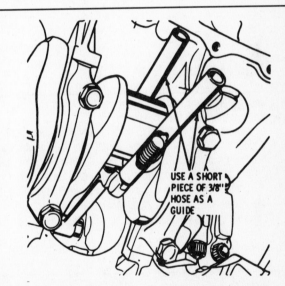

USE A SHORT PIECE OF 3/8" HOSE AS A GUIDE

Fig. 86 Always protect the crankshaft journals from scratches and dings—cover the connecting rod bolts with lengths of rubber hose or commercially available rod bolt covers

or quick drying paint for proper cylinder identification and cap-to-rod location.

6. Examine the cylinder bore above the ring travel. If a ridge exists, remove the ridge with a ridge reamer before attempting to remove the piston and rod assembly. Never cut into the ring travel area in excess of 0.8mm (0.0315 in.) when removing the ridges.

7. Remove the rod bearing cap and bearing.

8. Install a guide hose over threads of rod bolts. This is to prevent damage to bearing journal and rod bolt threads.

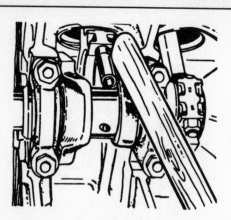

Fig. 87 Carefully push the piston out with a hammer handle or wooden dowel—never push on the soft bearing that sits in the center of the rod, as this will render it unusable

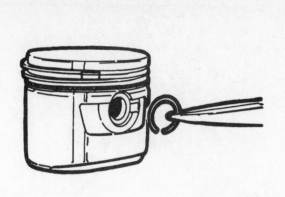

Fig. 88 Use needlenose or snapring pliers to remove the piston pin snaprings

9. Remove the rod and piston assembly through the top of the cylinder bore.

10. Remove the other rod and piston assemblies in the same manner.

PISTON PIN REPLACEMENT

♦ See Figure 88

Use care at all times when handling and servicing connecting rods and pistons. To prevent possible damage to these units, do not clamp the rod or piston in a vise since they may become distorted. Do not allow the pistons to strike against one another, against hard objects or bench surfaces, since distortion of the piston contour or nicks in the soft aluminum material may result.

1. Remove the piston rings using a suitable piston ring remover.

2. Remove the piston pin lockring, if used. Install the guide bushing of the Then, on all engines, press the piston pin out of the piston with tools designed for this purpose.

3. Install the piston and connecting rod assembly on a support, and place the assembly in an arbor press. Press the pin out of the connecting rod, using the appropriate piston pin tool.

4. Assembly is the reverse of disassembly. Use new lockrings where needed.

CLEANING AND INSPECTION

Connecting Rods

Wash connecting rods in cleaning solvent and dry with compressed air. Check for twisted or bent rods and inspect for nicks or cracks. Replace connecting rods that are damaged.

Pistons

Clean varnish from piston skirts and pins with a cleaning solvent. DO NOT WIRE BRUSH ANY PART OF THE PISTON. Clean

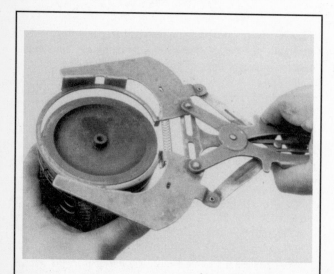

Use a ring expander tool to remove the piston rings

Clean the piston grooves using a ring groove cleaner

You can use a piece of an old ring to clean the piston grooves, BUT be careful, the ring is sharp

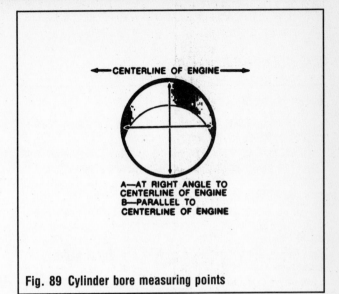

Fig. 89 Cylinder bore measuring points

Measure the piston's outer diameter using a micrometer

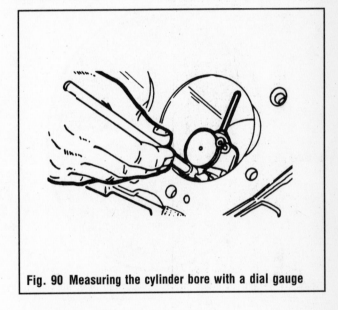

Fig. 90 Measuring the cylinder bore with a dial gauge

the ring grooves with a groove cleaner and make sure oil ring holes and slots are clean.

Inspect the piston for cracked ring lands, skirts or pin bosses, wavy or worn ring lands, scuffed or damaged skirts, eroded areas at the top of the piston. Replace pistons that are damaged or show signs of excessive wear. Inspect the grooves for nicks or burrs that might cause the rings to hang up.

Measure piston skirt (across center line of piston pin) and check piston clearance.

MEASURING THE OLD PISTONS

▶ See Figures 89 and 90

Check used piston-to-cylinder bore clearance as follows:
1. Measure the cylinder bore diameter with a telescope gauge.
2. Measure the piston diameter. When measuring the pistons for size or taper, measurements must be made with the piston pin removed.

3. Subtract the piston diameter from the cylinder bore diameter to determine piston-to-bore clearance.
4. Compare the piston-to-bore clearances obtained with those clearances recommended. Determine if the piston-to-bore clearance is in the acceptable range.
5. When measuring taper, the largest reading must be at the bottom of the skirt.

SELECTING NEW PISTONS

1. If the used piston is not acceptable, check the service piston size and determine if a new piston can be selected. Service pistons are available in standard, and oversizes of 0.25mm and 0.50mm.
2. If the cylinder bore must be reconditioned, measure the new piston diameter, then hone the cylinder bore to obtain the preferred clearance.

3. Select a new piston and mark the piston to identify the cylinder for which it was fitted.

CYLINDER HONING

◗ **See Figure 91**

1. When cylinders are being honed, follow the manufacturer's recommendations for the use of the hone.

2. Occasionally during the honing operation, the cylinder bore should be thoroughly cleaned and the selected piston checked for correct fit.

3. When finish-honing a cylinder bore, the hone should be moved up and down at a sufficient speed to obtain a very fine uniform surface finish in a cross-hatch pattern of approximately 45–65° included angle. The finish marks should be clean but not sharp, free from imbedded particles and torn or folded metal.

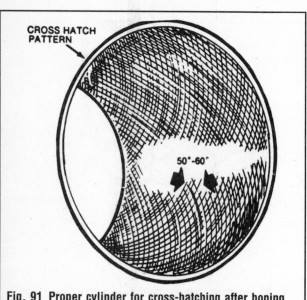

Fig. 91 Proper cylinder for cross-hatching after honing

A solid hone can also be used to cross-hatch the cylinder bore

Using a ball type cylinder hone is an easy way to hone the cylinder bore

As with a ball hone, work the hone carefully up and down the bore to achieve the desired results

4. Permanently mark the piston for the cylinder to which it has been fitted and proceed to hone the remaining cylinders.

➥**Handle pistons with care. Do not attempt to force pistons through cylinders until the cylinders have been honed to correct size. Pistons can be distorted through careless handling.**

5. Thoroughly clean the bores with hot water and detergent. Scrub well with a stiff bristle brush and rinse thoroughly with hot water. It is extremely essential that a good cleaning operation be performed. If any of the abrasive material is allowed to remain in the cylinder bores, it will rapidly wear the new rings and cylinder bores. The bores should be swabbed several times with light engine oil and a clean cloth and then wiped with a clean dry cloth. CYLINDERS SHOULD NOT BE CLEANED WITH KEROSENE OR GASOLINE. Clean the remainder of the cylinder block to remove the excess material spread during the honing operation.

CHECKING CYLINDER BORE

Cylinder bore size can be measured with inside micrometers or a cylinder gauge. The most wear will occur at the top of the ring travel.

Reconditioned cylinder bores should be held to not more than 0.025mm (0.00098 in.) taper.

If the cylinder bores are smooth, the cylinder walls should not be deglazed. If the cylinder walls are scored, the walls may have to be honed before installing new rings. It is important that reconditioned cylinder bores be thoroughly washed with a soap and water solution to remove all traces of abrasive material to eliminate premature wear.

PISTON RING REPLACEMENT

◗ **See Figures 92, 93 and 94**

The pistons have three rings (two compression rings and one oil ring). The oil ring consists of two rails and an expander.

For service ring specifications and detailed installation pro-

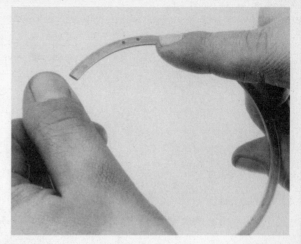

Most rings are marked to show which side should face upward

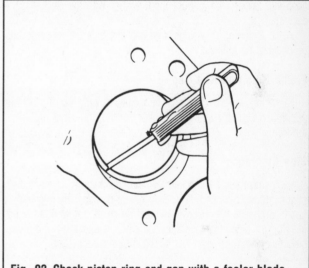

Fig. 92 Check piston ring end-gap with a feeler blade

A telescoping gauge may be used to measure the cylinder bore diameter

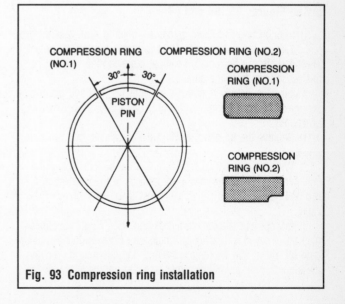

Fig. 93 Compression ring installation

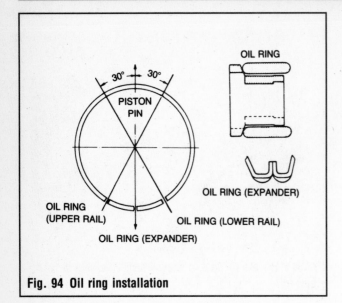

Fig. 94 Oil ring installation

ductions, refer to the instructions furnished with the parts package.

When installing new rings, ring gap and side clearance should be checked as follows:

Piston Ring and Rail Gap

Each ring and rail gap must be measured with the ring or rail positioned squarely and at the bottom of the ring-travel area of the bore.

Side Clearance

Each ring must be checked for side clearance in its respective piston groove by inserting a feeler gauge between the ring and its upper land. The piston grooves must be cleaned before checking the ring for side clearance specifications. To check oil ring side clearance, the oil rings must be installed on the piston.

ROD BEARING REPLACEMENT

◆ See Figures 95, 96 and 97

The connecting rod bearings are designed to have a slight projection above the rod and cap faces to insure a positive contact. The bearings can be replaced without removing the rod and piston assemblies from the engine.

If you have already removed the connecting rod and piston assemblies from the engine, follow only Steps 3–7 of the following procedure.

1. Remove the oil pan. See the Oil Pan procedures, earlier in this section.

2. With the connecting rod journal at the bottom, stamp the cylinder number on the machined surfaces of the connecting rod and cap for identification when installing, then remove the caps.

3. Inspect journals for roughness and wear. Slight roughness may be removed with a fine grit polishing cloth saturated with engine oil. Burrs may be removed with a fine oil stone by moving the stone on the journal circumference. Do not move the stone

Checking the ring-to-ring groove clearance

The notch on the the side of the bearing cap matches the groove on the bearing insert

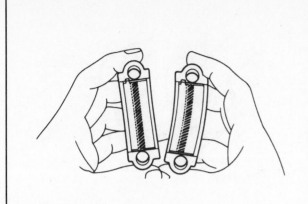

Fig. 95 Inspect the rod bearings for scuffing or other wear—also check the crankshaft journal

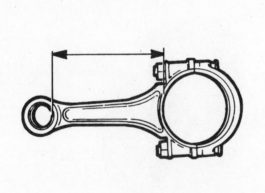

Fig. 96 Measure the connecting rod length at these points

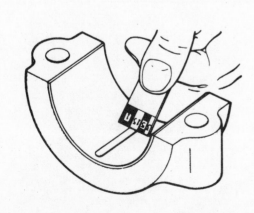

Fig. 97 Measuring the connecting rod bearing oil clearance with a strip of Plastigage® material

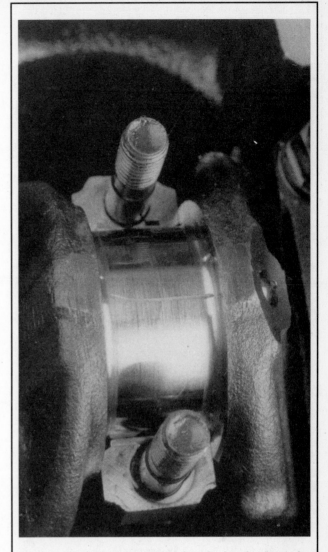

Apply a strip of gauging material to the bearing journal, then install and torque the cap

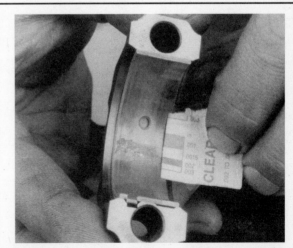

After the cap is removed again, use the scale supplied with the gauge material to check clearances

back and forth across the journal. If the journals are scored or ridged, the crankshaft must be replaced.

4. The connecting rod journals should be checked for out-of-round and correct size with a micrometer.

➡**Crankshaft rod journals will normally be standard size. If any undersized bearings are used, all will be 0.25mm undersize and 0.25mm will be stamped on the number 4 counterweight.**

If plastic gauging material is to be used:

5. Clean oil from the journal bearing cap, connecting rod and outer and inner surfaces of the bearing inserts. Position the insert so that the tang is properly aligned with the notch in the rod and cap.

6. Place a piece of plastic gauging material in the center of lower bearing shell.

7. Remove the bearing cap and determine the bearing clearances by comparing the width of the flattened plastic gauging material at its widest point with the graduation on the container. The number within the graduation on the envelope indicates the clearance in thousandths of an inch or millimeters. If this clearance is excessive, replace the bearing and recheck the clearance with the plastic gauging material. Undersized bearings are available in sizes of 0.25mm, 0.50mm and 0.75mm. Lubricate the bearing with engine oil before installation. Repeat Steps 2–7 on the remaining connecting rod bearings. All rods must be connected to their journals when rotating the crankshaft, to prevent engine damage.

INSTALLATION

◆ **See Figures 98 and 99**

1. Install some lengths of rubber tubing over the connecting rod bolts to prevent damage to the journals.
2. Apply engine oil to the rings and piston, then install a piston ring compressing tool on the piston.
3. Install the assembly in its respective cylinder bore.
4. Lubricate the crankshaft journal with engine oil and install

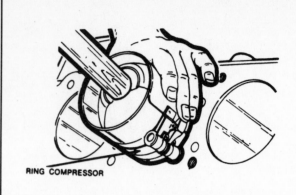

RING COMPRESSOR

Fig. 99 Using a wooden hammer handle, tap the piston down through the ring compressor and into the cylinder bore

Most pistons are marked to indicate positioning in the engine (usually a mark means the side facing front)

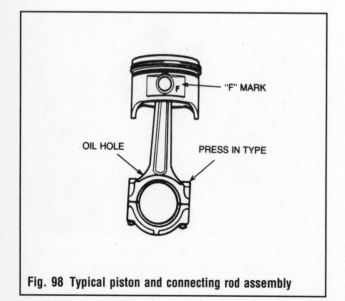

"F" MARK

OIL HOLE   PRESS IN TYPE

Fig. 98 Typical piston and connecting rod assembly

Installing the piston into the block using a ring compressor and the handle of a hammer

the connecting rod bearing and cap, with the bearing index tang in rod and cap on same side.

➡ **When more than one rod and piston assembly is being installed, the connecting rod cap attaching nuts should be tightened only enough to keep each rod in position until all have been installed. This will aid installation of the remaining piston assemblies.**

5. Torque the rod bolt nuts to specification. Using a feeler gauge and small prybar, check connecting rod side clearance.

6. Install all other parts in reverse order of removal.

7. Install the engine in the truck. See Engine Removal and Installation.

Cylinder Liners

REMOVAL & INSTALLATION

Diesel Engine Only

▶ **See Figures 100 and 101**

➡ **A hydraulic press and adapters are necessary for this procedure.**

1. Remove the engine.
2. Remove the head.
3. Remove the pistons and connecting rods.
4. r the crankshaft and bearings.
5. Remove the camshaft.
6. Mount the block in the holding fixture under the press ram, bottom side up.
7. Drive the liners from the block.
8. Check the block bore for scratches. Remove them with an oil-soaked fine emery paper.
9. Invert the block and press the new liners in from the top.

➡ **Normal pressing pressure is 2,200–6,600 lb. Press pressure higher than 6,600 lb. will distort the liner; pressures lower than 2,200 lb. will result in a loose fit.**

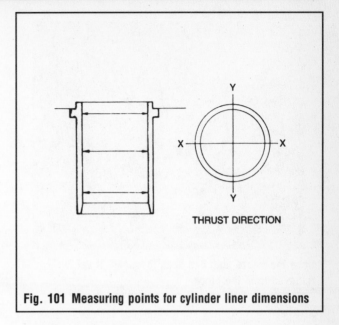

Fig. 101 Measuring points for cylinder liner dimensions

10. Once the liner is in place, check its protrusion above the head surface. Protrusion should be 0.66–0.78mm (0.02598–0.03071 in.).

11. Check the liner bore. Bore for a new liner should be 88.9mm ± 0.05mm (3.50 in. ± 0.00197 in.).

Freeze (Core) Plugs

REMOVAL & INSTALLATION

1. Drain the complete cooling system and engine block.
2. Drill or punch a hole in the center of the freeze plug and pull it out from the engine block with a slide hammer or equivalent.

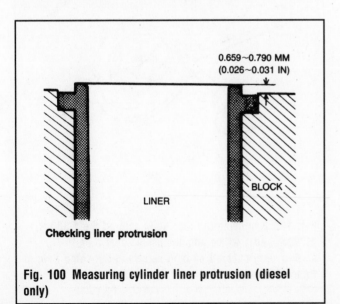

Fig. 100 Measuring cylinder liner protrusion (diesel only)

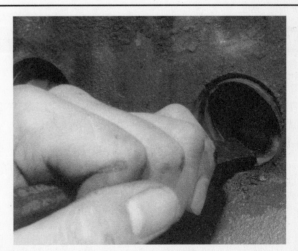

Using a punch and hammer, the freeze plug can be loosened in the block

Once the freeze plug has been loosened, it can be removed from the block

➡Stay away from the freeze plug location when working, as coolant will flow from the engine when the plug is removed.

3. Check the bore for roughness or burrs. If the bore is badly damaged, hone it and use an oversized freeze plug.

4. Coat the new freeze plug with sealer and drive into the correct position.

5. Refill the cooling system. Start the engine and check for coolant leaks.

Rear Main Oil Seal

REPLACEMENT

1,586cc, 1,796cc and 1,970cc Engines
▶ See Figures 102 and 103

If the rear main oil seal is being replaced independently of any other parts, it can be done with the engine in place. If the rear main oil seal and the rear main bearing are being replaced, together, the engine must be removed from the truck.

1. Remove the transmission.

2. On trucks with a manual transmission, remove the clutch disc, pressure plate and flywheel. On trucks with an automatic transmission, remove the drive plate.

3. Using an awl, punch two holes in the crankshaft rear oil seal. They should be punched on opposite sides of the crankshaft, just above the bearing cap-to-cylinder block split line.

4. Install a sheet metal screw in each hole. Pry against both screws at the same time to remove the oil seal. Do not scratch the oil seal surface on the crankshaft.

5. Clean the oil recess in the cylinder block and bearing cap. Clean the oil seal surface on the crankshaft.

6. Coat the oil seal surfaces with oil. Coat the oil surface and the seal surface on the crankshaft with Lubriplate®. Install the oil seal and be sure that it is not cocked. Be sure that the seal surface was not damaged.

7. Install the flywheel. Coat the threads of the flywheel or drive plate attaching bolts with oil resistant sealer. Torque the bolts to specifications in sequence across from each other.
- Flywheel:
  Gasoline engine—115–120 ft. lbs.
  Diesel engine—100–140 ft. lbs.
- Drive plate: 60–69 ft. lbs.

8. Install the clutch, pressure plate and transmission.

1,998cc Engine
▶ See Figures 104 and 105

1. Remove the transmission.

2. Remove the clutch assembly.

3. Remove the flywheel.

4. Remove the end plate.

5. The seal is located in the rear cover. Remove the rear cover. Discard the gasket.

6. Drive the old seal from the rear cover.

7. Apply clean engine oil to the outer rim of the new seal and the seal bore in the rear cover. Press the new seal into place.

8. Coat the seal lip with clean engine oil. Install the rear cover and new gasket. Torque the bolts to 72–102 in. lbs. (6–8.5 ft. lbs.).

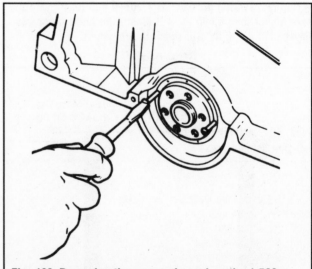

Fig. 102 Removing the rear main seal on the 1,586cc, 1,796cc and 1,970cc engines using sheet metal screws—pry outward on both screws at the same time to remove the seal

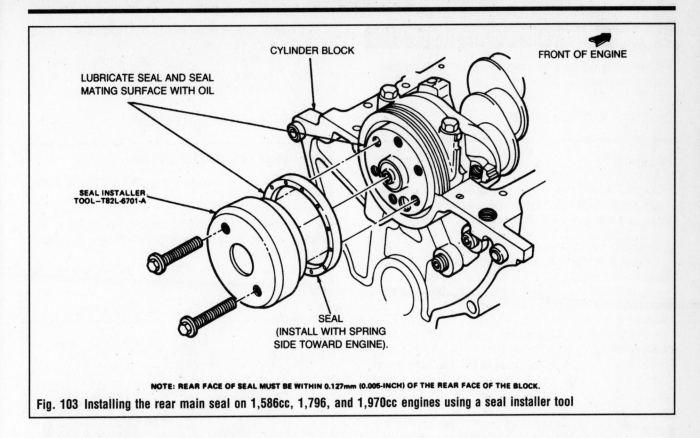

CYLINDER BLOCK

FRONT OF ENGINE

LUBRICATE SEAL AND SEAL
MATING SURFACE WITH OIL

SEAL INSTALLER
TOOL—T82L-6701-A

SEAL
(INSTALL WITH SPRING
SIDE TOWARD ENGINE).

NOTE: REAR FACE OF SEAL MUST BE WITHIN 0.127mm (0.005-INCH) OF THE REAR FACE OF THE BLOCK.

Fig. 103 Installing the rear main seal on 1,586cc, 1,796, and 1,970cc engines using a seal installer tool

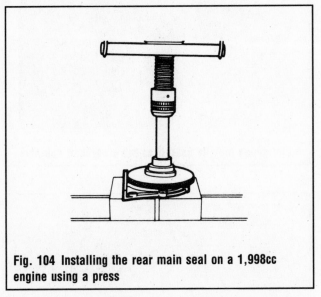

Fig. 104 Installing the rear main seal on a 1,998cc
engine using a press

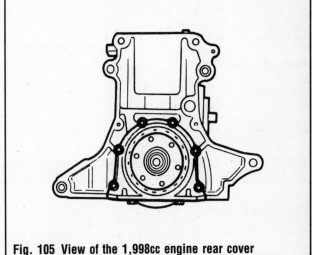

Fig. 105 View of the 1,998cc engine rear cover
installation

9. Using a sharp knife, cut away the part of the gasket that projects below the rear cover.
10. Install the end plate. Torque the bolts to 14–22 ft. lbs.
11. Install the flywheel.
12. Install the clutch assembly. See Chapter 7.
13. Install the transmission.

2,209cc Diesel Engine

1. Remove the transmission.
2. Remove the clutch assembly.

3. Remove the flywheel.
4. Remove the rear main seal housing.
5. Drive the old seal from the housing.
6. Clean the housing bore thoroughly.
7. Coat the outer edge of the new seal with gasket sealer.
8. Drive the new seal into the housing until it bottoms.
9. Coat the seal lip with clean engine oil and install the housing onto the engine. Torque the bolts, in a criss-cross pattern, to 10–14 ft. lbs.
10. Install all other parts in reverse of removal.

Flywheel/Flexplate and Ring Gear

➡**Flexplate is the term for a flywheel mated with an automatic transmission.**

REMOVAL & INSTALLATION

All Engines

➡**The ring gear is replaceable only on engines mated with a manual transmission. Engine with automatic transmissions have ring gears which are welded to the flexplate.**

1. Remove the transmission.
2. Remove the clutch, if equipped, or torque converter from the flywheel. The flywheel bolts should be loosened a little at a time in a cross pattern to avoid warping the flywheel. On trucks with manual transmission, replace the pilot bearing in the end of the crankshaft if removing the flywheel.
3. The flywheel should be checked for cracks and glazing. It can be resurfaced by a machine shop.
4. If the ring gear is to be replaced, drill a hole in the gear between two teeth, being careful not to contact the flywheel surface. Using a cold chisel at this point, crack the ring gear and remove it.
5. Polish the inner surface of the new ring gear and heat it in an oven to about 600°F (315°C). Quickly place the ring gear on the flywheel and tap it into place, making sure that it is fully seated.

➡**Never heat the ring gear past 800°F (426°C), or the tempering will be destroyed.**

6. Installation is the reverse of removal. To install the flywheel, first put it into position and then install the bolts loosely.
7. Torque the bolts a little at a time in a cross pattern, to the torque figure shown in the Torque Specifications Chart.

Crankshaft and Main Bearings

REMOVAL

1. Remove the engine assembly as previously outlined.
2. Remove the engine front cover.
3. Remove the timing chain/belt/gears and sprockets.
4. Remove the oil pan.
5. Remove the oil pump.
6. Remove the flywheel.
7. Stamp the cylinder number on the machined surfaces of the bolt bosses of the connecting rods and caps for identification when installing. If the pistons are to be removed from the connecting rod, mark the cylinder number on each piston with an indelible marker, silver pencil or quick drying paint for proper cylinder identification and cap to rod location.
8. Remove the connecting rod caps and store them so that they can be installed in their original positions.
9. Remove all the main bearing caps.

10. Note the position of the keyway in the crankshaft so it can be installed in the same position.
11. Lift the crankshaft out of the block. The rods will pivot to the center of the engine when the crankshaft is removed.
12. Remove the rear main oil seal.

INSPECTION AND INSTALLATION

♦ **See Figures 106, 107, 108 and 109**

1. Using a dial indicator, check the crankshaft journal runout. Measure the crankshaft journals with a micrometer to determine the correct size rod and main bearings to be used. Whenever a new or reconditioned crankshaft is installed, new connecting rod bearings and main bearings should be installed. See Main Bearings and Rod Bearings.
2. Clean all oil passages in the block (and crankshaft if it is being reused).

A dial gauge may be used to check crankshaft end-play

Carefully pry the shaft back and forth while reading the dial gauge for play

A dial gauge may also be used to check crankshaft run-out

Turn the crankshaft slowly by hand while checking the gauge

Mounting a dial gauge to read crankshaft run-out

➡️**A new rear main seal should be installed anytime the crankshaft is removed or replaced.**

3. Install sufficient oil pan bolts in the block to align with the connecting rod bolts. Use rubber bands between the bolts to position the connecting rods as required. Connecting rod position can be adjusted by increasing the tension on the rubber bands with additional turns around the pan bolts or thread protectors.

4. Position the upper half of main bearings in the block and lubricate them with engine oil.

5. Position crankshaft keyway in the same position as removed and lower it into block. The connecting rods will follow the crank pins into the correct position as the crankshaft is lowered.

6. Lubricate the thrust flanges with rebuilding oil. Install caps with the lower half of the bearings lubricated with engine oil. Lubricate the cap bolts with engine oil and install, but do not tighten.

7. With a block of wood, bump the shaft in each direction to

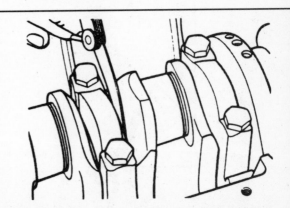

Fig. 106 Another method for checking crankshaft end-play is to use a feeler blade—gently pry the crankshaft in one direction and insert the feeler blade between the crankshaft and the thrust bearing. Check the crankshaft specifications chart for proper end-play

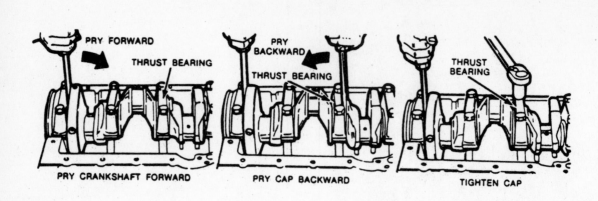

Fig. 107 Align the thrust bearing as illustrated. Torque the caps to specifications

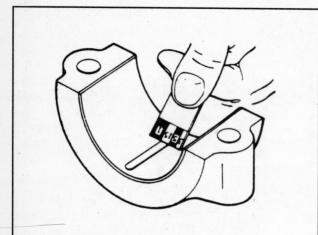

Fig. 108 Measure the main bearing clearance by comparing the flattened strip to the Plastigage® scale as shown

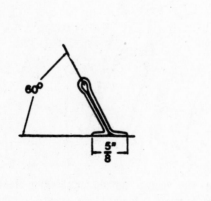

Fig. 109 Fabricate a roll-out pin as illustrated, if necessary

align the thrust flanges of the main bearing. After bumping the shaft in each direction, wedge the shaft to the front and hold it while torquing the thrust bearing cap bolts.

➡**In order to prevent the possibility of cylinder block and/or main bearing cap damage, the main bearing caps are to be tapped into their cylinder block cavity using a wood or rubber mallet before the bolts are installed. Do not use attaching bolts to pull the main bearing caps into their seats. Failure to observe this information may damage the cylinder block or a bearing cap.**

8. Torque all main bearing caps to specification. Check crankshaft end-play, using a flat feeler gauge.
9. Remove the connecting rod bolt thread protectors and lubricate the connecting rod bearings with engine oil.
10. Install the connecting rod bearing caps in their original position. Torque the nuts to specification.
11. Complete the installation by reversing the removal steps.

CHECKING BEARING CLEARANCE

1. Remove the bearing cap and wipe the oil from the crankshaft journal and the outer and inner surfaces of the bearing shell.
2. Place a piece of plastic gauging material in the center of the bearing.
3. Use a floor jack or other means to hold the crankshaft against the upper bearing shell. This is necessary to obtain accurate clearance readings when using plastic gauging material.
4. Install the bearing cap and bearing. Place engine oil on the cap bolts and install. Torque the bolts to specification.
5. Remove the bearing cap and determine the bearing clearance by comparing the width of the flattened plastic gauging material at its widest point with the graduations on the gauging material container. The number within the graduation on the envelope indicates the clearance in millimeters or thousandths of an inch. If the clearance is greater than allowed, REPLACE BOTH BEARING SHELLS AS A SET. Recheck the clearance after replacing the shells. (Refer to Main Bearing Replacement).

BEARING REPLACEMENT

Main bearing clearances must be corrected by the use of selective upper and lower shells. Undersized bearings are available in sizes of 0.25mm, 0.50mm and 0.75mm. UNDER NO CIRCUMSTANCES should the use of shims behind the shells to compensate for wear be attempted. To install the main bearing shells, proceed as follows:

1. Remove the oil pan as outlined below. On some models, the oil pump may also have to be removed.
2. Loosen all main bearing caps.
3. Remove the bearing cap and remove the lower shell.
4. Insert a flattened cotter pin or roll pin in the oil passage hole in the crankshaft, then rotate the crankshaft in the direction opposite to cranking rotation. The pin will contact the upper shell and roll it out.
5. The main bearing journals should be checked for roughness and wear. Slight roughness may be removed with a fine grit polishing cloth saturated with engine oil. Burrs may be removed with a fine oil stone. If the journals are scored or ridged, the crankshaft must be replaced.

The journals can be measured for out-of-round with the crankshaft installed by using a crankshaft caliper and inside micrometer or a main bearing micrometer. The upper bearing shell must be removed when measuring the crankshaft journals. Maximum out-of-round of the crankshaft journals must not exceed 0.050mm (0.00197 in.).

6. Clean the crankshaft journals and bearing caps thoroughly for installing new main bearings.
7. Apply clean engine oil or rebuilding oil, to the thrust flanges of bearing shells.
8. Place a new upper shell on the crankshaft journal with locating tang in the correct position and rotate the shaft to turn it into place using a cotter pin or roll pin as during removal.
9. Place a new bearing shell in the bearing cap.
10. Install a new oil seal in the rear main bearing cap and block.
11. Lubricate the main bearings with engine oil. Lubricate the thrust surface with lubricant rebuilding oil.
12. Lubricate the main bearing cap bolts with engine oil.

➡**In order to prevent the possibility of cylinder block and/or main bearing cap damage, the main bearing caps are to be tapped into their cylinder block cavity using a wood or rubber mallet before the attaching bolts are installed. Do not use attaching bolts to pull the main bearing caps into their seats. Failure to observe this information may damage the cylinder block or a bearing cap.**

13. Torque the main bearing cap bolts as specified.

ROTARY ENGINE MECHANICAL SERVICE

General Information

♦ **See Figure 110**

The Mazda rotary engine replaces conventional pistons with three-cornered rotors which have rounded sides. The rotors are mounted on a shaft which has eccentrics rather than crank throws.

The chamber in which the rotor travels is roughly oval shaped, but with the sides of the oval bowed in slightly. The technical name for this shape is a two lobe epitrochoid.

As the rotor travels its path in the chamber, it performs the same four functions as the piston in a regular four cycle engine:

1. Intake
2. Compression
3. Ignition
4. Exhaust

But all four functions in a rotary engine are happening concurrently, rather than in four separate stages.

Ignition of the compressed fuel/air mixture occurs each time a side of the rotor passes the spark plugs. Since the rotor has three sides there are three complete power impulses for each com-

How the Rotary Engine Works

1. INTAKE.
Fuel/air mixture is drawn into combustion chamber by revolving rotor through intake port (upper left). No valves or valve-operating mechanism needed.

2. COMPRESSION.
As rotor continues revolving, it reduces space in chamber containing fuel and air. This compresses mixture.

3. IGNITION.
Fuel/air mixture now fully compressed. Leading sparkplug fires. A split-second later, following plug fires to assure complete combustion.

4. EXHAUST.
Exploding mixture drives rotor, providing power. Rotor then expels gases through exhaust port.

Fig. 110 The rotary engine combustion cycle

plete revolution of the rotor. As it moves, the rotor experts pressure on the cam of the eccentric shaft, causing the shaft to turn.

Because there are three power pulses for every revolution of the rotor, the eccentric shaft must make three complete revolutions for every one revolution of the rotor. To maintain this ratio, the rotor has an internal gear that meshes with a fixed gear in a three-to-one ratio. If it was not for this gear arrangement, the rotor would spin freely and timing would be lost.

The Mazda rotary engine has two rotors mounted 60 degrees out of phase. This produces six power impulses for each complete revolution of both rotors and two power impulses for each revolution of the eccentric shaft.

Because of the number of power impulses for each revolution of the rotor and because all four functions are concurrent, the rotary engine is able to produce a much greater amount of power for its size and weight than a comparable reciprocating piston engine.

Instead of using valves to control the intake and exhaust operations, the rotor uncovers and covers ports on the wall of the chambers, as it turns. Thus, a complex valve train is unnecessary. The resulting elimination of parts further reduces the size and weight of the engine, as well as eliminating a major source of mechanical problems.

Spring loaded carbon seals are used to prevent loss of compression around the rotor apexes and cast iron seals are used to prevent loss of compression around the side faces of the rotor. These seals are equivalent to compression rings on a conventional piston, but must be more durable because of the high rotor rpm to which they are exposed.

Oil is controlled by means of circular seals mounted in two grooves on the side face of the rotor. These oil seals function to keep oil out of the combustion chamber and gasoline out of the crankcase, in a similar manner to the oil control ring on a piston.

The rotor housing is made of aluminum and the surfaces of the chamber are chrome plated.

Engine

REMOVAL & INSTALLATION

1. Scribe matchmarks on the hood and hinges. Remove the hood from the hinges.
2. Working from underneath the truck, remove the gravel shield then drain the cooling system.

✳✳ CAUTION

When draining engine coolant, keep in mind that cats and dogs are attracted to ethylene glycol antifreeze and could drink any that is left in an uncovered container or in puddles on the ground. This will prove fatal in sufficient quantity. Always drain coolant into a sealable container. Coolant should be reused unless it is contaminated or is several years old.

3. Drain the engine oil.
4. Disconnect the cable from the negative (−) battery terminal.

✳✳ CAUTION

The EPA warns that prolonged contact with used engine oil may cause a number of skin disorders, including cancer! You should make every effort to minimize you exposure to used engine oil. Protective gloves should be worn when changing the oil. Wash your hands and any other exposed skin areas as soon as possible after exposure to used engine oil. Soap and water, or waterless hand cleaner should be used.

5. Remove the air cleaner, bracket, and hoses.
6. Detach the accelerator cable, choke cable, and fuel lines from the carburetor.

✳✳ CAUTION

Never smoke when working around gasoline! Avoid all sources of sparks or ignition. Gasoline vapors are EXTREMELY volatile!

7. Remove the nuts which secure the thermostat housing. Disconnect the ground cable from the housing and install the housing again after the cable is removed.
8. Disconnect the power brake vacuum line from the intake manifold.
9. Remove the fan shroud securing bolts and then the shroud itself. Remove the bolts which secure the fan clutch to the eccentric shaft pulley. Withdraw the fan and clutch as a single unit.

✳✳ CAUTION

Keep the fan clutch in an upright position so that its fluid does not leak out.

10. Unfasten the clamps and remove both radiator hoses.
11. Note their respective positions and remove the spark plug cables. Disconnect the primary leads from the distributor and the distributor cap.
12. Detach all of the leads from the alternator, the water temperature sender, the oil pressure sender, and the starter motor.
13. Disconnect all of the wiring from the emission control system components.
14. Detach the heater hoses at the engine.
15. Detach the oil lines from the front and the rear of the engine.
16. Disconnect the battery cable from the positive (+) battery terminal and from the engine.
17. Unfasten the clutch slave cylinder retaining nuts from the clutch housing and tie the cylinder up and out of the way.

➡ Do not remove the hydraulic line from the slave cylinder.

18. Remove the exhaust pipe and the thermal reactor.

✳✳ CAUTION

Be sure that the thermal reactor has completely cooled; severe burns could result if it has not!

19. Remove the nuts and bolts, evenly and in two or three stages, which secure the clutch housing to the engine.
20. Support the transmission with a jack.
21. Remove the nuts from each of the engine mounts.
22. Attach a lifting sling to the lifting bracket on the rear of the engine housing.
23. Use a hoist to take up the slack on the sling.
24. Pull the engine forward until it clears the transmission input shaft. Lift the engine straight up and out of the truck.
25. Remove the hat stove from the exhaust manifold.
26. Remove the thermal reactor.
27. Mount the engine on a workstand.

To install:
28. Install the thermal reactor.
29. Install the hat stove on the exhaust manifold.
30. Lower the engine into the truck. Push it rearward to engage the transmission.
31. Install the nuts on the engine mounts. Torque them to 40 ft. lbs.
32. Install the nuts and bolts which secure the clutch housing to the engine. Torque them to 40 ft. lbs.
33. Remove the transmission jack.
34. Remove the shop crane.
35. Install the exhaust pipe and the thermal reactor. Torque the nuts to 40 ft. lbs.
36. Install the clutch slave cylinder.
37. Connect the battery cable.
38. Connect the oil lines at the front and the rear of the engine.
39. Connect the heater hoses at the engine.
40. Connect all of the wiring to the emission control system components.
41. Connect all of the leads to the alternator, the water temperature sender, the oil pressure sender, and the starter motor.
42. Install the spark plug cables.
43. Connect the primary leads at the distributor and the distributor cap.
44. Install both radiator hoses.
45. Install the fan and clutch.
46. Install the fan shroud.
47. Connect the power brake vacuum line at the intake manifold.
48. Install the thermostat housing and ground cable.
49. Connect the accelerator cable, choke cable, and fuel lines at the carburetor.
50. Install the air cleaner, bracket, and hoses.
51. Connect the cable to the negative (−) battery terminal.
52. Fill the cooling system.
53. Fill the engine with the proper amount of oil.
54. Install the gravel shield.
55. Install the hood.

Thermostat

♦ **See Figure 111**

REMOVAL & INSTALLATION

1. Drain the engine coolant into a large, clean container for reuse.

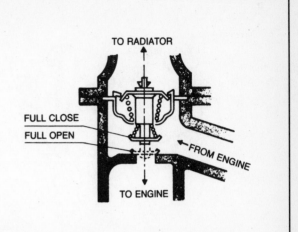

Fig. 111 View of the rotary engine's thermostat operation

✳✳ CAUTION

When draining engine coolant, keep in mind that cats and dogs are attracted to ethylene glycol antifreeze and could drink any that is left in an uncovered container or in puddles on the ground. This will prove fatal in sufficient quantity. Always drain coolant into a sealable container. Coolant should be reused unless it is contaminated or is several years old.

2. Remove the nuts which secure the thermostat housing to the water pump.
3. Lift the thermostat out.
4. Thermostat installation is performed in the reverse order of removal.

✳✳ WARNING

The thermostat is equipped with a plunger which covers and uncovers a bypass hole at its bottom. Because of its unusual construction, only the specified Mazda thermostat or an aftermarket thermostat equipped with this feature should be used for replacement. Use of a standard thermostat will cause the engine to overheat.

Intake Manifold

REMOVAL & INSTALLATION

♦ **See Figure 112**

To remove the intake manifold and carburetor assembly, with the engine remaining in the automobile, proceed in the following manner:
1. Perform Steps 2, 3, 4, 5, 7, and 13 of Engine Removal and Installation, above. Do not remove the engine. Do not drain the engine oil; merely remove the metering oil pump hose from the carburetor.
2. Perform Steps 2, 3, and 4 of Engine Disassembly, above.

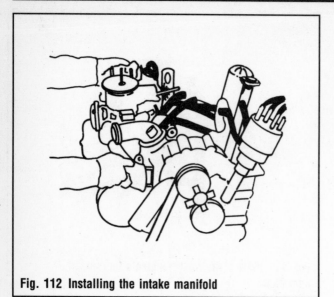

Fig. 112 Installing the intake manifold

3. Install the intake manifold and carburetor assembly in the reverse order of removal. Tighten the manifold securing nuts working from the inside out, and in two or three stages, to the specifications in the Torque Chart. Refill the cooling system.

Thermal Reactor

REMOVAL & INSTALLATION

▶ **See Figure 113**

✳✳ CAUTION

The thermal reactor operates at extremely high temperatures. Allow the engine to cool completely before attempting its removal.

To remove the thermal reactor, which replaces the exhaust manifold, proceed in the following manner:

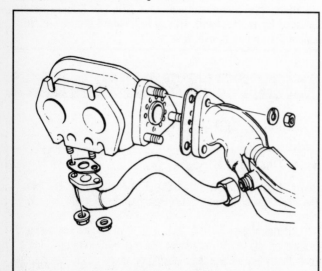

Fig. 113 View of the thermal reactor

1. Remove the air cleaner assembly from the carburetor.
2. Unbolt and remove the air injection pump, as outlined in Emission Controls.
3. Remove the intake manifold assembly, complete with carburetor.
4. Remove the heat stove from the thermal reactor.
5. Unfasten the thermal reactor securing nuts.

➡**The bottom nut is difficult to reach. Mazda makes a special wrench, part number 49 2133 001, to remove it. If the wrench is unavailable, a flexible drive metric socket wrench can be substituted.**

6. Lift the thermal reactor away from the engine.
7. Installation is the reverse of removal. Torque the nuts to 40 ft. lbs.

Radiator

▶ **See Figure 114**

REMOVAL & INSTALLATION

✳✳ CAUTION

Perform this operation when the engine has cooled completely.

1. Drain the engine coolant into a large, clean container so that it may be reused.

✳✳ CAUTION

When draining engine coolant, keep in mind that cats and dogs are attracted to ethylene glycol antifreeze and could drink any that is left in an uncovered container or in puddles on the ground. This will prove fatal in sufficient quantity. Always drain coolant into a sealable container. Coolant should be reused unless it is contaminated or is several years old.

2. Remove the nuts and bolts which attach the shroud to the radiator.
3. Remove the upper, lower and expansion tank hoses from the radiator.
4. Unfasten the bolts which attach the radiator to its mounting bracket. Remove the oil cooler nuts and bolts.
5. Withdraw the radiator from the truck.
6. Install the radiator in the reverse order of removal.

Oil Cooler

REMOVAL & INSTALLATION

▶ **See Figure 115**

1. Raise the truck and support it with jackstands.
2. Drain the engine oil.

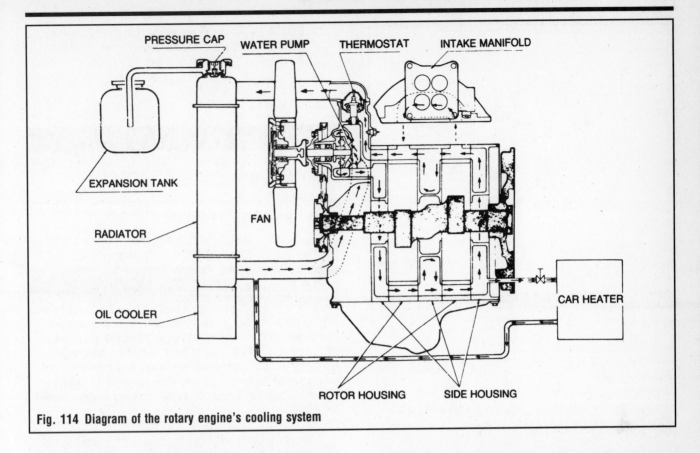

Fig. 114 Diagram of the rotary engine's cooling system

3. Unfasten the screws which retain the gravel shield and remove the shield.

4. Remove the oil lines from the oil cooler.

5. Unfasten the nuts which secure the oil cooler to the radiator.

6. Remove the oil cooler.

7. Examine the oil cooler for signs of leakage. Solder any leaks found. Blow the fins of the cooler clean with compressed air.

8. Installation is the reverse of removal.

Water Pump

♦ See Figure 116

REMOVAL & INSTALLATION

1. Drain the cooling system.

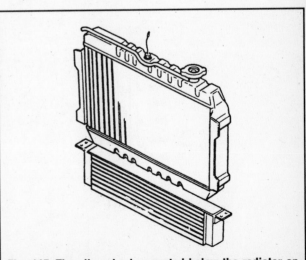

Fig. 115 The oil cooler is mounted below the radiator on rotary engine trucks

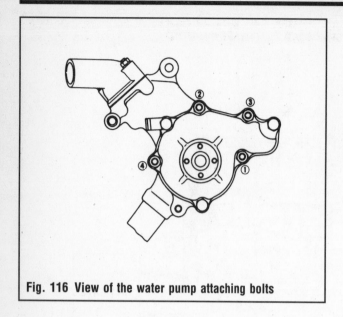

Fig. 116 View of the water pump attaching bolts

2. Remove the air cleaner.

3. Remove the bolts attaching the rear of the fan drive and remove the fan drive.

4. If necessary to disassemble the water pump, loosen the bolts attaching the water pump pulley to the water pump boss.

5. Remove the air pump and drive belt.

6. Remove the alternator and disconnect the drive belt.

7. If necessary, remove the water pump pulley and bolts.

8. Unbolt and remove the water pump.

9. Thoroughly clean the gasket mating surfaces of the pump and engine.

To install:

10. Install the water pump. Torque the bolts to 25 ft. lbs.

11. Install the water pump pulley and bolts.
12. Install the alternator and drive belt.
13. Install the air pump and drive belt.
14. Install the fan drive.
15. Install the air cleaner.
16. Fill the cooling system.

Oil Pan

REMOVAL & INSTALLATION

▶ **See Figures 117, 118 and 119**

1. Raise the front of the truck and support it with jackstands.
2. Remove the drain plug and drain the engine oil.

✳✳ CAUTION

The EPA warns that prolonged contact with used engine oil may cause a number of skin disorders, including cancer! You should make every effort to minimize you exposure to used engine oil. Protective gloves should be worn when changing the oil. Wash your hands and any other exposed skin areas as soon as possible after exposure to used engine oil. Soap and water, or waterless hand cleaner should be used.

3. Remove the nuts and bolts which secure the gravel shield and withdraw it from underneath the car.

4. Unfasten the retaining bolts and remove the oil pan with its gasket.

5. Oil pan installation is performed in the reverse order of removal. Coat both the oil pan flange and its mounting flange with sealer, prior to assembly. Torque the pan bolts to 84 in. lbs.

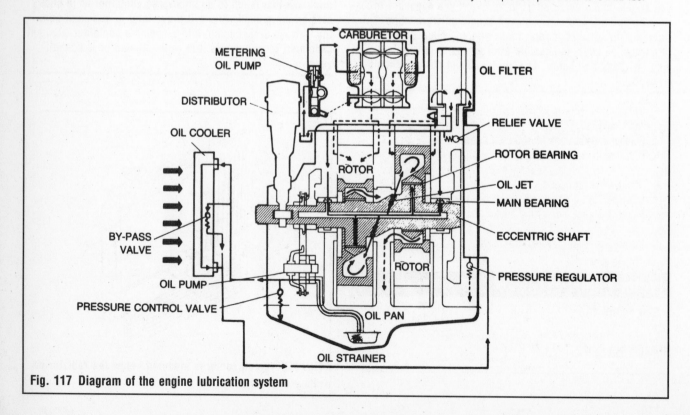

Fig. 117 Diagram of the engine lubrication system

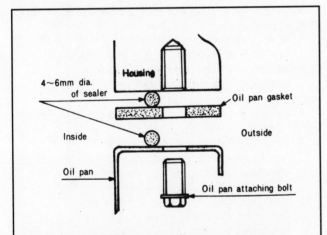

Fig. 118 Apply a continous bead of RTV sealant to the inside of the bolt holes on the oil pan mounting flange before installing the gasket

Fig. 119 Install the gasket to the oil pan mounting flange, then apply another continous bead of RTV sealant to the oil pan

Oil Pump

REMOVAL & INSTALLATION

A conventional oil pump, which is chain driven, circulates oil through the rotary engine. A full-flow filter is mounted on the top of the rear housing and an oil cooler is used to reduce the temperature of the engine oil.

An unusual feature of the rotary engine lubrication system is a metering oil pump which injects oil into the float chamber of the carburetor. Once there, it is mixed with the fuel which is to be burned, thus providing extra lubrication for the seals. The metering oil pump is designed to work only when the engine is operating under a load.

Oil pump removal and installation is contained in the Engine Overhaul section above. Perform only those steps needed in order to remove the oil pump.

Metering Oil Pump

OPERATION

◆ See Figures 120, 121 and 122

A metering oil pump, mounted on the top of the engine, is used to provide additional lubrication to the engine when it is operating under a load. The pump provides oil to the carburetor, where it is mixed in the float chamber with the fuel which is to be burned.

The metering pump is a plunger type and is controlled by throttle opening. A cam arrangement, connected to the carburetor throttle lever, operates a plunger. The plunger in turn, acts on a differential plunger, the stroke of which determines the amount of oil flow.

When the throttle opening is small, the amount of the plunger stroke is small; as the throttle opening increases, so does the amount of the plunger stroke.

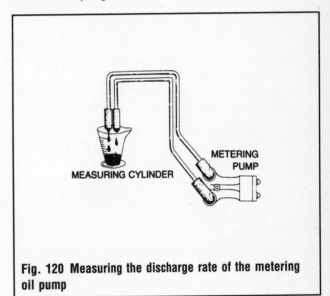

Fig. 120 Measuring the discharge rate of the metering oil pump

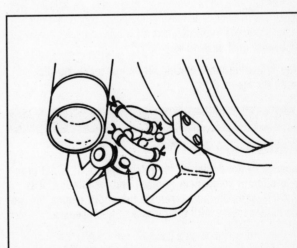

Fig. 121 Metering oil pump adjusting screw (small arrow, center)

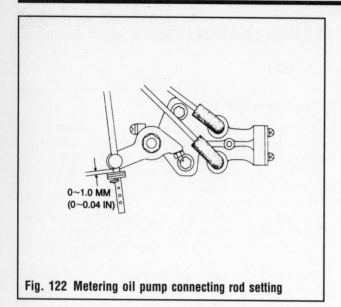

Fig. 122 Metering oil pump connecting rod setting

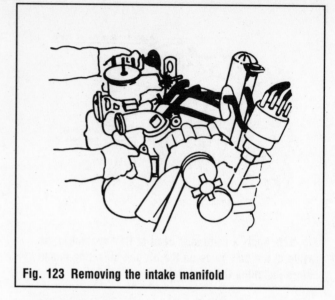

Fig. 123 Removing the intake manifold

TESTING

1. Disconnect the oil lines which run from the metering oil pump to the carburetor, at the carburetor end.
2. Use a container which has a scale calibrated in cubic centimeters (cc) to catch the pump discharge from the oil lines.

➡**Such a container is available from a scientific equipment supply house.**

3. Run the engine at 2,000 rpm for six minutes.
4. At the end of this time, 2.2cc of oil should be collected in the container. If not, adjust the pump as explained below.

ADJUSTMENTS

Rotate the adjusting screw on the metering oil pump to obtain the proper oil flow. Clockwise rotation of the screw increases the flow; counterclockwise rotation decreases the flow.

If necessary, the oil discharge rate may further be adjusted by changing the position of the cam in the pump connecting rod. The shorter the rod throw the more oil will be pumped. Adjust the throw by means of three holes provided.

➡**After adjusting the metering oil pump, check the discharge rate again.**

Engine Disassembly

◆ **See Figures 123 thru 131**

➡**Because of the design of the rotary engine, it is not practical to attempt component removal and installation. It is best to disassemble and assemble the entire engine, or, go as far as necessary with the disassembly procedure.**

1. Mount the engine on a stand.
2. Remove the oil hose support bracket from the front housing.
3. Disconnect the vacuum hoses, air hoses and remove the decel valve.

4. Remove the air pump and drive belt. Remove the air pump adjusting bar.
5. Remove the alternator and drive belt.
6. Disconnect the metering oil pump connecting rod, oil tubes and vacuum sensing tube from the carburetor.
7. Remove the carburetor and intake manifold as an assembly.
8. Remove the intake manifold gasket and two rubber rings. Discard them.
9. Remove the thermal reactor and gaskets.
10. Remove the spark plugs wires and distributor high tension leads, and remove the distributor from the front cover.
11. Remove the water pump and gasket.
12. Invert the engine on the stand.
13. Remove the oil pan and gasket.
14. Remove the oil pump screen and gasket.
15. Identify the front and rear rotor housing with a felt tip pen. These are common parts and must be identified to be reassembled in their respective locations.
16. Turn the engine on the stand so that the top of the engine is up.
17. Remove the engine mounting bracket from the front cover.
18. Hold the flywheel with a flywheel holder and remove the eccentric shaft pulley.
19. Turn the engine on a stand so that the front end of the engine is up.
20. Remove the front cover and gasket.
21. Remove the O-ring from the oil passage on the front housing.
22. Remove the oil slinger and distributor drive gear from the shaft.
23. Unbolt and remove the chain adjuster.
24. Remove the locknut and washer from the oil pump driven sprocket.
25. Slide the oil pump drive sprocket and driven sprocket together with the drive chain off the eccentric shaft and oil pump simultaneously.
26. Remove the keys from the eccentric and oil pump shafts.
27. Slide the balance weight, thrust washer and needle bearing from the shaft.

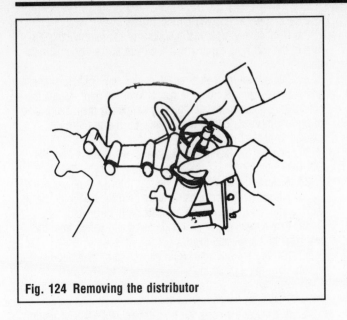

Fig. 124 Removing the distributor

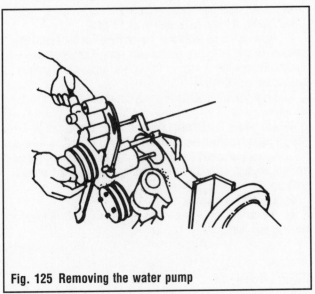

Fig. 125 Removing the water pump

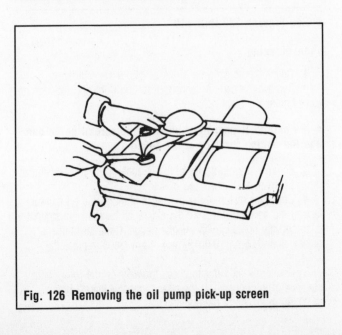

Fig. 126 Removing the oil pump pick-up screen

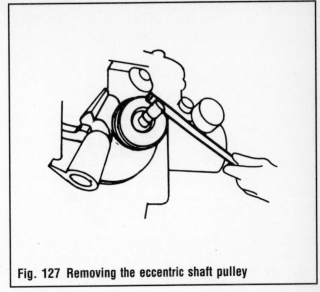

Fig. 127 Removing the eccentric shaft pulley

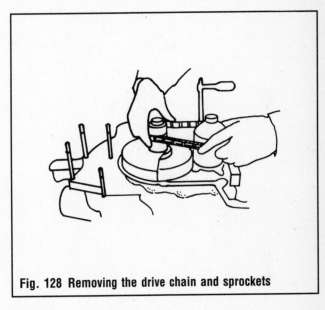

Fig. 128 Removing the drive chain and sprockets

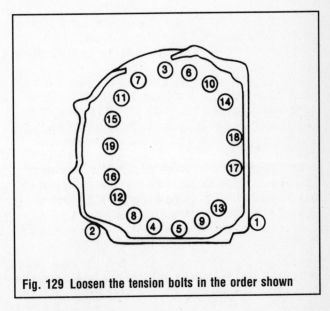

Fig. 129 Loosen the tension bolts in the order shown

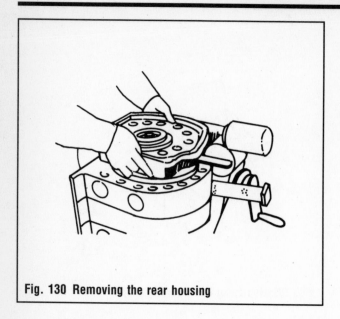

Fig. 130 Removing the rear housing

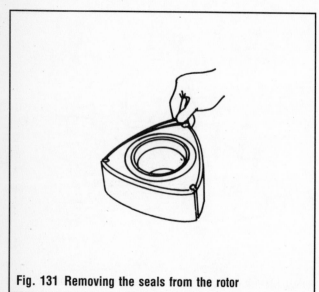

Fig. 131 Removing the seals from the rotor

28. Unbolt the bearing housing and slide the bearing housing, needle bearing, spacer and thrust plate off the shaft.

29. Turn the engine on the stand so that the top of the engine is up.

30. If equipped with a manual transmission, remove the clutch pressure plate and clutch disc. Loosen the pressure plate bolts evenly in small stages to prevent distortion and possible injury from the pressure plate flying off. Straighten the tab of the lockwasher and remove the flywheel nut. Remove the flywheel with a puller.

31. If equipped with an automatic transmission, remove the drive plate. Straighten the tab on the lockwasher and remove the counterweight nut, while holding the flywheel with a flywheel holder. Remove the counterweight using a puller.

32. Working at the rear of the engine, loosen the tension bolts in the sequence shown, and remove the tension bolts.

➡**Do not loosen the tension bolts one at a time. Loosen the bolts evenly in small stages to prevent distortion.**

33. Lift the rear housing off the shaft.

34. Remove any seals that are stuck to the rotor sliding surface of the rear housing and reinstall them in their original locations.

35. Remove all the corner seals, corner seal springs, side seal and side seal springs from the rear side of the rotor. Mazda has a special tray which holds all the seals and keeps them segregated to prevent mistakes during reassembly. Each seal groove is marked to prevent confusion.

36. Remove the two rubber seals and two O-rings from the rear rotor housing.

37. Remove the dowels from the rear rotor housing.

38. Lift the rear rotor housing away from the rear rotor, being very careful not to drop the apex seals on the rear rotor.

39. Remove each apex seal, side piece and spring from the rear rotor and segregate them.

40. Remove the rear rotor from the eccentric shaft and place it upside down on a clean rag.

41. Remove each seal and spring from the other side of the rotor and segregate these.

42. If some of the seals fall from the rotor, be careful not to change the original position of each seal.

43. Identify the rear rotor with a felt tip pen.

44. Remove the oil seals and the springs. Do not exert heavy pressure at only one place on the seal since it could be deformed. Replace the O-rings in the oil seal when the engine is overhauled.

45. Hold the intermediate housing down and remove the dowels from it.

46. Lift off the intermediate housing being careful not to damage the eccentric shaft. It should be removed by sliding it beyond the rear rotor journal on the eccentric shaft while holding the intermediate housing up and, at the same time, pushing the eccentric shaft up.

47. Lift out the eccentric shaft.

48. Repeat the above procedures to remove the front rotor housing and front rotor.

INSPECTION

➡ **See Figures 132 thru 140**

Front Housing

1. Check the housing for signs of gas or water leakage.

2. Remove the carbon deposits from the front housing with an extra fine emery cloth.

➡**If a carbon scraper must be used, be careful not to damage the mating surfaces of the housing.**

3. Remove any old sealer which is adhering to the housing using a brush or a cloth soaked in ketone.

4. Check for distortion by placing a straightedge on the surface of the housing. Measure the clearance between the straightedge and the housing with a feeler gauge. If the clearance is greater than 0.05mm (0.00197 in.) at any point, replace the housing.

5. Use a dial indicator to check for wear on the rotor contact surfaces of the housing. If the wear is greater than 0.10mm (0.00394 in.), replace the housing.

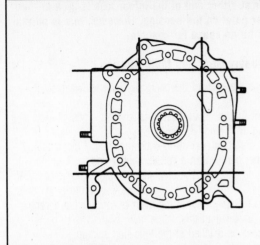

Fig. 132 Check the housing for warpage along these lines with a straightedge and feeler blade

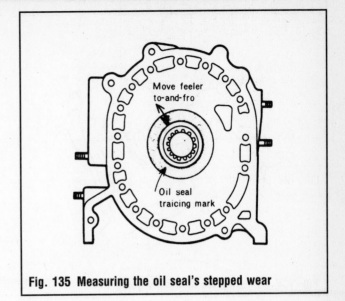

Fig. 135 Measuring the oil seal's stepped wear

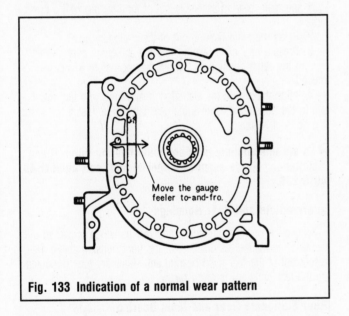

Fig. 133 Indication of a normal wear pattern

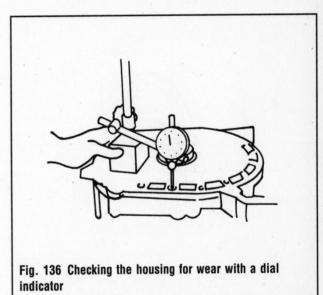

Fig. 136 Checking the housing for wear with a dial indicator

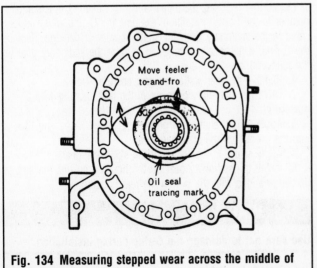

Fig. 134 Measuring stepped wear across the middle of the housing

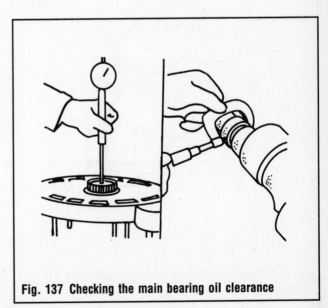

Fig. 137 Checking the main bearing oil clearance

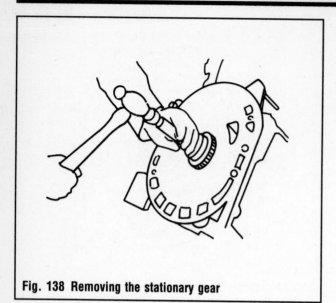

Fig. 138 Removing the stationary gear

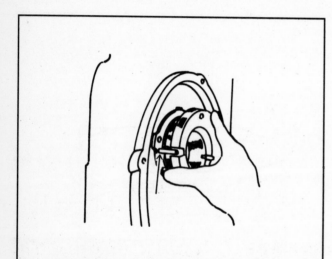

Fig. 139 Installing the stationary gear in the rear housing

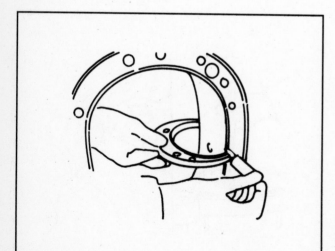

Fig. 140 Checking the rotor housing width using a micrometer

➡The wear at either end of the minor axis is greater than at any other point on the housing. However, this is normal and should be no cause for concern.

Front Stationary Gear and Main Bearing

1. Examine the teeth of the stationary gear for wear or damage.
2. Be sure that the main bearing shows no signs of excessive wear, scoring or flaking.
3. Check the main bearing-to-eccentric journal clearance by measuring the journal with a vernier caliper and the bearing with a pair of inside calipers. The clearance should be between 0.045–0.070mm (0.00177–0.00276 in.), and the wear limit is 0.010mm (0.000394 in.). Replace either the main bearing or the eccentric shaft if it is greater than this. If the main bearing is to be replaced, proceed as detailed in the following section.

Main Bearing Replacement

1. Unfasten the securing bolts, if used. Drive the stationary gear and main bearing assembly out of the housing with a brass drift.
2. Press the main bearing out of the stationary gear.
3. Press a new main bearing into the stationary gear so that it is in the same position as the old bearing before it was removed.
4. Align the slot in the stationary gear flange with the dowel pin in the housing and press the gear into place. Install the securing bolts, if required.

➡To aid in stationary gear and main bearing removal and installation, Mazda supplies a special tool, part number 49 0813 235.

Intermediate and Rear Housings

Inspection of the intermediate and rear housings is carried out in the same manner as detailed for the front housing above. Replacement of the rear main bearing and stationary gear (mounted on the rear housing) is given below.

Rear Stationary Gear and Main Bearing

Inspect the rear stationary gear and main bearing in a similar manner to the front. In addition, examine the O-ring which is located in the stationary gear, for signs of wear or damage. Replace the O-ring, if necessary. If required, replace the stationary gear in the following manner:

1. Remove the rear stationary gear securing bolts.
2. Drive the stationary gear out of the rear housing with a brass drift.
3. Apply a light coating of grease on a new O-ring and fit it into the groove on the stationary gear.
4. Apply sealer to the flange of the stationary gear.
5. Install the stationary gear on the housing so that the slot on its flange aligns with the pin on the rear housing.

✳✳ WARNING

Use care not to damage the O-ring during installation.

6. Tighten the stationary gear bolts evenly, and in several stages, to 15 ft. lbs.

Rotor Housings

1. Examine the inner margin of both housings for signs of gas or water leakage.

2. Wipe the inner surface of each housing with a clean cloth to remove the carbon deposits.

➡If the carbon deposits are stubborn, soak the cloth in a solution made for carbon removal. Do not scrape or sand the chrome plated surfaces of the rotor chamber.

3. Clean all of the rust deposits out of the cooling passages of each rotor housing.

4. Remove the old sealer with a cloth soaked in ketone.

5. Examine the chromium plate inner surfaces for scoring, flaking, or other signs of damage. If any are present, the housing must be replaced.

6. Check the rotor housing for distortion by placing a straightedge on the areas illustrated. If the distortion exceeds 0.04mm (0.00157 in.) have the housing refaced or replace it.

7. Measure the clearance between the straightedge and the housing with a feeler gauge. If the gap exceeds 0.05mm (0.00197 in.), replace the rotor housing.

8. Check the widths of both rotor housings, at a minimum of eight points near the trochoid surfaces of each housing, with a vernier caliper. If the difference between the maximum and minimum valves obtained is greater than 0.06mm (0.00236 in.), replace the housing. A housing in this conditions will be prone to gas and coolant leakage.

➡Standard rotor housing width is 70mm (2.7559 in.).

Rotors

1. Check the rotor for signs of blow-by around the side and corner seal areas.

2. The color of the carbon deposits on the rotor should be brown, just as in a piston engine.

➡Usually the carbon on the leading side of the rotor is brown, while the carbon on the trailing side tends toward black, as viewed from the direction of rotation.

3. Remove the carbon on the rotor with a scraper or extra fine emery paper. Use the scraper carefully when doing the seal grooves, so that no damage is done to them.

4. Wash the rotor in solvent and blow it dry with compressed air after removing the carbon.

5. Examine the internal gear for cracks or damaged teeth.

➡If the internal gear is damaged, the rotor and gear must be replaced as a single assembly.

6. With the oil seal removed, check the land protrusions by placing a straightedge over the lands. Measure the gap between the rotor surface and the straightedge with a feeler gauge. The standard specification is 0.10–0.20mm (0.00394–0.00787 in.); if it is less than this, the rotor must be replaced.

7. Check the gaps between the housing and the rotor on both sides:

    a. Measure the rotor width with a vernier caliper. The standard rotor width is 69.85mm (2.75 in.).

    b. Compare the rotor width with the width of the rotor housing measured above. The standard rotor housing width is 70mm (2.7559 in.).

    c. Replace the rotor if the difference between the two mea-

surements is not within 0.13–0.17mm (0.0052–0.0067 in.).

8. Check the rotor bearing for flaking, wearing, or scoring and proceed as indicated in the next section, if any of these are present.

The rotors are classified into five lettered grades, according to their weight. A letter between **A** and **E** is stamped on the internal gear side of the rotor. If it becomes necessary to replace a rotor, use one marked with a **C** because this is the standard replacement rotor.

Rotor Bearing Replacement

Special service tools are required to replace a rotor bearing. Replacement is also a tricky procedure which, if done improperly, could result in serious damage to the rotor and could even make replacement of the entire rotor necessary. Therefore, this service procedure is best left to an authorized service facility or a qualified machine shop.

Oil Seal Inspection

◆ **See Figure 141**

➡Inspect the oil seal while it is mounted in the rotor.

1. Examine the oil seal for signs of wear or damage.

2. Measure the width of the oil seal lip. If it is greater than 0.8mm (0.0315 in.), replace the oil seal.

3. Measure the protrusion of the oil seal, it should be greater than 0.5mm (0.0197 in.). Replace the seal, as detailed below, if it is not.

Oil Seal Replacement

➡Replace the rubber O-ring in the oil seal as a normal part of engine overhaul.

1. Pry the seal out gently by inserting a screwdriver in the slots on the rotor. Do not remove the seal by prying it at only one point as seal deformation will result.

✳✳ CAUTION

Be careful not to deform the lip of the oil seal if it is to be reinstalled.

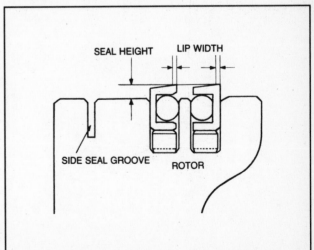

Fig. 141 Checking the oil seals for proper height and lip width

2. Fit both of the oil seal springs into their respective grooves, so that their ends are facing upward and their gaps are opposite each other on the rotor.

3. Insert a new rubber O-ring into each of the oil seals.

➡**Before installing the O-rings into the oil seals, fit each of the seals into its proper groove on the rotor. Check to see that all of the seals move smoothly and freely.**

4. Coat the oil seal groove and the oil seal with engine oil.

5. Gently press the oil seal into the groove with your fingers. Be careful not to distort the seal.

➡**Be sure that the white mark is on the bottom side of each seal when it is installed.**

6. Repeat the installation procedure for the oil seals on both sides of each rotor.

Apex Seals

♦ **See Figures 142, 143, 144, 145 and 145a**

✳✳ CAUTION

Although the apex seals are extremely durable when in service, they are easily broken when they are being handled. Be careful not to drop them.

1. Remove the carbon deposits from the apex seals and their springs. Do not use emery cloth on the seals as it will damage their finish.

2. Wash the seals and the springs in cleaning solution.

3. Check the apex seals for cracks and other signs of wear or damage.

4. Test the seal springs for weakness.

5. Use a micrometer to check the seal height. Replace any seal if its height is less than 7mm (0.276mm).

6. With a feeler gauge, check the side clearance between the apex seal and the groove in the rotor. Insert the gauge until its tip contacts the bottom of the groove. If the gap is greater than 0.15mm (0.0059 in.), replace the seal.

7. Check the gap between the apex seals and the side housing, in the following manner:

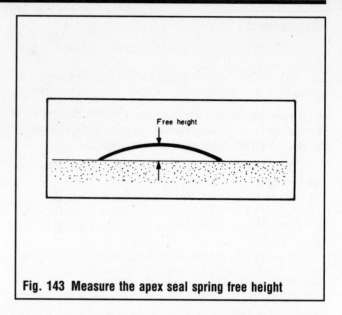

Fig. 143 Measure the apex seal spring free height

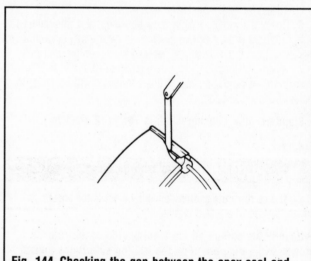

Fig. 144 Checking the gap between the apex seal and the groove

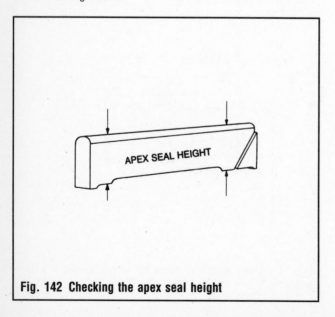

Fig. 142 Checking the apex seal height

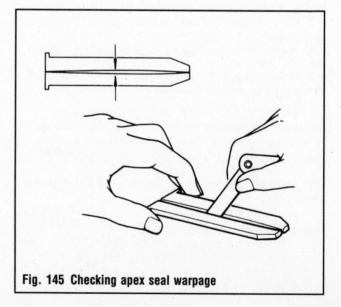

Fig. 145 Checking apex seal warpage

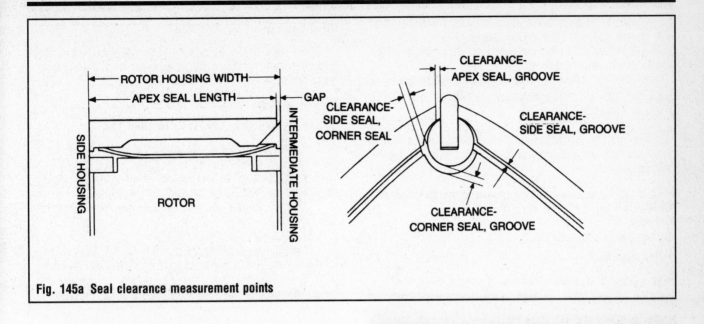

Fig. 145a Seal clearance measurement points

a. Use a vernier caliper to measure the length of each apex seal.

b. Compare this measurement to the minimum figure obtained when rotor housing width was being measured.

c. If the difference is more than 0.3mm (0.0118 in.), replace the seal. The standard gap is 0.13–0.17mm (0.0052–0.0067 in.).

d. If, on the other hand, the seal is too long, sand the ends of the seal with emery cloth until the proper length is reached.

✳✳ WARNING

Do not use the emery cloth on the faces of the seal!

Side Seals

1. Remove the carbon deposits from the side seals and their springs with a carbon scraper.

2. Check the protrusion of the side seals. It should be 0.5mm (0.0197 in.) or more.

3. Check the side seals for cracks or wear. Replace any of the seals found to be defective.

4. Check the clearance between the side seals and their grooves with a feeler gauge. Replace any side seals if they have a clearance of more than 0.10mm (0.00394 in.). The standard clearance is 0.05–0.08mm (0.00197–0.00315 in.).

5. Check the clearance between the side seals and the corner seals with both of them installed in the rotor.

a. Insert the gauge against the direction of the rotor's rotation.

b. Replace the side seal if the clearance is greater than 0.4mm (0.0157 in.).

6. If the side seal is replaced, adjust the clearance between it and the corner seal as follows:

a. File the side seal on its reverse side, in the same rotational direction of the rotor, along the outline made by the corner seal.

b. The clearance obtained should be 0.05–0.15mm (0.00197–0.0059 in.). If it exceeds this, the performance of the seals will deteriorate.

✳✳ WARNING

There are four different types of side seals, depending upon their location. Do not mix the seals up and be sure to use the proper type of seal for replacement!

Corner Seals

◆ **See Figure 146**

1. Clean the carbon deposits from the corner seals.

2. Examine each of the seals for wear or damage.

3. Check the corner seal protrusion from the rotor surface. It should be free to move under the finger pressure and protrude 0.5mm (0.0197 in.) or more.

4. Measure the clearance between the corner seal and its groove. The clearance should be 0.045–0.048mm (0.00177–0.001889 in.). The wear limit of the gap is 0.08mm (0.00315 in.).

5. If the wear is between the corner seal and the groove is uneven, check the clearance with the special bar limit gauge (Mazda

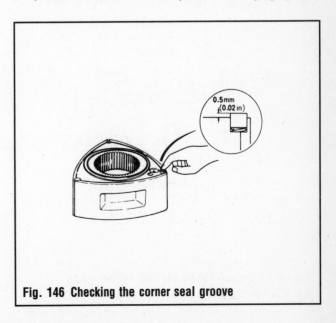

Fig. 146 Checking the corner seal groove

part number 49 0839 165). The gauge has a go end and a no go end. Use the gauge in the following manner:

a. If neither end of the gauge goes into the groove, the clearance is within specifications.

b. If the go end of the gauge fits into the groove, but the no go end does not, replace the corner seal with one that is 0.03mm oversize.

c. If both ends of the gauge fit into the groove, then the groove must be reamed out as detailed below. Replace the corner seal with one which is 0.0072 in. oversize, after completing reaming.

➡**Take the measurement of the groove in the direction of maximum wear, i.e., that of rotation.**

Corner Seal Groove Reaming

◗ **See Figure 147**

➡**This procedure requires the use of special tools; if attempted without them, damage to the rotor could result.**

1. Carefully remove all of the deposits which remain in the groove.

2. Fit the jig (Mazda part number 49 2113 030) over the rotor. Tighten its adjusting bar, being careful not to damage the rotor bearing or the apex seal grooves.

3. Use the corner seal groove reamer (Mazda part number 49 0839 170) to ream the groove.

4. Rotate the reamer at least 20 times while applying engine oil as a coolant.

➡**If engine oil is not used, it will be impossible to obtain the proper groove surfacing.**

5. Remove the reamer and the jig.

6. Repeat Steps 1–5 for each of the corner seal grooves.

7. Clean the rotor completely and check it for any signs of damage.

8. Fit a 0.2mm oversize corner seal into the groove and check its clearance. Clearance should be 0.02–0.05mm (0.000787–0.00197 in.).

Seal Springs

Check the seal springs for damage or weakness. Be exceptionally careful when checking the spring areas which contact either the rotor or the seal.

Eccentric Shaft

◗ **See Figures 148, 149, 150, 151 and 152**

1. Wash the eccentric shaft in solvent and blow its oil passages dry with compressed air.

2. Check the shaft for wear, cracks, or other signs of damage. Make sure that none of the oil passages are clogged.

3. Measure the shaft journals with a vernier caliper. The standard specifications are:
- Main journals—43mm (1.6929 in.)
- Rotor journals—74mm (2.9134 in.)

Replace the shaft if any of its journals show excessive wear.

4. Check eccentric shaft run-out by placing the shaft on V-blocks and using a dial indicator as shown. Rotate the shaft

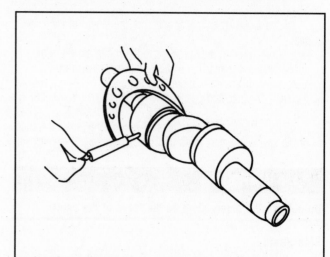

Fig. 148 Measuring the eccentric shaft rotor journal diameter

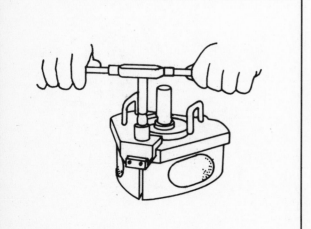

Fig. 147 Reaming the corner seal groove for an oversized corner seal

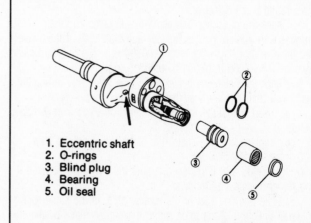

1. Eccentric shaft
2. O-rings
3. Blind plug
4. Bearing
5. Oil seal

Fig. 149 View of the eccentric shaft—arrow points to oil jet plug; remove it to check the spring and ball

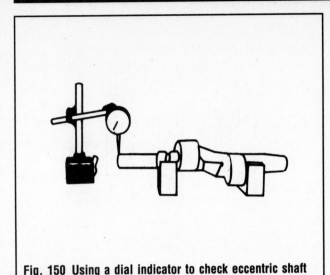

Fig. 150 Using a dial indicator to check eccentric shaft run-out

slowly and note the dial indicator reading. If run-out is more than 0.06mm (0.00236 in.), replace the eccentric shaft.

5. Check the blind plug at the end of the shaft. If it is loose or leaking, remove it with an allen wrench and replace the O-ring.

6. Check the operation of the needle roller bearing for smoothness by inserting a mainshaft into the bearing and rotating it. Examine the bearing for signs of wear or damage.

7. Replace the bearing if necessary, with the special tool, Mazda part number 49 0823 073 and 49 0823 072.

Engine Assembly

▶ **See Figures 153 thru 169**

1. Place the rotor in a rubber pad or cloth.

2. Install the oil seal rings in their respective grooves in the rotors with the edge of the spring in the stopper hole. The oil springs are painted cream or blue in color. The cream colored springs must be installed on the front faces of both rotors. The blue colored springs must be installed on the rear faces of both

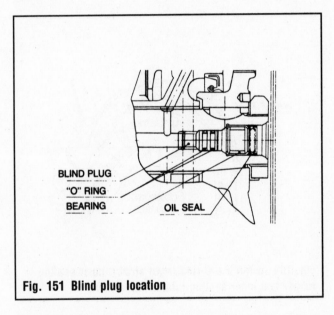

Fig. 151 Blind plug location

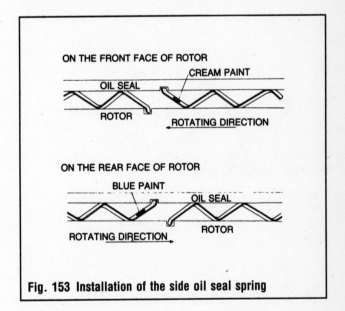

Fig. 153 Installation of the side oil seal spring

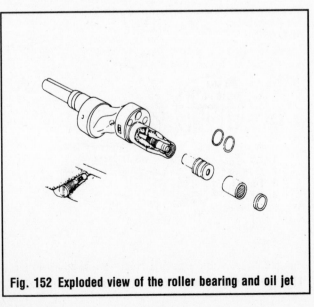

Fig. 152 Exploded view of the roller bearing and oil jet

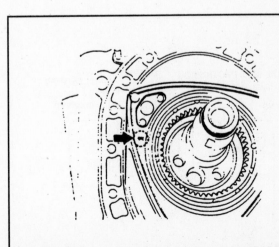

Fig. 154 Rotor, apex and side seals are identified by a number which corresponds to the number on each rotor face seal groove

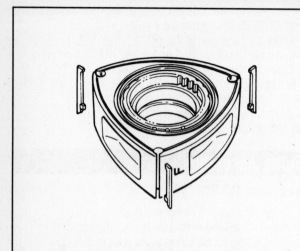

Fig. 155 Install the apex seals without springs or side pieces—"F" indicates the front rotor

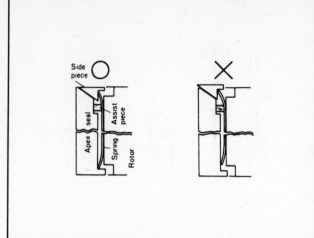

Fig. 158 Install the side piece as shown under "O"—the spring must butt against the apex seal lip

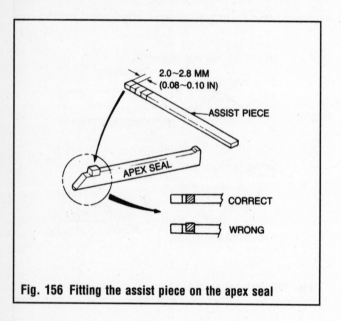

Fig. 156 Fitting the assist piece on the apex seal

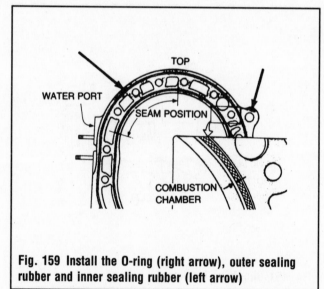

Fig. 159 Install the O-ring (right arrow), outer sealing rubber and inner sealing rubber (left arrow)

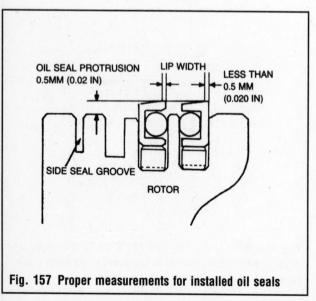

Fig. 157 Proper measurements for installed oil seals

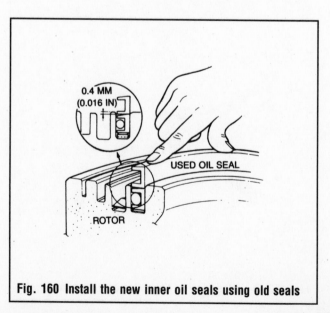

Fig. 160 Install the new inner oil seals using old seals

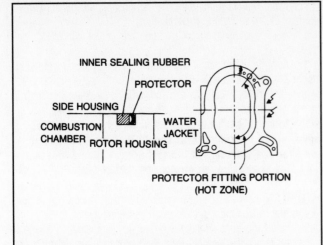

Fig. 161 Install the protector behind the inner sealing rubber in the area shown above and to the right

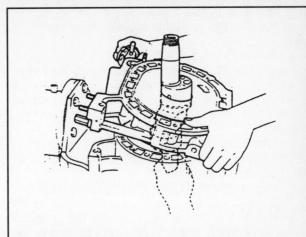

Fig. 164 Installing the intermediate housing—an extra hand to position and move the eccentric shaft aids in installation

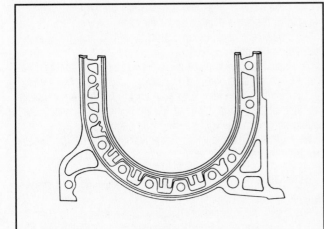

Fig. 162 Apply a sealing agent to the front side of the housing between the O-rings

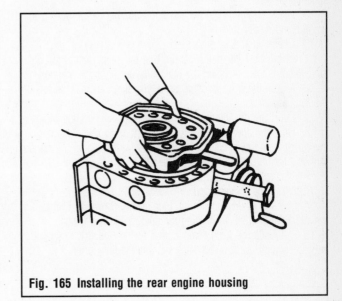

Fig. 165 Installing the rear engine housing

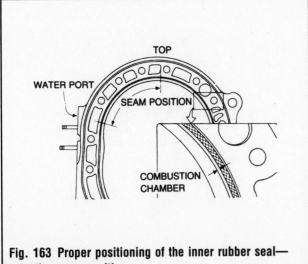

Fig. 163 Proper positioning of the inner rubber seal—note the seam position

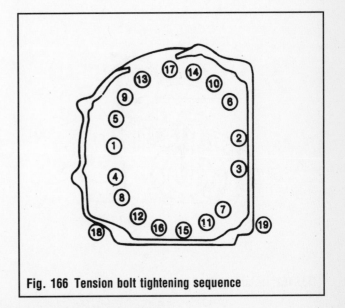

Fig. 166 Tension bolt tightening sequence

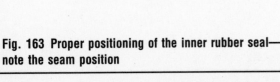

rotors. When installing each oil seal spring, the painted side (square side) of the spring must face upward (toward the oil seal).

3. Install a new O-ring in each groove. Place each oil seal in the groove so that the square edge of the spring fits in the stopper hole of the oil seal. Push the head of the oil seal slowly with the fingers, being careful that the seal is not deformed. Be sure that the oil seal moves smoothly in the grooves before installing the O-ring.

4. Lubricate each oil seal and groove with engine oil and check the movement of the seal. It should move freely when the head of the seal is pressed.

5. Check the oil seal protrusion and install the seals on the other side of each rotor.

6. Install the apex seals without springs and side pieces into their respective grooves so that each side piece positions on the side of each rotor.

7. Install the corner seal springs and corner seals into their respective grooves.

8. Install the side seal springs and side seals into their respective grooves.

9. Apply engine oil to each spring and check each spring for smooth movement.

10. Check each seal protrusion.

11. Invert the rotor being careful that the seals do not fall out, and install the oil seals on the other side in the same manner.

12. Mount the front housing on a workstand so that the top of the housing is up.

13. Lubricate the internal gear of the rotor with engine oil.

14. Hold the apex seals with used O-rings to keep the apex seals installed and place the rotor on the front housing. Be careful that you do not drop the seals. Turn the front housing so that the sliding surfaces faces upward.

15. Mesh the internal and stationary gears so that one of the rotor apexes is at any one of the four places shown and remove the old O-ring which is holding the apex seals in position.

16. Lubricate the front rotor journal of the eccentric shaft with engine oil and lubricate the eccentric shaft main journal.

17. Insert the eccentric shaft. Be careful that you do not damage the rotor bearing and main bearing.

18. Apply sealing agent to the front side of the front rotor housing.

19. Apply a light coat of petroleum jelly onto new O-rings and rubber seals (to prevent them from coming off) and install the O-rings and rubber seals on the front side of the rotor housing.

➡**The inner rubber seal is of the square type. The wider white line of the rubber seal should face the combustion chamber and the seam of the rubber seal should be positioned as shown. Do not stretch the rubber seal.**

20. If the engine is being overhauled, install the seal protector to only the inner rubber seal to improve durability.

21. Invert the front rotor housing, being careful not to let the rubber seals and O-rings fall from their grooves, and mount it on the front housing.

22. Lubricate the dowels with engine oil and insert them through the front rotor housing holes and into the front housing.

23. Apply sealer to the front side of the rotor housing.

24. Install new O-rings and rubber seals on the front rotor housing in the same manner as for the other side.

25. Insert each apex spring seal, making sure that the seal is installed in the proper direction.

26. Install each side piece in its original position and be sure that the springs seat on the side piece.

27. Lubricate the side pieces with engine oil. Make sure that the front rotor housing is free of foreign matter and lubricate the sliding surface of the front housing with engine oil.

28. Turn the front housing assembly with the rotor, so that the top of the housing is up. Pull the eccentric shaft about 25mm (1 in.).

29. Position the eccentric portion of the eccentric shaft diagonally, to the upper right.

30. Install the intermediate housing over the eccentric shaft onto the front rotor housing. Turn the engine so that the rear of the engine is up.

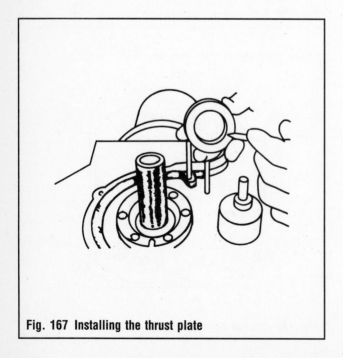

Fig. 167 Installing the thrust plate

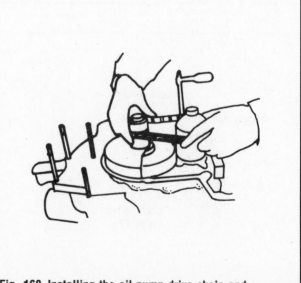

Fig. 168 Installing the oil pump drive chain and sprockets

31. Install the rear rotor and rear rotor housing following the same steps as for the front rotor and the front housing.

32. Turn the engine so that the rear of the engine is up.

33. Lubricate the stationary gear and main bearing.

34. Install the rear housing onto the rear rotor housing. If necessary, turn the rear rotor slightly to mesh the rear housing stationary gear with the rear rotor internal gear.

35. Install a new washer on each tension bolt, and lubricate each bolt with engine oil.

36. Install the tension bolts and tighten them evenly, in several stages following the sequence shown. The specified torque is 23–27 ft. lbs.

37. After tightening the bolts, turn the eccentric shaft to be sure that the shaft and rotors turn smoothly and easily.

38. Lubricate the oil seal in the rear housing.

39. On trucks with manual transmission, install the flywheel on the rear of the eccentric shaft so that the keyway of the flywheel fits the key on the shaft.

40. Apply sealer to both sides of the flywheel lockwasher and install the lockwasher.

41. Install the flywheel locknut. Hold the flywheel SECURELY and tighten the nut to THREE HUNDRED AND FIFTY ft. lbs. (350 ft. lbs.) of torque.

➡**350 ft. lbs. is a great deal of torque. In actual practice, it is practically impossible to accurately measure that much torque on the nut. At least a 3 ft. bar will be required to generate sufficient torque. Tighten it as tightly as possible, with no longer than 3 ft. of leverage. Be sure the engine is held SECURELY.**

42. On trucks with automatic transmission, install the key, counterweight, lockwasher and nut. Tighten the nut to 350 ft. lbs. SEE STEP 41 AND THE NOTE FOLLOWING STEP 41.

43. Turn the engine so that the front faces up.

44. Install the thrust plate with the tapered face down, and install the needle bearing on the eccentric shaft. Lubricate with engine oil.

45. Install the bearing housing on the front housing. Tighten

the bolts and bend up the lockwasher tabs. The spacer should be installed so that the center of the needle bearing comes to the center of the eccentric shaft and the spacer should be seated on the thrust plate.

46. Install the needle bearing on the shaft and lubricate it with engine oil.

47. Install the balancer and thrust washer on the eccentric shaft.

48. Install the oil pump drive chain over both of the sprockets. Install the sprocket and chain assembly over the eccentric shaft and oil pump shafts simultaneously. Install the key on the eccentric shaft.

➡**Be sure that both of the sprockets are engaged with the chain before installing them over the shafts.**

49. Install the distributor drive gear onto the eccentric shaft with the F mark on the gear facing the front of the engine. Slide the spacer and oil slinger onto the eccentric shaft.

50. Align the keyway and install the eccentric shaft pulley. Tighten the pulley bolt to 60 ft. lbs.

51. Turn the engine so that the top of the engine faces up.

52. Check eccentric shaft end-play in the following manner:

    a. Attach a dial indicator to the flywheel. Move the flywheel forward and backward.

    b. Note the reading on the dial indicator; it should be 0.04–0.07mm (0.00157–0.00276 in.).

    c. If the end-play is not within specifications, adjust it by replacing the front spacer. Spacers come in four sizes, ranging from 8.00–8.08mm. If necessary, a spacer can be ground on a surface plate with emery paper.

    d. Check the end-play again and, if it is now within specifications, proceed with the next step.

53. Remove the pulley from the front of the eccentric shaft. Tighten the oil pump drive sprocket nut and bend the locktabs on the lockwasher.

54. Fit a new O-ring over the front cover oil passages.

55. Install the chain tensioner and tighten its securing bolts.

56. Position the front cover gasket and the front cover on the front housing, then secure the front cover with its attachment bolts.

57. Install the eccentric shaft pulley again. Tighten its bolt to 60 ft. lbs.

58. Turn the engine so that the bottom faces up.

59. Cut off the excess gasket on the front cover along the mounting surface of the oil pan.

60. Install the oil strainer gasket and strainer on the front housing and tighten the attaching bolts.

61. Apply sealer to the joint surfaces of each housing.

62. Install the gasket and oil pan. Tighten the bolts evenly in two stages to 3.5 ft. lbs.

63. Turn the engine so that the top is up.

64. Install the water pump and gasket on the front housing. Tighten the attaching bolts.

65. Rotate the eccentric shaft until the yellow mark (leading side mark) aligns with the pointer on the front cover.

66. Align the marks on the distributor gear and housing and install the distributor so that the lockbolt is in the center of the slot.

67. Rotate the distributor until the leading points start to separate and tighten the distributor locknut.

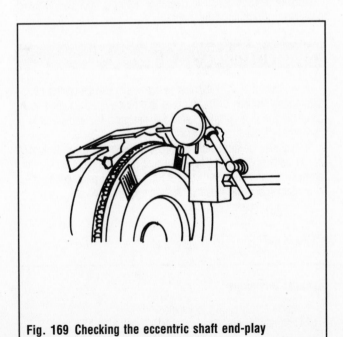

Fig. 169 Checking the eccentric shaft end-play

68. Install the gaskets and thermal reactor and tighten the attaching nuts.

69. Install the hot air duct.

70. Install the carburetor and intake manifold assembly with a new gasket. Tighten the attaching nuts.

71. Connect the oil tubes vacuum tube and metering oil pump connecting rod to the carburetor.

72. Install the decel valve and connect the vacuum lines, air hoses and wires.

73. Install the alternator bracket, alternator and bolt and check the clearance. If the clearance is more than 0.15mm (0.0059 in.), adjust the clearance using a shim. Shims are available in three sizes: 0.15mm, 0.30mm, and 0.50mm.

74. Install the alternator drive belt. Attach the alternator to the adjusting brace and adjust the belt tension to specification.

75. Install the air pump with the adjusting brace and install the air pump drive belt. Adjust the air pump drive belt to specifications.

76. Install the engine hanger bracket to the front cover.

77. Remove the engine from the stand.

78. Install the engine in the truck.

79. Fill the engine with fresh engine oil and install a new filter. Fill the engine with coolant. Start the engine, check the oil pressure, and warm it to normal operating temperature. Adjust the idle speed, timing and dwell. Recheck all capacities and refill if necessary. Check for leaks.

Flywheel

REMOVAL & INSTALLATION

1. Remove the transmission.
2. Remove the clutch assembly.
3. Attach a ring gear brake, 49-1881-060 to the engine.
4. Straighten the tabs of the lockwasher and remove the flywheel nut using wrench 49-0820-035.
5. Remove the flywheel with puller 49-0839-305A.

To install:

6. Apply engine oil to the rear housing seal.
7. Position the flywheel on the shaft, aligning the key and keyway.
8. Apply sealer to both sides of the lockwasher and place it on the shaft.
9. Install the nut and tighten it to 362 ft. lbs.
10. Bend the tabs of the lockwasher.
11. Install the clutch and transmission.

EXHAUST SYSTEM

General Information

➡**Safety glasses should be worn at all times when working on or near the exhaust system. Older exhaust systems will almost always be covered with loose rust particles which will shower you when disturbed. These particles are more than a nuisance and could injure your eye.**

Whenever working on the exhaust system always keep the following in mind:

• Check the complete exhaust system for open seams, holes loose connections, or other deterioration which could permit exhaust fumes to seep into the passenger compartment.

• The exhaust system is usually supported by free-hanging rubber mountings which permit some movement of the exhaust system, but does not permit transfer of noise and vibration into the passenger compartment. Do not replace the rubber mounts with solid ones.

• Before removing any component of the exhaust system, ALWAYS squirt a liquid rust dissolving agent onto the fasteners for ease of removal. A lot of knuckle skin will be saved by following this rule. It may even be wise to spray the fasteners and allow them to sit overnight.

✳✳ CAUTION

Allow the exhaust system to cool sufficiently before spraying a solvent exhaust fasteners. Some solvents are highly flammable and could ignite when sprayed on hot exhaust components.

• Annoying rattles and noise vibrations in the exhaust system are usually caused by misalignment of the parts. When aligning the system, leave all bolts and nuts loose until all parts are properly aligned, then tighten, working from front to rear.

• When installing exhaust system parts, make sure there is enough clearance between the hot exhaust parts and pipes and hoses that would be adversely affected by excessive heat. Also make sure there is adequate clearance from the floor pan to avoid possible overheating of the floor.

Special Tools

A number of special exhaust system tools can be rented from auto supply houses or local stores that rent special equipment. A common one is a tail pipe expander, designed to enable you to join pipes of identical diameter.

It may also be quite helpful to use solvents designed to loosen rusted bolts or flanges. Soaking rusted parts the night before you do the job can speed the work of freeing rusted parts considerably. Remember that these solvents are often flammable. Apply only to parts after they are cool!

COMPONENT REPLACEMENT

Exhaust Downpipe

1. Raise and truck on jackstands.
2. Saturate all bolts and nuts with penetrating lubricant.

3. Disconnect the downpipe from the manifold(s) and discard the seal.

4. Support the catalytic converter and disconnect the downpipe. Discard the gasket, if used.

5. Installation is the reverse of removal. Use new gaskets and seals. Tighten all fasteners to 23 ft. lbs. Make sure that there is sufficient clearance around all parts.

Catalytic Converter

1. Raise and truck on jackstands.
2. Saturate all bolts and nuts with penetrating lubricant.
3. Remove the converter-to-downpipe bolts.
4. Remove the converter-to-muffler inlet pipe bolts.
5. Installation is the reverse of removal. Use new gaskets. Torque the connections to 23 ft. lbs.

Muffler

1. Raise and truck on jackstands.
2. Saturate all bolts and nuts with penetrating lubricant.

3. Remove the converter-to-muffler pipe bolts.
4. Remove the muffler-to-silencer pipe bolts.
5. Remove all muffler hangers and lower the muffler from the truck.
6. Installation is the reverse of removal. Use new gaskets. Torque the bolts to 23 ft. lbs.

Silencer and Tailpipe

1. Raise and truck on jackstands.
2. Saturate all bolts and nuts with penetrating lubricant.
3. Remove the muffler-to-silencer pipe bolts.
4. Remove all silencer hangers and lower the silencer from the truck.
5. Installation is the reverse of removal. Use new gaskets. Torque the bolts to 23 ft. lbs.

USING A VACUUM GAUGE

White needle = steady needle   *Dark needle = drifting needle*

The vacuum gauge is one of the most useful and easy-to-use diagnostic tools. It is inexpensive, easy to hook up, and provides valuable information about the condition of your engine.

Indication: Normal engine in good condition

Gauge reading: Steady, from 17–22 in./Hg.

Indication: Sticking valve or ignition miss

Gauge reading: Needle fluctuates from 15–20 in./Hg. at idle

Indication: Late ignition or valve timing, low compression, stuck throttle valve, leaking carburetor or manifold gasket.

Gauge reading: Low (15–20 in./Hg.) but steady

Indication: Improper carburetor adjustment, or minor intake leak at carburetor or manifold

NOTE: Bad fuel injector O-rings may also cause this reading.

Gauge reading: Drifting needle

Indication: Weak valve springs, worn valve stem guides, or leaky cylinder head gasket (vibrating excessively at all speeds).

NOTE: A plugged catalytic converter may also cause this reading.

Gauge reading: Needle fluctuates as engine speed increases

Indication: Burnt valve or improper valve clearance. The needle will drop when the defective valve operates.

Gauge reading: Steady needle, but drops regularly

Indication: Choked muffler or obstruction in system. Speed up the engine. Choked muffler will exhibit a slow drop of vacuum to zero.

Gauge reading: Gradual drop in reading at idle

Indication: Worn valve guides

Gauge reading: Needle vibrates excessively at idle, but steadies as engine speed increases

Troubleshooting Engine Mechanical Problems

Problem	Cause	Solution
External oil leaks	• Cylinder head cover RTV sealant broken or improperly seated	• Replace sealant; inspect cylinder head cover sealant flange and cylinder head sealant surface for distortion and cracks
	• Oil filler cap leaking or missing	• Replace cap
	• Oil filter gasket broken or improperly seated	• Replace oil filter
	• Oil pan side gasket broken, improperly seated or opening in RTV sealant	• Replace gasket or repair opening in sealant; inspect oil pan gasket flange for distortion
	• Oil pan front oil seal broken or improperly seated	• Replace seal; inspect timing case cover and oil pan seal flange for distortion
	• Oil pan rear oil seal broken or improperly seated	• Replace seal; inspect oil pan rear oil seal flange; inspect rear main bearing cap for cracks, plugged oil return channels, or distortion in seal groove
	• Timing case cover oil seal broken or improperly seated	• Replace seal
	• Excess oil pressure because of restricted PCV valve	• Replace PCV valve
	• Oil pan drain plug loose or has stripped threads	• Repair as necessary and tighten
	• Rear oil gallery plug loose	• Use appropriate sealant on gallery plug and tighten
	• Rear camshaft plug loose or improperly seated	• Seat camshaft plug or replace and seal, as necessary
Excessive oil consumption	• Oil level too high	• Drain oil to specified level
	• Oil with wrong viscosity being used	• Replace with specified oil
	• PCV valve stuck closed	• Replace PCV valve
	• Valve stem oil deflectors (or seals) are damaged, missing, or incorrect type	• Replace valve stem oil deflectors
	• Valve stems or valve guides worn	• Measure stem-to-guide clearance and repair as necessary
	• Poorly fitted or missing valve cover baffles	• Replace valve cover
	• Piston rings broken or missing	• Replace broken or missing rings
	• Scuffed piston	• Replace piston
	• Incorrect piston ring gap	• Measure ring gap, repair as necessary
	• Piston rings sticking or excessively loose in grooves	• Measure ring side clearance, repair as necessary
	• Compression rings installed upside down	• Repair as necessary
	• Cylinder walls worn, scored, or glazed	• Repair as necessary

Troubleshooting Engine Mechanical Problems

Problem	Cause	Solution
Excessive oil consumption (cont.)	• Piston ring gaps not properly staggered	• Repair as necessary
	• Excessive main or connecting rod bearing clearance	• Measure bearing clearance, repair as necessary
No oil pressure	• Low oil level	• Add oil to correct level
	• Oil pressure gauge, warning lamp or sending unit inaccurate	• Replace oil pressure gauge or warning lamp
	• Oil pump malfunction	• Replace oil pump
	• Oil pressure relief valve sticking	• Remove and inspect oil pressure relief valve assembly
	• Oil passages on pressure side of pump obstructed	• Inspect oil passages for obstruction
	• Oil pickup screen or tube obstructed	• Inspect oil pickup for obstruction
	• Loose oil inlet tube	• Tighten or seal inlet tube
Low oil pressure	• Low oil level	• Add oil to correct level
	• Inaccurate gauge, warning lamp or sending unit	• Replace oil pressure gauge or warning lamp
	• Oil excessively thin because of dilution, poor quality, or improper grade	• Drain and refill crankcase with recommended oil
	• Excessive oil temperature	• Correct cause of overheating engine
	• Oil pressure relief spring weak or sticking	• Remove and inspect oil pressure relief valve assembly
	• Oil inlet tube and screen assembly has restriction or air leak	• Remove and inspect oil inlet tube and screen assembly. (Fill inlet tube with lacquer thinner to locate leaks.)
	• Excessive oil pump clearance	• Measure clearances
	• Excessive main, rod, or camshaft bearing clearance	• Measure bearing clearances, repair as necessary
High oil pressure	• Improper oil viscosity	• Drain and refill crankcase with correct viscosity oil
	• Oil pressure gauge or sending unit inaccurate	• Replace oil pressure gauge
	• Oil pressure relief valve sticking closed	• Remove and inspect oil pressure relief valve assembly
Main bearing noise	• Insufficient oil supply	• Inspect for low oil level and low oil pressure
	• Main bearing clearance excessive	• Measure main bearing clearance, repair as necessary
	• Bearing insert missing	• Replace missing insert
	• Crankshaft end-play excessive	• Measure end-play, repair as necessary
	• Improperly tightened main bearing cap bolts	• Tighten bolts with specified torque
	• Loose flywheel or drive plate	• Tighten flywheel or drive plate attaching bolts
	• Loose or damaged vibration damper	• Repair as necessary

Troubleshooting Engine Mechanical Problems

Problem	Cause	Solution
Connecting rod bearing noise	• Insufficient oil supply	• Inspect for low oil level and low oil pressure
	• Carbon build-up on piston	• Remove carbon from piston crown
	• Bearing clearance excessive or bearing missing	• Measure clearance, repair as necessary
	• Crankshaft connecting rod journal out-of-round	• Measure journal dimensions, repair or replace as necessary
	• Misaligned connecting rod or cap	• Repair as necessary
	• Connecting rod bolts tightened improperly	• Tighten bolts with specified torque
Piston noise	• Piston-to-cylinder wall clearance excessive (scuffed piston)	• Measure clearance and examine piston
	• Cylinder walls excessively tapered or out-of-round	• Measure cylinder wall dimensions, rebore cylinder
	• Piston ring broken	• Replace all rings on piston
	• Loose or seized piston pin	• Measure piston-to-pin clearance, repair as necessary
	• Connecting rods misaligned	• Measure rod alignment, straighten or replace
	• Piston ring side clearance excessively loose or tight	• Measure ring side clearance, repair as necessary
	• Carbon build-up on piston is excessive	• Remove carbon from piston
Valve actuating component noise	• Insufficient oil supply	• Check for: (a) Low oil level (b) Low oil pressure (c) Wrong hydraulic tappets (d) Restricted oil gallery (e) Excessive tappet to bore clearance
	• Rocker arms or pivots worn	• Replace worn rocker arms or pivots
	• Foreign objects or chips in hydraulic tappets	• Clean tappets
	• Excessive tappet leak-down	• Replace valve tappet
	• Tappet face worn	• Replace tappet; inspect corresponding cam lobe for wear
	• Broken or cocked valve springs	• Properly seat cocked springs; replace broken springs
	• Stem-to-guide clearance excessive	• Measure stem-to-guide clearance, repair as required
	• Valve bent	• Replace valve
	• Loose rocker arms	• Check and repair as necessary
	• Valve seat runout excessive	• Regrind valve seat/valves
	• Missing valve lock	• Install valve lock
	• Excessive engine oil	• Correct oil level

Troubleshooting Engine Performance

Problem	Cause	Solution
Hard starting (engine cranks normally)	• Faulty engine control system component	• Repair or replace as necessary
	• Faulty fuel pump	• Replace fuel pump
	• Faulty fuel system component	• Repair or replace as necessary
	• Faulty ignition coil	• Test and replace as necessary
	• Improper spark plug gap	• Adjust gap
	• Incorrect ignition timing	• Adjust timing
	• Incorrect valve timing	• Check valve timing; repair as necessary
Rough idle or stalling	• Incorrect curb or fast idle speed	• Adjust curb or fast idle speed (If possible)
	• Incorrect ignition timing	• Adjust timing to specification
	• Improper feedback system operation	• Refer to Chapter 4
	• Faulty EGR valve operation	• Test EGR system and replace as necessary
	• Faulty PCV valve air flow	• Test PCV valve and replace as necessary
	• Faulty TAC vacuum motor or valve	• Repair as necessary
	• Air leak into manifold vacuum	• Inspect manifold vacuum connections and repair as necessary
	• Faulty distributor rotor or cap	• Replace rotor or cap (Distributor systems only)
	• Improperly seated valves	• Test cylinder compression, repair as necessary
	• Incorrect ignition wiring	• Inspect wiring and correct as necessary
	• Faulty ignition coil	• Test coil and replace as necessary
	• Restricted air vent or idle passages	• Clean passages
	• Restricted air cleaner	• Clean or replace air cleaner filter element
Faulty low-speed operation	• Restricted idle air vents and passages	• Clean air vents and passages
	• Restricted air cleaner	• Clean or replace air cleaner filter element
	• Faulty spark plugs	• Clean or replace spark plugs
	• Dirty, corroded, or loose ignition secondary circuit wire connections	• Clean or tighten secondary circuit wire connections
	• Improper feedback system operation	• Refer to Chapter 4
	• Faulty ignition coil high voltage wire	• Replace ignition coil high voltage wire (Distributor systems only)
	• Faulty distributor cap	• Replace cap (Distributor systems only)
Faulty acceleration	• Incorrect ignition timing	• Adjust timing
	• Faulty fuel system component	• Repair or replace as necessary
	• Faulty spark plug(s)	• Clean or replace spark plug(s)
	• Improperly seated valves	• Test cylinder compression, repair as necessary
	• Faulty ignition coil	• Test coil and replace as necessary

Troubleshooting Engine Performance

Problem	Cause	Solution
Faulty acceleration (cont.)	• Improper feedback system operation	• Refer to Chapter 4
Faulty high speed operation	• Incorrect ignition timing • Faulty advance mechanism	• Adjust timing (if possible) • Check advance mechanism and repair as necessary (Distributor systems only)
	• Low fuel pump volume • Wrong spark plug air gap or wrong plug • Partially restricted exhaust manifold, exhaust pipe, catalytic converter, muffler, or tailpipe • Restricted vacuum passages • Restricted air cleaner • Faulty distributor rotor or cap • Faulty ignition coil • Improperly seated valve(s) • Faulty valve spring(s) • Incorrect valve timing • Intake manifold restricted • Worn distributor shaft • Improper feedback system operation	• Replace fuel pump • Adjust air gap or install correct plug • Eliminate restriction • Clean passages • Cleaner or replace filter element as necessary • Replace rotor or cap (Distributor systems only) • Test coil and replace as necessary • Test cylinder compression, repair as necessary • Inspect and test valve spring tension, replace as necessary • Check valve timing and repair as necessary • Remove restriction or replace manifold • Replace shaft (Distributor systems only) • Refer to Chapter 4
Misfire at all speeds	• Faulty spark plug(s) • Faulty spark plug wire(s) • Faulty distributor cap or rotor • Faulty ignition coil • Primary ignition circuit shorted or open intermittently • Improperly seated valve(s) • Faulty hydraulic tappet(s) • Improper feedback system operation • Faulty valve spring(s) • Worn camshaft lobes • Air leak into manifold • Fuel pump volume or pressure low • Blown cylinder head gasket • Intake or exhaust manifold passage(s) restricted	• Clean or relace spark plug(s) • Replace as necessary • Replace cap or rotor (Distributor systems only) • Test coil and replace as necessary • Troubleshoot primary circuit and repair as necessary • Test cylinder compression, repair as necessary • Clean or replace tappet(s) • Refer to Chapter 4 • Inspect and test valve spring tension, repair as necessary • Replace camshaft • Check manifold vacuum and repair as necessary • Replace fuel pump • Replace gasket • Pass chain through passage(s) and repair as necessary
Power not up to normal	• Incorrect ignition timing • Faulty distributor rotor	• Adjust timing • Replace rotor (Distributor systems only)

Troubleshooting Engine Performance

Problem	Cause	Solution
Power not up to normal (cont.)	• Incorrect spark plug gap • Faulty fuel pump • Faulty fuel pump • Incorrect valve timing • Faulty ignition coil • Faulty ignition wires • Improperly seated valves • Blown cylinder head gasket • Leaking piston rings • Improper feedback system operation	• Adjust gap • Replace fuel pump • Replace fuel pump • Check valve timing and repair as necessary • Test coil and replace as necessary • Test wires and replace as necessary • Test cylinder compression and repair as necessary • Replace gasket • Test compression and repair as necessary • Refer to Chapter 4
Intake backfire	• Improper ignition timing • Defective EGR component • Defective TAC vacuum motor or valve	• Adjust timing • Repair as necessary • Repair as necessary
Exhaust backfire	• Air leak into manifold vacuum • Faulty air injection diverter valve • Exhaust leak	• Check manifold vacuum and repair as necessary • Test diverter valve and replace as necessary • Locate and eliminate leak
Ping or spark knock	• Incorrect ignition timing • Distributor advance malfunction • Excessive combustion chamber deposits • Air leak into manifold vacuum • Excessively high compression • Fuel octane rating excessively low • Sharp edges in combustion chamber • EGR valve not functioning properly	• Adjust timing • Inspect advance mechanism and repair as necessary (Distributor systems only) • Remove with combustion chamber cleaner • Check manifold vacuum and repair as necessary • Test compression and repair as necessary • Try alternate fuel source • Grind smooth • Test EGR system and replace as necessary
Surging (at cruising to top speeds)	• Low fuel pump pressure or volume • Improper PCV valve air flow • Air leak into manifold vacuum • Incorrect spark advance • Restricted fuel filter • Restricted air cleaner • EGR valve not functioning properly • Improper feedback system operation	• Replace fuel pump • Test PCV valve and replace as necessary • Check manifold vacuum and repair as necessary • Test and replace as necessary • Replace fuel filter • Clean or replace air cleaner filter element • Test EGR system and replace as necessary • Refer to Chapter 4

Troubleshooting the Serpentine Drive Belt

Problem	Cause	Solution
Tension sheeting fabric failure (woven fabric on outside circumference of belt has cracked or separated from body of belt)	• Grooved or backside idler pulley diameters are less than minimum recommended • Tension sheeting contacting (rubbing) stationary object • Excessive heat causing woven fabric to age • Tension sheeting splice has fractured	• Replace pulley(s) not conforming to specification • Correct rubbing condition • Replace belt • Replace belt
Noise (objectional squeal, squeak, or rumble is heard or felt while drive belt is in operation)	• Belt slippage • Bearing noise • Belt misalignment • Belt-to-pulley mismatch • Driven component inducing vibration • System resonant frequency inducing vibration	• Adjust belt • Locate and repair • Align belt/pulley(s) • Install correct belt • Locate defective driven component and repair • Vary belt tension within specifications. Replace belt.
Rib chunking (one or more ribs has separated from belt body)	• Foreign objects imbedded in pulley grooves • Installation damage • Drive loads in excess of design specifications • Insufficient internal belt adhesion	• Remove foreign objects from pulley grooves • Replace belt • Adjust belt tension • Replace belt
Rib or belt wear (belt ribs contact bottom of pulley grooves)	• Pulley(s) misaligned • Mismatch of belt and pulley groove widths • Abrasive environment • Rusted pulley(s) • Sharp or jagged pulley groove tips • Rubber deteriorated	• Align pulley(s) • Replace belt • Replace belt • Clean rust from pulley(s) • Replace pulley • Replace belt
Longitudinal belt cracking (cracks between two ribs)	• Belt has mistracked from pulley groove • Pulley groove tip has worn away rubber-to-tensile member	• Replace belt • Replace belt
Belt slips	• Belt slipping because of insufficient tension • Belt or pulley subjected to substance (belt dressing, oil, ethylene glycol) that has reduced friction • Driven component bearing failure • Belt glazed and hardened from heat and excessive slippage	• Adjust tension • Replace belt and clean pulleys • Replace faulty component bearing • Replace belt
"Groove jumping" (belt does not maintain correct position on pulley, or turns over and/or runs off pulleys)	• Insufficient belt tension • Pulley(s) not within design tolerance • Foreign object(s) in grooves	• Adjust belt tension • Replace pulley(s) • Remove foreign objects from grooves

Troubleshooting the Serpentine Drive Belt

Problem	Cause	Solution
"Groove jumping" (belt does not maintain correct position on pulley, or turns over and/or runs off pulleys)	• Excessive belt speed • Pulley misalignment • Belt-to-pulley profile mismatched • Belt cordline is distorted	• Avoid excessive engine acceleration • Align pulley(s) • Install correct belt • Replace belt
Belt broken (Note: identify and correct problem before replacement belt is installed)	• Excessive tension • Tensile members damaged during belt installation • Belt turnover • Severe pulley misalignment • Bracket, pulley, or bearing failure	• Replace belt and adjust tension to specification • Replace belt • Replace belt • Align pulley(s) • Replace defective component and belt
Cord edge failure (tensile member exposed at edges of belt or separated from belt body)	• Excessive tension • Drive pulley misalignment • Belt contacting stationary object • Pulley irregularities • Improper pulley construction • Insufficient adhesion between tensile member and rubber matrix	• Adjust belt tension • Align pulley • Correct as necessary • Replace pulley • Replace pulley • Replace belt and adjust tension to specifications
Sporadic rib cracking (multiple cracks in belt ribs at random intervals)	• Ribbed pulley(s) diameter less than minimum specification • Backside bend flat pulley(s) diameter less than minimum • Excessive heat condition causing rubber to harden • Excessive belt thickness • Belt overcured • Excessive tension	• Replace pulley(s) • Replace pulley(s) • Correct heat condition as necessary • Replace belt • Replace belt • Adjust belt tension

Troubleshooting the Cooling System

Problem	Cause	Solution
High temperature gauge indication—overheating	• Coolant level low • Improper fan operation • Radiator hose(s) collapsed • Radiator airflow blocked	• Replenish coolant • Repair or replace as necessary • Replace hose(s) • Remove restriction (bug screen, fog lamps, etc.)
	• Faulty pressure cap • Ignition timing incorrect • Air trapped in cooling system • Heavy traffic driving	• Replace pressure cap • Adjust ignition timing • Purge air • Operate at fast idle in neutral intermittently to cool engine • Install proper component(s)
	• Incorrect cooling system component(s) installed • Faulty thermostat • Water pump shaft broken or impeller loose	• Replace thermostat • Replace water pump
	• Radiator tubes clogged • Cooling system clogged • Casting flash in cooling passages	• Flush radiator • Flush system • Repair or replace as necessary. Flash may be visible by removing cooling system components or removing core plugs.
	• Brakes dragging • Excessive engine friction • Antifreeze concentration over 68%	• Repair brakes • Repair engine • Lower antifreeze concentration percentage
	• Missing air seals • Faulty gauge or sending unit	• Replace air seals • Repair or replace faulty component
	• Loss of coolant flow caused by leakage or foaming • Viscous fan drive failed	• Repair or replace leaking component, replace coolant • Replace unit
Low temperature indication—undercooling	• Thermostat stuck open • Faulty gauge or sending unit	• Replace thermostat • Repair or replace faulty component
Coolant loss—boilover	• Overfilled cooling system	• Reduce coolant level to proper specification
	• Quick shutdown after hard (hot) run • Air in system resulting in occasional "burping" of coolant • Insufficient antifreeze allowing coolant boiling point to be too low	• Allow engine to run at fast idle prior to shutdown • Purge system • Add antifreeze to raise boiling point
	• Antifreeze deteriorated because of age or contamination	• Replace coolant
	• Leaks due to loose hose clamps, loose nuts, bolts, drain plugs, faulty hoses, or defective radiator	• Pressure test system to locate source of leak(s) then repair as necessary

Troubleshooting the Cooling System (cont.)

Problem	Cause	Solution
Coolant loss—boilover	• Faulty head gasket • Cracked head, manifold, or block • Faulty radiator cap	• Replace head gasket • Replace as necessary • Replace cap
Coolant entry into crankcase or cylinder(s)	• Faulty head gasket • Crack in head, manifold or block	• Replace head gasket • Replace as necessary
Coolant recovery system inoperative	• Coolant level low • Leak in system • Pressure cap not tight or seal missing, or leaking • Pressure cap defective • Overflow tube clogged or leaking • Recovery bottle vent restricted	• Replenish coolant to FULL mark • Pressure test to isolate leak and repair as necessary • Repair as necessary • Replace cap • Repair as necessary • Remove restriction
Noise	• Fan contacting shroud • Loose water pump impeller • Glazed fan belt • Loose fan belt • Rough surface on drive pulley • Water pump bearing worn • Belt alignment	• Reposition shroud and inspect engine mounts (on electric fans inspect assembly) • Replace pump • Apply silicone or replace belt • Adjust fan belt tension • Replace pulley • Remove belt to isolate. Replace pump. • Check pulley alignment. Repair as necessary.
No coolant flow through heater core	• Restricted return inlet in water pump • Heater hose collapsed or restricted • Restricted heater core • Restricted outlet in thermostat housing • Intake manifold bypass hole in cylinder head restricted • Faulty heater control valve • Intake manifold coolant passage restricted	• Remove restriction • Remove restriction or replace hose • Remove restriction or replace core • Remove flash or restriction • Remove restriction • Replace valve • Remove restriction or replace intake manifold

NOTE: *Immediately after shutdown, the engine enters a condition known as heat soak. This is caused by the cooling system being inoperative while engine temperature is still high. If coolant temperature rises above boiling point, expansion and pressure may push some coolant out of the radiator overflow tube. If this does not occur frequently it is considered normal.*

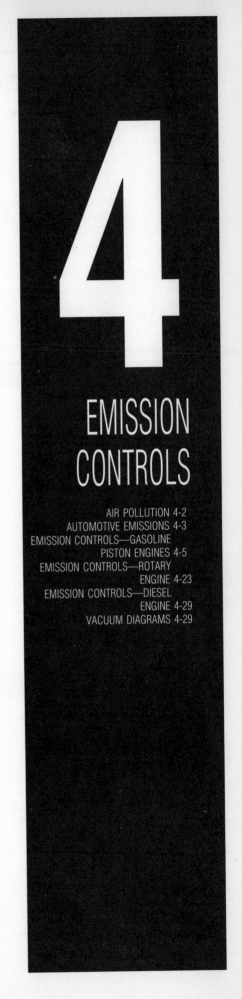

4

EMISSION CONTROLS

AIR POLLUTION

The earth's atmosphere, at or near sea level, consists approximately of 78 percent nitrogen, 21 percent oxygen and 1 percent other gases. If it were possible to remain in this state, 100 percent clean air would result. However, many varied sources allow other gases and particulates to mix with the clean air, causing our atmosphere to become unclean or polluted.

Some of these pollutants are visible while others are invisible, with each having the capability of causing distress to the eyes, ears, throat, skin and respiratory system. Should these pollutants become concentrated in a specific area and under certain conditions, death could result due to the displacement or chemical change of the oxygen content in the air. These pollutants can also cause great damage to the environment and to the many man made objects that are exposed to the elements.

To better understand the causes of air pollution, the pollutants can be categorized into 3 separate types, natural, industrial and automotive.

Natural Pollutants

Natural pollution has been present on earth since before man appeared and continues to be a factor when discussing air pollution, although it causes only a small percentage of the overall pollution problem. It is the direct result of decaying organic matter, wind born smoke and particulates from such natural events as plain and forest fires (ignited by heat or lightning), volcanic ash, sand and dust which can spread over a large area of the countryside.

Such a phenomenon of natural pollution has been seen in the form of volcanic eruptions, with the resulting plume of smoke, steam and volcanic ash blotting out the sun's rays as it spreads and rises higher into the atmosphere. As it travels into the atmosphere the upper air currents catch and carry the smoke and ash, while condensing the steam back into water vapor. As the water vapor, smoke and ash travel on their journey, the smoke dissipates into the atmosphere while the ash and moisture settle back to earth in a trail hundreds of miles long. In some cases, lives are lost and millions of dollars of property damage result.

Industrial Pollutants

Industrial pollution is caused primarily by industrial processes, the burning of coal, oil and natural gas, which in turn produce smoke and fumes. Because the burning fuels contain large amounts of sulfur, the principal ingredients of smoke and fumes are sulfur dioxide and particulate matter. This type of pollutant occurs most severely during still, damp and cool weather, such as at night. Even in its less severe form, this pollutant is not confined to just cities. Because of air movements, the pollutants move for miles over the surrounding countryside, leaving in its path a barren and unhealthy environment for all living things.

Working with Federal, State and Local mandated regulations and by carefully monitoring emissions, big business has greatly reduced the amount of pollutant introduced from its industrial sources, striving to obtain an acceptable level. Because of the mandated industrial emission clean up, many land areas and streams in and around the cities that were formerly barren of vegetation and life, have now begun to move back in the direction of nature's intended balance.

Automotive Pollutants

The third major source of air pollution is automotive emissions. The emissions from the internal combustion engines were not an appreciable problem years ago because of the small number of registered vehicles and the nation's small highway system. However, during the early 1950's, the trend of the American people was to move from the cities to the surrounding suburbs. This caused an immediate problem in transportation because the majority of suburbs were not afforded mass transit conveniences. This lack of transportation created an attractive market for the automobile manufacturers, which resulted in a dramatic increase in the number of vehicles produced and sold, along with a marked increase in highway construction between cities and the suburbs. Multi-vehicle families emerged with a growing emphasis placed on an individual vehicle per family member. As the increase in vehicle ownership and usage occurred, so did pollutant levels in and around the cities, as suburbanites drove daily to their businesses and employment, returning at the end of the day to their homes in the suburbs.

It was noted that a smoke and fog type haze was being formed and at times, remained in suspension over the cities, taking time to dissipate. At first this "smog," derived from the words "smoke" and "fog," was thought to result from industrial pollution but it was determined that automobile emissions shared the blame. It was discovered that when normal automobile emissions were exposed to sunlight for a period of time, complex chemical reactions would take place.

It is now known that smog is a photo chemical layer which develops when certain oxides of nitrogen (NOx) and unburned hydrocarbons (HC) from automobile emissions are exposed to sunlight. Pollution was more severe when smog would become stagnant over an area in which a warm layer of air settled over the top of the cooler air mass, trapping and holding the cooler mass at ground level. The trapped cooler air would keep the emissions from being dispersed and diluted through normal air flows. This type of air stagnation was given the name "Temperature Inversion."

TEMPERATURE INVERSION

In normal weather situations, surface air is warmed by heat radiating from the earth's surface and the sun's rays. This causes it to rise upward, into the atmosphere. Upon rising it will cool through a convection type heat exchange with the cooler upper air. As warm air rises, the surface pollutants are carried upward and dissipated into the atmosphere.

When a temperature inversion occurs, we find the higher air is no longer cooler, but is warmer than the surface air, causing the cooler surface air to become trapped. This warm air blanket can extend from above ground level to a few hundred or even a few thousand feet into the air. As the surface air is trapped, so are the pollutants, causing a severe smog condition. Should this stagnant air mass extend to a few thousand feet high, enough air movement with the inversion takes place to allow the smog layer to rise above ground level but the pollutants still cannot dissipate. This inversion can remain for days over an area, with the smog level only rising or lowering from ground level to a few hundred feet high. Meanwhile, the pollutant levels increase, causing eye irritation, respiratory problems, reduced visibility, plant damage and in some cases, even disease.

This inversion phenomenon was first noted in the Los Angeles, California area. The city lies in terrain resembling a basin and with certain weather conditions, a cold air mass is held in the basin while a warmer air mass covers it like a lid.

Because this type of condition was first documented as prevalent in the Los Angeles area, this type of trapped pollution was named Los Angeles Smog, although it occurs in other areas where a large concentration of automobiles are used and the air remains stagnant for any length of time.

HEAT TRANSFER

Consider the internal combustion engine as a machine in which raw materials must be placed so a finished product comes out. As in any machine operation, a certain amount of wasted material is formed. When we relate this to the internal combustion engine, we find that through the input of air and fuel, we obtain power during the combustion process to drive the vehicle. The by-product or waste of this power is, in part, heat and exhaust gases with which we must dispose.

The heat from the combustion process can rise to over 4000°F (2204°C). The dissipation of this heat is controlled by a ram air effect, the use of cooling fans to cause air flow and a liquid coolant solution surrounding the combustion area to transfer the heat of combustion through the cylinder walls and into the coolant. The coolant is then directed to a thin-finned, multi-tubed radiator, from which the excess heat is transferred to the atmosphere by 1 of the 3 heat transfer methods, conduction, convection or radiation.

The cooling of the combustion area is an important part in the control of exhaust emissions. To understand the behavior of the combustion and transfer of its heat, consider the air/fuel charge. It is ignited and the flame front burns progressively across the combustion chamber until the burning charge reaches the cylinder walls. Some of the fuel in contact with the walls is not hot enough to burn, thereby snuffing out or quenching the combustion process. This leaves unburned fuel in the combustion chamber. This unburned fuel is then forced out of the cylinder and into the exhaust system, along with the exhaust gases.

Many attempts have been made to minimize the amount of unburned fuel in the combustion chambers due to quenching, by increasing the coolant temperature and lessening the contact area of the coolant around the combustion area. However, design limitations within the combustion chambers prevent the complete burning of the air/fuel charge, so a certain amount of the unburned fuel is still expelled into the exhaust system, regardless of modifications to the engine.

AUTOMOTIVE EMISSIONS

Before emission controls were mandated on internal combustion engines, other sources of engine pollutants were discovered along with the exhaust emissions. It was determined that engine combustion exhaust produced approximately 60 percent of the total emission pollutants, fuel evaporation from the fuel tank and carburetor vents produced 20 percent, with the final 20 percent being produced through the crankcase as a by-product of the combustion process.

Exhaust Gases

The exhaust gases emitted into the atmosphere are a combination of burned and unburned fuel. To understand the exhaust emission and its composition, we must review some basic chemistry.

When the air/fuel mixture is introduced into the engine, we are mixing air, composed of nitrogen (78 percent), oxygen (21 percent) and other gases (1 percent) with the fuel, which is 100 percent hydrocarbons (HC), in a semi-controlled ratio. As the combustion process is accomplished, power is produced to move the vehicle while the heat of combustion is transferred to the cooling system. The exhaust gases are then composed of nitrogen, a diatomic gas (N_2), the same as was introduced in the engine, carbon dioxide (CO_2), the same gas that is used in beverage carbonation, and water vapor (H_2O). The nitrogen (N_2), for the most part, passes through the engine unchanged, while the oxygen (O_2) reacts (burns) with the hydrocarbons (HC) and produces the carbon dioxide (CO_2) and the water vapors (H_2O). If this chemical process would be the only process to take place, the exhaust emissions would be harmless. However, during the combustion process, other compounds are formed which are considered dangerous. These pollutants are hydrocarbons (HC), carbon monoxide (CO), oxides of nitrogen (NOx) oxides of sulfur (SOx) and engine particulates.

HYDROCARBONS

Hydrocarbons (HC) are essentially fuel which was not burned during the combustion process or which has escaped into the atmosphere through fuel evaporation. The main sources of incomplete combustion are rich air/fuel mixtures, low engine temperatures and improper spark timing. The main sources of hydrocarbon emission through fuel evaporation on most vehicles used to be the vehicle's fuel tank and carburetor float bowl.

To reduce combustion hydrocarbon emission, engine modifications were made to minimize dead space and surface area in the combustion chamber. In addition, the air/fuel mixture was made more lean through the improved control which feedback carburetion and fuel injection offers and by the addition of external controls to aid in further combustion of the hydrocarbons outside the engine. Two such methods were the addition of air injection systems, to inject fresh air into the exhaust manifolds and the installation of catalytic converters, units that are able to burn traces of hydrocarbons without affecting the internal combustion process or fuel economy.

To control hydrocarbon emissions through fuel evaporation, modifications were made to the fuel tank to allow storage of the fuel vapors during periods of engine shut-down. Modifications were also made to the air intake system so that at specific times during engine operation, these vapors may be purged and burned by blending them with the air/fuel mixture.

CARBON MONOXIDE

Carbon monoxide is formed when not enough oxygen is present during the combustion process to convert carbon (C) to carbon dioxide (CO_2). An increase in the carbon monoxide (CO) emission is normally accompanied by an increase in the hydrocarbon (HC) emission because of the lack of oxygen to completely burn all of the fuel mixture.

Carbon monoxide (CO) also increases the rate at which the photo chemical smog is formed by speeding up the conversion of nitric oxide (NO) to nitrogen dioxide (NO_2). To accomplish this, carbon monoxide (CO) combines with oxygen (O_2) and nitric oxide (NO) to produce carbon dioxide (CO_2) and nitrogen dioxide (NO_2). ($CO + O_2 + NO \quad CO_2 + NO_2$).

The dangers of carbon monoxide, which is an odorless and colorless toxic gas are many. When carbon monoxide is inhaled into the lungs and passed into the blood stream, oxygen is replaced by the carbon monoxide in the red blood cells, causing a reduction in the amount of oxygen supplied to the many parts of the body. This lack of oxygen causes headaches, lack of coordination, reduced mental alertness and, should the carbon monoxide concentration be high enough, death could result.

NITROGEN

Normally, nitrogen is an inert gas. When heated to approximately 2500°F (1371°C) through the combustion process, this gas becomes active and causes an increase in the nitric oxide (NO) emission.

Oxides of nitrogen (NOx) are composed of approximately 97–98 percent nitric oxide (NO). Nitric oxide is a colorless gas but when it is passed into the atmosphere, it combines with oxygen and forms nitrogen dioxide (NO_2). The nitrogen dioxide then combines with chemically active hydrocarbons (HC) and when in the presence of sunlight, causes the formation of photo-chemical smog.

Ozone

To further complicate matters, some of the nitrogen dioxide (NO_2) is broken apart by the sunlight to form nitric oxide and oxygen. (NO_2 + sunlight NO + O). This single atom of oxygen then combines with diatomic (meaning 2 atoms) oxygen (O_2) to form ozone (O_3). Ozone is one of the smells associated with smog. It has a pungent and offensive odor, irritates the eyes and lung tissues, affects the growth of plant life and causes rapid deterioration of rubber products. Ozone can be formed by sunlight as well as electrical discharge into the air.

The most common discharge area on the automobile engine is the secondary ignition electrical system, especially when inferior quality spark plug cables are used. As the surge of high voltage is routed through the secondary cable, the circuit builds up an electrical field around the wire, which acts upon the oxygen in the surrounding air to form the ozone. The faint glow along the cable with the engine running that may be visible on a dark night, is called the "corona discharge." It is the result of the electrical field passing from a high along the cable, to a low in the surrounding air, which forms the ozone gas. The combination of corona and ozone has been a major cause of cable deterioration. Recently, dif-

ferent and better quality insulating materials have lengthened the life of the electrical cables.

Although ozone at ground level can be harmful, ozone is beneficial to the earth's inhabitants. By having a concentrated ozone layer called the "ozonosphere," between 10 and 20 miles (16–32 km) up in the atmosphere, much of the ultra violet radiation from the sun's rays are absorbed and screened. If this ozone layer were not present, much of the earth's surface would be burned, dried and unfit for human life.

OXIDES OF SULFUR

Oxides of sulfur (SOx) were initially ignored in the exhaust system emissions, since the sulfur content of gasoline as a fuel is less than $\frac{1}{10}$ of 1 percent. Because of this small amount, it was felt that it contributed very little to the overall pollution problem. However, because of the difficulty in solving the sulfur emissions in industrial pollutions and the introduction of catalytic converter to the automobile exhaust systems, a change was mandated. The automobile exhaust system, when equipped with a catalytic converter, changes the sulfur dioxide (SO_2) into sulfur trioxide (SO_3).

When this combines with water vapors (H_2O), a sulfuric acid mist (H_2SO_4) is formed and is a very difficult pollutant to handle since it is extremely corrosive. This sulfuric acid mist that is formed, is the same mist that rises from the vents of an automobile battery when an active chemical reaction takes place within the battery cells.

When a large concentration of vehicles equipped with catalytic converters are operating in an area, this acid mist may rise and be distributed over a large ground area causing land, plant, crop, paint and building damage.

PARTICULATE MATTER

A certain amount of particulate matter is present in the burning of any fuel, with carbon constituting the largest percentage of the particulates. In gasoline, the remaining particulates are the burned remains of the various other compounds used in its manufacture. When a gasoline engine is in good internal condition, the particulate emissions are low but as the engine wears internally, the particulate emissions increase. By visually inspecting the tail pipe emissions, a determination can be made as to where an engine defect may exist. An engine with light gray or blue smoke emitting from the tail pipe normally indicates an increase in the oil consumption through burning due to internal engine wear. Black smoke would indicate a defective fuel delivery system, causing the engine to operate in a rich mode. Regardless of the color of the smoke, the internal part of the engine or the fuel delivery system should be repaired to prevent excess particulate emissions.

Diesel and turbine engines emit a darkened plume of smoke from the exhaust system because of the type of fuel used. Emission control regulations are mandated for this type of emission and more stringent measures are being used to prevent excess emission of the particulate matter. Electronic components are being introduced to control the injection of the fuel at precisely the proper time of piston travel, to achieve the optimum in fuel ignition and fuel usage. Other particulate after-burning components are being tested to achieve a cleaner emission.

Good grades of engine lubricating oils should be used, which meet the manufacturers specification. Cut-rate oils can contribute to the particulate emission problem because of their low flash or ignition temperature point. Such oils burn prematurely during the combustion process causing emission of particulate matter.

The cooling system is an important factor in the reduction of particulate matter. The optimum combustion will occur, with the cooling system operating at a temperature specified by the manufacturer. The cooling system must be maintained in the same manner as the engine oiling system, as each system is required to perform properly in order for the engine to operate efficiently for a long time.

Crankcase Emissions

Crankcase emissions are made up of water, acids, unburned fuel, oil fumes and particulates. These emissions are classified as hydrocarbons (HC) and are formed by the small amount of unburned, compressed air/fuel mixture entering the crankcase from the combustion area (between the cylinder walls and piston rings) during the compression and power strokes. The head of the compression and combustion help to form the remaining crankcase emissions.

Since the first engines, crankcase emissions were allowed into the atmosphere through a road draft tube, mounted on the lower side of the engine block. Fresh air came in through an open oil filler cap or breather. The air passed through the crankcase mixing with blow-by gases. The motion of the vehicle and the air blowing past the open end of the road draft tube caused a low pressure area (vacuum) at the end of the tube. Crankcase emissions were simply drawn out of the road draft tube into the air.

To control the crankcase emission, the road draft tube was deleted. A hose and/or tubing was routed from the crankcase to the intake manifold so the blow-by emission could be burned with the air/fuel mixture. However, it was found that intake manifold vacuum, used to draw the crankcase emissions into the manifold, would vary in strength at the wrong time and not allow the proper emission flow. A regulating valve was needed to control the flow of air through the crankcase.

Testing, showed the removal of the blow-by gases from the crankcase as quickly as possible, was most important to the longevity of the engine. Should large accumulations of blow-by gases remain and condense, dilution of the engine oil would occur to form water, soots, resins, acids and lead salts, resulting in the formation of sludge and varnishes. This condensation of the blow-by gases occurs more frequently on vehicles used in numerous starting and stopping conditions, excessive idling and when the engine is not allowed to attain normal operating temperature through short runs.

Evaporative Emissions

Gasoline fuel is a major source of pollution, before and after it is burned in the automobile engine. From the time the fuel is refined, stored, pumped and transported, again stored until it is pumped into the fuel tank of the vehicle, the gasoline gives off unburned hydrocarbons (HC) into the atmosphere. Through the redesign of storage areas and venting systems, the pollution factor was diminished, but not eliminated, from the refinery standpoint. However, the automobile still remained the primary source of vaporized, unburned hydrocarbon (HC) emissions.

Fuel pumped from an underground storage tank is cool but when exposed to a warmer ambient temperature, will expand. Before controls were mandated, an owner might fill the fuel tank with fuel from an underground storage tank and park the vehicle for some time in warm area, such as a parking lot. As the fuel would warm, it would expand and should no provisions or area be provided for the expansion, the fuel would spill out of the filler neck and onto the ground, causing hydrocarbon (HC) pollution and creating a severe fire hazard. To correct this condition, the vehicle manufacturers added overflow plumbing and/or gasoline tanks with built in expansion areas or domes.

However, this did not control the fuel vapor emission from the fuel tank. It was determined that most of the fuel evaporation occurred when the vehicle was stationary and the engine not operating. Most vehicles carry 5–25 gallons (19–95 liters) of gasoline. Should a large concentration of vehicles be parked in one area, such as a large parking lot, excessive fuel vapor emissions would take place, increasing as the temperature increases.

To prevent the vapor emission from escaping into the atmosphere, the fuel systems were designed to trap the vapors while the vehicle is stationary, by sealing the system from the atmosphere. A storage system is used to collect and hold the fuel vapors from the carburetor (if equipped) and the fuel tank when the engine is not operating. When the engine is started, the storage system is then purged of the fuel vapors, which are drawn into the engine and burned with the air/fuel mixture.

EMISSION CONTROLS—GASOLINE PISTON ENGINES

The B1600 uses four emission control systems:
• Throttle Positioner system
• Positive Crankcase Ventilation system
• Evaporative Emission Control system
• Thermactor Air Injection system.
The B1800 and B2000 employ seven basic systems:
• Thermactor Air Injection system
• Positive Crankcase Ventilation (PCV) system
• Evaporative Emission Control system
• Deceleration Control system
• Exhaust Gas Recirculation (EGR) is used on 1976 California Mazdas with manual transmission, and all 1977 and later models

• Catalytic Converter, used on some 1976–78 California trucks and most 1979 and later models
• Spark Delay system is used on 1977 and later 1.8 and 2.0 engines

Throttle Positioner System—B1600

The throttle positioner system consists of a servo diaphragm connected to the throttle lever and a vacuum control valve which controls intake manifold vacuum through the servo diaphragm.

TESTING THE SYSTEM

Servo Diaphragm

♦ See Figures 1 and 2

1. Start the engine and set the idle speed to 800 rpm. Stop the engine.
2. Disconnect the vacuum sensing tube between the servo diaphragm and the vacuum control valve at the servo diaphragm.
3. Remove the intake manifold suction hole plug.
4. Connect the intake manifold and the servo diaphragm with a tube so that the intake manifold vacuum goes directly to the servo diaphragm.
5. Connect a tachometer and remove the vacuum sensing tube between the carburetor and distributor.
6. Start the engine and read the speed. If the engine is running between 1,300–1,500 rpm, the servo diaphragm is operating normally. If the engine speed is 800–1,500 rpm, adjust the speed with the throttle opening screw. If the engine speed remains normal, about 800 rpm, the servo diaphragm is defective and should be replaced.

SERVICING

Servo Diaphragm Replacement

1. Remove the air cleaner.
2. Disconnect the vacuum sensing tube from the servo diaphragm.
3. Remove the cotter pin and link.
4. Loosen the locknut and remove the servo diaphragm.
5. Installation is the reverse of removal. Adjust the servo diaphragm.

Vacuum Control Valve Replacement

1. Remove the air cleaner.
2. Disconnect the vacuum sensing tubes from the vacuum control valve.
3. Unbolt and remove the vacuum control valve.
4. Installation is the reverse of removal.

ADJUSTMENTS

Throttle Opener

1. Install a tachometer on the engine.
2. Start the engine and set the idle speed.
3. Stop the engine.
4. Disconnect the vacuum sensing tube between the servo diaphragm and the vacuum control valve from the servo diaphragm.
5. Remove the plug from the intake manifold suction hole.
6. Attach a test tube between the intake manifold and the servo diaphragm to route intake manifold vacuum directly to the servo diaphragm.
7. Start the engine and note the speed.
8. Set the engine speed to 1,400 rpm using the throttle opener screw. Turning the adjusting screw clockwise increases engine speed.
9. Stop the engine and disconnect the tachometer. Reconnect all lines.

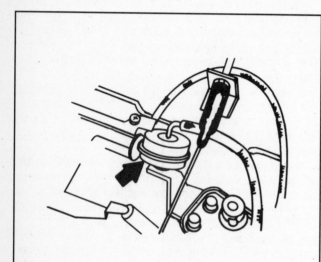

Fig. 1 View of the servo diaphragm (arrow), located on the intake manifold next to the carburetor

Positive Crankcase Ventilation (PCV) System

♦ See Figure 3

The function of the PCV valve is to divert blow-by gases from the crankcase to the intake manifold to be burned in the cylinders. The system consists of a PCV valve, an oil separator and the hoses necessary to connect the components.

Ventilating air is routed into the rocker cover from the air cleaner. The air is then moved to the oil separator and from the separator to the PCV valve. The PCV valve is operated by differences in air pressure between the intake manifold and the rocker cover.

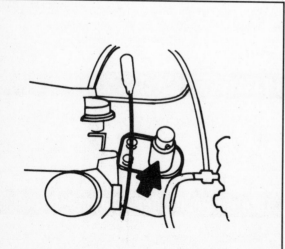

Fig. 2 View of the vacuum control valve, located next to the servo diaphragm and bolted to the intake manifold

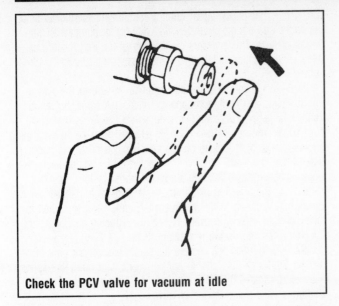

Check the PCV valve for vacuum at idle

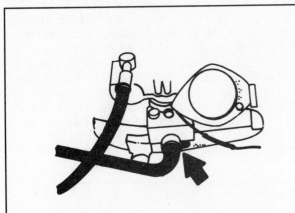

Fig. 3 View of the 1972–84 PCV valve, located on the intake manifold under the carburetor mounting flange—1986 models are located on the valve cover

TESTING

Standard Test

1. Remove the hose from the PCV valve.
2. Start the engine and run it at approximately 700–1,000 rpm.
3. Cover the end of the PCV valve with a finger. A distinct vacuum should be felt. If no vacuum is felt, replace the valve.

Alternate Test

Remove the valve from its fitting. Shake the valve. If a rattle is heard, the valve is probably functioning normally. If no rattle is heard, the valve is probably stuck (open or shut) and should be replaced.

REMOVAL & INSTALLATION

1. Remove the air cleaner, if necessary.
2. Disconnect the hose from the PCV valve.

Once its hose is disconnected, pull the PCV valve out of the valve cover—push-in style shown

3. Remove the valve from the intake manifold fitting.
4. Install the valve in the fitting.
5. Connect the hose to the valve.
6. Install the air cleaner, if removed.

Evaporative Emission Control System

The evaporative emission control system is designed to control the emission of gasoline vapors into the atmosphere. The system consists of a fuel tank, a condenser tank and a check valve. In 1977, the system was changed slightly to consist of a sealed fuel tank, a vapor controlling orifice in the line between the tank and the charcoal canister, and the canister. The check valve of the previous system was eliminated through the substitution of a filler cap with vacuum and pressure relief valves, and a fuel vapor valve on the tank.

When the engine is not running, fuel vapors are channeled to the condenser tank. The fuel returns to the fuel tank as the vapors condense. During periods of engine operation, fuel vapor that has not condensed in the condenser tank moves to the carbon canister. The stored vapors are removed from the charcoal by fresh air moving through the inlet hole in the bottom of the canister.

The check valve (1972–76), located between the condenser tank and the canister, allows fuel vapor and ventilation to flow during normal operation. If the system becomes clogged or frozen, the valve opens (by negative pressure in the fuel tank) to allow fuel to be drawn from the tank. The valve also opens to vent internal tank pressure under hot conditions. The fuel tank cap and fuel vapor valve replace the check valve in 1977 and later, and perform essentially the same functions.

The only service necessary for this system is replacement of the charcoal canister at regular intervals and inspection of the rubber hoses at the same time for cracks or breaks. Any deteriorated hoses should be replaced.

REMOVAL & INSTALLATION

Condenser Tank

1. Raise and support the rear of the truck.
2. Disconnect the hoses from the condenser tank.

3. Unbolt and remove the condenser tank.
4. Install the tank and tighten the bolts.
5. Connect the hoses to the tank.
6. Lower the truck.

Check Valve

1. Disconnect the hoses from the check valve.
2. Unscrew and remove the valve.
3. Position a new valve on the crossmember. Tighten the attaching screws.
4. Connect all hoses to the valve.

Air Injection System

▶ **See Figure 4**

Because of the many variables under which the engine operates, some hydrocarbon and carbon monoxide gases escape unburnt from the combustion chamber. To burn these gases more thoroughly, a belt-driven pump is used to supply fresh air to an air injection manifold located on the exhaust manifold. The injection of fresh air supports combustion of the hot unburned HC and CO gases within the exhaust manifold.

The Thermactor system, used on California trucks only in 1972 and 1973, and all trucks thereafter, consists of an air pump with relief valve, a check valve, four air injection nozzles (one for each cylinder) connected to an air injection manifold, an air by-pass valve, and hoses from 1972–74. The air pump pushes air through the one way check valve into the injection manifold and through the nozzles. The check valve prevents any backfire of gases into the system. An air by-pass valve is used to prevent air injection during cold choke operation. Pulling the choke cable closes both the choke and the air by-pass valve, venting all pumped air into the air cleaner. This prevents overheating of the rich mixture exhaust. The air pump relief valve vents excess pressure to the atmosphere.

1975–76 trucks use a slightly modified version of the system. The principle and main components remain the same, but an air control valve, incorporating two relief valves, replaces the air by-pass valve. The no. 1 relief valve is activated by a control unit (an engine rpm switch) located on the kick panel beneath the parking brake lever; the No. 2 relief valve is activated by engine vacuum. Below 4,000 rpm (4,300 with automatic transmission), no. 1 directs air to the injection manifold. Above that engine speed, no. 1 opens and vents air to the air cleaner. Number 2 opens when intake manifold vacuum exceeds 6.3 in.Hg, reducing air flow to the injection manifold during low engine loads.

1977–78 1,796cc engines are the same, except that only trucks sold in California have the air control valve, with one relief valve activated by intake manifold vacuum. In addition, trucks sold in California have a vacuum delay valve.

The systems used in 1979 and later are slightly different. 1,970cc engines sold for 49 States use do not have an air pump. Instead, air injection is controlled by exhaust system back pressure. The air injection pipe runs from the air cleaner case to the exhaust manifold. A one-way check valve is installed in the pipe. During periods of negative exhaust pulsation, air is drawn from the air cleaner, through the check valve, and into the exhaust manifold. During periods of positive exhaust back pressure (positive pulsation), the check valve closes and no air is drawn into the exhaust system.

Models sold in California have an air pump, a check valve, and

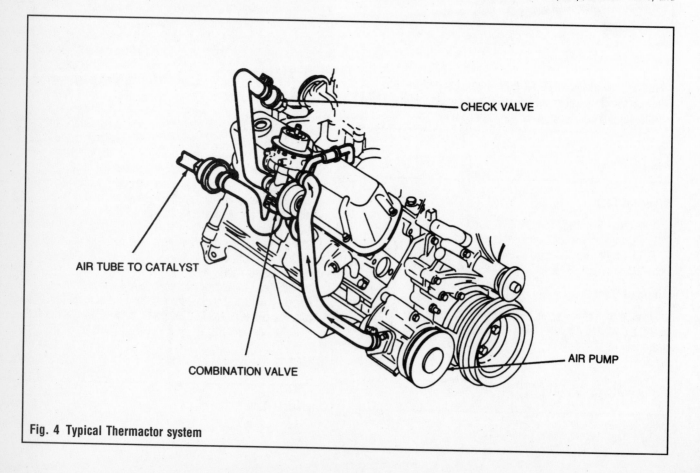

Fig. 4 Typical Thermactor system

CHECK VALVE

AIR TUBE TO CATALYST

COMBINATION VALVE

AIR PUMP

an air control valve. The air control valve has a no. 1 relief valve, activated by intake manifold vacuum, and a No. 2 relief valve, which modulates the amount of secondary air. The No. 2 relief valve is not used with automatic transmissions.

TESTING

Air Pump Drive Belt

Be sure that the air pump drive belt is adjusted to the proper tension. See Section 1.

Air Pump

▶ See Figure 5

1. Disconnect the air pump outlet hose from the air by-pass valve.

2. Connect a T-fitting and pressure gauge into the outlet line. The other end of the fitting should have a plug with an $^{11}/_{32}$" hole drilled through it.

3. Start the engine and run it briefly at 1,500 rpm. Be sure the choke is fully open (pushed in).

4. If the pressure reading is below 1 psi, replace the pump.

Air Pump Relief Valve

▶ See Figure 6

1. Operate the engine at idle.

2. Check the relief valve for airflow. No flow should be evi-

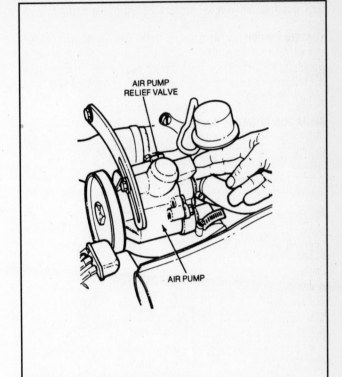

Fig. 6 Example of how to check the air pump relief valve

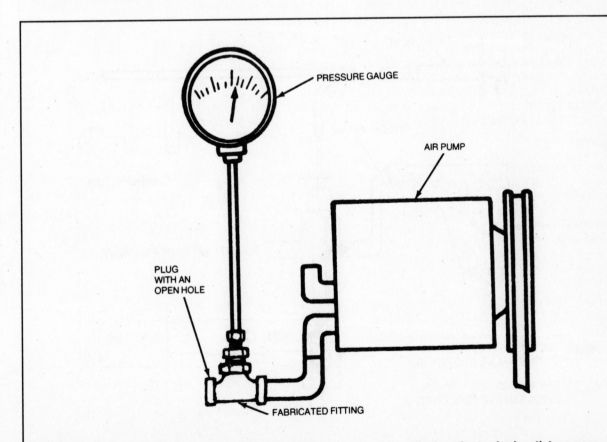

Fig. 5 An example of connecting an air pressure gauge to the air pump outlet in order to check outlet pressure—if the reading is under 1 psi, replace the pump

dent. If airflow out is noted, replace the relief valve and air pump.

3. Increase the engine speed to 3,000 rpm (4,500 rpm, 1978 and later). If air flows out of the relief valve, the valve is in good condition. If air does not flow from the relief valve, or if the valve is excessively noisy, the relief valve and air pump assembly should be replaced.

Air Manifold Check Valve

Remove the check valve from the air injection manifold. Blow through the valve from the intake side of the outlet side. Air should pass through the valve from the intake side only. If air passes through the valve from the outlet side, replace the valve.

Air Bypass Valve

1972–74 VEHICLES

▶ **See Figure 7**

1. Disconnect the air line at the check valve.
2. Push the choke knob all the way in.
3. Run the engine at 1,500 rpm.
4. Hold your hand over the end of the air pump air line. Air should flow from the hose.
5. Pull the choke knob all the way out. No air should flow from the air line.
6. If the valve is not operating properly, replace the valve.

Air Control Valve

1975–76 VEHICLES

1. Disconnect the outlet hose from the bottom of the air control valve at the air cleaner. Start the engine and let it idle. Air should not be discharged from the outlet.
2. Unplug the air control valve solenoid electrical connector. With the engine still idling, check for air discharge from the valve outlet.
3. Reconnect the electrical connectors. Increase the engine speed above 4,000 rpm (4,300 with automatic transmission), and check that air is discharged from the valve outlet. When the engine speed falls, the air discharge should stop.
4. If the valve is not operating properly, check the hoses for leaks, breaks, kinks, or improper connections. Replace the valve as necessary.

Control Unit

1975–76 VEHICLES

▶ **See Figures 8 and 9**

1. Attach a test light to the unit connector as shown.
2. Start the engine. The light should be on with the engine idling.
3. Increase the speed above 4,000 rpm (4,300 with automatic transmission). The light should go off.

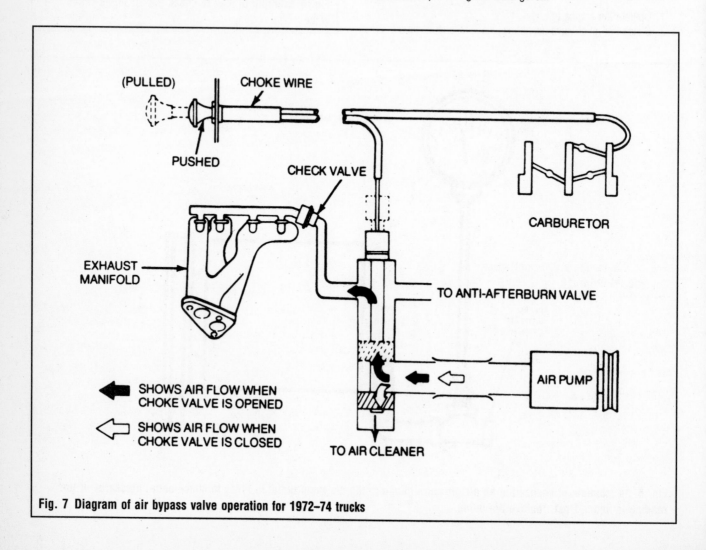

Fig. 7 Diagram of air bypass valve operation for 1972–74 trucks

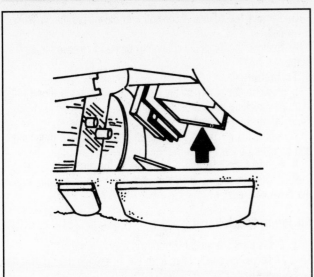

Fig. 8 The control unit is located on the kick panel, beneath the parking brake lever

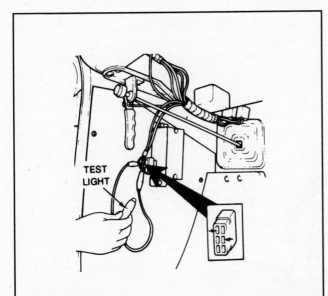

Fig. 9 Connecting a test light to the 1975–76 air injection control unit

4. If the light does not go off when specified, or does not remain on with the engine idling, replace the unit.

Air Control Valve

1977–78 VEHICLES

This procedure is for all 1,796cc engines. Only California trucks have this valve.

1. Disconnect the outlet hose at the bottom of the valve. Start the engine and let it idle.
2. Check that air is not discharged from the outlet.

3. Disconnect the small diameter hose from the top of the valve. Air should now be felt at the valve outlet.
4. If the valve is not operating properly, check the hoses for leaks, kinks, breaks, or improper connections, and inspect the check valve for proper operation. Replace the air control valve if necessary. Reconnect the hoses after the test.

Air Control Valve

1980 AND LATER VEHICLES WITH MANUAL TRANSMISSION

This test is for all 1980 models sold in California with a manual transmission.

1. Warm the engine to normal operating temperature, then shut it off.
2. Disconnect the air hose at the bottom of the air control valve. Start the engine and allow it to idle.
3. Disconnect the thin vacuum hose from the top of the air control valve. This is the hose which runs to the intake manifold. Air should be discharged from the air control valve outlet. Connect the hose again; the airflow from the outlet should stop.
4. Disconnect the vacuum sensing hose (which connects to the No. 2 relief valve on the side of the air control valve) at the T-fitting.
5. Obtain a T fitting and a length of vacuum hose. Disconnect the vacuum hose from the top of the air control valve (same hose as disconnected in Step 3). Connect this hose to the T-fitting and the hose fitting on the top of the air control valve from which the other length of hose (intake manifold vacuum hose) was just removed. You should now have a T-fitting with two hoses connected to it: one running from the top of the air control valve to the T-fitting, and the other running from the intake manifold to the T-fitting.
6. Connect the No. 2 relief valve vacuum hose (disconnect from its own T-fitting in Step 4) to the T-fitting. This will allow the No. 2 relief valve to be directly connected to intake manifold vacuum.
7. With the engine idling, air should be discharged from the outlet of the air control valve.
8. Disconnect and plug the vacuum hose from the No. 2 relief valve fitting (on the side of the air control valve). Airflow from the air control valve should stop.
9. If the air control valve does not operate correctly, replace it.

Check Valve

1979 AND LATER VEHICLES—49 STATES

This is a test for the check valve installed in the hose which runs from the air cleaner case to the exhaust manifold, on 1979 and later 49 State models without an air pump.

1. Warm the engine to normal operating temperature, then shut it off.
2. Disconnect the air hose from the check valve.
3. Start the engine and allow it to idle.
4. Place a finger over the check valve inlet; vacuum should be felt. If no air is being drawn into the valve, replace the valve.
5. Run the engine up to about 1,500 rpm. Check for exhaust gas leakage at the check valve air inlet fitting. If leakage is present, replace the valve.

ADJUSTMENTS

Air Pump Drive Belt

Adjustment of the air pump drive belt is covered in Section 1.

Air Bypass Valve

1972–74 VEHICLES

♦ **See Figure 10**

1. Push the choke handle all the way in. Be sure that the choke plate is fully open.
2. Loosen the cable retaining screw in the valve plunger and the screw in the cable retaining bracket.
3. Be sure that the plunger is fully bottomed.
4. Insert the cable in the plunger and tighten the retaining screw.
5. Push down on the cable as much as possible without bending the control wire, then tighten the bracket screw.
6. Pull the choke knob all the way out. The valve plunger should be pulled to the top of the bracket.

REMOVAL & INSTALLATION

Air Pump

1. Remove the battery, alternator and alternator drive belt.
2. Disconnect the inlet and outlet hoses from the air pump.

3. Remove the adjusting bar bolt and disengage the air pump drive belt.
4. Remove the air pump mounting bolt and remove the air pump.
   To install:
5. Position the pump on the mounting bracket and loosely install the attaching and adjusting bolts.
6. Install the air pump drive belt.
7. Adjust the air pump belt tension and tighten the mounting and adjusting bolts.
8. Connect the inlet and outlet lines to the air pump.
9. Install the battery, alternator and alternator drive belt. Adjust the drive belt tension.

Air Pump Check Valve

1. Disconnect the air hose from the check valve.
2. Unscrew the check valve from the air manifold.
   To install:
3. Screw the check valve into the air manifold. Tighten the check valve to 20 ft. lbs.
4. Connect the air hose to the check valve.

Air Manifold

1,796cc AND 1,970cc ENGINES

1. Remove the check valve.
2. Loosen the nuts securing the manifold to the cylinder head. Remove the nozzles from the manifold by removing the attaching nuts from the nozzles.
3. Unbolt and remove the manifold.

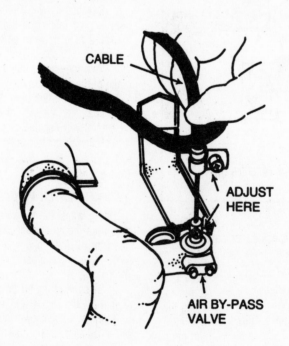

CABLE

ADJUST HERE

AIR BY-PASS VALVE

Fig. 10 View of the adjustment points on the air bypass valve for 1972–74 trucks

To install:

4. Install the nozzles in the manifold. Torque the nuts to 20 ft. lbs.

5. Install the manifold and torque the nuts to 15 ft. lbs.

6. Install the check valve.

Air Injection Nozzle

1,796cc AND 1,970cc ENGINES

1. Disconnect the air line from the check valve.

2. Remove the nozzles from the manifold by unscrewing the nuts.

3. Remove the heat stove from the exhaust manifold.

4. Remove the nozzles.

To install:

5. Install the nozzles. Torque the nuts to 20 ft. lbs.

6. Install the heat stove on the exhaust manifold.

7. Connect the air line to the manifold check valve.

Air Bypass Valve

1972–74 VEHICLES

1. Loosen the cable attaching screws at the valve plunger and cable retaining bracket.

2. Pull the cable out of the valve.

3. Unscrew and remove the valve from the mounting bracket.

To install:

4. Install the valve on the mounting bracket.

5. Push the choke knob all the way in.

6. Insert the end of the cable in the valve plunger and tighten the retaining screw.

7. Pull the cable to remove all slack between the plunger and cable bracket. Tighten the cable retaining screw at the bracket.

Deceleration Control System

The deceleration control system is designed to maintain a balance air/fuel mixture during periods of engine deceleration. Although the components used vary in some years, the basic theory remains the same: To more thoroughly burn or dilute the initial rich mixture formed when throttle is suddenly closed, and to smooth out the transition to a lean mixture by enriching the mixture slightly after the throttle has closed. Although the process may seem contradictory, they act in sequence to provide an overall ideal mixture.

The 1972 49 States and Canada Mazdas use a vacuum control valve, an accelerator switch, a servo diaphragm, and a set of spark retard points in the distributor. The vacuum control valve controls spark retard, through the ignition points, and throttle opening through the servo diaphragm, and a set of spark retard points in the distributor. The vacuum control valve controls spark retard, through the ignition points, and throttle opening through the servo diaphragm. During deceleration, the vacuum control valve applies vacuum to the servo diaphragm, slightly opening the primary throttle plate to admit additional fuel to the lean mixture. At the same time, it activates the retard points through a vacuum switch. At idle, the accelerator switch activates the retard points; above idle speed, the accelerator switch is off and the standard point set is used.

1972 Mazdas sold in California, and all 1973–74 Mazdas use

an anti-afterburn valve, and a coasting richer valve on the carburetor which is controlled by three switches: speedometer, accelerator, and clutch. 1975–76 Mazdas use the same system, but the clutch switch is not used. The anti-afterburn valve has a diaphragm controlled engine vacuum. During deceleration, the diaphragm lifts allow the air pump to inject air into the intake manifold. This dilutes the incoming rich mixture, preventing detonation in the exhaust system, which would occur if the injected air from the air pump were to burn this rich mixture in the exhaust manifold. The coasting richer valve acts to add additional fuel to the lean intake mixture as soon as the anti-afterburn valve has shut off. The speed, accelerator and clutch switches must be closed to allow the coasting richer valve to operate. The accelerator switch closes when the accelerator pedal is released. The speedometer switch closes when the truck speed is above 17–23 mph. The clutch switch, used from 1972–74, is closed when the clutch pedal is released.

1977–78 1,796cc 49 States and Canada Mazdas use an air bypass valve, a carburetor dashpot, and a throttle opener system comprised of a servo diaphragm connected to the throttle and a vacuum control valve. This is essentially the same as the 1972 49 States model. The air by-pass valve prevents afterburn in the exhaust by shutting off air to the exhaust manifold from the air pump during deceleration. The dashpot holds the throttle open slightly for an instant during sudden deceleration. The throttle opener system is the same as that used in the 1972 49 States models.

1977–78 California Mazdas use an anti-afterburn valve and a throttle opener system. The anti-afterburn valve is the same as that used from 1973–76, and the throttle opener is the same as that used in 1977–78 49 States models.

1979 and later 1,970cc 49 States models use an anti-afterburn valve and a throttle positioner. California models have an air by-pass valve and a throttle positioner. Canadian models have an air by-pass valve, a dashpot, and a throttle positioner.

On 1974 models with automatic transmission, a kick-down control system is used. Regardless of the gear selected, the transmission will not go above Second gear when the choke knob is pulled out.

TESTING

Combination Anti-Afterburn and Coasting Valve

1974 VEHICLES

1. Disconnect the hose which runs from the air cleaner to the combination valve at the air cleaner end.

2. Start the engine and run it at curb idle.

3. There should be no vacuum present at the end of the hose which you disconnect in Step 1.

4. Turn the engine off.

5. Disconnect the hose which runs from the coasting valve portion of the combination valve to the intake manifold from the coasting valve end and plug up the port.

6. Operate the engine at idle.

7. Disconnect the anti-afterburn valve solenoid connector.

8. Check for vacuum at the end of the hose which you disconnect in Step 1; there should be vacuum present. If not, the anti-afterburn valve is defective.

9. Turn the engine off. Reconnect the anti-afterburn valve electrical leads and the hose to the coasting valve.

10. Disconnect the intake manifold-to-anti-afterburn valve vacuum line at the valve end, and plug the vacuum fitting on the valve.

11. Start the engine and allow it to idle.

12. Disconnect the coasting valve solenoid at the multiconnector.

13. Hold your hand over the end of the vacuum line which you disconnected in Step 10. Vacuum should be felt; if not, replace the defective coasting valve.

14. Turn the engine off and reconnect the leads and hoses which were disconnected above.

Idle Switch

▶ **See Figure 11**

1. Unfasten the idle switch leads.
2. Connect the test meter to the switch terminals.
3. With the engine at idle, the meter should indicate a complete circuit.
4. Depress the plunger on the idle switch; the circuit should be broken (on meter reading). If the idle switch is not functioning properly, replace it with a new one.

Coolant Temperature Switch

1974–75 VEHICLES

➡**Start this test with the coolant temperature below 68°F (20°C).**

1. Disconnect the electrical lead from the temperature switch.
2. Connect a test light between one terminal of the switch and a 12v battery. Ground the other terminal.
3. The test light should light.
4. Start the engine and allow it to warm up. Once the engine reaches normal operating temperature, the test light should go out.
5. Replace the switch if it doesn't work as outlined.

Choke Switch (Semi-Automatic Choke)

1. Working underneath the instrument panel, disconnect the lead at the back of the choke switch.

2. Connect an ohmmeter to the terminals on the choke switch side of the connector.

3. With the choke knob on (off), the meter should show continuity (resistance reading).

4. Pull the choke knob out, about ½" for manual transmission trucks or 1" for automatics. The meter should show no continuity (read zero).

5. Replace the switch if defective.

Anti-Afterburn Valve

▶ **See Figure 12**

1. Remove the outlet hose from the anti-afterburn valve.

2. Hold a hand over the outlet fitting and raise the engine rpm. Quickly release the accelerator. Air should flow for approximately three seconds. If the valve passes air for more than three seconds, or does not pass air at all, it should be replaced.

Coasting Richer Valve (Deceleration Valve)

▶ **See Figure 13**

1. Remove the coasting richer valve from the carburetor.
2. Connect the coasting richer valve to the battery.
3. As power is applied to the valve, the solenoid plunger should be pulled into the valve body.
4. Reinstall the coasting richer valve. Connect a test light.
5. Raise the rear wheels and support the truck on stands. Block the front wheels.
6. Start the engine and raise the engine speed above 30 mph. Release the accelerator pedal. The test light should come ON and remain ON until the speed falls below 17–23 mph.
7. If the system is operating properly, no further tests are required. If not, proceed with the other tests.
8. Remove the stands and lower the truck. Disconnect the test light.

Clutch Switch

The clutch switch is activated by the clutch pedal. When checking the circuit, the test light should be ON when the clutch pedal is fully released, and should be OFF when the clutch pedal is fully depressed.

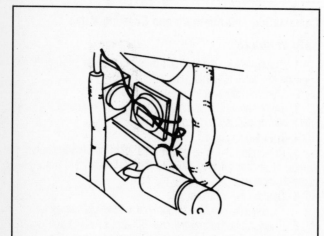

Fig. 11 View of the idle switch (arrow), located on the carburetor

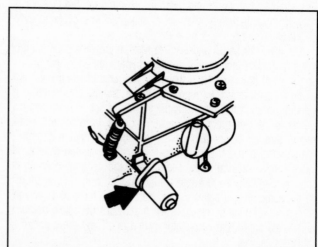

Fig. 12 View of the anti-afterburn valve, located on the intake manifold

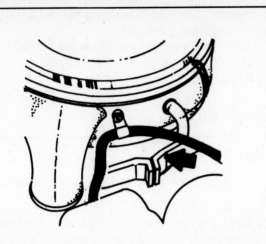

Fig. 13 View of the coasting richer valve, located on the carburetor

Accelerator Switch

▶ See Figure 14

The accelerator switch is actuated by a throttle lever link on the carburetor through 1978; the switch is located on the accelerator pedal on 1979 and later models. When checking the switch with a circuit tester, the test light should be ON when the accelerator pedal is fully released and should be OFF when the pedal is depressed.

Speed Switch

1. Remove the instrument cluster and attach a test light to the speedometer switch.
2. Reconnect the speedometer cable and ground wire.

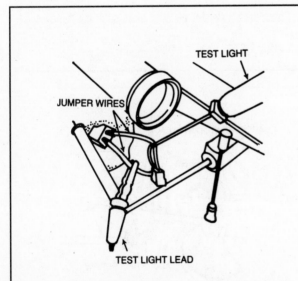

Fig. 14 Checking the accelerator switch with a test light—on 1972–78 trucks, the switch is located on the carburetor; on 1979 and later trucks, the switch is located on the arm of the accelerator pedal

3. Raise both wheels off the ground and support the truck on stands. Block the front wheels.
4. Start the engine.
5. Depress the accelerator pedal to accelerate the engine and confirm that the speed switch is ON at speeds of 17–23 mph and OFF at speeds below 17–23 mph.
6. If not, replace the switch.
7. Lower the truck and remove the test light. Reinstall the instrument cluster.

Speed Switch Relay

Check the speed switch relay with a test light to be sure that it is operating at 17–23 mph.

Three-Way Solenoid Valve

▶ See Figures 15 and 16

1,970cc ENGINES

1. Start the engine and allow it to reach normal operating temperature. Check the idle speed and adjust as necessary.

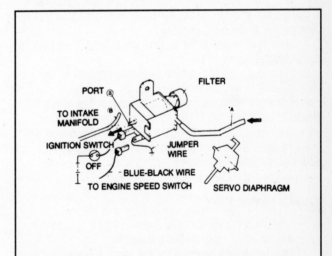

Fig. 15 Three-way solenoid valve check—with ignition switch OFF

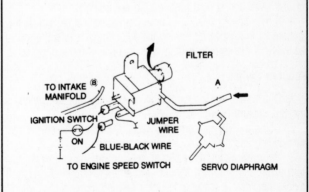

Fig. 16 Three-way solenoid valve check—with ignition switch ON

2. Disconnect the wire at the three way solenoid valve. This wire is coded either black with a white stripe or brown with a red stripe on some models.

3. When the wire is disconnected, the engine speed should increase to 1,000 rpm for 49 States trucks, or 1,100 rpm for California models.

4. If the engine speed does not increase, the three way solenoid valve or the servo diaphragm is not operating correctly. Check the servo diaphragm using the following procedure; if the servo diaphragm is operating correctly, the three way valve is faulty and should be replaced.

Servo Diaphragm

1. Start the engine and set the idle speed to specification.

2. Stop the engine and disconnect the vacuum line between the vacuum control valve and the diaphragm at the diaphragm.

3. Disconnect the vacuum line between the intake manifold and the vacuum control valve at the manifold on models through 1978. On 1979 and later models, disconnect the vacuum hose at the vacuum amplifier and the vacuum hose at the three way solenoid valve. Connect the vacuum hose from the servo diaphragm to the vacuum amplifier so that the intake manifold vacuum is applied directly to the servo diaphragm.

4. Disconnect and plug the vacuum line between the carburetor and distributor.

5. Connect a vacuum line from the intake manifold to the servo diaphragm on models through 1978.

6. Connect a tachometer and start the engine. The engine should idle at 1,300–1,500 rpm for models through 1978, or 900–1,100 rpm, 1979 (1,000–1,200 rpm for 1979 and later California models). If the engine speed is not correct, adjust by means of the servo diaphragm adjusting screw. If the correct speed is not obtainable, replace the diaphragm.

Vacuum Control Valve

1. Disconnect the vacuum hose between the vacuum control valve and the intake manifold at the manifold.

2. Attach a vacuum gauge in the line using a T-fitting.

3. Connect a tachometer to the engine. Start the engine and raise the speed to 3,000 rpm, then suddenly release the throttle. The vacuum reading should rise above 21.3 in.Hg, drop to that figure and hesitate there for one or two seconds, then drop to the normal idle vacuum of 16–18 in.Hg. Note that these readings are for sea level, and should be corrected accordingly.

4. If the vacuum reading is not within specification, adjust the vacuum control valve by turning the adjusting screw in the top of the valve. If the correct reading is unobtainable, replace the valve.

Vacuum Switch

1. Disconnect the vacuum hose between the vacuum switch and the vacuum control valve.

2. Using a T-fitting, connect a vacuum gauge between the vacuum switch and an external vacuum source.

3. Raise the vacuum reading above 8 in.Hg, then allow the vacuum to drop. The switch should click at approximately 6 in.Hg. If it does not, or if it clicks at a higher reading, replace the switch.

Air Bypass Valve

1. Disconnect the air hose from the side of the air by-pass valve.

2. Connect a tachometer to the engine. Start the engine and raise the speed above 2,000 rpm.

3. Release the throttle and check for air flow from the port on the side of the air by-pass valve. If there is no airflow, replace the valve.

ADJUSTMENTS

Dashpot

1. Check the engine idle speed and mixture, and adjust as necessary.

2. Remove the air cleaner.

3. With the tachometer still connected to the engine, loosen the dashpot locknut. Move the throttle lever and hold to maintain the engine speed at 2,400–2,600 rpm (2,100–2,300 rpm for California trucks).

4. Turn the dashpot until its rod contacts the throttle lever and tighten the locknut.

5. Move the throttle lever until it contacts the dashpot rod and recheck the engine speed. Repeat the adjustment if necessary.

Accelerator Switch
▶ **See Figure 17**

1972–78 VEHICLES

1. Be sure that the throttle valve is fully closed.

2. Loosen the switch adjusting screw and turn the switch off.

3. Gradually tighten the adjusting screw until the switch produces a clicking sound and is turned on.

4. Tighten the adjusting screw another 1½ turns.

1979 AND LATER VEHICLES

The accelerator switch is mounted on the arm of the accelerator pedal.

1. Check the accelerator pedal to make sure that it moves freely.

2. Loosen the accelerator switch locknut.

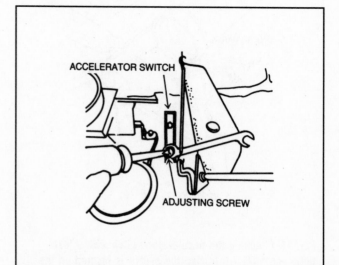

Fig. 17 Adjusting the accelerator switch

3. Gradually turn the adjusting screw until the accelerator switch clicks.

4. Tighten the locknut.

Idle Switch

1. Warm up the engine until the water temperature is at least 156°F (69°C).

2. Make sure that the mixture and idle speed are properly adjusted.

3. Adjust the idle speed to 1,075–1,100 rpm on models with manual transmission; 1,200–1,300 rpm on models with automatic transmission, by rotating the throttle adjusting screw.

4. Rotate the idle switch adjusting screw until the switch changes from OFF to ON position.

5. Slowly turn the idle switch adjusting screw back to the point where the switch just changes from ON to OFF.

6. Turn the throttle screw back so that the engine returns to idle.

➡Be sure that the idle switch goes on when the idle speed is still above 1,000 rpm.

REMOVAL & INSTALLATION

Speed Switch

The speed switch is integral with the speedometer head located in the instrument panel. To replace the speed switch, refer to Instrument Cluster Removal and Installation in Section 6.

Anti-Afterburn Valve

1. Remove the air cleaner assembly.
2. Disconnect the air hoses and vacuum lines from the valve.
3. Unfasten the solenoid wiring.
4. Remove the securing nuts and withdraw the valve.
5. Installation is performed in the reverse order of removal.

Coasting Valve

The coasting valve is removed and installed in the same manner as the anti-afterburn valve.

Idle Switch

1. Remove the coasting valve. See the section above.
2. Remove the carburetor as detailed in section 5.
3. Disconnect the wiring from the switch.
4. Unfasten the securing screws and remove the switch.
5. Installation is performed in the reverse order of removal. After installing the switch, adjust it as outlinedpreviously.

Air Supply Valve

1. Remove the air cleaner and the hot air duct.
2. Disconnect the air hose, the vacuum lines, and the solenoid wiring from the valve.
3. Unfasten the screws which secure the valve and remove it.
4. Air supply valve installation is performed in the reverse order of removal.

Coolant Temperature Switch

1. Drain the coolant from the radiator enough to bring the coolant level below the temperature switch.

✳✳ CAUTION

When draining engine coolant, keep in mind that cats and dogs are attracted to ethylene glycol antifreeze and could drink any that is left in an uncovered container or in puddles on the ground. This will prove fatal in sufficient quantity. Always drain coolant into a sealable container. Coolant should be reused unless it is contaminated or is several years old.

2. Remove the alternator and drive belt if they are in the way.
3. Disconnect the switch multiconnector.
4. Use an open-end wrench to remove the switch.
5. Installation is the reverse of removal.

Exhaust Gas Recirculation System

⬥ See Figures 18 and 18a

Oxides of nitrogen are formed under conditions of high temperatures and high pressure. By eliminating one of these conditions, the production of NOx is restricted. The exhaust gas recirculation system (EGR) reintroduces a small portion of the exhaust gases into the combustion chamber with the intake charge, thus reducing spark combustion temperature. The EGR system is used on 1976 Mazdas, and all 1977 and later trucks.

Components used through 1978 include an EGR control valve, a three-way solenoid valve, a vacuum amplifier, and a water thermo switch. The control valve, operated by engine vacuum, opens to allow exhaust gases into the intake manifold, and closes to shut them off. The solenoid valve regulates vacuum to the EGR valve, It is governed by the thermo switch. At coolant temperatures below 122°F (50°C)—131°F (55°C) for 1976 only—the thermo switch is closed. This closes the vacuum passage in the solenoid valve, cutting vacuum to the control valve which prevents exhaust recirculation when the engine is cold. At temperatures above 131°F (55°C), the thermo switch opens, allowing intake manifold vacuum to raise the control valve diaphragm, allowing recirculation of exhaust gases. The vacuum amplifier supplies varying amounts of vacuum to the control valve through the solenoid valve, opening or closing it during acceleration or at varying engine speeds.

A slightly different EGR system is used on 1979 and later models. Components include the EGR valve, a water thermo valve, and a vacuum amplifier. The three-way solenoid valve is used on 2.0 liter engines only. The EGR valve is the same vacuum operated unit used in earlier years, and operates in the same manner. The water thermo valve controls the EGR valve, except on California models; on California models, the thermo valve actuates the No. 2 relief valve in the air control valve, and the air control valve regulates the EGR vacuum signal. The thermo valve is closed when coolant temperatures are below 115°F (46°C). Above that temperature, the valve opens, allowing vacuum to be transmitted to the EGR valve. The vacuum amplifier performs the same function as in earlier years.

➡**1,970 Mazdas sold in California (1979–80) have two water thermo valves. One is for the EGR system and the other is for the Spark Timing Control System. The thermo valve used in the EGR system has two vacuum hoses; one runs to the vacuum amplifier, and the other runs to the EGR valve.**

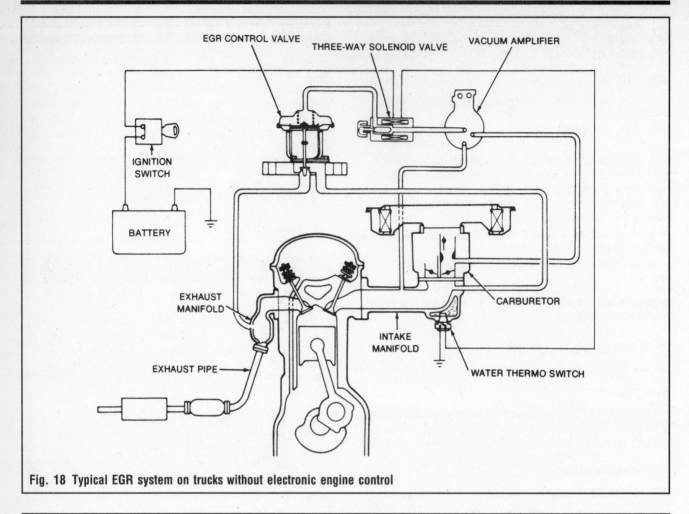

EGR CONTROL VALVE THREE-WAY SOLENOID VALVE VACUUM AMPLIFIER

IGNITION SWITCH

BATTERY

EXHAUST MANIFOLD

EXHAUST PIPE

INTAKE MANIFOLD

CARBURETOR

WATER THERMO SWITCH

Fig. 18 Typical EGR system on trucks without electronic engine control

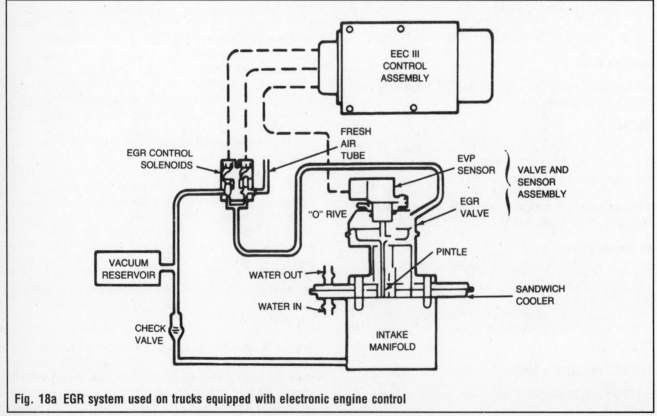

EEC III CONTROL ASSEMBLY

EGR CONTROL SOLENOIDS

FRESH AIR TUBE

EVP SENSOR

VALVE AND SENSOR ASSEMBLY

EGR VALVE

"O" RIVE

VACUUM RESERVOIR

WATER OUT

WATER IN

PINTLE

SANDWICH COOLER

CHECK VALVE

INTAKE MANIFOLD

Fig. 18a EGR system used on trucks equipped with electronic engine control

EGR CONTROL VALVE TEST

▶ **See Figure 19**

1. Start the engine and allow it to idle.

2. On 1976 trucks, disconnect the vacuum hose from the EGR valve. Disconnect the intake manifold vacuum hose from the vacuum amplifier, and connect it to the EGR valve.

3. On 1977–78 trucks, disconnect the vacuum hose which runs from the EGR valve to the three-way solenoid valve at the solenoid valve. Disconnect the intake manifold vacuum hose at the manifold, and connect the EGR valve vacuum hose to the intake manifold fitting.

4. On 1979 and later models, disconnect the vacuum hose from the water thermo valve. The valve is installed in the intake manifold. Disconnect the intake manifold vacuum hose and connect the EGR valve vacuum hose to the intake manifold vacuum fitting.

5. The engine should stall or idle roughly. If it does not, shut off the engine and remove the EGR valve and pipe from the engine. Clean the passages of the valve and pipe with a brush and a wire. Reinstall the parts and repeat the test.

6. If the test is not successful, replace the EGR valve. When engine stall or idle roughness occurs with the manifold vacuum hose connected to the EGR valve, return the hoses to their original positions.

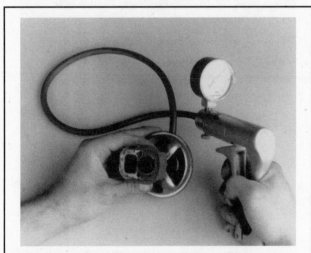

Some EGR valves may be tested using a vacuum pump by watching for diaphragm movement

Example of a thermal vacuum valve

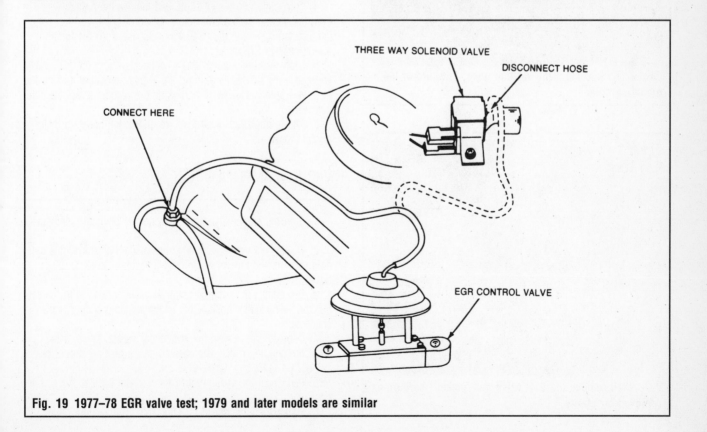

Fig. 19 1977–78 EGR valve test; 1979 and later models are similar

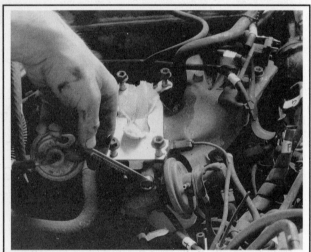

The EGR valve (arrow) is hidden under vacuum lines and can be tough to reach

Disconnect and label the vacuum hose, and loosen the mounting bolts . . .

. . . then remove the EGR valve and gasket—carburetor removed for clarity

THREE-WAY SOLENOID VALVE TEST

1. Disconnect the electrical connectors from the thermo switch. Connect a jumper wire between the connectors to simulate a complete circuit.
2. Turn the ignition switch ON.

A manifold vacuum gauge can be used to check a variety of vacuum-controlled components

3. Disconnect the vacuum hose from the EGR valve and blow into the hose. Air should be discharged from the three-way solenoid valve relief port. If it is not, replace the three-way valve.
4. Turn the ignition switch off, and remove the jumper wire from the thermo switch connectors. Disconnect the vacuum amplifier vacuum line from the three-way solenoid. Turn the ignition switch back to ON.
5. Blow into the vacuum line disconnected from the EGR valve, and check for air discharge from the vacuum amplifier port on the three-way solenoid valve. If there is no discharge, replace the solenoid valve.
6. After completion of all tests, reconnect the hoses to their original locations.

VACUUM AMPLIFIER TEST

1. Start the engine and warm it to normal operating temperature.
2. Disconnect the vacuum amplifier vacuum hose from the solenoid valve or thermo valve. Connect a vacuum gauge to this hose.
3. Disconnect the vacuum amplifier vacuum hose from the carburetor. The vacuum hose to the intake manifold should remain connected.
4. Depress and release the accelerator several times, then allow the engine to idle. The vacuum gauge reading should be 2.0 ± .04 in.Hg.
5. Reconnect the vacuum amplifier vacuum hose to the carburetor.
6. Increase engine speed to 3,500 rpm. The vacuum gauge

reading should be 3.54 in.Hg. If the vacuum amplifier does not test properly, replace it.

7. After all tests are completed, return the hoses to their original positions.

WATER THERMO VALVE TEST

1. Drain the cooling system until the coolant level is below the intake manifold. Remove the water thermo valve from the manifold.

✳✳ CAUTION

When draining engine coolant, keep in mind that cats and dogs are attracted to ethylene glycol antifreeze and could drink any that is left in an uncovered container or in puddles on the ground. This will prove fatal in sufficient quantity. Always drain coolant into a sealable container. Coolant should be reused unless it is contaminated or is several years old.

2. Place a valve in a container of water. Attach a length of vacuum hose to each of the two fittings.

3. Gradually heat the water while observing the temperature.

4. By blowing through one of the vacuum hoses, you will be able to tell when the valve opens. The valve should block the passage of air until the water temperature reaches approximately 115°F (46°C). If this is not the case, the valve is faulty and must be replaced.

EGR Warning Light

RESETTING

1976 Vehicles

1976 Mazdas with EGR are equipped with a maintenance warming light on the instrument panel, which lights every 12,500 miles. The light indicates that the EGR system should be checked for proper operation, using the procedures outlined. The EGR valve should be removed and cleaned every 25,000 miles.

The switch controlling the light is installed behind the speedometer. To reset the switch after the maintenance has been performed, remove the cover from the switch, and move the switch knob to the opposite position.

Catalytic Converter

The 1976 and later trucks sold in California and almost all 1979 and later trucks have a catalytic converter installed in the exhaust system to aid in the reduction of HC and CO emissions. The only exceptions are some 1979–80 models sold in Canada.

The catalytic converter is a muffler-shaped device located between the exhaust manifold and the muffler. It is filled with beads containing platinum and palladium which, through catalytic action, enables the HC and CO gases to be converted into water vapor (H_2O) and carbon dioxide (CO_2). The converter has a warning system (1976 only), consisting of a thermo sensor inserted into the

side of the converter, which monitors temperatures, and a warming light on the instrument panel which lights when the sensor detects converter temperatures exceeding 1,742°F (950°C). The converter should be inspected periodically for cracks, corrosion, and any signs of external burning, and replaced as required.

WARNING SYSTEM TEST

1976 Vehicles

1. Turn the ignition switch ON. The warning light on the instrument panel should light. Start the engine. The warning light should go off.

2. If the light does not light, check the bulb. If burned out, replace and retest the system.

3. If the light does not go out after the engine has started, shut off the engine and tilt the seatback forward.

4. Disconnect the thermo sensor wire electrical connectors.

5. Using an ohmmeter, check the thermo sensor circuit for continuity, on the sensor side of the wiring. If there is no continuity, replace the sensor. Reconnect the wires and repeat the test.

REMOVAL & INSTALLATION

1. Raise the truck and support it on safety stands.

✳✳ CAUTION

Be very careful when working on or near the converter. External temperatures can reach 1,500°F (815°C) and more, causing severe burns. Removal or installation should only be performed on a cold exhaust system.

2. Loosen the nut and remove the thermo sensor from the side of the converter (1976 models).

3. Remove the front and rear flange attaching nuts.

4. Remove the nut and rubber support which secures the converter bracket, and remove the converter.

5. Installation is the reverse of removal.

Oxygen Sensor

The oxygen sensor monitors the density of the oxygen in the exhaust gas. The sensor consists of a closed-end tube made of ceramic zirconia and other components. Porous platinum electrodes cover the tubes inner and outer surfaces. The tubes outer surface is exposed to the exhaust gases in the exhaust manifold, while its inner surface is exposed to normal air.

REMOVAL & INSTALLATION

The oxygen sensor is installed in the exhaust manifold and is removed in the same manner as a spark plug. Always remove electrical connection before trying to remove the sensor. Exercise care when handling the sensor do not drop or handle the sensor roughly; the electrical connector and louvered end must be kept free of grease and dirt. If a anti-seize compound is used in installation, make sure to coat just the threads of the sensor and care

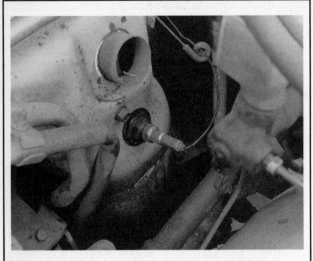

Disconnect the wire leading to the oxygen sensor . . .

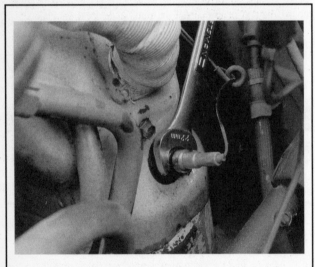

. . . then loosen and remove the sensor

should be used not to get compound on the sensor itself. You should disconnect the negative battery cable when servicing the oxygen sensor.

Spark Timing Control System

A spark delay system is used on 1977–78 1,796cc engines, and 1979 and later 1,970cc engines. Its purpose is to reduce the formation of CO and NO_2 emissions by delaying the vacuum advance to the distributor during normal acceleration. The system consists of a spark delay valve installed in the vacuum hose between the carburetor and the distributor vacuum advance diaphragm, on all 1977–78 models, as well as 1979 and later 49 States models. The spark delay valve is installed in the vacuum line between the water thermo valve and the distributor diaphragm on 1979 and later models sold in California. The water thermo valve is installed in the intake manifold. The spark delay valve has an internal restrictor to slow the air flow in one direction and a check valve which allows air to flow freely in the opposite direction.

SYSTEM TESTING

▶ **See Figure 20**

1. Remove the air cleaner. Disconnect the vacuum hose from the distributor.
2. On 1977–78 models, disconnect the vacuum control valve hose at the intake manifold fitting, and install the distributor hose on that fitting. On 1979 and later 49 States models, disconnect the anti-afterburn valve line at the intake manifold fitting and install the distributor vacuum line to the intake manifold fitting. On 1979 and later California models, disconnect the air bypass valve hose from the intake manifold fitting and install the distributor vacuum line to the intake manifold fitting.
3. Remove the vacuum hose from the carburetor side of the spark delay valve. Plug this hose, and attach a vacuum gauge to the delay valve.
4. Start the engine and allow it to idle.
5. Disconnect the vacuum hose from the intake manifold fitting (the hose from the spark delay valve to the distributor which has been connected to the intake manifold in Step 2) and note the time for the vacuum gauge reading to drop to 11.8 in. Hg. It should drop to this figure within 2–7 seconds (1–10 seconds on California models), 1977–78, or 4–6 seconds, 1979 and later. If the reading is not correct, replace the spark delay valve.
6. After all tests have been completed, return the hoses to their original positions.

DISTRIBUTOR SOLENOID VALVE TEST

1. Start the engine and allow it to idle.
2. Separate the connector at the distributor solenoid valve and apply battery power to the terminals to energize the valve.
3. Disconnect the vacuum hose from the vacuum advance unit. There should be no vacuum at the hose.
4. Remove the battery power to the solenoid valve. The valve is operating properly if air is drawn (by vacuum) into the vacuum hose as soon as power is removed.

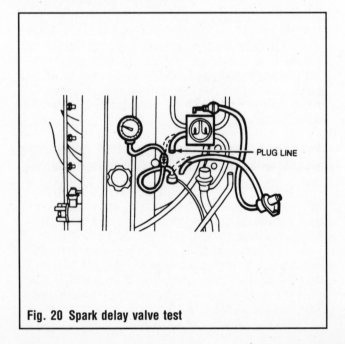

Fig. 20 Spark delay valve test

WATER THERMO SWITCH TEST

1. Remove the switch.
2. Connect an ohmmeter across the switch terminals and place the sensor in water. Heat the water gradually. Using a thermometer check the water temperature as it is heated.
3. Note the temperature at which continuity exists between both poles. The specified temperature is 131°F (55°C). If the temperature is not within specifications, replace the switch.

TIMER TEST

1. Remove the timer.
2. Connect suitable test wires to terminals A, B, and C, respectively.
3. Connect a test wire with a 30KΩ resistor to terminal D.
4. Connect a test wire with a 3.4w lamp to terminal E.
5. Connect the positive test lead of a voltmeter to terminal D and the negative lead to the battery negative terminal.
6. Connect test wires A, D, and E to the positive terminal. Do not connect Terminal B in this step.
7. Connect the wire from terminal C to the battery negative terminal.
8. Check the voltmeter reading. It should read about 6v or above.

9. Connect the test wire from terminal B to the positive battery terminal. At the moment the connection is complete, the voltmeter should read less than 1 volt, and the lamp will light. Maintain this connection for 2 minutes. The voltmeter should read about 8v.

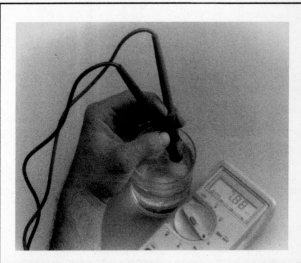

Submerge the end of the temperature sensor in cold or hot water and check resistance

EMISSION CONTROLS—ROTARY ENGINE

Positive Crankcase Ventilation (PCV) System

The positive crankcase ventilation (PCV) valve is located on the intake manifold below the carburetor. In this case, the word "crankcase" is not quite correct, as the Mazda rotary engine has no crankcase in the normal sense of the term. Rather, the valve, which is operated by intake manifold vacuum, is used to meter the flow of fuel and air vapors through the rotor housings.

TESTING AND REPLACEMENT

The procedures for PCV valve testing and replacement may be found under Routine Maintenance, in Section 1.

Air Injection System

The air injection system used on the Mazda rotary engine differs from the type used on a conventional piston engine in two respects:

1. Air is not only supplied to burn the gases in the exhaust ports, but it is also used to cool the thermal reactor.
2. A three-way air control valve is used in place of the conventional anti-backfire and diverter valves. It contains an air cut-out valve, a relief valve, and a safety valve.

Air is supplied to the system by a normal vane type air pump.

The air flows from the pump to the air control valve, where it is routed to the air injection nozzles to cool the thermal reactor or, in the case of a system malfunction, to the air cleaner. A check valve, located beneath the air control valve seat, prevents the back-flow of hot exhaust gases into the air injection system in case of air pressure loss.

Air injection nozzles are used to feed air into the exhaust ports, just as in a conventional piston engine.

TESTING

Air Pump

♦ **See Figure 21**

1. Check the air pump drive belt tension by applying 22 lbs. of pressure halfway between the water pump and air pump pulleys. The belt should deflect 6–9mm (0.236–0.354 in.). Adjust the belt if necessary, or replace it if it is cracked or worn.
2. Turn the pump by hand. If it has seized, the drive belt will slip, producing noise.

➡**Disregard any chirping squealing, or rolling sounds coming from inside the pump; these are normal when it is being turned by hand.**

3. Check the hoses and connections for leaks. Hissing or a blast of air is indicative of a leak. Soapy water, applied around the area in question, is a good method of detecting leaks.
4. Connect a pressure gauge between the air pump and the air control valve with a T-fitting.

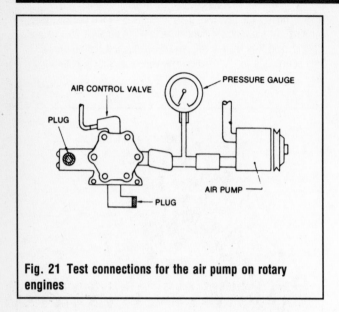

Fig. 21 Test connections for the air pump on rotary engines

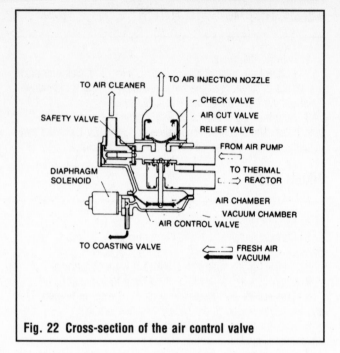

Fig. 22 Cross-section of the air control valve

5. Plug the other hose connections (outlets) on the air control valve, as illustrated.

❋❋ CAUTION

Be careful not to touch the thermal reactor; severe burns will result.

6. With the engine at normal idle speed, the pressure gauge should read 0.48–0.68 psi. Replace the air pump if it is less than this.
7. If the air pump is not defective, leave the pressure gauge connected but unplug the connections at the air control valve and proceed with the next test.

Air Control Valve

♦ **See Figures 22 and 23**

❋❋ CAUTION

When testing the air control valve, avoid touching the thermal reactor as severe burns will result.

1. Test the air control valve solenoid as follows:
   a. Turn the ignition switch off and on. A click should be heard coming from the solenoid. If no sound is audible, check the solenoid wiring.
   b. If no defect is found in the solenoid wiring, connect the solenoid directly to the truck's battery. If the solenoid still does not click, it is defective and must be replaced. If the solenoid works, then check the components of the air flow control system. See below.
2. Start the engine and run it at idle speed. The pressure gauge should still read 0.37–0.75 psi. No air should leak from the two outlets which were unplugged.
3. Increase the engine speed to 3,500 rpm for manual transmissions; 3,000 rpm for automatic transmissions. The pressure gauge should now read 1.2–2.8 psi and the two outlets still should not be leaking air.

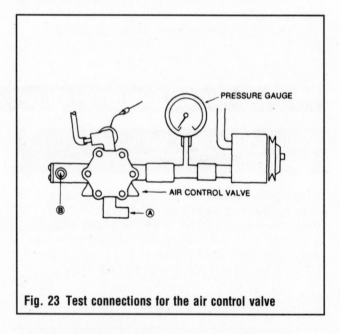

Fig. 23 Test connections for the air control valve

4. Return the engine to idle.
5. Disconnect the solenoid wiring. Air should now flow from the outlet marked A in the illustration, but not from the outlet marked B. The pressure gauge reading should remain the same as in Step 2.
6. Reconnect the solenoid.
7. If the relief valve is faulty, air sent from the air pump will flow into the cooling passages of the thermal reactor when the engine is at idle speed.
8. If the safety valve is faulty, air will flow into the air cleaner when the engine is idling.
9. Replace the air control valve if it fails to pass any one of the above tests. Remember to disconnect the pressure gauge.

Check Valve

▶ **See Figure 24**

1. Remove the check valve, as detailed below.
2. Depress the valve plate to see if it will seat properly.
3. Measure the free length of the valve spring; it should be 31mm (1.22 in.) on trucks with manual transmission; 19mm (0.748 in.) on trucks with automatic transmission.
4. Measure the installed length of the spring; it should be 17mm (0.669 in.). Replace the check valve if it is not up to specifications.

REMOVAL & INSTALLATION

Air Pump

1. Remove the air cleaner assembly from the carburetor.
2. Loosen, but do not remove, the adjusting link bolt.

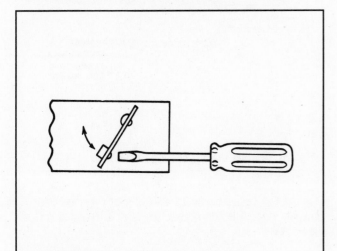

Fig. 24 Check the one-way valve operation, as illustrated

3. Push the pump toward the engine to slacken belt tension and remove drive belt.
4. Disconnect the air supply hoses from the pump.
5. Unfasten the pump securing bolts and remove the pump.

✲✲ WARNING

Do not pry on the air pump housing during removal and do not clamp the housing in a vise once the pump has been removed. Any type of heavy pressure applied to the housing will distort it.

6. Installation is performed in the reverse order of removal. Adjust the belt tension by moving the air pump to the specification given in the Testing section, above.

Air Control Valve

✲✲ CAUTION

Remove the air control valve only after the thermal reactor has cooled sufficiently to prevent the danger of a serious burn.

1. Remove the air cleaner assembly.
2. Unfasten the leads from the air control valve solenoid.
3. Disconnect the air hoses from the valve.
4. Loosen the screws which secure the air control valve and remove the valve.
5. Valve installation is performed in the reverse order of removal.

Check Valve

1. Perform the air control valve removal procedure, detailed above. Be sure to pay attention to the CAUTION.
2. Remove the check valve seat.
3. Withdraw the valve plate and spring.
4. Install the check valve in the reverse order of removal.

Air Injection System Diagnosis Chart

Problem	Cause	Cure
Noisy drive belt	Loose belt	Tighten belt
	Seized pump	Replace pump
Noisy pump	Leaking hose	Find and fix leak
	Loose hose	Tighten clamp
	Hose rubbing	Reposition
	Air control valve failure	Replace
	Check valve failure	Replace
	Pump mounting loose	Tighten mounting bolts
	Defective pump	Replace
No air supply	Loose belt	Tighten belt
	Leaking hose	Find and fix leak
	Air control valve failure	Replace
	Check valve failure	Replace
	Defective pump	Replace
Exhaust backfire	Vacuum or air leaks	Find and fix
	Air control valve failure	Replace
	Sticking choke	Repair
	Choke setting too rich	Adjust

Air Injection Nozzle

1. Remove the gravel shield from underneath the truck.
2. Perform the oil pan removal procedure as detailed in "Engine Lubrication," above.
3. Unbolt the air injection nozzles from both of the rotor housings.
4. Nozzle installation is performed in the reverse order of removal.

Altitude Compensator

▶ **See Figure 25**

1974–75 Rotary Pick-Ups have an altitude compensator which provides air to lean out the overly rich mixture which occurs at high altitudes.

TESTING

1. Detach the air intake hose from the altitude compensator.
2. Start the engine and run it at idle.
3. Hold your finger over the altitude compensator air intake; the engine speed should decrease. If it doesn't, replace the compensator.
4. Reconnect the air intake hose, if the compensator is in good working order.

REMOVAL & INSTALLATION

1. Disconnect both hoses from the altitude compensator. Be sure to note their positions for correct hook-up.
2. Unfasten the altitude compensator securing bolts.
3. Remove the compensator from its bracket.
4. Installation is the reverse of removal.

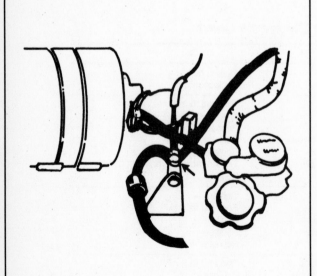

Fig. 25 Typical altitude compensator (arrow)

Thermal Reactor

▶ **See Figure 26**

A thermal reactor is used in place of a conventional exhaust manifold. It is used to oxidize unburned hydrocarbons and carbon monoxide before they can be released into the atmosphere.

If the engine speed exceeds 4,000 rpm, or if the truck is decelerating, the air control valve diverts air into passages in the thermal reactor housing in order to cool the reactor.

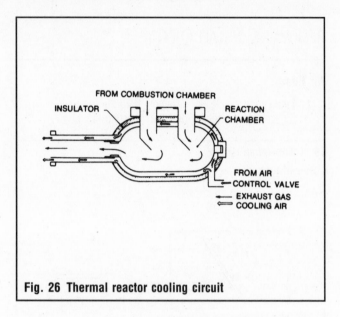

Fig. 26 Thermal reactor cooling circuit

A one-way valve prevents hot exhaust gases from the flowing back into the air injection system. The valve is located at the reactor air intake.

INSPECTION

❊❊ CAUTION

Perform thermal reactor inspection only after the reactor has cooled sufficiently to prevent the danger of being severely burned.

1. Examine the reactor housing for cracks or other signs of damage.
2. Remove the air supply hose from the one-way valve. Insert a screwdriver into the valve and test the butterfly for smooth operation. Replace the valve if necessary.
3. If the valve is functioning properly, connect the hose to it.

➡**Remember to check the components of the air injection system which are related to the thermal reactor.**

REMOVAL & INSTALLATION

Thermal reactor removal and installation are given in the Engine Mechanical section of Section 3.

Airflow Control System

The airflow control system consists of a thermosensor, thermodetector, vacuum switch and a control box.

The system determines when the trailing distributor should be used, depending upon engine temperature and speed (rpm). The airflow control system also operates the solenoid on the airflow control valve.

When the engine is cold, the thermosensor sends a signal to the control box which, in turn, activates the distributor. The thermodetector is used to keep the thermosensor from being influenced by ambient temperatures. This ensures easier cold starting and better drivability. The thermosensor and control box are located, in order, beneath the dash, next to the fuse box, and behind the grille.

TESTING

No. 1 Thermosensor
◆ **See Figure 27**

➡**Begin this test procedure with the engine cold.**

1. Remove the air cleaner.
2. Examine the no. 1 thermosensor, which is located next to the thermostat housing, for leakage around the boot and for signs of wax leakage.
3. Disconnect the multiconnector from the thermosensor and place the prods of an ohmmeter on the thermosensor terminals. The ohmmeter should read over 7kΩ with the engine cold and less than 2.3kΩ after the engine has been warmed up.
4. Replace the thermosensor with a new one, if the reading on the ohmmeter is not within specifications.
5. If the no. 1 thermosensor is functioning properly, proceed with the appropriate test for the thermodetector below.

Thermodetector

Use the following chart to determine the correct ohmmeter reading for the ambient temperature at the time of the test:

Thermodetector Resistence Specifications

Ambient Temperature Degrees F	Resistence K[om] [+ −] 5%
[N−]4	10.0
+32	3.0
+68	1.2
+105	0.5

No. 1 Control Box
◆ **See Figures 28, 29 and 30**

➡**If all of the other components of the airflow control system are functioning properly and the system wiring and vacuum lines are in good condition, then the fault probably lies in the no. 1 control box. Perform the following tests to verify this.**

1. Disconnect the no. 1 thermosensor. Disconnect the idle switch multiconnector.
2. Start the engine and run it to the speeds specified below. The timing light should come on in these speed ranges:
   • Manual Transmission: 3,600–4,400 rpm
   • Automatic Transmission: 4,300–5,300 rpm

➡**These speeds should be held for an instant only.**

3. Connect an ammeter to the air control valve solenoid leads and to ground.

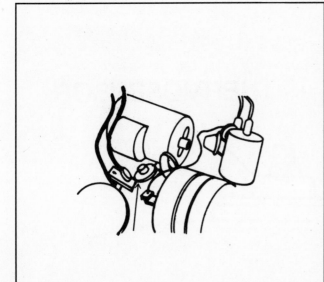

Fig. 27 The No. 1 thermosensor is located next to the thermostat housing

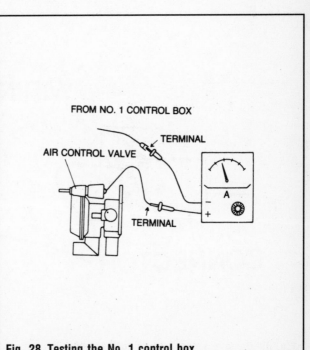

FROM NO. 1 CONTROL BOX

TERMINAL

AIR CONTROL VALVE

TERMINAL

Fig. 28 Testing the No. 1 control box

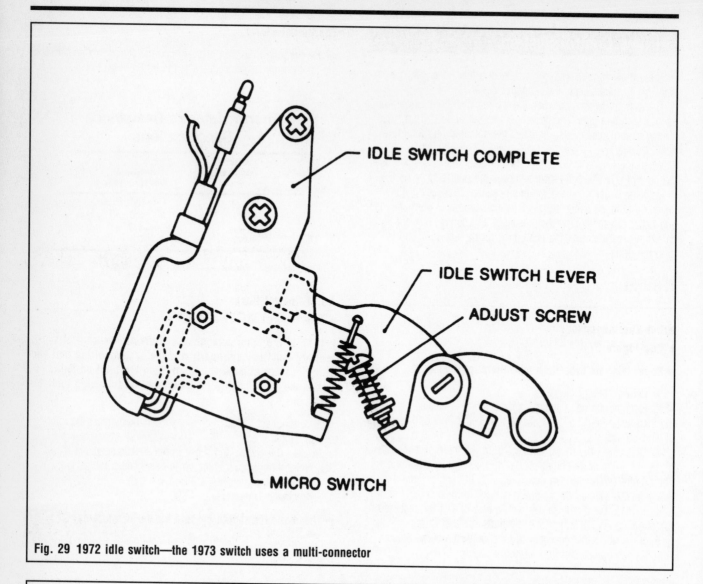

Fig. 29 1972 idle switch—the 1973 switch uses a multi-connector

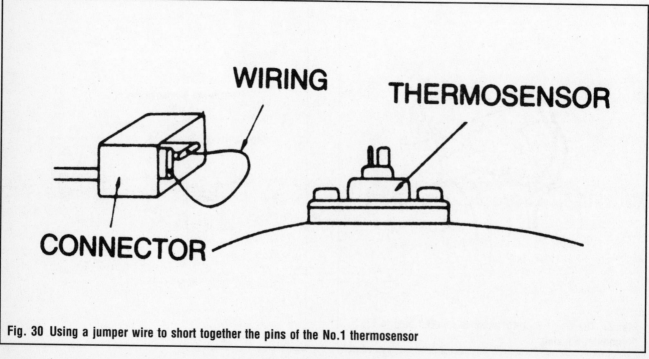

Fig. 30 Using a jumper wire to short together the pins of the No.1 thermosensor

a. Current should flow when the engine speed is between 900–4,000 ± 200 rpm, manual or 7,500–5,200, automatic.

b. Current flow should cease above 3,600–4,400 rpm, manual transmission or 4,300–5,300 rpm, automatic transmission.

4. Short together the pins of the no. 1 thermosensor multiconnector with a jumper wire. Connect the timing light to the trailing side of the distributor, if it is not already in place.

a. The timing light should go on when the engine is below 3,600–4,400 rpm, automatic, or below 4,300–5,200 rpm, manual.

b. On automatic transmission equipped models, connect an ammeter to the air control valve solenoid. Current should flow to the solenoid when the engine speed is below 3,400 ± 200 rpm and should cease flowing above this speed.

5. Remove the jumper wire from the multiconnector and re-connect the No. 1 thermosensor. Reconnect the vacuum switch if it was disconnected.

6. Connect the prods of the ammeter to the coasting valve solenoid terminals.

➡**For a further description of coasting valve operation, see Deceleration Control Systems.**

7. No current should flow to the solenoid with the engine at idle. Increase the engine speed; current should begin flowing between 1,250 and 1,500 rpm. Decrease engine speed; current should cease flowing between 1,300 and 1,100 rpm for manual transmissions; 1,400 rpm for automatic transmissions. If the no. 1 control box proves to be defective, replace it. Remember to disconnect all of the test equipment and reconnect the system components when the tests are completed.

REMOVAL & INSTALLATION

No. 1 Thermosensor

1. Remove the air cleaner assembly.
2. If necessary, remove the starter motor as detailed under Engine Electrical.
3. Unplug the thermosensor multiconnector.
4. Withdraw the boot from the thermosensor.
5. Unfasten its securing nuts and remove the switch.
6. Installation is the reverse of removal.

Control Box

1974–75 VEHICLES

✳✳ WARNING

Be sure that the ignition switch is turned off to prevent damage to the control box!

1. Working from underneath the instrument panel, locate and disconnect the control box multiconnector.
2. Remove the screws which secure the control box.
3. Remove the control box.
4. Installation is performed in the reverse order of removal.

Other Components

Any of the other components used in the airflow control system are removed by unfastening their multiconnectors and removing the screws which secure them.

EMISSION CONTROLS—DIESEL ENGINE

The diesel has only 2 basic emission control systems: a crankcase ventilation system, and a system which maintains a slight vacuum in the intake manifold, known as the Intake Shutter Valve System. The only maintenance required of the crankcase ventilation system is to occasionally check the cleanliness of the inside of the hose.

Intake Shutter Valve System

The intake shutter valve system may require checking of the vacuum it generates and adjustment of the diaphragm that operates the air shutter. To check, remove the plug in the intake manifold. Install an adapter with metric threads in place of the plug, and connect a vacuum gauge. Disconnect the electrical connector at the 3-way valve. Then, start the engine and run it at idle. Now, read the vacuum gauge. It should read approx. 16.92 in.Hg.

If the reading is not correct, adjust the adjusting screw on the shutter valve (located just to the right of the vacuum gauge on the air intake). Then, stop the engine, reconnect the electrical connector, and replace the plug in the intake manifold.

VACUUM DIAGRAMS

Following are vacuum diagrams for most of the engine and emissions package combinations covered by this manual. Because vacuum circuits will vary based on various engine and vehicle options, always refer first to the vehicle emission control information label, if present. Should the label be missing, or should vehicle be equipped with a different engine from the vehicle's original equipment, refer to the diagrams below for the same or similar configuration.

If you wish to obtain a replacement emissions label, most manufacturers make the labels available for purchase. The labels can usually be ordered from a local dealer.

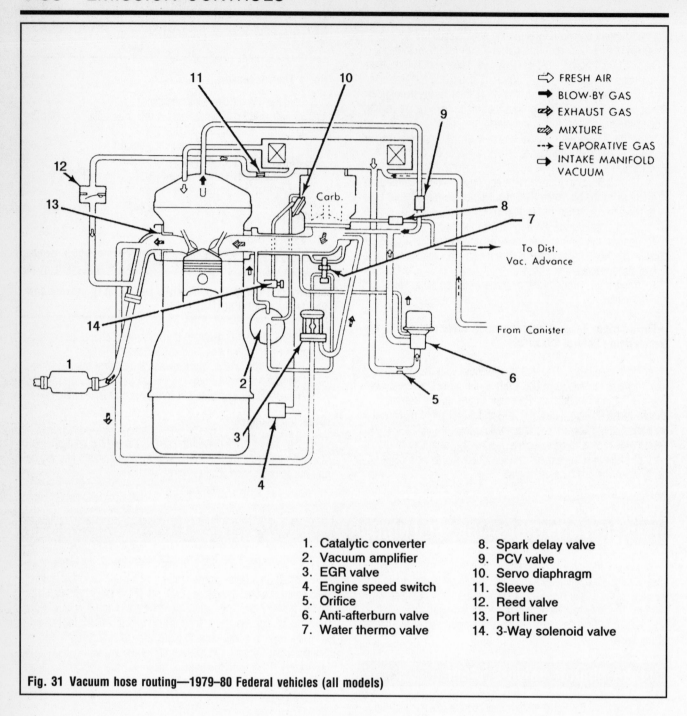

FRESH AIR

BLOW-BY GAS

EXHAUST GAS

MIXTURE

EVAPORATIVE GAS

INTAKE MANIFOLD VACUUM

Carb.

To Dist. Vac. Advance

From Canister

1. Catalytic converter
2. Vacuum amplifier
3. EGR valve
4. Engine speed switch
5. Orifice
6. Anti-afterburn valve
7. Water thermo valve
8. Spark delay valve
9. PCV valve
10. Servo diaphragm
11. Sleeve
12. Reed valve
13. Port liner
14. 3-Way solenoid valve

Fig. 31 Vacuum hose routing—1979–80 Federal vehicles (all models)

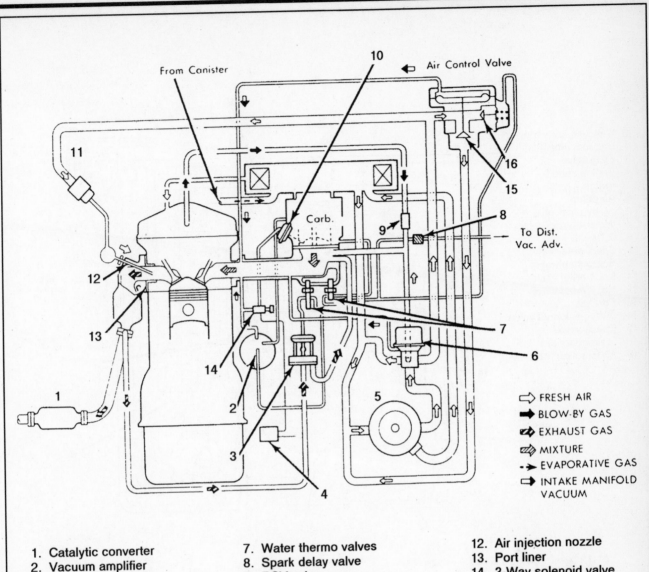

From Canister

10

Air Control Valve

Carb.

To Dist.
Vac. Adv.

⇨ FRESH AIR
➡ BLOW-BY GAS
🖎 EXHAUST GAS
🖎 MIXTURE
⇢ EVAPORATIVE GAS
⇨ INTAKE MANIFOLD
   VACUUM

1. Catalytic converter
2. Vacuum amplifier
3. EGR valve
4. Engine speed switch
5. Air pump
6. Air bypass valve

7. Water thermo valves
8. Spark delay valve
9. PCV valve
10. Servo diaphragm
11. Check valve (secondary air)

12. Air injection nozzle
13. Port liner
14. 3-Way solenoid valve
15. No. 1 relief valve
16. No. 2 relief valve

Fig. 32 Vacuum hose routing—1979 California vehicles (all models)

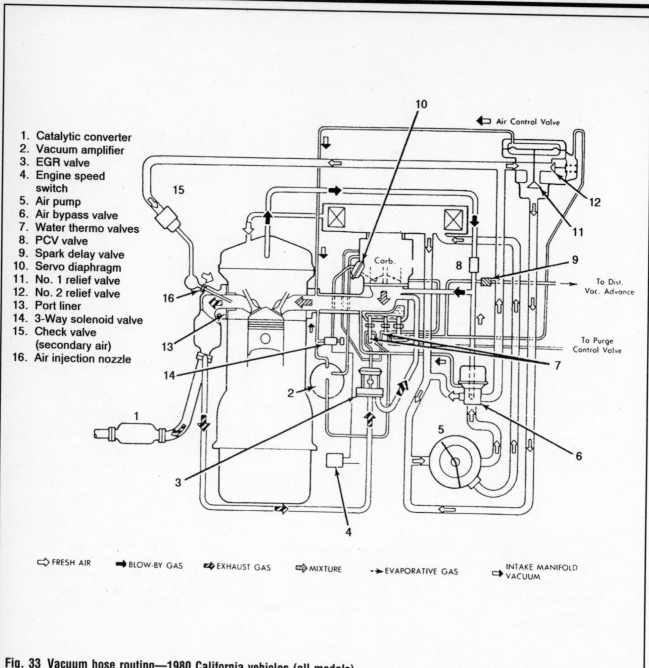

1. Catalytic converter
2. Vacuum amplifier
3. EGR valve
4. Engine speed switch
5. Air pump
6. Air bypass valve
7. Water thermo valves
8. PCV valve
9. Spark delay valve
10. Servo diaphragm
11. No. 1 relief valve
12. No. 2 relief valve
13. Port liner
14. 3-Way solenoid valve
15. Check valve (secondary air)
16. Air injection nozzle

Air Control Valve

Carb.

To Dist. Vac. Advance

To Purge Control Valve

⇨ FRESH AIR   ➡ BLOW-BY GAS   ⇶ EXHAUST GAS   ⇶ MIXTURE   ⇢ EVAPORATIVE GAS   ⇨ INTAKE MANIFOLD VACUUM

Fig. 33 Vacuum hose routing—1980 California vehicles (all models)

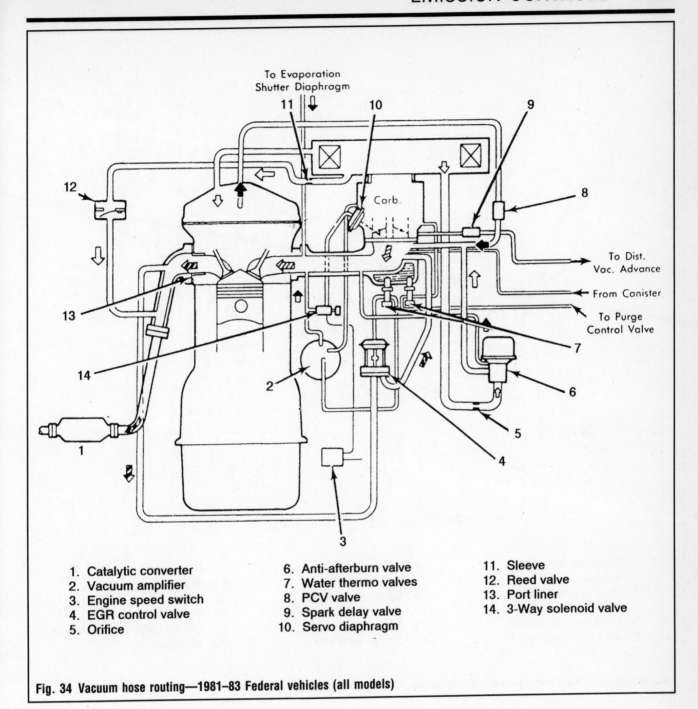

Fig. 34 Vacuum hose routing—1981–83 Federal vehicles (all models)

1. Catalytic converter
2. Vacuum amplifier
3. Engine speed switch
4. EGR control valve
5. Orifice
6. Anti-afterburn valve
7. Water thermo valves
8. PCV valve
9. Spark delay valve
10. Servo diaphragm
11. Sleeve
12. Reed valve
13. Port liner
14. 3-Way solenoid valve

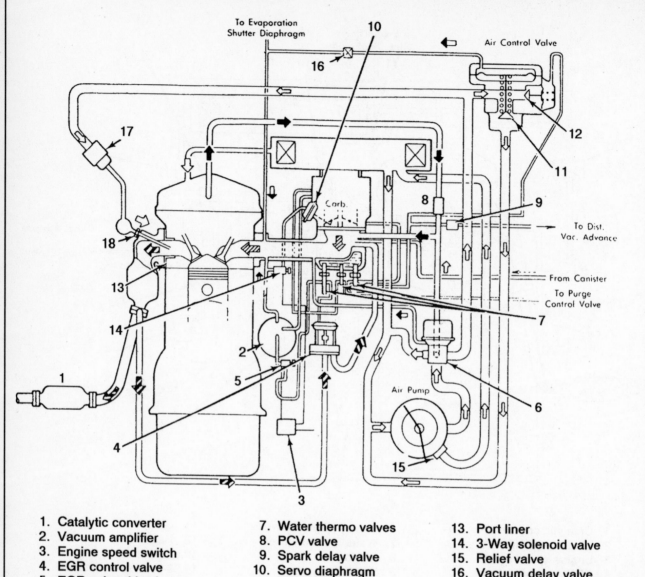

1. Catalytic converter
2. Vacuum amplifier
3. Engine speed switch
4. EGR control valve
5. EGR solenoid valve
6. Air bypass valve
7. Water thermo valves
8. PCV valve
9. Spark delay valve
10. Servo diaphragm
11. No. 1 relief valve
12. No. 2 relief valve
13. Port liner
14. 3-Way solenoid valve
15. Relief valve
16. Vacuum delay valve
17. Check valve (secondary air)
18. Air injection

Fig. 35 Vacuum hose routing—1981–82 California vehicles (all models)

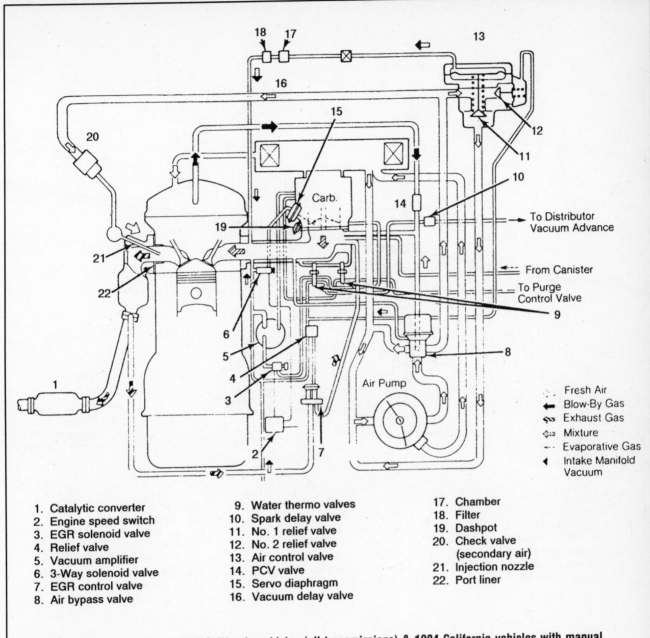

1. Catalytic converter
2. Engine speed switch
3. EGR solenoid valve
4. Relief valve
5. Vacuum amplifier
6. 3-Way solenoid valve
7. EGR control valve
8. Air bypass valve
9. Water thermo valves
10. Spark delay valve
11. No. 1 relief valve
12. No. 2 relief valve
13. Air control valve
14. PCV valve
15. Servo diaphragm
16. Vacuum delay valve
17. Chamber
18. Filter
19. Dashpot
20. Check valve (secondary air)
21. Injection nozzle
22. Port liner

Fresh Air
Blow-By Gas
Exhaust Gas
Mixture
Evaporative Gas
Intake Manifold Vacuum

To Distributor Vacuum Advance
From Canister
To Purge Control Valve

Fig. 36 Vacuum hose routing—1983 California vehicles (all transmissions) & 1984 California vehicles with manual transmission

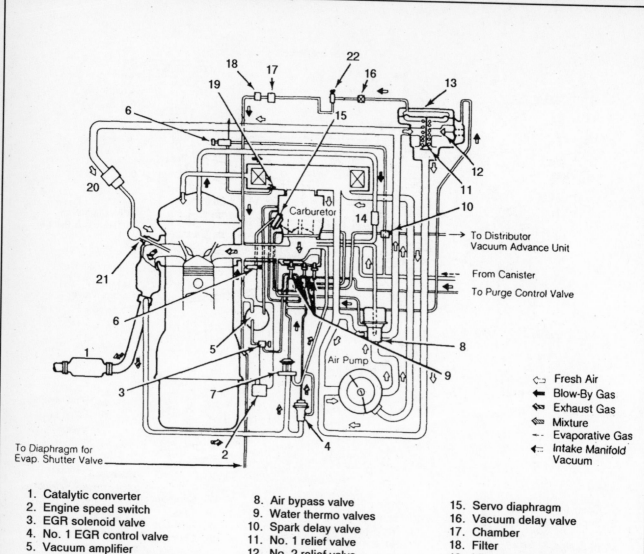

Fresh Air
Blow-By Gas
Exhaust Gas
Mixture
Evaporative Gas
Intake Manifold Vacuum

To Distributor Vacuum Advance Unit

From Canister
To Purge Control Valve

To Diaphragm for Evap. Shutter Valve

1. Catalytic converter
2. Engine speed switch
3. EGR solenoid valve
4. No. 1 EGR control valve
5. Vacuum amplifier
6. 3-Way solenoid valve
7. No. 2 EGR control valve
8. Air bypass valve
9. Water thermo valves
10. Spark delay valve
11. No. 1 relief valve
12. No. 2 relief valve
13. Air control valve
14. PCV valve
15. Servo diaphragm
16. Vacuum delay valve
17. Chamber
18. Filter
19. Idle compensator
20. Check valve (secondary air)
21. Air injection nozzle
22. ACV solenoid valve

Fig. 37 Vacuum hose routing—1984 California vehicles with automatic transmission

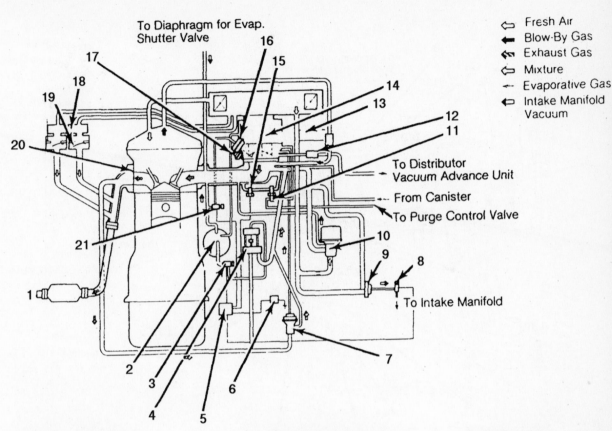

To Diaphragm for Evap.
Shutter Valve

⇐ Fresh Air
← Blow-By Gas
⇐ Exhaust Gas
⇐ Mixture
⇠ Evaporative Gas
⇐ Intake Manifold
Vacuum

To Distributor
Vacuum Advance Unit
From Canister
To Purge Control Valve
To Intake Manifold

1. Catalytic converter
2. Vacuum amplifier
3. EGR solenoid valve
4. No. 2 EGR control valve
5. Engine speed unit
6. Water thermo switch
7. No. 1 EGR control valve

8. Air shut solenoid valve
9. Air shut valve
10. Anti-afterburn valve
11. Water thermo valve
12. Spark delay valve
(except high altitude)
13. PCV valve

14. Carburetor
15. Water thermo switch
16. Servo diaphragm
17. Dashpot
18. Air chamber
19. Reed valve
20. Port liner
21. 3-Way solenoid valve

Fig. 38 Vacuum hose routing—1984 Federal vehicles with manual transmission

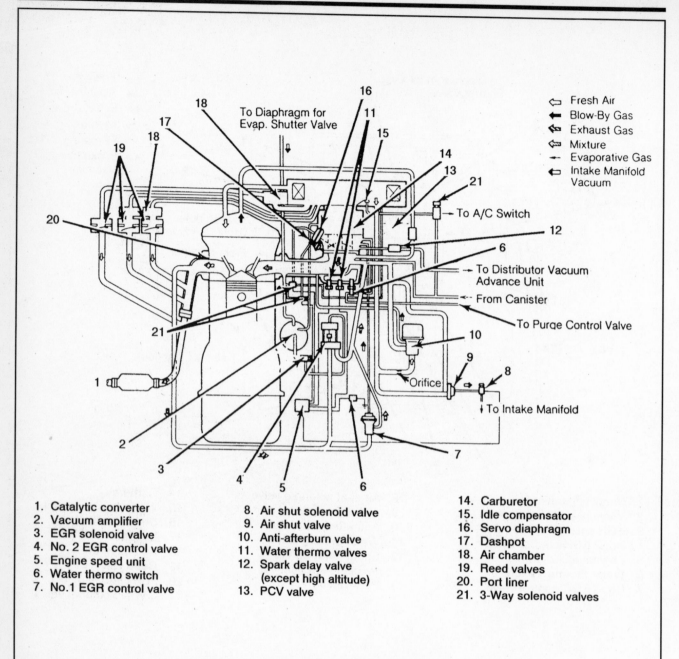

Fresh Air
Blow-By Gas
Exhaust Gas
Mixture
Evaporative Gas
Intake Manifold Vacuum

To Diaphragm for Evap. Shutter Valve

To A/C Switch

To Distributor Vacuum Advance Unit
From Canister
To Purge Control Valve

Orifice

To Intake Manifold

1. Catalytic converter
2. Vacuum amplifier
3. EGR solenoid valve
4. No. 2 EGR control valve
5. Engine speed unit
6. Water thermo switch
7. No.1 EGR control valve
8. Air shut solenoid valve
9. Air shut valve
10. Anti-afterburn valve
11. Water thermo valves
12. Spark delay valve (except high altitude)
13. PCV valve
14. Carburetor
15. Idle compensator
16. Servo diaphragm
17. Dashpot
18. Air chamber
19. Reed valves
20. Port liner
21. 3-Way solenoid valves

Fig. 39 Vacuum hose routing—1984 Federal vehicles with automatic transmission

1. Distributor
2. Fuel tank
3. Evaporative canister
4. Rear catalytic converter (except some Canadian)
5. No. 2 purge control valve
6. No. 1 purge control valve
7. EGR control valve
8. Water thermosensor
9. Duty solenoid valve
10. Vacuum check valve
11. Water thermo valve
12. PTC heater
13. PCV valve
14. Oxygen sensor
15. Front catalytic converter
16. Reed valves
17. Air chamber
18. No.2 control valve
19. ACV solenoid
20. No. 1 air control valve
21. High altitude compensator (Federal models only)
22. Vacuum sensor
23. Vacuum switch
24. Idle compensator
25. Coasting richer
26. Idle switch
27. Control valve
28. Air vent solenoid valve
29. Control unit

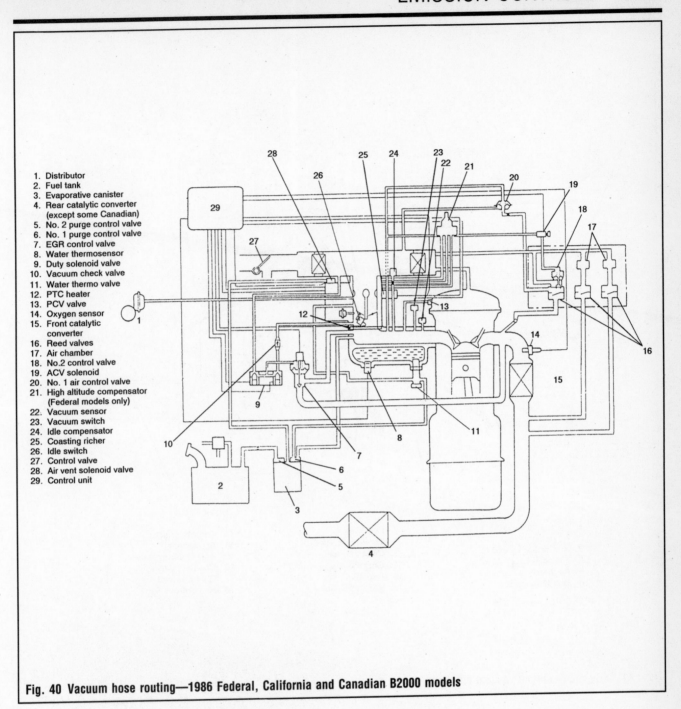

Fig. 40 Vacuum hose routing—1986 Federal, California and Canadian B2000 models

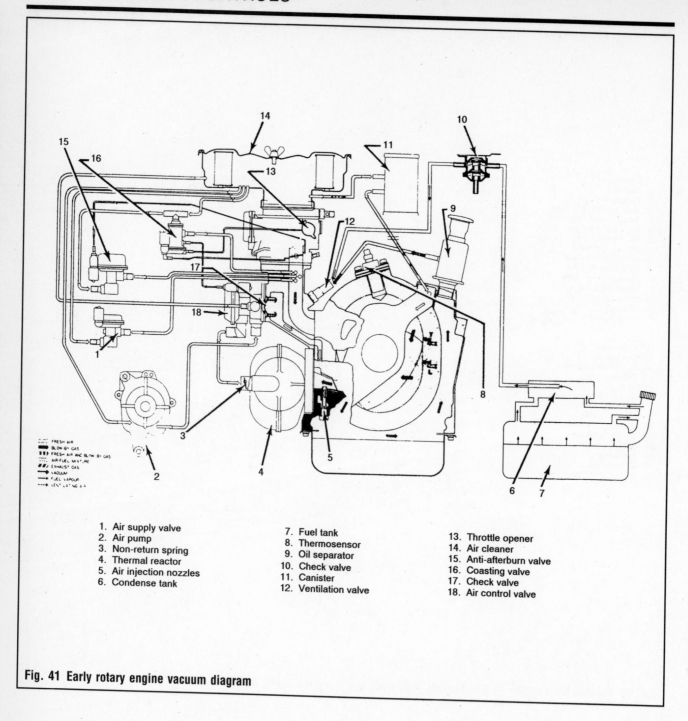

Fig. 41 Early rotary engine vacuum diagram

1. Air supply valve
2. Air pump
3. Non-return spring
4. Thermal reactor
5. Air injection nozzles
6. Condense tank

7. Fuel tank
8. Thermosensor
9. Oil separator
10. Check valve
11. Canister
12. Ventilation valve

13. Throttle opener
14. Air cleaner
15. Anti-afterburn valve
16. Coasting valve
17. Check valve
18. Air control valve

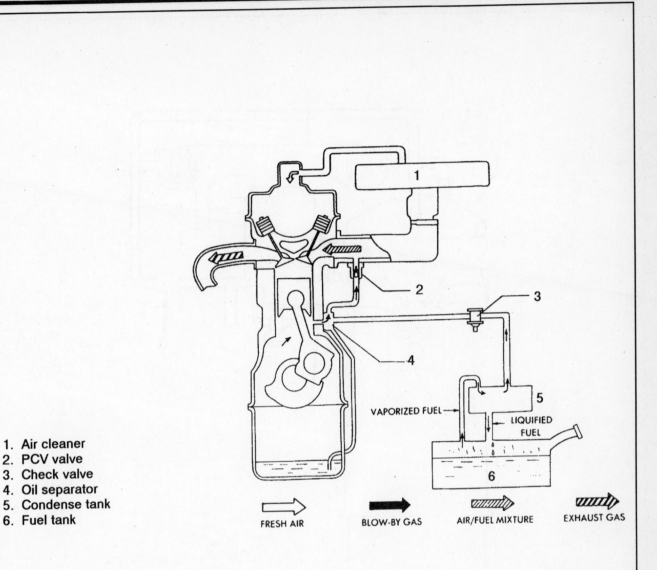

1. Air cleaner
2. PCV valve
3. Check valve
4. Oil separator
5. Condense tank
6. Fuel tank

VAPORIZED FUEL

LIQUIFIED FUEL

FRESH AIR   BLOW-BY GAS   AIR/FUEL MIXTURE   EXHAUST GAS

Fig. 42 1972–74 Piston engine PCV & Evaporative systems

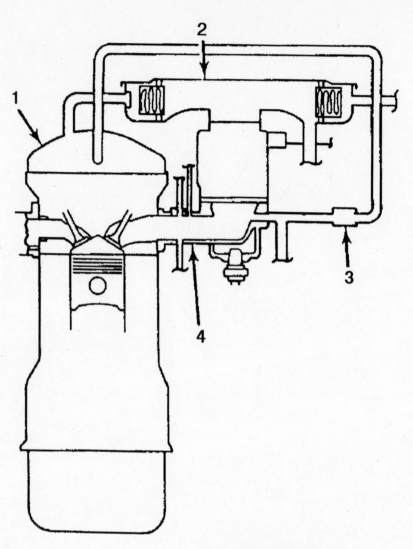

1. Rocker cover
2. Air cleaner
3. PCV valve
4. Intake manifold

Fig. 43 1975–78 Piston engine PCV system

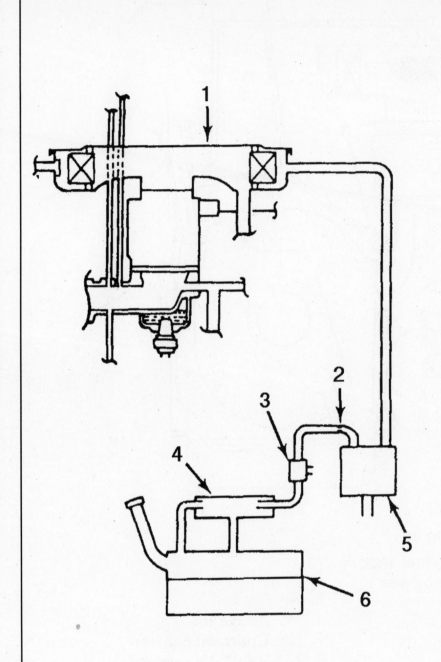

1. Air cleaner
2. Orifice
3. Check valve
4. Vapor separator
5. Carbon canister
6. Fuel tank

Fig. 44 1975–78 Piston engine evaporative system

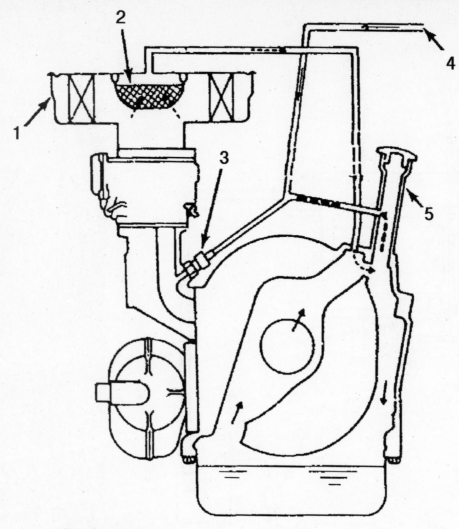

→ Fuel vapor

---→ Ventilating air

--→ Fresh air, fuel vapor
and blow-by gas

1. Air cleaner
2. Charcoal canister
3. Ventilation valve
4. From fuel tank
5. Oil fill tube

Fig. 45 1974–77 Rotary engine PCV system

5

FUEL SYSTEM

BASIC FUEL SYSTEM DIAGNOSIS

When there is a problem starting or driving a vehicle, two of the most important checks involve the ignition and the fuel systems. The questions most mechanics attempt to answer first, "is there spark?" and "is there fuel?" will often lead to solving most basic problems. For ignition system diagnosis and testing, please refer to the information on engine electrical components and ignition systems found earlier in this manual. If the ignition system checks out (there is spark), then you must determine if the fuel system is operating properly (is there fuel?).

CARBURETED FUEL SYSTEM

Electric Fuel Pump

On all models through 1984, the pump is mounted on the left frame rail adjacent to the fuel tank.

TESTING

To determine that the fuel pump is in good operating condition, test for both volume and pressure should be performed. The tests are performed with the fuel pump installed, and the engine at normal operating temperature and idle speed.

Be sure that the fuel filter has been changed within the specified interval. If in doubt, install a new filter.

Pressure Test
▶ **See Figure 1**

1. Remove the air cleaner.
2. Disconnect the fuel inlet line at the carburetor.
3. Connect a pressure gauge, a restrictor and a flexible hose between the fuel filter and the carburetor. Position the flexible hose and restrictor so that the fuel can be discharged into a suitable graduated container.
4. Before taking a pressure reading, operate the engine at idle speed and vent the system into the container by momentarily opening the hose restrictor.
5. Close the hose restrictor and allow the pressure to stabilize and note the reading. It should be 2.8–3.6 psi or 3.6–5.0 psi on the Rotary Pick-Up.

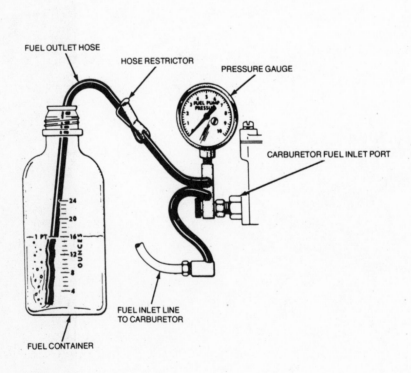

Fig. 1 Pressure and volume testing the electric fuel pump

6. If the pump pressure is not within specifications, and the fuel filter and fuel lines are not blocked, the pump is malfunctioning and should be replaced.

7. If the pressure is within specifications, perform the volume test.

Volume Test

1. Open the hose restrictor and expel the fuel into the container, while observing the time required to discharge 1 pint. Close the restrictor. Fuel pump volume should be approximately 2 pints/minute or 1.2 quarts/minutes on the Rotary Pick-Up.

2. If the pump volume is below specifications, repeat the test using an auxiliary fuel supply and a new filter. If the pump volume meets specifications while using an auxiliary fuel supply, check for a restriction in the fuel lines.

REMOVAL & INSTALLATION

1. Remove the fuel pump shield from the frame. Disconnect the electrical leads from the pump.

2. Disconnect the inlet and outlet lines from the pump. Plug the lines.

3. Unbolt and remove the pump from its mounting bracket.

4. Position the fuel pump on the mounting bracket and install the bolts. Be sure that both mounting surfaces are clean.

5. Connect the inlet and outlet hoses.

6. Connect the electrical leads to the pump.

7. Install the fuel pump shield.

Mechanical Fuel Pump

♦ **See Figure 2**

All 1986 models use a mechanically driven fuel pump, mounted on the left front of the cylinder head, driven by the camshaft.

TESTING

Pressure Test

1. Disconnect the pump-to-carburetor hose at the carburetor. Connect a pressure gauge.

2. Disconnect the fuel return hose from the pump and plug the pump return and the return port on the carburetor.

3. Run the engine at idle and check the pressure. Pressure should be 3.9–4.4 psi. If not, replace the pump.

REMOVAL & INSTALLATION

1. Disconnect the outlet, inlet and return hoses at the pump.

2. Unbolt and remove the pump and insulator. Discard the gaskets.

3. Installation is the reverse of removal. Use new gaskets coated with sealer.

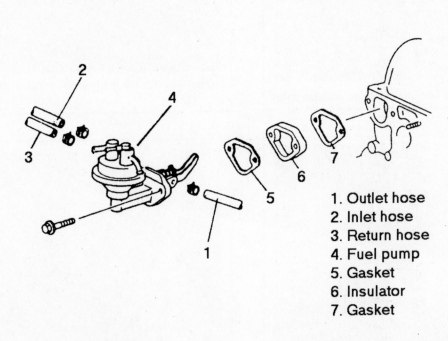

1. Outlet hose
2. Inlet hose
3. Return hose
4. Fuel pump
5. Gasket
6. Insulator
7. Gasket

Fig. 2 Exploded view of the mechanical fuel pump mounting—(1) fuel hoses (2) return line (3) fuel pump assembly. Note the spacer plate between the fuel pump gaskets

Label all fuel lines connected to the fuel pump . . .

. . . then remove the fuel lines

. . . and clamp off the fuel lines to avoid gasoline spills

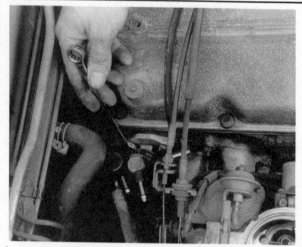

Loosen and remove the two fuel pump mounting bolts . . .

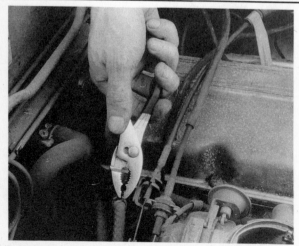

Release the spring clamps and slide them down the hose . . .

. . . and pull the fuel pump out of the cylinder head

Carburetor

The Mazda Rotary Pick-Up uses a 4-barrel downdraft carburetor, while the piston engines use 2-barrel downdraft units.

ADJUSTMENTS

Float and Fuel Level

1,586cc, 1,796cc AND 1,970cc ENGINES

◗ **See Figures 3, 4 and 5**

1. With the engine running, check the fuel level in the sight glass (in the fuel bowl).
2. If the fuel level is not at the specified mark on the sight glass, remove the carburetor from the truck.

Fig. 5 Bend the tang to adjust the float level—bend point (A) to correct float level and point (B) to correct float drop on 1,586cc, 1,796cc and 1,970cc engines

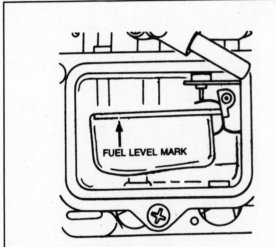

Fig. 3 Fuel level mark on the sight glass of 1,586cc, 1,796cc and 1,970cc engines

3. Remove the fuel bowl cover.
4. Invert the carburetor and lower the float until the tang on the float just contacts the needle valve.
5. Measure the clearance between the float and the edge of the bowl. Clearance should be:
   - 1,586cc—0.65mm (0.0256 in.)
   - 1,796cc—0.60mm (0.0236 in.)
   - 1,970cc—0.85mm (0.0334 in.)
6. If the clearance is not as specified, bend the float seal lip until the proper clearance is obtained.
7. Turn the carburetor right side up and measure the clearance between the bottom of the float and the bowl. Clearance should be:
   - 1,586cc and 1,796cc—1.2mm (0.0472 in.)
   - 1,970cc—1.0mm (0.0394 in.)
8. If not, bend the float stopper until the correct clearance is obtained.
9. Install the fuel bowl cover.
10. Reinstall the carburetor on the truck.
11. Recheck the fuel level at the sight glass.

1,998cc ENGINE

◗ **See Figures 6 and 7**

1. Remove the air horn from the carburetor.
2. Turn the air horn upside down on a level surface. Allow the float to hang under its own weight.
3. Measure the clearance between the float and the air horn gasket surface. The gap should be 11.5–12.5mm (0.4528–0.4921 in.). If not, bend the float seat lip to obtain the correct gap.
4. Turn the air horn right side up and allow the float to hang under its own weight.
5. Measure the gap between the BOTTOM of the float and the air horn gasket surface. The gap should be 46.0–47.0mm (1.811–1.850 in.). If not, bend the float stopper until it is.

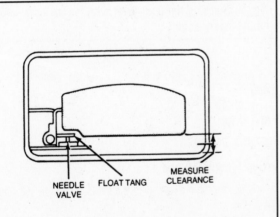

Fig. 4 Float level adjustment. Measure the clearance between the float and the edge of the bowl on 1,586cc, 1,796cc and 1,970cc engines

NEEDLE VALVE   FLOAT TANG   MEASURE CLEARANCE

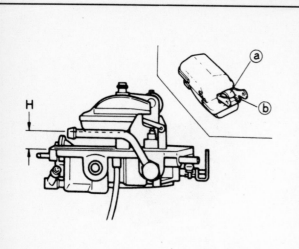

Fig. 6 1,998cc engine float level adjustment—bend point (a) to correct float level and point (b) to correct float drop

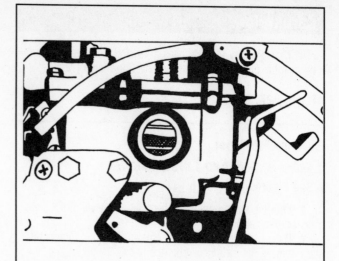

Fig. 8 Checking the fuel level in the sight glass on the rotary engine

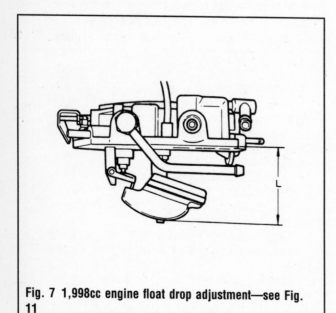

Fig. 7 1,998cc engine float drop adjustment—see Fig. 11

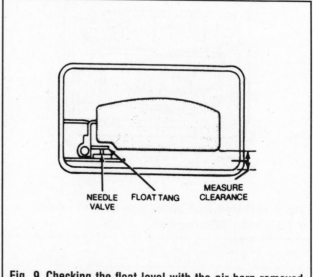

Fig. 9 Checking the float level with the air horn removed on the rotary engine

Float Level

ROTARY ENGINE

♦ See Figures 8 and 9

1. With the engine running, check the fuel level in the sight glass, using a mirror.
2. If the fuel levels are not within the specified marks on the sight glass, remove the air horn with the floats.
3. Invert the air horn and let the float hang so that it just contacts the needle valve.
4. Measure the clearance between the float and the air horn gasket, which should be 1.1mm (0.0433 in.). Bend the float seat lip to adjust the clearance if necessary.

5. Install the air horn and recheck the fuel levels in the sight glass.

Float Drop

ROTARY ENGINE

♦ See Figures 10 and 11

1. Remove the air horn with the floats and allow the floats to hang free.
2. Measure the clearance between the bottom of the float and the air horn gasket. The clearance should be 51.5–52.5mm (2.028–2.067 in.).
3. If not, adjust the distance by bending the float stopper.

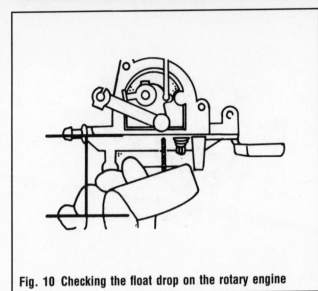

Fig. 10 Checking the float drop on the rotary engine

Fig. 12 1,586cc engine fast idle adjusting screw location (inset-arrow)

Fig. 11 Rotary engine float adjustment points—point (A) is for float level adjustment and point (B) is for float drop adjustment

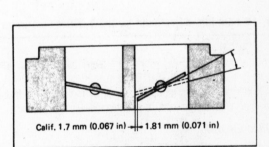

Calif. 1.7 mm (0.067 in) → ⊢ 1.81 mm (0.071 in)

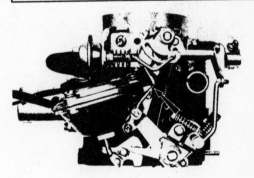

Fig. 13 Fast idle adjustment points for 1,796cc engine carburetors. Bend the link at the point indicated by the arrow

4. Install the air horn and recheck the fuel level in the sight glass.

Fast Idle

1,586cc ENGINE

▶ See Figure 12

The fast idle can be adjusted by turning the fast idle adjusting screw. Check the choke plate for free operation.

1,796cc ENGINE

▶ See Figure 13

1. Remove the air cleaner.
2. With the choke plate fully closed, measure the clearance between the primary throttle plate and the wall of the throttle bore. The clearance should measure 1.6–1.7mm (0.0629–0.0669 in.) through 1976, and 1.8mm (0.0708 in.) in 1977–78, or 2.5mm (0.0984 in.) for 1977–78 California models.
3. If the clearance is not as specified, bend the fast idle lever

where it contacts the throttle lever tang until the proper clearance is obtained.

4. Install the air cleaner.

1,970cc ENGINE

◆ **See Figure 14**

1. Close the choke fully.
2. Place the fast idle adjusting screw on the first step of the fast idle cam.
3. Check the clearance between the throttle plate and the in-

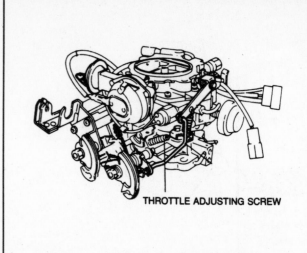

THROTTLE ADJUSTING SCREW

Fig. 16 Throttle adjusting screw on the 1,998cc engine

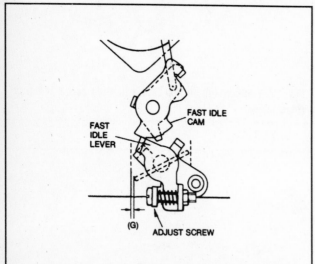

Fig. 14 Fast idle adjustment for the 1,970cc carburetor

side of the throttle wall (G) with a wire feeler gauge. It should measure 1.3–1.5mm (0.0512–0.0590 in.).

4. If the clearance is incorrect, adjust by means of the fast idle screw, clockwise to increase or counterclockwise to decrease.

1,998cc ENGINE

◆ **See Figures 15 and 16**

1. Set the fast idle cam so that the fast idle lever rests on the second step of the cam.

2. Adjust the clearance between the air horn wall and the lower edge of the throttle plates, (G) by turning the fast idle adjusting screw. Clearance should be 0.75–1.13mm (0.0295–0.0445 in.)

ROTARY ENGINE

◆ **See Figure 17**

1. Pull the choke knob all the way out.
2. Measure the clearance between the primary throttle plate and the wall of the primary throttle bore. The clearance can be measured with a suitable drill bit.
3. The clearance should be 1.0–1.3mm (#61–#55 drill) for trucks with manual transmission, or 1.2–1.5mm (#55–#53 drill) for trucks with automatic transmission.

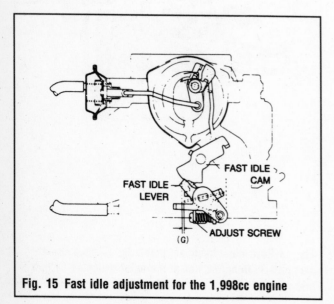

Fig. 15 Fast idle adjustment for the 1,998cc engine

Fig. 17 Fast idle adjustment on the rotary engine carburetor. Bend the rod at the point indicated by the arrow until the proper rpm is attained

4. If the clearance is not as specified, adjust the fast idle by bending the connecting rod to obtain the proper clearance.

Accelerator Linkage

1,586cc ENGINE

Inspect the throttle linkage for free operation. Remove the air cleaner. With the accelerator fully depressed, the position of the throttle plates should be vertical.

1,796cc AND 1,970cc ENGINES

1. Loosen the locknuts on the longer linkage rod and rotate both ends in the sockets until the proper accelerator travel from idle to wide-open throttle is obtained.
2. Tighten the locknuts to set the adjustment.

1,998cc ENGINE

▶ **See Figure 18**

1. Check the cable deflection at the carburetor. Deflection should be 1.0–3.0mm (0.0394–0.1181 in.). If not, adjust it by turning the adjusting nut at the bracket near the carburetor.

Accelerator cable adjustments are made using the adjuster nuts (arrows)—vehicles not equipped with cruise control have only one cable

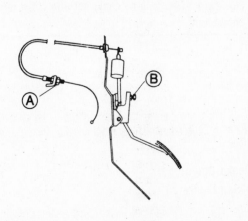

Fig. 18 Throttle cable adjustment points for the 1,998cc engine

2. Depress the accelerator pedal to the floor. The throttle plates should be vertical. If not, adjust their position by turning the adjusting nut on the accelerator pedal bracket.

Secondary Throttle Valve

ALL MODELS

▶ **See Figure 19**

The clearance between the primary throttle valve and the air horn wall, when the secondary throttle valve just starts to open should be:
- 1,586cc—5.00–5.60mm (0.1968–0.2204 in.)
- 1,796cc—4.70–5.30mm (0.1850–0.2086 in.)
- 1,970cc—6.10–6.85mm (0.2402–0.2697 in.)
- 1,998cc—7.30–8.30mm (0.2874–0.3268 in.)

If not, bend the fast idle link (1972–84) or the tab B (1986 illustrated).

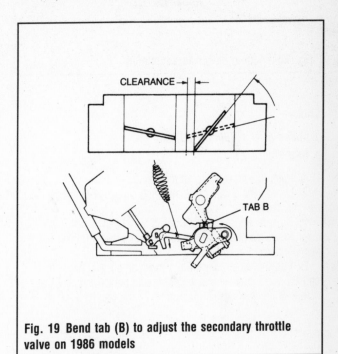

Fig. 19 Bend tab (B) to adjust the secondary throttle valve on 1986 models

Vacuum Pulldown

1976–78 VEHICLES

▶ **See Figure 20**

1. On California Mazdas, unplug the electrical connectors from the water thermo switch and connect a jumper wire between the connectors. Turn the ignition switch on.
2. Pull the choke knob out to fully close the choke.
3. Disconnect the vacuum source to the pulldown diaphragm.
4. Connect an external vacuum source to the pulldown diaphragm. Gradually apply vacuum. The pulldown should start to operate (open the choke) at 5.9–7.5 in.Hg.
5. Increase the vacuum to 9.8–12.0 in.Hg. Check the clearance between the carburetor air horn wall and the choke plate using a wire gauge. The clearance should measure 1.5–2.0mm (0.059–0.787 in.) for 1976; 1.6–1.9mm (0.063–0.075 in.) for 1977–78.
6. Adjust the clearance if necessary by bending the pulldown connecting rod.

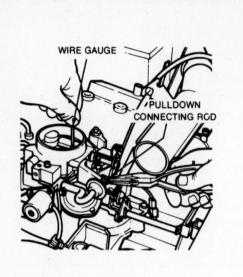

Fig. 20 Vacuum pulldown adjustment

Choke

1,586cc AND 1,796cc ENGINES

▶ **See Figure 21**

1. Push the choke knob all the way in.
2. Loosen the choke cable attaching screws at the choke lever and the choke cable bracket.
3. Be sure that the choke plate is fully open.
4. Insert the choke cable into the choke lever. Tighten the attaching screw.
5. Pull the cable outward to remove all slack between the choke lever and choke cable bracket and tighten the attaching screw at the choke cable bracket.

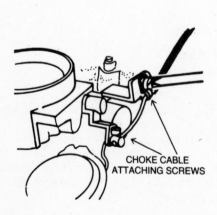

Fig. 21 Choke adjustment for 1,586cc and 1,796cc engine carburetors

6. Operate the choke to be sure that there is no binding and that it is operating properly.

1,970cc ENGINE

There are four adjustments to be made to the choke in these years; choke/throttle valve opening adjustment; choke diaphragm adjustment; choke unloader adjustment; and choke thermostat (bimetal) adjustment.

Choke/Throttle Valve Opening Angle

▶ **See Figure 22**

1. Adjust the fast idle cam as previously outlines before making this adjustment.
2. Place the fast idle screw on the second step of the fast idle cam.

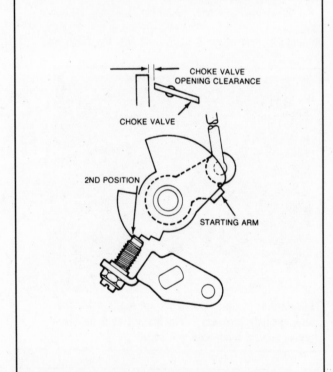

Fig. 22 1,970cc engine choke throttle valve opening adjustment

3. Measure the clearance between the edge of the choke plate and the throttle bore with a wire gauge. Clearance should be 0.4–0.7mm (0.0157–0.0276 in.).
4. If the clearance is incorrect, adjust by bending the starting arm. If a large adjustment is required, the choke rod can be bent slightly.

Choke Diaphragm

▶ **See Figure 23**

1. Remove the vacuum hose from the choke diaphragm. Attach a vacuum pump to the diaphragm fitting and apply approximately 15.6 in. Hg to the diaphragm.
2. Check to see that the fast idle screw is on the first step of the fast idle cam.

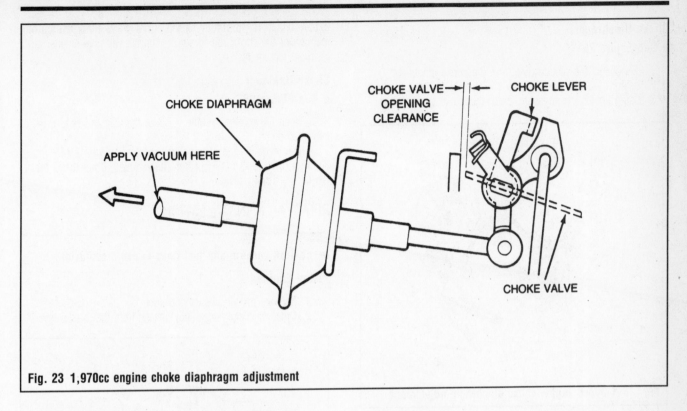

Fig. 23 1,970cc engine choke diaphragm adjustment

3. Press on the choke plate slightly to settle it. Measure the clearance between the edge of the choke plate and the throttle bore. Clearance should be 1.2–1.7mm (0.047–0.067 in.).

4. If the clearance is incorrect, adjust by bending the choke lever.

Choke Unloader
▶ **See Figure 24**

1. Close the choke plate fully. Open the throttle plate fully.

2. Measure the clearance between the edge of the choke plate and the throttle bore with a wire gauge. Clearance should be 2.0–2.5mm (0.0787–0.9843 in.).

3. If the clearance is incorrect, bend the choke unloader adjusting nail (tang).

Thermostat
▶ **See Figure 25**

1. The index mark on the thermostat cover should be aligned with the center mark on the choke housing.

2. Adjust by loosening the thermostat cover retaining screws slightly and shifting the position of the cover. Tighten the screws after adjustment.

1,998cc ENGINE

Three choke related adjustments are performed on these units.

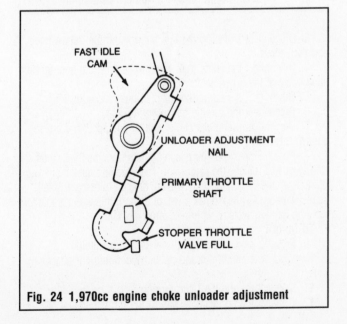

Fig. 24 1,970cc engine choke unloader adjustment

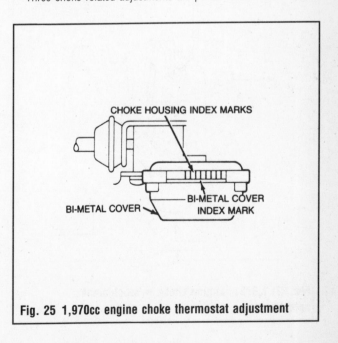

Fig. 25 1,970cc engine choke thermostat adjustment

Choke Diaphragm

▶ **See Figure 26**

1. Disconnect the vacuum line from the choke diaphragm unit.
2. Using a vacuum pump, apply 15.7 in. Hg to the diaphragm.
3. Using light finger pressure, close the choke valve. Check

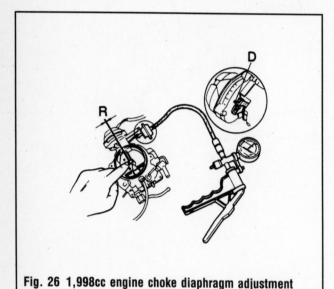

Fig. 26 1,998cc engine choke diaphragm adjustment

the clearance at the upper edge of the choke valve. Clearance should be 1.6–2.1mm (0.063–0.083 in.).

4. If not, bend the tab on the choke lever to adjust it.

Choke Valve Clearance

▶ **See Figure 27**

1. Position the fast idle lever on the second step of the fast idle cam.
2. The leading edge of the choke valve should be 0.60–1.0mm

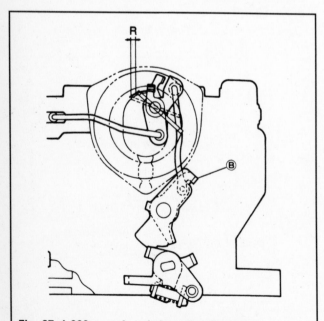

Fig. 27 1,998cc engine choke valve clearance adjustment

(0.024–0.039 in.) from fully closed. If not, bend either the tab on the cam or the choke rod to adjust. The tab will give smaller adjustment increments.

Choke Unloader

▶ **See Figure 28**

1. Open the primary throttle valve all the way and hold it in this position.
2. The leading edge of the choke valve should be 2.74–3.60mm (0.1079–0.1417 in.) from fully closed. If not, bend the tab on the throttle lever.

REMOVAL & INSTALLATION

➡ **Label all vacuum and fuel lines to avoid confusion.**

Piston Engines

1. Remove the air cleaner and duct.
2. Disconnect the accelerator linkage from the throttle lever.

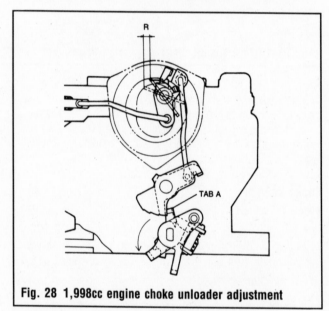

Fig. 28 1,998cc engine choke unloader adjustment

3. Disconnect and plug the fuel supply and fuel return lines and plug these.
4. Disconnect the leads from the throttle solenoid and deceleration valve at the quick-disconnects.
5. Disconnect the carburetor-to-distributor vacuum line.
6. Disconnect the throttle return spring.
7. Disconnect the choke cable, and, if equipped, the cruise control cable.
8. Remove the carburetor attaching nuts from the intake manifold studs and remove the carburetor. The attaching nuts are tucked underneath the carburetor body and are difficult to reach; a small socket with an "L" shaped hex drive, or a short, thin wrench sold for work on ignition systems will make removal easier.

To install:

9. Install a new carburetor gasket on the manifold.
10. Install the carburetor and tighten the carburetor attaching nuts.
11. Connect the throttle return spring.
12. Connect the accelerator shaft to the throttle shaft.

Label and remove all vacuum lines to the carburetor . . .

. . . then remove the cables from the throttle shaft

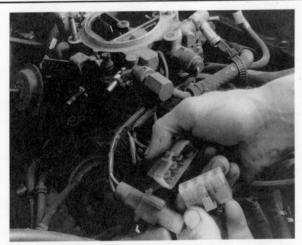

. . . then label and remove all electrical connections to the carburetor

Loosen and remove the carburetor mounting bolts . . .

Remove any clips retaining the accelerator cables and pull them free of their brackets . . .

. . . and lift off the carburetor assembly

13. Connect the electrical leads to the throttle solenoid and deceleration valve.

14. Connect the distributor vacuum line.

15. Connect the fuel supply and fuel return lines.

16. Connect and adjust the choke cable and, if equipped, the cruise control cable.

17. Install the air cleaner and duct.

18. Start the engine and check for fuel leaks.

Rotary Engine

1. Remove the air cleaner assembly, complete with its hoses and mounting bracket.

2. Detach the choke and accelerator cables from the carburetor.

3. Disconnect the fuel and vacuum lines from the carburetor.

4. Remove the oil line which runs to the metering oil pump, at the carburetor.

5. Unfasten the idle sensor switch wiring, if so equipped.

6. Remove the carburetor attaching nuts and/or bolts, gasket or heat insulator, and remove the carburetor.

7. Installation is performed in the reverse order of removal. Use a new gasket. Fill the float bowl with gasoline to aid in engine starting.

OVERHAUL

◗ See Figures 29 thru 33a

The following instructions are general overhaul procedures. Most good carburetor rebuilding kits come replete with exploded views and specific instructions.

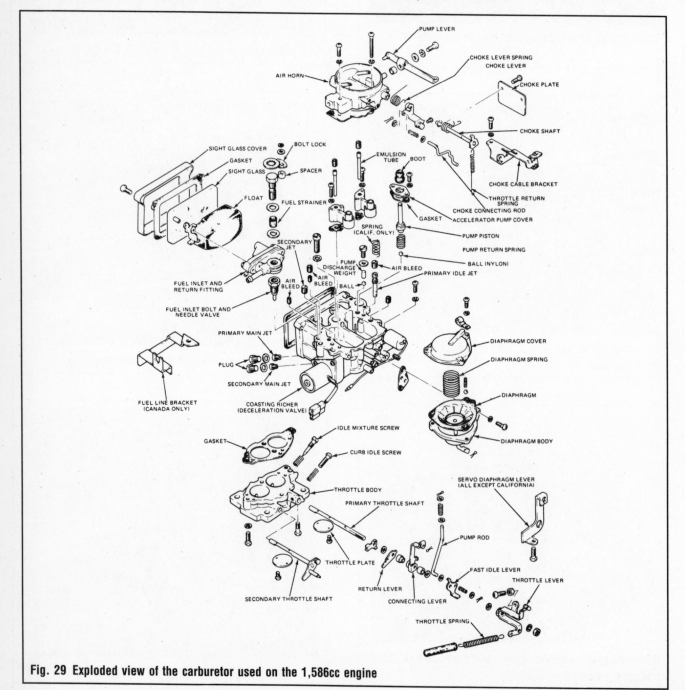

Fig. 29 Exploded view of the carburetor used on the 1,586cc engine

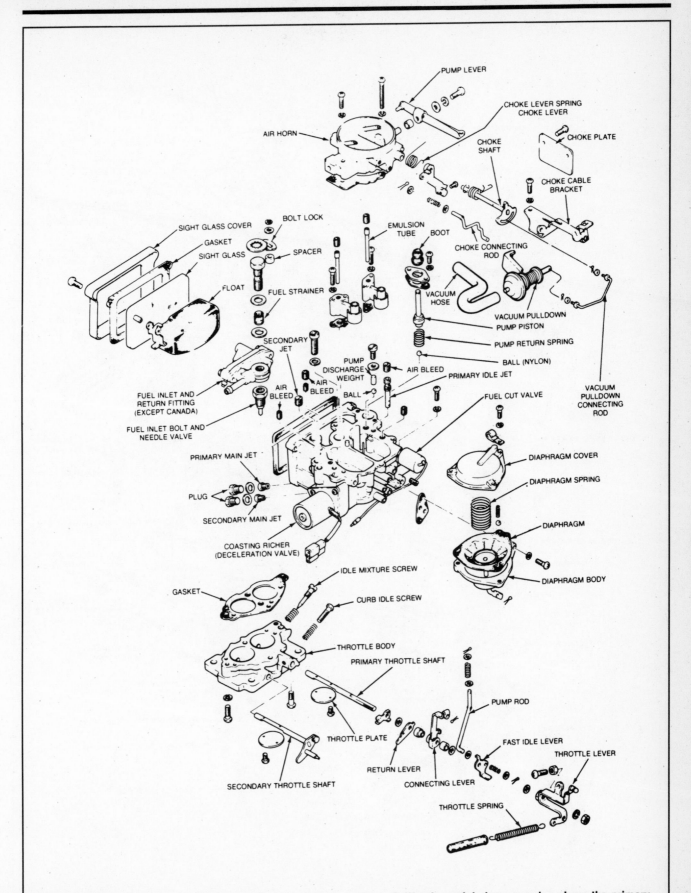

Fig. 30 Exploded view of the carburetor used on the 1,796cc engine—California models have a spring above the primary idle jet air bleed

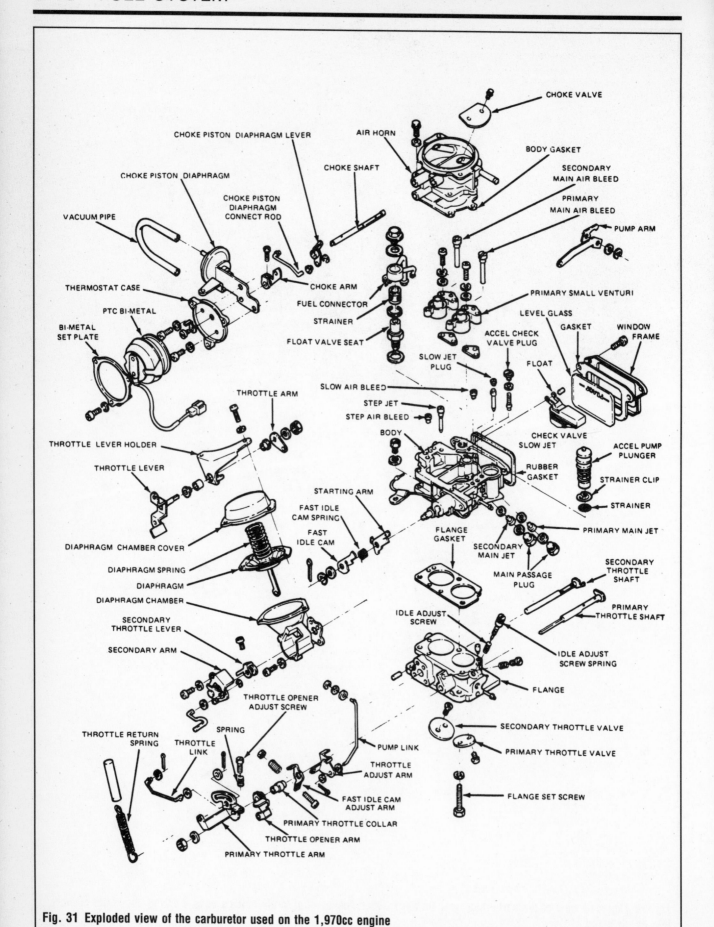

Fig. 31 Exploded view of the carburetor used on the 1,970cc engine

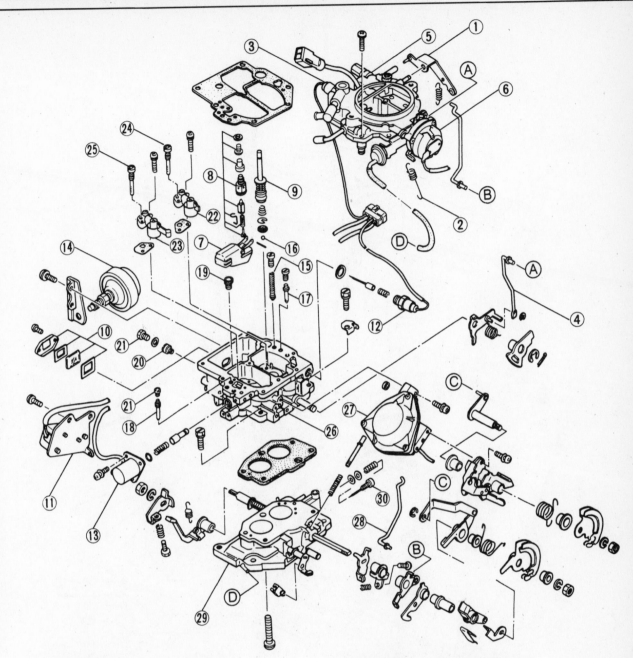

1. Accelerator pump connecting rod
2. Connect spring
3. Air vent solenoid valve
4. Choke rod
5. Air horn
6. Automatic choke assembly
7. Float
8. Needle valve assembly
9. Accelerator pump
10. Fuel bowl sight glass
11. Idle switch
12. Slow fuel cut solenoid valve
13. Coasting richer solenoid valve
14. Dash pot
15. Accelerator pump outlet check ball

16. Accelerator pump inlet check ball
17. Slow jet
18. Step jet
19. Primary main jet
20. Secondary main jet
21. Plug
22. Primary ventury & nozzle
23. Secondary ventury & nozzle
24. Primary main air bleed
25. Secondary main air bleed
26. Main body
27. Vacuum diaphragm
28. Throttle link
29. Throttle body
30. Mixture adjusting screw

Fig. 32 Exploded view of the carburetor used on the 1,998cc engine

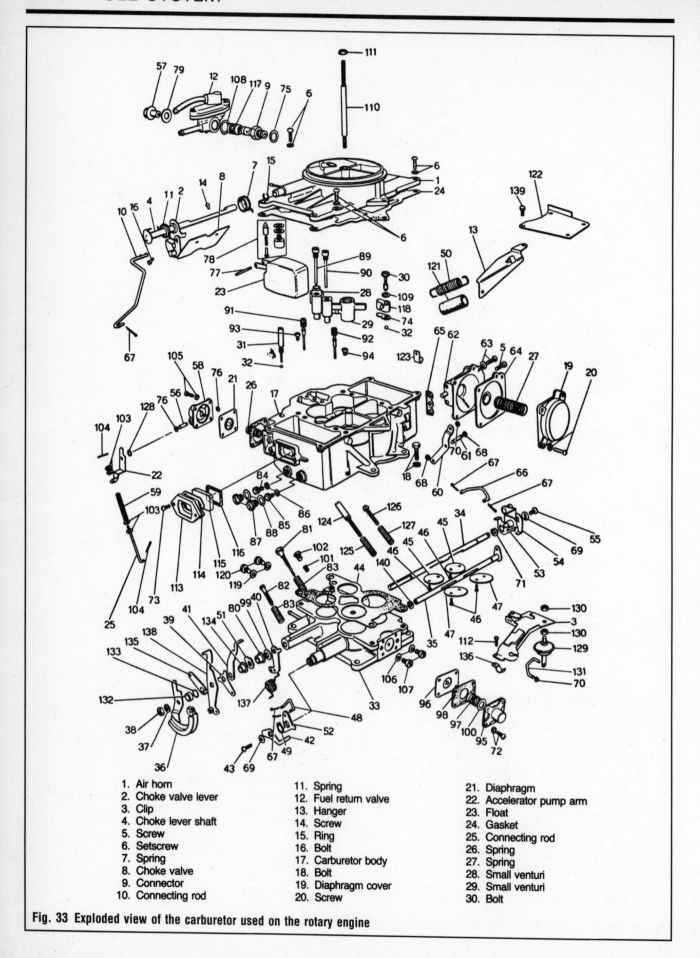

1. Air horn
2. Choke valve lever
3. Clip
4. Choke lever shaft
5. Screw
6. Setscrew
7. Spring
8. Choke valve
9. Connector
10. Connecting rod
11. Spring
12. Fuel return valve
13. Hanger
14. Screw
15. Ring
16. Bolt
17. Carburetor body
18. Bolt
19. Diaphragm cover
20. Screw
21. Diaphragm
22. Accelerator pump arm
23. Float
24. Gasket
25. Connecting rod
26. Spring
27. Spring
28. Small venturi
29. Small venturi
30. Bolt

Fig. 33 Exploded view of the carburetor used on the rotary engine

31. Check ball plug
32. Steel ball
33. Flange
34. Throttle shaft
35. Throttle shaft
36. Throttle lever
37. Spring washer
38. Nut
39. Lock
40. Adjusting arm
41. Starting lever
42. Arm
43. Screw
44. Gasket
45. Valve
46. Screw
47. Throttle valve
48. Throttle lever link
49. Ring
50. Throttle return spring
51. Arm
52. Retainer
53. Metering pump lever
54. Metering pump arm
55. Screw
56. Pin
57. Union bolt
58. Cover
59. Diaphragm spring
60. Diaphragm lever
61. Diaphragm pin
62. Diaphragm chamber
63. Screw
64. Diaphragm
65. Gasket
66. Connecting rod
67. Pin

68. Ring
69. Washer
70. Diaphragm stop ring
71. Diaphragm stop ring
72. Screw
73. Level gauge screw
74. Gasket
75. Gasket
76. Stop ring
77. Float pin
78. Needle valve seat
79. Gasket
80. Collar
81. Throttle adjusting screw
82. Idle adjusting screw
83. Spring
84. Main jet
85. Main jet
86. Gasket
87. Plug
88. Gasket
89. Air bleed
90. Air bleed
91. Slow jet
92. Step jet
93. Air bleed screw
94. Air bleed step
95. Cover
96. Diaphragm
97. Spring
98. Gasket
99. Washer
100. Shim
101. Jet
102. Bleed plug
103. Retainer
104. Pin

105. Screw
106. Gasket
107. Plug
108. Gasket
109. Gasket
110. Bolt
111. Nut
112. Screw
113. Cover
114. Gasket
115. Sight glass
116. Gasket
117. Filter
118. Accelerator nozzle
119. Gasket
120. Plug
121. Cover
122. Coasting valve bracket
123. Clip
124. Screw
125. Spring
126. Screw
127. Spring
128. Shim
129. Throttle positioner
130. Nut
131. Rod
132. Collar
133. Shim
134. Collar
135. Arm
136. Plate
137. Retaining spring
138. Lever
139. Setscrew
140. Ring

Fig. 33a Key list for the carburetor used on the rotary engine (continued)

Efficient carburetion depends greatly on careful cleaning and inspection during overhaul, since dirt, gum, water, or varnish in or on the carburetor parts are often responsible for poor performance.

Overhaul your carburetor in a clean, dust-free area. Carefully disassemble the carburetor, referring often to the exploded views. Keep all similar and look alike parts segregated during disassembly and cleaning to avoid accidental interchange during assembly. Make a note of all jet sizes.

When the carburetor is disassembled, wash all parts (except diaphragms, electric choke units, pump plunger, and any other plastic, leather, fiber or rubber parts) in clean carburetor solvent. Do not leave parts in the solvent any longer than is necessary to sufficiently loosen the deposits. Excessive cleaning may remove the special finish from the float bowl and choke valve bodies, leaving these parts unfit for service. Rinse all parts in clean solvent and blow them dry with compressed air or allow them to airdry. Wipe clean all cork, plastic, leather, and fiber parts with a clean, lint-free cloth.

Blow out all passages and jets with compressed air and be sure that there are no restrictions or blockages. Never use wire or similar tools to clean jets, fuel passages, or air bleeds. Clean all jets and valves separately to avoid accidental interchange.

Check all parts for wear or damage. If wear or damage is found, replace the defective parts. Especially check the following:

1. Check the float needle and seat for wear. If wear is found, replace the complete assembly.

2. Check the float hinge pin for wear and the float(s) for dents or distortion. Replace the float if fuel has leaked into it.

3. Check the throttle and choke shaft bores for wear or an out-of-round condition. Damage or wear to the throttle arm, shaft, or shaft bore will often require replacement of the throttle body. These parts require a close tolerance of fit; wear may allow air leakage, which could affect starting and idling.

➡**Throttle shafts and bushings are not included in overhaul kits. They can be purchased separately.**

4. Inspect the idle mixture adjusting needles for burrs or grooves. Any such condition requires replacement of the needle, since you will not be able to obtain a satisfactory idle.

5. Test the accelerator pump check valves. They should pass air one way but not the other. Test for proper seating by blowing and sucking on the valve. Replace the valve if necessary. If the valve is satisfactory, wash the valve again to remove breath moisture.

6. Check the bowl cover for warped surfaces with a straightedge.

7. Closely inspect the valves and seats for wear or damage, replacing as necessary.

8. After the carburetor is assembled, check the choke valve for freedom of operation.

Carburetor overhaul kits are recommended for each overhaul. These kits contain all gaskets and new parts to replace those that deteriorate most rapidly. Failure to replace all parts supplied with the kit (especially gaskets) can result in poor performance later.

Some carburetor manufacturers supply overhaul kits of three basic types: minor repair; major repair; and gasket kits. Basically, they contain the following:

Minor Repair Kits:
- All gaskets
- Float needle valve
- Volume control screw
- All diaphragms
- Spring for the pump diaphragm

Major Repair Kits:
- All jet and gaskets
- All diaphragms
- Float needle valve
- Volume control screw
- Pump ball valve
- Main jet carrier
- Float
- Complete intermediate rod
- Intermediate pump lever
- Complete injector tube
- Some cover hold-down screws and washers

Gasket Kits:
- All gaskets

After cleaning and checking all components, reassemble the carburetor, using new parts and referring to the exploded view. When reassembling, make sure that all screws and jets are tight in their seats, but do not overtighten as the tips will be distorted. Tighten all screws gradually, in rotation. Do not tighten needle valves into their seats; uneven jetting will result. Always use new gaskets. Be sure to adjust the float lever when reassembling.

DIESEL FUEL SYSTEM

Troubleshooting

Use the accompanying chart to find the cause of fuel system related problems.

Fuel Filter and Priming Pump

REMOVAL & INSTALLATION

1. Disconnect both battery ground cables.
2. Disconnect and cap the filter lines.
3. The filter is removed with a band wrench.

4. Remove the two bolts attaching the priming pump to its bracket and lift off the pump.
5. Unbolt and remove the bracket from the engine.
6. Installation is the reverse of removal. Apply clean fuel to the filter O-ring prior to installation. Loosen the vent screw and prime the pump to expel air. Close the vent screw.

Injection Pump

REMOVAL & INSTALLATION

◆ **See Figures 34 and 35**

1. Disconnect both battery ground cables.
2. Remove the radiator fan and shroud.

Diesel Fuel System Troubleshooting

Problem	Possible Causes	Remedy
Hard Starting	Clogged fuel filter	Replace
	Water or air in the fuel filter	Replace
	Faulty fuel cut-off solenoid	Replace
	Incorrect injection timing	Adjust
	Air in the injection pump	Repair
	Incorrect stop lever position	Adjust
	Mechanical problems in the injection pump	Replace
	Seized injector needle valve	Replace
	Fuel leakage at the injector nozzle	Replace
	Incorrect injector opening pressure	Repair
	Bad glow plug	Replace
Rough Idle	Clogged fuel filter	Replace
	Water or air in the fuel filter	Replace
	Faulty fuel cut-off solenoid	Replace
	Incorrect injection timing	Adjust
	Air in the injection pump	Repair
	Incorrect stop lever position	Adjust
	Mechanical problems in the injection pump	Replace
	Seized injector needle valve	Replace
	Fuel leakage at the injector nozzle	Replace
	Incorrect injector opening pressure	Repair
	Loose or incorrectly installed injector	Replace
	Bad injector copper washer	Replace
	Cracked or leaking injection lines	Replace
	Incorrect idle speed adjustment	Adjust
Engine Knock	Incorrect injection timing	Adjust
	Poor quality fuel	Replace
	Incorrect injector opening pressure	Repair
	Seized injector needle valve	Replace
	Fuel leakage at the injector nozzle	Replace
High Fuel Consumption	Incorrect idle speed adjustment	Adjust
	Incorrect injection timing	Adjust
	Fuel leakage at the injector nozzle	Replace
	Incorrect injector opening pressure	Repair
	Loose or incorrectly installed injector	Replace
	Bad injector copper washer	Replace
	Cracked or leaking injection lines	Replace
	Clogged fuel filter	Replace
	Clogged air cleaner	Replace
Poor Acceleration	Clogged air cleaner	Replace
	Seized injector needle valve	Replace
	Fuel leakage at the injector nozzle	Replace
	Faulty fuel cut-off solenoid	Replace
	Incorrect injection timing	Adjust
	Air in the injection pump	Repair
	Incorrect stop lever position	Adjust
	Mechanical problems in the injection pump	Replace
	Cracked or leaking injection lines	Replace
	Water or air in the fuel filter	Replace

3. Remove the air conditioning compressor/power steering drive belt and idler pulley.

4. Remove the injection pump cover and gasket.

5. Turn the crankshaft until the injection pump drive gear keyway is at TDC.

6. Remove the large nut and washer attaching the drive gear to the injection pump.

➡ **Be careful! It's easy to accidentally drop the washer into the timing case.**

7. Remove the intake hose from the air cleaner and manifold.

8. Disconnect the throttle cable and, if equipped, the cruise control cable, from the pump.

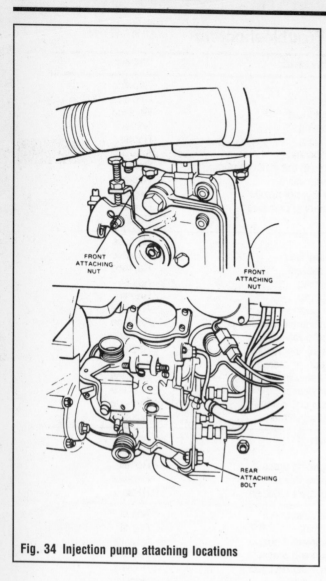

Fig. 34 Injection pump attaching locations

FRONT ATTACHING NUT

FRONT ATTACHING NUT

REAR ATTACHING BOLT

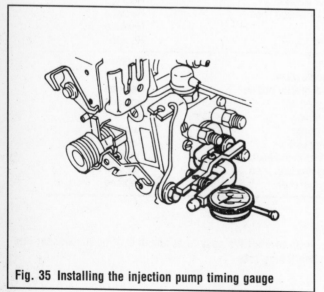

Fig. 35 Installing the injection pump timing gauge

9. Disconnect the fuel inlet line from the pump. Cap the line and pump fitting immediately.

10. Disconnect the fuel shut-off solenoid lead at the pump.

11. Disconnect the injection lines from the nozzle and pump. Cap the lines, nozzles and pump openings immediately.

12. Disconnect the lower fuel return line at the pump and fuel hoses. Cap all openings.

13. Loosen the lower no.3 intake port nut and remove the fuel return line.

14. Remove the two nuts attaching the injection pump to the front timing gear cover, and the one bolt attaching the pump to the rear support bracket.

15. Install a gear and hub remover in the drive gear cover and attach it to the injection pump drive gear. Rotate the screw clockwise until the gear separates from the pump. Remove the pump.

➡**When removing the pump, be careful to avoid dropping the pump shaft key into the timing case. Disconnect the cold start cable before lifting the pump clear of the engine, and reconnect it when lowering the pump into place for installation.**

To install:

16. Install the pump in the case, aligning the key with the keyway in the gear.

17. Install the nuts and washers attaching the pump and draw the pump into position. Do not tighten the fasteners completely, at this time.

18. Install the bolt attaching the pump to the rear support. Install the washer and nut attaching the pump to the drive gear. Torque the nut to 50 ft. lbs.

19. Install the pump drive gear cover and new gasket.

20. Adjust the injection timing as described above.

21. Connect all other components in the reverse of their removal order. Bleed the system through the priming pump, as described above. Run the engine and check for leaks.

INJECTION TIMING

◗ **See Figures 36, 37 and 38**

➡**A static timing gauge adapter and metric dial indicator are necessary for this procedure.**

1. Disconnect the battery ground cables.

2. Remove the distributor head plug bolt from the injection pump.

3. Install the timing gauge adapter and metric dial indicator so that the indicator pointer is in contact with the injection pump plunger and the gauge reads 2.0mm (0.0787 in.).

4. Align the 2° ATDC mark on the crankshaft pulley with the indicator on the timing gear case cover.

5. Slowly turn the engine counterclockwise until the dial indicator pointer stops moving (approximately 30–50° pulley travel).

6. Adjust the dial indicator to 0. Confirm that the dial indicator does not move from 0, by rotating the crankshaft slightly from right to left.

7. Turn the crankshaft clockwise until the timing mark is once again aligned with the cover pointer. The dial indicator should

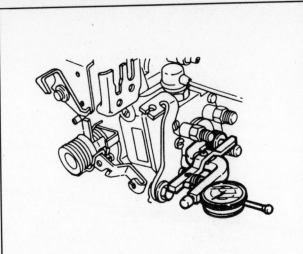

Fig. 36 Installing the injection pump timing gauge

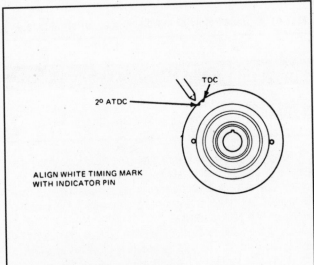

Fig. 37 Aligning the timing mark

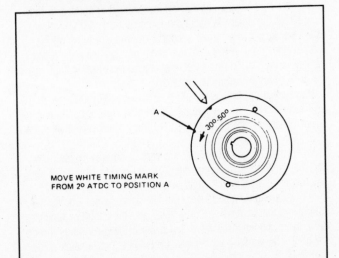

Fig. 38 Moving the crankshaft pulley timing mark

read 1mm ± 0.02mm (0.0394 in. ± 0.00079 in.). If not, proceed to Step 8.

8. Loosen the injection pump mounting nuts and bolts.

9. Rotate the pump counterclockwise past the correct timing position, then clockwise until timing is correct.

10. Repeat the timing check to make sure the adjustment is correct.

Fuel Injectors

REMOVAL & INSTALLATION

▶ **See Figure 39**

➡**A 27mm deep well socket is necessary for this procedure.**

1. Disconnect both battery ground cables.

2. Disconnect the injection lines at the nozzle and pump. Cap all openings immediately.

3. Remove the fuel return line and gaskets.

4. Unbolt the fuel line heater from the head and position it out of the way.

5. Unscrew the nozzles.

6. Remove the copper washer and steel gasket from the nozzle. Discard them.

7. Clean the nozzles and seats with a cleaning kit made for diesel nozzles.

8. Using new gaskets and washers, install the nozzles in the head. Torque them to 50 ft. lbs.

➡**The gaskets are installed with the blue side up.**

9. Install all other parts in reverse of their removal order.

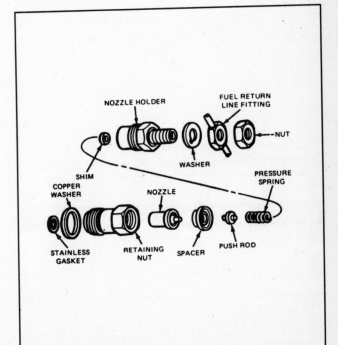

Fig. 39 Exploded view of the diesel engine fuel injector

Water Separator

DRAINING

▶ **See Figure 40**

1. Loosen the drain plug and allow the water to drain out.
2. If the water won't drain freely, or at all, loosen the vent plug on the priming pump.
3. When the water has drained, prime the system with the priming pump. Bleed the system at the priming pump.

REMOVAL & INSTALLATION

1. Disconnect the wiring.
2. Disconnect and cap the fuel lines.
3. Remove the protective cover.
4. Unbolt and remove the separator.
5. Installation is the reverse of removal. Bleed the system.

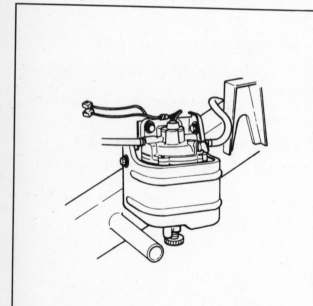

Fig. 40 Diesel water separator. Drain the water by loosening the drain plug on the bottom of the separator

Fuel Cut-Off Solenoid

▶ **See Figure 41**

REMOVAL & INSTALLATION

1. Disconnect the battery ground cables.
2. Disconnect the wiring.
3. Unscrew the cut-off solenoid and discard the O-ring.
4. Installation is the reverse of removal. Use a new O-ring coated with clean diesel fuel.

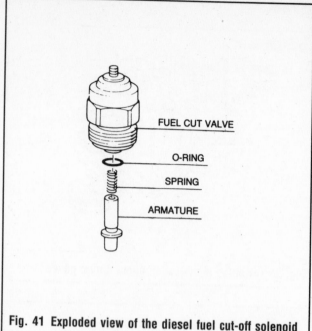

Fig. 41 Exploded view of the diesel fuel cut-off solenoid

Glow Plugs

OPERATION

This engine uses a quick start glow plug system, enabling the operator to start the engine relatively quickly after the key-on sequence. One glow plug per cylinder is used, controlled by a control module, two relays, a resistor, a coolant temperature switch, and clutch and neutral switches.

Relay, power, and feedback circuits are protected by fusible links in the harness. The control module is protected by a 10A fuse in the fuse panel.

When the ignition switch is turned ON, a Wait-to-Start signal appears near the cold start knob on the instrument panel. At this time, relay no.1 closes and full system voltage is applied to the glow plugs. If coolant temperature is below 86°F (30°C), relay no.2 also closes. After three seconds, the module turns off the Wait-to-Start light. If the operator does not start the engine and the key is left ON, the no.1 relay opens and cuts off voltage to the glow plugs within three seconds.

However, if coolant temperature is below 86°F (30°C) when the no.1 relay opens, the no.2 relay will remain closed, continuing reduced voltage to the glow plugs until the ignition switch is turned OFF.

When the engine is cranked, the control module cycles relay no.1 intermittently, providing the glow plugs with between 4 and 12v, depending on which replay is closed.

Once the engine has started, the alternator output signals the control module to open the no.1 relay and the afterglow function takes over, supplying between 4 and 5v to the glow plugs through the no.2 relay as long as the coolant temperature remains below 86°F (30°C).

Once the truck is in motion, the clutch and neutral switches close, opening the no.2 relay if the temperature switch hasn't already done so.

TESTING

▶ **See Figure 42**

1. Disconnect the leads from each glow plug. Connect one lead of an ohmmeter to the glow plug terminal and the other lead to a good ground. Set the ohmmeter on the X1 scale.

2. If the ohmmeter indicates less than 1Ω, the problem is not with the glow plug. If the ohmmeter indicates greater than 1Ω, replace the glow plug and retest.

REMOVAL & INSTALLATION

1. Disconnect the battery ground cables.
2. Disconnect the glow plug harness.

3. Using a 12mm deep well socket, unscrew the glow plugs.
4. Installation is the reverse of removal. Torque the glow plugs to 11–15 ft. lbs.

Cold Start Device

ADJUSTMENT

▶ **See Figures 43 and 44**

1. Disconnect the cable from the advance lever on the pump.
2. Pull the control knob under the dash to the full out position.
3. Connect a tachometer to the engine.

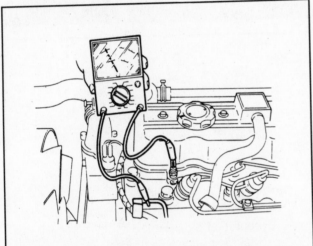

Fig. 42 Using an ohmmeter to test glow plugs—if the reading is greater than 1 ohm, replace the glow plug

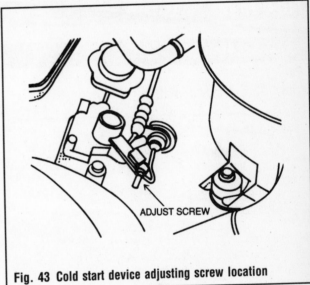

Fig. 43 Cold start device adjusting screw location

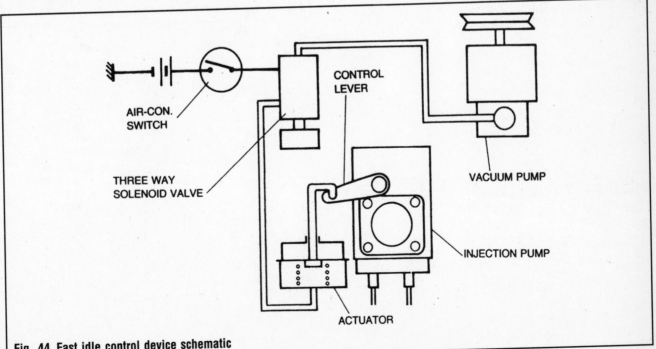

Fig. 44 Fast idle control device schematic

4. Start the engine and push the advance lever all the way to the stopper. Connect the cable.

5. Turn the adjusting screw until engine speed is 1,150–1,250 rpm.

Fast Idle Control Device

TESTING

With Air Conditioning Only

When the air conditioning compressor cycles on, the vacuum pump signals the three-way solenoid valve, which in turn applies vacuum to a vacuum diaphragm unit connected to a control lever on the injection pump. Engine speed should be held at 700 rpm or increase to no more than 750 rpm. If engine speed drops below 700 rpm with the air conditioning compressor on, there is a leak in the vacuum circuit.

FUEL TANK

Tank Assembly

REMOVAL & INSTALLATION

▶ **See Figure 45**

1. Raise and support the rear of the truck.
2. Remove the fuel tank drain plug and drain the gasoline into a metal container.
3. Install the drain plug.
4. Disconnect and plug the fuel pump line at the tank.
5. Disconnect the line from the condenser tank or vapor valve at the fuel tank.
6. If so equipped, disconnect the fuel return line.
7. Disconnect the fuel sending unit lead and the electrical connector.
8. Remove the fuel tank attaching bolts at the mounting bracket and lower the tank.
9. Installation is the reverse of removal.

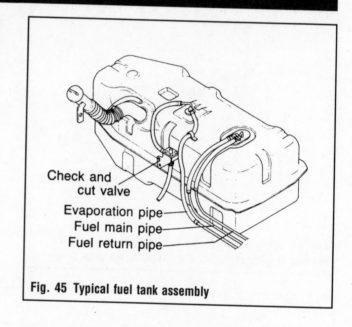

Check and
cut valve
Evaporation pipe
Fuel main pipe
Fuel return pipe

Fig. 45 Typical fuel tank assembly

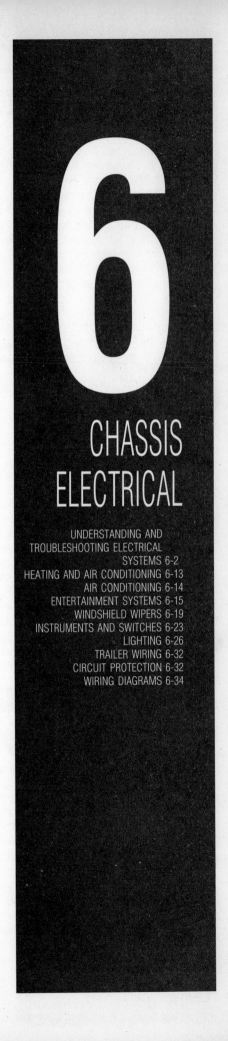

6

CHASSIS ELECTRICAL

UNDERSTANDING AND TROUBLESHOOTING ELECTRICAL SYSTEMS

Over the years import and domestic manufacturers have incorporated electronic control systems into their production lines. In fact, electronic control systems are so prevalent that all new cars and trucks built today are equipped with at least one on-board computer. These electronic components (with no moving parts) should theoretically last the life of the vehicle, provided that nothing external happens to damage the circuits or memory chips.

While it is true that electronic components should never wear out, in the real world malfunctions do occur. It is also true that any computer-based system is extremely sensitive to electrical voltages and cannot tolerate careless or haphazard testing/service procedures. An inexperienced individual can literally cause major damage looking for a minor problem by using the wrong kind of test equipment or connecting test leads/connectors with the ignition switch **ON**. When selecting test equipment, make sure the manufacturer's instructions state that the tester is compatible with whatever type of system is being serviced. Read all instructions carefully and double check all test points before installing probes or making any test connections.

The following section outlines basic diagnosis techniques for dealing with automotive electrical systems. Along with a general explanation of the various types of test equipment available to aid in servicing modern automotive systems, basic repair techniques for wiring harnesses and connectors are also given. Read the basic information before attempting any repairs or testing. This will provide the background of information necessary to avoid the most common and obvious mistakes that can cost both time and money. Although the replacement and testing procedures are simple in themselves, the systems are not, and unless one has a thorough understanding of all components and their function within a particular system, the logical test sequence these systems demand cannot be followed. Minor malfunctions can make a big difference, so it is important to know how each component affects the operation of the overall system in order to find the ultimate cause of a problem without replacing good components unnecessarily. It is not enough to use the correct test equipment; the test equipment must be used correctly.

Safety Precautions

✳✳ CAUTION

Whenever working on or around any electrical or electronic systems, always observe these general precautions to prevent the possibility of personal injury or damage to electronic components.

• Never install or remove battery cables with the key **ON** or the engine running. Jumper cables should be connected with the key **OFF** to avoid power surges that can damage electronic control units. Engines equipped with computer controlled systems should avoid both giving and getting jump starts due to the possibility of serious damage to components from arcing in the engine compartment if connections are made with the ignition **ON**.

• Always remove the battery cables before charging the battery. Never use a high output charger on an installed battery or attempt to use any type of "hot shot" (24 volt) starting aid.

• Exercise care when inserting test probes into connectors to insure good contact without damaging the connector or spreading the pins. Always probe connectors from the rear (wire) side, NOT the pin side, to avoid accidental shorting of terminals during test procedures.

• Never remove or attach wiring harness connectors with the ignition switch **ON**, especially to an electronic control unit.

• Do not drop any components during service procedures and never apply 12 volts directly to any component (like a solenoid or relay) unless instructed specifically to do so. Some component electrical windings are designed to safely handle only 4 or 5 volts and can be destroyed in seconds if 12 volts are applied directly to the connector.

• Remove the electronic control unit if the vehicle is to be placed in an environment where temperatures exceed approximately 176°F (80°C), such as a paint spray booth or when arc/gas welding near the control unit location.

Understanding Basic Electricity

Understanding the basic theory of electricity makes electrical troubleshooting much easier. Several gauges are used in electrical troubleshooting to see inside the circuit being tested. Without a basic understanding, it will be difficult to understand testing procedures.

THE WATER ANALOGY

Electricity is the flow of electrons—hypothetical particles thought to constitute the basic stuff of electricity. Many people have been taught electrical theory using an analogy with water. In a comparison with water flowing in a pipe, the electrons would be the water. As the flow of water can be measured, the flow of electricity can be measured. The unit of measurement is amperes, frequently abbreviated amps. An ammeter will measure the actual amount of current flowing in the circuit.

Just as the water pressure is measured in units such as pounds per square inch, electrical pressure is measured in volts. When a voltmeter's two probes are placed on two live portions of an electrical circuit with different electrical pressures, current will flow through the voltmeter and produce a reading which indicates the difference in electrical pressure between the two parts of the circuit.

While increasing the voltage in a circuit will increase the flow of current, the actual flow depends not only on voltage, but on the resistance of the circuit. The standard unit for measuring circuit resistance is an ohm, measured by an ohmmeter. The ohmmeter is somewhat similar to an ammeter, but incorporates its own source of power so that a standard voltage is always present.

CIRCUITS

An actual electric circuit consists of four basic parts. These are: the power source, such as a generator or battery; a hot wire, which conducts the electricity under a relatively high voltage to the component supplied by the circuit; the load, such as a lamp, motor, resistor or relay coil; and the ground wire, which carries the current back to the source under very low voltage. In such a circuit the bulk of the resistance exists between the point where the hot wire is connected to the load, and the point where the load is grounded. In an automobile, the vehicle's frame or body, which is made of steel, is used as a part of the ground circuit for many of the electrical devices.

Remember that, in electrical testing, the voltmeter is connected in parallel with the circuit being tested (without disconnecting any wires) and measures the difference in voltage between the locations of the two probes; that the ammeter is connected in series with the load (the circuit is separated at one point and the ammeter inserted so it becomes a part of the circuit); and the ohmmeter is self-powered, so that all the power in the circuit should be off and the portion of the circuit to be measured contacted at either end by one of the probes of the meter.

For any electrical system to operate, it must make a complete circuit. This simply means that the power flow from the battery must make a complete circle. When an electrical component is operating, power flows from the battery to the component, passes through the component causing it to perform it to function (such as lighting a light bulb) and then returns to the battery through the ground of the circuit. This ground is usually (but not always) the metal part of the vehicle on which the electrical component is mounted.

Perhaps the easiest way to visualize this is to think of connecting a light bulb with two wires attached to it to your vehicle's battery. The battery in your vehicle has two posts (negative and positive). If one of the two wires attached to the light bulb was attached to the negative post of the battery and the other wire was attached to the positive post of the battery, you would have a complete circuit. Current from the battery would flow out one post, through the wire attached to it and then to the light bulb, where it would pass through causing it to light. It would then leave the light bulb, travel through the other wire, and return to the other post of the battery.

AUTOMOTIVE CIRCUITS

The normal automotive circuit differs from this simple example in two ways. First, instead of having a return wire from the bulb to the battery, the light bulb return the current to the battery through the chassis of the vehicle. Since the negative battery cable is attached to the chassis and the chassis is made of electrically conductive metal, the chassis of the vehicle can serve as a ground wire to complete the circuit. Secondly, most automotive circuits contain switches to turn components on and off.

Some electrical components which require a large amount of current to operate also have a relay in their circuit. Since these circuits carry a large amount of current, the thickness of the wire in the circuit (gauge size) is also greater. If this large wire were connected from the component to the control switch on the instrument panel, and then back to the component, a voltage drop would occur in the circuit. To prevent this potential drop in voltage, an electromagnetic switch (relay) is used. The large wires in the circuit are connected from the vehicle battery to one side of the relay, and from the opposite side of the relay to the component. The relay is normally open, preventing current from passing through the circuit. An additional, smaller wire is connected from the relay to the control switch for the circuit. When the control switch is turned on, it grounds the smaller wire from the relay and completes the circuit.

SHORT CIRCUITS

If you were to disconnect the light bulb (from the previous example of a light-bulb being connected to the battery by two wires) from the wires and touch the two wires together (please take our word for this; don't try it), the result will be a shower of sparks. A similar thing happens (on a smaller scale) when the power supply wire to a component or the electrical component itself becomes grounded before the normal ground connection for the circuit. To prevent damage to the system, the fuse for the circuit blows to interrupt the circuit—protecting the components from damage. Because grounding a wire from a power source makes a complete circuit—less the required component to use the power—the phenomenon is called a short circuit. The most common causes of short circuits are: the rubber insulation on a wire breaking or rubbing through to expose the current carrying core of the wire to a metal part of the car, or a shorted switch.

Some electrical systems on the vehicle are protected by a circuit breaker which is, basically, a self-repairing fuse. When either of the described events takes place in a system which is protected by a circuit breaker, the circuit breaker opens the circuit the same way a fuse does. However, when either the short is removed from the circuit or the surge subsides, the circuit breaker resets itself and does not have to be replaced as a fuse does.

Troubleshooting

When diagnosing a specific problem, organized troubleshooting is a must. The complexity of a modern automobile demands that you approach any problem in a logical, organized manner. There are certain troubleshooting techniques that are standard:

1. Establish when the problem occurs. Does the problem appear only under certain conditions? Were there any noises, odors, or other unusual symptoms?

2. Isolate the problem area. To do this, make some simple tests and observations; then eliminate the systems that are working properly. Check for obvious problems such as broken wires, dirty connections or split/disconnected vacuum hoses. Always check the obvious before assuming something complicated is the cause.

3. Test for problems systematically to determine the cause once the problem area is isolated. Are all the components functioning properly? Is there power going to electrical switches and motors? Is there vacuum at vacuum switches and/or actuators? Is there a mechanical problem such as bent linkage or loose mounting screws? Performing careful, systematic checks will often turn up most causes on the first inspection without wasting time checking components that have little or no relationship to the problem.

4. Test all repairs after the work is done to make sure that the problem is fixed. Some causes can be traced to more than one component, so a careful verification of repair work is important in order to pick up additional malfunctions that may cause a problem to reappear or a different problem to arise. A blown fuse, for example, is a simple problem that may require more than another

fuse to repair. If you don't look for a problem that caused a fuse to blow, a shorted wire (for example) may go undetected.

Experience has shown that most problems tend to be the result of a fairly simple and obvious cause, such as loose or corroded connectors or air leaks in the intake system. This makes careful inspection of components during testing essential to quick and accurate troubleshooting.

BASIC TROUBLESHOOTING THEORY

Electrical problems generally fall into one of three areas:
• The component that is not functioning is not receiving current.
• The component itself is not functioning.
• The component is not properly grounded.

Problems that fall into the first category are by far the most complicated. It is the current supply system to the component which contains all the switches, relay, fuses, etc.

The electrical system can be checked with a test light and a jumper wire. A test light is a device that looks like a pointed screwdriver with a wire attached to it. It has a light bulb in its handle. A jumper wire is a piece of insulated wire with an alligator clip attached to each end.

If a light bulb is not working, you must follow a systematic plan to determine which of the three causes is the villain.

1. Turn on the switch that controls the inoperable bulb.

2. Disconnect the power supply wire from the bulb.

3. Attach the ground wire to the test light to a good metal ground.

4. Touch the probe end of the test light to the end of the power supply wire that was disconnected from the bulb. If the bulb is receiving current, the test light will go on.

➡**If the bulb is one which works only when the ignition key is turned on (turn signal), make sure the key is turned on.**

If the test light does not go on, then the problem is in the circuit between the battery and the bulb. As mentioned before, this includes all the switches, fuses, and relays in the system. Turn to a wiring diagram and find the bulb on the diagram. Follow the wire that runs back to the battery. The problem is an open circuit between the battery and the bulb. If the fuse is blown and, when replaced, immediately blows again, there is a short circuit in the system which must be located and repaired. If there is a switch in the system, bypass it with a jumper wire. This is done by connecting one end of the jumper wire to the power supply wire into the switch and the other end of the jumper wire to the wire coming out of the switch. If the test light illuminates with the jumper wire installed, the switch or whatever was bypassed is defective.

➡**Never substitute the jumper wire for the bulb, as the bulb is the component required to use the power from the power source.**

5. If the bulb in the test light goes on, then the current is getting to the bulb that is not working in the car. This eliminates the first of the three possible causes. Connect the power supply wire and connect a jumper wire from the bulb to a good metal ground. Do this with the switch which controls the bulb works with jumper wire installed, then it has a bad ground. This is usually caused by the metal area on which the bulb mounts to the vehicle being coated with some type of foreign matter.

6. If neither test located the source of the trouble, then the light bulb itself is defective.

The above test procedure can be applied to any of the components of the chassis electrical system by substituting the component that is not working for the light bulb. Remember that for any electrical system to work, all connections must be clean and tight.

TEST EQUIPMENT

➡**Pinpointing the exact cause of trouble in an electrical system can sometimes only be accomplished by the use of special test equipment. The following describes different types of commonly used test equipment and explains how to use them in diagnosis. In addition to the information covered below, the tool manufacturer's instructions booklet (provided with the tester) should be read and clearly understood before attempting any test procedures.**

Jumper Wires

Jumper wires are simple, yet extremely valuable, pieces of test equipment. They are basically test wires which are used to bypass sections of a circuit. The simplest type of jumper wire is a length of multi-strand wire with an alligator clip at each end. Jumper wires are usually fabricated from lengths of standard automotive wire and whatever type of connector (alligator clip, spade connector or pin connector) that is required for the particular vehicle being tested. The well equipped tool box will have several different styles of jumper wires in several different lengths. Some jumper wires are made with three or more terminals coming from a common splice for special purpose testing. In cramped, hard-to-reach areas it is advisable to have insulated boots over the jumper wire terminals in order to prevent accidental grounding, sparks, and possible fire, especially when testing fuel system components.

Jumper wires are used primarily to locate open electrical circuits, on either the ground $(-)$ side of the circuit or on the hot $(+)$ side. If an electrical component fails to operate, connect the jumper wire between the component and a good ground. If the component operates only with the jumper installed, the ground circuit is open. If the ground circuit is good, but the component does not operate, the circuit between the power feed and component may be open. By moving the jumper wire successively back from the lamp toward the power source, you can isolate the area of the circuit where the open is located. When the component stops functioning, or the power is cut off, the open is in the segment of wire between the jumper and the point previously tested.

You can sometimes connect the jumper wire directly from the battery to the hot terminal of the component, but first make sure the component uses 12 volts in operation. Some electrical components, such as fuel injectors, are designed to operate on about 4 volts and running 12 volts directly to the injector terminals can cause damage.

By inserting an in-line fuse holder between a set of test leads, a fused jumper wire can be used for bypassing open circuits. Use a 5 amp fuse to provide protection against voltage spikes. When in doubt, use a voltmeter to check the voltage input to the component and measure how much voltage is normally being applied.

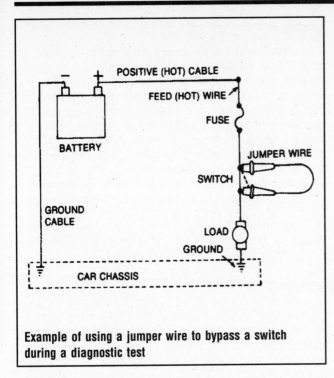

Example of using a jumper wire to bypass a switch during a diagnostic test

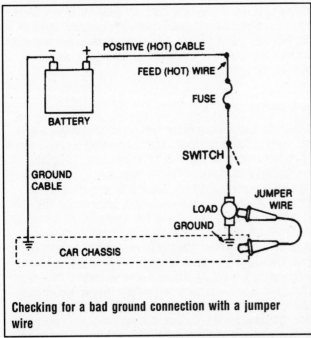

Checking for a bad ground connection with a jumper wire

✳✳ CAUTION

Never use jumpers made from wire that is of lighter gauge than that which is used in the circuit under test. If the jumper wire is of too small a gauge, it may overheat and possibly melt. Never use jumpers to bypass high resistance loads in a circuit. Bypassing resistances, in effect, creates a short circuit. This may, in turn, cause damage and fire. Jumper wires should only be used to bypass lengths of wire.

Unpowered Test Lights

The 12 volt test light is used to check circuits and components while electrical current is flowing through them. It is used for voltage and ground tests. Twelve volt test lights come in different styles but all have three main parts; a ground clip, a probe, and a light. The most commonly used 12 volt test lights have pick-type probes. To use a 12 volt test light, connect the ground clip to a good ground and probe wherever necessary with the pick. The pick should be sharp so that it can be probed into tight spaces.

✳✳ CAUTION

Do not use a test light to probe electronic ignition spark plug or coil wires. Never use a pick-type test light to probe wiring on computer controlled systems unless specifically instructed to do so. Any wire insulation that is pierced by the test light probe should be taped and sealed with silicone after testing.

Like the jumper wire, the 12 volt test light is used to isolate opens in circuits. But, whereas the jumper wire is used to bypass the open to operate the load, the 12 volt test light is used to locate the presence of voltage in a circuit. If the test light glows, you know that there is power up to that point; if the 12 volt test light does not glow when its probe is inserted into the wire or connector, you know that there is an open circuit (no power). Move the test light in successive steps back toward the power source until the light in the handle does glow. When it glows, the open is between the probe and point which was probed previously.

➡ **The test light does not detect that 12 volts (or any particular amount of voltage) is present; it only detects that some voltage is present. It is advisable before using the test light to touch its terminals across the battery posts to make sure the light is operating properly.**

Self-Powered Test Lights

The self-powered test light usually contains a 1.5 volt penlight battery. One type of self-powered test light is similar in design to the 12 volt unit. This type has both the battery and the light in the handle, along with a pick-type probe tip. The second type has the light toward the open tip, so that the light illuminates the contact point. The self-powered test light is a dual purpose piece of test equipment. It can be used to test for either open or short circuits when power is isolated from the circuit (continuity test). A powered test light should not be used on any computer controlled system or component unless specifically instructed to do so. Many engine sensors can be destroyed by even this small amount of voltage applied directly to the terminals.

Voltmeters

A voltmeter is used to measure voltage at any point in a circuit, or to measure the voltage drop across any part of a circuit. It can also be used to check continuity in a wire or circuit by indicating current flow from one end to the other. Analog voltmeters usually have various scales on the meter dial and a selector switch to allow the selection of different voltages. The voltmeter has a positive and a negative lead. To avoid damage to the meter, always connect the negative lead to the negative (−) side of the circuit (to ground or nearest the ground side of the circuit) and connect the positive lead to the positive (+) side of the circuit (to the power source or the nearest power source). Note that the negative voltmeter lead will always be black and that the positive voltmeter will always be some color other than black (usually red).

Depending on how the voltmeter is connected into the circuit, it has several uses. A voltmeter can be connected either in parallel or in series with a circuit and it has a very high resistance to current flow. When connected in parallel, only a small amount of current will flow through the voltmeter current path; the rest will flow through the normal circuit current path and the circuit will work normally. When the voltmeter is connected in series with a circuit, only a small amount of current can flow through the circuit. The circuit will not work properly, but the voltmeter reading will show if the circuit is complete or not.

Ohmmeters

The ohmmeter is designed to read resistance (which is measured in ohms or Ω) in a circuit or component. Although there are several different styles of ohmmeters, all analog meters will usually have a selector switch which permits the measurement of different ranges of resistance (usually the selector switch allows the multiplication of the meter reading by 10, 100, 1000, and 10,000). A calibration knob allows the meter to be set at zero for accurate measurement. Since all ohmmeters are powered by an internal battery, the ohmmeter can be used as a self-powered test light. When the ohmmeter is connected, current from the ohmmeter flows through the circuit or component being tested. Since the ohmmeter's internal resistance and voltage are known values, the amount of current flow through the meter depends on the resistance of the circuit or component being tested.

The ohmmeter can be used to perform a continuity test for opens or shorts (either by observation of the meter needle or as a self-powered test light), and to read actual resistance in a circuit. It should be noted that the ohmmeter is used to check the resistance of a component or wire while there is no voltage applied to the circuit. Current flow from an outside voltage source (such as the vehicle battery) can damage the ohmmeter, so the circuit or component should be isolated from the vehicle electrical system before any testing is done. Since the ohmmeter uses its own voltage source, either lead can be connected to any test point.

➡️**When checking diodes or other solid state components, the ohmmeter leads can only be connected one way in order to measure current flow in a single direction. Make sure the positive (+) and negative (−) terminal connections are as described in the test procedures to verify the one-way diode operation.**

In using the meter for making continuity checks, do not be concerned with the actual resistance readings. Zero resistance, or any ohm reading, indicates continuity in the circuit. Infinite resistance indicates an open in the circuit. A high resistance reading where there should be none indicates a problem in the circuit. Checks for short circuits are made in the same manner as checks for open circuits except that the circuit must be isolated from both power and normal ground. Infinite resistance indicates no continuity to ground, while zero resistance indicates a dead short to ground.

Ammeters

An ammeter measures the amount of current flowing through a circuit in units called amperes or amps. Amperes are units of electron flow which indicate how fast the electrons are flowing through the circuit. Since Ohms Law dictates that current flow in a circuit is equal to the circuit voltage divided by the total circuit resistance, increasing voltage also increases the current level (amps). Likewise, any decrease in resistance will increase the amount of amps in a circuit. At normal operating voltage, most circuits have a characteristic amount of amperes, called "current draw" which can be measured using an ammeter. By referring to a specified current draw rating, measuring the amperes, and comparing the two values, one can determine what is happening within the circuit to aid in diagnosis. An open circuit, for example, will not allow any current to flow so the ammeter reading will be zero. More current flows through a heavily loaded circuit or when the charging system is operating.

An ammeter is always connected in series with the circuit being tested. All of the current that normally flows through the circuit must also flow through the ammeter; if there is any other path for the current to follow, the ammeter reading will not be accurate. The ammeter itself has very little resistance to current flow and therefore will not affect the circuit, but it will measure current draw only when the circuit is closed and electricity is flowing. Excessive current draw can blow fuses and drain the battery, while a reduced current draw can cause motors to run slowly, lights to dim and other components to not operate properly. The ammeter can help diagnose these conditions by locating the cause of the high or low reading.

Multimeters

Different combinations of test meters can be built into a single unit designed for specific tests. Some of the more common combination test devices are known as Volt/Amp testers, Tach/Dwell meters, or Digital Multimeters. The Volt/Amp tester is used for charging system, starting system or battery tests and consists of a voltmeter, an ammeter and a variable resistance carbon pile. The voltmeter will usually have at least two ranges for use with 6, 12 and/or 24 volt systems. The ammeter also has more than one range for testing various levels of battery loads and starter current draw. The carbon pile can be adjusted to offer different amounts of resistance. The Volt/Amp tester has heavy leads to carry large amounts of current and many later models have an inductive ammeter pickup that clamps around the wire to simplify test connections. On some models, the ammeter also has a zero-center scale to allow testing of charging and starting systems without switching leads or polarity. A digital multimeter is a voltmeter, ammeter and ohmmeter combined in an instrument which gives a digital readout. These are often used when testing solid state circuits because of their high input impedance (usually 10 megohms or more).

The tach/dwell meter that combines a tachometer and a dwell (cam angle) meter is a specialized kind of voltmeter. The tachometer scale is marked to show engine speed in rpm and the dwell scale is marked to show degrees of distributor shaft rotation. In most electronic ignition systems, dwell is determined by the control unit, but the dwell meter can also be used to check the duty cycle (operation) of some electronic engine control systems. Some tach/dwell meters are powered by an internal battery, while others take their power from the vehicle battery in use. The battery powered testers usually require calibration (much like an ohmmeter) before testing.

TESTING

Open Circuits

To use the self-powered test light or a multimeter to check for open circuits, first isolate the circuit from the vehicle's 12 volt power source by disconnecting the battery or wiring harness connector. Connect the test light or ohmmeter ground clip to a good ground and probe sections of the circuit sequentially with the test light. (start from either end of the circuit). If the light is out/or there is infinite resistance, the open is between the probe and the circuit ground. If the light is on/or the meter shows continuity, the open is between the probe and end of the circuit toward the power source.

Short Circuits

By isolating the circuit both from power and from ground, and using a self-powered test light or multimeter, you can check for shorts to ground in the circuit. Isolate the circuit from power and ground. Connect the test light or ohmmeter ground clip to a good ground and probe any easy-to-reach test point in the circuit. If the light comes on or there is continuity, there is a short somewhere in the circuit. To isolate the short, probe a test point at either end of the isolated circuit (the light should be on/there should be continuity). Leave the test light probe engaged and open connectors, switches, remove parts, etc., sequentially, until the light goes out/continuity is broken. When the light goes out, the short is between the last circuit component opened and the previous circuit opened.

➡**The battery in the test light and does not provide much current. A weak battery may not provide enough power to illuminate the test light even when a complete circuit is made (especially if there are high resistances in the circuit). Always make sure that the test battery is strong. To check the battery, briefly touch the ground clip to the probe; if the light glows brightly the battery is strong enough for testing. Never use a self-powered test light to perform checks for opens or shorts when power is applied to the electrical system under test. The 12 volt vehicle power will quickly burn out the light bulb in the test light.**

Available Voltage Measurement

Set the voltmeter selector switch to the 20V position and connect the meter negative lead to the negative post of the battery. Connect the positive meter lead to the positive post of the battery and turn the ignition switch **ON** to provide a load. Read the voltage on the meter or digital display. A well charged battery should register over 12 volts. If the meter reads below 11.5 volts, the battery power may be insufficient to operate the electrical system properly. This test determines voltage available from the battery and should be the first step in any electrical trouble diagnosis procedure. Many electrical problems, especially on computer controlled systems, can be caused by a low state of charge in the battery. Excessive corrosion at the battery cable terminals can cause

a poor contact that will prevent proper charging and full battery current flow.

Normal battery voltage is 12 volts when fully charged. When the battery is supplying current to one or more circuits it is said to be "under load." When everything is off the electrical system is under a "no-load" condition. A fully charged battery may show about 12.5 volts at no load; will drop to 12 volts under medium load; and will drop even lower under heavy load. If the battery is partially discharged the voltage decrease under heavy load may be excessive, even though the battery shows 12 volts or more at no load. When allowed to discharge further, the battery's available voltage under load will decrease more severely. For this reason, it is important that the battery be fully charged during all testing procedures to avoid errors in diagnosis and incorrect test results.

Voltage Drop

When current flows through a resistance, the voltage beyond the resistance is reduced (the larger the current, the greater the reduction in voltage). When no current is flowing, there is no voltage drop because there is no current flow. All points in the circuit which are connected to the power source are at the same voltage as the power source. The total voltage drop always equals the total source voltage. In a long circuit with many connectors, a series of small, unwanted voltage drops due to corrosion at the connectors can add up to a total loss of voltage which impairs the operation of the normal loads in the circuit. The maximum allowable voltage drop under load is critical, especially if there is m than one high resistance problem in a circuit because all voltage drops are cumulative. A small drop is normal due to the resistance of the conductors.

INDIRECT COMPUTATION OF VOLTAGE DROPS

1. Set the voltmeter selector switch to the 20 volt position.
2. Connect the meter negative lead to a good ground.
3. While operating the circuit, probe all loads in the circuit with the positive meter lead and observe the voltage readings. A drop should be noticed after the first load. But, there should be little or no voltage drop before the first load.

DIRECT MEASUREMENT OF VOLTAGE DROPS

1. Set the voltmeter switch to the 20 volt position.
2. Connect the voltmeter negative lead to the ground side of the load to be measured.
3. Connect the positive lead to the positive side of the resistance or load to be measured.
4. Read the voltage drop directly on the 20 volt scale.

Too high a voltage indicates too high a resistance. If, for example, a blower motor runs too slowly, you can determine if perhaps there is too high a resistance in the resistor pack. By taking voltage drop readings in all parts of the circuit, you can isolate the problem. Too low a voltage drop indicates too low a resistance. Take the blower motor for example again. If a blower motor runs too fast in the MED and/or LOW position, the problem might be isolated in the resistor pack by taking voltage drop readings in all parts of the circuit to locate a possibly shorted resistor.

HIGH RESISTANCE TESTING

1. Set the voltmeter selector switch to the 4 volt position.
2. Connect the voltmeter positive lead to the positive post of the battery.

3. Turn on the headlights and heater blower to provide a load.

4. Probe various points in the circuit with the negative voltmeter lead.

5. Read the voltage drop on the 4 volt scale. Some average maximum allowable voltage drops are:

- FUSE PANEL: 0.7 volts
- IGNITION SWITCH: 0.5 volts
- HEADLIGHT SWITCH: 0.7 volts
- IGNITION COIL (+): 0.5 volts
- ANY OTHER LOAD: 1.3 volts

➡**Voltage drops are all measured while a load is operating; without current flow, there will be no voltage drop.**

Resistance Measurement

The batteries in an ohmmeter will weaken with age and temperature, so the ohmmeter must be calibrated or "zeroed" before taking measurements. To zero the meter, place the selector switch in its lowest range and touch the two ohmmeter leads together. Turn the calibration knob until the meter needle is exactly on zero.

➡**All analog (needle) type ohmmeters must be zeroed before use, but some digital ohmmeter models are automatically calibrated when the switch is turned on. Self-calibrating digital ohmmeters do not have an adjusting knob, but its a good idea to check for a zero readout before use by touching the leads together. All computer controlled systems require the use of a digital ohmmeter with at least 10 megohms impedance for testing. Before any test procedures are attempted, make sure the ohmmeter used is compatible with the electrical system or damage to the on-board computer could result.**

To measure resistance, first isolate the circuit from the vehicle power source by disconnecting the battery cables or the harness connector. Make sure the key is **OFF** when disconnecting any components or the battery. Where necessary, also isolate at least one side of the circuit to be checked in order to avoid reading parallel resistances. Parallel circuit resistances will always give a lower reading than the actual resistance of either of the branches. When measuring the resistance of parallel circuits, the total resistance will always be lower than the smallest resistance in the circuit. Connect the meter leads to both sides of the circuit (wire or component) and read the actual measured ohms on the meter scale. Make sure the selector switch is set to the proper ohm scale for the circuit being tested to avoid misreading the ohmmeter test value.

❋❋ WARNING

Never use an ohmmeter with power applied to the circuit. Like the self-powered test light, the ohmmeter is designed to operate on its own power supply. The normal 12 volt automotive electrical system current could damage the meter!

Wiring Harnesses

The average automobile contains about ½ mile of wiring, with hundreds of individual connections. To protect the many wires from damage and to keep them from becoming a confusing tangle, they are organized into bundles, enclosed in plastic or taped together and called wiring harnesses. Different harnesses serve different parts of the vehicle. Individual wires are color coded to help trace them through a harness where sections are hidden from view.

Automotive wiring or circuit conductors can be in any one of three forms:

1. Single strand wire
2. Multi-strand wire
3. Printed circuitry

Single strand wire has a solid metal core and is usually used inside such components as alternators, motors, relays and other devices. Multi-strand wire has a core made of many small strands of wire twisted together into a single conductor. Most of the wiring in an automotive electrical system is made up of multi-strand wire, either as a single conductor or grouped together in a harness. All wiring is color coded on the insulator, either as a solid color or as a colored wire with an identification stripe. A printed circuit is a thin film of copper or other conductor that is printed on an insulator backing. Occasionally, a printed circuit is sandwiched between two sheets of plastic for more protection and flexibility. A complete printed circuit, consisting of conductors, insulating material and connectors for lamps or other components is called a printed circuit board. Printed circuitry is used in place of individual wires or harnesses in places where space is limited, such as behind instrument panels.

Since automotive electrical systems are very sensitive to changes in resistance, the selection of properly sized wires is critical when systems are repaired. A loose or corroded connection or a replacement wire that is too small for the circuit will add extra resistance and an additional voltage drop to the circuit. A ten percent voltage drop can result in slow or erratic motor operation, for example, even though the circuit is complete. The wire gauge number is an expression of the cross-section area of the conductor. The most common system for expressing wire size is the American Wire Gauge (AWG) system.

Gauge numbers are assigned to conductors of various cross-section areas. As gauge number increases, area decreases and the conductor becomes smaller. A 5 gauge conductor is smaller than a 1 gauge conductor and a 10 gauge is smaller than a 5 gauge. As the cross-section area of a conductor decreases, resistance increases and so does the gauge number. A conductor with a higher gauge number will carry less current than a conductor with a lower gauge number.

➡**Gauge wire size refers to the size of the conductor, not the size of the complete wire. It is possible to have two wires of the same gauge with different diameters because one may have thicker insulation than the other.**

12 volt automotive electrical systems generally use 10, 12, 14, 16 and 18 gauge wire. Main power distribution circuits and larger accessories usually use 10 and 12 gauge wire. Battery cables are usually 4 or 6 gauge, although 1 and 2 gauge wires are occasionally used. Wire length must also be considered when making repairs to a circuit. As conductor length increases, so does resistance. An 18 gauge wire, for example, can carry a 10 amp load for 10 feet without excessive voltage drop; however if a 15 foot wire is required for the same 10 amp load, it must be a 16 gauge wire.

An electrical schematic shows the electrical current paths when a circuit is operating properly. It is essential to understand how a circuit works before trying to figure out why it doesn't. Schematics break the entire electrical system down into individual circuits and show only one particular circuit. In a schematic, no attempt is made to represent wiring and components as they physically appear on the vehicle; switches and other components are shown as simply as possible. Face views of harness connectors show the cavity or terminal locations in all multi-pin connectors to help locate test points.

If you need to backprobe a connector while it is on the component, the order of the terminals must be mentally reversed. The wire color code can help in this situation, as well as a keyway, lock tab or other reference mark.

WIRING REPAIR

Soldering is a quick, efficient method of joining metals permanently. Everyone who has the occasion to make wiring repairs should know how to solder. Electrical connections that are soldered are far less likely to come apart and will conduct electricity much better than connections that are only "pig-tailed" together. The most popular (and preferred) method of soldering is with an electrical soldering gun. Soldering irons are available in many sizes and wattage ratings. Irons with higher wattage ratings deliver higher temperatures and recover lost heat faster. A small soldering iron rated for no more than 50 watts is recommended, especially on electrical systems where excess heat can damage the components being soldered.

There are three ingredients necessary for successful soldering; proper flux, good solder and sufficient heat. A soldering flux is necessary to clean the metal of tarnish, prepare it for soldering and to enable the solder to spread into tiny crevices. When soldering, always use a rosin core solder which is non-corrosive and will not attract moisture once the job is finished. Other types of flux (acid core) will leave a residue that will attract moisture and cause the wires to corrode. Tin is a unique metal with a low melting point. In a molten state, it dissolves and alloys easily with many metals. Solder is made by mixing tin with lead. The most common proportions are 40/60, 50/50 and 60/40, with the percentage of tin listed first. Low priced solders usually contain less tin, making them very difficult for a beginner to use because more heat is required to melt the solder. A common solder is 40/60 which is well suited for all-around general use, but 60/40 melts easier and is preferred for electrical work.

Soldering Techniques

Successful soldering requires that the metals to be joined be heated to a temperature that will melt the solder, usually 360–460°F (182–238°C). Contrary to popular belief, the purpose of the soldering iron is not to melt the solder itself, but to heat the parts being soldered to a temperature high enough to melt the solder when it is touched to the work. Melting flux-cored solder on the soldering iron will usually destroy the effectiveness of the flux.

➡**Soldering tips are made of copper for good heat conductivity, but must be "tinned" regularly for quick transference of heat to the project and to prevent the solder from sticking to the iron. To "tin" the iron, simply heat it and touch the flux-cored solder to the tip; the solder will flow over the hot tip. Wipe the excess off with a clean rag, but be careful as the iron will be hot.**

After some use, the tip may become pitted. If so, simply dress the tip smooth with a smooth file and "tin" the tip again. Flux-cored solder will remove oxides but rust, bits of insulation and oil or grease must be removed with a wire brush or emery cloth. For

maximum strength in soldered parts, the joint must start off clean and tight. Weak joints will result in gaps too wide for the solder to bridge.

If a separate soldering flux is used, it should be brushed or swabbed on only those areas that are to be soldered. Most solders contain a core of flux and separate fluxing is unnecessary. Hold the work to be soldered firmly. It is best to solder on a wooden board, because a metal vise will only rob the piece to be soldered of heat and make it difficult to melt the solder. Hold the soldering tip with the broadest face against the work to be soldered. Apply solder under the tip close to the work, using enough solder to give a heavy film between the iron and the piece being soldered, while moving slowly and making sure the solder melts properly. Keep the work level or the solder will run to the lowest part and favor the thicker parts, because these require more heat to melt the solder. If the soldering tip overheats (the solder coating on the face of the tip burns up), it should be retinned. Once the soldering is completed, let the soldered joint stand until cool. Tape and seal all soldered wire splices after the repair has cooled.

Wire Harness Connectors

Most connectors in the engine compartment or that are otherwise exposed to the elements are protected against moisture and dirt which could create oxidation and deposits on the terminals.

These special connectors are weather-proof. All repairs require the use of a special terminal and the tool required to service it. This tool is used to remove the pin and sleeve terminals. If removal is attempted with an ordinary pick, there is a good chance that the terminal will be bent or deformed. Unlike standard blade type terminals, these weather-proof terminals cannot be straightened once they are bent. Make certain that the connectors are properly seated and all of the sealing rings are in place when connecting leads. On some models, a hinge-type flap provides a backup or secondary locking feature for the terminals. Most secondary locks are used to improve connector reliability by retaining the terminals if the small terminal lock tangs are not positioned properly.

Molded-on connectors require complete replacement of the connection. This means splicing a new connector assembly into the harness. All splices should be soldered to insure proper contact. Use care when probing the connections or replacing terminals in them as it is possible to short between opposite terminals. If this happens to the wrong terminal pair, it is possible to damage certain components. Always use jumper wires between connectors for circuit checking and never probe through weatherproof seals.

Open circuits are often difficult to locate by sight because corrosion or terminal misalignment are hidden by the connectors. Merely wiggling a connector on a sensor or in the wiring harness may correct the open circuit condition. This should always be considered when an open circuit or a failed sensor is indicated. Intermittent problems may also be caused by oxidized or loose connections. When using a circuit tester for diagnosis, always probe connections from the wire side. Be careful not to damage sealed connectors with test probes.

All wiring harnesses should be replaced with identical parts, using the same gauge wire and connectors. When signal wires are spliced into a harness, use wire with high temperature insulation only. It is seldom necessary to replace a complete harness. If replacement is necessary, pay close attention to insure proper harness routing. Secure the harness with suitable plastic wire clamps to prevent vibrations from causing the harness to wear in spots or contact any hot components.

➡**Weatherproof connectors cannot be replaced with standard connectors. Instructions are provided with replacement connector and terminal packages. Some wire harnesses have mounting indicators (usually pieces of colored tape) to mark where the harness is to be secured.**

In making wiring repairs, its important that you always replace damaged wires with wiring of the same gauge as the wire being replaced. The heavier the wire, the smaller the gauge number. Wires are color-coded to aid in identification and whenever possible the same color coded wire should be used for replacement. A wire stripping and crimping tool is necessary to install solderless terminal connectors. Test all crimps by pulling on the wires; it should not be possible to pull the wires out of a good crimp.

Wires which are open, exposed or otherwise damaged are repaired by simple splicing. Where possible, if the wiring harness is accessible and the damaged place in the wire can be located, it is best to open the harness and check for all possible damage. In an inaccessible harness, the wire must be bypassed with a new insert, usually taped to the outside of the old harness.

When replacing fusible links, be sure to use fusible link wire, NOT ordinary automotive wire. Make sure the fusible segment is of the same gauge and construction as the one being replaced and double the stripped end when crimping the terminal connector for a good contact. The melted (open) fusible link segment of the wiring harness should be cut off as close to the harness as possible, then a new segment spliced in as described. In the case of a damaged fusible link that feeds two harness wires, the harness connections should be replaced with two fusible link wires so that each circuit will have its own separate protection.

➡**Most of the problems caused in the wiring harness are due to bad ground connections. Always check all vehicle ground connections for corrosion or looseness before performing any power feed checks to eliminate the chance of a bad ground affecting the circuit.**

Hard-Shell Connectors

Unlike molded connectors, the terminal contacts in hard-shell connectors can be replaced. Weatherproof hard-shell connectors with the leads molded into the shell have non-replaceable terminal ends. Replacement usually involves the use of a special terminal removal tool that depresses the locking tangs (barbs) on the connector terminal and allows the connector to be removed from the rear of the shell. The connector shell should be replaced if it shows any evidence of burning, melting, cracks, or breaks. Replace individual terminals that are burnt, corroded, distorted or loose.

➡**The insulation crimp must be tight to prevent the insulation from sliding back on the wire when the wire is pulled. The insulation must be visibly compressed under the crimp tabs, and the ends of the crimp should be turned in for a firm grip on the insulation.**

The wire crimp must be made with all wire strands inside the crimp. The terminal must be fully compressed on the wire strands with the ends of the crimp tabs turned in to make a firm grip on the wire. Check all connections with an ohmmeter to insure a good contact. There should be no measurable resistance between the wire and the terminal when connected.

Fusible Links

The fuse link is a short length of special, Hypalon (high temperature) insulated wire, integral with the engine compartment wiring harness and should not be confused with standard wire. It is several wire gauges smaller than the circuit which it protects. Under no circumstances should a fuse link replacement repair be made using a length of standard wire cut from bulk stock or from another wiring harness.

To repair any blown fuse link use the following procedure:

1. Determine which circuit is damaged, its location and the cause of the open fuse link. If the damaged fuse link is one of three fed by a common No. 10 or 12 gauge feed wire, determine the specific affected circuit.

2. Disconnect the negative battery cable.

3. Cut the damaged fuse link from the wiring harness and discard it. If the fuse link is one of three circuits fed by a single feed wire, cut it out of the harness at each splice end and discard it.

4. Identify and procure the proper fuse link with butt connectors for attaching the fuse link to the harness.

➡**Heat shrink tubing must be slipped over the wire before crimping and soldering the connection.**

5. To repair any fuse link in a 3-link group with one feed:

   a. After cutting the open link out of the harness, cut each of the remaining undamaged fuse links close to the feed wire weld.

   b. Strip approximately ½ in. (13mm) of insulation from the detached ends of the two good fuse links. Insert two wire ends into one end of a butt connector, then carefully push one stripped end of the replacement fuse link into the same end of the butt connector and crimp all three firmly together.

➡**Care must be taken when fitting the three fuse links into the butt connector as the internal diameter is a snug fit for three wires. Make sure to use a proper crimping tool. Pliers, side cutters, etc. will not apply the proper crimp to retain the wires and withstand a pull test.**

   c. After crimping the butt connector to the three fuse links, cut the weld portion from the feed wire and strip approximately ½ in. (13mm) of insulation from the cut end. Insert the stripped end into the open end of the butt connector and crimp very firmly.

   d. To attach the remaining end of the replacement fuse link, strip approximately ½ in. (13mm) of insulation from the wire end of the circuit from which the blown fuse link was removed, and firmly crimp a butt connector or equivalent to the stripped wire. Then, insert the end of the replacement link into the other end of the butt connector and crimp firmly.

   e. Using rosin core solder with a consistency of 60 percent tin and 40 percent lead, solder the connectors and the wires at the repairs then insulate with electrical tape or heat shrink tubing.

6. To replace any fuse link on a single circuit in a harness, cut out the damaged portion, strip approximately ½ in. (13mm) of insulation from the two wire ends and attach the appropriate replacement fuse link to the stripped wire ends with two proper size butt connectors. Solder the connectors and wires, then insulate.

7. To repair any fuse link which has an eyelet terminal on one end such as the charging circuit, cut off the open fuse link behind the weld, strip approximately ½ in. (13mm) of insulation from the cut end and attach the appropriate new eyelet fuse link to the cut stripped wire with an appropriate size butt connector. Solder the connectors and wires at the repair, then insulate.

8. Connect the negative battery cable to the battery and test the system for proper operation.

REMOVE EXISTING VINYL TUBE SHIELDING
REINSTALL OVER FUSE LINK BEFORE CRIMPING
FUSE LINK TO WIRE ENDS

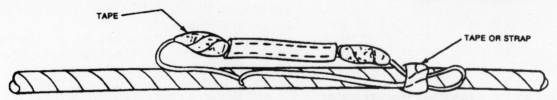

TAPE

TAPE OR STRAP

TYPICAL REPAIR USING THE SPECIAL #17 GA. (9.00" LONG-YELLOW) FUSE LINK REQUIRED FOR THE AIR/COND.
CIRCUITS (2) #687E and #261A LOCATED IN THE ENGINE COMPARTMENT

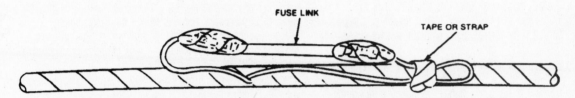

FUSE LINK

TAPE OR STRAP

TYPICAL REPAIR FOR ANY IN-LINE FUSE LINK USING THE SPECIFIED GAUGE FUSE LINK FOR THE SPECIFIC CIRCUIT

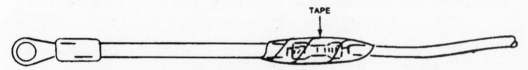

TAPE

TYPICAL REPAIR USING THE EYELET TERMINAL FUSE LINK OF THE SPECIFIED GAUGE FOR ATTACHMENT TO A CIRCUIT WIRE END

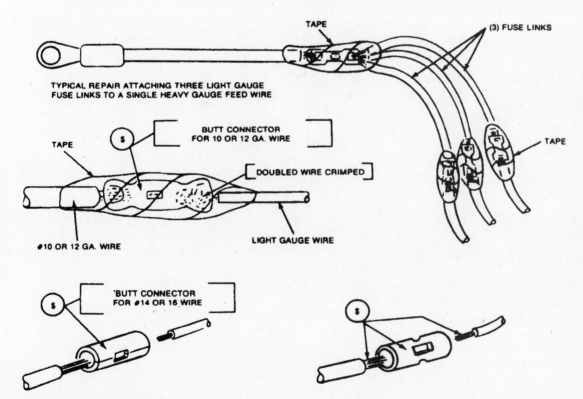

TAPE

(3) FUSE LINKS

TYPICAL REPAIR ATTACHING THREE LIGHT GAUGE
FUSE LINKS TO A SINGLE HEAVY GAUGE FEED WIRE

TAPE

TAPE

$ BUTT CONNECTOR
FOR 10 OR 12 GA. WIRE

DOUBLED WIRE CRIMPED

#10 OR 12 GA. WIRE

LIGHT GAUGE WIRE

$ 'BUTT CONNECTOR
FOR #14 OR 16 WIRE

$

FUSIBLE LINK REPAIR PROCEDURE

General fusible link repair—never replace a fusible link with regular wire or a fusible link rated at a higher amperage than the one being replaced

➡**Do not mistake a resistor wire for a fuse link. The resistor wire is generally longer and has print stating, "Resistor-don't cut or splice."**

When attaching a single No. 16, 17, 18 or 20 gauge fuse link to a heavy gauge wire, always double the stripped wire end of the fuse link before inserting and crimping it into the butt connector for positive wire retention.

Add-On Electrical Equipment

The electrical system in your vehicle is designed to perform under reasonable operating conditions without interference between components. Before any additional electrical equipment is installed, it is recommended that you consult your dealer or a reputable repair facility that is familiar with the vehicle and its systems.

If the vehicle is equipped with mobile radio equipment and/or mobile telephone, it may have an effect upon the operation of any on-board computer control modules. Radio Frequency Interference (RFI) from the communications system can be picked up by the vehicle's wiring harnesses and conducted into the control module, giving it the wrong messages at the wrong time. Although well shielded against RFI, the computer should be further protected by taking the following measures:

• Install the antenna as far as possible from the control module. For instance, if the module is located behind the center console area, then the antenna should be mounted at the rear of the vehicle.

• Keep the antenna wiring a minimum of eight inches away from any wiring running to control modules and from the module itself. NEVER wind the antenna wire around any other wiring.

• Mount the equipment as far from the control module as possible. Be very careful during installation not to drill through any wires or short a wire harness with a mounting screw.

• Insure that the electrical feed wire(s) to the equipment are properly and tightly connected. Loose connectors can cause interference.

• Make certain that the equipment is properly grounded to the vehicle. Poor grounding can damage expensive equipment.

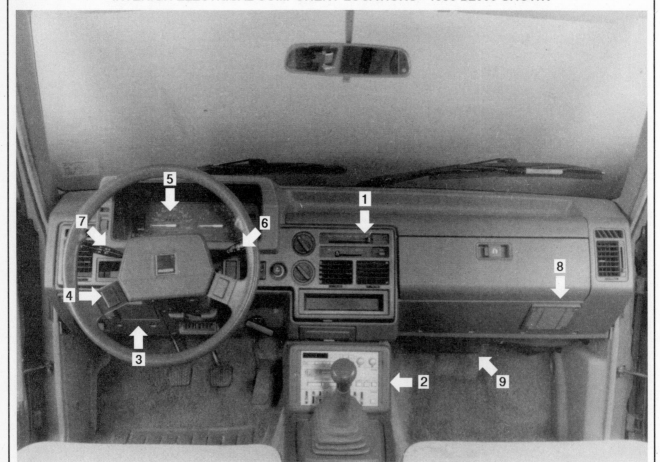

INTERIOR ELECTRICAL COMPONENT LOCATIONS - 1986 B2000 SHOWN

1. Climate controls
2. Radio pod
3. Fuse access panel
4. Horn button
5. Instrument cluster
6. Wiper control switch
7. Combination switch
8. Radio speaker
9. Heater assembly

HEATING AND AIR CONDITIONING

Heater Assembly

REMOVAL & INSTALLATION

1. Disconnect the battery ground cable.
2. Drain the cooling system.

❄❄ CAUTION

When draining engine coolant, keep in mind that cats and dogs are attracted to ethylene glycol antifreeze and could drink any that is left in an uncovered container or in puddles on the ground. This will prove fatal in sufficient quantity. Always drain coolant into a sealable container. Coolant should be reused unless it is contaminated or is several years old.

3. Remove the water valve shield at the left side of the heater.
4. Disconnect the two hoses from the left side of the heater.
5. At the heat-defroster door, the water valve and the outside recirculation door, disengage the control cable housing from the mounting clip on the heater. Disconnect each of the three cable wires from the crank arms.
6. Disconnect the fan motor electrical lead.
7. Remove the glove compartment for clearance.
8. Working inside the engine compartment, remove the two retaining nuts and the single bolt and washer which hold the heater to the firewall. Later models also have a retaining bolt inside the passenger compartment which must be removed.
9. Disconnect the two defroster ducts from the heater and remove the heater.
To install:
10. Install the heater on the dash so that the heater duct indexes with the air intake duct and the two mounting studs enter their respective holes.
11. From the engine side of the firewall, install the nuts on the mounting studs. While an assistant holds the heater in position, install the mounting bolt.
12. Connect the defroster ducts.
13. Connect the heat-defrost door control cable to the door crank arm. Set the control lever (upper) in the HEAT position and turn the crank arm toward the mounting clip as far as it will go. Engage the cable housing in the clip and install the screw in the clip.
14. Connect the water valve control cable wire to the crank arm on the water valve lever. Locate the cable housing in the mounting clip. Set the control lever in the HOT position and pull the valve plunger and lever to the full outward position. This will move the lever crank arm toward the cable mounting clip as far as it will go. Tighten the clip and screw.
15. Insert the outside recirculation door control cable into the hole in the door crank arm. Bend the wire over and tighten the screw Set the center control lever in the REC position and turn

the door crank arm toward the mounting clip as far as it will go. Engage the cable housing in the clip and install the screw in the clip.
16. Connect the fan motor electrical lead.
17. Connect the two hoses to the heater core tubes, at the left side of the heater, and tighten the clamp.
18. Install the water valve shield and tighten the three screws (left side of the heater).
19. Refill the cooling system and connect the battery ground cable.
20. Run the engine and check for leaks. Check the operation of the heater.
21. Replace the glove compartment.

Heater Motor and Blower Fan

REMOVAL & INSTALLATION

1. Remove the heater assembly.
2. Remove the five screws and separate the halves of the heater assembly.
3. Loosen the fan retaining nut. Lightly tap on the nut to loosen the fan. Remove the fan and nut from the motor shaft.
4. Remove the three motor-to-case retaining screws and disconnect the bullet connector to the resistor and ground screw.
5. Rotate the motor and remove it from the case.
To install:
6. Install the motor in the case, rotating it slightly.
7. Install the retaining screws and connect the bullet connector and ground wire.
8. Install the fan on the shaft and install the nut.
9. Assemble the halves together and install the five retaining screws.
10. Install the heater in the trucks. Check the operation of the heater.

Heater Core

REMOVAL & INSTALLATION

1. Remove the heater from the truck.
2. Remove the five screws and separate the halves of the case.
3. Loosen the hose clamps and slide the heater core from the case.
4. Slide the replacement core into the case. At the same time, connect the core tube to the water valve tube with the short hose and clamps.
5. Assemble the halves of the heater and install the five screws.
6. Install the heater in the truck. Check the operation of the heater.

AIR CONDITIONING

Compressor

REMOVAL & INSTALLATION

✳✳ CAUTION

Please refer to Section 1 before discharging the compressor or disconnecting air conditioning lines. Damage to the air conditioning system or personal injury could result. Consult your local laws concerning refrigerant discharge and recycling. In many areas it may be illegal for anyone but a certified technician to service the A/C system. Always use an approved recovery station when discharging the air conditioning.

1. Run the engine at fast idle for ten minutes with the air conditioning unit ON, then stop the engine.
2. Disconnect the negative battery cable and discharge the system as described in Section 1.
3. Disconnect the wire from the magnetic clutch.
4. Disconnect the suction and discharge hoses from the compressor and plug the ends of the hoses to prevent the entry of moisture and contamination. Always use a back-up wrench on the fittings!
5. Loosen the compressor mounting bolts and slip the drive belt from the pulley.
6. Remove the mounting bolts and remove the compressor from the vehicle.
To install:
7. Position the compressor onto its mounting and install the mounting bolts. Place the drive belt onto the pulley.
8. Connect the suction and discharge hoses to the compressor and adjust the drive belt tension. Always use a back-up wrench on the fittings!
9. Connect the magnetic clutch wire.
10. Evacuate and charge the system as described in Section 1.
11. Connect the negative battery cable.

Condenser

REMOVAL & INSTALLATION

✳✳ CAUTION

Please refer to Section 1 before discharging the compressor or disconnecting air conditioning lines. Damage to the air conditioning system or personal injury could result. Consult your local laws concerning refrigerant discharge and recycling. In many areas it may be illegal for anyone but a certified technician to service the A/C system. Always use an approved recovery station when discharging the air conditioning.

1. Disconnect the negative battery cable. Discharge the refrigerant system. See Section 1.
2. Remove the air cleaner assembly.
3. As required, remove the front grille, air seal cover and side lamps. Remove the clamps and the hood lock brace, if installed.
4. Disconnect and plug the condenser inlet, outlet and liquid lines to prevent the entry of moisture and dirt.
5. Remove the necessary components (such as the cooling fan) in order to gain access to the condenser mounting bolts.
6. Remove the condenser mounting bolts. Remove the condensor from the vehicle.
To install:
7. Lower the condenser into the vehicle and secure it with the mounting bolts. Reinstall all other parts.
8. Connect the suction, discharge and liquid lines to the condenser.
9. Install the hood lock brace and the clamps, if removed. Install the air seal and the front grille and side lamps.

➡**If a new condensor was installed, add approximately 30cc of clean compressor oil to the unit.**

10. Install the air cleaner assembly. Connect the negative battery cable.
11. Evacuate, charge and test the system as described in Section 1.

Evaporator Core

REMOVAL & INSTALLATION

✳✳ CAUTION

Please refer to Section 1 before discharging the compressor or disconnecting air conditioning lines. Damage to the air conditioning system or personal injury could result. Consult your local laws concerning refrigerant discharge and recycling. In many areas it may be illegal for anyone but a certified technician to service the A/C system. Always use an approved recovery station when discharging the air conditioning.

1. Discharge the refrigerant system. See Section 1.
2. Disconnect the battery ground cable.
3. Drain the cooling system.

✳✳ CAUTION

When draining engine coolant, keep in mind that cats and dogs are attracted to ethylene glycol antifreeze and could drink any that is left in an uncovered container or in puddles on the ground. This will prove fatal in sufficient quantity. Always drain coolant into a sealable container. Coolant should be reused unless it is contaminated or is several years old.

4. Remove the water valve shield at the left side of the heater.

5. Disconnect the two hoses from the left side of the heater.

6. Using a back-up wrench, disconnect the refrigerant lines at the core connectors. Plug all openings at once!

7. At the heat-defroster door, the water valve and the outside recirculation door, disengage the control cable housing from the mounting clip on the heater. Disconnect each of the three cable wires from the crank arms.

8. Disconnect the fan motor electrical lead.

9. Remove the glove compartment for clearance.

10. Working inside the engine compartment, remove the fasteners which hold the heater/evaporator case to the firewall. Later models also have a retaining bolt inside the passenger compartment which must be removed.

11. Disconnect the defroster ducts from the heater/evaporator case and remove the unit.

To install:

12. Install the unit on the firewall so that the heater duct indexes with the air intake duct and the two mounting studs enter their respective holes.

13. From the engine side of the firewall, install the fasteners. While an assistant holds the unit in position, install the mounting bolts.

14. Connect the defroster ducts.

15. Connect the heat-defrost door control cable to the door crank arm. Set the control lever (upper) in the HEAT position and turn the crank arm toward the mounting clip as far as it will go. Engage the cable housing in the clip and install the screw in the clip.

16. Connect the water valve control cable wire to the crank arm on the water valve lever. Locate the cable housing in the mounting clip. Set the control lever in the HOT position and pull the valve plunger and lever to the full outward position. This will move the lever crank arm toward the cable mounting clip as far as it will go. Tighten the clip and screw.

17. Insert the outside recirculation door control cable into the hole in the door crank arm. Bend the wire over and tighten the screw Set the center control lever in the REC position and turn the door crank arm toward the mounting clip as far as it will go. Engage the cable housing in the clip and install the screw in the clip.

18. Connect the fan motor electrical lead.

19. Using a back-up wrench and new O-rings coated with clean refrigerant oil, connect the refrigerant lines to the core tubes.

20. Connect the two hoses to the heater core tubes, at the left side of the heater, and tighten the clamp.

21. Install the water valve shield and tighten the three screws (left side of the heater).

22. Refill the cooling system and connect the battery ground cable.

23. Evacuate, charge and leak-test the refrigerant system. See Section 1.

24. Run the engine and check for leaks. Check the operation of the heater.

25. Replace the glove compartment.

ENTERTAINMENT SYSTEMS

Radio

♦ **See Figures 1, 2 and 2a**

For best FM reception, adjust the antenna to a height of 31 inches. For best AM reception, extend the antenna to its full height.

✳✳ WARNING

Never operate the radio with the speaker lead or antenna disconnected! Operation of the radio without a load will damage the amplifier's output transistors. If a replacement speaker is installed, be sure it is of the same impedance (resistance in ohms) as the original.

REMOVAL & INSTALLATION

1972–78 Vehicles

1. Remove the ash tray, ash tray retainer and rear retainer support. Remove the heater control knobs, heater control bezel and right-hand defroster hose.

2. Remove the heater control and position it to the left.

3. Remove the radio chassis rear support bracket.

4. Bend the bracket down 90°.

5. Remove the radio knobs, attaching nuts and bezel.

6. Pull the chassis forward until the control shafts clear the holes in the instrument panel. Disconnect the speaker wires, power lead and antenna lead. Rotate the chassis so that the control shafts point upward and lower the radio.

To install:

7. Install the radio vertically, with the control shafts pointed upward.

8. Connect the speaker wires, power lead and antenna cable.

9. Slide the chassis upward and position it with the control shafts in the holes in the instrument panel.

10. Install the radio attaching nuts, and control knobs.

11. Bend the bracket on the dash panel back into position.

12. Install the radio rear support nut to the ash tray retainer rear support.

13. Install the ash tray retainer, heater control bezel and knobs, ash tray, and right-hand defroster hose.

1979–84 Vehicles

1. Disconnect the negative battery cable.

2. Pull off the heater control knobs, the instrument light brightness control knob, and the radio knobs.

3. Remove the ring nut and fiber washer for the brightness

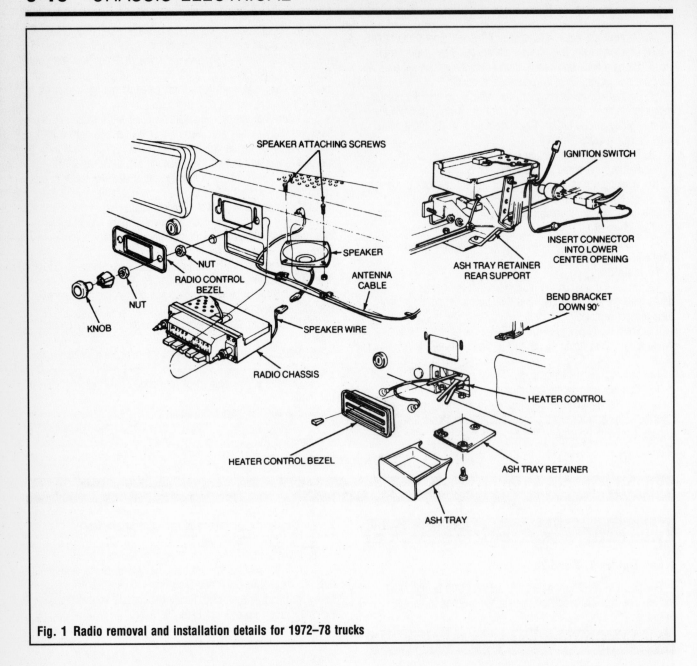

Fig. 1 Radio removal and installation details for 1972–78 trucks

control. Remove the radio attaching nuts (shaft nuts). Remove the four screws from the meter hood (instrument trim panel) and remove the hood.

4. Slide the radio to the left until the rear support pin clears the support bracket. Pull the radio out from the instrument panel far enough to gain access to the wires at the rear of the radio chassis.

5. Disconnect the power lead, speaker leads and the antenna cable. Remove the radio.

To install:

6. Connect the wires to the radio.

7. Slide the radio into place. Move the radio to the left, engage the support pin with its bracket, then slide the radio to the right.

8. Install the meter hood, inserting the radio shafts and heater knobs through it as it is fitted into place. Install the four retaining screws but do not tighten them yet.

9. Install the washer and ring nut for the brightness control. Install the radio shaft nuts loosely. Tighten the meter hood screws, then tighten the radio shaft nuts.

10. Install the knobs. Connect the negative battery cable.

1986 Vehicles

1. Disconnect the battery ground.

2. Disconnect the antenna lead, wiring and speaker connectors behind the radio.

3. Remove the radio pod mounting screws and lift out the unit.

4. Installation is the reverse of removal.

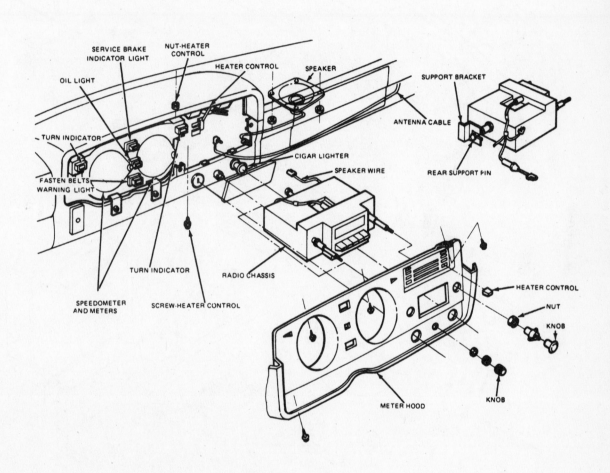

Fig. 2 Radio removal and installation details for 1979–84 trucks

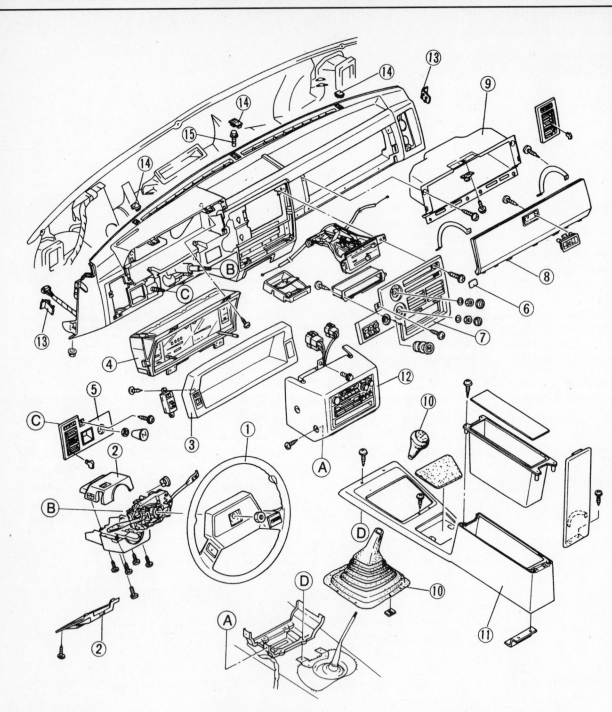

1. Steering wheel
2. Column cover
   (upper and lower)
3. Meter hood
4. Meter
5. Side panel
6. Hole cover
7. Center panel

8. Glove box lid
9. Glove box
10. Change knob and boot
11. Console box
12. Radio assembly
13. Side hole covers
    (right and left)

14. Hole cover uppers
15. Bolts

Fig. 2a Exploded view of the 1986 dashboard—the radio pod is mounted to floor bracket (A) and to the dashboard by the ashtray

WINDSHIELD WIPERS

Windshield Wiper Blade and Arm

REMOVAL & INSTALLATION

▶ **See Figures 3 and 4**

1. To remove the blade and arm, unscrew the retaining nut and pry the blade and arm from the pivot shaft. The shaft and arm are serrated to provide for adjustment of the wiper pattern on the glass.

2. To set the arms back in the proper park position, turn the wiper switch on and allow the motor to cycle three or four times. Then turn off the wiper switch (do not turn off the wiper motor with the ignition key). This will place the wiper shafts in the proper park position.

3. Install the blade and arm on the shaft and install the retaining nut. The blades and arms should be positioned according to the illustration.

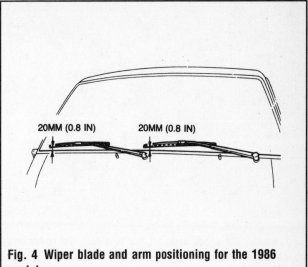

Fig. 4 Wiper blade and arm positioning for the 1986 model

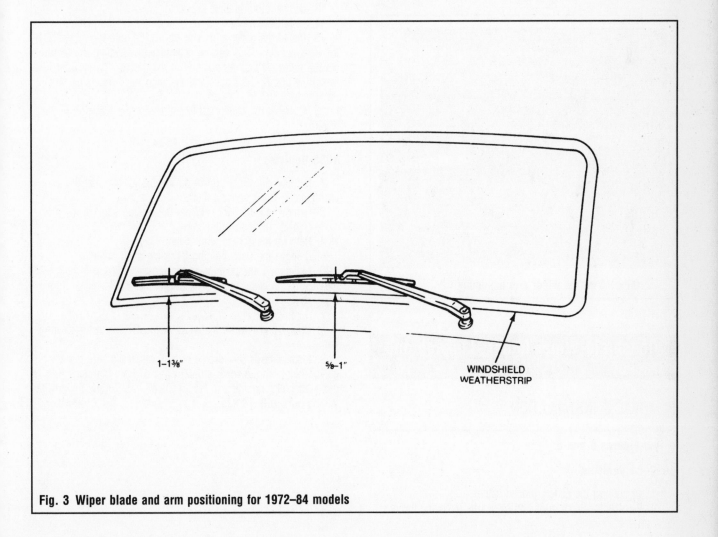

Fig. 3 Wiper blade and arm positioning for 1972–84 models

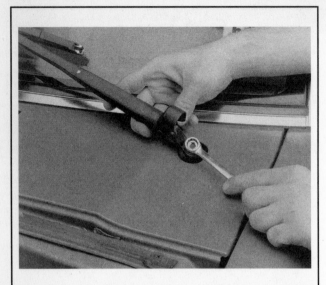

To remove the wiper arm, lift the retaining nut cover and loosen the retaining nut . . .

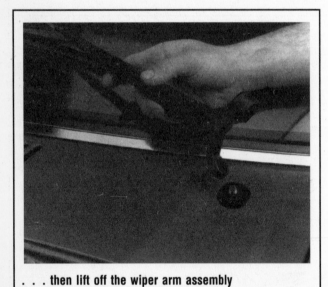

. . . then lift off the wiper arm assembly

Windshield Wiper Motor, Linkage and Bracket

REMOVAL & INSTALLATION

♦ **See Figures 5 and 6**

1972–84 Vehicles

1. Disconnect the battery ground cable.
2. Remove the wiper arms and blades by removing the retaining nuts.

3. Remove the rubber cap, nut, tapered spacer and rubber grommet from each pivot shaft.
4. Remove the two motor and bracket retaining bolts and washers.
5. Disconnect the wiper motor leads at the multiple connector.
6. Remove the motor and bracket assembly. Note the position of the ground washer and the rubber washer at the bracket mounting holes. Remove the plastic water shield.
7. To disconnect the motor from the bracket, remove the retaining clip that holds the linkage to the motor output arm. Note the position of the washers before removing the motor from the bracket.
8. Remove the four motor-to-bracket retaining bolts and remove the motor.

To assemble:
9. Install the wiper motor on the bracket and install the four retaining bolts.
10. Install the washers and position the linkage on the motor output arm. Install the retaining clip.
11. Install the plastic water shield.

To install:
12. Install the motor and bracket assembly in the truck.
13. Connect the multiple connector.
14. Install the washers, spacers and nuts on the pivot shafts.
15. Install the wiper arms and blades. Be sure the motor is in the Park position. This can be determined by cycling the motor several times. Adjust the position of the wipers. The clearance between the tips of the blades and the windshield moulding should be 20mm (0.787 in.) at park.
16. Connect the battery cable and check the operation of the wipers.

1986 Vehicles

1. Remove the wiper arm/blade assembly. Note that the arms are different. Don't confuse them.
2. Remove the rubber seal from the leading edge of the cowl.
3. Unbolt and remove the cowl.
4. Remove the access hole covers.
5. Remove the bolts holding the wiper shaft drives.
6. Matchmark the position of the wiper crank arm in relation to the face of the wiper motor. Disconnect the wiper linkage from the wiper motor crank arm.
7. Remove the wiper linkage.
8. Unbolt and remove the wiper motor. Disconnect the wiring harness.
9. Installation is the reverse of removal. Make sure that the parked height of the wiper arms, measured from the blade tips to the windshield moulding is 20mm (0.787 in.). Torque the arm retaining nuts to 8–10 ft.lb.

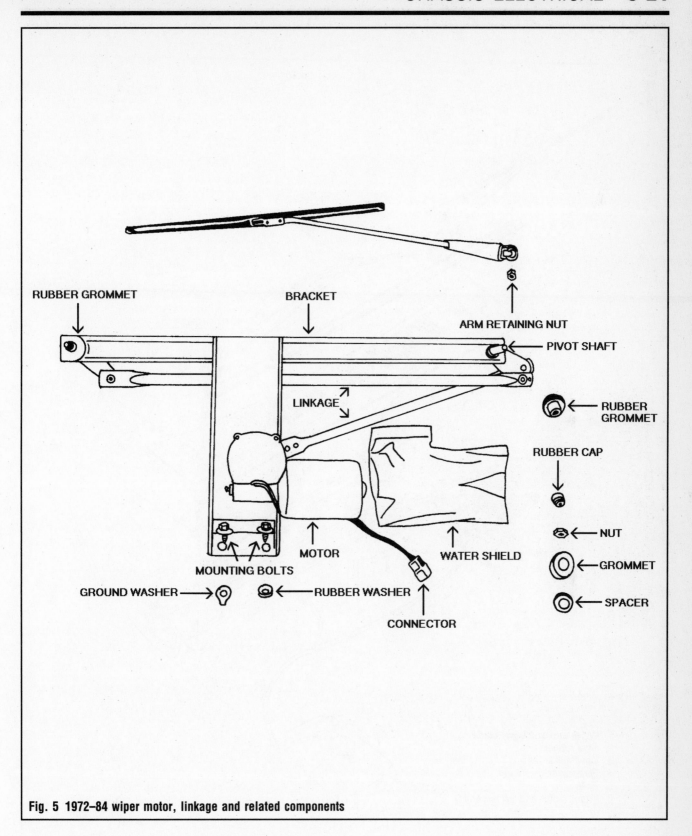

Fig. 5 1972–84 wiper motor, linkage and related components

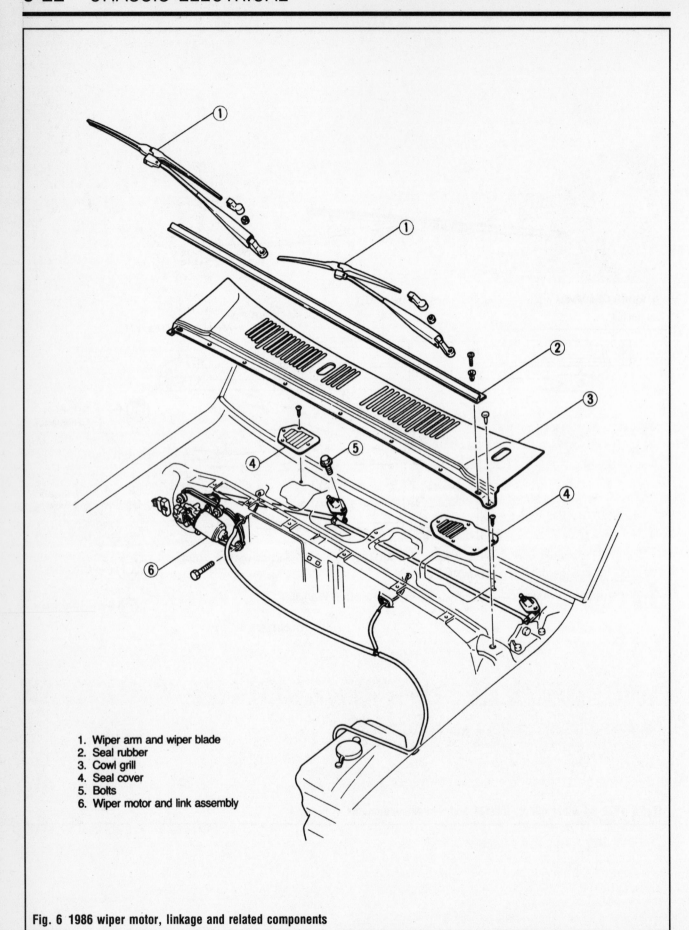

1. Wiper arm and wiper blade
2. Seal rubber
3. Cowl grill
4. Seal cover
5. Bolts
6. Wiper motor and link assembly

Fig. 6 1986 wiper motor, linkage and related components

To remove the wiper motor, detach the electrical connector . . .

. . . pull out gently on the wiper motor assembly and pry off the linkage . . .

. . . loosen the wiper motor retaining bolts . . .

. . . and remove the wiper motor assembly

INSTRUMENTS AND SWITCHES

Instrument Cluster

REMOVAL & INSTALLATION

1972–84 Vehicles

1. Disconnect the battery ground cable.
2. On 1979 and later models only, the meter hood (instrument cluster trim panel) must be removed for access to the cluster. See Steps 1–3 of the 1979 and later radio removal and installation procedure for details on meter hood removal.
3. Remove the screws holding the cluster to the instrument panel.

4. Pull the cluster rearward enough to gain access to the cluster assembly.
5. Reach behind the cluster and disconnect the speedometer cable.
6. Pull the multiple connector from the printed circuit.
7. Note the position of the two ammeter leads and disconnect them.
8. Remove the screw attaching the ground wire to the rear of the cluster. On trucks equipped with a coasting richer valve, remove the two connectors at the speedometer sensor switch.
9. Remove the instrument cluster.
To install:
10. Position the cluster assembly near the opening and connect the ground lead.
11. Connect the two ammeter lads to the ammeter.

12. Install the multiple connector at the rear of the cluster. On trucks equipped with a coasting richer valve, connect the two wires to the speedometer speed sensor.

13. Connect the speedometer cable to the speedometer head.

14. Install the four attaching screws.

15. On 1979 and later models, replace the meter hood.

16. Connect the battery cable.

17. Run the engine and check the operation of all gauges.

1986 Vehicles

▶ **See Figures 7 and 8**

1. Disconnect the battery ground cable.

2. Reach behind the cluster and disconnect the speedometer cable.

3. Remove the screws attaching the cluster hood and carefully lift the hood off.

4. Remove the screw attaching the cluster pod to the dash panel and pull the pod out toward you, gradually. Reach behind the pod and disconnect the wiring connectors.

5. Remove the trip meter knob, and, on clusters w/tachometer, the clock adjust knob.

6. Remove the screws retaining the lens cover and lift off the cover.

7. Remove the screws retaining the cluster bezel and lift off the bezel.

8. Lift out the warning light plate.

9. On clusters wo/tachometer, remove, in order:
- fuel gauge
- speedometer
- temperature gauge
- printed circuit board

10. On cluster w/tachometer, remove, in order:
- speedometer
- digital clock
- tachometer
- fuel gauge
- temperature gauge
- printed circuit board

11. Installation is the reverse of removal.

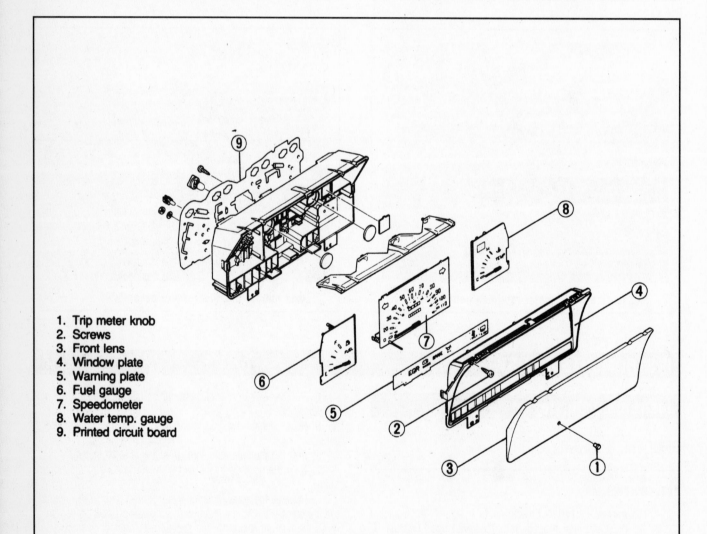

1. Trip meter knob
2. Screws
3. Front lens
4. Window plate
5. Warning plate
6. Fuel gauge
7. Speedometer
8. Water temp. gauge
9. Printed circuit board

Fig. 7 Standard instrument cluster for 1986 vehicles

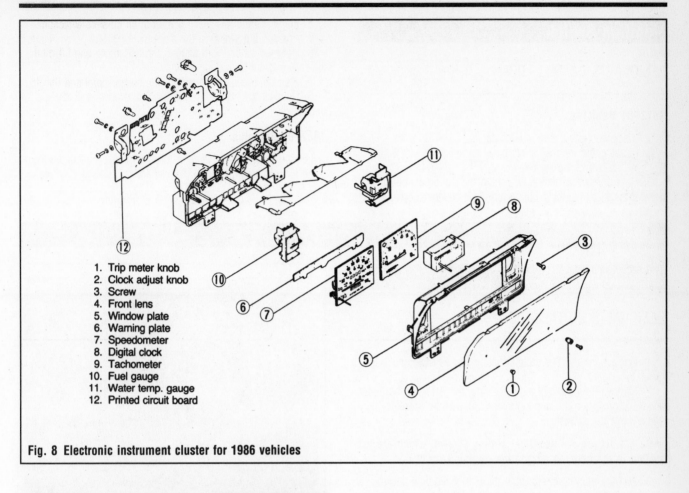

1. Trip meter knob
2. Clock adjust knob
3. Screw
4. Front lens
5. Window plate
6. Warning plate
7. Speedometer
8. Digital clock
9. Tachometer
10. Fuel gauge
11. Water temp. gauge
12. Printed circuit board

Fig. 8 Electronic instrument cluster for 1986 vehicles

Windshield Wiper Switch

REMOVAL & INSTALLATION

The windshield wiper switch is part of the multi-function switch mounted in the steering column. For service procedures, see Section 8.

Headlight Switch

REMOVAL & INSTALLATION

The switch is part of the multi-function switch mounted in the steering column. For service procedures, see Section 8.

Speedometer Cable

REMOVAL & INSTALLATION

◆ **See Figure 9**

1. Remove the instrument cluster.
2. Remove the old cable by pulling it out from the speedometer end of the cable housing. If the old cable is broken, the speed-ometer cable will have to be disconnected from the transmission and the broken piece removed from the transmission end.
3. Lubricate the lower ¾ of the new cable with speedometer cable lubricant, and feed the cable into the housing.
4. Connect the speedometer cable to the speedometer, and to the transmission if disconnected there.
5. Replace the instrument cluster.

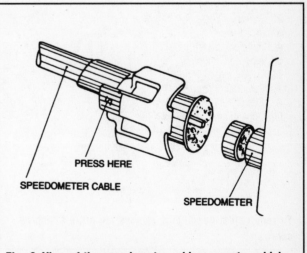

PRESS HERE
SPEEDOMETER CABLE
SPEEDOMETER

Fig. 9 View of the speedometer cable connector which is attached to the speedometer

Ignition Switch

REMOVAL & INSTALLATION

1972–81 Vehicles

1. Disconnect the battery ground cable.
2. Reach under the instrument panel and pull the wire connector from the rear of the switch.
3. Hold the switch body from behind the instrument panel and remove the black retaining nut by turning it counterclockwise.

4. Remove the switch from the rear of the instrument panel.
5. Position the switch in the instrument panel.
6. Hold the switch from behind the instrument panel. Install the retaining nut by turning it clockwise.
7. Plug the multiple connector into the back of the switch.
8. Connect the battery ground cable and check the operation of the switch.

1982–86 Vehicles

Ignition switches and ignition locks on these models are located in the steering column. For service procedures, see Section 8.

LIGHTING

Headlights

REMOVAL & INSTALLATION

1. Remove the radiator grille attaching screws and remove the grille.
2. Remove the headlight bulb trim ring, by removing the three screws and rotating the ring clockwise. Support the headlight bulb and remove the trim ring.

➡**Do not disturb the headlight aiming screws, which are installed in the housing next to the retaining screws.**

3. Pull the plug connector from the rear of the bulb and remove the bulb.
To install:
4. Connect the plug connector to the rear of a new headlight.

. . . and the grille

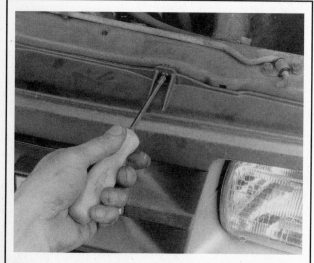

To remove the headlights, remove the grille attaching screws . . .

Loosen the trim ring retaining bolts (Do NOT disturb the 2 headlight aiming screws; located at the center of the top and side of the trim ring) . . .

. . . and remove the trim ring

5. Install the headlight in the housing, and locate the bulb tabs in the slots and the housing.

6. Position the trim ring over the bulb and loosely install the retaining screws. Rotate the ring counterclockwise to lock it in position. Tighten the three attaching screws. Check the headlight operation.

7. Install the grille.

8. Have the headlight aim checked.

Front Combination Lights

REMOVAL & INSTALLATION

1. Remove the lens mounting screws and pull off the lens.

2. Carefully push in on the bulb and twist it counterclockwise to remove it.

3. Installation is the reverse of removal.

Pull off the electrical connector from the back of the bulb . . .

To change the front combination light bulbs, unfasten the lens mounting screws . . .

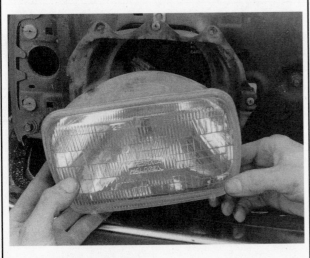

. . . and remove the bulb

. . . and remove the lens . . .

. . . then remove the bulb by pushing in and twisting it counterclockwise

. . . and remove the lens . . .

Front Turn Signal Lights

REMOVAL & INSTALLATION

1. Remove the lens mounting screws and pull off the lens.
2. Carefully push in on the bulb and twist it counterclockwise to remove it.
3. Installation is the reverse of removal.

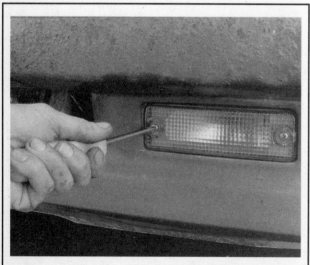

To change the front turn signal bulbs, remove the lens mounting screws . . .

. . . then remove the bulb by pushing in and twisting it counterclockwise

Rear Combination Lights

REMOVAL & INSTALLATION

1. Remove the lens mounting screws and pull off the lens.
2. Carefully push in on the bulb and twist it counterclockwise to remove it.
3. Installation is the reverse of removal.

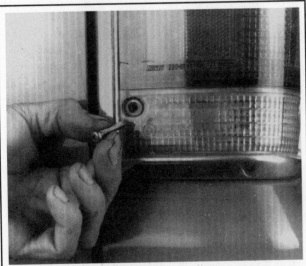

To replace the rear combination light bulbs, loosen the lens retaining screws . . .

. . . then remove the screws . . .

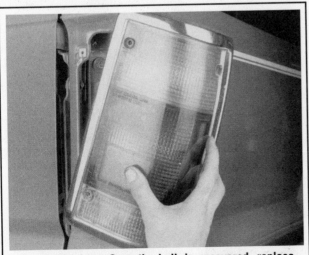

. . . and the lens. Once the bulb is uncovered, replace it by pushing in and twisting counterclockwise

License Plate Lights

REMOVAL & INSTALLATION

1. Remove the lens mounting screws and pull off the lens.
2. Carefully push in on the bulb and twist it counterclockwise to remove it.
3. Installation is the reverse of removal.

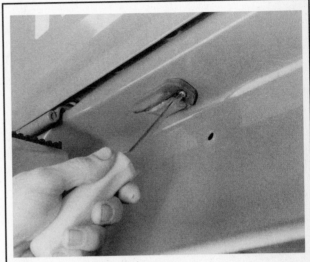

To replace the rear license plate bulb, remove the lens mounting screws . . .

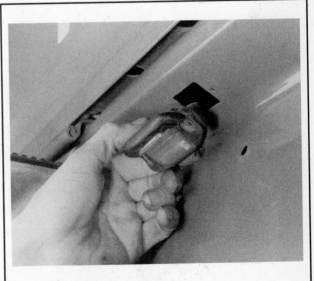

. . . and pull out the assembly

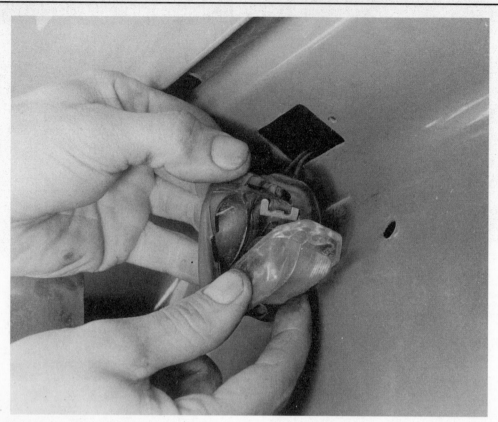

Remove the lens from the rubber boot . . .

. . . then remove the bulb by pushing in and twisting it counterclockwise

Light Bulb Chart

This chart gives the common sizes for these models,
however, always check owners manual when possible
All Specifications given in watts

| Years | Head Light (Hi/Lo) | Front | | License Plate Light | Interior (Dome) Light | Rear | | | Side Marker Frt. & Rear | Instrument Panel Light |
		Parking	Turn Signal			Parking/ Brake	Turn Signal	Back-up Light		
72–80	①	8	27	6	5	8/27	27	27	3.8	3.4
81–84	65/55	8	27	6	5	8/27	27	27	3.8	3.4
86	②	8	27	6	10	8/27	27	27	8	3.4

① Type 1 bulb: 37.5 watts
　 Type 2 bulb: 50/37.5 watts
② Standard bulb: 65/55 watts
　 Halogen bulb: 65/35 watts

Dome Light

REMOVAL & INSTALLATION

1. Pull the dome light lens off of the dome light housing.
2. Grab hold of the bulb and pull it free.
3. Push new bulb into place and snap lens back over housing.
4. Cab-plus models have an additional dome light in the center of the headliner, however replacement is identical.

. . . then pull out the bulb—make sure the switch is in the off position

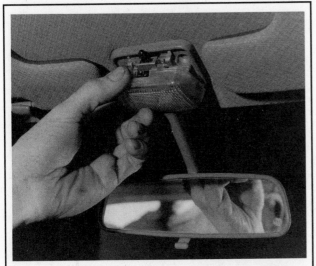

Pull down on the dome light lens to remove the lens cover . . .

TRAILER WIRING

Wiring the vehicle for towing is fairly easy. There are a number of good wiring kits available and these should be used, rather than trying to design your own.

All trailers will need brake lights and turn signals as well as tail lights and side marker lights. Most areas require extra marker lights for overwide trailers. Also, most areas have recently required back-up lights for trailers, and most trailer manufacturers have been building trailers with back-up lights for several years.

Additionally, some Class I, most Class II and just about all Class III trailers will have electric brakes. Add to this number an accessories wire, to operate trailer internal equipment or to charge the trailer's battery, and you can have as many as seven wires in the harness.

Determine the equipment on your trailer and buy the wiring kit necessary. The kit will contain all the wires needed, plus a plug adapter set which includes the female plug, mounted on the bumper or hitch, and the male plug, wired into, or plugged into the trailer harness.

When installing the kit, follow the manufacturer's instructions.

The color coding of the wires is usually standard throughout the industry. One point to note: some domestic vehicles, and most imported vehicles, have separate turn signals. On most domestic vehicles, the brake lights and rear turn signals operate with the same bulb. For those vehicles with separate turn signals, you can purchase an isolation unit so that the brake lights won't blink whenever the turn signals are operated, or, you can go to your local electronics supply house and buy four diodes to wire in series with the brake and turn signal bulbs. Diodes will isolate the brake and turn signals. The choice is yours. The isolation units are simple and quick to install, but far more expensive than the diodes. The diodes, however, require more work to install properly, since they require the cutting of each bulb's wire and soldering in place of the diode.

One, final point, the best kits are those with a spring loaded cover on the vehicle mounted socket. This cover prevents dirt and moisture from corroding the terminals. Never let the vehicle socket hang loosely; always mount it securely to the bumper or hitch.

CIRCUIT PROTECTION

The fuse box, on trucks through 1984, is located on the left side of the engine compartment near the windshield.

On 1986 pick-ups, the fuse box is located under the instrument panel, on the left of the driver.

On 1972–76 models, there is a 40 amp master fuse located underneath a plastic cover on the right-hand fender apron in the engine compartment, just behind the battery tray support. To replace it, first disconnect the battery ground cable. Then remove the plastic cover and the fuse.

1986 trucks have a master fuse block located under a protective cover on the right fender apron just behind the battery. This fuse block contains a 30 amp and an 80 amp fuse. The 30 amp fuse can be removed without disturbing the fuse block by simply pulling it out and pushing a new on in. To remove the 80 amp fuse, you'll have to remove the fuse block, remove the cover, unscrew the wiring terminal and pull out the fuse.

The master fuse(s) protects the entire electrical system; all systems will be dead if it has blown.

1977–84 trucks have a fusible link instead of the master fuse. The fusible link is a length of wire specially designed to melt under excessive electrical loads. It protects the entire electrical system. Replacements are made by splicing a new section into place. To replace the fusible link, first disconnect the battery negative cable. Then remove the old link and replace it with a link of similar capacity, available at your dealer.

When a fuse blows out, inspect the electrical system for shorts or other faults. Fuses of specified capacity should be installed in

their respective positions. Oversize fuses will allow excessive current to flow and should not be used.

Spare fuses should be kept in a vinyl bag in the glove compartment.

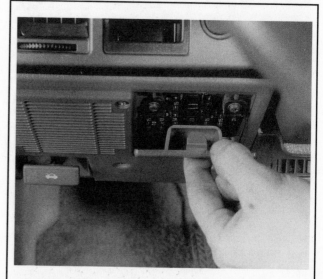

To replace a blown fuse, open the fuse panel cover . . .

. . . then remove the fuse with a fuse removal/
installation tool, or a pair of pliers—1986 model shown,
earlier models have the fuse panel located in the engine
compartment

To replace the master fuse(s), loosen . . .

. . . and remove the negative battery terminal from the
battery . . .

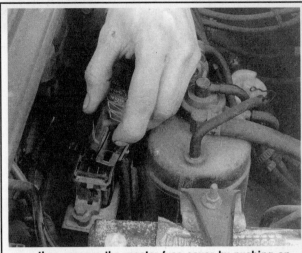

. . . then remove the master fuse cover by pushing on
the lock and pulling up

Pull upwards on the fuse to remove it—some models
secure the fuse with screws which must be removed for
replacement

Flashers and Relays

The hazard warning flasher is located to the left of the steering
column, beneath the instrument panel, and is secured by a clamp
and one screw. To remove it, simply unplug the electrical connector, loosen the screw, and slide the flasher out of the clamp. The
turn signal flasher is located to the right of the steering column,
beneath the instrument panel, and is secured in the same way as
the hazard flasher.

The turn the signal relay is located to the immediate right of
the hazard flasher, and is secured by two screws. To remove it,
unplug the electrical connector and remove the screws.

WIRING DIAGRAMS

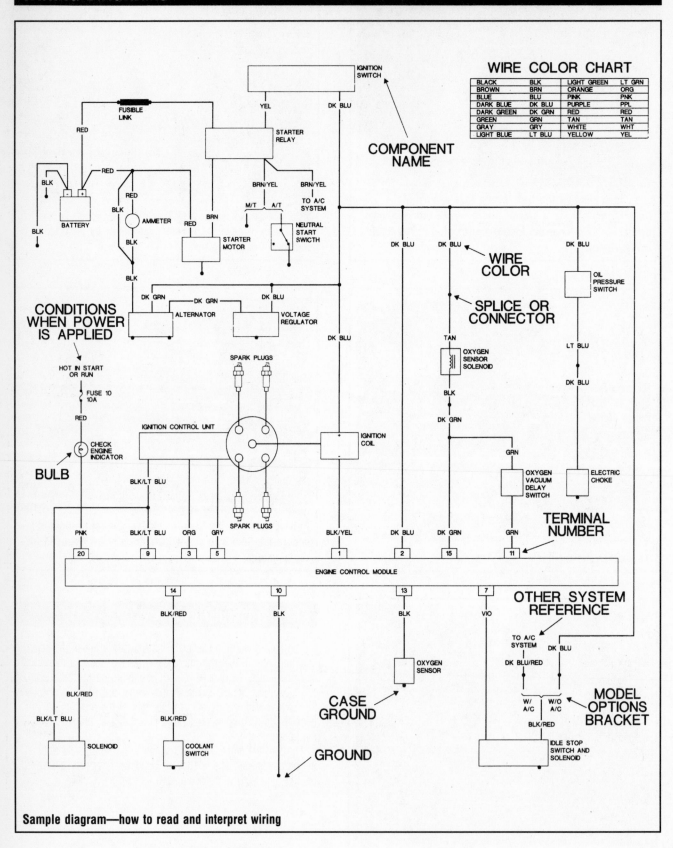

Sample diagram—how to read and interpret wiring

WIRING DIAGRAM SYMBOLS

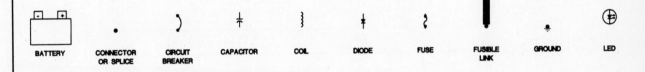

BATTERY   CONNECTOR OR SPLICE   CIRCUIT BREAKER   CAPACITOR   COIL   DIODE   FUSE   FUSIBLE LINK   GROUND   LED

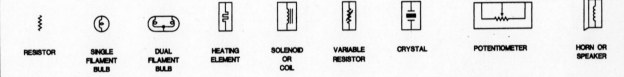

RESISTOR   SINGLE FILAMENT BULB   DUAL FILAMENT BULB   HEATING ELEMENT   SOLENOID OR COIL   VARIABLE RESISTOR   CRYSTAL   POTENTIOMETER   HORN OR SPEAKER

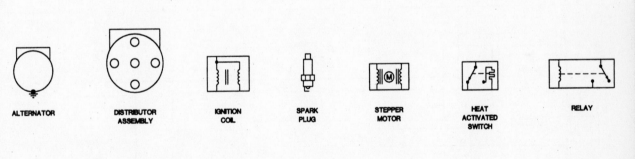

ALTERNATOR   DISTRIBUTOR ASSEMBLY   IGNITION COIL   SPARK PLUG   STEPPER MOTOR   HEAT ACTIVATED SWITCH   RELAY

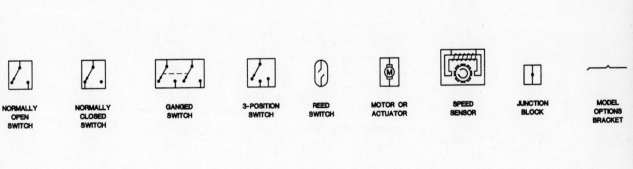

NORMALLY OPEN SWITCH   NORMALLY CLOSED SWITCH   GANGED SWITCH   3-POSITION SWITCH   REED SWITCH   MOTOR OR ACTUATOR   SPEED SENSOR   JUNCTION BLOCK   MODEL OPTIONS BRACKET

Common wiring diagram symbols

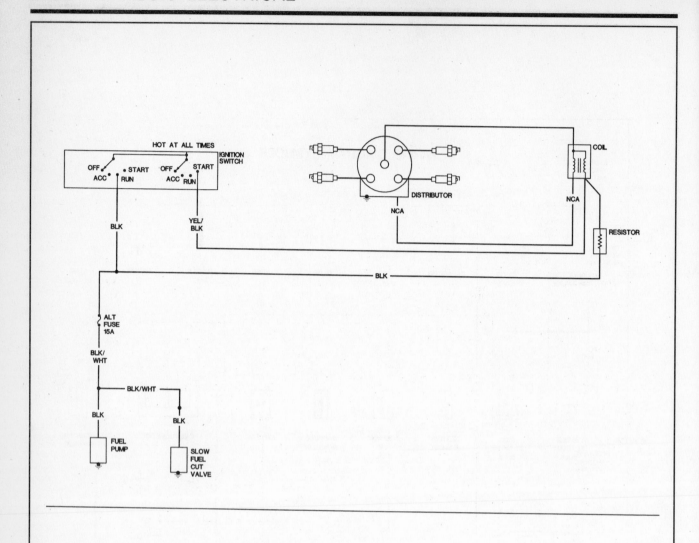

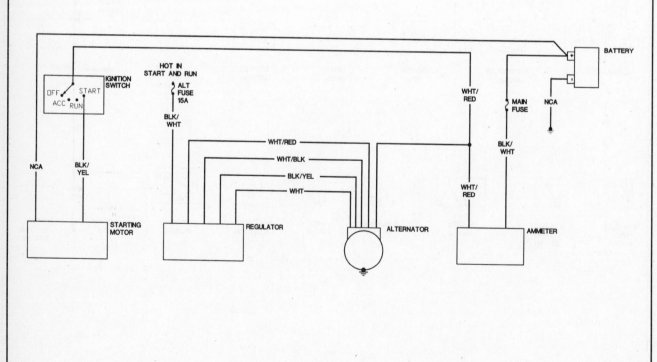

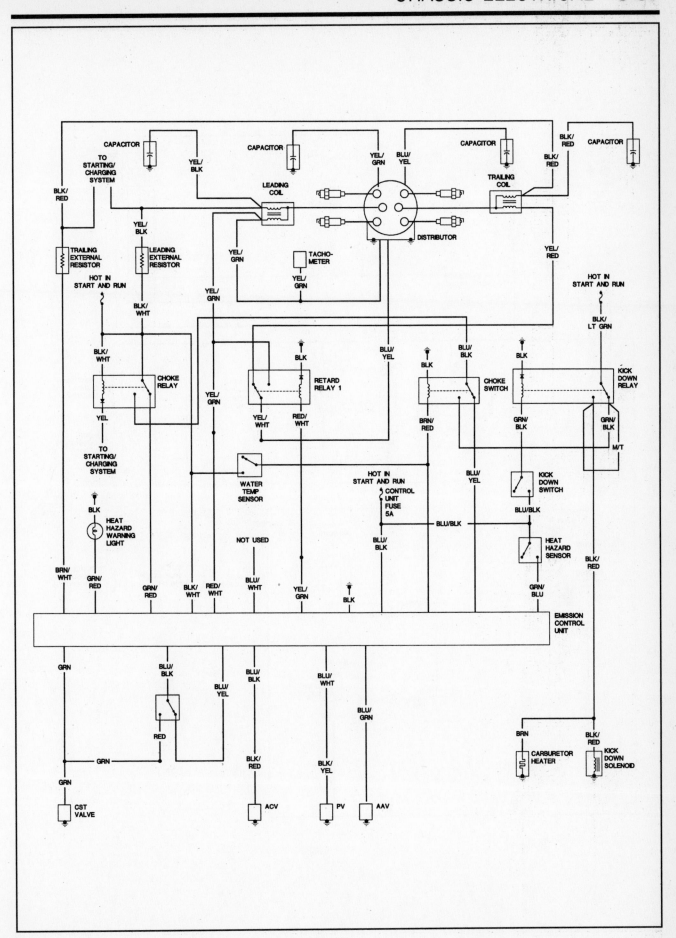

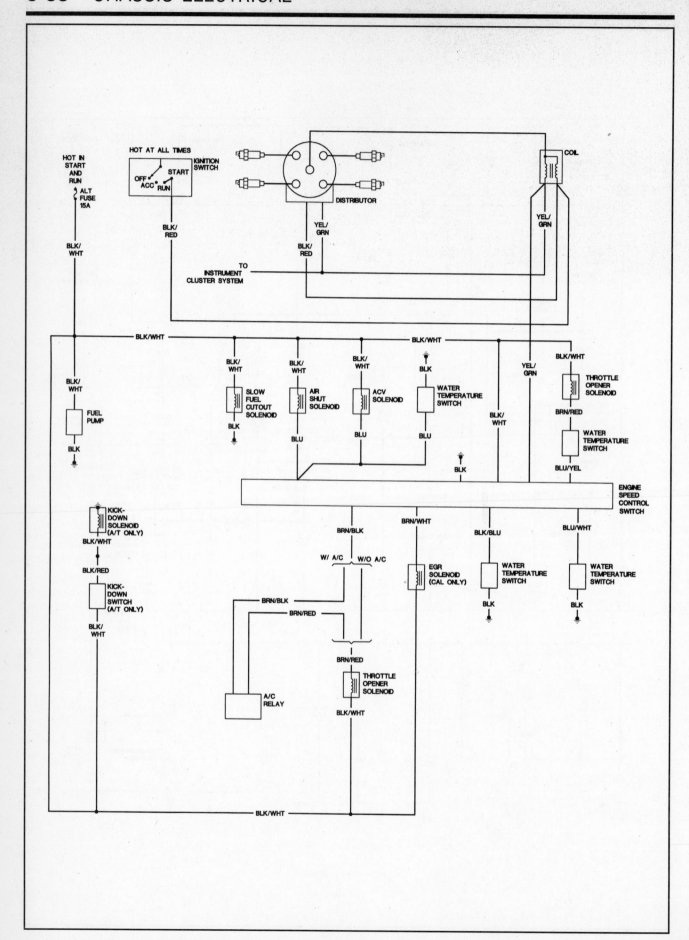

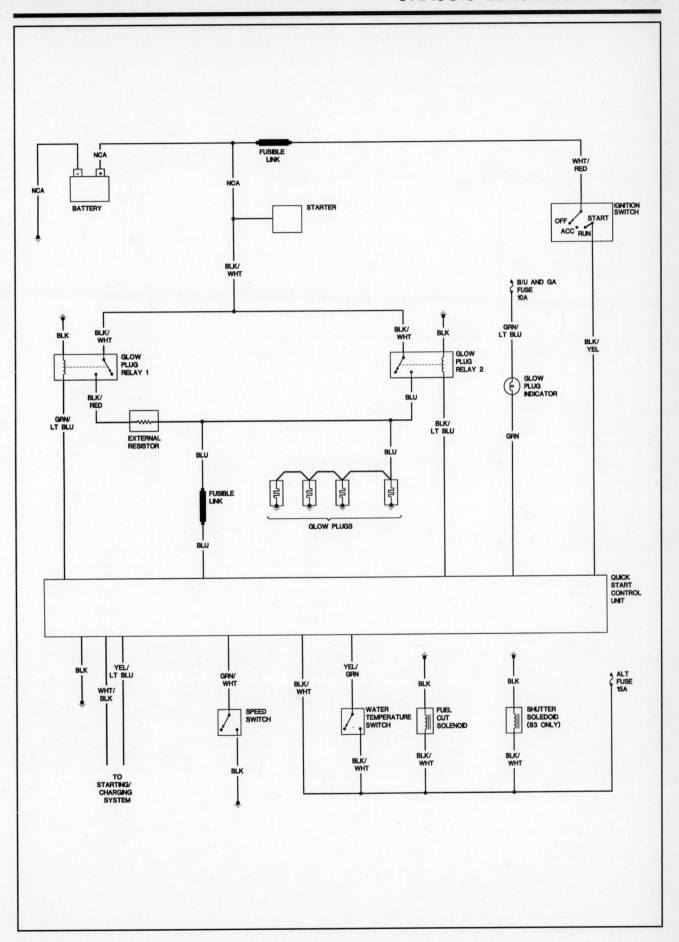

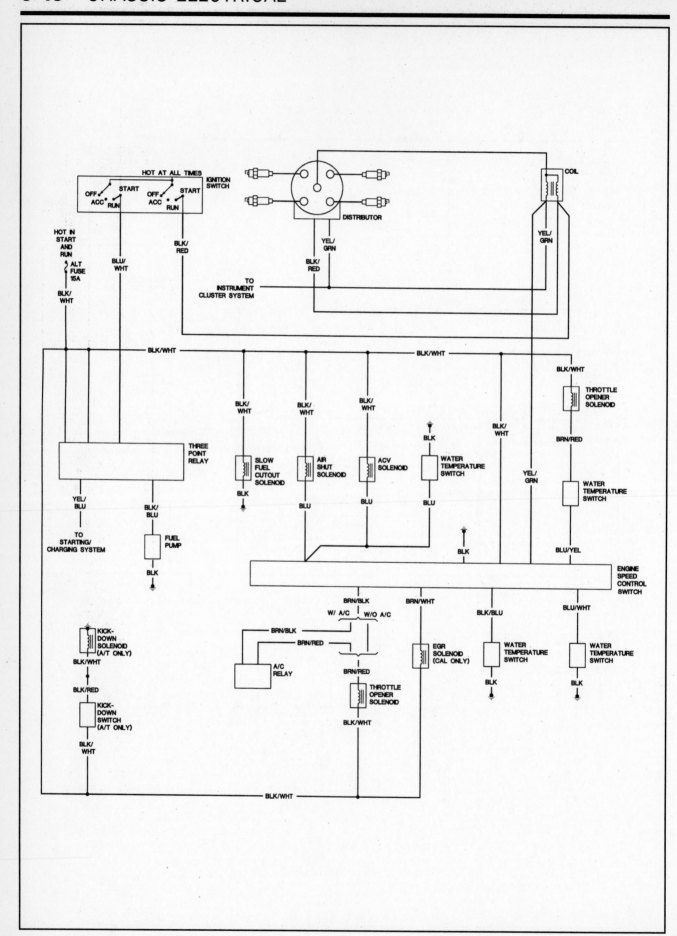

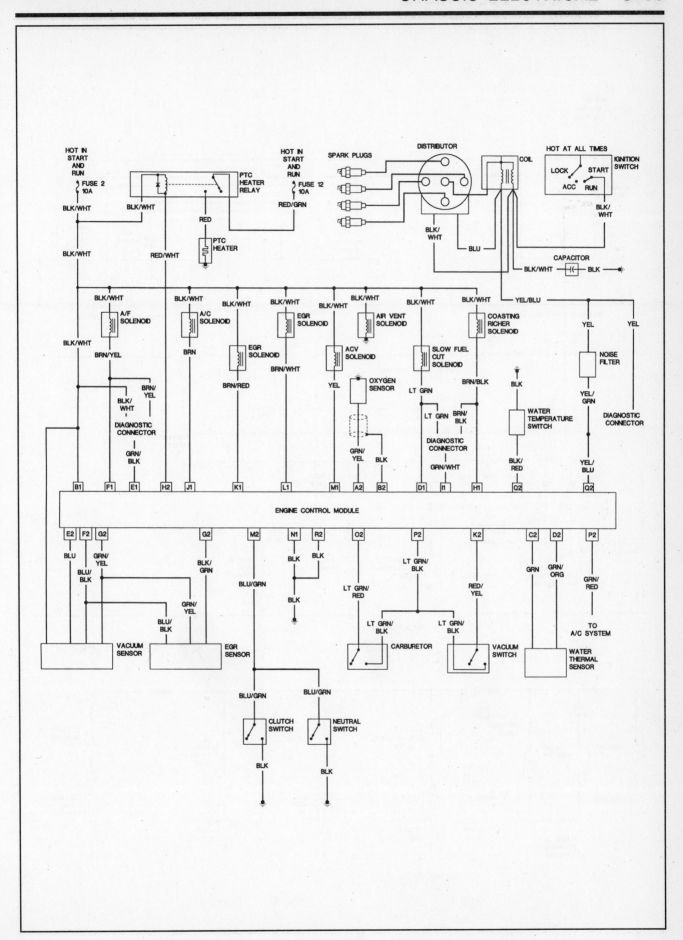

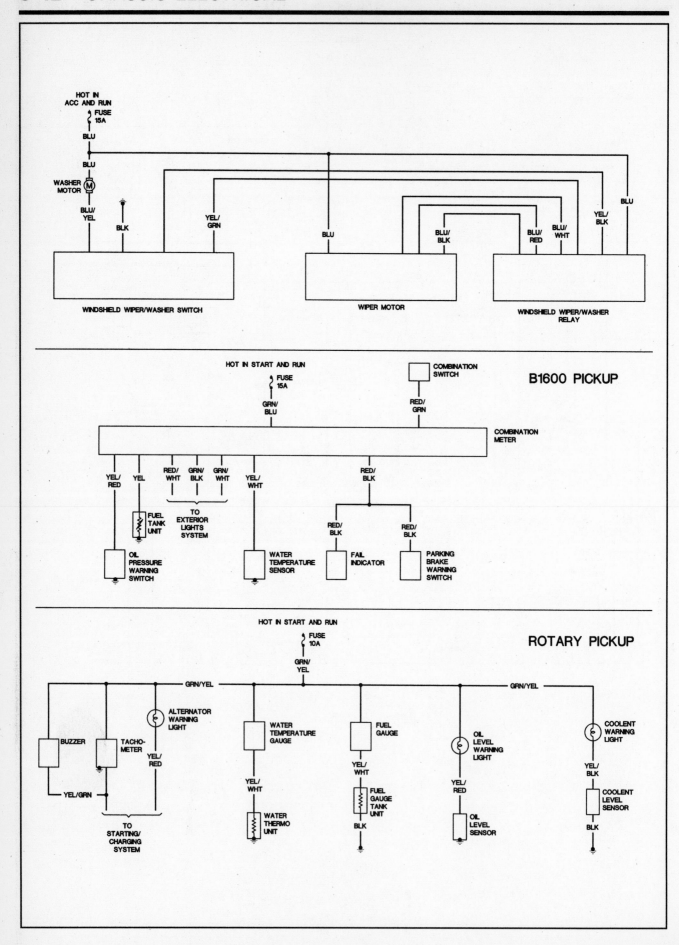

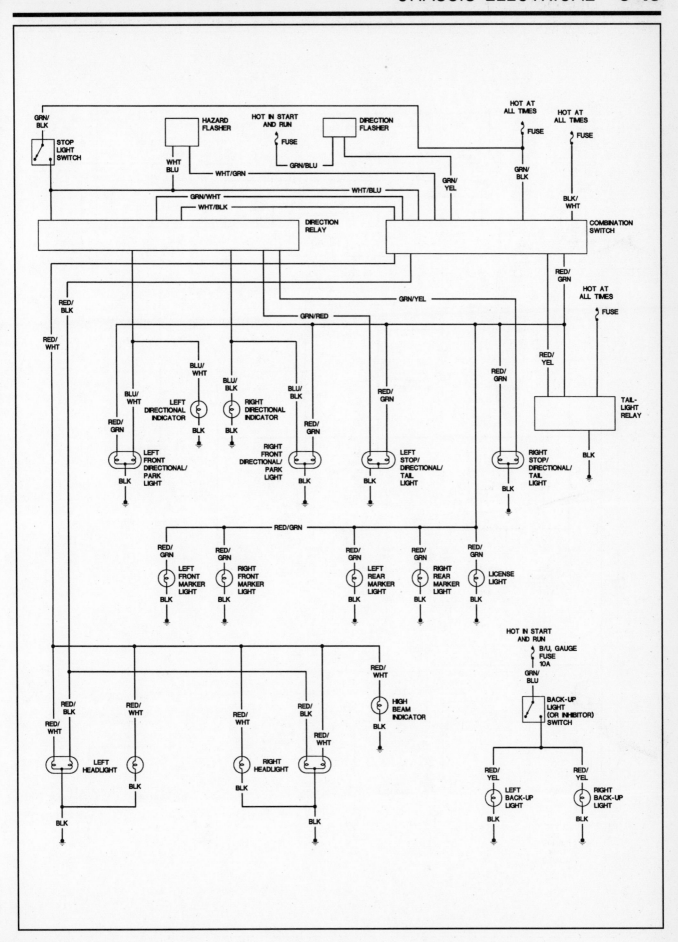

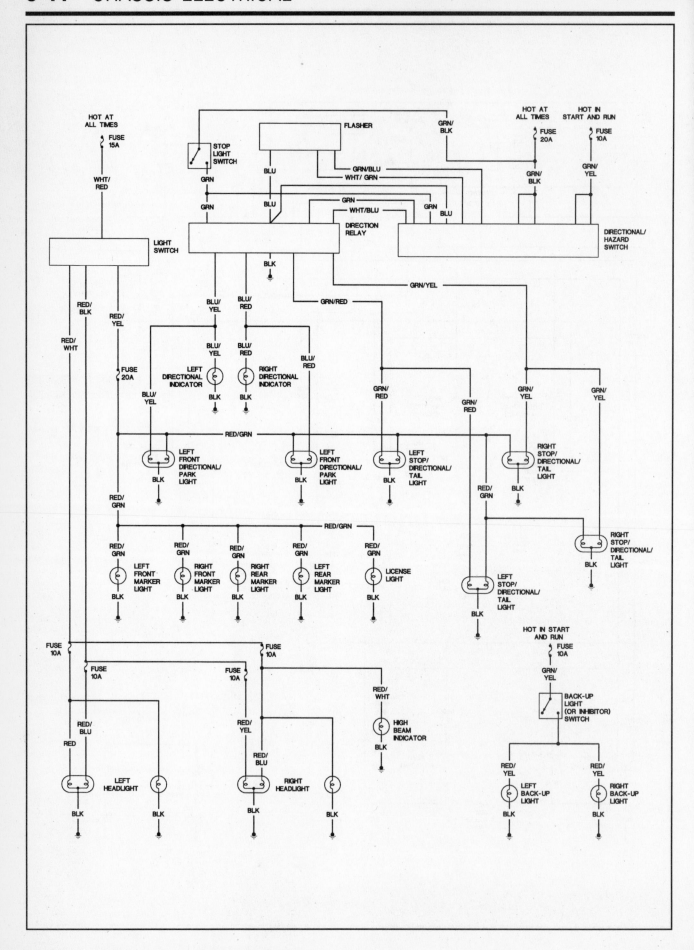

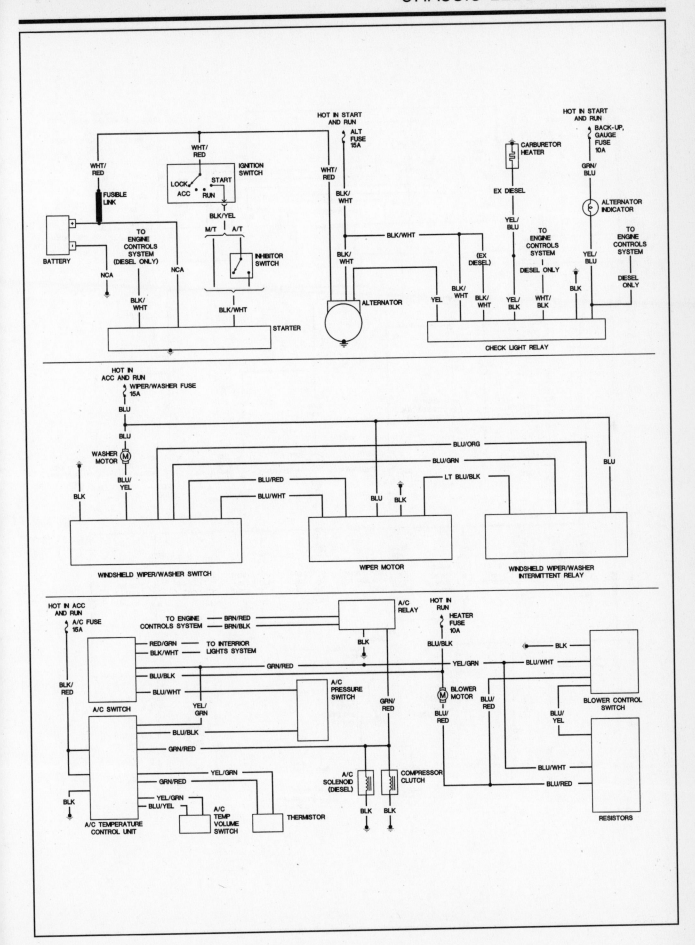

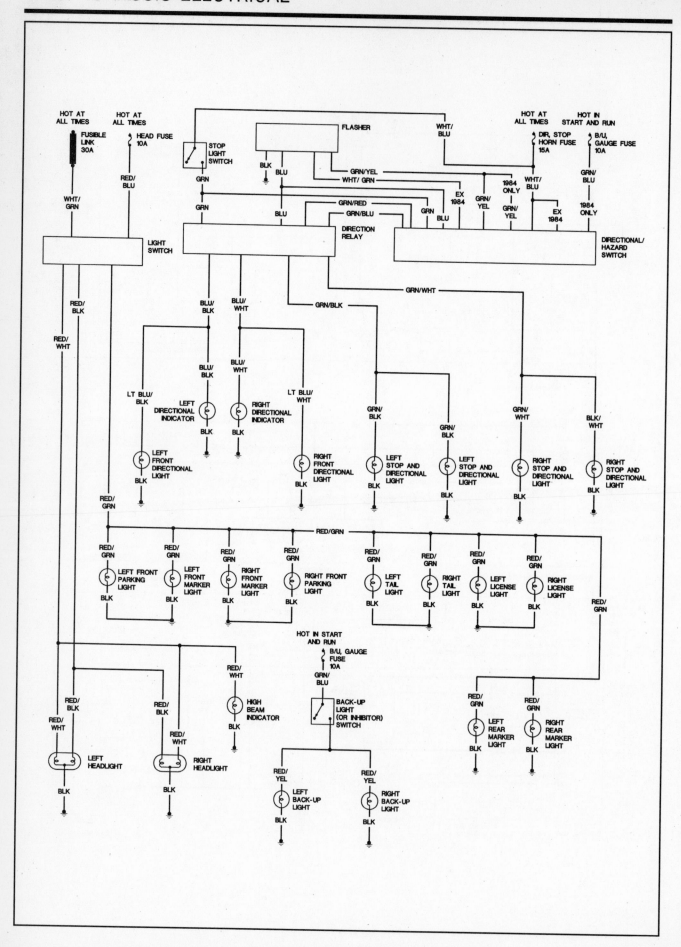

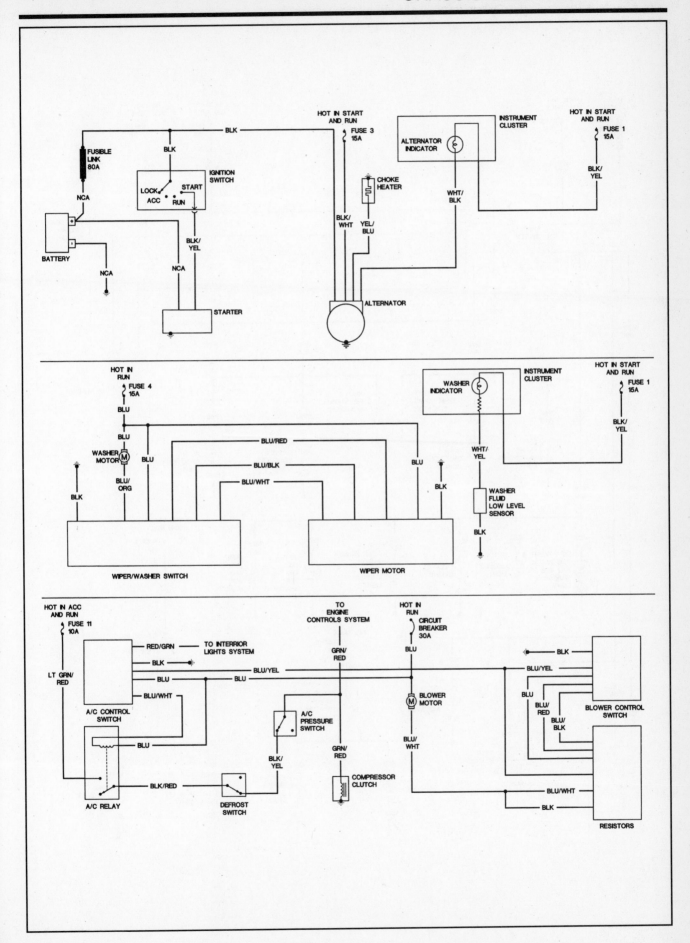

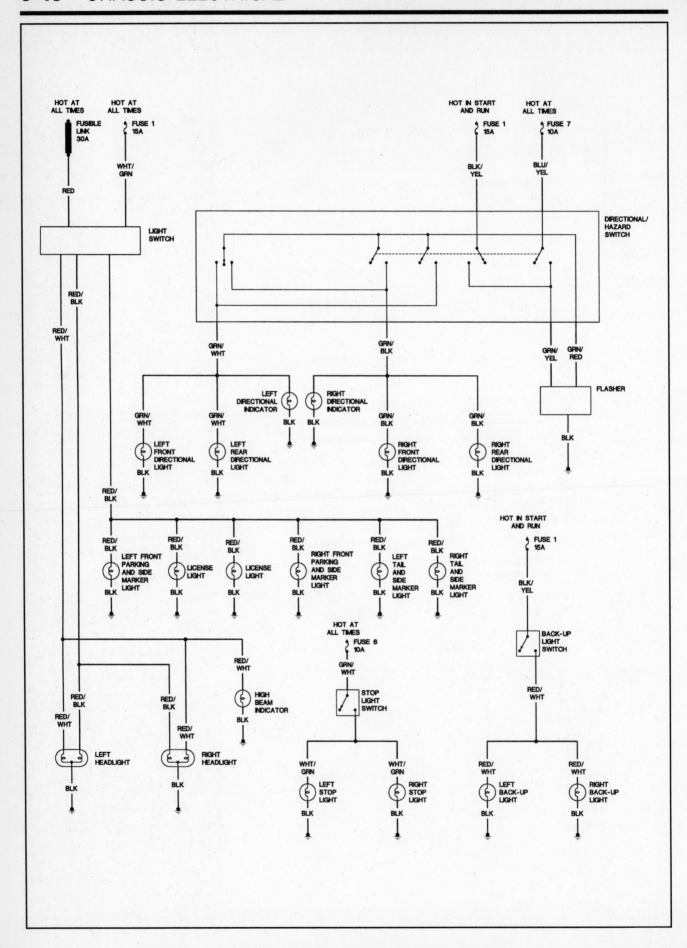

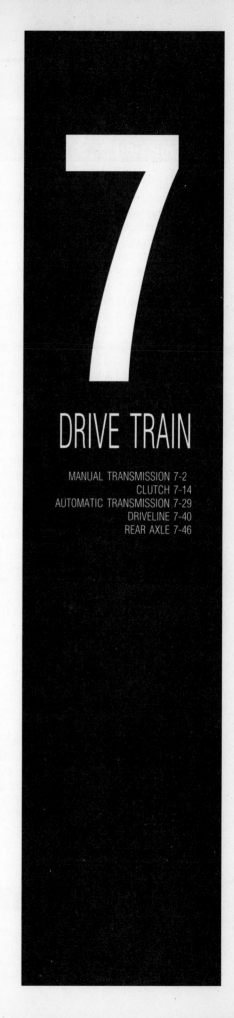

7
DRIVE TRAIN

MANUAL TRANSMISSION

Understanding the Manual Transmission

Because of the way an internal combustion engine breathes, it can produce torque (or twisting force) only within a narrow speed range. Most overhead valve pushrod engines must turn at about 2500 rpm to produce their peak torque. Often by 4500 rpm, they are producing so little torque that continued increases in engine speed produce no power increases.

The torque peak on overhead camshaft engines is, generally, much higher, but much narrower.

The manual transmission and clutch are employed to vary the relationship between engine RPM and the speed of the wheels so that adequate power can be produced under all circumstances. The clutch allows engine torque to be applied to the transmission input shaft gradually, due to mechanical slippage. The vehicle can, consequently, be started smoothly from a full stop.

The transmission changes the ratio between the rotating speeds of the engine and the wheels by the use of gears. 4-speed or 5-speed transmissions are most common. The lower gears allow full engine power to be applied to the rear wheels during acceleration at low speeds.

The clutch driveplate is a thin disc, the center of which is splined to the transmission input shaft. Both sides of the disc are covered with a layer of material which is similar to brake lining and which is capable of allowing slippage without roughness or excessive noise.

The clutch cover is bolted to the engine flywheel and incorporates a diaphragm spring which provides the pressure to engage the clutch. The cover also houses the pressure plate. When the clutch pedal is released, the driven disc is sandwiched between the pressure plate and the smooth surface of the flywheel, thus forcing the disc to turn at the same speed as the engine crankshaft.

The transmission contains a mainshaft which passes all the way through the transmission, from the clutch to the driveshaft. This shaft is separated at one point, so that front and rear portions can turn at different speeds.

Power is transmitted by a countershaft in the lower gears and reverse. The gears of the countershaft mesh with gears on the mainshaft, allowing power to be carried from one to the other. Countershaft gears are often integral with that shaft, while several of the mainshaft gears can either rotate independently of the shaft or be locked to it. Shifting from one gear to the next causes one of the gears to be freed from rotating with the shaft and locks another to it. Gears are locked and unlocked by internal dog clutches which slide between the center of the gear and the shaft. The forward gears usually employ synchronizers; friction members which smoothly bring gear and shaft to the same speed before the toothed dog clutches are engaged.

Transmission Applications

The 4-speed manual transmission, used from 1972 through 1984, is synchronized in all forward gears. The transmission case is of light metal construction, manufactured as two mated halves. There is no external shift linkage; all the shifting mechanisms are contained within the case. There are no linkage or shifter adjustments.

An optional 5-speed manual, first available in 1976 and used through 1984, has the same ratio in the first four gears as the 4-speed, but has an overdrive 5th gear with a 0.875:1 ratio. It is synchronized in all forward gears. The transmission case is cast aluminum, with a bottom cover and removable clutch and extension housings. The gearshift lever is connected directly to the shift forks; thus, there is no external linkage, and no adjustments are necessary.

In 1986 a completely different unit was introduced. This transmission is a 4-speed unit which, in its optional form, is converted to a 5-speed overdrive gearbox with the addition of an intermediate housing containing the overdrive gearing.

Back-Up Light Switch

REMOVAL & INSTALLATION

The switch is located on the upper left rear of the transmission case. To replace it, disconnect the wiring and unscrew the switch from the case. Don't lose the washer.

Transmission Assembly

REMOVAL & INSTALLATION

B1600

♦ See Figure 1

1. Raise and support the truck. Drain the lubricant from the transmission.
2. Disconnect the ground wire from the battery.
3. Remove the gearshift lever boot.
4. Unbolt the cover plate from the gearshift lever retainer.
5. Pull the gearshift lever, shim and bushing straight up and away from the gearshift lever retainer.
6. Disconnect the wires from the starter motor and back-up light switch.
7. Disconnect the speedometer cable from the extension housing.
8. Remove the driveshaft.
9. Unbolt the exhaust pipe from the bracket on the transmission case.
10. Disconnect the exhaust pipe at the exhaust manifold.
11. Unhook the clutch release fork return spring and remove the clutch release cylinder from the clutch housing.
12. Remove the starter.
13. Support the transmission with a jack.
14. Unbolt the transmission from the rear of the engine.
15. Place a jack under the engine, protecting the oil pan with a block of wood.
16. Unbolt the transmission from the crossmember.
17. Unbolt and remove the crossmember.
18. Lower the jack and slide the transmission rearward until the mainshaft clears the clutch disc.

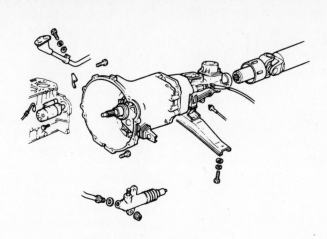

Fig. 1 Typical 1972–84 piston engine manual transmission mounting

19. Remove the transmission from under the truck.

To install:

20. Position the transmission under the truck.

21. Raise the jack and slide the transmission forward until the mainshaft enters the clutch disc.

22. Install the crossmember. Torque the bolts to 50 ft. lbs.

23. Bolt the transmission to the crossmember. Torque the bolts to 45 ft. lbs.

24. Remove the jack from under the engine.

25. Bolt the transmission to the rear of the engine. Torque the bolts to 45 ft. lbs.

26. Remove the transmission jack.

27. Install the starter.

28. Install the clutch release cylinder.

29. Connect the exhaust pipe at the exhaust manifold.

30. Connect the exhaust pipe bracket on the transmission case.

31. Install the driveshaft.

32. Connect the speedometer cable.

33. Connect the wires at the starter motor and back-up light switch.

34. Install the gearshift lever.

35. Install the gearshift lever boot.

36. Connect the ground wire to the battery.

37. Fill the transmission.

B1800, B2200 Diesel and 1979–84 B2000

1. Put the gearshift in Neutral.

2. Lift up the boot covering the shift lever and detach the gearshift tower from the extension housing. Remove the shift lever, tower and gasket as an assembly.

3. Cover the opening in the case with a heavy rag to keep dirt out.

4. Remove the negative battery cable. Raise and support the truck.

5. Disconnect the driveshaft at the rear axle.

6. Remove the driveshaft center bearing support and pull the driveshaft rearward to disconnect the driveshaft from the transmission. Install a plug in the extension housing to prevent lubricant from leaking out.

7. Remove the exhaust pipe brackets from the transmission case.

8. Disconnect the exhaust pipe hanger from the clutch housing.

9. Disconnect the exhaust pipe at the manifold and muffler and remove the exhaust pipe-resonator assembly or catalytic converter.

10. Unhook the clutch release lever return spring. Remove the clutch release cylinder and secure it out of the way.

11. Remove the speedometer cable from the extension housing.

12. Disconnect the starter motor and backup light wires.

13. Protect the oil pan with a block of wood and support the engine with a jack. Support the transmission with a separate jack.

14. Remove the starter.

15. Unbolt the transmission from the engine rear plate.

16. Unbolt the transmission mount from the crossmember.

17. Remove the crossmember.

18. Work the clutch housing off the locating dowels. Slide the transmission rearward until the input shaft spline clears the clutch disc.

19. Remove the transmission from the truck.

20. Be sure that all mating surfaces are free of dirt, burrs and paint.

To install:

21. Lift the transmission into place and start the input shaft into the clutch disc. Be sure that the splines align and move the transmission forward until the clutch housing seats on the locating dowels of the engine rear plate.

22. Bolt the clutch housing to the rear plate. Torque the bolts to 45 ft. lbs.

23. Install the starter motor.

24. Raise the engine and install the rear crossmember. Torque the bolts to 50 ft. lbs.

25. Install the rear transmission mount on the crossmember. Bolt the transmission to the rear mount. Torque the bolts to 45 ft. lbs.

26. Remove the jacks.

27. Install the driveshaft in the transmission extension housing. Install the center bearing.

28. Connect the driveshaft to the rear axle flange.

29. Install the exhaust pipe and resonator.
30. Connect the exhaust pipe to the flywheel housing and transmission brackets.
31. Connect the starter and back-up light wires.
32. Install the clutch release cylinder.
33. Adjust the clutch release lever free travel. Connect the return spring.
34. Connect the speedometer cable.
35. Fill the transmission with lubricant.
36. Lower the truck.
37. Install the shift tower and gasket. Install the boot.
38. Road test the truck and check for leaks.

1986 B2000

♦ **See Figure 2**

1. Disconnect the battery ground cable.
2. Raise and support the truck on jackstands.
3. Drain the transmission oil.
4. Remove the gearshift knob, remove the shift console attaching screws, and lift off the console.
5. Remove the shift lever-to-extension housing attaching bolts and remove the shift lever.
6. Remove the driveshaft.
7. Disconnect the speedometer cable from the transmission.
8. Disconnect the wiring at the starter and remove the starter.
9. Disconnect and tag all wiring at the transmission.
10. Disconnect the parking brake return spring, and disconnect the parking brake cables.
11. Remove the clutch slave cylinder.
12. Remove the transmission front support bracket.
13. Disconnect the exhaust pipe at the transmission and manifold.
14. Support the weight of the transmission with a floor jack or transmission jack.
15. Remove the transmission crossmember.

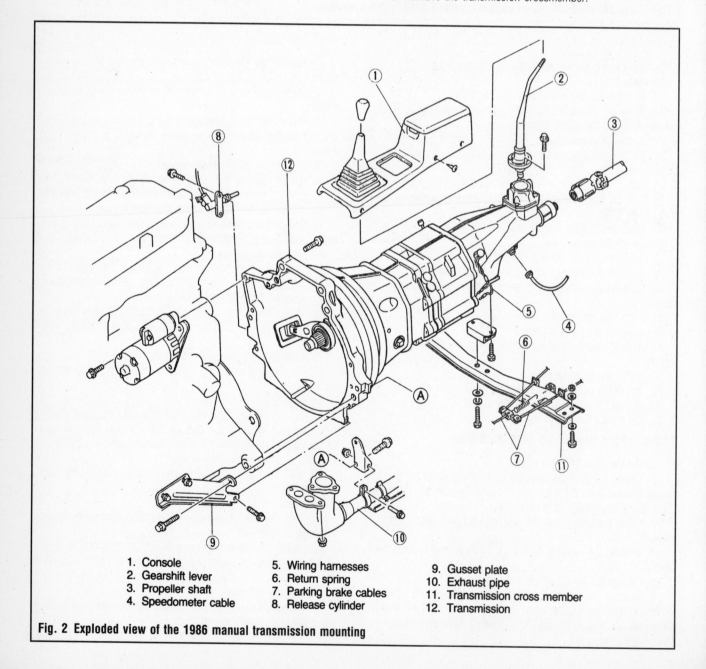

1. Console
2. Gearshift lever
3. Propeller shaft
4. Speedometer cable
5. Wiring harnesses
6. Return spring
7. Parking brake cables
8. Release cylinder
9. Gusset plate
10. Exhaust pipe
11. Transmission cross member
12. Transmission

Fig. 2 Exploded view of the 1986 manual transmission mounting

16. Lower the transmission to get access to the top bolts and remove the transmission-to-engine bolts.

17. Pull the transmission straight back and away from the engine. When clear, lower it and remove it from under the truck.

To install:

18. Position the transmission under the truck.

19. Raise the transmission and slide it forward until the mainshaft enters the clutch disc. The transmission should align with the locating dowels and sit flush with the engine. Install the transmission-to-engine bolts. Torque the transmission-to-engine bolts to 60–65 ft. lbs.

20. Install the transmission crossmember. Torque the bolts to 50 ft. lbs.

21. Remove the transmission jack.

22. Connect the exhaust pipe at the transmission and manifold.

23. Install the transmission front support bracket.

24. Install the clutch slave cylinder.

25. Connect the parking brake return spring, and connect the parking brake cables.

26. Connect all wiring at the transmission.

27. Install the starter.

28. Connect the speedometer cable.

29. Install the driveshaft.

30. Install the shift lever. Torque the gearshift lever bolts to 6–8 ft. lbs.

31. Install the shift console and shifter knob.

32. Fill the transmission.

33. Lower the truck.

34. Connect the battery ground cable.

Rotary Engine Models

▶ **See Figure 3**

1. Remove the knob from the gearshift lever.

2. Remove the gearshift lever.

3. Unbolt the retainer cover from the gearshift lever retainer.

4. Pull the gearshift lever, shim and bushing straight up and away from the gearshift lever retainer.

5. Disconnect the battery ground wire.

6. Remove the bolt attaching the power brake vacuum pipe to the clutch housing.

7. Disconnect the ground strap from the transmission case.

8. Remove the clutch release cylinder.

9. Remove the one upper bolt holding the starter and the three upper bolts and nuts securing the transmission to the engine.

10. Raise and support the truck.

11. Disconnect the wires from the starter motor and the back-up light switch wires.

12. Unbolt and remove the heat insulator from the front exhaust pipe.

13. Disconnect the exhaust pipe from the brackets.

14. Disconnect the exhaust pipe front flange from the exhaust manifold. Remove the front exhaust pipe.

15. Remove the driveshaft.

16. Insert a transmission oil plug into the extension housing.

17. Remove the starter.

18. Install a jack under the engine and support the engine.

19. Unbolt the transmission support from the body.

20. Remove the two lower bolts holding the transmission to the engine.

21. Slide the transmission rearward until the mainshaft clears the clutch disc and remove the transmission from under the truck.

22. Installation is the reverse of removal.

OVERHAUL

1972–84 4-Speed Transmission

DISASSEMBLY

The clutch housing, split transmission case, and extension housing are all made of aluminum.

1. Drain the oil.

2. Remove the clutch housing, bearing retainer, release bearing, and release fork.

3. Remove the speedometer shaft sleeve and driven gear.

4. Remove the extension housing.

5. Remove the back-up light switch.

6. Separate the case halves. Do not pry apart.

7. Measure gear backlash. The backlash for all gears should be 0.1–0.2mm (0.0039–0.0079 in.).

8. Remove the countergear set from the right-hand half of the case.

9. Use a magnet to remove the ball from the second countergear bearing.

10. Withdraw the input and the output shafts as a unit.

11. Use a punch to drive the three slotted spring pins out of the shift forks and shift fork shafts.

➡**The slotted pin cannot always be fully removed from the first/second shift fork; however, the shift fork can still be withdrawn. Do not try to force the pin out, as damage to the transmission case could result.**

12. Remove the case cover and the three detent balls and springs.

13. Remove the shift fork shafts in the following order: First/second shaft. Pin. Reverse shift fork shaft. Third/fourth shaft. Pin.

14. Measure the thrust clearance of the reverse idler gear. The specified clearance is 0.05–0.50mm (0.0019–0.0197 in.).

15. Remove the idler shaft. Remove the gear and washer.

16. Measure the thrust clearance of the gears on the output shaft:

- 1st, 2nd, 4th—0.15–0.25mm (0.0059–0.0098 in.)
- 3rd—0.15–0.30mm (0.0059–0.0118 in.)
- Reverse—0.20–0.30mm (0.0079–0.0118 in.)

17. Disassemble the components of the output shaft. Replace the front bearing, if it is rough or noisy. Use a drift and a press. Remove the snapring first. For bearing installation, replacement snaprings are available in a range of sizes 2.35–2.60mm (0.0925–0.1023 in.) to obtain minimum axial play between the input shaft and the bearing.

ASSEMBLY

1. Assemble the components of the synchronizer hubs, and the output shaft.

2. Install the rear bushing on the output shaft, being careful to install it in the proper direction.

3. Install the ball into the groove of the bushing and slide the bushing over the shaft.

4. Install the needle roller bearing, reverse gear, the ball and the reverse gear synchronizer hub.

5. Install the following items on the output shaft of the four-

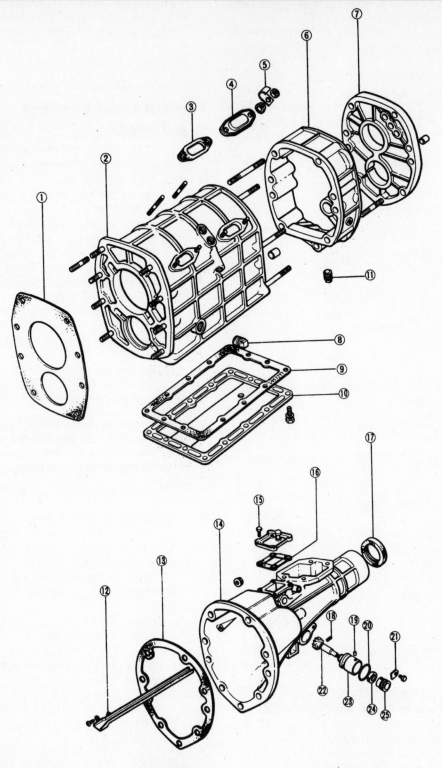

Fig. 3 Exploded view of the rotary engine transmission

1. Gasket
2. Transmission case
3. Gasket
4. Blind cover
5. Clip
6. Intermediate housing
7. Rear bearing housing
8. Oil plug
9. Gasket
10. Under cover
11. Oil plug
12. Oil pass
13. Gasket
14. Extension housing
15. Blind cover
16. Gasket
17. Oil seal
18. Pin
19. Pin
20. O ring
21. Lock plate
22. Speedometer driven gear
23. Sleeve
24. Oil seal
25. Cable joint

speed transmission, in the order indicated: Large-diameter reverse gear spacer. Long spacer. Shims.

6. Install the shims and the nut on the end of the output shaft.

➡**If the original nut is being used, change the number of shims to alter the locking portion of the nut.**

7. Check the thrust clearance of each gear.

8. Working from the rear of the output shaft, install 3rd gear, synchronizer, spacer, and 3rd/4th synchronizer hub (should face forward).

9. Select a snapring to obtain a thrust clearance of less than 0.05mm (0.0197 in.) for the 3rd/4th synchronizer hub.

10. Assemble the following from the rear of the output shaft: snapring. Key. Speedometer drive gear. snapring.

11. Check thrust clearance of gears.

12. Install the fork and shaft assembly in the transmission case.

13. Insert the straight pins in the grooves on either side of the third/fourth shift shaft.

14. Assemble the first/second gear shaft and fork.

15. Perform Step 11 for the reverse shift fork shaft.

16. Insert the three detent balls, followed by their springs.

17. Place the cover gasket on the case and install the cover.

18. Use a punch to drive a slotted spring pin into each shift fork to secure it.

19. Assemble the input and output shafts.

20. Install the shift forks into their respective grooves on the input/output shaft assembly.

21. Install the shaft assembly in the right-hand half of the transmission case, so that the snapring is positioned firmly against the front surface of the transmission case.

22. Apply grease to the countergear rear bearing lockball. Insert the ball into the hole in the rear bearing outer race.

23. Place the countergear assembly into the right-hand half of the transmission case. Mate the lockball with the hole in the transmission case. Place the bearing snapring firmly against the front surface of the transmission case.

24. Install the reverse idler gear.

25. Install the washers, so that their protrusions align with the grooves in the transmission case.

26. Install the shaft into the case and through the gears and washers.

27. Align the grooves in the idler shaft with the hole in the shaft boss. Install the retaining bolt and washer into the boss.

28. Apply a light coating of liquid sealer over the joint surfaces of the transmission case halves.

✳✳ CAUTION

Do not apply sealer to the ½ in. hole for the back-up light switch.

29. Align the transmission case locating pins with their holes and assemble the halves of the case.

➡**There are four different bolt lengths, do not install the wrong bolt in the wrong hole.**

30. Insert the ball, spring, and washer in the back-up light switch hole. Screw in the switch assembly.

31. Install the gasket and bolt the extension housing to the rear of the transmission.

32. Install the speedometer shaft sleeve and drive gear.

33. Apply grease to the conical springs. Install one spring over the input shaft bearing and the other over the countershaft bearing. Install the spacer over the countershaft bearing spring, after coating the spacer with grease.

34. Install the gasket and the clutch housing.

1976–84 5-Speed Transmission

DISASSEMBLY

1. Pull the release fork outward until the spring clip of the fork releases from the ball pivot.

2. Remove the fork and release bearing.

3. Remove the clutch housing shim and gasket.

4. Remove the gearshift lever retainer and gasket.

5. Remove the spring and steel ball, select lock spindle and spring from the gearshift lever retainer.

6. Remove the extension housing with the control lever end down to the left as far as it will go.

7. Remove the control lever end, key and control rod.

8. Remove the lock plate and speedometer gear.

9. Remove the back-up light switch.

10. Remove the snapring and slide the speedometer drive gear from the mainshaft.

11. Remove the bottom cover and gasket.

12. Remove the shift rod ends.

13. Remove the rear bearing housing.

14. Remove the snapring and remove the mainshaft rear bearing, thrust washer and race.

15. Using the puller, remove the washer and countershaft rear bearing.

16. Remove the counter fifth gear.

17. Remove the intermediate housing.

18. Remove the springs and shift locking balls.

19. Remove the two blind covers and gaskets from the case.

20. Remove the reverse/fifth shift rod, fork and interlock pin.

21. Remove the first/second and third/fourth shift forks, rods and interlock pins.

22. Remove the snapring and slide the washer, fifth gear and synchronizer ring from the mainshaft. Also, remove the steel ball and needle bearing.

23. Lock the rotation of the mainshaft with second and reverse.

24. Remove the locknut and slide the reverse/fifth clutch hub and sleeve assembly, synchronizer ring, reverse gear and needle bearing from the mainshaft.

25. Remove the spacer and counter reverse gear from the countershaft.

26. Remove the reverse idler gear, thrust washers and shaft from the transmission case.

27. Remove the bearing rear cover plate.

28. Remove the snapring from the front end of the countershaft and install Mazda tool number 49 0839 445 synchronizer ring holder or its equivalent between the fourth synchronizer ring and the synchromesh gear on the main driveshaft.

29. Remove the countershaft front bearing.

30. Remove the adjusting shim from the countershaft front bearing bore.

31. Remove the countershaft center bearing outer race.

32. With a special puller and attachment, remove the mainshaft front bearing, thrust washer and inner race along with the adjusting shim from the mainshaft front bearing bore.

33. Remove the snapring, and remove the main driveshaft bearing.

34. Remove the countershaft center bearing inner race with the puller.

35. Separate the input shaft from the mainshaft and remove the input shaft.

36. Remove the synchronizer ring and needle bearing from the input shaft.

37. Remove the mainshaft assembly.

38. Remove the first/second and third/fourth shift forks from the case.

39. Remove the snapring and slide the third/fourth clutch hub and sleeve assembly, synchronizer ring and third gear from the mainshaft.

40. Remove the thrust washer, first gear and needle bearing from the rear of the mainshaft.

41. Press out the needle bearing inner race, synchronizer ring, first and second clutch hub, sleeve assembly, synchronizer ring and second gear from the mainshaft.

ASSEMBLY

1. Install the third/fourth clutch hub into the sleeve, place the three keys into the clutch hub slots and install the springs onto the hub.

2. Assemble the first/second and reverse/fifth clutch hub and sleeve.

3. Install the needle bearing, second gear, synchronizer ring, and first/second clutch assembly on the rear section of the mainshaft.

4. Press on the first gear needle bearing inner race.

5. Install the third gear and synchronizer ring onto the front section of the mainshaft.

6. Install the third/fourth clutch assembly onto the mainshaft.

7. Install the snapring on the mainshaft.

8. Install the needle bearing, synchronizer ring, first gear and thrust washer on the mainshaft.

9. Install the mainshaft assembly.

10. Install the needle bearing on the front end of the mainshaft.

11. Install the first/second and third/fourth shift forks in their respective clutch sleeves.

12. Check the mainshaft bearing end-play. Check the depth of the mainshaft bearing bore in the case. Measure the mainshaft bearing height. The difference indicates the required adjusting shim to give a total end-play of less than 0.1mm (0.0039 in.).

13. Install the synchronizer ring holder tool between the fourth synchronizer ring and the synchromesh gear on the input shaft.

14. Position the shims and mainshaft bearing in the bore and install with a press.

15. Install the input shaft bearing in the same way.

16. Check the countershaft front bearing end-play in the same way as the mainshaft bearing end-play.

17. Install the front bearing snapring.

18. Press the countershaft center bearing into position.

19. Install the bearing cover plate.

20. Install the reverse idler gearshaft, thrust washers and reverse idler gear.

21. Install the counter reverse gear and spacer on the rear end on the countershaft.

22. Install the thrust washer and press the needle bearing inner race of the reverse gear on the mainshaft.

23. Install the needle bearing, reverse gear, synchronizer ring, reverse/fifth clutch assembly and new mainshaft locknut on the mainshaft.

24. Lock the mainshaft with the second and reverse gears. Tighten the locknut.

25. Install the needle bearing, synchronizer ring and fifth gear on the mainshaft.

26. Install the thrust washer, steel ball and snapring on the mainshaft.

27. Check the thrust washer-to-snapring clearance. It should be 0.10–0.30mm (0.0039–0.0118 in.).

28. Install the first/second shift rod through the holes in the case and fork.

29. Install the interlock pin with a special installer and guide.

30. Install the third/fourth shift rod through the holes in the case and fork.

31. Align the holes and install the lockbolts of each shift fork and rod.

32. Install the interlock pin as above.

33. Position the reverse/fifth shift fork on the clutch sleeve and install the shift rod.

34. Tighten the lockbolt.

35. Install the three shift locking balls, springs and cap bolts.

36. Place the third/fourth clutch sleeve in third gear.

37. Check the clearance between the synchronizer key and the exposed edge of the synchronizer ring with a feeler gauge. The gap should be 0.66–2.00mm (0.0259–0.0787 in.). Adjust by varying thrust washers.

38. Install the two blind covers and gaskets.

39. Install the undercover and gasket.

40. Apply a thin coat of sealer to the mating edges and install the intermediate housing on the transmission case. Align the lockbolt holes of the housing and reverse idler gearshaft, install and tighten the lockbolt.

41. Position the counter fifth gear and bearing to the rear end of the countershaft and install with a press.

42. Install the thrust washer and snapring.

43. Check the clearance between the washer and snapring. Clearance should be less than 0.1mm (0.0039 in.).

44. Install the mainshaft rear bearing.

45. Install the thrust washer and snapring.

46. Check the thrust washer-to-snapring clearance. Clearance should be less than 0.15mm (0.0059 in.).

47. Apply a thin coat of sealing agent to the mating surfaces and install the bearing housing on the intermediate housing.

48. Install the shift rod ends on their respective rods.

49. Install the speedometer drive gear and steel ball on the mainshaft. Secure it with a snapring.

50. Install a speedometer driven gear assembly on the extension housing and secure it with the bolt and lock plate.

51. Insert the control rod through the holes from the front side of the extension housing.

52. Align the key and insert the control lever end in the control rod.

53. Install the bolt and tighten it to 20–30 ft. lbs.

54. Install the back-up light switch.

55. Place the gasket on the case and install the extension hous-

ing with the control lever end down and as far to the left as it will go.

56. Insert the select lock spindle and spring from the underside of the shift lever retainer.

57. Install the steel ball and spring in alignment with the spindle groove and install the spring cap bolt.

58. Install the gearshift lever retainer and gasket on the extension housing.

59. Check the bearing end-play. Measure the depth of the bearing bore in the housing. Measure the height of the bearing protrusion. The difference indicates the thickness of the shim needed. The end-play should be less than 0.1mm (0.0039 in.).

60. Place the gasket on the front side of the case. Apply lubricant to the lip of the oil seal and install the clutch housing on the case.

61. Install the release bearing and fork on the clutch housing.

1986 4-Speed Transmission

DISASSEMBLY

▶ **See Figure 4**

1. Remove the throwout bearing return spring, throwout bearing, and the release fork.
2. Remove the bearing housing.
3. Remove the input shaft and countershaft snaprings.
4. Remove the floorshift lever retainer, complete with gasket.
5. Unfasten the cap bolt and withdraw the spring, steel ball, select lock pin and spring from the retainer.
6. Remove the extension housing. Turn the control lever as far left as it will go and slide the extension housing off the output shaft.

7. Remove the spring seat and spring from the end of the shift control lever.

8. Loosen the spring cap and withdraw the spring and plunger from their bore.

9. Remove the control rod and boss from the extension housing.

10. Remove the speedometer driven gear. Remove the back-up light switch.

11. Remove the speedometer drive gear.

12. Tap the front ends of the input shaft and countershaft with a plastic hammer; then remove the intermediate housing assembly from the transmission case.

13. Remove the three cap bolts; then withdraw the springs and lockballs.

14. Remove the reverse shift rod, reverse idler gear, and shift lever.

15. Remove the setscrews from all the shift forks and push the shift rods rearward to remove them. Remove the shift forks.

16. Withdraw the reverse shift rod lockball, spring, and interlock pins from the intermediate housing.

17. Remove reverse gear and key from the output shaft.

18. Remove the reverse countergear.

19. Remove the countershaft and output shaft from the intermediate housing.

20. Remove the bearings from the intermediate housing and transmission case.

21. Remove the snapring from the output shaft.

22. Slide the third/fourth clutch hub, sleeve, synchronizer ring, and third gear off the output shaft.

23. Remove the thrust washer, first gear, sleeve, synchronizer ring, and second gear from the rear of the output shaft.

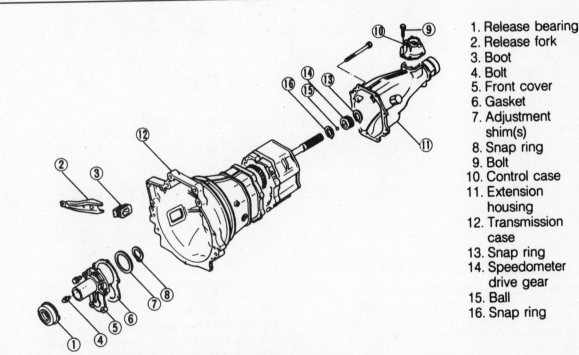

1. Release bearing
2. Release fork
3. Boot
4. Bolt
5. Front cover
6. Gasket
7. Adjustment shim(s)
8. Snap ring
9. Bolt
10. Control case
11. Extension housing
12. Transmission case
13. Snap ring
14. Speedometer drive gear
15. Ball
16. Snap ring

Fig. 4 Exploded view of the 1986 transmission front and rear housing parts

ASSEMBLY

▶ **See Figures 5, 6, 7 and 8**

1. Install the third/fourth synchronizer clutch hub on the sleeve. Place the three synchronizer keys in the clutch hub key slots. Install the key springs with their open ends 120° apart.

2. Install third gear and the synchronizer ring on the front of the output shaft. Install the third/fourth clutch hub assembly on the output shaft. Be sure that the larger boss faces the front of the shaft.

3. Secure the gear and synchronizer with the snapring.

4. Perform Step 1 to the first/second synchronizer assembly.

5. Position the synchronizer ring on second gear. Slide second gear on the output shaft so that the synchronizer ring faces the rear of the shaft.

6. Install the first/second clutch hub assembly on the output shaft so that its oil grooves face the front of the shaft. Engage the keys in the notches on the second gear synchronizer ring.

7. Slide the first gear sleeve onto the output shaft. Position the synchronizer ring on first gear. Install the first gear on the output shaft so that the synchronizer ring faces frontward. Rotate the first gear as required to engage the notches in the synchronizer ring with the keys in the clutch hub.

8. Slip the thrust washer on the rear of the output shaft. Install the needle bearing on the front of the output shaft.

9. Install the synchronizer ring on fourth gear and install the input shaft on the front of the output shaft.

10. Press the countershaft rear bearing and shim into the intermediate housing, then press the countershaft into the rear bearing.

11. Keep the thrust washer and first gear from falling off the output shaft by supporting the shaft. Install the output shaft on the intermediate housing. Be sure that each output shaft gear engages with its opposite number on the countershaft.

12. Tap the output shaft bearing and shim into the intermediate housing with a plastic hammer. Install the cover.

13. Install reverse gear on the output shaft and secure it with its key.

➡**The chamfer on the teeth of both the reverse gear and the reverse countergear should face rearward.**

14. Install the reverse countergear.

15. Install the lockball and spring into the bore in the intermediate housing. Depress the ball with a screwdriver.

16. Install the reverse shift rod, lever, and idler gear at the same time. Place the reverse shift rod in the neutral position.

17. Align the bores and insert the shift interlock pin.

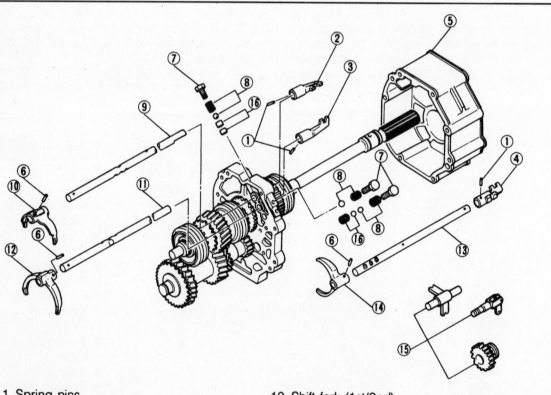

1. Spring pins
2. Shift rod end (1st/2nd)
3. Shift rod end (3rd/4th)   5-speed
4. Shift rod end (5th/reverse)   transmission
5. Intermediate housing   only
6. Spring pins
7. Cap plugs
8. Springs and balls
9. Shift rod (1st/2nd)
10. Shift fork (1st/2nd)
11. Shift rod (3rd/4th)
12. Shift fork (3rd/4th)
13. Shift rod (5th/reverse)   5-speed
14. Shift fork (5th/reverse)   transmission only
15. Shift rod, shift lever,   4-speed
     reverse idle gear   transmission only
16. Springs, balls (5th), interlock pins

Fig. 5 Exploded view of the 1986 transmission 4 and 5-speed shift forks and shift rods

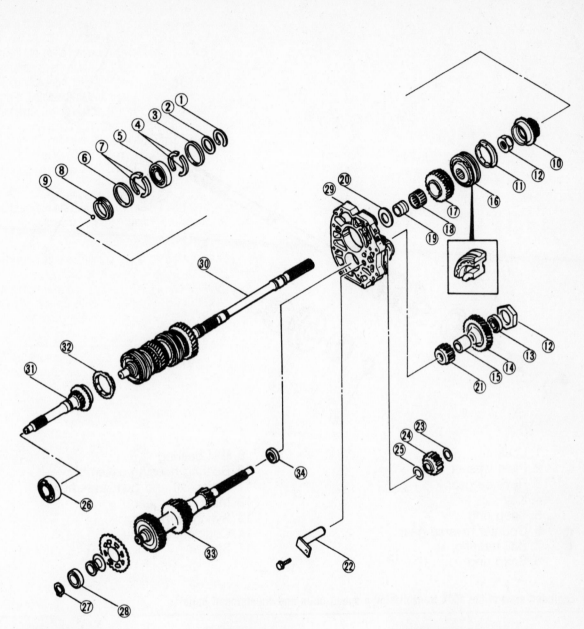

1. Snap ring
2. Washer
3. Retaining ring
4. C washers
5. Ball bearing
6. Retaining ring
7. C washers
8. Thrust lock washer
9. Ball
10. 5th gear
11. Synchronizer ring
12. Locknuts
13. Ball bearing
14. Counter gear
15. Spacer
16. Clutch.hub assembly (5th/reverse)
17. Reverse gear
18. Needle bearing
19. Inner race
20. Washer
21. Counter reverse gear
22. Reverse idle gear shaft
23. Washer
24. Reverse idle gear
25. Washer
26. Ball bearing
27. Snap ring
28. Ball bearing
29. Bearing housing assembly
30. Mainshaft and gear assembly
31. Main drive gear
32. Synchronizer ring
33. Countershaft gear
34. Spacer

Fig. 6 Exploded view of the 1986 transmission 4 and 5-speed main and countershaft parts

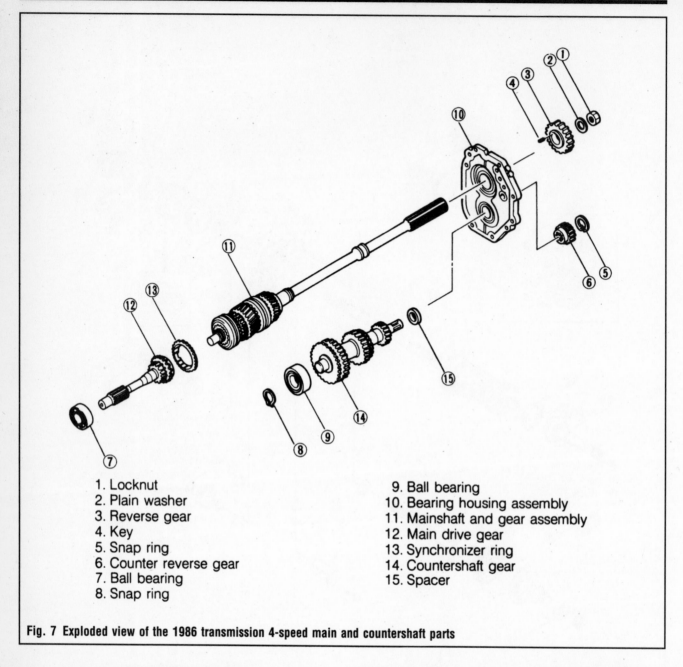

1. Locknut
2. Plain washer
3. Reverse gear
4. Key
5. Snap ring
6. Counter reverse gear
7. Ball bearing
8. Snap ring

9. Ball bearing
10. Bearing housing assembly
11. Mainshaft and gear assembly
12. Main drive gear
13. Synchronizer ring
14. Countershaft gear
15. Spacer

Fig. 7 Exploded view of the 1986 transmission 4-speed main and countershaft parts

18. Install the third/fourth shift rod into the intermediate housing and shift bores. Place the shift rod in Neutral.

19. Install the next interlock pin in the bore.

20. Install the first/second shift rod.

21. Install the lockballs and springs in their bores. Install the cap bolt.

22. Install the speedometer drive gear and lockball on the output shaft, and install its snapring.

23. Apply sealer to the mating surfaces of the intermediate housing. Install the intermediate housing in the transmission case.

24. Install the input shaft and countershaft front bearings in the transmission case.

25. Secure the speedometer driven gear.

26. Install the control rod through the holes in the front of the extension housing.

27. Align the key with the keyway and install the yoke on the end of the control rod. Install the yoke lockbolt.

28. Fit the plunger and spring into the extension housing bore and secure with the spring cap.

29. Turn the control rod all the way to the left and install the extension housing on the intermediate housing.

30. Insert the spring and select lockpin inside the gearshift retainer. Align the steel ball and spring with the lockpin slot, and secure it with the spring cap.

31. Install the spring and spring seat in the control rod yoke.

32. Install the gearshift lever retainer over its gasket on the extension housing.

33. Lubricate the lip of the front bearing cover oil seal and secure the cover on the transmission case.

34. Check the clearance between the front bearing cover and bearing. It should be less than 0.15mm (0.0059 in.). If it is not within specifications insert additional adjusting shims. The shims are available in 0.15mm or 0.30mm sizes.

35. Install the throwout bearing, return spring and release fork.

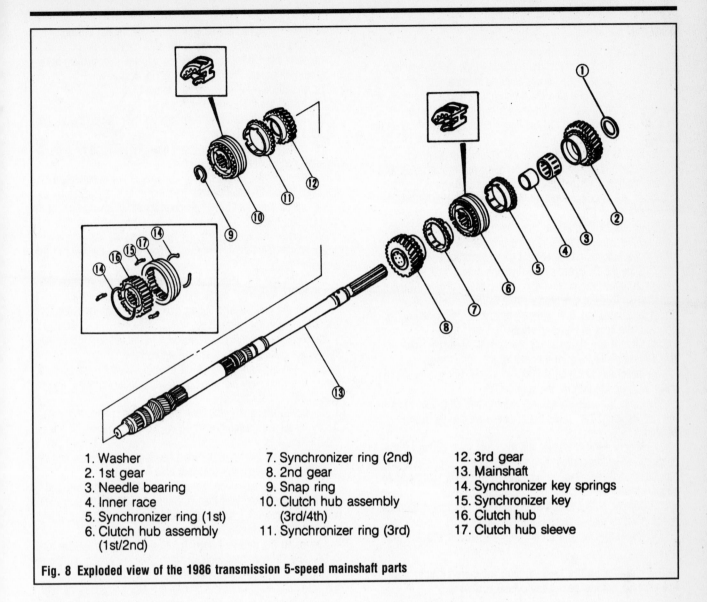

1. Washer
2. 1st gear
3. Needle bearing
4. Inner race
5. Synchronizer ring (1st)
6. Clutch hub assembly (1st/2nd)
7. Synchronizer ring (2nd)
8. 2nd gear
9. Snap ring
10. Clutch hub assembly (3rd/4th)
11. Synchronizer ring (3rd)
12. 3rd gear
13. Mainshaft
14. Synchronizer key springs
15. Synchronizer key
16. Clutch hub
17. Clutch hub sleeve

Fig. 8 Exploded view of the 1986 transmission 5-speed mainshaft parts

1986 5-Speed Transmission

DISASSEMBLY

1. Remove the throwout bearing return spring, throwout bearing, and the release fork.
2. Remove the bearing housing.
3. Remove the input shaft and countershaft snaprings.
4. Remove the floorshift lever retainer, complete with gasket.
5. Unfasten the cap bolt and withdraw the spring, steel ball, select lock pin and spring from the retainer.
6. Remove the extension housing. Turn the control lever as far left as it will go and slide the extension housing off the output shaft.
7. Remove the spring seat and spring from the end of the shift control lever.
8. Loosen the spring cap and withdraw the spring and plunger from their bore.
9. Remove the control rod and boss from the extension housing.
10. Remove the speedometer driven gear. Remove the back-up light switch.
11. Remove the speedometer drive gear.

12. Tap the front ends of the input shaft and countershaft with a plastic hammer; then remove the intermediate housing assembly from the transmission case.
13. Remove the three cap bolts; then withdraw the springs and lockballs.
14. Remove the reverse shift rod, reverse idler gear, and shift lever.
15. Remove the setscrews from all the shift forks and push the shift rods rearward to remove them. Remove the shift forks.
16. Withdraw the reverse shift rod lockball, spring, and interlock pins from the intermediate housing.
17. Remove reverse gear and key from the output shaft.
18. Remove the reverse countergear.
19. Remove the countershaft and output shaft from the intermediate housing.
20. Remove the bearings from the intermediate housing and transmission case.
21. Remove the snapring from the output shaft.
22. Slide the third/fourth clutch hub, sleeve, synchronizer ring, and third gear off the output shaft.
23. Remove the thrust washer, first gear, sleeve, synchronizer ring, and second gear from the rear of the output shaft.

ASSEMBLY

1. Install the third/fourth synchronizer clutch hub on the sleeve. Place the three synchronizer keys in the clutch hub key slots. Install the key springs with their open ends 120° apart.

2. Install third gear and the synchronizer ring on the front of the output shaft. Install the third/fourth clutch hub assembly on the output shaft. Be sure that the larger boss faces the front of the shaft.

3. Secure the gear and synchronizer with the snapring.

4. Perform Step 1 to the first/second synchronizer assembly.

5. Position the synchronizer ring on second gear. Slide second gear on the output shaft so that the synchronizer ring faces the rear of the shaft.

6. Install the first/second clutch hub assembly on the output shaft so that its oil grooves face the front of the shaft. Engage the keys in the notches on the second gear synchronizer ring.

7. Slide the first gear sleeve onto the output shaft. Position the synchronizer ring on first gear. Install the first gear on the output shaft so that the synchronizer ring faces frontward. Rotate the first gear as required to engage the notches in the synchronizer ring with the keys in the clutch hub.

8. Slip the thrust washer on the rear of the output shaft. Install the needle bearing on the front of the output shaft.

9. Install the synchronizer ring on fourth gear and install the input shaft on the front of the output shaft.

10. Press the countershaft rear bearing and shim into the intermediate housing, then press the countershaft into the rear bearing.

11. Keep the thrust washer and first gear from falling off the output shaft by supporting the shaft. Install the output shaft on the intermediate housing. Be sure that each output shaft gear engages with its opposite number on the countershaft.

12. Tap the output shaft bearing and shim into the intermediate housing with a plastic hammer. Install the cover.

13. Install reverse gear on the output shaft and secure it with its key.

➡**The chamfer on the teeth of both the reverse gear and the reverse countergear should face rearward.**

14. Install the reverse countergear.

15. Install the lockball and spring into the bore in the intermediate housing. Depress the ball with a screwdriver.

16. Install the reverse shift rod, lever, and idler gear at the same time. Place the reverse shift rod in the neutral position.

17. Align the bores and insert the shift interlock pin.

18. Install the third/fourth shift rod into the intermediate housing and shift bores. Place the shift rod in Neutral.

19. Install the next interlock pin in the bore.

20. Install the first/second shift rod.

21. Install the lockballs and springs in their bores. Install the cap bolt.

22. Install the speedometer drive gear and lockball on the output shaft, and install its snapring.

23. Apply sealer to the mating surfaces of the intermediate housing. Install the intermediate housing in the transmission case.

24. Install the input shaft and countershaft front bearings in the transmission case.

25. Secure the speedometer driven gear.

26. Install the control rod through the holes in the front of the extension housing.

27. Align the key with the keyway and install the yoke on the end of the control rod. Install the yoke lockbolt.

28. Fit the plunger and spring into the extension housing bore and secure with the spring cap.

29. Turn the control rod all the way to the left and install the extension housing on the intermediate housing.

30. Insert the spring and select lockpin inside the gearshift retainer. Align the steel ball and spring with the lockpin slot, and secure it with the spring cap.

31. Install the spring and spring seat in the control rod yoke.

32. Install the gearshift lever retainer over its gasket on the extension housing.

33. Lubricate the lip of the front bearing cover oil seal and secure the cover on the transmission case.

34. Check the clearance between the front bearing cover and bearing. It should be less than 0.15mm (0.0059 in.). If it is not within specifications insert additional adjusting shims. The shims are available in 0.15mm or 0.30mm sizes.

35. Install the throwout bearing, return spring and release fork.

36. The 5th gear housing can be removed by taking out the retaining bolts. The housing will have to be lightly tapped with a soft-faced hammer. The removal of the housing exposes the 5th/reverse synchronizer assembly, the reverse countergear, the countershaft and mainshaft bearings. The bearings are pulled from the shafts and then the gears can be removed. Assembly is the reverse of disassembly.

CLUTCH

Understanding the Clutch

The purpose of the clutch is to disconnect and connect engine power at the transmission. A vehicle at rest requires a lot of engine torque to get all that weight moving. An internal combustion engine does not develop a high starting torque (unlike steam engines) so it must be allowed to operate without any load until it builds up enough torque to move the vehicle. To a point, torque increases with engine rpm. The clutch allows the engine to build up torque by physically disconnecting the engine from the transmission, relieving the engine of any load or resistance.

The transfer of engine power to the transmission (the load) must be smooth and gradual; if it weren't, drive line components would wear out or break quickly. This gradual power transfer is made possible by gradually releasing the clutch pedal. The clutch disc and pressure plate are the connecting link between the engine and transmission. When the clutch pedal is released, the disc and plate contact each other (the clutch is engaged) physically joining the engine and transmission. When the pedal is pushed in, the disc and plate separate (the clutch is disengaged) disconnecting the engine from the transmission.

Most clutch assemblies consists of the flywheel, the clutch disc, the clutch pressure plate, the throw out bearing and fork, the actuating linkage and the pedal. The flywheel and clutch pressure plate (driving members) are connected to the engine crankshaft and rotate with it. The clutch disc is located between the flywheel and pressure plate, and is splined to the transmission shaft. A driving member is one that is attached to the engine and transfers engine power to a driven member (clutch disc) on the transmission shaft. A driving member (pressure plate) rotates (drives) a driven member (clutch disc) on contact and, in so doing, turns the transmission shaft.

There is a circular diaphragm spring within the pressure plate cover (transmission side). In a relaxed state (when the clutch pedal is fully released) this spring is convex; that is, it is dished outward toward the transmission. Pushing in the clutch pedal actuates the attached linkage. Connected to the other end of this is the throw out fork, which hold the throw out bearing. When the clutch pedal is depressed, the clutch linkage pushes the fork and bearing forward to contact the diaphragm spring of the pressure plate. The outer edges of the spring are secured to the pressure plate and are pivoted on rings so that when the center of the spring is compressed by the throw out bearing, the outer edges bow outward and, by so doing, pull the pressure plate in the same direction away from the clutch disc. This action separates the disc from the plate, disengaging the clutch and allowing the transmission to be shifted into another gear. A coil type clutch return spring attached to the clutch pedal arm permits full release of the pedal. Releasing the pedal pulls the throw out bearing away from the diaphragm spring resulting in a reversal of spring position. As bearing pressure is gradually released from the spring center, the outer edges of the spring bow outward, pushing the pressure plate into closer contact with the clutch disc. As the disc and plate move closer together, friction between the two increases and slippage is reduced until, when full spring pressure is applied (by fully releasing the pedal) the speed of the disc and plate are the same. This stops all slipping, creating a direct connection between the plate and disc which results in the transfer of power from the engine to the transmission. The clutch disc is now rotating with the pressure plate at engine speed and, because it is splined to the transmission shaft, the shaft now turns at the same engine speed.

The clutch is operating properly if:

1. It will stall the engine when released with the vehicle held stationary.

2. The shift lever can be moved freely between 1st and reverse gears when the vehicle is stationary and the clutch disengaged.

General Information

The clutch is a dry single disc type, consisting of a clutch disc, clutch cover and pressure plate and a clutch release mechanism. It is hydraulically operated by a firewall mounted master cylinder and a clutch release slave cylinder mounted on the clutch housing.

✳✳ CAUTION

The clutch driven disc may contain asbestos, which has been determined to be a cancer causing agent. Never clean clutch surfaces with compressed air! Avoid inhaling any dust from any clutch surface! When cleaning clutch surfaces, use a commercially available brake cleaning fluid.

Adjustments

▶ **See Figure 9**

CLUTCH PEDAL FREE-PLAY

1972–75 Vehicles

The free-play of the clutch pedal before the pushrod contacts the piston in the master cylinder should be 0.5–3.0mm (0.0197–0.1181 in.). To adjust the free-play, loosen the locknut and turn the pushrod until the proper adjustment is obtained. Tighten the locknut after the adjustment is complete.

1976–86 Vehicles

The clutch pedal free-play is measured from the top of the pedal pad at rest to the point at which it stops when the pushrod hits the master cylinder piston. Free-play is adjusted by loosening the locknut on the pushrod and adjusting the pushrod length by rotating the rod. The clutch should have a free travel, measured at the pedal pad, of 0.6–3.0mm (0.0236–0.1181 in.) for 1976–84, 5–13mm (0.197–0.512 in.) for 1986 trucks. Tighten the locknut when the adjustment is complete.

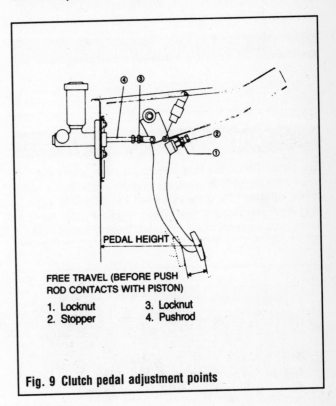

PEDAL HEIGHT

FREE TRAVEL (BEFORE PUSH ROD CONTACTS WITH PISTON)

1. Locknut   3. Locknut
2. Stopper   4. Pushrod

Fig. 9 Clutch pedal adjustment points

PEDAL HEIGHT

Pedal height is measured from the top of the pedal at rest, to the floor board, horizontally behind the pedal. Adjustment is made by loosening the locknut on the pedal stopper and turning the adjusting bolt. Pedal height should be:

- 1972–81—215mm (8.465 in.)
- 1982–84
  - Gasoline engine—205mm (8.071 in.)
  - Diesel engine—215mm (8.465 in.)
- 1986—215mm (8.465 in.)

CLUTCH RELEASE LEVER

1972–75 Vehicles

➡This adjustment must be maintained to prevent release bearing and clutch damage.

1. Raise and support the truck.
2. Disconnect the release lever return spring at the lever.
3. Loosen the locknut and rotate the adjusting nut until a clearance of 3.5–4.5mm (0.138–0.177 in.) is obtained between the bullet nosed end of the adjusting nut and the release lever.
4. Tighten the locknut and hook the return spring.
5. Lower the truck.

1976–86 Vehicles

No adjustment is possible on 1976 and later trucks. Instead, the stroke can be checked by raising the truck and moving the release rod. If the stroke measures less than 5mm (0.197 in.), the clutch pedal should be replaced.

Release Lever and Bearing

REMOVAL & INSTALLATION

❈❈ CAUTION

The clutch driven disc may contain asbestos, which has been determined to be a cancer causing agent. Never clean clutch surfaces with compressed air! Avoid inhaling any dust from any clutch surface! When cleaning clutch surfaces, use a commercially available brake cleaning fluid.

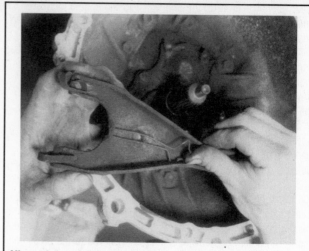

View of the clutch release fork; check this for signs of damage

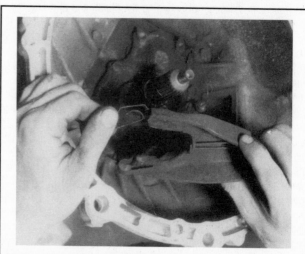

View of the clutch release fork bearing clips; make sure these are not bent or broken

Grease the clutch release fork ball

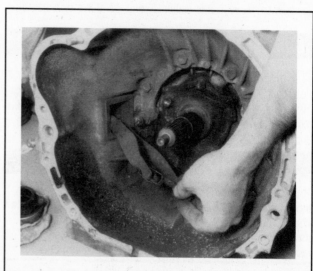

Removing the clutch release fork bearing clips

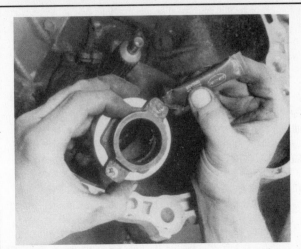

Grease the throwout bearing assembly at the outer contact points

View of the clutch release fork assembly installed; be sure all parts move freely

Grease the throwout bearing assembly at the inner contact points

➡The transmission must be removed to perform the following steps.

1. Most earlier models have a spring attached to the release bearing (throwout bearing) collar. If present, remove this spring. The release lever (fork) is retained by either a spring (earlier models) or a spring clip (1976 and later). Remove the spring and pull the fork from the pivot pin.

2. Remove the lever, dust cover boot and the release (throwout) bearing.

3. Inspect the parts carefully. Wipe off all the oil and dirt from the bearing, but do not soak it in solvent; it is prelubricated. Any burrs should be smoothed with crocus cloth. If burrs are present, inspect the transmission input shaft bearing retainer, and smooth any scoring with crocus cloth.

4. Coat the bearing retainer with a thin film of lithium base grease. Apply a thin film of this grease to both sides of the fork at contact points. Also lightly coat the release bearing surface where it contacts the pressure plate fingers.

5. Fill the grease groove inside the bearing hub with the lithium grease. Do not use polyethylene grease. Clean any excess grease from the bore of the hub, because excess grease will eventually work its way into the clutch disc.

6. Before installing the bearing, hold the inner race and rotate the outer race, applying pressure. If the rotation is noisy or rough, replace the bearing. Bearing failure is generally caused by improper free-play settings at the release cylinder or pedal. Riding the pedal can reduce clearance, causing the bearing to constantly spin, increasing wear. The bearing can also fail due to release lever misalignment (bent out of plane or not centered on the housing bracket) or misalignment between the engine and transmission.

7. Apply a thin film of lithium grease to the input shaft bearing retainer portion of the clutch housing.

8. Dab the end of the pivot pin with grease, and drive the release lever onto it. Apply a thin film of grease to the contact points of the release lever, and install the release bearing. Hook the release collar spring back into place (if applicable).

9. Check the operation of the release bearing hub. It should slide freely on the input shaft bearing retainer.

10. Install the dust boot.

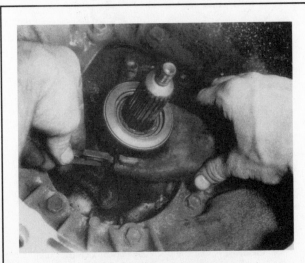

Installing the clutch release fork bearing clip

Driven Disc and Pressure Plate

REMOVAL & INSTALLATION

♦ **See Figures 10, 11, 12, 13 and 14**

❋❋ CAUTION

The clutch driven disc may contain asbestos, which has been determined to be a cancer causing agent. Never clean clutch surfaces with compressed air! Avoid inhaling any dust from any clutch surface! When cleaning clutch surfaces, use a commercially available brake cleaning fluid.

All Models

1. Remove the transmission.
2. Remove the four attaching and two pilot bolts holding the clutch cover to the flywheel. Loosen the bolts evenly and a turn or two at a time. If the clutch cover is to be reinstalled, mark the flywheel and clutch cover to show the location of the two pilot holes.
3. Remove the clutch disc.
4. Install the clutch disc on the flywheel. Do not touch the facing or allow the facing to come in contact with grease or oil. The clutch disc can be aligned using a tool made for that purpose, or with an old mainshaft.
5. Install the clutch cover on the flywheel and install the four standard bolts and the two pilot bolts.
6. To avoid distorting the pressure plate, tighten the bolts evenly a few turns at a time until they are all tight.
7. Torque the bolts to 13–20 ft.lbs. using a crossing pattern.
8. Remove the aligning tool.
9. Apply a light film of lubricant to the release bearing, release lever contact area on the release bearing hub and to the input shaft bearing retainer.
10. Install the transmission.
11. Check the operation of the clutch and if necessary, adjust the pedal free-play and the release lever.

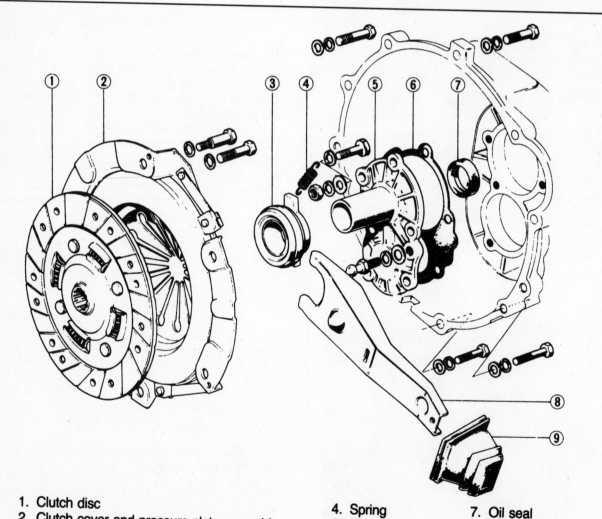

1. Clutch disc
2. Clutch cover and pressure plate assembly
3. Release bearing
4. Spring
5. Front cover
6. Gasket
7. Oil seal
8. Release fork
9. Dust cover

Fig. 10 1972–75 piston engine clutch assembly

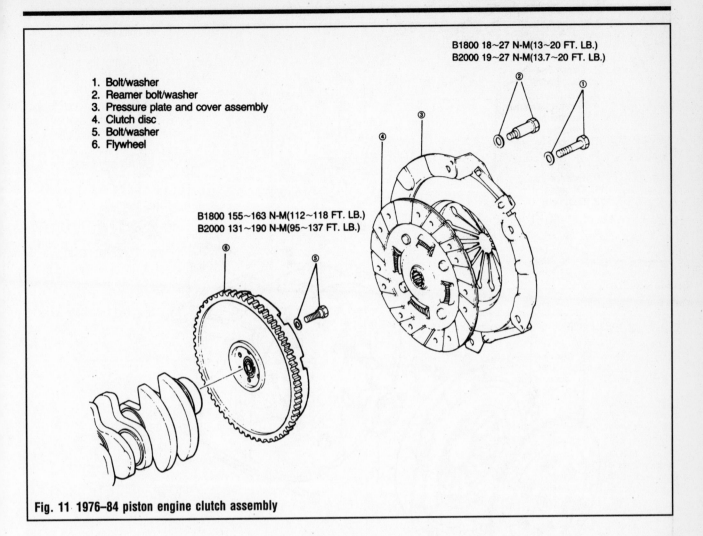

1. Bolt/washer
2. Reamer bolt/washer
3. Pressure plate and cover assembly
4. Clutch disc
5. Bolt/washer
6. Flywheel

B1800 18~27 N-M(13~20 FT. LB.)
B2000 19~27 N-M(13.7~20 FT. LB.)

B1800 155~163 N-M(112~118 FT. LB.)
B2000 131~190 N-M(95~137 FT. LB.)

Fig. 11 1976–84 piston engine clutch assembly

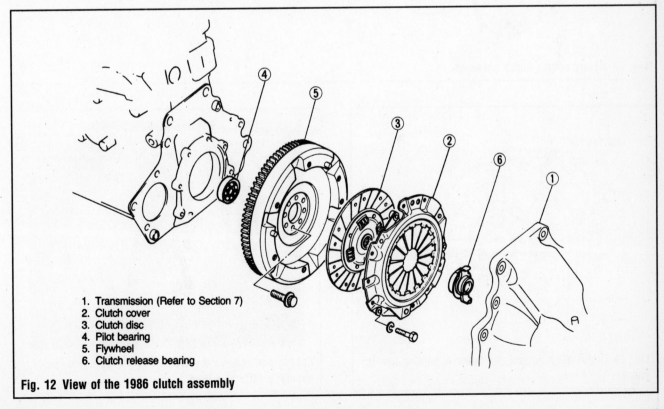

1. Transmission (Refer to Section 7)
2. Clutch cover
3. Clutch disc
4. Pilot bearing
5. Flywheel
6. Clutch release bearing

Fig. 12 View of the 1986 clutch assembly

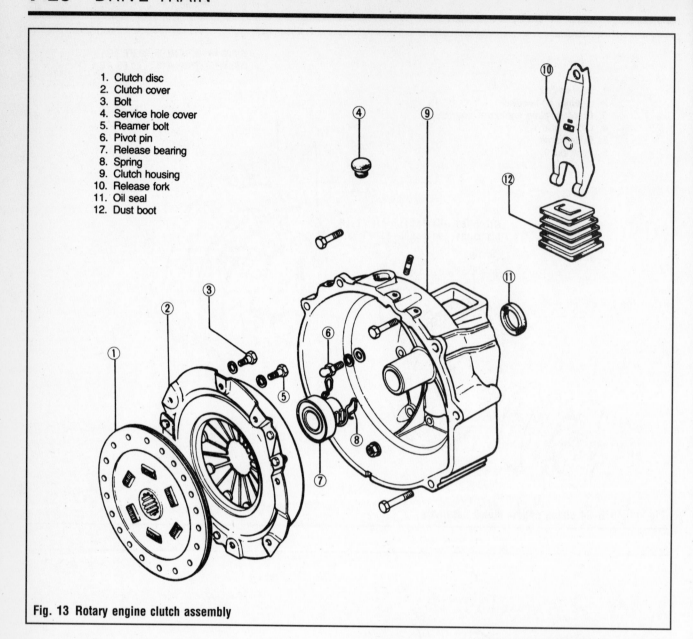

1. Clutch disc
2. Clutch cover
3. Bolt
4. Service hole cover
5. Reamer bolt
6. Pivot pin
7. Release bearing
8. Spring
9. Clutch housing
10. Release fork
11. Oil seal
12. Dust boot

Fig. 13 Rotary engine clutch assembly

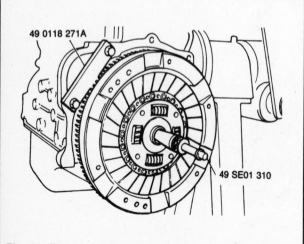

49 0118 271A

49 SE01 310

Fig. 14 Clutch aligning tool and flywheel holding tool in place

Loosen and remove the clutch and pressure plate bolts evenly, a little at a time . . .

Removing the clutch and pressure plate assembly

Check across the flywheel surface, it should be flat

. . . then carefully remove the clutch and pressure plate assembly from the flywheel

If necessary, lock the flywheel in place and remove the retaining bolts . . .

View of the flywheel once the clutch assembly is removed

. . . then remove the flywheel from the crankshaft in order replace it or have it machined

Upon installation, it is usually a good idea to apply a thread-locking compound to the flywheel bolts

Typical clutch alignment tool, note how the splines match the transmission's input shaft

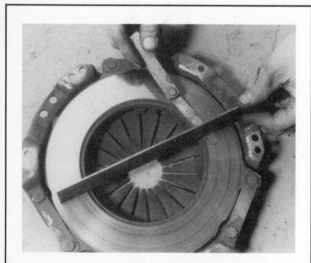

Check the pressure plate for excessive wear

Install a clutch alignment arbor, to align the clutch assembly during installation

Be sure that the flywheel surface is clean, before installing the clutch

Clutch plate installed with the arbor in place

Clutch plate and pressure plate installed with the alignment arbor in place

Install the clutch assembly bolts and tighten in steps, using an X pattern

Pressure plate-to-flywheel bolt holes should align

Be sure to use a torque wrench to tighten all bolts

You may want to use a thread locking compound on the clutch assembly bolts

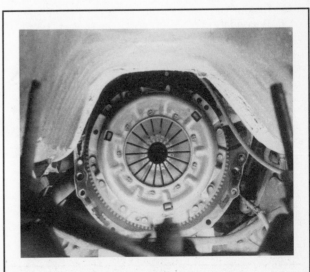

View of the clutch and pressure plate assembly

Master Cylinder

REMOVAL & INSTALLATION

All Models

1. Disconnect and plug the fluid outlet line at the outlet fitting on the master cylinder one-way valve.

2. Remove the nuts and bolts attaching the master cylinder to the firewall.

3. Remove the cylinder straight out away from the firewall.

4. Start the pedal pushrod into the master cylinder and position the master cylinder on the firewall.

5. Install the attaching nuts and bolts. Torque the nuts to 12–17 ft. lbs.

6. Connect the fluid outlet line to the master cylinder fitting.

7. Bleed the hydraulic system.

8. Check the clutch pedal free-travel and adjust as necessary.

OVERHAUL

1972–84 Vehicles
♦ **See Figures 15, 16, 17 and 18**

1. Remove the master cylinder.

2. Clean the outside of the cylinder thoroughly and drain the fluid.

3. On models through 1975, remove the dust cover.

4. Pry out the piston stop ring and remove the stop washer.

5. Remove the piston, piston cup and spring from the cylinder.

6. On all models except the 1976–78 B1800, carefully remove and disassemble the one-way valve.

7. Clean all parts thoroughly using clean brake fluid.

8. Discard any worn, damaged or misshapen parts.

9. Check the piston-to-bore clearance. Clearance should be 0.15mm (0.0059 in.). If clearance exceeds this figure, replace the unit.

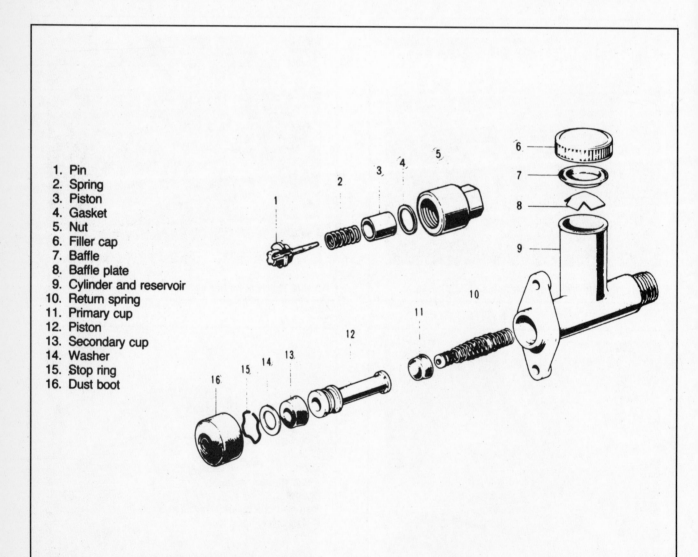

1. Pin
2. Spring
3. Piston
4. Gasket
5. Nut
6. Filler cap
7. Baffle
8. Baffle plate
9. Cylinder and reservoir
10. Return spring
11. Primary cup
12. Piston
13. Secondary cup
14. Washer
15. Stop ring
16. Dust boot

Fig. 15 1972–75 piston engine clutch master cylinder

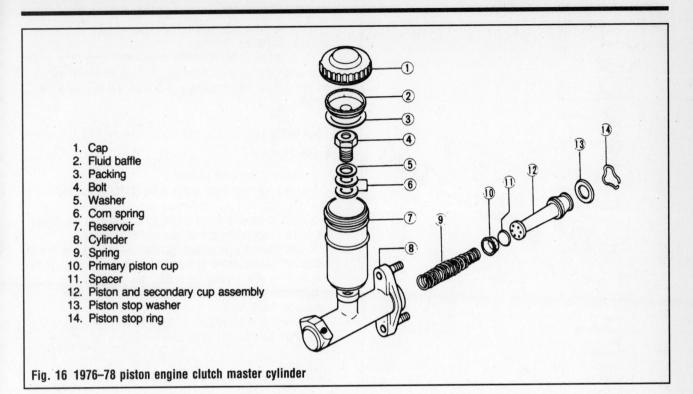

1. Cap
2. Fluid baffle
3. Packing
4. Bolt
5. Washer
6. Corn spring
7. Reservoir
8. Cylinder
9. Spring
10. Primary piston cup
11. Spacer
12. Piston and secondary cup assembly
13. Piston stop washer
14. Piston stop ring

Fig. 16 1976–78 piston engine clutch master cylinder

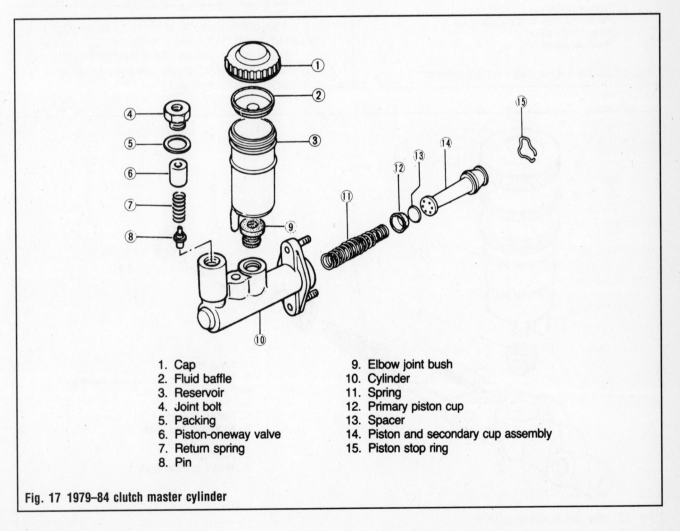

1. Cap	9. Elbow joint bush
2. Fluid baffle	10. Cylinder
3. Reservoir	11. Spring
4. Joint bolt	12. Primary piston cup
5. Packing	13. Spacer
6. Piston-oneway valve	14. Piston and secondary cup assembly
7. Return spring	15. Piston stop ring
8. Pin	

Fig. 17 1979–84 clutch master cylinder

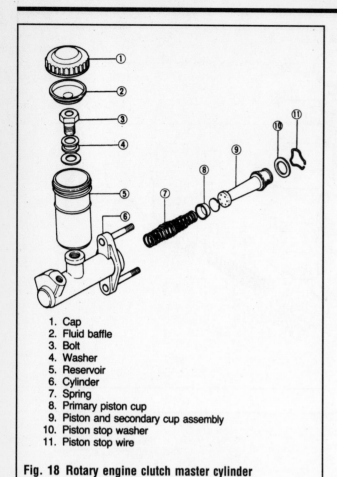

1. Cap
2. Fluid baffle
3. Bolt
4. Washer
5. Reservoir
6. Cylinder
7. Spring
8. Primary piston cup
9. Piston and secondary cup assembly
10. Piston stop washer
11. Piston stop wire

Fig. 18 Rotary engine clutch master cylinder

10. If the cylinder bore is lightly scored or brinnelled, it may be honed to restore the finish.

11. Assembly is the reverse of disassembly. Coat all parts with clean brake fluid prior to assembly. On 1976–78 B1800 models, be sure that the compensating port is open. Fill and bleed the system.

1986 Vehicles
♦ See Figure 19

1. Remove the master cylinder.
2. Using snapring pliers, press down on the piston and remove the snapring from the cylinder bore.
3. Remove the piston and secondary cup, primary cup protector, primary cup, return spring, reservoir and bushing.
4. The secondary piston and cup must be blown out with compressed air applied to the fluid pipe hole. Be careful to cover the bore opening with a heavy rag to catch the piston.
5. Inspect all parts for wear or damage. Clean all parts in clean brake fluid.
6. Assembly is the reverse of disassembly. Coat all parts with clean brake fluid prior to assembly.

ONE-WAY VALVE REMOVAL & INSTALLATION

A one-way valve is used on all master cylinders except 1976–78 1.8 liter models, which have a compensating port instead.
1. Remove the cap from the side of the master cylinder.
2. Remove the washer, one-way valve, and the spring.
3. Installation is the reverse.

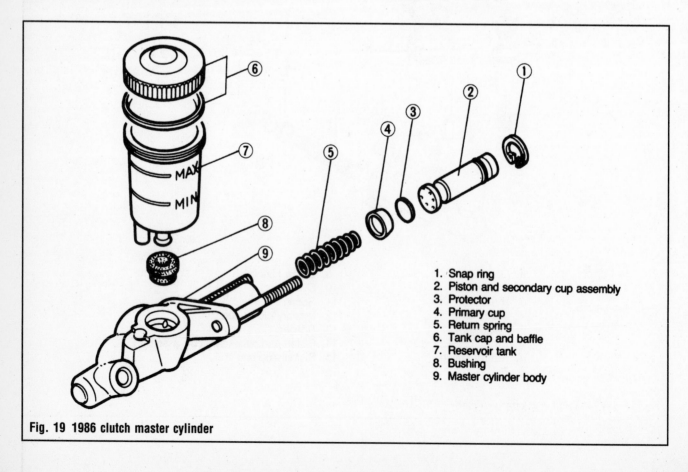

1. Snap ring
2. Piston and secondary cup assembly
3. Protector
4. Primary cup
5. Return spring
6. Tank cap and baffle
7. Reservoir tank
8. Bushing
9. Master cylinder body

Fig. 19 1986 clutch master cylinder

Slave Cylinder

REMOVAL & INSTALLATION

1972–84 Vehicles

1. Disconnect and plug the line at the cylinder.
2. On models through 1975, unhook the release lever return spring. On 1976 and later models, unhook the lever from the pushrod.
3. Remove the nuts and washers attaching the slave cylinder to the clutch housing.
4. Installation is the reverse of removal. Torque the mounting nuts to 12–17 ft. lbs. Fill and bleed the system.

1986 Vehicles

1. Raise and support the front end on jackstands.
2. Back off the flare nut on the fluid pipe to free the slave cylinder hose.
3. Pull off the hose-to-bracket retaining clip and pull the hose from the bracket. Cap the pipe to prevent fluid loss.
4. Unbolt and remove the slave cylinder.
5. Installation is the reverse of removal. Torque the bolt to 12–17 ft. lbs.

OVERHAUL

1972–84 Vehicles

♦ **See Figures 20, 21 and 22**

1. Remove the cylinder.
2. Clean the outside thoroughly.

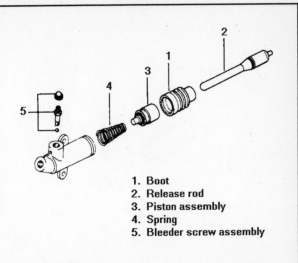

1. Boot
2. Release rod
3. Piston assembly
4. Spring
5. Bleeder screw assembly

Fig. 21 1979–84 clutch slave cylinder—(1) Boot, (2) Release rod, (3) Piston assembly, (4) Spring, (5) Bleeder screw components

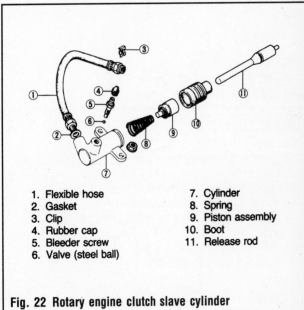

1. Flexible hose
2. Gasket
3. Clip
4. Rubber cap
5. Bleeder screw
6. Valve (steel ball)
7. Cylinder
8. Spring
9. Piston assembly
10. Boot
11. Release rod

Fig. 22 Rotary engine clutch slave cylinder

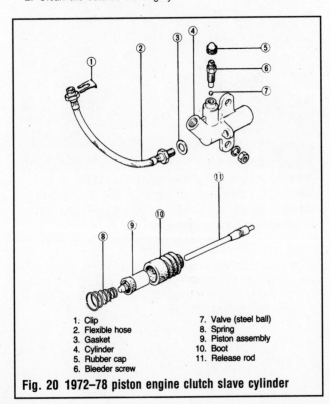

1. Clip
2. Flexible hose
3. Gasket
4. Cylinder
5. Rubber cap
6. Bleeder screw
7. Valve (steel ball)
8. Spring
9. Piston assembly
10. Boot
11. Release rod

Fig. 20 1972–78 piston engine clutch slave cylinder

3. Remove the dust cover and release rod.
4. Remove the piston from the cylinder.
5. Disassemble the bleeder valve.
6. Discard any worn, damaged or distorted parts.
7. Clean all parts in clean brake fluid.
8. The cylinder bore may be honed to remove slight surface damage.
9. Assembly is the reverse of disassembly. Coat all parts in clean brake fluid prior to assembly.

1986 Vehicles

♦ **See Figure 23**

1. Remove the cylinder.
2. Clean the outside thoroughly.
3. Remove the dust cover and release rod.
4. Remove the piston from the cylinder.

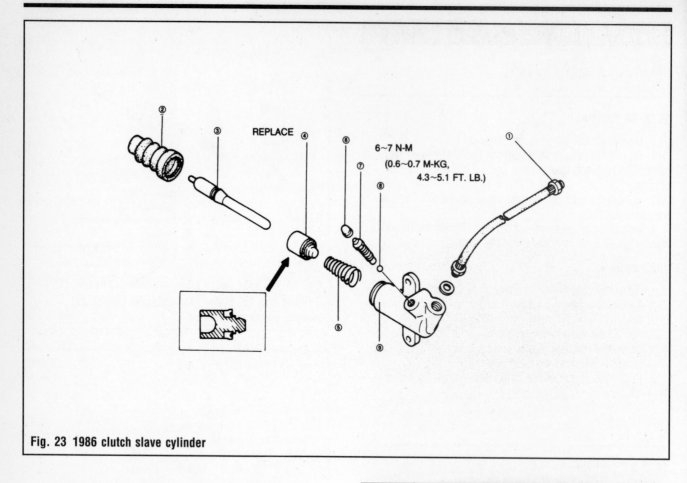

Fig. 23 1986 clutch slave cylinder

5. Remove the return spring.

6. Remove the bleeder screw and the small steel check ball underneath it.

7. Discard any worn, damaged or distorted parts.

8. Clean all parts in clean brake fluid.

9. The cylinder bore may be honed to remove slight surface damage.

10. Assembly is the reverse of disassembly. Coat all parts in clean brake fluid prior to assembly.

BLEEDING THE HYDRAULIC SYSTEM

The clutch hydraulic system must be bled whenever the line has been disconnected or air has entered the system.

To bleed the system, remove the rubber cap from the bleeder valve and attach a rubber hose to the valve. Submerge the other end of the hose in a large jar of clean brake fluid. Open the bleeder valve. Depress the clutch pedal and allow it to return slowly. Continue this pumping action and watch the jar of brake fluid. When air bubbles stop appearing, close the bleeder valve and remove the tube.

During the bleeding process, the master cylinder must be kept at least ¾ full. After the bleeding operation is finished, install the

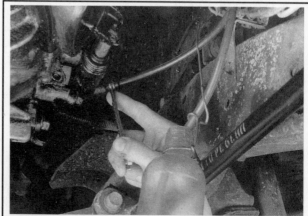

Bleeding the clutch hydraulic system is similar to bleeding the brake hydraulic system. Use clear plastic tubing hooked to the bleeder screw with the open end submerged in a catch can/bottle

cap on the bleeder valve and fill the master cylinder to the proper level. Always use fresh brake fluid, and above all, do not use the fluid that was in the jar for bleeding, since it contains air. Install the master cylinder reservoir cap.

Troubleshooting Basic Clutch Problems

Problem	Cause
Excessive clutch noise	Throwout bearing noises are more audible at the lower end of pedal travel. The usual causes are: • Riding the clutch • Too little pedal free-play • Lack of bearing lubrication A bad clutch shaft pilot bearing will make a high pitched squeal, when the clutch is disengaged and the transmission is in gear or within the first 2″ of pedal travel. The bearing must be replaced. Noise from the clutch linkage is a clicking or snapping that can be heard or felt as the pedal is moved completely up or down. This usually requires lubrication. Transmitted engine noises are amplified by the clutch housing and heard in the passenger compartment. They are usually the result of insufficient pedal free-play and can be changed by manipulating the clutch pedal.
Clutch slips (the car does not move as it should when the clutch is engaged)	This is usually most noticeable when pulling away from a standing start. A severe test is to start the engine, apply the brakes, shift into high gear and SLOWLY release the clutch pedal. A healthy clutch will stall the engine. If it slips it may be due to: • A worn pressure plate or clutch plate • Oil soaked clutch plate • Insufficient pedal free-play
Clutch drags or fails to release	The clutch disc and some transmission gears spin briefly after clutch disengagement. Under normal conditions in average temperatures, 3 seconds is maximum spin-time. Failure to release properly can be caused by: • Too light transmission lubricant or low lubricant level • Improperly adjusted clutch linkage
Low clutch life	Low clutch life is usually a result of poor driving habits or heavy duty use. Riding the clutch, pulling heavy loads, holding the car on a grade with the clutch instead of the brakes and rapid clutch engagement all contribute to low clutch life.

AUTOMATIC TRANSMISSION

Understanding Automatic Transmissions

The automatic transmission allows engine torque and power to be transmitted to the rear wheels within a narrow range of engine operating speeds. It will allow the engine to turn fast enough to produce plenty of power and torque at very low speeds, while keeping it at a sensible rpm at high vehicle speeds (and it does this job without driver assistance). The transmission uses a light fluid as the medium for the transmission of power. This fluid also works in the operation of various hydraulic control circuits and as a lubricant. Because the transmission fluid performs all of these functions, trouble within the unit can easily travel from one part to another. For this reason, and because of the complexity and unusual operating principles of the transmission, a very sound understanding of the basic principles of operation will simplify troubleshooting.

TORQUE CONVERTER

The torque converter replaces the conventional clutch. It has three functions:

1. It allows the engine to idle with the vehicle at a standstill, even with the transmission in gear.

2. It allows the transmission to shift from range-to-range smoothly, without requiring that the driver close the throttle during the shift.

3. It multiplies engine torque to an increasing extent as vehicle speed drops and throttle opening is increased. This has the effect of making the transmission more responsive and reduces the amount of shifting required.

The torque converter is a metal case which is shaped like a sphere that has been flattened on opposite sides. It is bolted to the rear end of the engine's crankshaft. Generally, the entire metal case rotates at engine speed and serves as the engine's flywheel.

The case contains three sets of blades. One set is attached directly to the case. This set forms the torus or pump. Another set is directly connected to the output shaft, and forms the turbine. The third set is mounted on a hub which, in turn, is mounted on a stationary shaft through a one-way clutch. This third set is known as the stator.

A pump, which is driven by the converter hub at engine speed, keeps the torque converter full of transmission fluid at all times. Fluid flows continuously through the unit to provide cooling.

Under low speed acceleration, the torque converter functions as follows:

The torus is turning faster than the turbine. It picks up fluid at the center of the converter and, through centrifugal force, slings it outward. Since the outer edge of the converter moves faster than the portions at the center, the fluid picks up speed.

The fluid then enters the outer edge of the turbine blades. It then travels back toward the center of the converter case along the turbine blades. In impinging upon the turbine blades, the fluid loses the energy picked up in the torus.

If the fluid was now returned directly into the torus, both halves of the converter would have to turn at approximately the same speed at all times, and torque input and output would both be the same.

In flowing through the torus and turbine, the fluid picks up two types of flow, or flow in two separate directions. It flows through the turbine blades, and it spins with the engine. The stator, whose blades are stationary when the vehicle is being accelerated at low speeds, converts one type of flow into another. Instead of allowing the fluid to flow straight back into the torus, the stator's curved blades turn the fluid almost 90° toward the direction of rotation of the engine. Thus the fluid does not flow as fast toward the torus, but is already spinning when the torus picks it up. This has the effect of allowing the torus to turn much faster than the turbine. This difference in speed may be compared to the difference in speed between the smaller and larger gears in any gear train. The result is that engine power output is higher, and engine torque is multiplied.

As the speed of the turbine increases, the fluid spins faster and faster in the direction of engine rotation. As a result, the ability of the stator to redirect the fluid flow is reduced. Under cruising conditions, the stator is eventually forced to rotate on its one-way

clutch in the direction of engine rotation. Under these conditions, the torque converter begins to behave almost like a solid shaft, with the torus and turbine speeds being almost equal.

PLANETARY GEARBOX

The ability of the torque converter to multiply engine torque is limited. Also, the unit tends to be more efficient when the turbine is rotating at relatively high speeds. Therefore, a planetary gearbox is used to carry the power output of the turbine to the driveshaft.

Planetary gears function very similarly to conventional transmission gears. However, their construction is different in that three elements make up one gear system, and, in that all three elements are different from one another. The three elements are: an outer gear that is shaped like a hoop, with teeth cut into the inner surface; a sun gear, mounted on a shaft and located at the very center of the outer gear; and a set of three planet gears, held by pins in a ring-like planet carrier, meshing with both the sun gear and the outer gear. Either the outer gear or the sun gear may be held stationary, providing more than one possible torque multiplication factor for each set of gears. Also, if all three gears are forced to rotate at the same speed, the gearset forms, in effect, a solid shaft.

Most automatics use the planetary gears to provide various reductions ratios. Bands and clutches are used to hold various portions of the gearsets to the transmission case or to the shaft on which they are mounted. Shifting is accomplished, then, by changing the portion of each planetary gearset which is held to the transmission case or to the shaft.

SERVOS AND ACCUMULATORS

The servos are hydraulic pistons and cylinders. They resemble the hydraulic actuators used on many other machines, such as bulldozers. Hydraulic fluid enters the cylinder, under pressure, and forces the piston to move to engage the band or clutches.

The accumulators are used to cushion the engagement of the

The torque converter housing is rotated by the engine's crankshaft, and turns the impeller—The impeller then spins the turbine, which gives motion to the turbine shaft, driving the gears

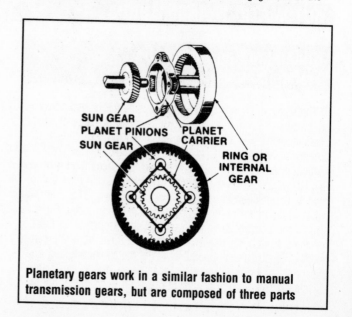

Planetary gears work in a similar fashion to manual transmission gears, but are composed of three parts

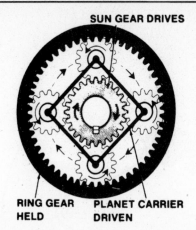

Planetary gears in the minimum reduction (drive) range. The ring gear is allowed to revolve, providing a higher gear ratio

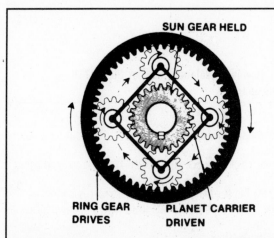

Planetary gears in the minimum reduction (drive) range. The ring gear is allowed to revolve, providing a higher gear ratio

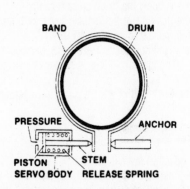

Servos, operated by pressure, are used to apply or release the bands, to either hold the ring gear or allow it to rotate

servos. The transmission fluid must pass through the accumulator on the way to the servo. The accumulator housing contains a thin piston which is sprung away from the discharge passage of the accumulator. When fluid passes through the accumulator on the way to the servo, it must move the piston against spring pressure, and this action smooths out the action of the servo.

HYDRAULIC CONTROL SYSTEM

The hydraulic pressure used to operate the servos comes from the main transmission oil pump. This fluid is channeled to the various servos through the shift valves. There is generally a manual shift valve which is operated by the transmission selector lever and an automatic shift valve for each automatic upshift the transmission provides.

➡**Many new transmissions are electronically controlled. On these models, electrical solenoids are used to better control the hydraulic fluid. Usually, the solenoids are regulated by an electronic control module.**

There are two pressures which affect the operation of these valves. One is the governor pressure which is effected by vehicle speed. The other is the modulator pressure which is effected by intake manifold vacuum or throttle position. Governor pressure rises with an increase in vehicle speed, and modulator pressure rises as the throttle is opened wider. By responding to these two pressures, the shift valves cause the upshift points to be delayed with increased throttle opening to make the best use of the engine's power output.

Most transmissions also make use of an auxiliary circuit for downshifting. This circuit may be actuated by the throttle linkage the vacuum line which actuates the modulator, by a cable or by a solenoid. It applies pressure to a special downshift surface on the shift valve or valves.

The transmission modulator also governs the line pressure, used to actuate the servos. In this way, the clutches and bands will be actuated with a force matching the torque output of the engine.

Transmission Applications

An automatic transmission was first used on the Rotary Pick-Up in 1974. This unit was the 3-speed JATCO R3A.

The first automatic in a piston engined truck was the JATCO 3N71B, 3-speed unit used in the 1984 B2000. No automatics were offered again until 1987.

Fluid Pan

REMOVAL & INSTALLATION

1. Raise and support the truck on jackstands.
2. Place a drain pan under the transmission.
3. Remove all the pan bolts except the two at the front. Loosen these slightly and allow the fluid to drain. The pan may have to be carefully pried loose.
4. Remove the pan. Discard the gasket.
5. Clean the pan thoroughly in a safe solvent.

6. Installation is the reverse of removal. Torque the bolts to 5 ft. lbs.

Adjustments

KICKDOWN SWITCH

♦ **See Figures 24, 25 and 26**

1. Make sure that the accelerator pedal travels its entire stroke properly.

2. Turn the ignition switch to **ON,** but don't start the truck.

3. Depress the accelerator pedal as far as possible. As the throttle nears the wide open position, the contact point of the kick-down switch should close with a light click from the solenoid.

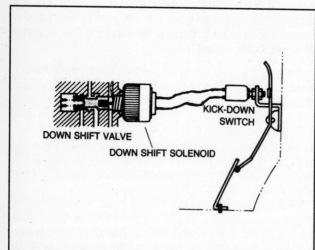

Fig. 24 Kickdown and downshift adjustment for the R3A automatic transmission

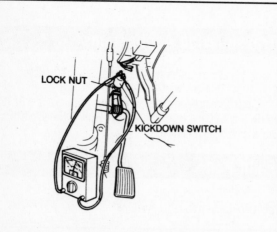

Fig. 25 Kickdown switch check for the 3N71B automatic transmission

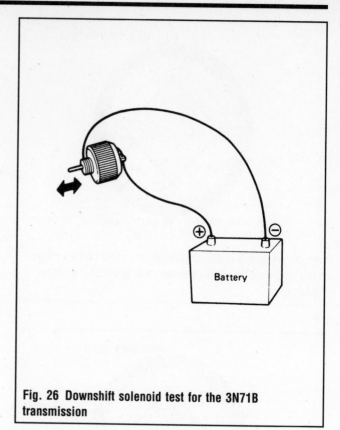

Fig. 26 Downshift solenoid test for the 3N71B transmission

The kickdown switch should begin operation at about ⅞ of full pedal stroke.

4. If not, loosen the kickdown switch attaching nut and adjust the switch.

5. Tighten the attaching nut when adjustment is correct.

6. If the switch cannot be made to operate properly, replace it.

SHIFT LINKAGE

R3A

♦ **See Figure 27**

1. Put the shift lever in **NEUTRAL.**

2. Raise and support the truck on jackstands.

3. Adjust the position of the manual lever by turning the T-joint so that the manual lever is in **NEUTRAL.**

4. Shift the gearshift lever to PARK and make sure that the parking pawl is engaged and there is no looseness in the linkage.

5. Lower the truck and check transmission operation.

3N71B

♦ **See Figures 28 and 29**

1. Put the gearshift lever in Neutral.

2. Raise and support the truck.

3. Disconnect the T-joint from the lower end of the selector lever operating arm.

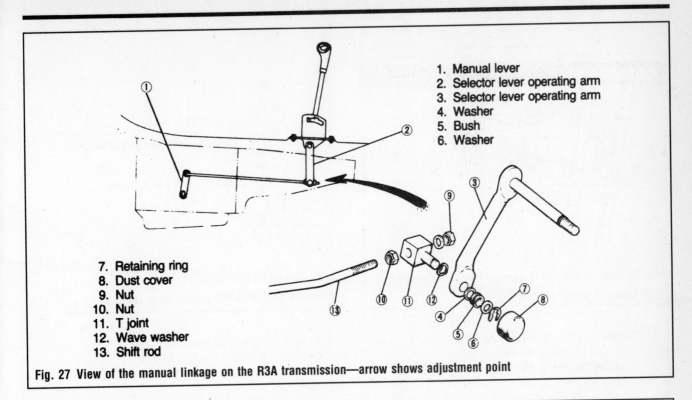

1. Manual lever
2. Selector lever operating arm
3. Selector lever operating arm
4. Washer
5. Bush
6. Washer

7. Retaining ring
8. Dust cover
9. Nut
10. Nut
11. T joint
12. Wave washer
13. Shift rod

Fig. 27 View of the manual linkage on the R3A transmission—arrow shows adjustment point

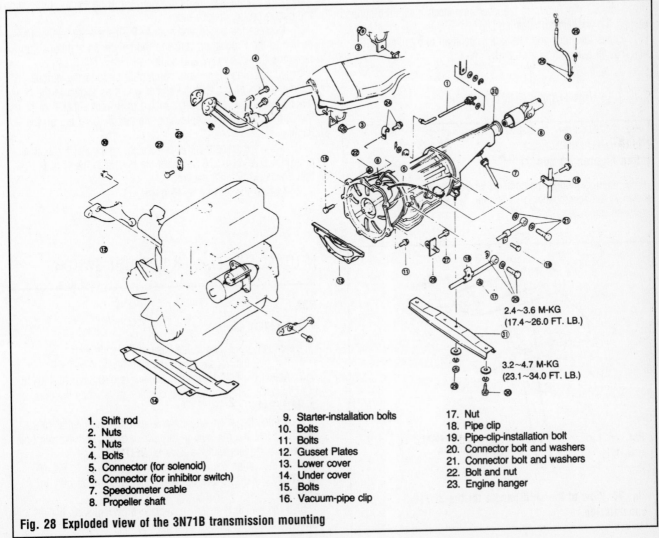

2.4~3.6 M-KG
(17.4~26.0 FT. LB.)

3.2~4.7 M-KG
(23.1~34.0 FT. LB.)

1. Shift rod	9. Starter-installation bolts	17. Nut
2. Nuts	10. Bolts	18. Pipe clip
3. Nuts	11. Bolts	19. Pipe-clip-installation bolt
4. Bolts	12. Gusset Plates	20. Connector bolt and washers
5. Connector (for solenoid)	13. Lower cover	21. Connector bolt and washers
6. Connector (for inhibitor switch)	14. Under cover	22. Bolt and nut
7. Speedometer cable	15. Bolts	23. Engine hanger
8. Propeller shaft	16. Vacuum-pipe clip	

Fig. 28 Exploded view of the 3N71B transmission mounting

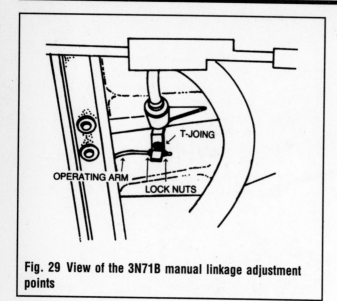

Fig. 29 View of the 3N71B manual linkage adjustment points

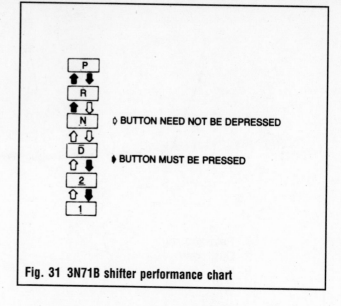

◊ BUTTON NEED NOT BE DEPRESSED

♦ BUTTON MUST BE PRESSED

Fig. 31 3N71B shifter performance chart

4. Move the transmission manual lever to Neutral, the 3rd detent position from the rear of the transmission.

5. Loosen the two T-joint retaining nuts and adjust the T-joint so that it freely enters the hole of the lever. Tighten the retaining nuts to secure the adjustment.

6. Connect the T-joint to the lever and attach it with the spring washer, flat washer and retaining clip.

7. Lower the truck and check the operation of the linkage. Be sure that all gears engage properly.

SHIFT LEVER HANDLE INTERLOCK

3N71B

♦ See Figures 30 and 31

The interlock should be adjusted when it does not perform as shown in the accompanying illustration, or, whenever the handle has been removed.

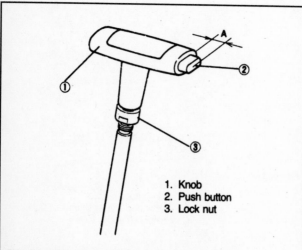

1. Knob
2. Push button
3. Lock nut

Fig. 30 View of the shift handle for the 3N71B transmission

1. Back off the locknut below the handle.

2. Position the shifter in either **N** or **D**.

3. Screw in the handle until no play is felt at the interlock button.

4. Turn the handle one additional turn, if necessary, to position the button on the driver's side.

5. Depress the button and shift to **P.** If the lever cannot be moved to the P position, screw in the handle an additional turn, repeating the shift move and additional turn, until P can be engaged smoothly. From this point, shift through the various positions, confirming that the shifter works as shown in the illustration. If the lever can be shifted to R from either P or N, or into 2 from D, without depressing the button, back out on the handle.

6. When the adjustment is completed, check that the button protrudes 6.0mm (0.236 in.) from the handle in the N or P position. Recheck the shift pattern.

7. Tighten the locknut to 15 ft. lbs.

NEUTRAL SAFETY/BACK-UP LIGHT SWITCH

R3A

♦ See Figure 32

The switch is located at the base of the shift lever.

1. Remove the housing from the shift lever.

2. Adjust the shift lever so that there is 0–0.3mm (0–0.0118 in.) clearance between the pin and guide plate when the lever is in **NEUTRAL.**

3. Loosen the retaining screws and adjust the neutral safety switch so that the pin hole in the switch aligns with the pin hole in the sliding plate with the lever in **NEUTRAL.**

4. At this point, the engine should start only in PARK or **NEUTRAL,** and the back-up lights should come on only in REVERSE.

5. If the switch is defective, replace it by removing the retaining screws and disconnecting the wiring.

Fig. 32 Neutral safety/back-up light switch adjustment on the R3A transmission

3N71B

♦ **See Figure 33**

The switch is located on the right side of the transmission case.

1. Adjust the shift linkage.

2. Place the transmission shift rod in Neutral (3rd detent from the rear of the transmission).

3. Remove the transmission shift rod retaining nut and disconnect the rod from the switch.

4. Loosen the switch attaching bolts. Remove the screw from the alignment pin hole at the bottom of the switch.

5. Rotate the switch and insert an alignment pin, 1.5mm (0.059 in.) diameter into the alignment pin hole and internal rotor.

6. Tighten the two switch attaching bolts and remove the alignment pin.

7. Reinstall the alignment pin hole screw in the switch body.

8. Connect the shift rod.

9. Check the operation of the switch. The engine should start, only with the transmission selector lever in Neutral or Park. The back-up lights should come on, only with the lever in Reverse.

10. If the switch is defective, replace it by simply removing the attaching screws and disconnecting the wiring.

INTERMEDIATE BAND

R3A and 3N71B

♦ **See Figures 34 and 35**

1. Raise and support the truck.

2. Place a drain pan under the transmission and loosen the pan attaching bolts to drain the fluid. Finally remove all the bolts except the two at the front.

3. When the fluid has drained, remove and thoroughly clean the pan.

4. Discard the pan gasket.

5. Loosen the brake band adjusting screw locknut and tighten the adjusting screw to 9–11 ft. lbs.

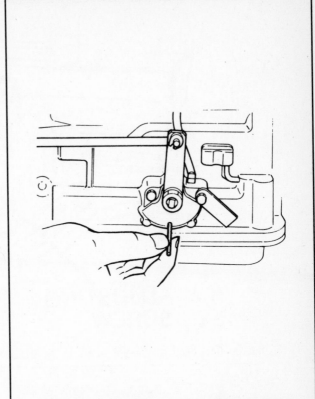

Fig. 33 Neutral safety/back-up light switch adjustment on the 3N71B transmission

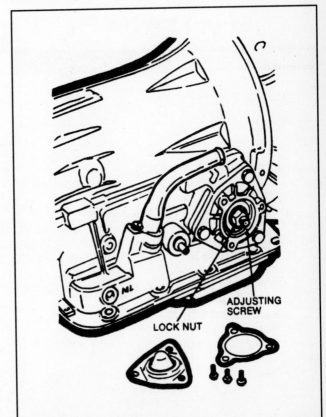

Fig. 34 Intermediate band adjustment points on the R3A transmission

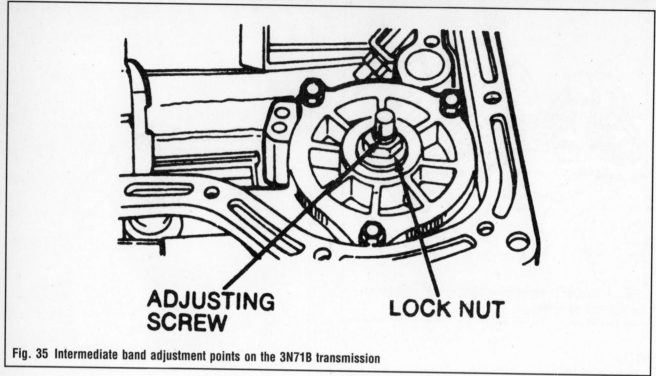

Fig. 35 Intermediate band adjustment points on the 3N71B transmission

6. Back the adjusting screw off two turns.

7. Hold the adjusting screw locknut to 22–29 ft. lbs.

8. Install a new pan gasket and install the pan on the transmission.

9. Lower the truck and fill the transmission with fluid.

Transmission Assembly

REMOVAL & INSTALLATION

R3A

1. Disconnect the battery ground.

2. Disconnect the power brake vacuum line from the converter housing.

3. Raise and support the truck on jackstands.

4. Remove the bell housing access cover and remove the four converter-to-drive plate bolts by turning the drive plate until the bolt appears and holding the drive pulley lockbolt with a wrench.

5. Remove the heat insulator from the exhaust pipe.

6. Disconnect the exhaust pipe at the manifold and the muffler and remove the pipe.

7. Remove the underbody heat shield.

8. Remove the driveshaft.

9. Disconnect the speedometer cable from the extension housing.

10. Disconnect the shift linkage at the transmission.

11. Remove the starter as explained in Chapter 3.

12. Remove the converter housing cover.

13. Support the transmission with a floor jack. Remove the transmission crossmember.

14. Lower the transmission slightly and remove the vacuum fitting bolt from the intake manifold.

15. Remove the vacuum line clips from the length of the transmission.

16. Disconnect and tag all wiring from the transmission.

17. Disconnect and plug the cooling lines from the transmission.

18. Remove the transmission-to-engine bolts.

19. Raise the transmission to its normal position and slide it rearward. It may be necessary to carefully pry the transmission from the engine. Be careful! The torque converter will come off with the transmission, but can easily fall.

20. Lower the jack once the unit is clear.

21. Check the converter drive plate runout. Runout should be less than 0.3mm (0.0118 in.). If not, replace the drive plate.

22. If the converter was removed and installed, check the distance between the flat face of the converter and the mating surface of the housing. Distance should be 20mm (0.787 in.). If not, remove and install the converter in a different position.

To install:

23. Raise the transmission to its normal position and slide it forward.

24. Install the transmission-to-engine bolts. Torque the bolts to 40 ft. lbs.

25. Connect the cooling lines.

26. Connect all wiring.

27. Install the vacuum line clips.

28. Install the vacuum fitting bolt in the intake manifold.

29. Install the transmission crossmember. Torque the bolts to 50 ft. lbs.

30. Bolt the transmission to the jack. Torque the bolts to 40 ft. lbs.

31. Remove the jack.

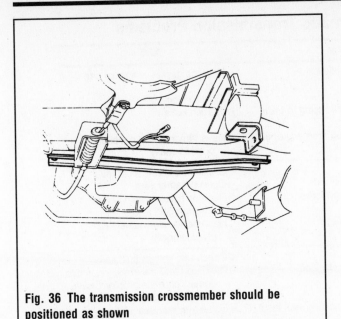

Fig. 36 The transmission crossmember should be positioned as shown

32. Install the converter housing cover.
33. Install the starter.
34. Connect the shift linkage at the transmission.
35. Connect the speedometer cable.
36. Install the driveshaft.
37. Install the underbody heat shield.
38. Connect the exhaust pipe at the manifold and the muffler.
39. Install the heat insulator.
40. Install the four converter-to-drive plate bolts by turning the drive plate until the bolt hole appears, and holding the drive pulley lockbolt with a wrench. Torque the bolts to 40 ft. lbs.
41. Install the bellhousing access cover.
42. Adjust the shift linkage.
43. Lower the truck.
44. Connect the power brake vacuum line at the converter housing.
45. Connect the battery ground.

3N71B

▶ **See Figure 36**

1. Disconnect the negative cable from the battery.
2. Raise and support the truck.
3. Drain the transmission fluid but do not remove the pan. After the fluid has drained, install a few bolts to hold the pan in place, temporarily.
4. Remove the exhaust pipe bracket bolt from the right side of the converter housing.
5. Remove the exhaust pipe flange bolts from the rear of the resonator or catalytic converter, and disconnect the pipe.
6. Disconnect the driveshaft from the rear axle flange.
7. Remove the driveshaft center bearing support nuts, washers, and lockwashers. Lower the driveshaft and remove it from transmission.
8. Disconnect the speedometer cable.
9. Disconnect the shift rod from the manual lever.
10. Remove the vacuum hose from the diaphragm. Disconnect

the electrical connectors from the downshift solenoid and inhibitor switch, and remove their wires from the clip.
11. Disconnect and plug the cooler lines from the radiator at the transmission. Use a flare nut wrench if one is available.
12. Remove the access cover from the lower front of the converter housing.
13. Matchmark the drive plate (flywheel) and torque converter for reassembly. Remove the four bolts holding the torque converter to the drive plate.
14. Remove the bolts connecting the crossmember to the transmission.
15. Support the transmission with a jack. Remove the crossmember-to-frame bolts, and remove the crossmember.
16. Make sure that the transmission is securely supported. Secure it to the jack with a safety chain, if necessary.
17. Lower the transmission to provide working clearance, and remove the starter.
18. Remove the converter housing-to-engine bolts.
19. Remove the fluid filler tube.
20. With a prybar, exert light pressure between the converter and the drive plate to prevent the converter from disengaging from the transmission as it is removed.
21. Lower the transmission and converter as an assembly. Be careful not to let the converter fall out.

To install:

22. Place the transmission on the jack. Be sure that the converter is properly installed.
23. Raise the transmission into place. Install the converter housing-to-engine bolts, and torque in two stages to 23–34 ft. lbs.
24. Lower the transmission on the jack and install the starter.
25. Install the fluid filler tube with a new O-ring.
26. Raise the transmission slightly, and install the crossmember to the frame. Tighten the bolts to 23–34 ft. lbs.
27. Lower the transmission and install the transmission-to-crossmember bolts. Tighten to 23–34 ft. lbs.
28. Align the matchmarks made earlier on the torque converter and drive plate. Install the four attaching bolts and torque to 25–36 ft. lbs. in three stages.
29. Install the access cover. Remove the jack.
30. Connect the cooler lines.
31. Install the electrical connectors to the switch and solenoid, and replace the wires in the clip. Install the diaphragm vacuum hose.
32. Connect the shift rod to the lever.
33. Reconnect the speedometer cable.
34. Insert the driveshaft into the transmission. Install the center bearing support. Bolt the driveshaft to the rear of the axle flange.
35. Connect the exhaust pipe to the resonator or catalytic converter, using a new gasket. Reinstall the exhaust pipe clamp onto the converter housing, and torque the bolt to 10–15 ft. lbs.
36. Install a new pan gasket and the fluid pan, if this has not already been done.
37. Lower the truck. Connect the battery cable. Fill the transmission through the dipstick tube with the specified fluid, being careful not to overfill, and check for leaks.

Troubleshooting Basic Automatic Transmission Problems

Problem	Cause	Solution
Fluid leakage	• Defective pan gasket	• Replace gasket or tighten pan bolts
	• Loose filler tube	• Tighten tube nut
	• Loose extension housing to transmission case	• Tighten bolts
	• Converter housing area leakage	• Have transmission checked professionally
Fluid flows out the oil filler tube	• High fluid level	• Check and correct fluid level
	• Breather vent clogged	• Open breather vent
	• Clogged oil filter or screen	• Replace filter or clean screen (change fluid also)
	• Internal fluid leakage	• Have transmission checked professionally
Transmission overheats (this is usually accompanied by a strong burned odor to the fluid)	• Low fluid level	• Check and correct fluid level
	• Fluid cooler lines clogged	• Drain and refill transmission. If this doesn't cure the problem, have cooler lines cleared or replaced.
	• Heavy pulling or hauling with insufficient cooling	• Install a transmission oil cooler
	• Faulty oil pump, internal slippage	• Have transmission checked professionally
Buzzing or whining noise	• Low fluid level	• Check and correct fluid level
	• Defective torque converter, scored gears	• Have transmission checked professionally
No forward or reverse gears or slippage in one or more gears	• Low fluid level	• Check and correct fluid level
	• Defective vacuum or linkage controls, internal clutch or band failure	• Have unit checked professionally
Delayed or erratic shift	• Low fluid level	• Check and correct fluid level
	• Broken vacuum lines	• Repair or replace lines
	• Internal malfunction	• Have transmission checked professionally

Transmission Fluid Indications

The appearance and odor of the transmission fluid can give valuable clues to the overall condition of the transmission. Always note the appearance of the fluid when you check the fluid level or change the fluid. Rub a small amount of fluid between your fingers to feel for grit and smell the fluid on the dipstick.

If the fluid appears:	It indicates:
Clear and red colored	• Normal operation
Discolored (extremely dark red or brownish) or smells burned	• Band or clutch pack failure, usually caused by an overheated transmission. Hauling very heavy loads with insufficient power or failure to change the fluid, often result in overheating. Do not confuse this appearance with newer fluids that have a darker red color and a strong odor (though not a burned odor).
Foamy or aerated (light in color and full of bubbles)	• The level is too high (gear train is churning oil) • An internal air leak (air is mixing with the fluid). Have the transmission checked professionally.
Solid residue in the fluid	• Defective bands, clutch pack or bearings. Bits of band material or metal abrasives are clinging to the dipstick. Have the transmission checked professionally.
Varnish coating on the dipstick	• The transmission fluid is overheating

Lockup Torque Converter Service Diagnosis

Problem	Cause	Solution

No lockup	• Faulty oil pump
	• Sticking governor valve
	• Valve body malfunction
	   (a) Stuck switch valve
	   (b) Stuck lockup valve
	   (c) Stuck fail-safe valve
	• Failed locking clutch
	• Leaking turbine hub seal
	• Faulty input shaft or seal ring
		• Replace oil pump
		• Repair or replace as necessary
		• Repair or replace valve body or its internal components as necessary
		
		• Replace torque converter
		• Replace torque converter
		• Repair or replace as necessary

Will not unlock	• Sticking governor valve
	• Valve body malfunction
	   (a) Stuck switch valve
	   (b) Stuck lockup valve
	   (c) Stuck fail-safe valve
		• Repair or replace as necessary
		• Repair or replace valve body or its internal components as necessary

Stays locked up at too low a speed in direct	• Sticking governor valve
	• Valve body malfunction
	   (a) Stuck switch valve
	   (b) Stuck lockup valve
	   (c) Stuck fail-safe valve
		• Repair or replace as necessary
		• Repair or replace valve body or its internal components as necessary

Locks up or drags in low or second	• Faulty oil pump
	• Valve body malfunction
	   (a) Stuck switch valve
	   (b) Stuck fail-safe valve
		• Replace oil pump
		• Repair or replace valve body or its internal components as necessary

Sluggish or stalls in reverse	• Faulty oil pump
	• Plugged cooler, cooler lines or fittings
	• Valve body malfunction
	   (a) Stuck switch valve
	   (b) Faulty input shaft or seal ring
		• Replace oil pump as necessary
		• Flush or replace cooler and flush lines and fittings
		• Repair or replace valve body or its internal components as necessary

Loud chatter during lockup engagement (cold)	• Faulty torque converter • Failed locking clutch • Leaking turbine hub seal	• Replace torque converter • Replace torque converter • Replace torque converter
Vibration or shudder during lockup engagement	• Faulty oil pump • Valve body malfunction • Faulty torque converter • Engine needs tune-up	• Repair or replace oil pump as necessary • Repair or replace valve body or its internal components as necessary • Replace torque converter • Tune engine
Vibration after lockup engagement	• Faulty torque converter • Exhaust system strikes underbody • Engine needs tune-up • Throttle linkage misadjusted	• Replace torque converter • Align exhaust system • Tune engine • Adjust throttle linkage
Vibration when revved in neutral Overheating: oil blows out of dip stick tube or pump seal	• Torque converter out of balance • Plugged cooler, cooler lines or fittings • Stuck switch valve	• Replace torque converter • Flush or replace cooler and flush lines and fittings • Repair switch valve in valve body or replace valve body
Shudder after lockup engagement	• Faulty oil pump • Plugged cooler, cooler lines or fittings • Valve body malfunction • Faulty torque converter • Fail locking clutch • Exhaust system strikes underbody • Engine needs tune-up • Throttle linkage misadjusted	• Replace oil pump • Flush or replace cooler and flush lines and fittings • Repair or replace valve body or its internal components as necessary • Replace torque converter • Replace torque converter • Align exhaust system • Tune engine • Adjust throttle linkage

DRIVELINE

A 2-piece driveshaft is used on all models through 1976. Some 1977 and later models use a one piece driveshaft with U-joints at each end.

The 2-piece driveshaft assembly consists of the front shaft, the rear shaft, a center support bearing and U-joints and yokes. The rear end of the driveshaft is attached to a companion flange at the rear axle through a U-joint, and, at the front, to the mainshaft by means of a sliding yoke. This arrangement provides for fore-aft movement of the driveshaft as the truck moves up and down. The center of the driveshaft is supported by the bearing attached to the underside of the truck.

Driveshaft and U-Joints

REMOVAL & INSTALLATION

▶ **See Figures 37 thru 42**

1. Matchmark the rear U-joint with the rear companion flange. Remove the bolts attaching the driveshaft to the rear companion flange.

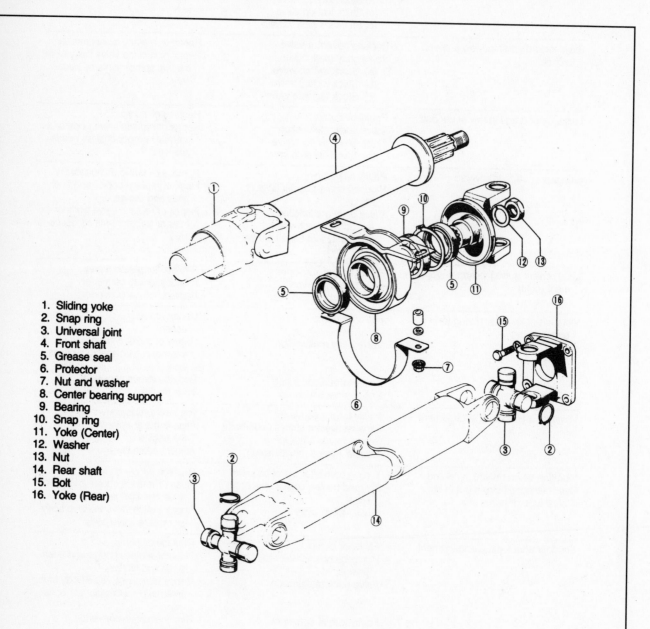

1. Sliding yoke
2. Snap ring
3. Universal joint
4. Front shaft
5. Grease seal
6. Protector
7. Nut and washer
8. Center bearing support
9. Bearing
10. Snap ring
11. Yoke (Center)
12. Washer
13. Nut
14. Rear shaft
15. Bolt
16. Yoke (Rear)

Fig. 37 1972–76 driveshaft components

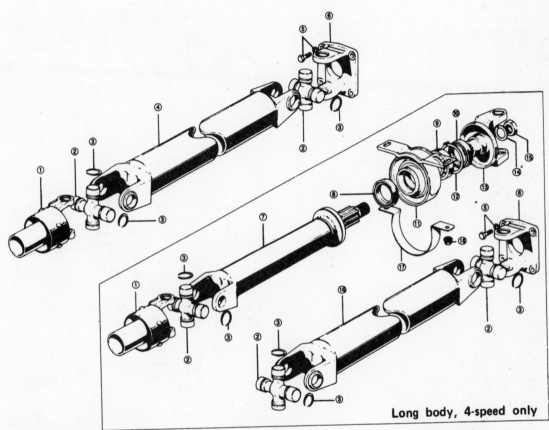

Long body, 4-speed only

1. Sliding yoke
2. Universal joint
3. Snap ring
4. Propeller shaft
5. Bolt and washer
6. Yoke (Rear)
7. Front shaft
8. Oil seal
9. Bearing
10. Oil seal
11. Center bearing support
12. Snap ring
13. Yoke (Center)
14. Washer
15. Nut
16. Rear shaft
17. Protector
18. Flange nut

Fig. 38 1977–83 driveshaft components

1. Yoke
2. Universal joint set
3. Propeller shaft
4. Universal joint yoke
5. Protector
6. Snap ring
7. Support
8. Ball bearing
9. Oil seal
10. Yoke

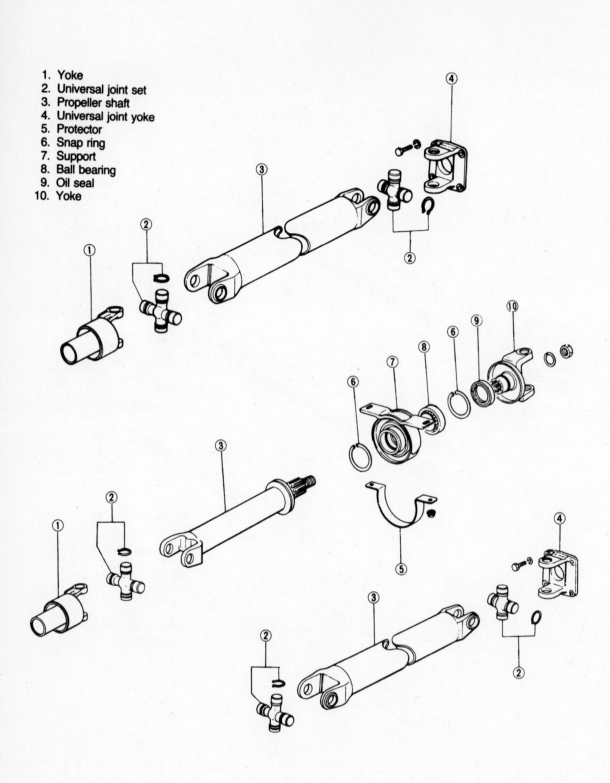

Fig. 39 1984 driveshaft components

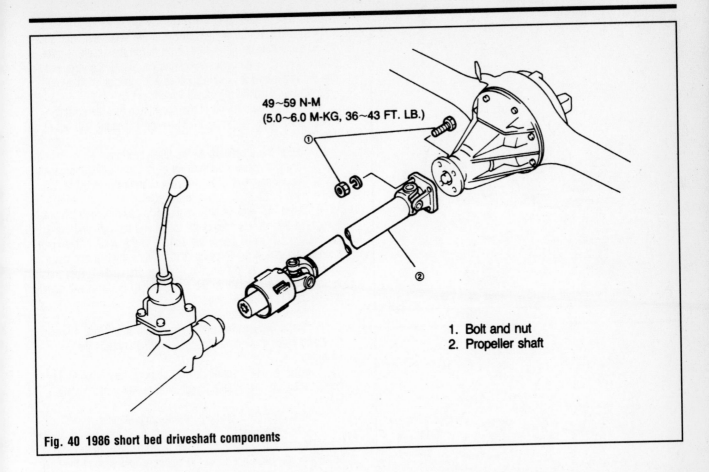

49~59 N-M
(5.0~6.0 M-KG, 36~43 FT. LB.)

1. Bolt and nut
2. Propeller shaft

Fig. 40 1986 short bed driveshaft components

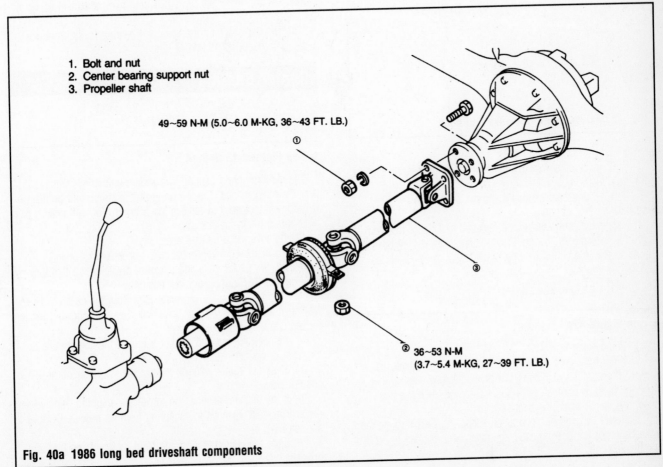

1. Bolt and nut
2. Center bearing support nut
3. Propeller shaft

49~59 N-M (5.0~6.0 M-KG, 36~43 FT. LB.)

36~53 N-M
(3.7~5.4 M-KG, 27~39 FT. LB.)

Fig. 40a 1986 long bed driveshaft components

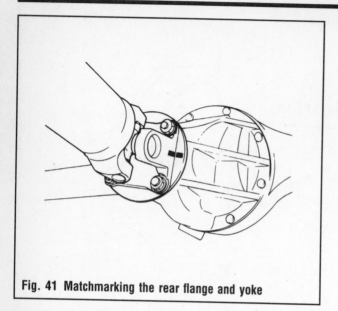

Fig. 41 Matchmarking the rear flange and yoke

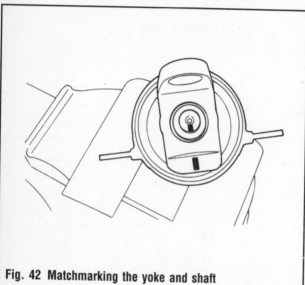

Fig. 42 Matchmarking the yoke and shaft

2. On 2-piece units, remove the center support bearing bracket from the underbody.

3. Pull the driveshaft rearward and out of the transmission. Plug the rear seal opening.

4. Installation is the reverse of removal. Make sure that you align the matchmarks. Torque the rear companion flange bolts to 39–47 ft. lbs.; the center bearing bracket nuts to 27–38 ft. lbs.

U-JOINT REPLACEMENT

▶ **See Figure 42a**

1. Remove the driveshaft.

2. If the front yoke is to be disassembled, matchmark the driveshaft and sliding splined yoke (transmission yoke) so that driveline balance is preserved upon reassembly. Remove the snaprings which retain the bearing caps.

3. Select two sockets, one small enough to pass through the yoke holes for the bearing caps, the other large enough to receive the bearing cap.

4. Using a vise or a press, position the small and large sockets on either side of the U-joint. Press in on the smaller socket so that it presses the opposite bearing cap out of the yoke and into the larger socket. If the cap does not come all the way out, grasp it with a pair of pliers and work it out.

5. Reverse the position of the sockets so that the smaller socket presses on the cross. Press the other bearing cap out of the yoke.

6. Repeat the procedure on the other bearings.

7. To install, grease the bearing caps and needles thoroughly if they are not pregreased. Start a new bearing cap into one side of the yoke. Position the cross in the yoke.

8. Select two sockets small enough to pass through the yoke holes. Put the sockets against the cross and the cap, and press the bearing cap ¼ in. below the surface of the yoke. If there is a sudden increase in the force needed to press the cap into place, or if the cross starts to bind, the bearings are cocked. They must be removed and restarted in the yoke. Failure to do so will greatly reduce the life of the bearing.

9. Install a new snapring.

10. Start a new bearing into the opposite side. Place a socket on it and press in until the opposite bearing contacts the snapring.

11. Install a new snapring. It may be necessary to grind the facing surface of the snapring slightly to permit easier installation.

12. Install the other bearings in the same manner.

13. Check the joint for free movement. If binding exists, smack the yoke ears with a brass or plastic faced hammer to seat the bearing needles. Do not strike the bearings, and support the shaft firmly. Do not install the driveshaft until free movement exists at all joints.

14. The nut attaching the yoke and bearing to the front coupling is torqued to 115–130 ft. lbs.

Center Bearing

REMOVAL & INSTALLATION

▶ **See Figures 43 and 44**

The center support bearing is a sealed unit which requires no periodic maintenance. The following procedure should be used if it becomes necessary to replace the bearing. You will need a pair of snapring pliers for this job.

1. Remove the driveshaft assembly.

2. To maintain driveline balance, matchmark the rear driveshaft, the center yoke and the front driveshaft so that they may be installed in their original positions.

3. Remove the center universal joint from the center yoke, leaving it attached to the rear driveshaft. See the following section for the correct procedure.

4. Remove the nut and washer securing the center yoke to the front driveshaft.

5. Slide the center yoke off the splines. The rear oil seal should slide off with it.

6. If the oil has remained on top of the snapring, remove and discard the seal. Remove the snapring from its groove. Remove the bearing.

7. Slide the center support and front oil seal from the front driveshaft. Discard the seal.

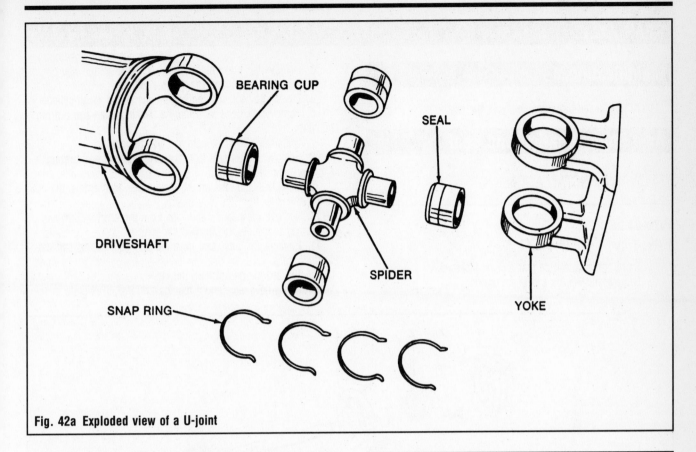

Fig. 42a Exploded view of a U-joint

BEARING CUP

SEAL

SPIDER

DRIVESHAFT

YOKE

SNAP RING

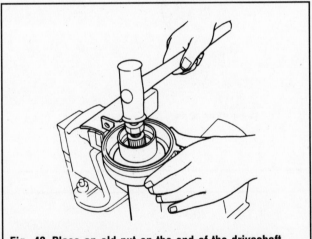

Fig. 43 Place an old nut on the end of the driveshaft and tap the nut lightly to force off the center support and bearing assembly

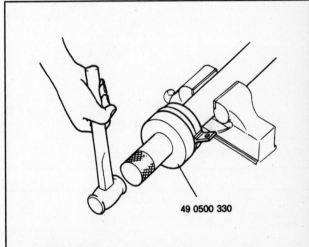

49 0500 330

Fig. 44 Installing the center support and bearing assembly

8. Install the new bearing into the center support. Secure it with the snapring.

9. Apply a coat of grease to the lips of the new oil seals, and install them into the center support on either side of the bearing.

10. Coat the splines of the front driveshaft with grease. Install the center support assembly and the center yoke onto the front driveshaft, being sure to match up the marks made during disassembly.

11. Install the washer and nut. Torque the nut to 116–130 ft. lbs.

12. Check that the center support assembly rotates smoothly around the driveshaft.

13. Align the mating marks on the center yoke and the rear driveshaft, and assemble the center universal joint.

14. Install the driveshaft. Be sure that the rear yoke and the axle flange realigned properly.

REAR AXLE

Identification

Mazda uses a removable carrier type rear axle.

Axle Shaft, Bearing and Seal

REMOVAL & INSTALLATION

1972–84 Vehicles

▶ **See Figures 45, 46 and 47**

1. Raise and support the rear end on jackstands.
2. Remove the wheels and brake drums.

3. Remove the brake shoes.
4. Remove the parking brake cable retainer.
5. Disconnect and cap the brake lines at the wheel cylinders.
6. Remove the bolts securing the backing plate and bearing housing.
7. Slide the axle shaft from the axle housing.
8. Remove the oil seal from the axle housing and discard it. A puller may be necessary.
9. Straighten the tabs on the lockwasher and remove the nut and lockwasher from the axle shaft.
10. Remove the bearing and race from the shaft. A puller or press may be necessary. Discard the spacer.
11. Remove the outer seal from the bearing housing and discard it.
12. Discard the gasket from the baffle.
13. Using new seals and a new gasket, install all parts in re-

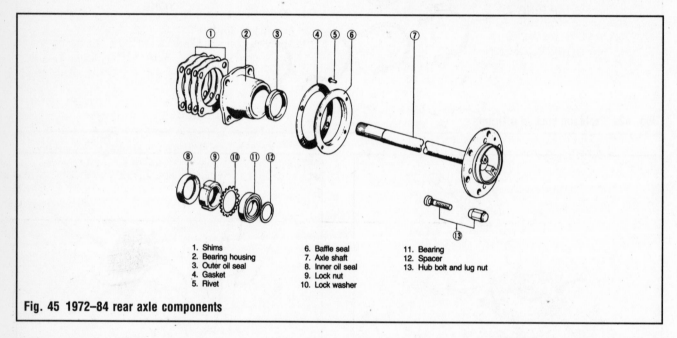

1. Shims
2. Bearing housing
3. Outer oil seal
4. Gasket
5. Rivet
6. Baffle seal
7. Axle shaft
8. Inner oil seal
9. Lock nut
10. Lock washer
11. Bearing
12. Spacer
13. Hub bolt and lug nut

Fig. 45 1972–84 rear axle components

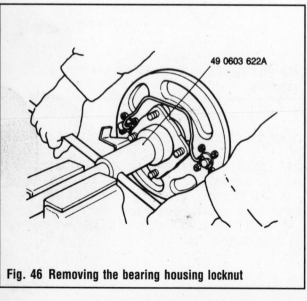

49 0603 622A

Fig. 46 Removing the bearing housing locknut

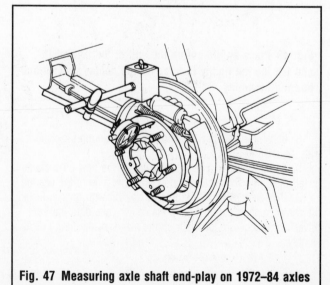

Fig. 47 Measuring axle shaft end-play on 1972–84 axles

verse order of removal. Temporarily install the bearing/backing plate bolts, torquing them to 16 ft. lbs. Don't install the brake shoes or drum yet.

14. Using a dial indicator mounted as shown, check axle shaft end-play. If only one shaft has been removed, end-play should be 0.05–0.15mm (0.00197–0.0059 in.). If both shaft have been removed, check end-play immediately after the first shaft has been replaced. End-play should be 0.66–0.84mm (0.0259–0.0330 in.). Install the second shaft and check that end-play. Second shaft end-play should be 0.05–0.15mm (0.00197–0.0059 in.). If end-play at any step is not within specifications, shims are available.

15. After end-play is adjusted, torque the bearing retainer/backing plate bolts to 40–50 ft. lbs. and assemble all remaining parts.

1986 Vehicles

▶ **See Figures 48 thru 58**

➡**A bearing puller and a press are necessary for this procedure.**

1. Raise and support the rear end on jackstands.
2. Remove the wheel and brake drum.
3. Remove the brake shoes.
4. Remove the parking brake cable retainer.
5. Disconnect and cap the brake lines at the wheel cylinders.
6. Remove the bolts securing the backing plate and bearing housing.
7. Slide the axle shaft from the axle housing. Be careful to avoid damaging the oil seal with the shaft.
8. If the seal in the axle housing is damaged in any way, it must be replaced. The seal can be removed using a slide hammer and adapter.
9. Remove two of the backing plate bolts, diagonally from each other.

10. Using a grinding wheel, grind down the bearing retaining collar in one spot, until about 5mm (0.197 in.) remains before you get to the axle shaft. Place a chisel at this point and break the collar. Be careful to avoid damaging the shaft.

✳✳ CAUTION

Wear some kind of protective goggles when grinding the collar and breaking the collar from the shaft!

11. Using a press or puller, remove the hub and bearing assembly from the shaft. Remove the spacer from the shaft.
12. Remove the bearing and seal from the hub.
13. Using a drift, tap the race from the hub.
14. Check all parts for wear or damage. If either race is to be replaced, both must be replaced. The race in the axle housing can be removed with a slide hammer and adapter. It's a good idea to replace the bearing and races as a set. It's also a good idea to replace the seals, regardless of what other service is being performed.
15. The outer race must be installed using an arbor press. The inner race can be driven into place in the axle housing.
16. Pack the hub with lithium based wheel bearing grease.
17. Tap a new oil seal into the axle housing until it is flush with the end of the housing. Coat the seal lip with wheel bearing grease.
18. Install a new spacer on the shaft with the larger flat surface up.
19. Install a new seal in the hub.
20. Thoroughly pack the bearing with clean, lithium based, wheel bearing grease. If one is available, use a grease gun adapter meant for packing bearings. These are available at all auto parts stores.

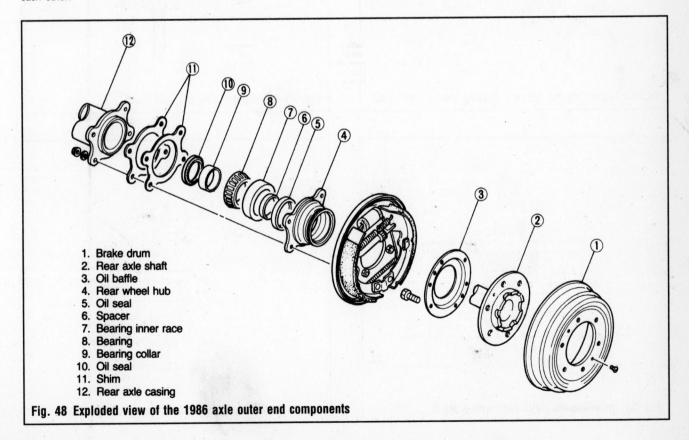

1. Brake drum
2. Rear axle shaft
3. Oil baffle
4. Rear wheel hub
5. Oil seal
6. Spacer
7. Bearing inner race
8. Bearing
9. Bearing collar
10. Oil seal
11. Shim
12. Rear axle casing

Fig. 48 Exploded view of the 1986 axle outer end components

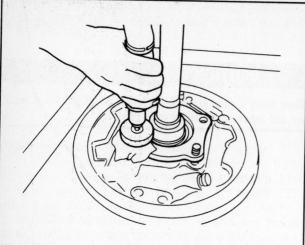

Fig. 49 Grinding down the bearing retaining collar on a 1986 axle

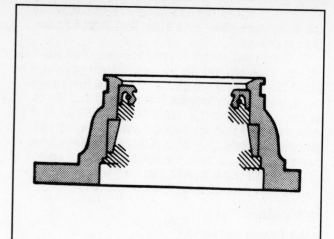

Fig. 52 Pack the hub at the shaded areas with lithium based wheel bearing grease

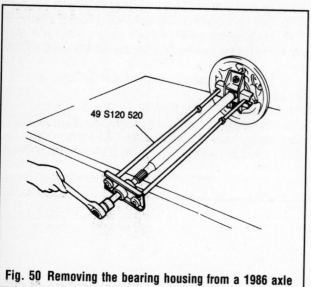

Fig. 50 Removing the bearing housing from a 1986 axle

49 S120 520

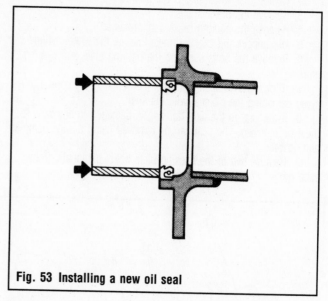

Fig. 53 Installing a new oil seal

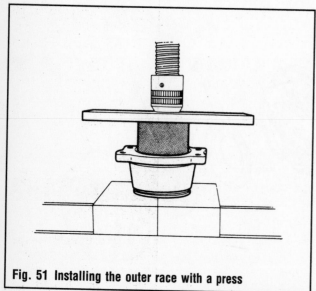

Fig. 51 Installing the outer race with a press

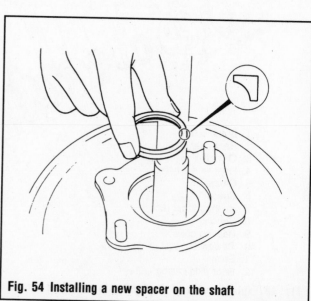

Fig. 54 Installing a new spacer on the shaft

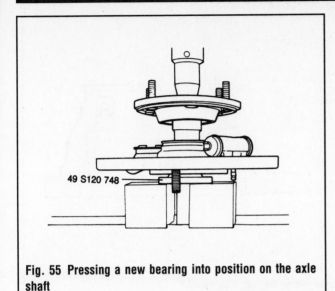

Fig. 55 Pressing a new bearing into position on the axle shaft

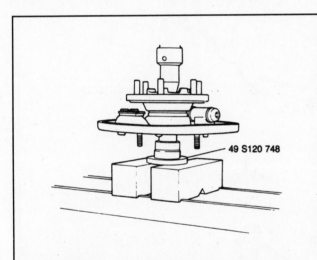

Fig. 56 Pressing a new retaining collar into position on the axle shaft

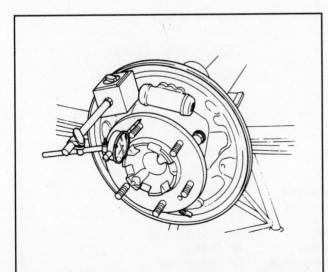

Fig. 57 Checking the axle shaft end-play on a 1986 axle

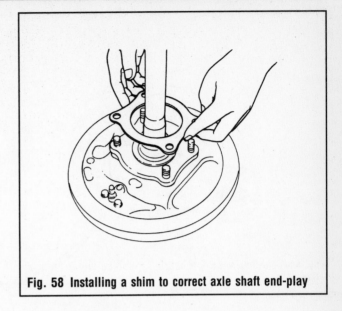

Fig. 58 Installing a shim to correct axle shaft end-play

21. Place the bearing in the hub, and, using a press, press the hub and bearing assembly onto the shaft.

22. Press the new collar onto the shaft. The press pressure for the collar is critical. Press pressures should be 9,240–13,420 lbs.

23. Install one shaft in the housing being very careful to avoid damaging the inner seal.

24. If only one shaft was being serviced, the other must now be removed to check bearing play on the serviced axle. If both shafts were removed, leave the other one out for now.

25. Tighten the backing plate bolts on the one installed axle to 80 ft. lbs.

26. Mount a dial indicator on the backing plate, with the pointer resting on the axle shaft flange. Check the axial play. Standard bearing play should be 0.65–0.95mm (0.0256–0.0374 in.).

27. If play is not within specifications, shims are available for correcting it. See the table below:

Shim Selection Chart

Part Number	Thickness mm (in.)
S083 26 165	0.10 (0.004)
S083 26 166	0.15 (0.006)
S083 26 167	0.50 (0.020)
S083 23 168	0.75 (0.030)

28. Install the other shaft and torque the backing plate bolts. Check the play as on the first shaft. Play should be 0.05–0.25mm (0.0019–0.0098 in.). If not, correct it with shims.

29. Install the brake drums and wheels. Bleed the brake system.

Differential Carrier

◗ **See Figure 59**

➡Differential service is best left to those extremely familiar with their vagaries and idiosyncrasies. A great many specialized tools are required as well as a good deal of experience.

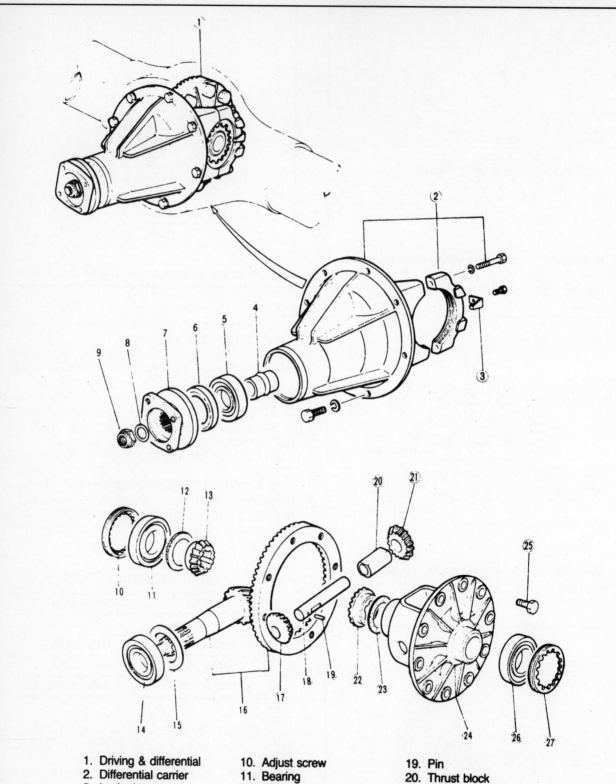

Fig. 59 Exploded view of the differential carrier components

1. Driving & differential
2. Differential carrier
3. Lock plate
4. Distance piece
5. Front pinion bearing
6. Oil seal
7. Companion flange
8. Washer
9. Lock nut
10. Adjust screw
11. Bearing
12. Washer
13. Differential side gear
14. Rear pinion bearing
15. Spacer
16. Final gear set
17. Differential pinion
18. Differential pinion shaft
19. Pin
20. Thrust block
21. Differential pinion
22. Differential side gear
23. Washer
24. Case
25. Ring gear bolt
26. Bearing
27. Adjust screw

REMOVAL & INSTALLATION

1. Raise the vehicle and support it safely with jackstands.

2. Remove the differential drain plug and drain the lubricant from the differential. Install the plug after all of the fluid has drained.

3. Remove the axle shafts as previously outlined.

4. Remove the driveshaft(s) as previously outlined.

5. Remove the carrier-to-differential housing retaining fasteners and remove the carrier assembly from the housing.

6. Clean the carrier and axle housing mating surfaces.

7. If the differential originally used a gasket between the carrier and the differential housing, replace the gasket. If the unit had no gasket, apply a thin film of oil-resistant silicone sealer to the mating surfaces of both the carrier and the housing and allow the sealer to set according to the manufacturer's instructions.

8. Place the carrier assembly onto the housing and install the carrier-to-housing fasteners. Torque the fasteners to 12–17 ft. lbs.

9. Install the driveshaft(s) and axle shafts as previously outlined.

10. Install the brake drums and wheels.

11. Fill the differential with the proper amount of SAE 80W-90 fluid (see the Capacities Chart).

Axle Housing

REMOVAL & INSTALLATION

1. Raise and support the truck on jackstands, allowing the rear axle to hang freely.

2. Remove the wheels.

3. Support the weight of the axle with a floor jack.

4. Disconnect the shock absorbers.

5. Remove the axle-to-spring U-bolts.

6. Disconnect the brake line hose at the junction block. Plug the line.

7. Lower the axle and remove it.

8. Installation is the reverse of removal. Torque the U-bolt nuts to 58 ft. lbs. Torque the shock absorber lower bolts to 58 ft. lbs. Bleed the brakes.

Pinion Seal

REMOVAL & INSTALLATION

♦ **See Figures 60, 61 and 62**

1. Raise and support the front end on jackstands.

2. Matchmark and remove the driveshaft.

3. Remove the wheels and brake calipers.

4. Using an in. lbs. torque wrench on the companion flange nut, measure the rotational torque of the differential and note the reading.

5. Hold the companion flange from turning and remove the locknut.

6. Using a puller, remove the companion flange.

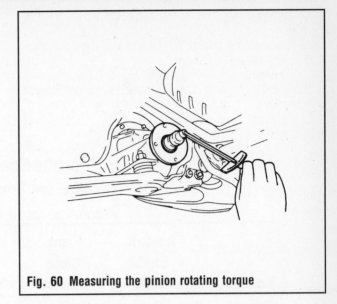

Fig. 60 Measuring the pinion rotating torque

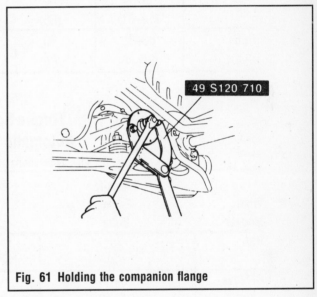

Fig. 61 Holding the companion flange

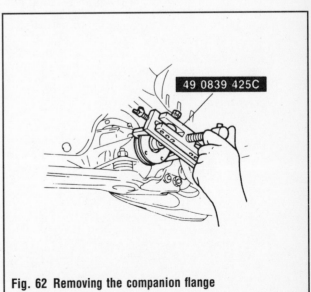

Fig. 62 Removing the companion flange

7. Using a center punch to deform the seal and pry it out of the bore.

8. Coat the outer edge of the new seal with sealer and drive it into place with a seal driver.

9. Coat the seal lip with clean gear oil.

10. Coat the companion flange with chassis lube and install it.

11. Install the nut and tighten it until the previously noted rotational torque is achieved. Torque on the nut should not exceed 130 ft. lbs.

12. Install the driveshaft.

13. Replace any lost gear oil.

Torque Specifications
Manual Transmission

All specifications are given in ft. lbs. (Nm)

Years	Trans.-to -Engine Bolts	Trans. Cross Memeber	Clutch Pressure Plate	Attaching Bolts	
				Clutch Master Cyl.	Clutch Slave Cyl.
1972–84	40–45 (54–61)	50 (68)	13–20 (18–26)	12–17 (16–23)	12–17 (16–23)
1986	60–65 (81–88)	50 (68)	13–20 (18–26)	12–17 (16–23)	12–17 (16–23)

Torque Specifications
Automatic Transmission

All specifications are given in ft. lbs. (Nm)

Trans. Models	Trans.-to -Engine Bolts	Torque Converter Bolts	Trans. Cross Member
R3A	40 (54)	40 (54)	50 (68)
3N71B	23–34 (31–46)	25–36 (34–49)	23–34 (31–46)

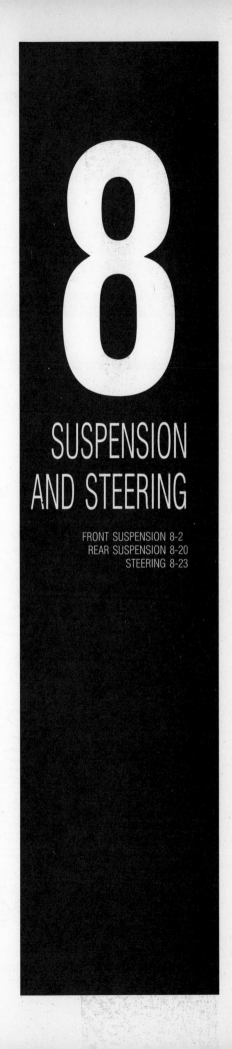

8

SUSPENSION
AND STEERING

FRONT SUSPENSION

▶ **See Figures 1 and 2**

On 1972–84 trucks, the front suspension consists of a wishbone-type, upper and lower control arm assembly with coil spring. Suspension travel is dampened by double acting shock absorbers.

1986 pick-ups use a torsion bar type front suspension, with upper and lower control arms. The lower control arm is further located by tension rods extending to the frame forward of the axle. Conventional, double-acting shock absorbers are employed to dampen motion. A stabilizer bar is standard equipment.

Shock Absorbers

TESTING

The easiest way to check the performance of your shocks is to go to one corner of the truck and start it bouncing up and down.

Get it going as much as you can and then release it. It should stop bouncing in less than two full bounces.

REMOVAL & INSTALLATION

▶ **See Figures 3, 4 and 5**

1. Raise and support the front end on jackstands.
2. Remove the upper end nut, bushings and washers from the shock stem.
3. Remove the lower end attaching bolts.
4. Remove the shock from beneath the lower control arm.
5. Installation is the reverse of removal. Tighten the lower bolts to 25 ft. lbs. on 1972–84 trucks, and 55–59 ft. lbs. on 1986 trucks. Tighten the upper nut until 6mm (0.236 in.) of thread is visible above the locknut on the Rotary Pick-Up, B1800, and 1979–84 B2000, or 3mm (0.118 in.) on the B1600. On 1986 trucks, tighten the upper nut to 17–25 ft. lbs. At this point, 7mm (0.276 in.) of thread should be visible above the nut.

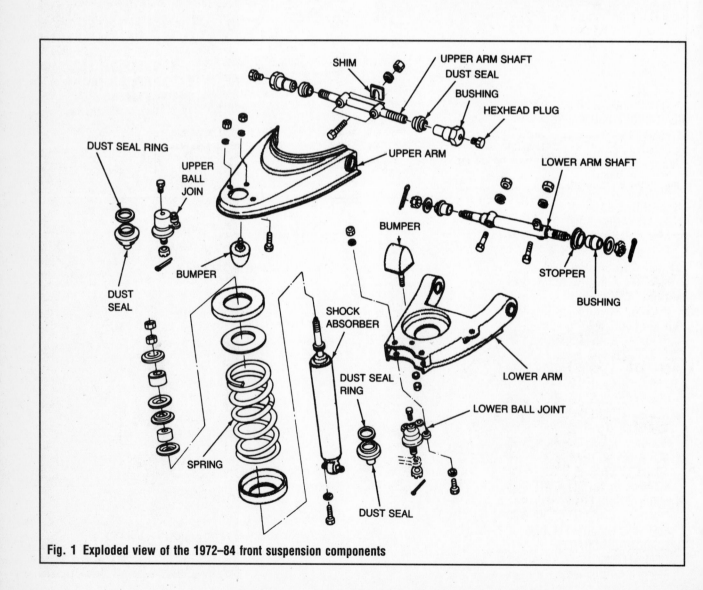

Fig. 1 Exploded view of the 1972–84 front suspension components

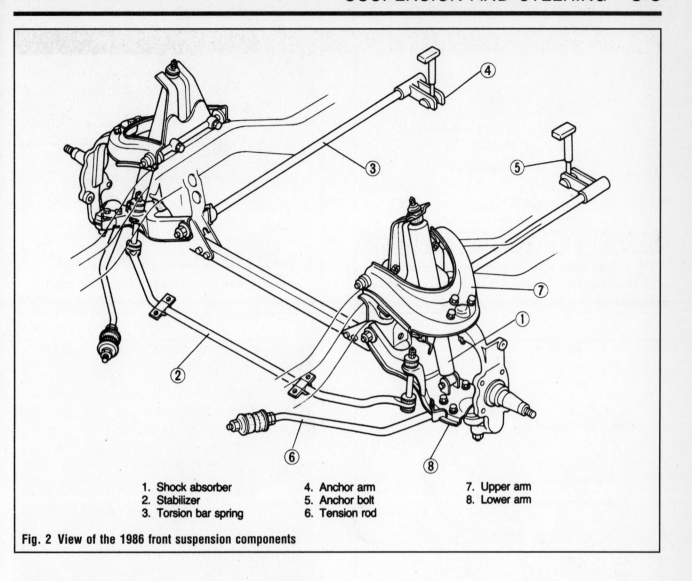

1. Shock absorber
2. Stabilizer
3. Torsion bar spring
4. Anchor arm
5. Anchor bolt
6. Tension rod
7. Upper arm
8. Lower arm

Fig. 2 View of the 1986 front suspension components

Underside view of the front suspension—B2000 shown

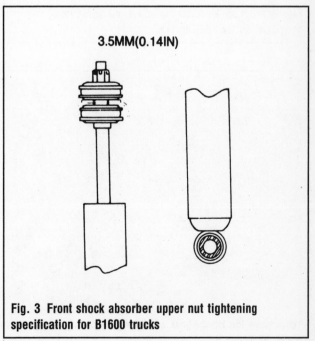

3.5MM(0.14IN)

Fig. 3 Front shock absorber upper nut tightening specification for B1600 trucks

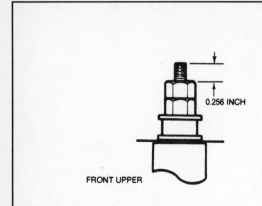

Fig. 4 Front shock absorber upper nut tightening specifications for the rotary pick-up, B1800, and 1979–84 B2000 trucks

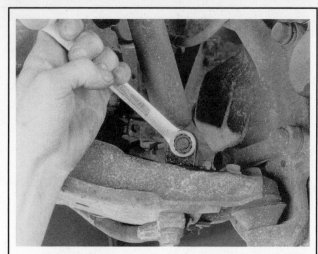

. . . then remove the lower shock absorber mounting bolt

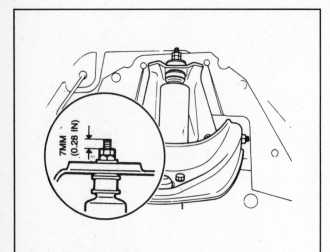

Fig. 5 Front shock absorber upper nut tightening specification for 1986 trucks

Spraying the bolts with a rust penetrating product may aid in removal

To remove the front shock absorber, loosen the upper shock absorber mounting nut (arrow) . . .

Coil Springs

REMOVAL & INSTALLATION

1972–84 Vehicles

✸✸ CAUTION

The spring is under a great deal of tension! It's best to use a coil spring compressor when removing the spring. Mishandling the spring could cause it to fly out of its mounting, causing a great deal of personal damage!

1. Raise and support the front end on jackstands under the frame.
2. Remove the wheel.
3. Remove the shock absorber. Install the spring compressor.

4. Remove the stabilizer bar.

5. Support the lower arm with a floor jack.

6. Disconnect the upper and lower ball joints from the knuckle by removing the cotter pins and nuts and separating the ball joints with a ball joint separator tool.

7. Remove the upper control arm as described below.

8. Slowly lower the jack and remove the spring. Release the compressor to remove spring tension.

9. Installation is the reverse of removal. It's best to replace springs in pairs, however, spacers are available to equalize road height.

Torsion Bar and Lower Control Arm

REMOVAL & INSTALLATION

♦ **See Figures 6 thru 16**

1986 Vehicles

➡**Special tools are necessary for this procedure.**

1. Raise and support the front end on jackstands under the frame.

2. Remove the wheel.

3. Remove the cotter pin and nut from the lower ball joint.

4. Remove the lower shock absorber bolt.

5. Matchmark the anchor arm bolt and anchor swivel and remove the bolt and swivel.

6. Matchmark the torsion bar and anchor arm and the torsion bar and torque plate.

7. Remove the anchor arm and torsion bar from the torque plate. Separate the anchor arm from the torsion bar.

8. Unbolt and remove the torque plate.

9. Remove the lower arm-to-frame bolt. Separate the lower arm from the frame bracket with bushing puller/installer 49 0727 575.

10. Unbolt the tension rod from the lower arm and frame and remove it.

➡**Don't change the position of the double nut at the rear of the tension rod bushing, since it would affect caster.**

11. Remove the stabilizer bar bolt, bushing, retainer and nut and remove the stabilizer bar.

12. Using a ball joint separator, separate the lower ball joint from the knuckle. Remove the lower control arm.

13. Inspect all parts for wear or damage. Replace any suspect parts. Using a spring scale and adapter 49 0180 510B, check the ball joint preload. Pull scale reading should be 39.6 lb. or less. Measure the preload after first shaking the ball joint stud 3 or 4 times to make sure it is free.

To install:

14. Install the lower arm on the frame bracket and hand-tighten the nut.

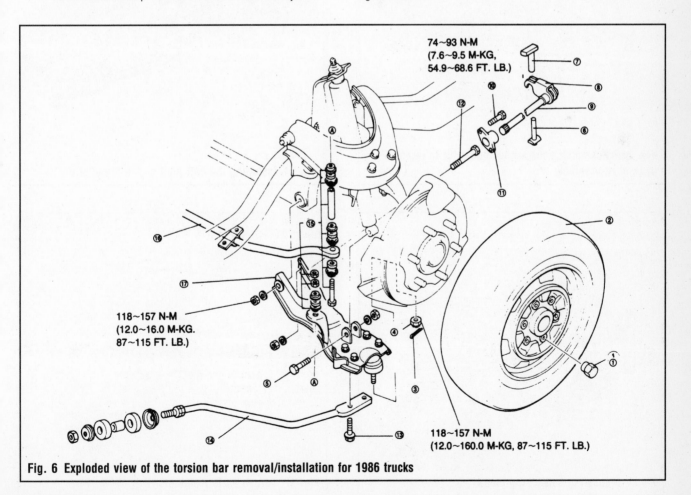

74~93 N-M
(7.6~9.5 M-KG,
54.9~68.6 FT. LB.)

118~157 N-M
(12.0~16.0 M-KG.
87~115 FT. LB.)

118~157 N-M
(12.0~160.0 M-KG, 87~115 FT. LB.)

Fig. 6 Exploded view of the torsion bar removal/installation for 1986 trucks

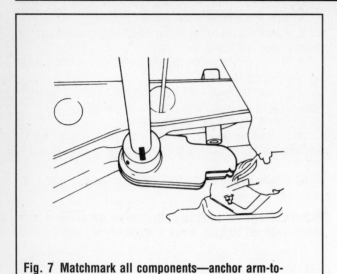

Fig. 7 Matchmark all components—anchor arm-to-torsion bar shown

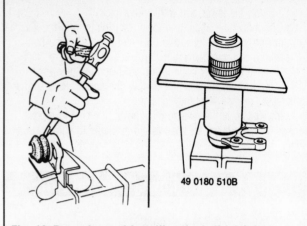

49 0180 510B

Fig. 10 Removing and installing the ball joint dust boot—always inspect all parts for wear and visible damage, and replace as needed

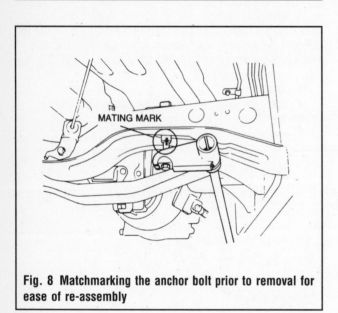

MATING MARK

Fig. 8 Matchmarking the anchor bolt prior to removal for ease of re-assembly

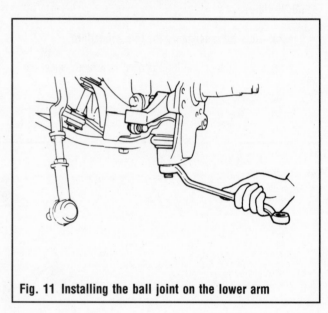

Fig. 11 Installing the ball joint on the lower arm

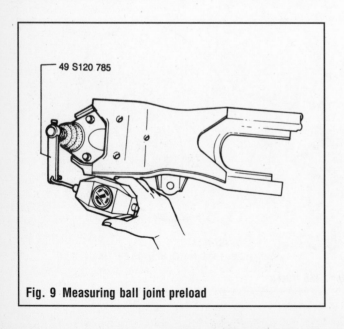

49 S120 785

Fig. 9 Measuring ball joint preload

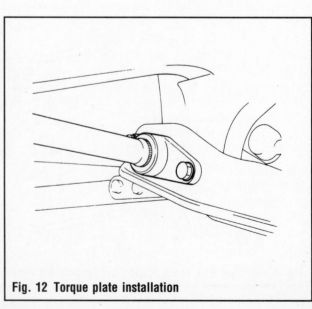

Fig. 12 Torque plate installation

15. Install the lower ball joint on the knuckle and torque the nut to 115 ft. lbs. Install the cotter pin.

16. Tighten the lower arm-to-frame nut to 115 ft. lbs.

17. Position the torque plate and tighten the bolt to 68 ft. lbs.

18. Coat the splines on the torsion bar with lithium based wheel bearing grease. Check the ends of the torsion bar. The bars are marked **L** for left and **R** for right. Don't confuse them. Align the matchmarks and install the torsion bar in the torque plate.

19. Coat the splines on the torsion bar with lithium based grease. Align the matchmarks and install the anchor arm on the torsion bar.

20. Install the anchor bolt and swivel and tighten the bolt until the matchmarks are mated.

21. Install the tension rod. Torque the bushing end nut to 90 ft. lbs.; the lower arm end bolts to 85 ft. lbs.

22. Install the stabilizer bar. Torque the bolt to 19 ft. lbs.

23. Install the shock absorber bolt. Torque the bolt to 55–59 ft. lbs.

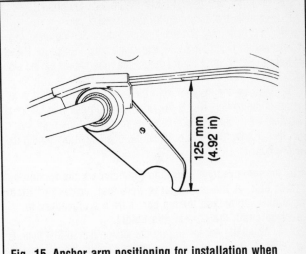

Fig. 15 Anchor arm positioning for installation when matchmarks aren't present

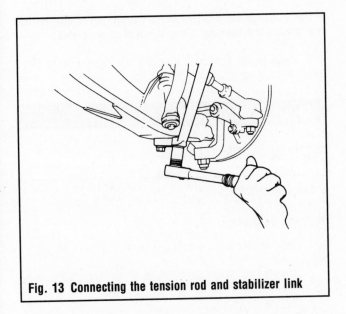

Fig. 13 Connecting the tension rod and stabilizer link

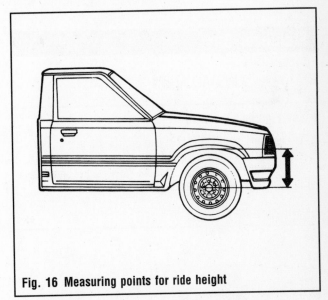

Fig. 16 Measuring points for ride height

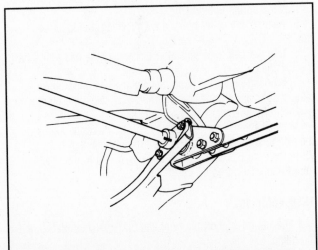

Fig. 14 Connecting the torsion bar to the torque plate— align the matchmarks made prior to disassembly

After removing the cotter pin, loosen the lower ball joint-to-control arm nut—do NOT remove the nut unless the lower control arm is safely supported

24. Install the wheels and lower the truck to the ground.
25. Retorque the lower arm-to-frame bracket nut.
26. Check the front and rear tire pressures. Set the pressures to what are specified on the vehicle rating plate, except for P-metric radials. Set them at the maximum pressure shown on the side wall.

27. Measure the distance from the center of the wheel hub to the lip of the fender. This is the ride height. Proper ride height is obtained when the difference between the left and the right side is less than 10mm (0.394 in.). Adjust the ride height by turning the anchor bolt.

➡**If, for some reason, you didn't matchmark the torsion bar anchor bolt, or the matchmarks were lost, or you're installing a new, unmarked torsion bar, here's a procedure to help you attain the correct ride height:**

a. Install the anchor arm on the torsion bar so that there is 125mm (4.92 in.) between the lowest point on the arm and the crossmember directly above it.

b. Tighten the anchor bolt until the anchor arm contacts the swivel. Then, tighten the bolt an additional 45mm (1.77 in.) travel.

Stabilizer Bar

REMOVAL & INSTALLATION

♦ **See Figures 17 and 18**

1. Raise and support the front end on jackstands.
2. Unbolt the stabilizer bar-to-frame clamps.
3. Unbolt the stabilizer bar from the lower control arms. Keep all the bushings, washers and spacers in order.

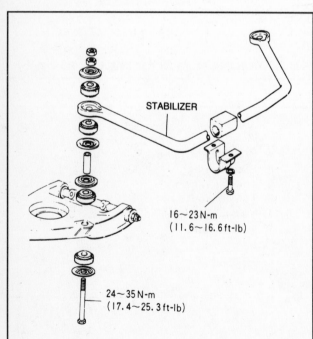

STABILIZER

16~23 N-m
(11.6~16.6 ft-lb)

24~35 N-m
(17.4~25.3 ft-lb)

Fig. 17 Exploded view of the 1972–84 models' stabilizer bar and end link

4. Check all parts for wear or damage and replace anything which looks suspicious.
5. Installation is the reverse of removal. Tighten all fasteners lightly, then torque them to specifications with the wheels on the ground.
   - Stabilizer bar-to-control arm nut:
     1972–84: 25 ft. lbs.
     1986: 34 ft. lbs.
   - Stabilizer-to-frame clamp bolts: 16 ft. lbs.

Tension Rod

REMOVAL & INSTALLATION

1986 Vehicles

1. Unbolt the tension rod from the lower arm and frame and remove it.

➡**Don't change the position of the double nut at the rear of the tension rod bushing, since it would affect caster.**

2. Install the tension rod. Torque the bushing end nut to 90 ft. lbs.; the lower arm end bolts to 85 ft. lbs.

Upper Control Arm

REMOVAL & INSTALLATION

♦ **See Figure 18a**

1972–84 Vehicles

1. Raise and support the front end on jackstands under the frame.
2. Using a floor jack, raise the lower control arm until the upper control arm is off the bumper stop.
3. Remove the wheel.
4. Place a chain through the coil spring as a safety measure, or install a spring compressor.
5. Remove the cotter pin and nut retaining the upper ball joint.
6. Using a ball joint separator, disconnect the ball joint from the spindle.
7. Working under the hood, remove the two upper arm retaining bolts and lift the arm from the truck. Note the number and position of any shims.
8. Installation is the reverse of removal. Place the shims in their original locations. Torque the two arm retaining bolts to 65–75 ft. lbs.; the ball joint-to-arm bolts to 15–20 ft. lbs.; the ball joint-to-spindle nut to 40–55 ft. lbs.

1986 Vehicles

1. Raise and support the front end on jackstands placed under the frame.
2. Remove the wheels. Support the lower arm with a floor jack.

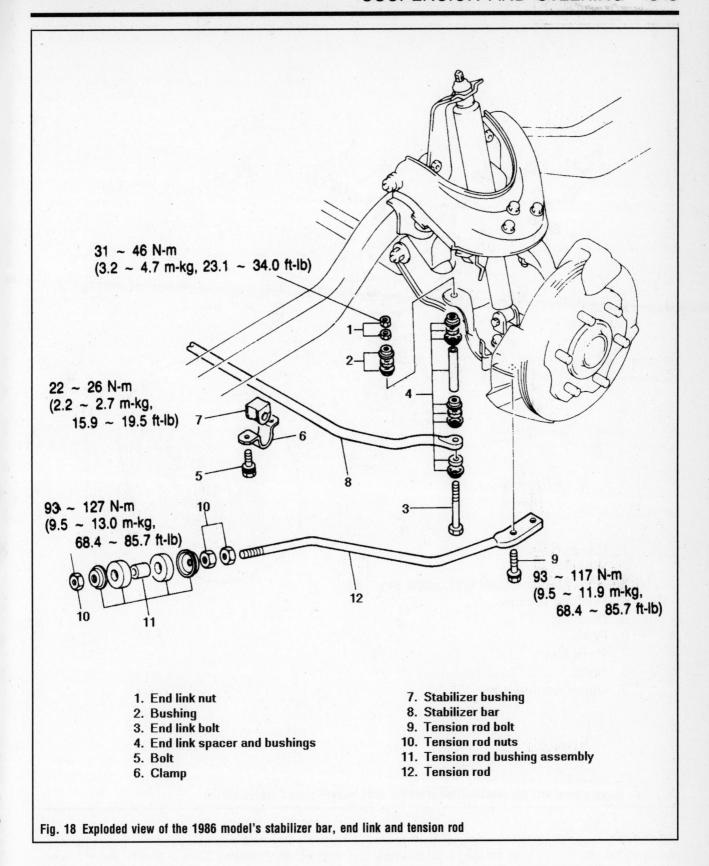

31 ~ 46 N-m
(3.2 ~ 4.7 m-kg, 23.1 ~ 34.0 ft-lb)

22 ~ 26 N-m
(2.2 ~ 2.7 m-kg,
15.9 ~ 19.5 ft-lb)

93 ~ 127 N-m
(9.5 ~ 13.0 m-kg,
68.4 ~ 85.7 ft-lb)

93 ~ 117 N-m
(9.5 ~ 11.9 m-kg,
68.4 ~ 85.7 ft-lb)

1. End link nut
2. Bushing
3. End link bolt
4. End link spacer and bushings
5. Bolt
6. Clamp
7. Stabilizer bushing
8. Stabilizer bar
9. Tension rod bolt
10. Tension rod nuts
11. Tension rod bushing assembly
12. Tension rod

Fig. 18 Exploded view of the 1986 model's stabilizer bar, end link and tension rod

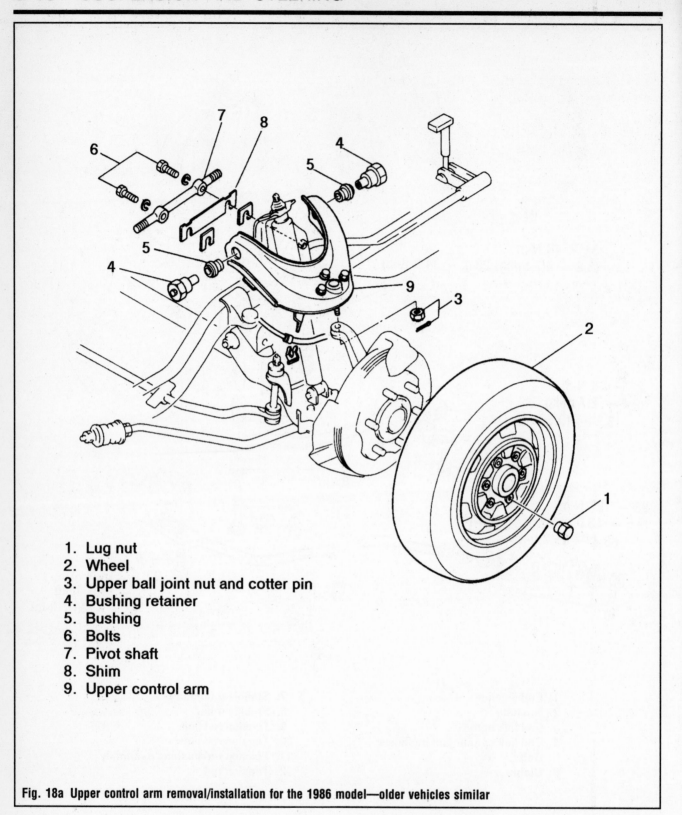

1. Lug nut
2. Wheel
3. Upper ball joint nut and cotter pin
4. Bushing retainer
5. Bushing
6. Bolts
7. Pivot shaft
8. Shim
9. Upper control arm

Fig. 18a Upper control arm removal/installation for the 1986 model—older vehicles similar

3. Remove the cotter pin and nut from the upper ball joint and separate the ball joint from the upper arm using a ball joint separator tool.

4. Remove the bushings and dust seals from the ends of the upper arm shaft.

5. Remove the nuts and bolts that retain the upper arm shaft to the support bracket. Note the number and location of the shims

under the nuts. These must be installed in their exact locations for proper wheel alignment. Check all parts for wear or damage. Replace any suspect parts. Check the ball joint preload with a pull scale and adapter 49 0180 510B. Shake the ball joint stud a few times to make sure that it is free, then take the reading. The pull scale reading should be 40 lb. or less.

6. Installation is the reverse of removal. Torque the upper arm

shaft mounting bolts to 60–68 ft. lbs.; the ball joint nut to 30–37 ft. lbs.

Lower Control Arm

REMOVAL & INSTALLATION

1972–84 Vehicles

1. Raise the front end and support it on jackstands under the frame.
2. Remove the wheels.
3. Remove the lower shock absorber bolts and push the shock up, out of the way.
4. Disconnect the front stabilizer bar from the control arms.
5. Place a floor jack under the lower arm and raise the arm to compress the spring. Install a safety chain or spring compressor.
6. Unbolt the ball joint from the lower arm.
7. Pull the spindle and ball joint away from the arm.
8. Carefully lower the jack. The spring is under pressure, so be very careful that it is secured with the chain or spring compressor.
9. Remove the three lower control arm retaining bolts and lift the arm from the frame.
10. When installing the arm, safety chain the spring to the arm prior to installing the arm, or use a spring compressor. When the arm is in position, loosely install the ball joint bolts and remove the chain or compressor, then, tighten the ball joint nut to 70 ft. lbs.; the three ball joint retaining nuts to 70 ft. lbs. Install all other parts in reverse order of removal.
11. Have the front end alignment checked.

Upper Ball Joint

INSPECTION

1. Inspect the dust seals. If cracked or brittle, replace them.
2. Check end-play of the ball joints. If end-play exceeds 0.10mm (0.0039 in.), it is defective.

REMOVAL & INSTALLATION

1972–84 Vehicles

1. Raise and support the front end on jackstands under the frame.
2. Using a floor jack, raise the lower control arm until the upper control arm is off the bumper stop.
3. Remove the wheel.
4. Place a chain through the coil spring as a safety measure, or install a spring compressor.
5. Remove the cotter pin and nut retaining the upper ball joint.
6. Using a ball joint separator, disconnect the ball joint from the spindle.
7. Working under the hood, remove the two upper arm re-

taining bolts and lift the arm from the truck. Note the number and position of any shims.
8. Unbolt and remove the ball joint from the arm.
9. Installation is the reverse of removal. Place the shims in their original locations. Torque the two arm retaining bolts to 65–75 ft. lbs.; the ball joint-to-arm bolts to 15–20 ft. lbs.; the ball joint-to-spindle nut to 40–55 ft. lbs.

1986 Vehicles

1. Raise and support the front end on jackstands placed under the frame.
2. Remove the wheels. Support the lower arm with a floor jack.
3. Remove the cotter pin and nut from the upper ball joint and separate the ball joint from the knuckle using a ball joint separator tool.
4. Remove the bushings and dust seals from the ends of the upper arm shaft.
5. Remove the nuts and bolts that retain the upper arm shaft to the support bracket. Note the number and location of the shims under the nuts. These must be installed in their exact locations for proper wheel alignment. Check all parts for wear or damage. Replace any suspect parts. Check the ball joint preload with a pull scale and adapter 49 0180 510B. Shake the ball joint stud a few times to make sure that it is free, then take the reading. The pull scale reading should be 40 lb. or less.
6. Unbolt and remove the ball joint from the arm.
7. Installation is the reverse of removal. Torque the upper arm shaft mounting bolts to 60–68 ft. lbs.; the ball joint-to-arm bolts to 15–20 ft. lbs.; the ball joint nut to 30–37 ft. lbs.

Lower Ball Joint

INSPECTION

1. Inspect the dust seals. If cracked or brittle, replace them.
2. Check end-play of the ball joint. If end-play exceeds 0.10mm (0.0039 in.), it is defective.

REMOVAL & INSTALLATION

1972–84 Vehicles

1. Raise the front end and support it on jackstands under the frame.
2. Remove the wheels.
3. Remove the lower shock absorber bolts and push the shock up, out of the way.
4. Disconnect the front stabilizer bar from the control arms.
5. Place a floor jack under the lower arm and raise the arm to compress the spring. Install a safety chain or spring compressor.
6. Remove the ball joint nut.
7. Unbolt the ball joint from the lower arm.
8. Carefully lower the jack. The spring is under pressure, so be very careful that it is secured with the chain or spring compressor.
9. Remove the ball joint nut and separate the ball joint from the arm with a separator.
10. When installing the arm, safety chain the spring to the arm

prior to installing the arm, or use a spring compressor. When the arm is in position, loosely install the ball joint bolts and remove the chain or compressor, then, tighten the ball joint nut to 70 ft. lbs.; the three ball joint retaining nuts to 70 ft. lbs. Install all other parts in reverse order of removal.

11. Have the front end alignment checked.

1986 Vehicles

➡**Special tools are necessary for this procedure.**

1. Raise and support the front end on jackstands under the frame.

2. Remove the wheel.

3. Remove the cotter pin and nut from the lower ball joint.

4. Remove the lower shock absorber bolt.

5. Matchmark the anchor arm bolt and anchor swivel and remove the bolt and swivel.

6. Matchmark the torsion bar and anchor arm and the torsion bar and torque plate.

7. Remove the anchor arm and torsion bar from the torque plate. Separate the anchor arm from the torsion bar.

8. Unbolt and remove the torque plate.

9. Remove the lower arm-to-frame bolt. Separate the lower arm from the frame bracket with bushing puller/installer 49 0727 575.

10. Unbolt the tension rod from the lower arm and frame and remove it.

➡**Don't change the position of the double nut at the rear of the tension rod bushing, since it would affect caster.**

11. Remove the stabilizer bar bolt, bushing, retainer and nut and remove the stabilizer bar.

12. Using a ball joint separator, separate the lower ball joint from the knuckle. Remove the lower control arm.

13. Inspect all parts for wear or damage. Replace any suspect parts. Using a spring scale and adapter 49 0180 510B, check the ball joint preload. Pull scale reading should be 39.6 lb. or less. Measure the preload after first shaking the ball joint stud 3 or 4 times to make sure it is free.

14. Unbolt the ball joint from the lower arm.

To install:

15. Install a new ball joint in the arm. Torque the nuts to 70 ft. lbs.

16. Install the lower arm on the frame bracket and hand-tighten the nut.

17. Install the lower ball joint on the knuckle and torque the nut to 115 ft. lbs. Install the cotter pin.

18. Tighten the lower arm-to-frame nut to 115 ft. lbs.

19. Position the torque plate and tighten the bolt to 68 ft. lbs.

20. Coat the splines on the torsion bar with lithium based wheel bearing grease. Check the ends of the torsion bar. The bars are marked **L** for left and **R** for right. Don't confuse them. Align the matchmarks and install the torsion bar in the torque plate.

21. Coat the splines on the torsion bar with lithium based grease. Align the matchmarks and install the anchor arm on the torsion bar.

22. Install the anchor bolt and swivel and tighten the bolt until the matchmarks are mated.

23. Install the tension rod. Torque the bushing end nut to 90 ft. lbs.; the lower arm end bolts to 85 ft. lbs.

24. Install the stabilizer bar. Torque the bolt to 19 ft. lbs.

25. Install the shock absorber bolt. Torque the bolt to 55–59 ft. lbs.

26. Install the wheels and lower the truck to the ground.

27. Retorque the lower arm-to-frame bracket nut.

28. Check the front and rear tire pressures. Set the pressures to what are specified on the vehicle rating plate, except for P-metric radials. Set them at the maximum pressure shown on the side wall.

29. Measure the distance from the center of the wheel hub to the lip of the fender. This is the ride height. Proper ride height is obtained when the difference between the left and the right side is less than 10mm (0.394 in.). Adjust the ride height by turning the anchor bolt.

➡**If, for some reason, you didn't matchmark the torsion bar anchor bolt, or the matchmarks were lost, or you're installing a new, unmarked torsion bar, here's a procedure to help you attain the correct ride height:**

a. Install the anchor arm on the torsion bar so that there is 125mm (4.92 in.) between the lowest point on the arm and the crossmember directly above it.

b. Tighten the anchor bolt until the anchor arm contacts the swivel. Then, tighten the bolt an additional 45mm (1.77 in.) travel.

Knuckle and Spindle

REMOVAL & INSTALLATION

◆ **See Figures 19 thru 37**

✳✳ CAUTION

The coil spring on 1972–84 models is under great tension! Use a coil spring compressor for safety's sake.

1. Raise and support the front end on jackstands.

2. Remove the wheels.

3. Remove the brake drums or calipers. Suspend the calipers out of the way with a wire. Don't disconnect the brake line.

4. Remove the hub and bearings.

5. Remove the tie rod-to-knuckle nut, and, using a ball joint separator, remove the tie rod end from the knuckle.

6. On models through 1984, remove the shock absorber.

7. On models through 1984, install a spring compressor on the coil spring.

8. Support the lower arm with a floor jack.

9. Remove the cotter pin and nut from the lower ball joint, and, using a ball joint separator, disconnect the lower ball joint from the knuckle.

10. Remove the cotter pin and nut from the upper ball joint, and, using a ball joint separator, disconnect the upper ball joint from the knuckle.

11. Pull the knuckle and spindle assembly from the control arms.

12. The knuckle arm may now be removed.

13. Clean and inspect all parts for wear or damage. Replace parts as necessary.

14. Secure the knuckle in a vise and install the knuckle arm. Torque the bolts to 70–74 ft. lbs.

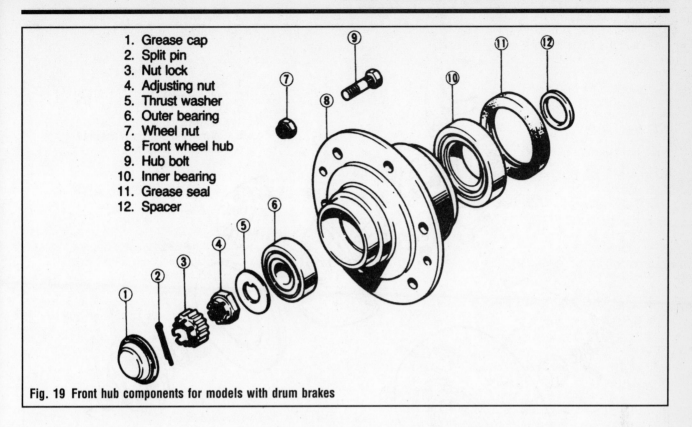

1. Grease cap
2. Split pin
3. Nut lock
4. Adjusting nut
5. Thrust washer
6. Outer bearing
7. Wheel nut
8. Front wheel hub
9. Hub bolt
10. Inner bearing
11. Grease seal
12. Spacer

Fig. 19 Front hub components for models with drum brakes

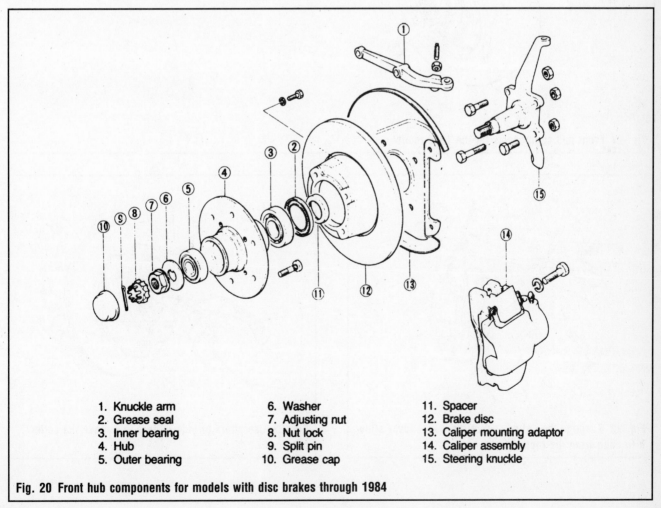

1. Knuckle arm	6. Washer	11. Spacer
2. Grease seal	7. Adjusting nut	12. Brake disc
3. Inner bearing	8. Nut lock	13. Caliper mounting adaptor
4. Hub	9. Split pin	14. Caliper assembly
5. Outer bearing	10. Grease cap	15. Steering knuckle

Fig. 20 Front hub components for models with disc brakes through 1984

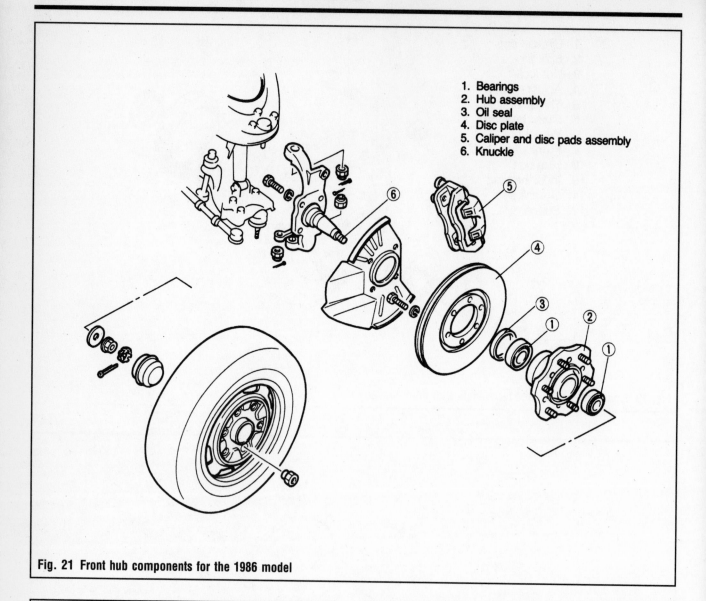

1. Bearings
2. Hub assembly
3. Oil seal
4. Disc plate
5. Caliper and disc pads assembly
6. Knuckle

Fig. 21 Front hub components for the 1986 model

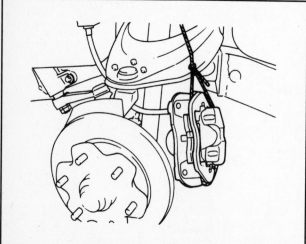

Fig. 22 Suspend the caliper out of the way—never allow it to hang from the rubber brake hose

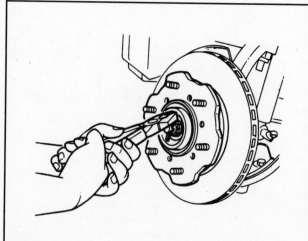

Fig. 23 Use pliers or side-cutters to remove the cotter pin

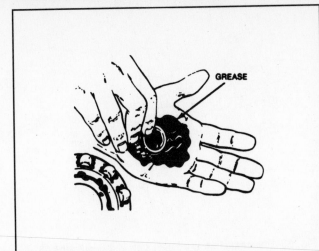

Fig. 24 Pack the wheel bearings thoroughly with clean grease

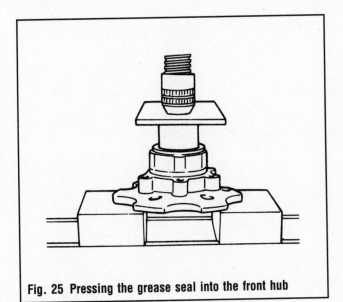

Fig. 25 Pressing the grease seal into the front hub

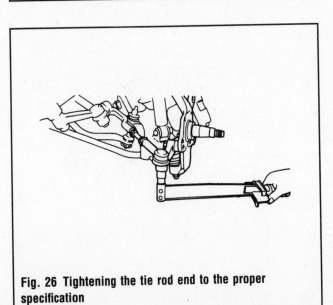

Fig. 26 Tightening the tie rod end to the proper specification

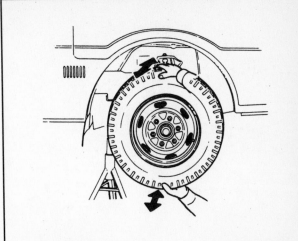

Fig. 27 Rock the tire from the top and bottom to check bearing axial play

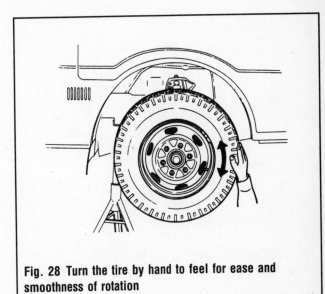

Fig. 28 Turn the tire by hand to feel for ease and smoothness of rotation

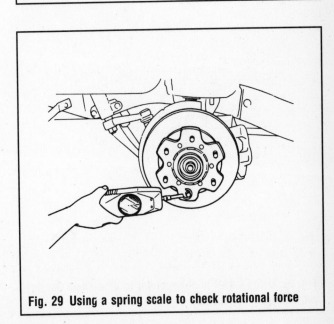

Fig. 29 Using a spring scale to check rotational force

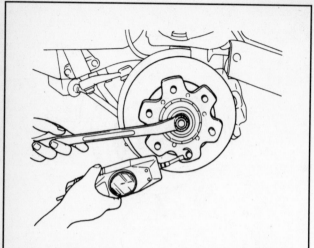

Fig. 30 Adjust rotational force by loosening or tightening the spindle nut

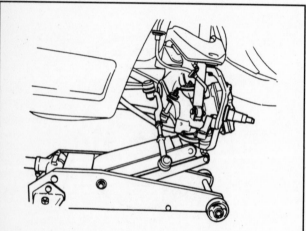

Fig. 31 When disconnecting any suspension components, it's a good idea to support the lower control arm

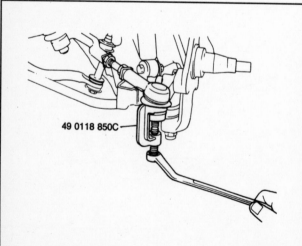

Fig. 32 Using a ball joint separator to disconnect the tie rod end from the knuckle

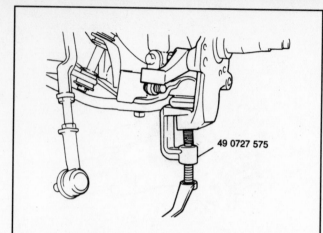

Fig. 33 Disconnecting the lower ball joint—be sure to support the lower control arm, as there is a great deal of spring pressure pushing on it

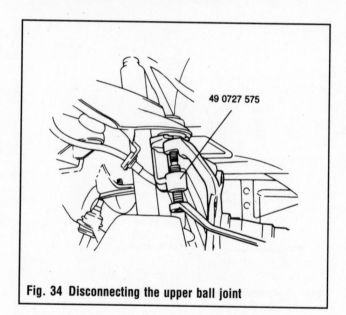

Fig. 34 Disconnecting the upper ball joint

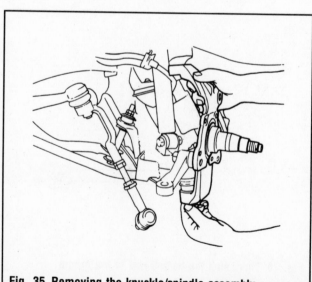

Fig. 35 Removing the knuckle/spindle assembly

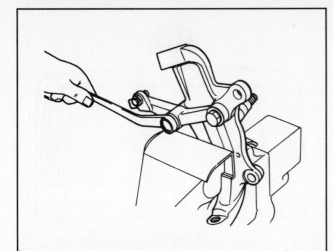

Fig. 36 Carefully clamp the spindle in a vise and unbolt the knuckle arm from the spindle

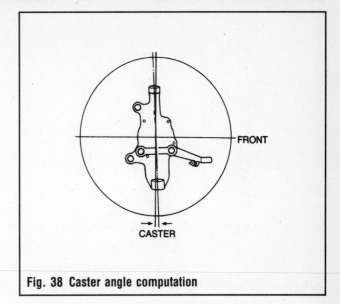

Fig. 38 Caster angle computation

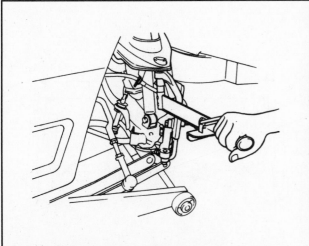

Fig. 37 After installation, tighten the upper and lower ball joint nuts to the proper specification

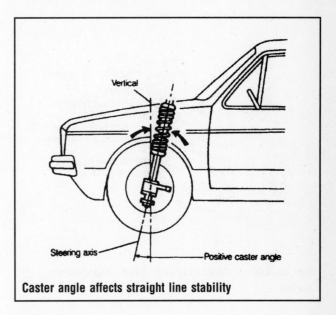

Caster angle affects straight line stability

15. Installation of the knuckle assembly is the reverse of removal. Observe the following torques.
- Upper ball joint-to-knuckle:
  1972–84—50–55 ft. lbs.
  1986—35–38 ft. lbs.
- Lower ball joint-to-knuckle:
  1972–84—70 ft. lbs.
  1986—116 ft. lbs.
- Tie rod end-to-knuckle: 22–29 ft. lbs.

Front End Alignment

CASTER

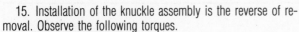 **See Figure 38**

Caster is the forward or rearward tilt of the upper ball joint. Rearward tilt is positive caster; forward tilt is negative caster.

Caster is adjusted by changing the shims between the upper arm shaft and the frame, or, by turning the shaft until the correct angle is obtained.

CAMBER

▶ **See Figures 39 and 40**

Camber is the outward or inward tilting of the wheels at the top. Camber is adjusted by adding or subtracting the shims between the upper arm shaft and the frame. Shims are available in thicknesses of 1.0mm, 1.5mm, 2.0mm, and 3.0mm.

TOE-IN

▶ **See Figures 41 and 42**

Toe-in is the amount, measured in fractions of an inch, that the wheels are closer together in the front than the rear.

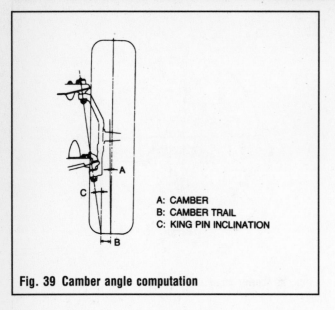

A: CAMBER
B: CAMBER TRAIL
C: KING PIN INCLINATION

Fig. 39 Camber angle computation

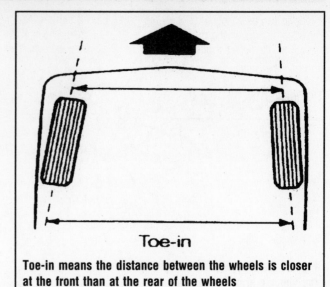

Toe-in

Toe-in means the distance between the wheels is closer at the front than at the rear of the wheels

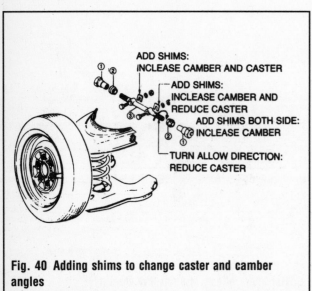

ADD SHIMS:
INCLEASE CAMBER AND CASTER

ADD SHIMS:
INCLEASE CAMBER AND
REDUCE CASTER

ADD SHIMS BOTH SIDE:
INCLEASE CAMBER

TURN ALLOW DIRECTION:
REDUCE CASTER

Fig. 40 Adding shims to change caster and camber angles

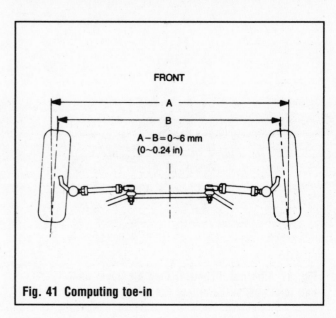

FRONT

A

B

A − B = 0~6 mm
(0~0.24 in)

Fig. 41 Computing toe-in

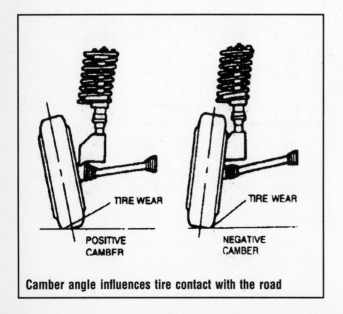

TIRE WEAR

TIRE WEAR

POSITIVE
CAMBER

NEGATIVE
CAMBER

Camber angle influences tire contact with the road

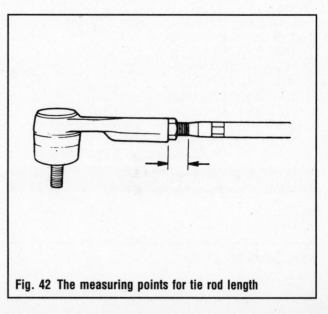

Fig. 42 The measuring points for tie rod length

Toe-in can be changed by changing the length of the tie rods. Threaded sleeves on the rods are provided for this purpose. The clamps on the tie rods must be positioned to prevent interference with the center link on the Rotary Pick-Up.

TURNING ANGLE

▶ **See Figure 43**

Turning stop screws are located at the steering knuckle. If necessary, the screws can be adjusted.

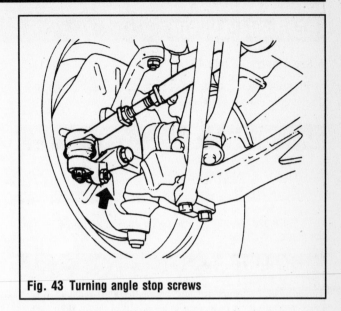

Fig. 43 Turning angle stop screws

Wheel Alignment Specifications

Model/ Years	Caster		Toe-in (in.)	Camber		Kingpin (deg.)
	Range	Pref.		Range	Pref.	
B1600	0.66P to 1.33P	1P	0 to 0.24	1.05P to 2.72P	1.38P	7.62
B1800	0.66P to 1.33P	1P	0 to 0.24	0.42P to 1.25P	0.75P	8.25
B2000 1979–84	0.66P to 1.33P	1P	0 to 0.24	0.42P to 1.25P	0.75P	8.25
B2000 1986	①	②	0 to 0.24	0.33P to 1.25P	0.75P	8.25
B2200 Diesel	0.66P to 1.33P	1P	0 to 0.24	0.42P to 1.25P	0.75P	8.25
Rotary Pick-up 1972–75	0.87P to 1.53P	1.20P	0 to 0.24	0.08N to 0.58P	0.25P	8.75
Rotary Pick-up 1976–77	1.62P to 2.75P	1.95P	0.12 out to 0.12 in	0.08N to 0.58P	0.25P	8.75

① Manual steering: 0.083P to 0.58P
   Power steering: 1.08P to 2.58P
② Manual steering: 0.83P
   Power steering: 1.83P

REAR SUSPENSION

▶ **See Figures 44 and 45**

The suspension is made up of semi-eliptical leaf springs and double action shock absorbers.

Leaf Springs

REMOVAL & INSTALLATION

1. Raise and support the rear of the truck on jackstands under the frame.

✳ CAUTION

The rear leaf springs are under considerable tension. Be very careful when removing and installing them; they can exert enough force to cause serious injuries.

2. Place a floor jack under the rear axle to take up its weight.
3. Disconnect the lower end of the shock absorbers.
4. Remove the spring U-bolts and plate.
5. Remove the spring front bolt.
6. Remove the rear shackle nuts and the shackle.
7. Lift the spring from the truck.
8. Installation is the reverse of removal. Hand-tighten all fasteners until the truck is back on the ground. When the truck is rest-

Underside view of the rear suspension

ing on its wheels, then torque the nuts and bolts. Observe the following torques:
- Spring rear shackle nuts:
  Rotary pick-up: 76 ft. lbs.
  All others: 58 ft. lbs.
- 2-wheel drive U-bolt nuts: 58 ft. lbs.
- Front spring pin nut:

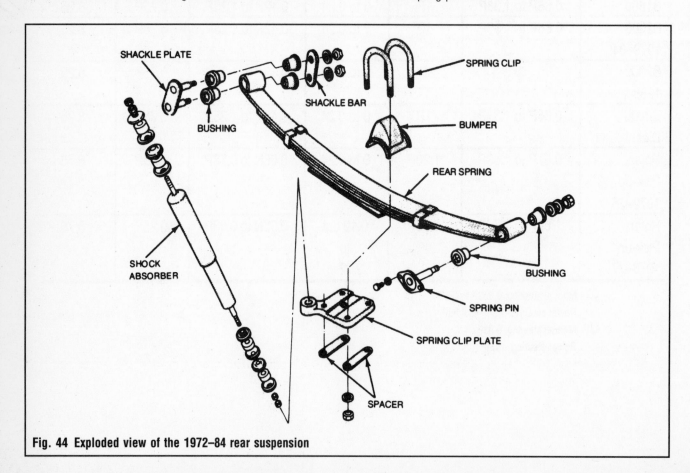

Fig. 44 Exploded view of the 1972–84 rear suspension

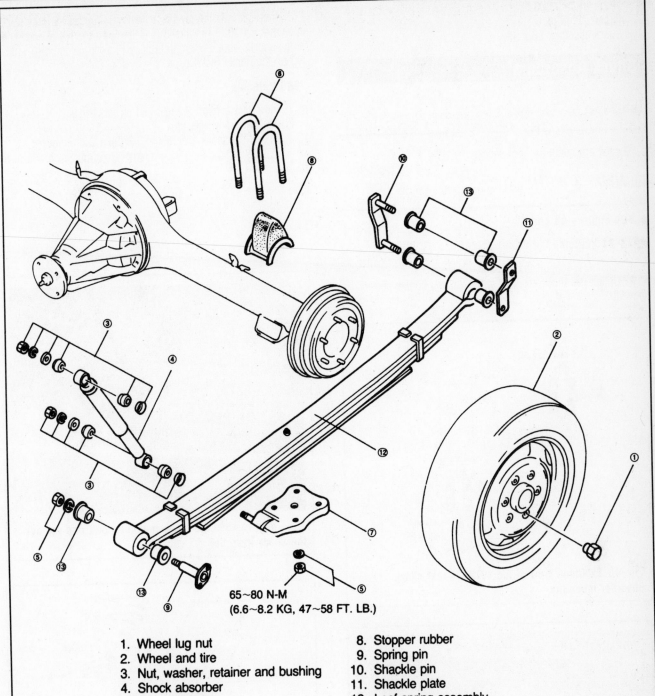

65~80 N-M
(6.6~8.2 KG, 47~58 FT. LB.)

1. Wheel lug nut
2. Wheel and tire
3. Nut, washer, retainer and bushing
4. Shock absorber
5. Nut and washer
6. U-bolts
7. Set plate
8. Stopper rubber
9. Spring pin
10. Shackle pin
11. Shackle plate
12. Leaf spring assembly
13. Bushings

Fig. 45 Exploded view of the 1986 rear suspension

Through 1984: 76 ft. lbs.
1986: 72 ft. lbs.
• Shock absorber: 58 ft. lbs.

Shock Absorbers

TESTING

See the procedure for front shocks.

REMOVAL & INSTALLATION

▶ **See Figures 46 and 47**

1972–84 Vehicles

1. Raise and support the truck on jackstands.
2. Unbolt the shock absorber at the top and bottom and remove it.

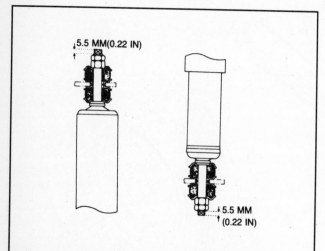

Fig. 46 Exploded view of the 1972–84 rear shock absorber mounting

To remove the rear shock absorber, remove the upper shock absorber mounting bolt . . .

3. Installation is the reverse of removal. Tighten the nuts so that 6mm (0.236 in.) of thread is visible past the nut at each end of the shocks on all except the Rotary Pick-Up, or 3mm (0.118 in.) on the Rotary Pick-Up.

1986 Vehicles

1. Raise and support the rear end on jackstands.
2. Remove the wheels.
3. Unbolt the shock absorber at each end and remove it.
4. Installation is the reverse of removal. Torque each bolt to 58 ft. lbs.

. . . then remove the lower mounting bolt and remove the shock absorber

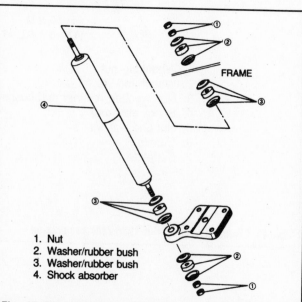

1. Nut
2. Washer/rubber bush
3. Washer/rubber bush
4. Shock absorber

Fig. 47 Rear shock absorber upper nut tightening specification for 1972–84 trucks

STEERING

▶ **See Figures 48, 49 and 50**

The steering system consists of a recirculating ball nut gear unit.

Steering Wheel

REMOVAL & INSTALLATION

1. Disconnect the battery ground.
2. On the B1600, turn the horn button counterclockwise and remove it. On all other models, pull the steering wheel pad straight up to remove it, then remove the horn button and contact.
3. Remove the horn contact spring.
4. Matchmark the steering wheel and shaft.
5. Remove the wheel attaching nut and pull the wheel with a steering wheel puller.

6. Installation is the reverse of removal. Align the marks and tighten the nut to 25 ft. lbs. on 1972–84 models; 35 ft. lbs. on 1986 models.

CHECKING FREE-PLAY

Steering wheel free-play is measured from any point on the outer circumference of the wheel. Free-play in either direction must not exceed 13–26mm (0.512–1.024 in.) on 1972–84 models and 6–19mm (0.236–0.748 in.) on 1986 models. If it does, check for:

a. worn ball joints
b. worn idler arm bushings
c. loose wheel bearings
d. worn or out-of-adjustment steering gear

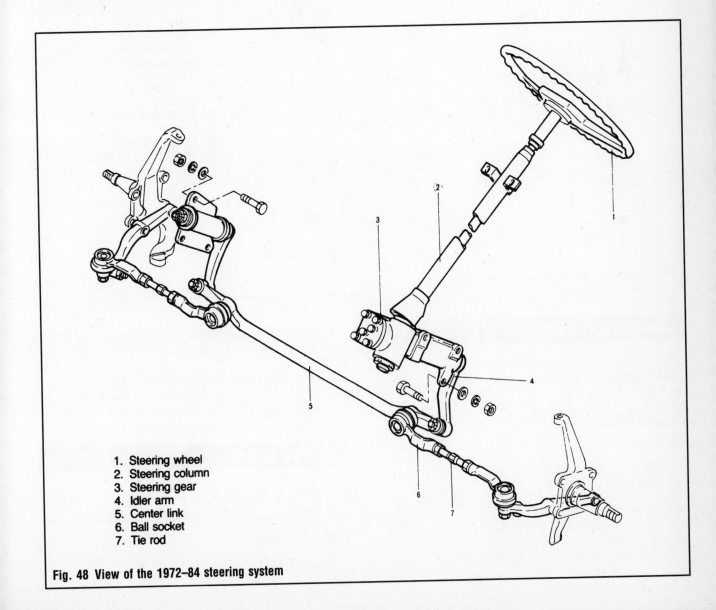

1. Steering wheel
2. Steering column
3. Steering gear
4. Idler arm
5. Center link
6. Ball socket
7. Tie rod

Fig. 48 View of the 1972–84 steering system

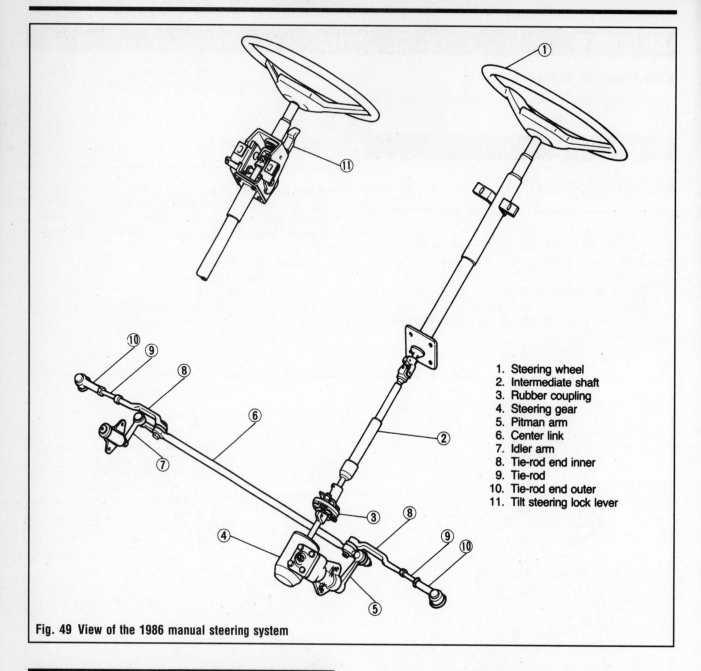

1. Steering wheel
2. Intermediate shaft
3. Rubber coupling
4. Steering gear
5. Pitman arm
6. Center link
7. Idler arm
8. Tie-rod end inner
9. Tie-rod
10. Tie-rod end outer
11. Tilt steering lock lever

Fig. 49 View of the 1986 manual steering system

Combination Switch

The combination turn signal, windshield wiper, and headlight switch is mounted on the steering column, and must be replaced as an assembly.

REMOVAL & INSTALLATION

1. Disconnect the negative battery cable.
2. Remove the steering wheel.
3. Remove the "Lights-Hazard" Indicator and the steering column shroud.
4. Unplug the electrical multiple connectors at the base of the steering column.
5. Pull the headlight knob from its shaft.

6. Remove the snapring, which retains the switch, from the steering shaft. Pull the turn indicator canceling cam from the shaft.
7. Remove the single retaining bolt near the bottom of the switch. Remove the complete switch from the column.
8. Installation is the reverse of removal. Check the operation of the switch before installing the steering wheel.

Ignition Switch

REMOVAL & INSTALLATION

1982–84 Vehicles

1. Disconnect the negative battery terminal.
2. Remove the steering wheel.

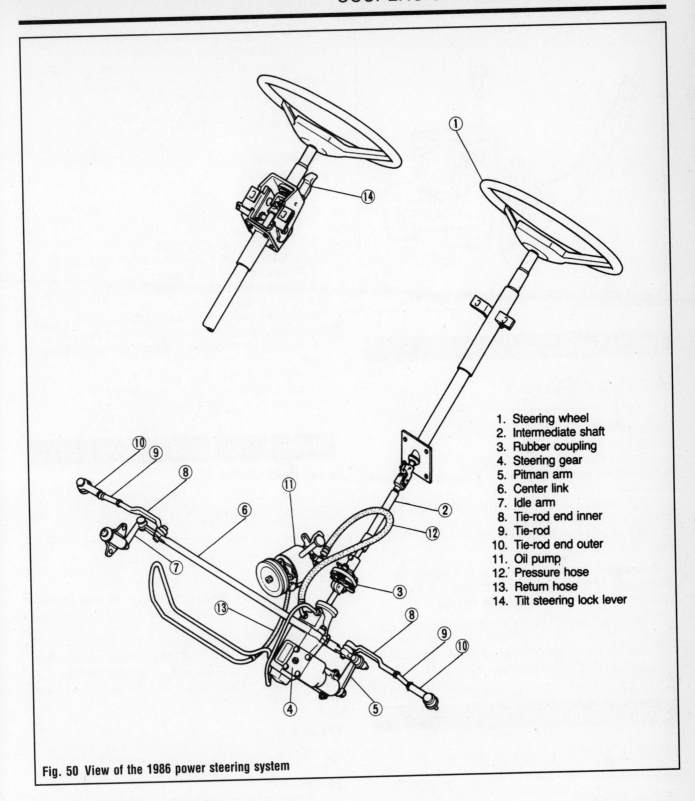

Fig. 50 View of the 1986 power steering system

1. Steering wheel
2. Intermediate shaft
3. Rubber coupling
4. Steering gear
5. Pitman arm
6. Center link
7. Idle arm
8. Tie-rod end inner
9. Tie-rod
10. Tie-rod end outer
11. Oil pump
12. Pressure hose
13. Return hose
14. Tilt steering lock lever

3. Remove the steering column shroud.

4. Disconnect the multiple connectors at the base of the combination switch.

5. Remove the switch retaining snapring. Pull the turn signal indicator canceling cam off the shaft.

6. Remove the switch retaining bolt and remove the complete switch from the column.

7. Installation is the reverse of removal.

1986 Vehicles

▶ **See Figure 51**

1. Disconnect the battery ground cable.
2. Remove the steering column covers.
3. Disconnect the wiring harness connector at the switch.
4. Remove the attaching screw and lift out the switch.
5. Installation is the reverse of removal.

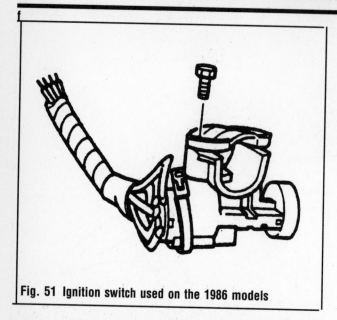

Fig. 51 Ignition switch used on the 1986 models

Ignition Lock

REMOVAL & INSTALLATION

1. Disconnect the negative battery terminal.
2. Remove the steering wheel.
3. Remove the steering column shroud.
4. Disconnect the multiple connectors at the base of the combination switch.
5. Remove the switch retaining snapring. Pull the turn signal indicator canceling cam off the shaft.
6. Remove the switch retaining bolt and remove the complete switch from the column.

➡ **Make a groove on the head of the bolts attaching the steering lock body to the column shaft using a saw. A screwdriver can be used to loosen the screws.**

7. Remove the steering lock attaching bolts. Remove the steering lock.
8. Installation is the reverse of removal. During installation position a new steering lock on the column shaft. Tighten the bolts until the heads break off.

Steering Column

REMOVAL & INSTALLATION

1972–84 Vehicles

1. Disconnect the battery ground.
2. Remove the steering wheel.
3. Remove the column cover.
4. Remove the combination switch.
5. Remove the column bracket-to-instrument panel bolts.
6. Remove the carpet and insulator.
7. Remove the floor panel opening cover bolts and pull the jacket off the steering shaft.

8. Remove the bolt at the steering shaft-to-wormshaft coupling and pull the column up and out of the truck.
9. Installation is the reverse of removal. Observe the following torques:
- Coupling bolt: 20 ft. lbs.
- Column bracket: 19 ft. lbs.
- Steering wheel nut: 29 ft. lbs.

1986 Vehicles

◆ **See Figure 52**

1. Disconnect the battery ground.
2. Remove the steering wheel.
3. Remove the column cover.
4. Remove the combination switch.
5. Remove the column bracket-to-instrument panel bolts.
6. Remove the carpet and insulator.
7. Remove the floor panel opening cover bolts and pull the jacket off the steering shaft.
8. Remove the bolt at the steering shaft-to-intermediate shaft coupling bolt and pull the column up and out of the truck.
9. Installation is the reverse of removal. Observe the following torque:
- Coupling bolt: 18 ft. lbs.
- Column bracket: 16 ft. lbs.
- Steering wheel nut: 36 ft. lbs.

Steering Linkage

◆ **See Figures 53 thru 61**

REMOVAL & INSTALLATION

Idler Arm

1. Raise and support the front end on jackstands.
2. Remove the idler arm-to-center link nut and cotter pin. Disconnect the center link from the idler arm using a ball joint separator.
3. Unbolt and remove the idler arm.
4. Installation is the reverse of removal. Torque the center link nut to 58 ft. lbs. on 1972–84 trucks, or 36 ft. lbs. on 1986 trucks, the frame mounting bolts to 40 ft. lbs. on 1972–84 trucks, or 69 ft. lbs. on 1986 trucks.

Pitman Arm

1. Raise and support the front end on jackstands.
2. Remove the cotter pin and nut attaching the center link to the Pitman arm.
3. Disconnect the center link from the Pitman arm with a ball joint separator.
4. Matchmark the Pitman arm and sector shaft.
5. Remove the Pitman arm-to-sector shaft nut and remove the Pitman arm. It may be necessary to use a puller.
6. Installation is the reverse of removal. Make sure you align the matchmarks. Tighten the Pitman arm-to-sector shaft nut to 130 ft. lbs.; the Pitman arm-to-center link nut to 32 ft. lbs. on 1972–86 trucks. If the cotter pin does not align, tighten the nut to make it line up; never loosen it!

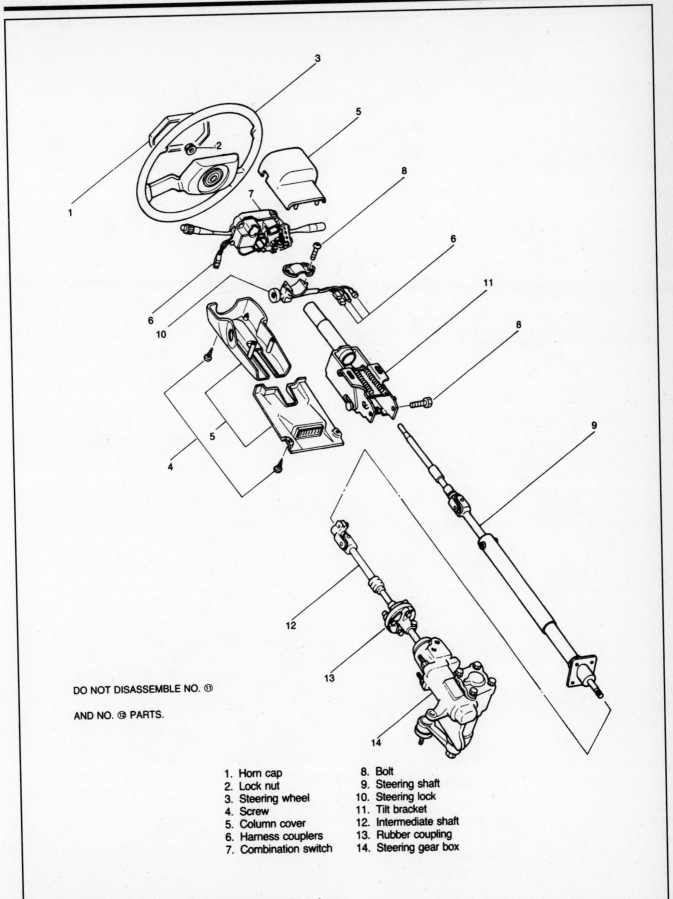

DO NOT DISASSEMBLE NO. ⑪

AND NO. ⑫ PARTS.

1. Horn cap
2. Lock nut
3. Steering wheel
4. Screw
5. Column cover
6. Harness couplers
7. Combination switch
8. Bolt
9. Steering shaft
10. Steering lock
11. Tilt bracket
12. Intermediate shaft
13. Rubber coupling
14. Steering gear box

Fig. 52 Exploded view of the 1986 steering gear and column

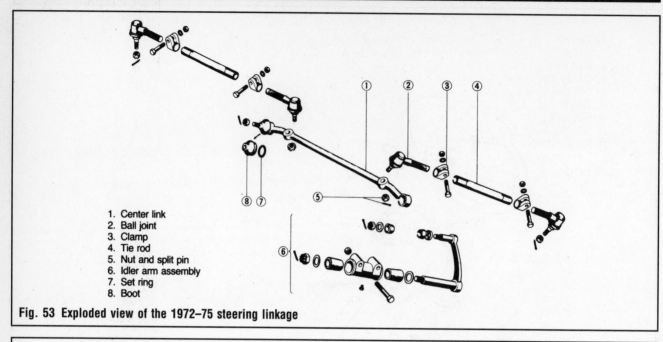

1. Center link
2. Ball joint
3. Clamp
4. Tie rod
5. Nut and split pin
6. Idler arm assembly
7. Set ring
8. Boot

Fig. 53 Exploded view of the 1972–75 steering linkage

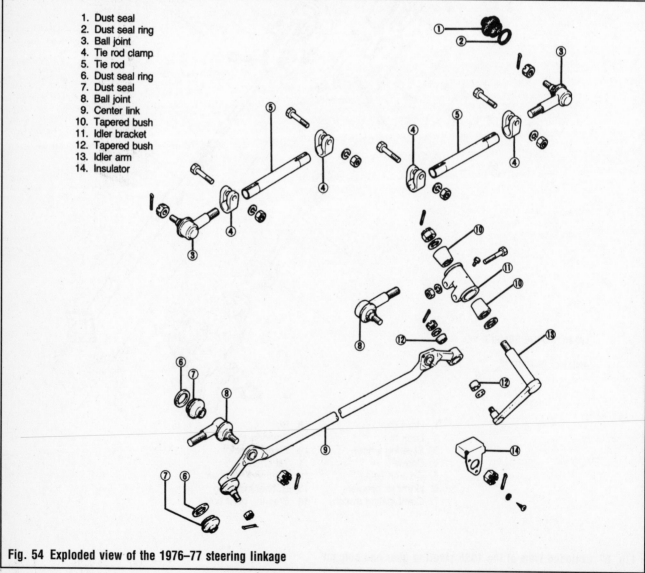

1. Dust seal
2. Dust seal ring
3. Ball joint
4. Tie rod clamp
5. Tie rod
6. Dust seal ring
7. Dust seal
8. Ball joint
9. Center link
10. Tapered bush
11. Idler bracket
12. Tapered bush
13. Idler arm
14. Insulator

Fig. 54 Exploded view of the 1976–77 steering linkage

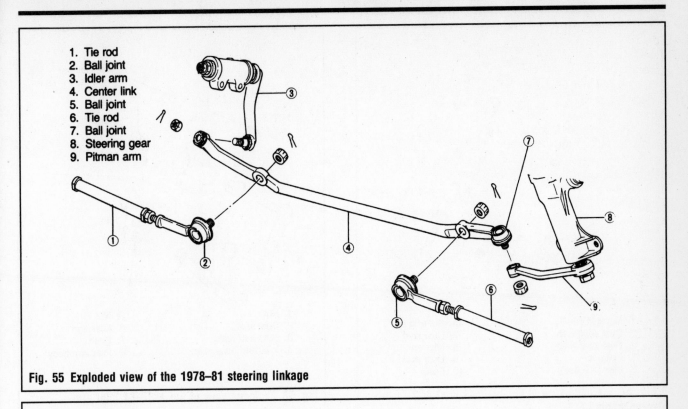

1. Tie rod
2. Ball joint
3. Idler arm
4. Center link
5. Ball joint
6. Tie rod
7. Ball joint
8. Steering gear
9. Pitman arm

Fig. 55 Exploded view of the 1978–81 steering linkage

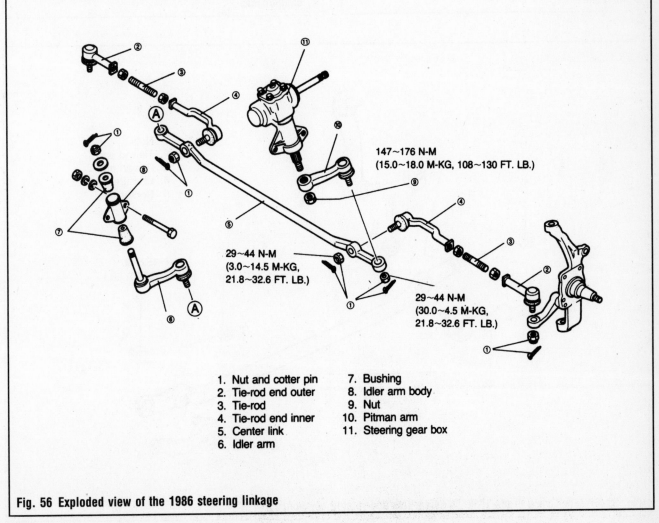

147~176 N-M
(15.0~18.0 M-KG, 108~130 FT. LB.)

29~44 N-M
(3.0~14.5 M-KG, 21.8~32.6 FT. LB.)

29~44 N-M
(30.0~4.5 M-KG, 21.8~32.6 FT. LB.)

1. Nut and cotter pin
2. Tie-rod end outer
3. Tie-rod
4. Tie-rod end inner
5. Center link
6. Idler arm
7. Bushing
8. Idler arm body
9. Nut
10. Pitman arm
11. Steering gear box

Fig. 56 Exploded view of the 1986 steering linkage

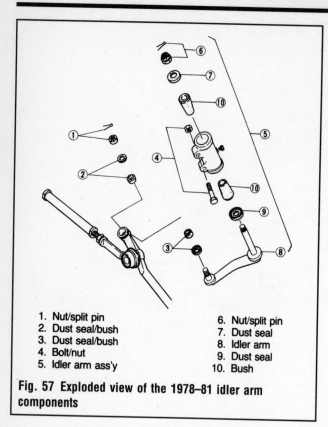

1. Nut/split pin
2. Dust seal/bush
3. Dust seal/bush
4. Bolt/nut
5. Idler arm ass'y
6. Nut/split pin
7. Dust seal
8. Idler arm
9. Dust seal
10. Bush

Fig. 57 Exploded view of the 1978–81 idler arm components

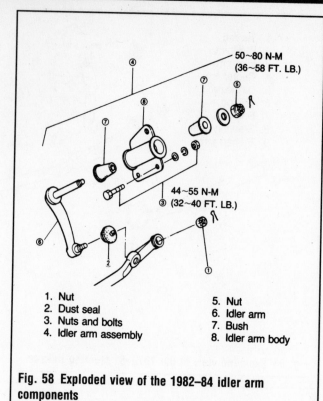

50~80 N-M
(36~58 FT. LB.)

44~55 N-M
(32~40 FT. LB.)

1. Nut
2. Dust seal
3. Nuts and bolts
4. Idler arm assembly
5. Nut
6. Idler arm
7. Bush
8. Idler arm body

Fig. 58 Exploded view of the 1982–84 idler arm components

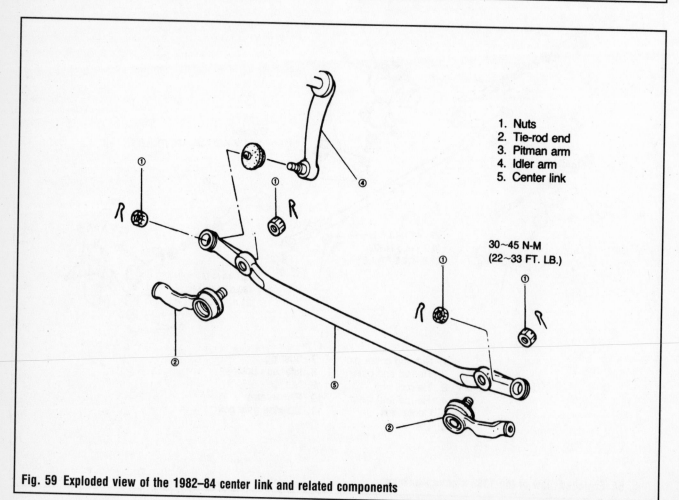

1. Nuts
2. Tie-rod end
3. Pitman arm
4. Idler arm
5. Center link

30~45 N-M
(22~33 FT. LB.)

Fig. 59 Exploded view of the 1982–84 center link and related components

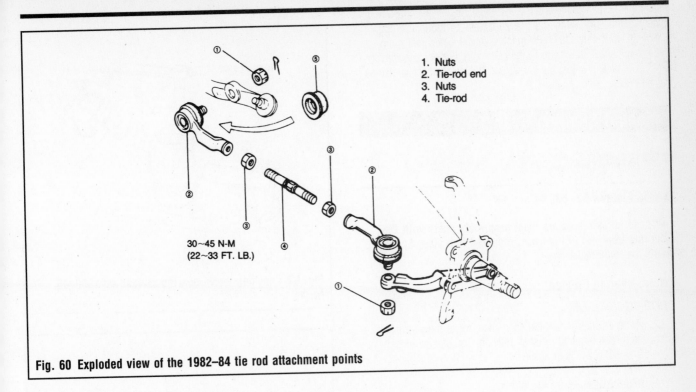

1. Nuts
2. Tie-rod end
3. Nuts
4. Tie-rod

30~45 N-M
(22~33 FT. LB.)

Fig. 60 Exploded view of the 1982–84 tie rod attachment points

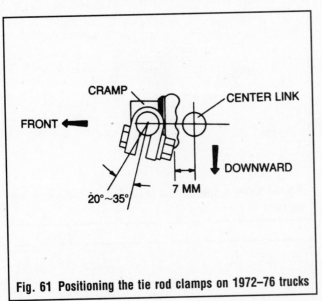

Fig. 61 Positioning the tie rod clamps on 1972–76 trucks

Center Link

1. Raise and support the front end on jackstands.
2. Disconnect the center link at the tie rods, Pitman arm and idler arm.
3. Installation is the reverse of removal. Tighten all of the nuts to:
   - 1972–75
     Pitman arm nut: 28 ft. lbs.
     Idler arm nut: 47 ft. lbs.
     Tie rod nut: 25 ft. lbs.
   - 1976–84
     Idler arm nut: 58 ft. lbs.
     All others: 29 ft. lbs.
   - 1986 all nuts: 32 ft. lbs.

Tie Rod Ends

1. Loosen the tie rod clamp nuts (jam nuts, 1977 and later).
2. Remove and discard the cotter pin from the ball socket end, and remove the nut.
3. Use a ball joint puller to loosen the ball socket stud from the center link. Remove the stud from the kingpin steering arm in the same way.
4. Unscrew the tie rod end from the threaded sleeve, counting the number of threads until it's off. The threads may be left or right-hand threads. Tighten the jam nuts to 58 ft. lbs.
5. To install, lightly coat the threads with grease, and turn the new end in as many turns as were required to remove it. This will give the approximate correct toe-in.
6. Install the ball socket studs into center link and kingpin

It's a good idea to matchmark all adjusting points on the tie rods before removal of any one component—this will help to maintain the same alignment settings

steering arm. Tighten the nuts to 25 ft. lbs. for models through 1976; 32 ft. lbs. for 1977–86 models. Install a new cotter pin. You may tighten the nut to fit the cotter pin, but don't loosen it.

7. Check and adjust the toe-in, and tighten the tie rod clamps or jam nuts.

Manual Steering Gear

ADJUSTMENTS

♦ See Figures 62, 63, 64 and 65

➡These adjustments are most accurately made with the steering gear out of the truck, mounted in a vise. Special tools are required.

Worm Bearing Preload

1972–81 VEHICLES

1. Using an inch pound torque wrench, rotate the wormshaft. Note the torque required for shaft rotation. Torque should be:
• 1979–81: 5.2–7.8 in. lbs.
• 1978: 7.9–10.4 in. lbs.
• 1976–77: 0.9–3.5 in. lbs.
• 1972–75: 7.9–10.4 in. lbs.
2. If not, remove the end cover and correct it by adding or removing shims under the cover. Shims are available in sizes of 0.050mm, 0.060mm, 0.070mm, 0.075mm, 0.080mm, 0.100mm and 0.200mm.

1982–86 VEHICLES

1. Install a spring scale and adapter 49 0180 510B to the wormshaft. Rotating torque should be ½–1 lb.
2. If not, loosen the wormshaft locknut and, using spanner 49 UB39 585, turn the adjuster until preload is within specifications.
3. Using wrench 49 1391 580, or equivalent, tighten the locknut to 140 ft. lbs.

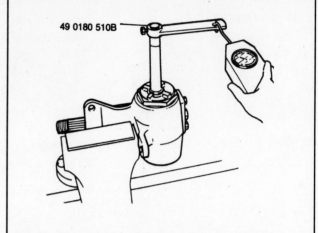

Fig. 63 Checking worm bearing preload on 1982–86 trucks

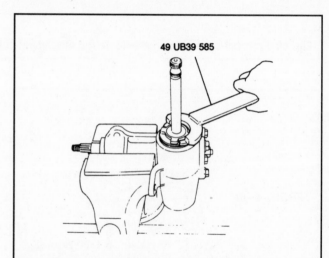

Fig. 64 Using a special tool to tighten the locknut on the adjuster

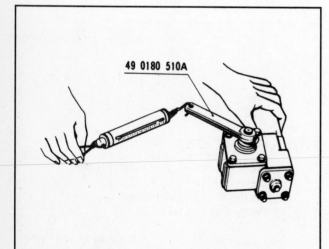

Fig. 62 Checking worm bearing preload on 1972–81 trucks

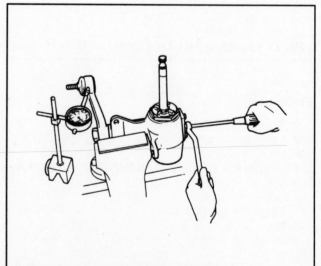

Fig. 65 Checking and adjusting backlash

Sector Shaft Clearance

1982–86 VEHICLES

1. Set the adjusting screw and shim in the T-groove on the top of the sector shaft, and measure the axial clearance. Proper clearance should be 0–0.1mm (0–0.0039 in.).

2. If the clearance is excessive, adjust it with different shims. Shims are available in 0.05mm increments from 1.95–2.10mm for 1982–86 trucks.

Backlash

1. Mount a dial indicator next to the vise, with the pointer on the end of the Pitman arm. With the gear in what would be the straight ahead position, backlash should be 0.

2. If not, adjust it using the adjusting screw on top of the gear. Hold the screw with a screwdriver and loosen the locknut. Turn the screw until backlash is correct. Make sure that the Pitman arm is in the position it would be with the wheels straight ahead.

3. When backlash is correct, hold the screw and tighten the locknut.

REMOVAL & INSTALLATION

1972–75 B1600

1. Remove the steering wheel as outlined above.
2. Remove the light switch knob.
3. Remove the steering column covers.
4. Remove the stop ring, cancelling cam and spring from the end of the column.
5. Disconnect the combination switch wiring.
6. Remove the combination switch from the column.
7. Remove the steering column support bracket.
8. Loosen the nut securing the bottom of the steering column jacket and pull the jacket off of the shaft.
9. Remove the dust cover from the firewall at the bottom of the shaft.
10. Raise and support the front end on jackstands.
11. Remove the left front wheel.
12. Using a floor jack, raise the lower control arm until the upper control arm is off the bumper stop.
13. Place a chain through the coil spring as a safety measure, or install a spring compressor.
14. Remove the cotter pin and nut retaining the upper ball joint.
15. Using a ball joint separator, disconnect the ball joint from the spindle.
16. Working under the hood, remove the two upper arm retaining bolts and lift the arm from the truck. Note the number and position of any shims.
17. Disconnect the center link from the Pitman arm.
18. Unbolt the steering gear from the frame. Lift the gear off of the frame, noting the position of the shim for installation.
19. Installation is the reverse of removal. Mount the steering gear, placing the shim in its original position. Place the upper control arm shaft shims in their original locations. Observe the following torques:
   - Steering gear-to-frame: 40 ft. lbs.
   - Upper control arm shaft bolts: 65–75 ft. lbs.
   - Ball joint-to-knuckle: 40–55 ft. lbs.
   - Center link-to-Pitman arm: 30 ft. lbs.
   - Pitman arm-to-sector shaft: 130 ft. lbs.
   - Steering wheel nut: 22–29 ft. lbs.

1976–77 B1600

1. Raise and support the front end on jackstands. Remove the left front wheel.
2. Loosen the bolt securing the wormshaft to the steering shaft joint.
3. Remove the cotter pin and nut securing the Pitman arm to the center link and separate the Pitman arm from the link with a ball joint tool.
4. Remove the speedometer cable from the clips securing it to the steering gear housing and power brake booster.
4. Unbolt the steering gear from the frame.
5. If the Pitman arm is to be removed from the sector shaft, first matchmark their positions, relative to each other.
6. Installation is the reverse of removal. Observe the following torques:
   - Steering gear-to-frame: 40 ft. lbs.
   - Wormshaft-to-steering shaft yoke: 28 ft. lbs.
   - Pitman arm-to-sector shaft: 139 ft. lbs.
   - Pitman arm-to-center link: 30 ft. lbs.

Rotary Pick-Up

1. Raise and support the front end on jackstands. Remove the left front wheel.
2. Loosen the bolt securing the wormshaft to the steering shaft joint.
3. Remove the cotter pin and nut securing the Pitman arm to the center link and separate the Pitman arm from the link with a ball joint tool.
4. Unbolt and remove the insulator from the Pitman arm.
5. Unbolt the steering gear from the frame.
6. If the Pitman arm is to be removed from the sector shaft, first matchmark their positions, relative to each other.
7. Installation is the reverse of removal. Observe the following torques:
   - Steering gear-to-frame: 40 ft. lbs.
   - Wormshaft-to-steering shaft yoke: 28 ft. lbs.
   - Pitman arm-to-sector shaft: 139 ft. lbs.
   - Pitman arm-to-center link: 30 ft. lbs.

B1800 and 1979–81 B2000

1. Remove the steering wheel as outlined above.
2. Remove the light switch knob.
3. Remove the steering column covers.
4. Remove the stop ring, cancelling cam and spring from the end of the column.
5. Disconnect the combination switch wiring.

6. Remove the combination switch from the column.

7. Remove the steering column support bracket.

8. Loosen the nut securing the bottom of the steering column jacket and pull the jacket off of the shaft.

9. Remove the dust cover from the firewall at the bottom of the shaft.

10. Raise and support the front end on jackstands.

11. Remove the left front wheel. Remove the air cleaner.

12. Disconnect the fluid pipe at the clutch master cylinder, and cap the openings.

13. Disconnect the fluid pipes at the brake master cylinder, and cap the openings.

14. Remove the brake master cylinder.

15. Disconnect the pushrod at the pedal.

16. Unbolt and remove the power booster from the firewall.

17. Drain the cooling system.

❊❊ CAUTION

When draining the coolant, keep in mind that cats and dogs are attracted by the ethelyne glycol antifreeze, and are quite likely to drink any that is left in an uncovered container or in puddles on the ground. This will prove fatal in sufficient quantity. Always drain the coolant into a sealable container. Coolant should be reused unless it is contaminated or several years old.

18. Disconnect the EGR pipe.

19. Remove the accelerator linkage.

20. Disconnect the choke cable and fuel line. Plug the fuel line.

21. Disconnect the PCV valve hose.

22. Disconnect the heater return hose and by-pass hose.

23. Remove the intake manifold-to-cylinder head attaching nuts.

24. Remove the manifold and carburetor as an assembly.

25. Clean the gasket mating surfaces.

26. Using a floor jack, raise the lower control arm until the upper control arm is off the bumper stop.

27. Place a chain through the coil spring as a safety measure, or install a spring compressor.

28. Remove the cotter pin and nut retaining the upper ball joint.

29. Using a ball joint separator, disconnect the ball joint from the spindle.

30. Working under the hood, remove the two upper arm retaining bolts and lift the arm from the truck. Note the number and position of any shims.

31. Disconnect the center link from the Pitman arm.

32. Unbolt the steering gear from the frame. Lift the gear off of the frame, noting the position of the shim for installation.

33. Installation of the steering gear and control arm is the reverse of removal. Mount the steering gear, placing the shim in its original position. Place the upper control arm shaft shims in their original locations. When installing the brake booster, check the clearance between the master cylinder piston and the power booster pushrod. Clearance should be 0.10–0.50mm (0.0039–0.0197 in.). If not, adjust it at the pushrod. Observe the following torques:

- Steering gear-to-frame: 40 ft. lbs.
- Wormshaft-to-steering shaft yoke: 20 ft. lbs.
- Upper control arm shaft bolts: 65–75 ft. lbs.
- Ball joint-to-knuckle: 40–55 ft. lbs.
- Center link-to-Pitman arm: 30 ft. lbs.
- Pitman arm-to-sector shaft: 130 ft. lbs.
- Steering wheel nut: 22–29 ft. lbs.
- Power brake booster-to-firewall: 17 ft. lbs.
- Master Cylinder-to-booster: 15 ft. lbs.

34. Install a new gasket and the manifold on the studs. Torque the attaching nuts to specification, working from the center outward.

35. Connect the PCV valve hose to the manifold.

36. Connect the by-pass and heater return hoses.

37. Install the accelerator linkage.

38. Connect the fuel line and choke cable.

39. Replace the air cleaner.

40. Fill the cooling system. Bleed the brakes and clutch. Run the engine and check for leaks.

1982–84 B2000 and B2200

1. Remove the steering wheel as outlined above.

2. Remove the steering column covers.

3. Remove the stop ring, cancelling cam and spring from the end of the column.

4. Disconnect the combination switch wiring.

5. Remove the combination switch from the column.

6. Remove the steering column support bracket.

7. Loosen the nut securing the bottom of the steering column jacket and pull the jacket off of the shaft.

8. Remove the dust cover from the firewall at the bottom of the shaft.

9. Remove the bolt securing the yoke joint to the wormshaft and remove the steering shaft.

10. Remove the air cleaner.

11. On trucks with column shift, unbolt the lower bracket from the gear select rod and the shift rod.

12. Remove the lower bracket from the steering gear.

13. Remove the brake lines from the master cylinder and cap the lines.

14. Unbolt and remove the master cylinder from the firewall or power booster. These trucks have a remotely mounted reservoir, so the lines will have to be unclipped and plugged.

15. Remove the cotter pin and nut and disconnect the center link from the Pitman arm using a ball joint tool.

16. Remove the cotter pin and nut, matchmark the Pitman arm and sector shaft and disconnect the Pitman arm from the sector shaft using a ball joint tool.

17. Unbolt the steering gear from the frame, noting the position of any shim that might be installed.

18. Installation is the reverse of removal. Mount the steering gear, placing the shim in its original position. Observe the following torques:

- Steering gear-to-frame: 40 ft. lbs.
- Center link-to-Pitman arm: 30 ft. lbs.
- Pitman arm-to-sector shaft: 130 ft. lbs.
- Steering wheel nut: 22–29 ft. lbs.
- Master Cylinder-to-booster: 15 ft. lbs.
- Wormshaft-to-steering shaft yoke: 20 ft. lbs.

1986 B2000

1. Raise and support the front end on jackstands.
2. Remove the pinch bolt securing the wormshaft to the steering shaft coupling.
3. Remove the cotter pin and nut securing the Pitman arm to the center link and separate the Pitman arm from the link with a ball joint tool.
4. Unbolt the steering gear from the frame.
5. If the Pitman arm is to be removed from the sector shaft, first matchmark their positions, relative to each other.
6. Installation is the reverse of removal. Observe the following torques:
- Steering gear-to-frame: 40 ft. lbs.
- Wormshaft-to-steering shaft yoke: 28 ft. lbs.
- Pitman arm-to-sector shaft: 139 ft. lbs.
- Pitman arm-to-center link: 30 ft. lbs.

Power Steering Gear

ADJUSTMENT

Wormshaft Preload

▶ **See Figures 66 and 67**

1. With the steering gear mounted in a vise, and the Pitman are positioned in a "wheels straight ahead" position, attach a spring scale and adapter 49 0180 510B to the wormshaft.
2. Check the rotating torque of the wormshaft. Rotating torque should be 2.2 lbs. or less and at least ½ to 1 lb. higher than what the rotating torque is at a point 360° from straight ahead.
3. If preload is not correct, hold the adjusting screw on top of the gear with a screwdriver and loosen the locknut. Turn the adjusting screw to obtain the correct preload.
4. When preload is correct, hold the adjusting screw and tighten the locknut to 35 ft. lbs. Make sure that the adjusting screw does not move while the locknut is being tightened.

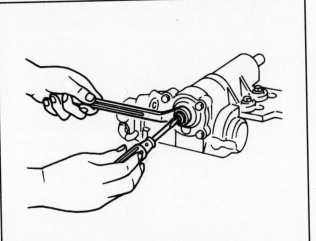

Fig. 66 Power steering gear preload adjustment

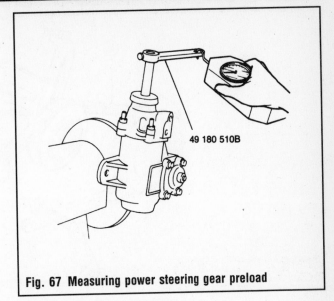

49 180 510B

Fig. 67 Measuring power steering gear preload

REMOVAL & INSTALLATION

1. Raise and support the front end on jackstands.
2. Disconnect the pressure and return lines at the gear box. Have a drain pan underneath to catch the fluid.
3. Remove the pinch bolt securing the wormshaft to the steering shaft coupling.
4. Remove the cotter pin and nut securing the Pitman arm to the center link and separate the Pitman arm from the link with a ball joint tool.
5. Unbolt the steering gear from the frame.
6. If the Pitman arm is to be removed from the sector shaft, first matchmark their positions, relative to each other.
7. Installation is the reverse of removal. Observe the following torques:
- Pressure line: 26 ft. lbs.
- Return line: 35 ft. lbs.
- Steering gear-to-frame: 40 ft. lbs.
- Wormshaft-to-steering shaft yoke: 28 ft. lbs.
- Pitman arm-to-sector shaft: 139 ft. lbs.
- Pitman arm-to-center link: 30 ft. lbs.

Power Steering Pump

REMOVAL & INSTALLATION

▶ **See Figure 68**

1. Raise and support the front end on jackstands.
2. Remove the power steering pump pulley nut.
3. Loosen the drive belt tensioner pulley and remove the belt.
4. Remove the pulley from the pump.
5. Position a drain pan under the pump and disconnect the hoses.
6. Remove the bracket-to-pump bolts and remove the pump from the truck.
7. Installation is the reverse of removal. Adjust the belt to give ½" deflection along its longest straight run. Bleed the system.

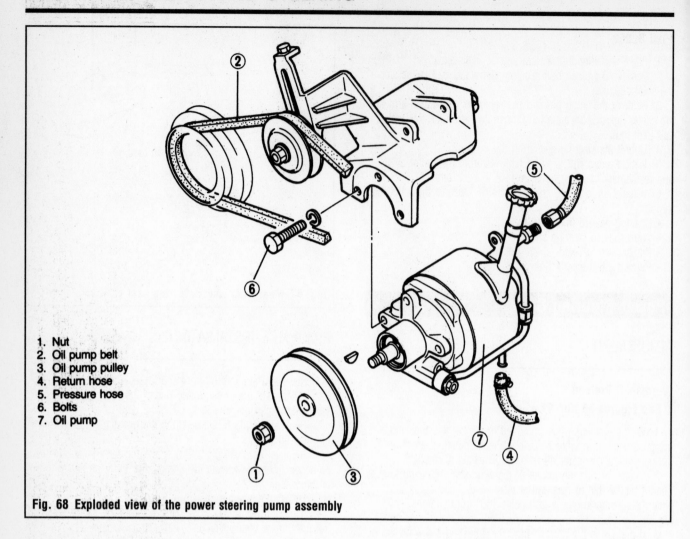

1. Nut
2. Oil pump belt
3. Oil pump pulley
4. Return hose
5. Pressure hose
6. Bolts
7. Oil pump

Fig. 68 Exploded view of the power steering pump assembly

BLEEDING THE SYSTEM

1. Raise and support the front end on jackstands.
2. Check the fluid level and fill it, if necessary.
3. Start the engine and let it idle. Turn the steering wheel lock-to-lock, several times. Recheck the fluid level.
4. Lower the truck to the ground.

5. With the engine idling, turn the wheel lock-to-lock several times again. If noise is heard in the fluid lines, air is present.
6. Put the wheels in the straight ahead position and shut off the engine.
7. Check the fluid level. If it is higher than when you last checked it, air is in the system. Repeat Step 5. Keep repeating Step 5 until no air is present.

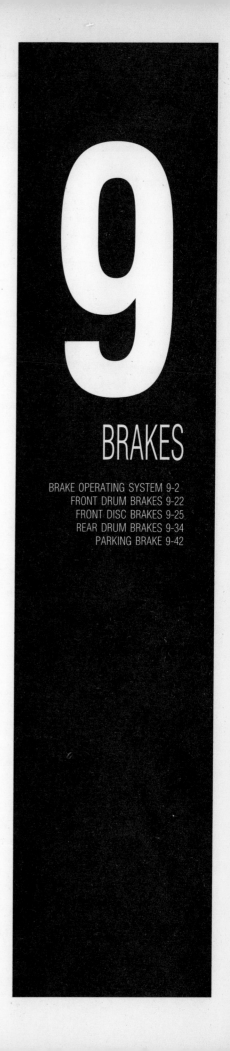

9
BRAKES

BRAKE OPERATING SYSTEM

Basic Operating Principles

◆ **See Figures 1 thru 6**

Hydraulic systems are used to actuate the brakes of all modern automobiles. The system transports the power required to force the frictional surfaces of the braking system together from the pedal to the individual brake units at each wheel. A hydraulic system is used for two reasons.

First, fluid under pressure can be carried to all parts of an automobile by small pipes and flexible hoses without taking up a significant amount of room or posing routing problems.

Second, a great mechanical advantage can be given to the brake pedal end of the system, and the foot pressure required to actuate the brakes can be reduced by making the surface area of

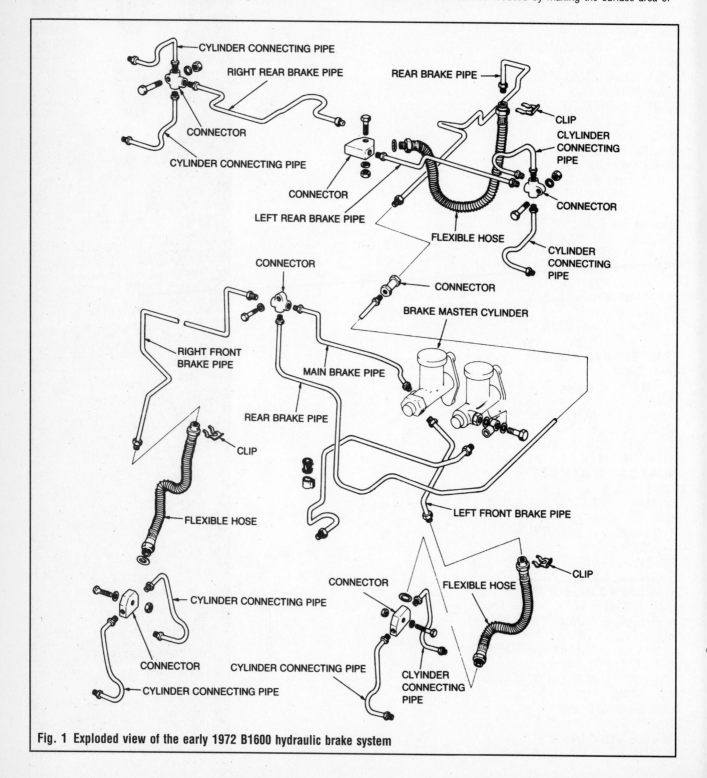

Fig. 1 Exploded view of the early 1972 B1600 hydraulic brake system

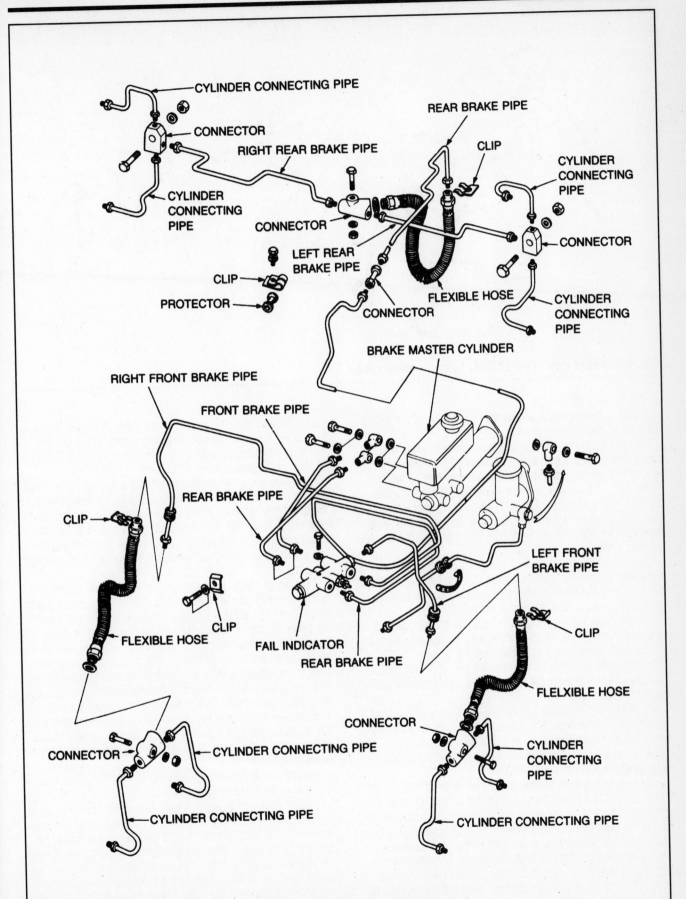

Fig. 2 Exploded view of the late 1972 through 1975 B1600 hydraulic brake system

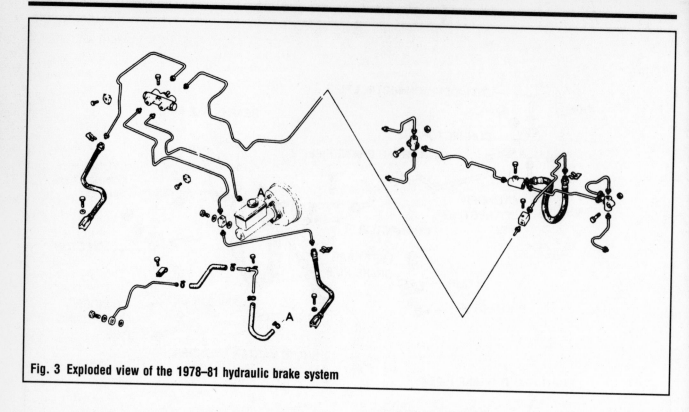

Fig. 3 Exploded view of the 1978–81 hydraulic brake system

the master cylinder pistons smaller than that of any of the pistons in the wheel cylinders or calipers.

The master cylinder consists of a fluid reservoir along with a double cylinder and piston assembly. Double type master cylinders are designed to separate the front and rear braking systems hydraulically in case of a leak. The master cylinder coverts mechanical motion from the pedal into hydraulic pressure within the lines. This pressure is translated back into mechanical motion at the wheels by either the wheel cylinder (drum brakes) or the caliper (disc brakes).

Steel lines carry the brake fluid to a point on the vehicle's frame near each of the vehicle's wheels. The fluid is then carried to the calipers and wheel cylinders by flexible tubes in order to allow for suspension and steering movements.

In drum brake systems, each wheel cylinder contains two pistons, one at either end, which push outward in opposite directions and force the brake shoe into contact with the drum.

In disc brake systems, the cylinders are part of the calipers. At least one cylinder in each caliper is used to force the brake pads against the disc.

All pistons employ some type of seal, usually made of rubber, to minimize fluid leakage. A rubber dust boot seals the outer end of the cylinder against dust and dirt. The boot fits around the outer end of the piston on disc brake calipers, and around the brake actuating rod on wheel cylinders.

The hydraulic system operates as follows: When at rest, the entire system, from the piston(s) in the master cylinder to those in the wheel cylinders or calipers, is full of brake fluid. Upon application of the brake pedal, fluid trapped in front of the master cylinder piston(s) is forced through the lines to the wheel cylinders. Here, it forces the pistons outward, in the case of drum brakes, and inward toward the disc, in the case of disc brakes. The motion of the pistons is opposed by return springs mounted outside the cylinders in drum brakes, and by spring seals, in disc brakes.

Upon release of the brake pedal, a spring located inside the master cylinder immediately returns the master cylinder pistons to the normal position. The pistons contain check valves and the master cylinder has compensating ports drilled in it. These are uncovered as the pistons reach their normal position. The piston check valves allow fluid to flow toward the wheel cylinders or calipers as the pistons withdraw. Then, as the return springs force the brake pads or shoes into the released position, the excess fluid reservoir through the compensating ports. It is during the time the pedal is in the released position that any fluid that has leaked out of the system will be replaced through the compensating ports.

Dual circuit master cylinders employ two pistons, located one behind the other, in the same cylinder. The primary piston is actuated directly by mechanical linkage from the brake pedal through the power booster. The secondary piston is actuated by fluid trapped between the two pistons. If a leak develops in front of the secondary piston, it moves forward until it bottoms against the front of the master cylinder, and the fluid trapped between the pistons will operate the rear brakes. If the rear brakes develop a leak, the primary piston will move forward until direct contact with the secondary piston takes place, and it will force the secondary piston to actuate the front brakes. In either case, the brake pedal moves farther when the brakes are applied, and less braking power is available.

All dual circuit systems use a switch to warn the driver when only half of the brake system is operational. This switch is usually located in a valve body which is mounted on the firewall or the frame below the master cylinder. A hydraulic piston receives pressure from both circuits, each circuit's pressure being applied to one end of the piston. When the pressures are in balance, the piston remains stationary. When one circuit has a leak, however, the greater pressure in that circuit during application of the brakes will push the piston to one side, closing the switch and activating the brake warning light.

In disc brake systems, this valve body also contains a metering

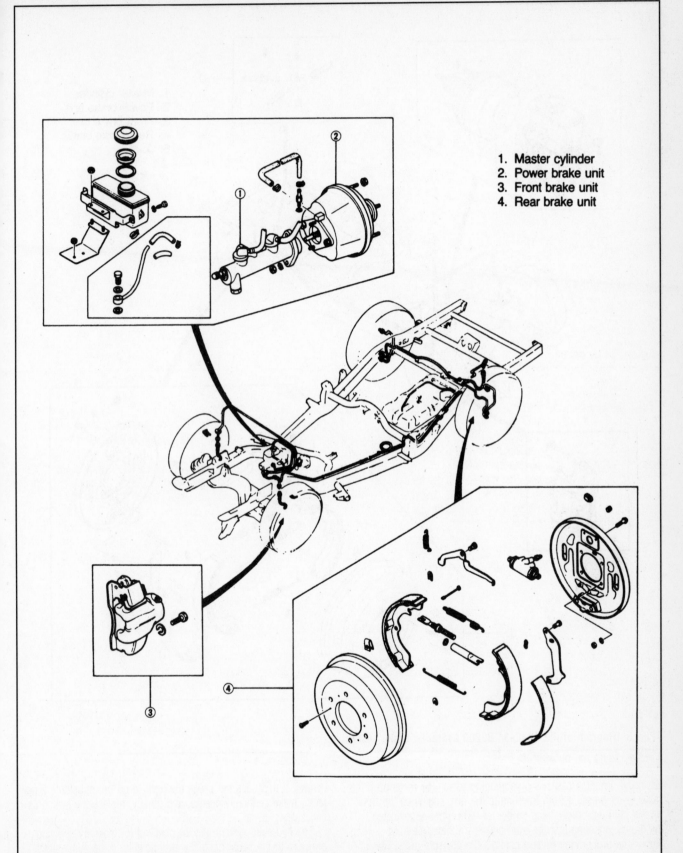

1. Master cylinder
2. Power brake unit
3. Front brake unit
4. Rear brake unit

Fig. 4 Diagram of the 1982–84 B2000 hydraulic brake system

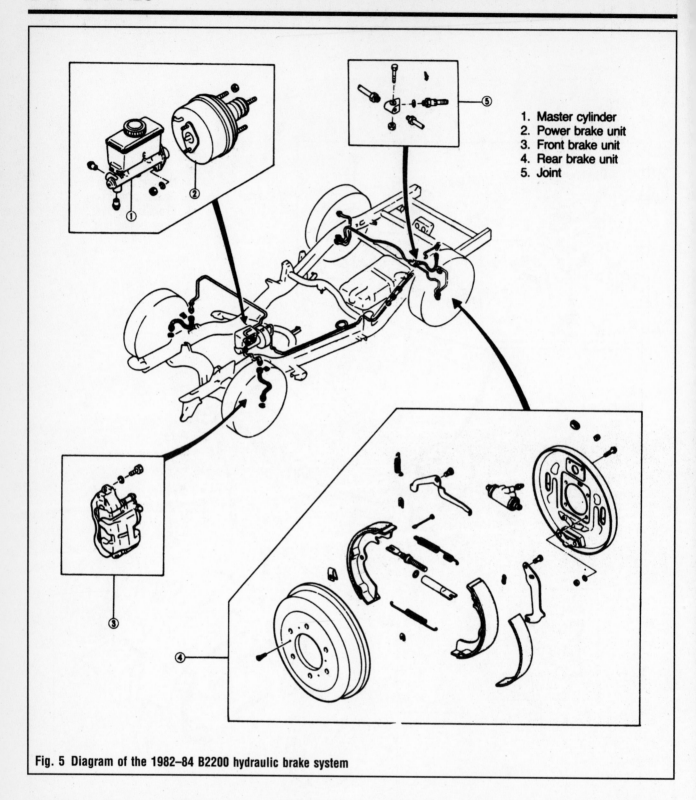

1. Master cylinder
2. Power brake unit
3. Front brake unit
4. Rear brake unit
5. Joint

Fig. 5 Diagram of the 1982–84 B2200 hydraulic brake system

valve and, in some cases, a proportioning valve. The metering valve keeps pressure from traveling to the disc brakes on the front wheels until the brake shoes on the rear wheels have contacted the drums, ensuring that the front brakes will never be used alone. The proportioning valve controls the pressure to the rear brakes to lessen the chance of rear wheel lock-up during very hard braking.

Warning lights may be tested by depressing the brake pedal and holding it while opening one of the wheel cylinder bleeder screws. If this does not cause the light to go on, substitute a new lamp, make continuity checks, and, finally, replace the switch as necessary.

The hydraulic system may be checked for leaks by applying pressure to the pedal gradually and steadily. If the pedal sinks very slowly to the floor, the system has a leak. This is not to be confused with a springy or spongy feel due to the compression of air within the lines. If the system leaks, there will be a gradual change in the position of the pedal with a constant pressure.

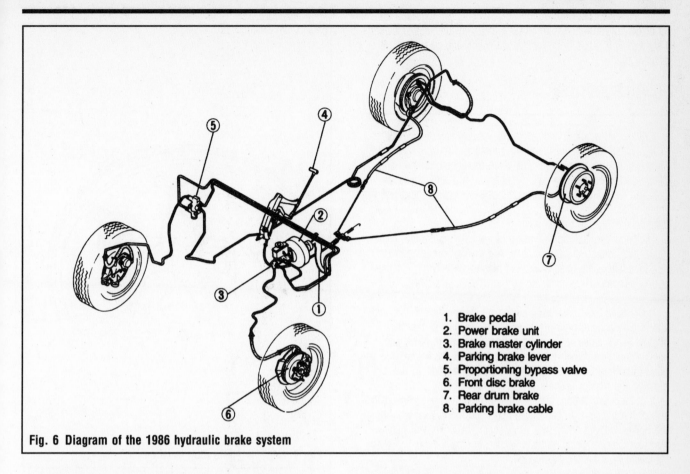

1. Brake pedal
2. Power brake unit
3. Brake master cylinder
4. Parking brake lever
5. Proportioning bypass valve
6. Front disc brake
7. Rear drum brake
8. Parking brake cable

Fig. 6 Diagram of the 1986 hydraulic brake system

Check for leaks along all lines and at wheel cylinders. If no external leaks are apparent, the problem is inside the master cylinder.

DISC BRAKES

Instead of the traditional expanding brakes that press outward against a circular drum, disc brake systems utilize a disc (rotor) with brake pads positioned on either side of it. An easily-seen analogy is the hand brake arrangement on a bicycle. The pads squeeze onto the rim of the bike wheel, slowing its motion. Automobile disc brakes use the identical principle but apply the braking effort to a separate disc instead of the wheel.

The disc (rotor) is a casting, usually equipped with cooling fins between the two braking surfaces. This enables air to circulate between the braking surfaces making them less sensitive to heat buildup and more resistant to fade. Dirt and water do not drastically affect braking action since contaminants are thrown off by the centrifugal action of the rotor or scraped off the by the pads. Also, the equal clamping action of the two brake pads tends to ensure uniform, straight line stops. Disc brakes are inherently self-adjusting. There are three general types of disc brake:
1. A fixed caliper.
2. A floating caliper.
3. A sliding caliper.

The fixed caliper design uses two pistons mounted on either side of the rotor (in each side of the caliper). The caliper is mounted rigidly and does not move.

The sliding and floating designs are quite similar. In fact, these two types are often lumped together. In both designs, the pad on

the inside of the rotor is moved into contact with the rotor by hydraulic force. The caliper, which is not held in a fixed position, moves slightly, bringing the outside pad into contact with the rotor. There are various methods of attaching floating calipers. Some pivot at the bottom or top, and some slide on mounting bolts. In any event, the end result is the same.

DRUM BRAKES

Drum brakes employ two brake shoes mounted on a stationary backing plate. These shoes are positioned inside a circular drum which rotates with the wheel assembly. The shoes are held in place by springs. This allows them to slide toward the drums (when they are applied) while keeping the linings and drums in alignment. The shoes are actuated by a wheel cylinder which is mounted at the top of the backing plate. When the brakes are applied, hydraulic pressure forces the wheel cylinder's actuating links outward. Since these links bear directly against the top of the brake shoes, the tops of the shoes are then forced against the inner side of the drum. This action forces the bottoms of the two shoes to contact the brake drum by rotating the entire assembly slightly (known as servo action). When pressure within the wheel cylinder is relaxed, return springs pull the shoes back away from the drum.

Most modern drum brakes are designed to self-adjust themselves during application when the vehicle is moving in reverse. This motion causes both shoes to rotate very slightly with the drum, rocking an adjusting lever, thereby causing rotation of the adjusting screw. Some drum brake systems are designed to self-adjust during application whenever the brakes are applied. This on-board adjustment system reduces the need for maintenance adjustments and keeps both the brake function and pedal feel satisfactory.

POWER BOOSTERS

Virtually all modern vehicles use a vacuum assisted power brake system to multiply the braking force and reduce pedal effort. Since vacuum is always available when the engine is operating, the system is simple and efficient. A vacuum diaphragm is located on the front of the master cylinder and assists the driver in applying the brakes, reducing both the effort and travel he must put into moving the brake pedal.

The vacuum diaphragm housing is normally connected to the intake manifold by a vacuum hose. A check valve is placed at the point where the hose enters the diaphragm housing, so that during periods of low manifold vacuum brakes assist will not be lost.

Depressing the brake pedal closes off the vacuum source and allows atmospheric pressure to enter on one side of the diaphragm. This causes the master cylinder pistons to move and apply the brakes. When the brake pedal is released, vacuum is applied to both sides of the diaphragm and springs return the diaphragm and master cylinder pistons to the released position.

If the vacuum supply fails, the brake pedal rod will contact the end of the master cylinder actuator rod and the system will apply the brakes without any power assistance. The driver will notice that much higher pedal effort is needed to stop the car and that the pedal feels harder than usual.

Vacuum Leak Test

1. Operate the engine at idle without touching the brake pedal for at least one minute.
2. Turn off the engine and wait one minute.
3. Test for the presence of assist vacuum by depressing the brake pedal and releasing it several times. If vacuum is present in the system, light application will produce less and less pedal travel. If there is no vacuum, air is leaking into the system.

System Operation Test

1. With the engine **OFF**, pump the brake pedal until the supply vacuum is entirely gone.
2. Put light, steady pressure on the brake pedal.
3. Start the engine and let it idle. If the system is operating correctly, the brake pedal should fall toward the floor if the constant pressure is maintained.

Power brake systems may be tested for hydraulic leaks just as ordinary systems are tested.

ADJUSTMENTS

▶ **See Figures 7 and 8**

FRONT DRUM BRAKES

The brakes should be cool before adjustment.
1. Raise and support the front end on jackstands.
2. Remove the adjuster slot plugs from the backing plates.
3. Insert a brake adjusting tool in the slot and engage the star-

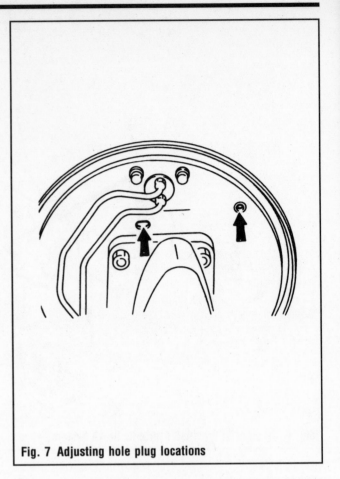

Fig. 7 Adjusting hole plug locations

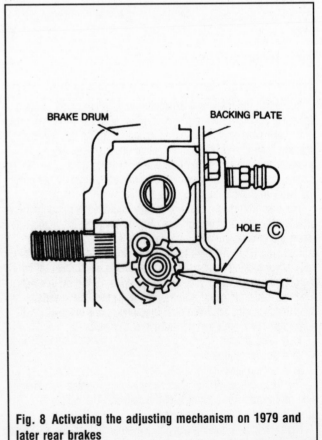

Fig. 8 Activating the adjusting mechanism on 1979 and later rear brakes

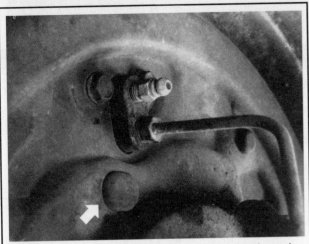

Adjust rear brakes by removing the rubber plug (arrow) and inserting a brake adjuster spoon. Turn the starwheel until the wheel locks up, then back it off three to five turns—the wheel should spin freely (no drag)

wheel. Rotate the starwheel until the drum is locked by the brake shoes, then back it off 5 notches. Repeat this for each starwheel.

4. When adjustment is complete, check that the wheels rotate freely, with no drag.

REAR DRUM BRAKES

1972–78 Vehicles

The brakes should be cool prior to adjustment.
1. Raise and support the rear end on jackstands.
2. Release the parking brake.
3. Disconnect the parking brake equalizer clevis pin.
4. Remove the adjusting slot plugs from the backing plates.
5. Insert a brake adjusting tool into the lower slot and engage the starwheel.
6. Turn the starwheel until the brake shoes lock the wheel, then back it off 5 notches.
7. Repeat this procedure for the top starwheel, then continue on to the other wheel and adjust those brakes in the same sequence.
8. When adjustment is complete, make sure that each wheel rotates freely, with no drag.

1979–86 Vehicles

The rear drum brakes are self-adjusting on 1979 and later models. Manual adjustment is required only when the brake shoes have been replaced, or when the length of the self-adjusting rod has been changes for some reason. The brakes should be cold (room temperature).
1. If the shoe retaining spring has been removed, first retract the pushrod fully (drum removed).
2. Raise and support the rear of the truck. The wheels must be free to turn.
3. Make sure the parking brake is fully released.
4. Remove the two adjusting hole plugs from the brake backing plate.
5. An arrow stamped on the backing plate indicates the direc-

tion to turn the adjuster starwheel to expand the shoes. Insert a brake spoon through the adjuster hole and turn the starwheel until the brakes are locked.
6. Insert a drift through the other adjuster hole. Use the drift to hold the pole lever of the self-adjuster firmly. Back off the starwheel three or four notches; the wheel should rotate freely (no drag).
7. Repeat the adjustment on the other wheel. Make sure the adjustment is exactly the same. Road test for equal brake action and readjust as necessary.

DISC BRAKES

Disc brakes require no adjustments.

BRAKE PEDAL FREE-PLAY

◆ **See Figure 9**

On trucks with power brakes, depress the pedal a few times to dispel all vacuum from the booster.

Using the top of the pedal pad as a reference point, there should be 7.0–9.0mm (0.276–0.354 in.) on trucks through 1984 with power brakes, 4.0–7.0mm (0.157–0.276 in.) on 1986 trucks

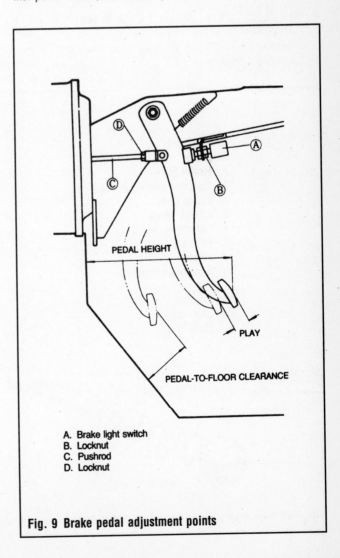

A. Brake light switch
B. Locknut
C. Pushrod
D. Locknut

Fig. 9 Brake pedal adjustment points

with power brakes, and a little less than 3mm (0.118 in.) free-play before the pushrod contacts the master cylinder piston on models with non-power brakes.

1. Loosen the locknut on the master cylinder pushrod at the clevis.

2. Turn the pushrod to obtain the proper free-play, then tighten the nut.

BRAKE PEDAL HEIGHT

Pedal height is measured from the center of the pedal pad surface, horizontally to the firewall. On the Rotary Pick-Up, pedal height should be 190mm (7.48 in.). On piston engine trucks through 1984, pedal height should be 205mm (8.07 in.). On 1986 pick-ups, pedal height should be 209–214mm (8.23–8.43 in.).

If not, loosen the stop light switch locknut and turn the switch until the proper height is obtained. Tighten the locknut.

Brake Light Switch

REMOVAL & INSTALLATION

The switch is located at the top of the brake pedal.

1. Disconnect the wiring from the switch.

2. Loosen the locknut and adjusting nut and unscrew the switch from the bracket.

3. Installation is the reverse of removal. Adjust the brake pedal.

Master Cylinder

♦ **See Figures 10 thru 19**

REMOVAL & INSTALLATION

1. Remove the brake lines from the master cylinder and cap the lines.

2. On 1986 models, disconnect the fluid level sensor coupling.

3. Unbolt and remove the master cylinder from the firewall or power booster. 1977–84 models have a remotely mounted reservoir, so the lines will have to be unclipped and plugged.

✳✳ WARNING

Clean, high quality brake fluid is essential to the safe and proper operation of the brake system. You should always buy the highest quality brake fluid that is available. If the brake fluid becomes contaminated, drain and flush the system, then refill the master cylinder with new fluid. Never re-use any brake fluid. Any brake fluid that is removed from the system should be discarded.

4. Installation is the reverse of removal. Torque the mounting nuts to 15 ft. lbs.

5. Bleed the system.

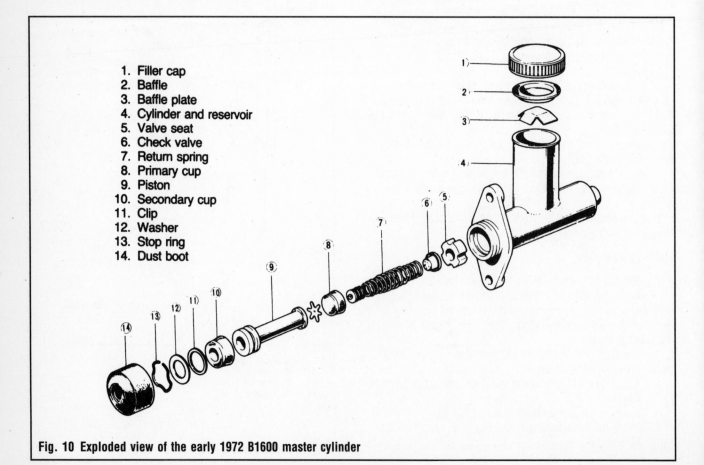

1. Filler cap
2. Baffle
3. Baffle plate
4. Cylinder and reservoir
5. Valve seat
6. Check valve
7. Return spring
8. Primary cup
9. Piston
10. Secondary cup
11. Clip
12. Washer
13. Stop ring
14. Dust boot

Fig. 10 Exploded view of the early 1972 B1600 master cylinder

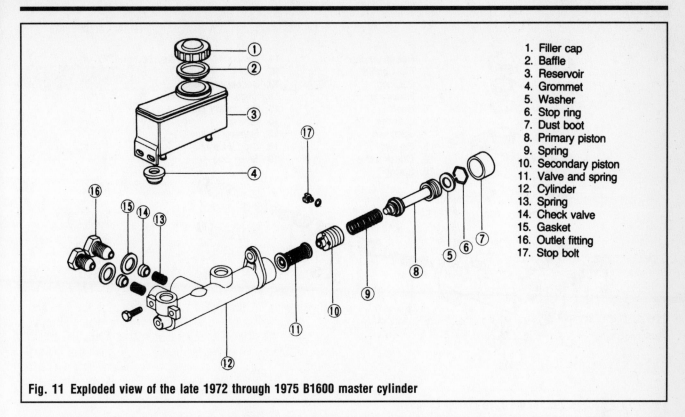

1. Filler cap
2. Baffle
3. Reservoir
4. Grommet
5. Washer
6. Stop ring
7. Dust boot
8. Primary piston
9. Spring
10. Secondary piston
11. Valve and spring
12. Cylinder
13. Spring
14. Check valve
15. Gasket
16. Outlet fitting
17. Stop bolt

Fig. 11 Exploded view of the late 1972 through 1975 B1600 master cylinder

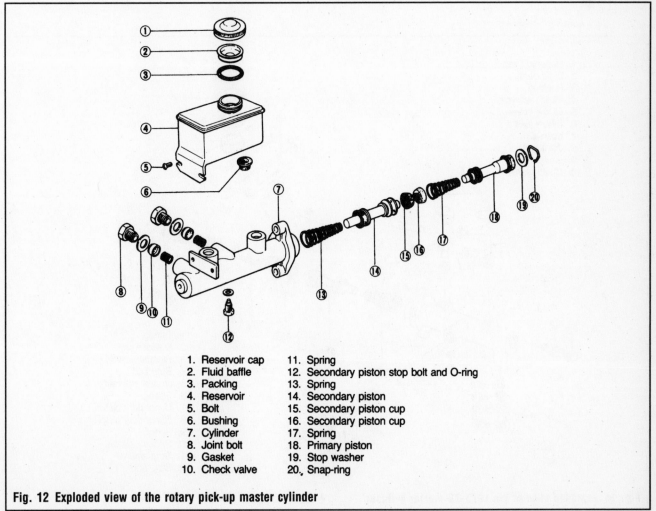

1. Reservoir cap
2. Fluid baffle
3. Packing
4. Reservoir
5. Bolt
6. Bushing
7. Cylinder
8. Joint bolt
9. Gasket
10. Check valve
11. Spring
12. Secondary piston stop bolt and O-ring
13. Spring
14. Secondary piston
15. Secondary piston cup
16. Secondary piston cup
17. Spring
18. Primary piston
19. Stop washer
20. Snap-ring

Fig. 12 Exploded view of the rotary pick-up master cylinder

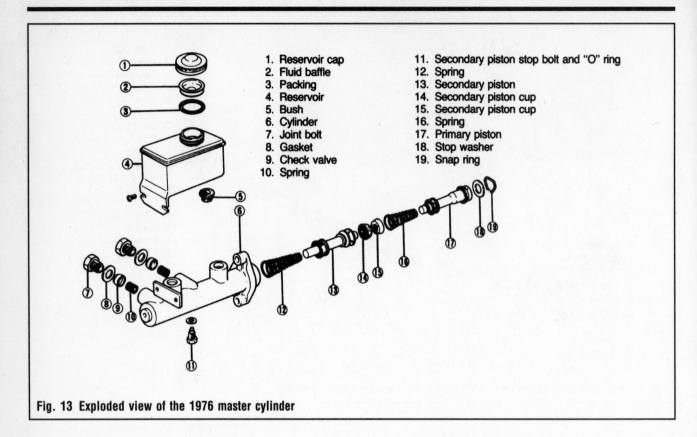

1. Reservoir cap
2. Fluid baffle
3. Packing
4. Reservoir
5. Bush
6. Cylinder
7. Joint bolt
8. Gasket
9. Check valve
10. Spring

11. Secondary piston stop bolt and "O" ring
12. Spring
13. Secondary piston
14. Secondary piston cup
15. Secondary piston cup
16. Spring
17. Primary piston
18. Stop washer
19. Snap ring

Fig. 13 Exploded view of the 1976 master cylinder

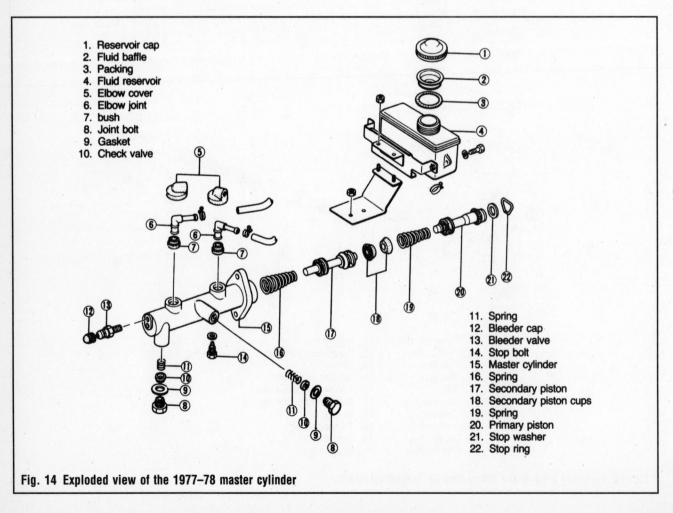

1. Reservoir cap
2. Fluid baffle
3. Packing
4. Fluid reservoir
5. Elbow cover
6. Elbow joint
7. bush
8. Joint bolt
9. Gasket
10. Check valve

11. Spring
12. Bleeder cap
13. Bleeder valve
14. Stop bolt
15. Master cylinder
16. Spring
17. Secondary piston
18. Secondary piston cups
19. Spring
20. Primary piston
21. Stop washer
22. Stop ring

Fig. 14 Exploded view of the 1977–78 master cylinder

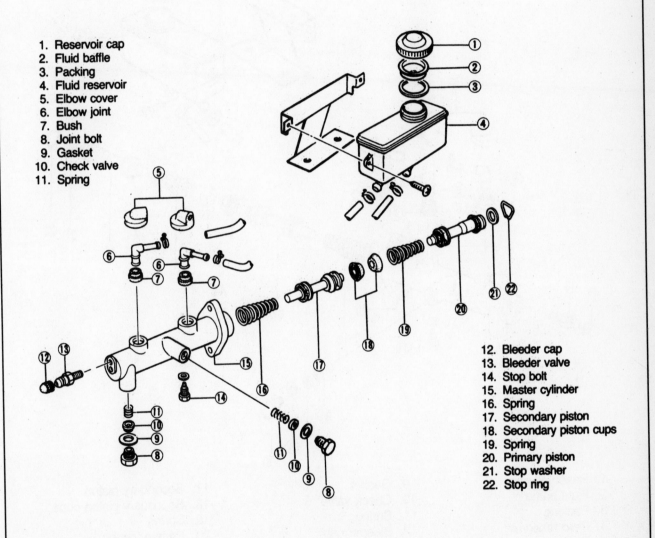

1. Reservoir cap
2. Fluid baffle
3. Packing
4. Fluid reservoir
5. Elbow cover
6. Elbow joint
7. Bush
8. Joint bolt
9. Gasket
10. Check valve
11. Spring

12. Bleeder cap
13. Bleeder valve
14. Stop bolt
15. Master cylinder
16. Spring
17. Secondary piston
18. Secondary piston cups
19. Spring
20. Primary piston
21. Stop washer
22. Stop ring

Fig. 15 Exploded view of the 1979–80 master cylinder

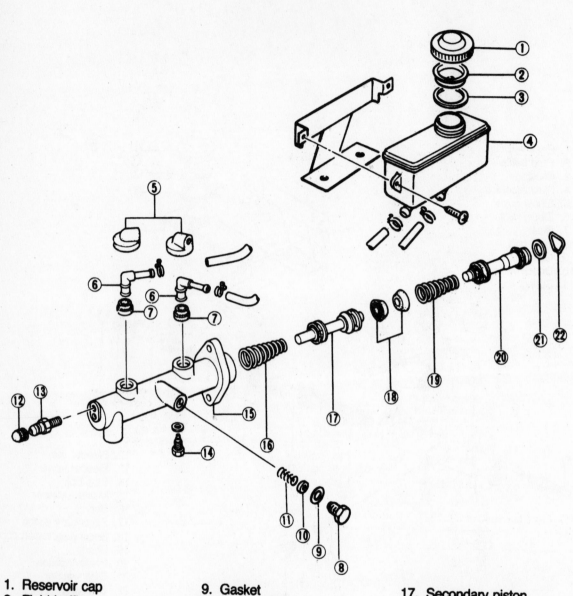

1. Reservoir cap
2. Fluid baffle
3. Packing
4. Fluid reservoir
5. Elbow cover
6. Elbow joint
7. Bush
8. Joint bolt

9. Gasket
10. Check valve
11. Spring
12. Bleeder cap
13. Bleeder valve
14. Stop bolt
15. Master cylinder
16. Spring

17. Secondary piston
18. Secondary piston cups
19. Spring
20. Primary piston
21. Stop washer
22. Stop ring

Fig. 16 Exploded view of the 1981 master cylinder

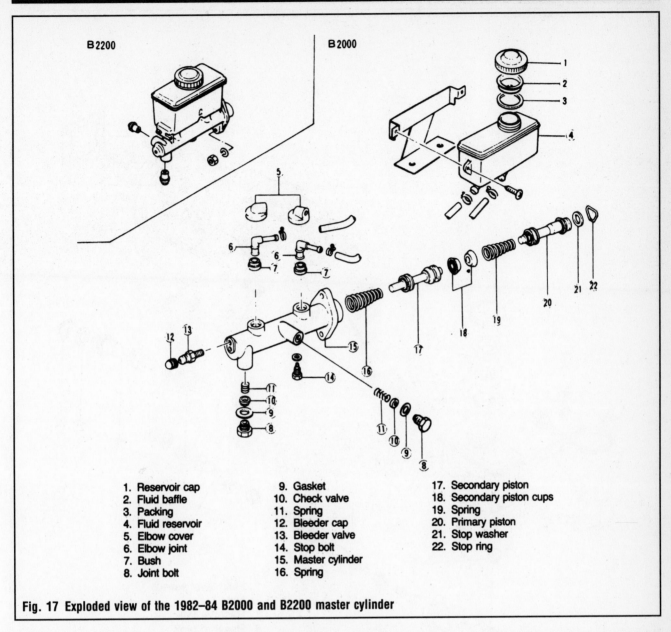

1. Reservoir cap
2. Fluid baffle
3. Packing
4. Fluid reservoir
5. Elbow cover
6. Elbow joint
7. Bush
8. Joint bolt
9. Gasket
10. Check valve
11. Spring
12. Bleeder cap
13. Bleeder valve
14. Stop bolt
15. Master cylinder
16. Spring
17. Secondary piston
18. Secondary piston cups
19. Spring
20. Primary piston
21. Stop washer
22. Stop ring

Fig. 17 Exploded view of the 1982–84 B2000 and B2200 master cylinder

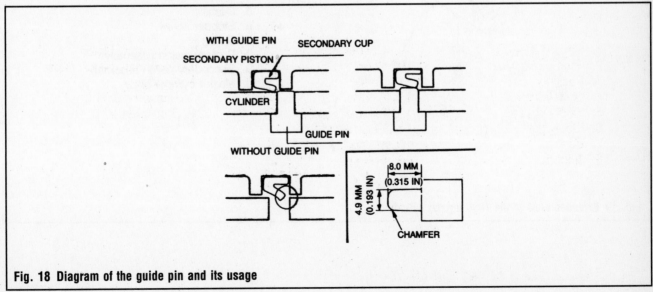

Fig. 18 Diagram of the guide pin and its usage

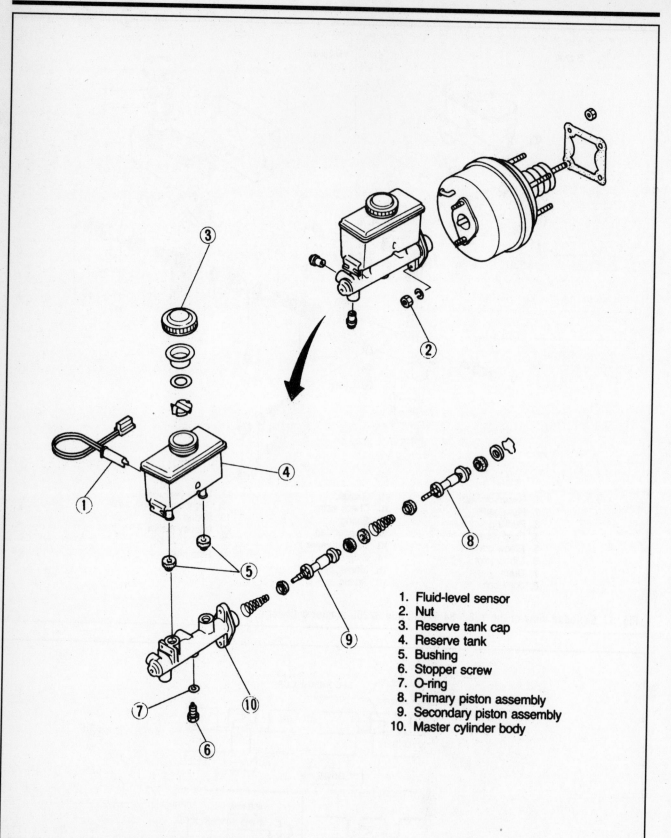

1. Fluid-level sensor
2. Nut
3. Reserve tank cap
4. Reserve tank
5. Bushing
6. Stopper screw
7. O-ring
8. Primary piston assembly
9. Secondary piston assembly
10. Master cylinder body

Fig. 19 Exploded view of the 1986 master cylinder

To remove the master cylinder, remove the brake lines connected to the master cylinder . . .

. . . then unbolt the master cylinder attaching nuts

On 1986 models, also unplug the fluid level sensor wire

Finally lift the master cylinder off the mounting studs

OVERHAUL

1972–84 Vehicles

1. Remove the master cylinder.
2. Drain the fluid. On models through 1976, remove the reservoir.
3. Remove the reservoir grommets from the master cylinder body on models through 1976 or elbow connectors on 1977–84 models.
4. Remove the dust boot.
5. Depress the piston and remove the piston stop ring from the cylinder.
6. Remove the piston stop washer, primary piston, and spring.
7. Loosen, but do not remove, the secondary piston stop screw.
8. Push the secondary piston inward, then remove the stop screw. Insert a guide pin in its place, and remove the secondary piston.
9. Remove the outlet port fittings, check valves and springs.
10. Clean all parts in clean brake fluid.
11. Inspect all parts for wear or damage. Replace any worn, discolored, misshapen or suspect part. The cylinder bore may be honed to remove light scoring, pitting or discoloration. If honing cannot polish the interior, discard the cylinder. Check the piston-to-bore clearance. If the clearance exceeds 0.15mm (0.0059 in.), replace the cylinder.
12. Assembly is the reverse of disassembly. Coat all parts in clean brake fluid before assembly. Use the guide pin to aid in installing the secondary piston. Refill the master cylinder and pump the piston several times, until fluid flows from each outlet port.

1986 Vehicles

1. Rock the reservoir from side-to-side to remove it from the master cylinder.

2. Remove the reservoir grommets.

3. Remove the piston stopper screw from the bottom of the master cylinder.

4. Depress the piston and remove the snapring.

5. Remove the primary piston assembly.

6. Remove the secondary piston assembly. Compressed air applied to the rearmost fluid port may be necessary to remove the secondary piston. If so, place a heavy rag over the cylinder bore to catch the piston.

7. Clean all parts in clean brake fluid.

8. Inspect all parts for wear or damage. Replace any worn, discolored, misshapen or suspect part. The cylinder bore may be honed to remove light scoring, pitting or discoloration. If honing cannot polish the interior, discard the cylinder. Check the piston-to-bore clearance. If the clearance exceeds 0.12mm (0.0047 in.), replace the cylinder.

Power Brake Booster

REMOVAL & INSTALLATION

▶ **See Figures 20 and 21**

1. Remove the master cylinder.
2. Disconnect the pushrod at the pedal.

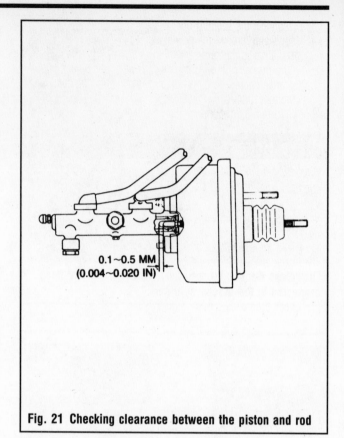

0.1~0.5 MM
(0.004~0.020 IN)

Fig. 21 Checking clearance between the piston and rod

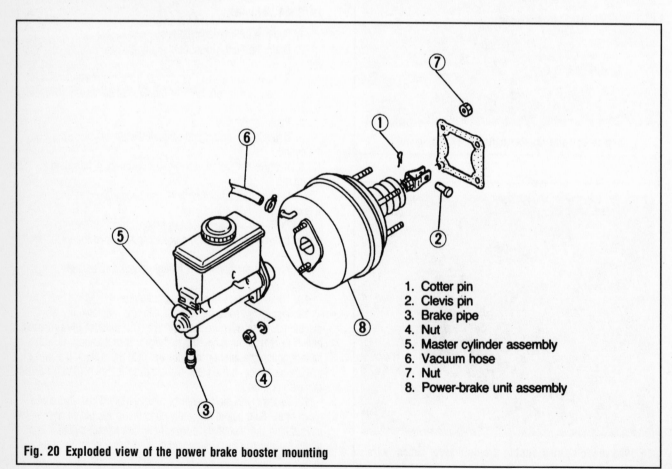

1. Cotter pin
2. Clevis pin
3. Brake pipe
4. Nut
5. Master cylinder assembly
6. Vacuum hose
7. Nut
8. Power-brake unit assembly

Fig. 20 Exploded view of the power brake booster mounting

3. Disconnect the vacuum line at the booster.

4. Unbolt and remove the power booster from the firewall.

5. Installation is the reverse of removal. Check the clearance between the master cylinder piston and the power booster pushrod. Clearance should be 0.10–0.50mm (0.0039–0.0197 in.) on trucks through 1984; 0 on 1986 trucks. If not, adjust it at the pushrod. Torque the mounting nuts to 17 ft. lbs.

Brake Hoses

INSPECTION & REPLACEMENT

▶ **See Figure 22**

1. Clean the brake hose thoroughly before inspecting it.

2. Check all flexible hoses for any signs of swelling, cracking or brittleness. Replace any hose that shows any of these symptoms.

3. Check the hoses for any sign that they are rubbing against

. . . **and remove the attaching bolt from the hose fitting**

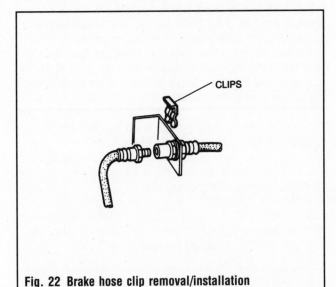

Fig. 22 Brake hose clip removal/installation

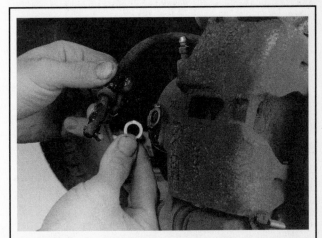

Pay attention to these copper gaskets which seal the bolt to the hose and the hose to the brake connection—be sure the sealing surfaces are free of any grit or dirt

To remove the flexible rubber brake hoses, loosen . . .

any other component. If shiny marks or scuffing is found, determine what the hose is rubbing against and correct the problem. If scuffing has removed *any* material from the hose, replace it.

4. Check brake pipes for corrosion or dents. Replace any damaged pipe.

5. Check all connections for signs of leakage. Check threads for damage.

6. When disconnecting hoses and pipes, remove the retaining clip AFTER loosening the flare nut at the joint. When tightening fittings, install the clip, THEN, tighten the flare nut.

7. When installing a hose, make sure it is not twisted. Make absolutely certain, especially in the case of the hoses connected to the front calipers or wheel cylinders, that they will not come into contact with any other component with the front wheels in any position. Observe the following torques when installing lines:

• Flexible hose-to-caliper or wheel cylinder: 16–19 ft. lbs.

• Flare nuts: 10–15 ft. lbs.

✳✳ WARNING

Clean, high quality brake fluid is essential to the safe and proper operation of the brake system. You should always buy the highest quality brake fluid that is available. If the brake fluid becomes contaminated, drain and flush the system, then refill the master cylinder with new fluid. Never reuse any brake fluid. Any brake fluid that is removed from the system should be discarded.

8. When any brake line is opened, the system must be bled when the job is done.

Pressure Differential Valve

▶ **See Figure 23**

REMOVAL & INSTALLATION

1. Disconnect the brake warning light switch connector, at the switch.
2. Disconnect the brake lines at the valve, and plug the lines.
3. Unbolt and remove the valve.
4. Installation is the reverse of removal. Bleed the system.

CENTERING THE PRESSURE DIFFERENTIAL VALVE

After the brake system has been opened for repairs, or bled, the brake light will remain on. The pressure differential valve must be centered to make the light go off.
1. Turn the ignition switch **ON,** but don't start the engine.
2. Make sure that the master cylinder reservoirs are filled.
3. Slowly depress the brake pedal. The valve should center itself and the light go off. If not, bleed the brakes again and repeat the above procedure.

Bleeding the Brake System

The hydraulic brake system must be free of air to operate properly. Air can enter the system when hydraulic parts are disconnected for servicing or replacement, or when the fluid level in the master cylinder reservoirs is very low. Air in the system will give the brake pedal a spongy feeling upon application.

The quickest and easiest of the two ways for system bleeding is the pressure method, but special equipment is needed to externally pressurize the hydraulic system. The other, more commonly used method of brake bleeding is done manually.

BLEEDING SEQUENCE

▶ **See Figures 24, 25 and 26**

✳✳ WARNING

Clean, high quality brake fluid is essential to the safe and proper operation of the brake system. You should always buy the highest quality brake fluid that is available. If the brake fluid becomes contaminated, drain and flush the system, then refill the master cylinder with new fluid. Never reuse any brake fluid. Any brake fluid that is removed from the system should be discarded.

1. Master cylinder. If the cylinder is not equipped with bleeder screws, open the brake line(s) to the wheels slightly while pressure is applied to the brake pedal. Be sure to tighten the line before the brake pedal is released. The procedure for bench bleeding the master cylinder is covered below.
2. Pressure Differential Valve: If equipped with a bleeder screw.
3. Front/Back Split Systems: Start with the wheel farthest away from the master cylinder, usually the right rear wheel. Bleed the other rear wheel then the right front and left front.

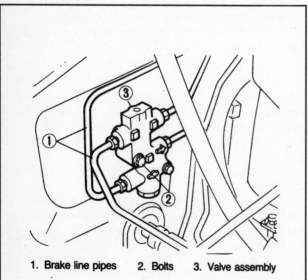

1. Brake line pipes 2. Bolts 3. Valve assembly

Fig. 23 Typical pressure differential valve

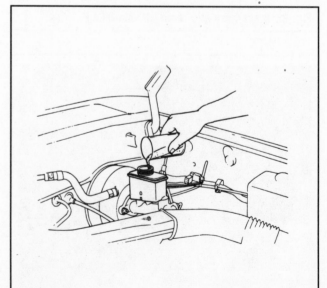

Fig. 24 Fill the master cylinder before bleeding the brake system

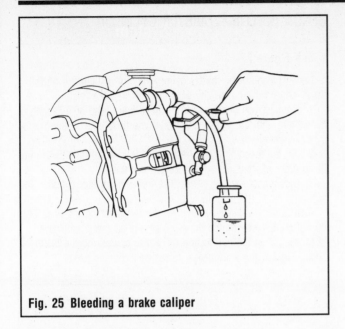

Fig. 25 Bleeding a brake caliper

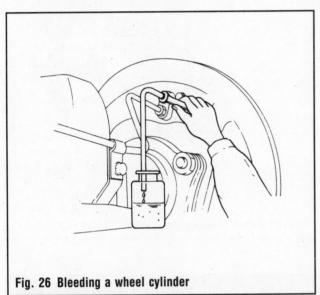

Fig. 26 Bleeding a wheel cylinder

✳✳ CAUTION

Do not allow brake fluid to spill on the truck's finish, it will remove the paint. Flush the area with water.

MANUAL BLEEDING

✳✳ WARNING

Clean, high quality brake fluid is essential to the safe and proper operation of the brake system. You should always buy the highest quality brake fluid that is available. If the brake fluid becomes contaminated, drain and flush the system, then refill the master cylinder with new fluid. Never reuse any brake fluid. Any brake fluid that is removed from the system should be discarded.

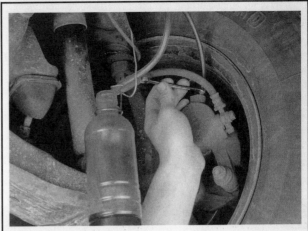

Bleed the brakes as shown—start at the farthest bleeder screw from the master cylinder (usually the passenger side rear) and work your way forward

1. Clean the bleed screw at each wheel.
2. Start with the wheel farthest from the master cylinder (right rear).
3. Attach a small rubber hose to the bleed screw and place the end in a container of clear brake fluid.
4. Fill the master cylinder with brake fluid. (Check often during bleeding). Have an assistant slowly pump up the brake pedal and hold pressure.
5. Open the bleed screw about one-quarter turn, press the brake pedal to the floor, close the bleed screw and slowly release the pedal. Continue until no more air bubbles are forced from the cylinder on application of the brake pedal.
6. Repeat procedure on remaining wheel cylinders and calipers, still working from cylinder/caliper farthest from the master cylinder.

Master cylinders equipped with bleed screws may be bled independently. When bleeding the Bendix-type dual master cylinder it is necessary to solidly cap one reservoir section while bleeding the other to prevent pressure loss through the cap vent hole.

✳✳ CAUTION

The bleeder valve at the wheel cylinder must be closed at the end of each stroke, and before the brake pedal is released, to insure that no air can enter the system. It is also important that the brake pedal be returned to the full up position so the piston in the master cylinder moves back enough to clear the bypass outlets.

PRESSURE BLEEDING DISC BRAKES

✳✳ CAUTION

Special adapters are required when pressure bleeding cylinders with plastic reservoirs.

Pressure bleeding equipment should be diaphragm type; placing a diaphragm between the pressurized air supply and the brake fluid. This prevents moisture and other contaminants from entering the hydraulic system.

➡️Some front disc/rear drum equipped vehicles use a metering valve which closes off pressure to the front brakes under certain conditions. These systems contain manual release actuators, which must be engaged to pressure bleed the front brakes.

1. Connect the tank hydraulic hose and adapter to the master cylinder.
2. Close hydraulic valve on the bleeder equipment.
3. Apply air pressure to the bleeder equipment.

✳✳ CAUTION

Follow equipment manufacturer's recommendations for correct air pressure.

4. Open the valve to bleed air out of the pressure hose to the master cylinder.

➡️Never bleed this system using the secondary piston stop-screw on the bottom of many master cylinders.

5. Open the hydraulic valve and bleed each wheel cylinder and caliper. Bleed rear brake system first when bleeding both front and rear systems.

FLUSHING HYDRAULIC BRAKE SYSTEMS

Hydraulic brake systems must be totally flushed if the fluid becomes contaminated with water, dirt or other corrosive chemicals. To flush, simply bleed the entire system until all fluid has been replaced with the correct type of new fluid.

FRONT DRUM BRAKES

✳✳ CAUTION

Brake shoes contain asbestos, which has been determined to be a cancer causing agent. Never clean the brake surfaces with compressed air! Avoid inhaling any dust from any brake surface! When cleaning brake surfaces, use a commercially available brake cleaning fluid.

Brake Drum

REMOVAL & INSTALLATION

▶ **See Figure 28**

1. Raise and support the front end on jackstands.
2. Remove the wheel.
3. Remove the drum attaching screws and insert them in the

BENCH BLEEDING MASTER CYLINDER

▶ **See Figure 27**

Bench bleeding the master cylinder before installing it on the truck reduces the possibility of getting air into the lines.

1. Connect two short pieces of brake line to the outlet fittings, bend them until the free end is below the fluid level in the master cylinder reservoirs.
2. Fill the reservoirs with fresh brake fluid. Pump the piston until no more air bubbles appear in the reservoir(s).
3. Disconnect the two short lines, refill the master cylinder and securely install the cylinder cap(s).
4. Install the master cylinder on the truck. Attach the lines but do not completely tighten them. Force any air that might have been trapped in the connection by slowly depressing the brake pedal. Tighten the lines before releasing the brake pedal.

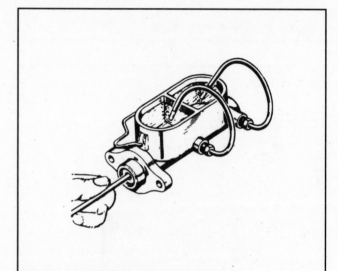

Fig. 27 Bench bleeding the master cylinder

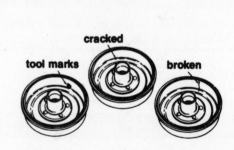

Fig. 28 Check the drums for tool marks or small cracks which can be machined out by a brake shop—replace broken drums

threaded holes in the drum. Turn the screws inward, evenly, to force the rum off the hub.

4. Thoroughly inspect the drum. Discard a cracked drum. If the drum is suspected of being out of round, or shows signs of wear or has a ridged or rough surface, have it turned on a lathe at a machine shop. The maximum oversize is stamped into the drum.

5. Installation is the reverse of removal. Make sure that the holes are aligned for the attaching screws. Tighten the screws evenly to install the drum.

Brake Shoes

REMOVAL & INSTALLATION

▶ **See Figures 29, 30 and 31**

The purchase of an inexpensive brake spring tool will make this job a lot easier.

1. Raise and support the front end on jackstands.
2. Remove the drums.
3. Remove the retracting springs.
4. Remove the hold-down springs and guide pins by turning the collars 90° with a pliers, or spring tool, releasing the springs.
5. Remove the shoes, noting in which place the shoe with the longer lining is installed.
6. Inspect the shoes for cracks, heat checking or contamination by oil or grease. Minimum lining thickness is 1.00mm (0.039

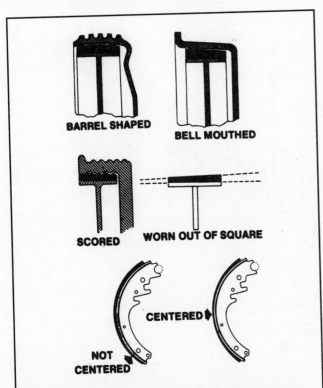

Fig. 29 Improperly worn linings are cause for concern, especially if braking is unstable and/or excessively noisy. Compare lining and drum wear patterns—the drum wear pattern is more important, since it causes the lining wear pattern

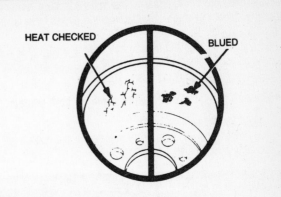

Fig. 30 A severely heat checked or blued drum, and charred or heavily glazed linings, are signs of overheating—the brake shoes should be replaced and the problem diagnosed and corrected

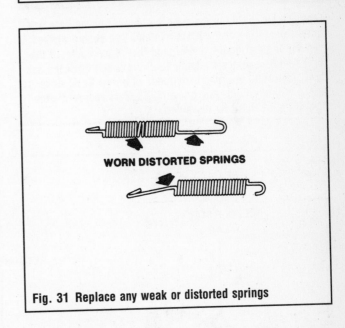

Fig. 31 Replace any weak or distorted springs

in.). If heat checking or discoloration is noted, the wheel cylinder are probably at fault and will have to be rebuilt or replaced.

➡**Never replace the shoes on one side of the truck, only! Always replace shoes on both sides!**

7. Clean the backing plate with an approved cleaning fluid.
8. Lubricated the threads of the starwheel with lithium based or silicone based grease. Apply a small dab of lithium or silicone based grease to the pads on which the brake shoes ride.

To install:

9. Transfer the parking brake lever to the new shoe.
10. Position the shoes on the backing plate.
11. Connect the parking brake cable to the lever.
12. Install the hold-down springs and guide pins.
13. Install the adjusting pawl and spring.
14. Install the adjusting screw assembly.
15. Install the retracting springs.
16. Install the drums.
17. Working through the 2 holes in the backing plate, reach

through the hole in the center with a brake adjusting spoon and turn the star-wheel screw until the wheel is locked, that is, it can't be turned by hand.

18. Reach through the outside hole with a small bar and hold off the adjusting pawl while backing off the star-wheel about 6–7 clicks, or until the wheel is free to rotate.

➡**The adjustment should be the same on both wheels.**

19. Adjust the parking brake.
20. Operate the brake pedal a few times. If the brakes feel at all spongy, bleed the system.

Wheel Cylinder

REMOVAL & INSTALLATION

✴✴ WARNING

Clean, high quality brake fluid is essential to the safe and proper operation of the brake system. You should always buy the highest quality brake fluid that is available. If the brake fluid becomes contaminated, drain and flush the system, then refill the master cylinder with new fluid. Never re-use any brake fluid. Any brake fluid that is removed from the system should be discarded.

1. Raise and support the front end on jackstands.
2. Remove the brake drum and shoes.
3. Disconnect the brake line at the wheel cylinder and plug it.
4. Remove the attaching nuts from behind the backing plate and remove the wheel cylinder.
5. Installation is the reverse of removal.

OVERHAUL

◆ **See Figure 32**

1. Remove the wheel cylinder.
2. Remove the piston and adjusting screw, then remove the boot and adjuster.
3. Using compressed air in the inlet port, blow out the piston cup, expander and spring.
4. Clean all parts in clean brake fluid.
5. Inspect all parts for wear or damage. Replace any worn, discolored, misshapen or suspect part. The cylinder bore may be honed to remove light scoring, pitting or discoloration. If honing cannot polish the interior, discard the cylinder. Check the piston-to-bore clearance. If the clearance exceeds 0.15mm (0.0059 in.), replace the cylinder.
6. Assembly is the reverse of disassembly. Coat all parts in clean brake fluid before assembly.
7. Install the wheel cylinder and all other parts. Bleed the system.

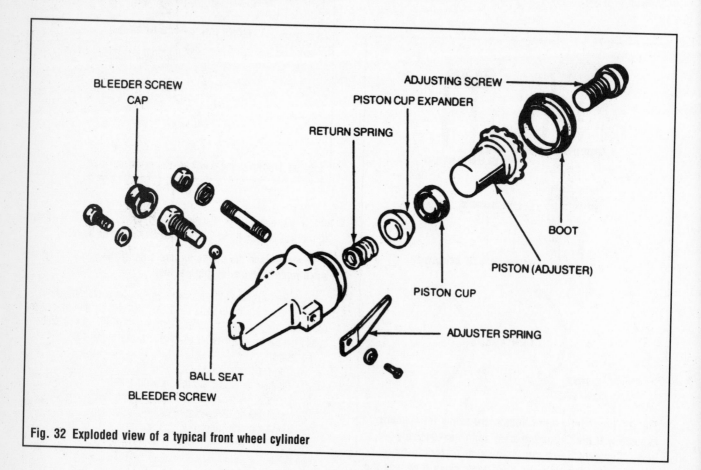

Fig. 32 Exploded view of a typical front wheel cylinder

FRONT DISC BRAKES

✷✷ CAUTION

Brake shoes may contain asbestos, which has been determined to be a cancer causing agent. Never clean the brake surfaces with compressed air! Avoid inhaling any dust from any brake surface! When cleaning brake surfaces, use a commercially available brake cleaning fluid.

Brake Pads

REMOVAL & INSTALLATION

▶ **See Figures 33, 34 and 35**

➡Minimum thickness of the pad lining and backing plate combined should be 7mm (0.276 in.).

Through 1984

1. Raise and support the front end on jackstands.
2. Remove the wheels.

3. Remove the caliper retaining pins and hold-down plates.
4. Lift off the caliper, remove the anti-rattle clips and remove the pads.
5. Remove about ½ of the fluid from the front brake reservoir of the master cylinder.
6. Position a large C-clamp on the caliper and force the piston back into its bore.
7. Installation is the reverse of removal. Shims are used behind the pads on these trucks from the factory. These shims should be discarded and replaced with new ones at each pad change. Some aftermarket pads are too thick to use these shims. In that case, don't try to force new shims in place. Do without them. Refill the master cylinder reservoir. Pump the brake pedal a few times to restore pressure.

1986 Vehicles

1. Raise and support the front end on jackstands.
2. Remove the wheels.
3. Remove the caliper lockpin bolts.
4. Lift off the caliper and remove the brake pads.

1. Brake rotor
2. Brake caliper
3. Caliper bracket
4. Rubber brake hose
5. Wheel hub
6. Splash shield

Front brake overall view

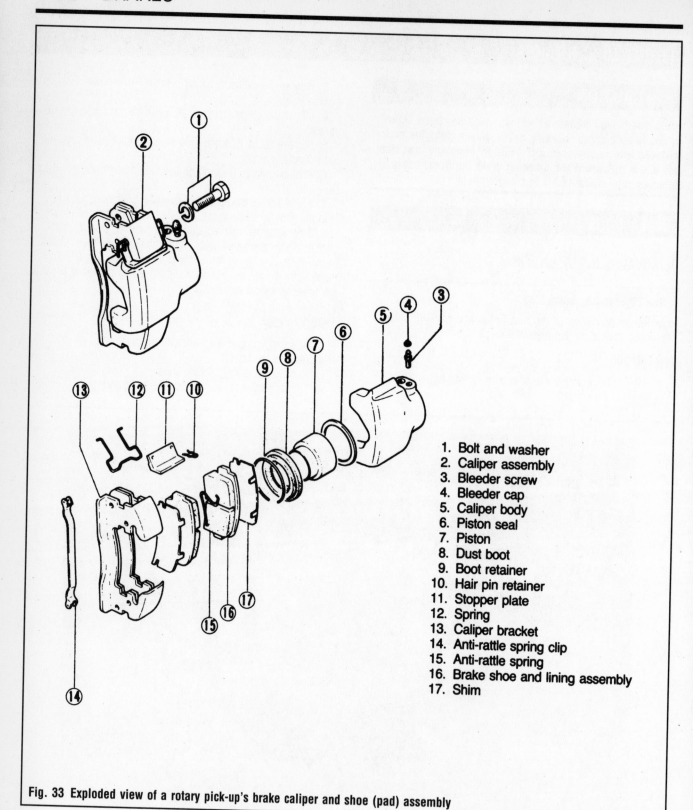

1. Bolt and washer
2. Caliper assembly
3. Bleeder screw
4. Bleeder cap
5. Caliper body
6. Piston seal
7. Piston
8. Dust boot
9. Boot retainer
10. Hair pin retainer
11. Stopper plate
12. Spring
13. Caliper bracket
14. Anti-rattle spring clip
15. Anti-rattle spring
16. Brake shoe and lining assembly
17. Shim

Fig. 33 Exploded view of a rotary pick-up's brake caliper and shoe (pad) assembly

5. Remove about ½ of the fluid from the front brake reservoir of the master cylinder.

6. Position a large C-clamp on the caliper and force the piston back into its bore.

7. Install new pads in the caliper. Shims are used behind the pads on these trucks from the factory. These shims should be discarded and replaced with new ones at each pad change. Some aftermarket pads are too thick to use these shims. In that case, don't try to force new shims in place. Do without them.

8. Position the caliper on the mounting support, install the lockpins and tighten them to 30 ft. lbs.

9. Install the wheels, lower the truck to the ground and refill the master cylinder. Pump the brake pedal a few times to restore pressure.

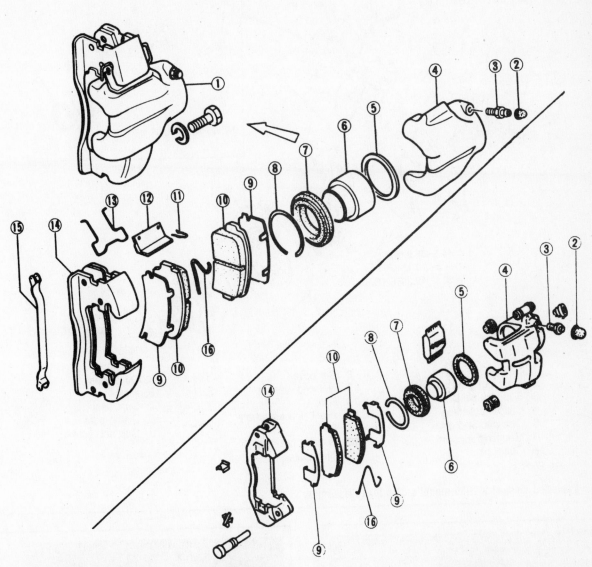

1. Caliper assembly
2. Bleeder cap
3. Bleeder screw
4. Caliper body
5. Piston seal
6. Piston

7. Dust boot
8. Boot retainer
9. Shim
10. Brake shoe and lining assembly
11. Locking clip
12. Stopper plate

13. Spring
14. Caliper bracket
15. Anti-rattle spring clip
16. Anti-rattle spring

Fig. 34 Exploded views of the B1800 and 1979–84 B2000 (top) and B2200 (bottom) brake caliper and shoe (pad) assemblies

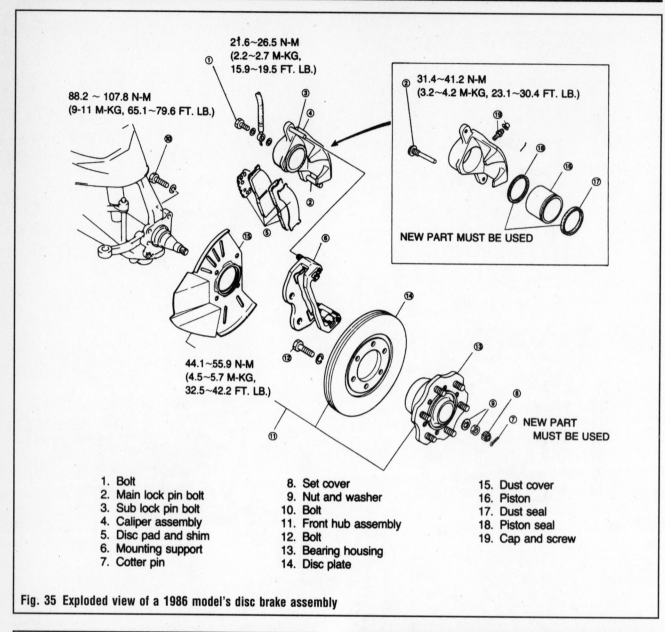

21.6~26.5 N-M
(2.2~2.7 M-KG,
15.9~19.5 FT. LB.)

88.2 ~ 107.8 N-M
(9-11 M-KG, 65.1~79.6 FT. LB.)

31.4~41.2 N-M
(3.2~4.2 M-KG, 23.1~30.4 FT. LB.)

NEW PART MUST BE USED

44.1~55.9 N-M
(4.5~5.7 M-KG,
32.5~42.2 FT. LB.)

NEW PART
MUST BE USED

1. Bolt
2. Main lock pin bolt
3. Sub lock pin bolt
4. Caliper assembly
5. Disc pad and shim
6. Mounting support
7. Cotter pin
8. Set cover
9. Nut and washer
10. Bolt
11. Front hub assembly
12. Bolt
13. Bearing housing
14. Disc plate
15. Dust cover
16. Piston
17. Dust seal
18. Piston seal
19. Cap and screw

Fig. 35 Exploded view of a 1986 model's disc brake assembly

To aid in caliper removal for changing the brake pads, place a large C-clamp over the caliper as shown, and tighten the clamp slightly to release static pressure on the pads

Remove the lower caliper mounting bolt and loosen the upper bolt . . .

. . . then pivot the caliper slowly . . .

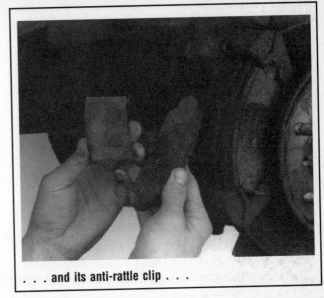

. . . and its anti-rattle clip . . .

. . . until it is clear of the brake pads (some models may require you to remove the upper bolt and then lift the caliper off the pads)

. . . followed by the outer brake pad . . .

Remove the inner brake pad . . .

. . . and its anti-rattle clip

Make sure the caliper piston is fully seated in the caliper before attempting to install the new pads—using an old brake pad with the large C-clamp will protect the caliper piston from damage

Brake Caliper

REMOVAL & INSTALLATION

1. Follow the preceding procedure for removing the brake pads.
2. Disconnect the brake line at the caliper and plug the line.
3. Installation is the reverse of removal. Bleed the brakes.

OVERHAUL

▶ **See Figures 36 thru 40**

1. Remove the caliper.
2. Place a thin piece of wood in the caliper, in front of the

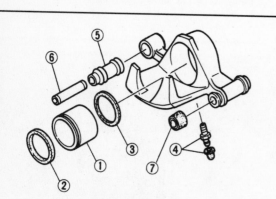

1. Piston
2. Dust seal
3. Piston seal
4. Bleeder screw and cap
5. Pin boot
6. Pin
7. Bushing

Fig. 36 Exploded view of the caliper components

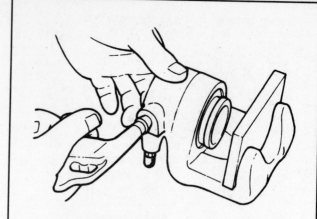

Fig. 37 Use compressed air to force the piston out of the caliper housing—a block of wood is positioned to catch the piston

Fig. 38 Pry out the dust seal

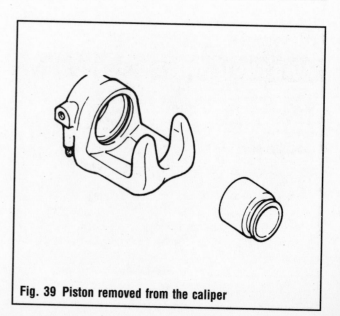

Fig. 39 Piston removed from the caliper

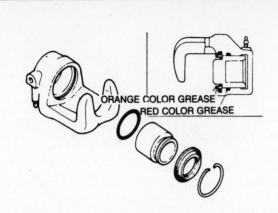

Fig. 40 Exploded view of the piston components—inset shows location of the color coded grease application points

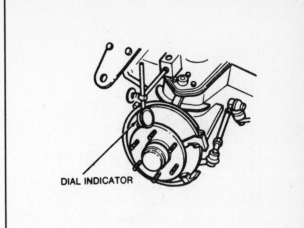

Fig. 41 Use a dial indicator to check disc run-out

piston. Apply enough compressed air through the brake line inlet hole to force the piston out of the caliper. Don't try to catch the piston with your fingers. A set of mashed fingers will result. It's also a good idea to wear safety glasses, as a spray of brake fluid will often result. If the piston is seized, try tapping around the caliper while applying pressure. If that doesn't work, fill the caliper with a rust dissolving agent such as Liquid Wrench® or WD-40® and let it stand for a while.

3. Discard all rubber parts.
4. Remove the bleeder screw.
5. Clean all parts in clean brake fluid. Inspect the piston and bore for any signs of wear, damage or heat discoloration. Minor damage can be corrected with light polishing using a crocus cloth.
6. Rebuilding kits are equipped with two kinds of grease, color coded orange and red. See the illustration for application details. Install a new seal, lubricated with clean brake fluid, on the piston. Be sure that the seal is not twisted!
7. Lubricate the piston and bore with clean brake fluid and insert the piston in the bore.
8. Install a new dust boot and retainer.
9. Install the bleeder screw.
10. Install the caliper in reverse of removal.

Brake Disc (Rotor)

REMOVAL & INSTALLATION

♦ **See Figures 41 thru 52**

1. Raise and support the front end on jackstands.
2. Remove the wheel.
3. Remove the grease cap, cotter pin, hub nut and flat washer.
4. Remove the caliper and suspend it out of the way without disconnecting the brake line. At this point, check the disc runout using a dial indicator. Slowly pull the hub from the spindle, positioning your hand to catch the outer bearing.
5. Matchmark the hub and rotor. Unbolt the rotor from the hub.

Fig. 42 Using a micrometer to measure the rotor thickness

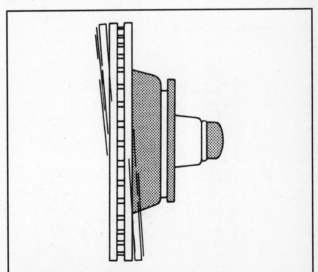

Fig. 43 Example of excessive run-out, which can cause brake pedal pulsation

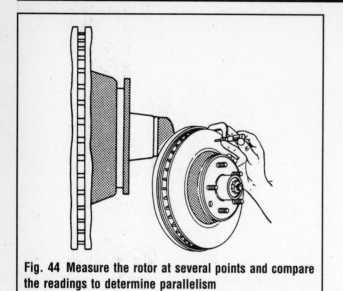

Fig. 44 Measure the rotor at several points and compare the readings to determine parallelism

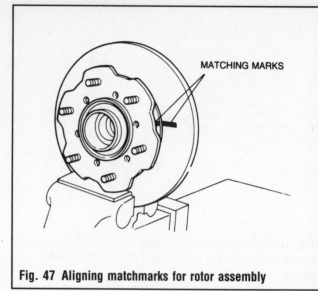

MATCHING MARKS

Fig. 47 Aligning matchmarks for rotor assembly

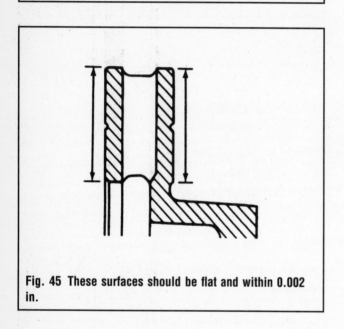

Fig. 45 These surfaces should be flat and within 0.002 in.

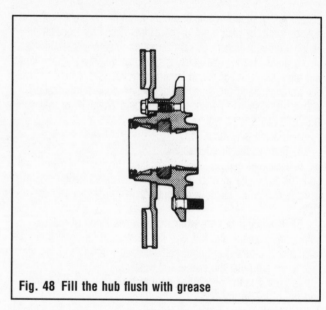

Fig. 48 Fill the hub flush with grease

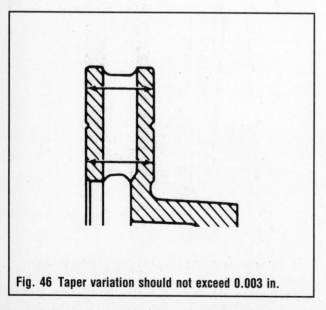

Fig. 46 Taper variation should not exceed 0.003 in.

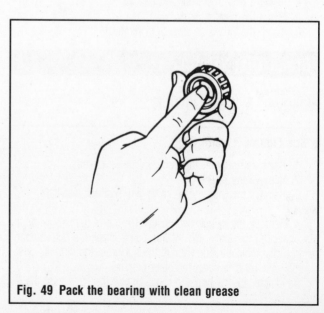

Fig. 49 Pack the bearing with clean grease

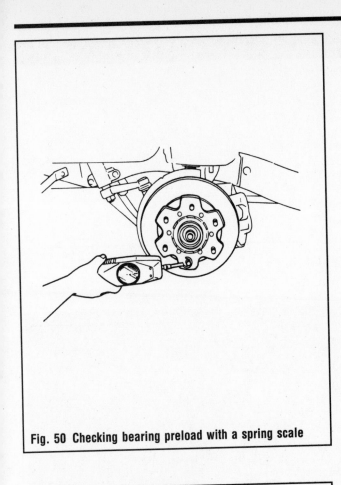

Fig. 50 Checking bearing preload with a spring scale

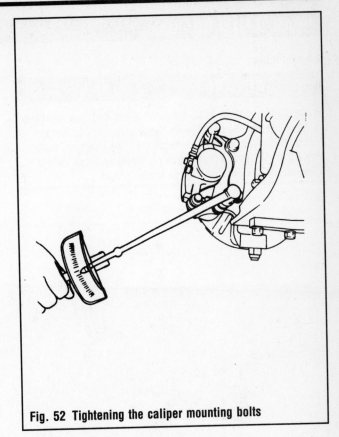

Fig. 52 Tightening the caliper mounting bolts

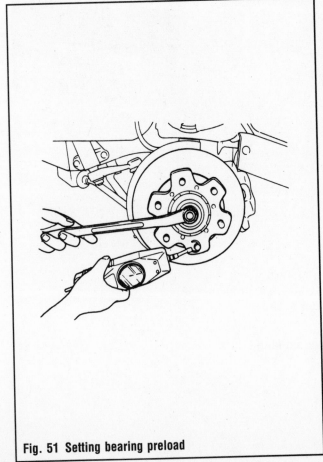

Fig. 51 Setting bearing preload

6. Inspect the rotor for any signs of wear, damage, roughness, ridges, pitting or heat discoloration. If heat discoloration is noted, you probably have a problem with the caliper piston seizing. Rebuild the caliper. Check the rotor thickness. To correct most of the above problems, have the rotor turned at a machine shop. Minimum rotor thickness is 11mm (0.433 in.).

7. When installing the rotor, make sure that the matchmarks are aligned. Tighten the rotor-to-hub bolts to 40 ft. lbs.

8. Pack the inside of the hub with clean wheel bearing grease until it is flush packed.

9. Pack the bearing with clean grease, making sure that it is thoroughly packed. Special devices are sold for packing bearings. They are inexpensive and readily available. If you don't have one, just make certain that the bearing is as full of grease as possible by working it in with your fingers.

10. If removed, install the inner bearing and seal. Drive the seal into place carefully until it is seated.

11. Install the spacer and the hub on the spindle.

12. Install the outer bearing, flat washer and hub nut. Torque the nut to 22 ft. lbs. and turn the hub 2 or 3 times to seat the bearings. Back off the nut until it is loose. Rock the hub back and forth to make sure the pads are not causing any drag on the rotor. It may be necessary to force the inner pad back using a C-clamp.

13. Attach a spring scale to a wheel lug.

14. Pull the scale horizontally and check the force needed to start the wheel turning. The force should be 1.3–2.4 lbs. If the reading is not correct, tighten or loosen the hub nut until the correct pull rating is obtained.

15. Install the nut cap, cotter pin and grease cap. Install the wheel.

REAR DRUM BRAKES

▶ See Figures 53, 54 and 55

✳✳ CAUTION

Brake shoes contain asbestos, which has been determined to be a cancer causing agent. Never clean the brake surfaces with compressed air! Avoid inhaling any dust from any brake surface! When cleaning brake surfaces, use a commercially available brake cleaning fluid.

1. Drum attaching screw
2. Rubber brake hose
3. Maximum drum diameter marking
4. Brake drum

Rear brake overall view

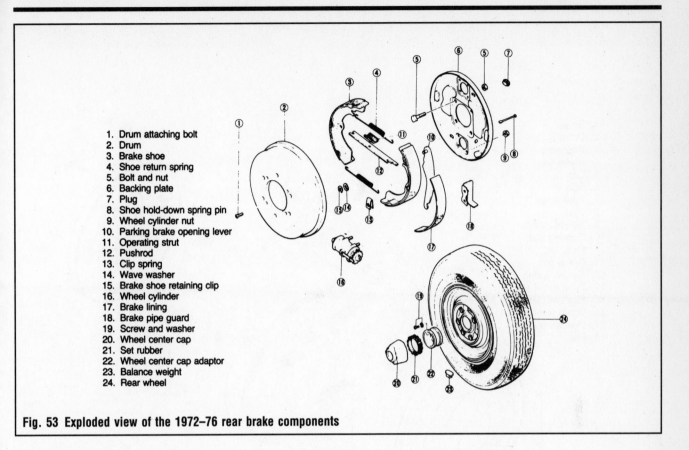

1. Drum attaching bolt
2. Drum
3. Brake shoe
4. Shoe return spring
5. Bolt and nut
6. Backing plate
7. Plug
8. Shoe hold-down spring pin
9. Wheel cylinder nut
10. Parking brake opening lever
11. Operating strut
12. Pushrod
13. Clip spring
14. Wave washer
15. Brake shoe retaining clip
16. Wheel cylinder
17. Brake lining
18. Brake pipe guard
19. Screw and washer
20. Wheel center cap
21. Set rubber
22. Wheel center cap adaptor
23. Balance weight
24. Rear wheel

Fig. 53 Exploded view of the 1972–76 rear brake components

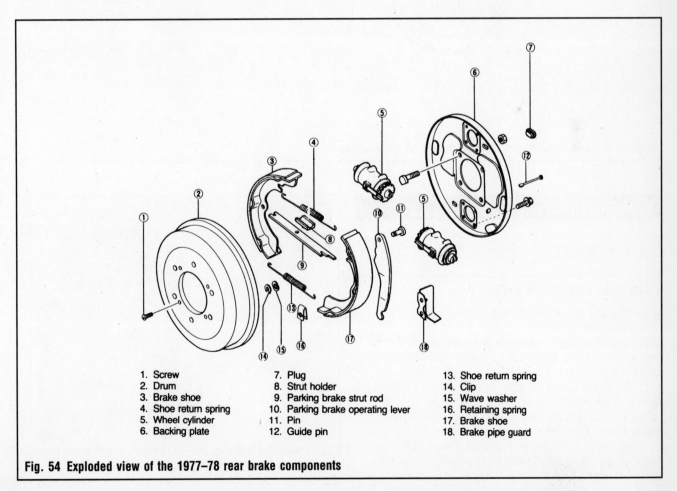

1. Screw	7. Plug	13. Shoe return spring
2. Drum	8. Strut holder	14. Clip
3. Brake shoe	9. Parking brake strut rod	15. Wave washer
4. Shoe return spring	10. Parking brake operating lever	16. Retaining spring
5. Wheel cylinder	11. Pin	17. Brake shoe
6. Backing plate	12. Guide pin	18. Brake pipe guard

Fig. 54 Exploded view of the 1977–78 rear brake components

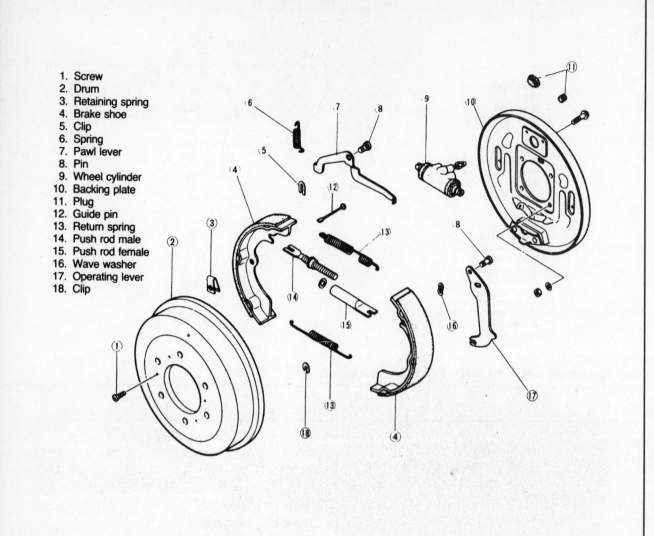

1. Screw
2. Drum
3. Retaining spring
4. Brake shoe
5. Clip
6. Spring
7. Pawl lever
8. Pin
9. Wheel cylinder
10. Backing plate
11. Plug
12. Guide pin
13. Return spring
14. Push rod male
15. Push rod female
16. Wave washer
17. Operating lever
18. Clip

Fig. 55 Exploded view of the 1979–86 rear brake components

Brake Drums

REMOVAL & INSTALLATION

▶ **See Figures 56, 57, 58 and 59**

1. Raise and support the rear end on jackstands.
2. Remove the wheels.
3. Remove the drum attaching screws and insert them in the threaded holes in the drum. Turn the screws inward, evenly, to force the rum off the hub.
4. Thoroughly inspect the drum. Discard a cracked drum. If the drum is suspected of being out of round, or shows signs of wear or has a ridged or rough surface, have it turned on a lathe at a machine shop. The maximum oversize is stamped into the drum.
5. Installation is the reverse of removal. Make sure that the holes are aligned for the attaching screws. Tighten the screws evenly to install the drum.

To remove the brake drums, matchmark the drum to the center hub, then remove the drum attaching screws . . .

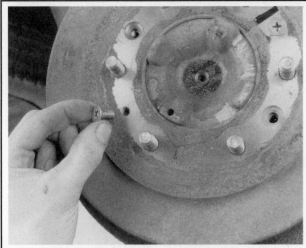

. . . and insert them into the threaded holes in the drum—tighten the screws evenly to draw the drum off the hub

Fig. 57 If a tool mark ridge is visible in the drum, measure the inside diameter to determine if the drum is over the maximum allowable size; if so, the drum must be replaced

Once it is free of the center hub, grasp the drum and pull it free of the rear axle

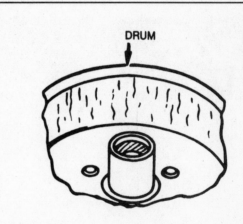

Fig. 58 Look for small heat checks that may be able to be machined out of the drum—excessive checking may require replacement

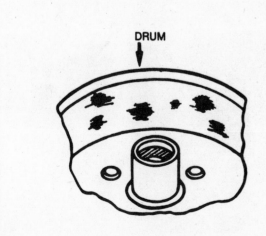

Fig. 56 Look for hard or chill spots on the drum surface

Fig. 59 If the drum is in good condition, lightly sand the inside surface to deglaze the drum

Brake Shoes

REMOVAL & INSTALLATION

◆ See Figure 60

The purchase of an inexpensive brake spring tool will make this job a lot easier.

1. Raise and support the rear end on jackstands.

✳✳ CAUTION

Brake shoes contain asbestos, which has been determined to be a cancer causing agent. Never clean the brake surfaces with compressed air! Avoid inhaling any dust from any brake surface! When cleaning brake surfaces, use a commercially available brake cleaning fluid.

Remove the brake shoe retracting springs . . .

Rear brake assembly overall view

. . . and the hold-down spring clips

To replace the rear brake shoes, start by cleaning the brake assembly; follow all local rules and regulations, as well as the cleaning product's directions—NEVER use compressed air to blow off brake dust

Grasp the brake shoes and spread them apart until they clear the anchor plate at the bottom center . . .

. . . then disconnect the parking brake cable from the parking brake lever. An extra pair of hands may help ease the removal of the parking brake cable

Finally, remove the brake shoes—shown here with the top retracting spring and brake adjuster, which were hidden previously by the axle flange

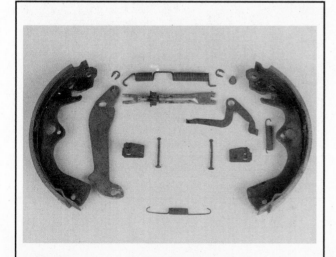

Rear brake shoe assembly—exploded view

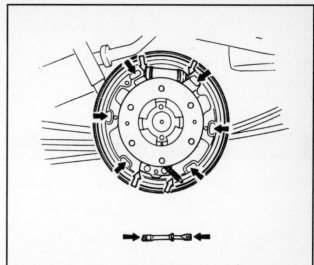

Fig. 60 Lubrication points prior to installing the brake shoes—take care not to get any grease on the shoes or drum

2. Remove the drums.

3. Remove the retracting springs.

4. Remove the hold-down springs and guide pins by turning the collars 90° with a pliers, or spring tool, releasing the springs.

5. Remove the parking brake link and disconnect the parking brake cable from the lever.

6. Remove the adjusting pawl and spring.

7. Remove the shoes, noting in which place the shoe with the longer lining is installed.

8. Inspect the shoes for cracks, heat checking or contamination by oil or grease. Minimum lining thickness is 1.00mm (0.039 in.). If heat checking or discoloration is noted, the wheel cylinders are probably at fault and will have to be rebuilt or replaced.

➡Never replace the shoes on one side of the truck, only! Always replace shoes on both sides!

9. Clean the backing plate with an approved cleaning fluid.

10. Lubricate the threads of the starwheel with lithium based or silicone based grease. Apply a small dab of lithium or silicone based grease to the pads on which the brake shoes ride.

To install:

11. Transfer the parking brake lever to the new shoe.

12. Position the shoes on the backing plate.

13. Connect the parking brake cable to the lever.

14. Install the hold-down springs and guide pins.

15. Install the adjusting pawl and spring.

16. Install the adjusting screw assembly.

17. Install the retracting springs.

18. Install the drums.

19. Working through the 2 holes in the backing plate, reach through the hole in the center with a brake adjusting spoon and turn the starwheel screw until the wheel is locked, that is, it can't be turned by hand.

20. Reach through the outside hole with a small bar and hold off the adjusting pawl while backing off the star-wheel about 6–7 clicks, or until the wheel is free to rotate.

➡**The adjustment should be the same on both wheels.**

21. Adjust the parking brake.
22. Operate the brake pedal a few times. If the brakes feel at all spongy, bleed the system.

Wheel Cylinder

REMOVAL & INSTALLATION

1. Raise and support the rear end on jackstands.
2. Remove the brake drum and shoes.
3. Disconnect and plug the brake line(s) at the wheel cylinder.
4. Remove the attaching nuts from behind the backing plate and remove the wheel cylinder.
5. Installation is the reverse of removal.

OVERHAUL

▶ **See Figures 61 and 62**

1. Remove the wheel cylinder.
2. Remove the piston and adjusting screw, then remove the boot and adjuster.
3. Using compressed air in the inlet port, blow out the piston cup, expander and spring.
4. Clean all parts in clean brake fluid.

5. Inspect all parts for wear or damage. Replace any worn, discolored, misshapen or suspect part. The cylinder bore may be honed to remove light scoring, pitting or discoloration. If honing cannot polish the interior, discard the cylinder. Check the piston-to-bore clearance. If the clearance exceeds 0.15mm (0.0059 in.), replace the cylinder.

6. Assembly is the reverse of disassembly. Coat all parts in clean brake fluid before assembly.

7. Install the wheel cylinder and all other parts. Bleed the system.

. . . **remove the two attaching bolts** . . .

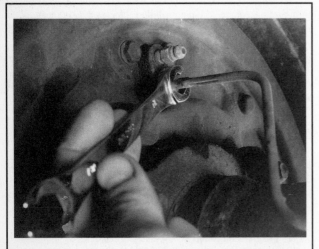

To remove the rear wheel cylinder, remove the brake shoes and unbolt the brake line attached to the back of the wheel cylinder, . . .

. . . **and lift the wheel cylinder off the brake backing plate**

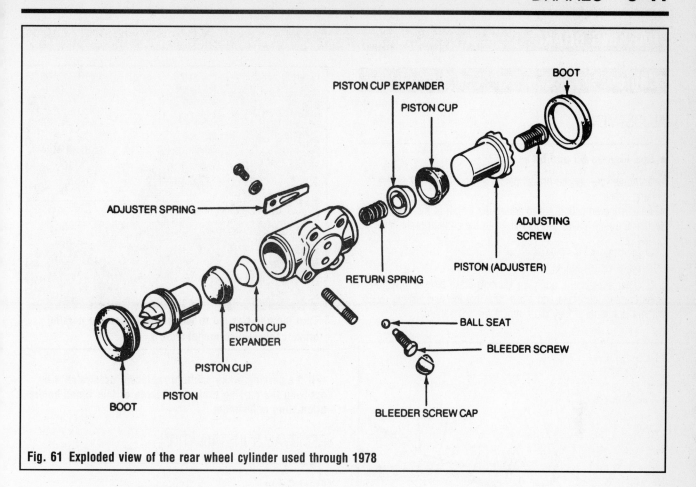

Fig. 61 Exploded view of the rear wheel cylinder used through 1978

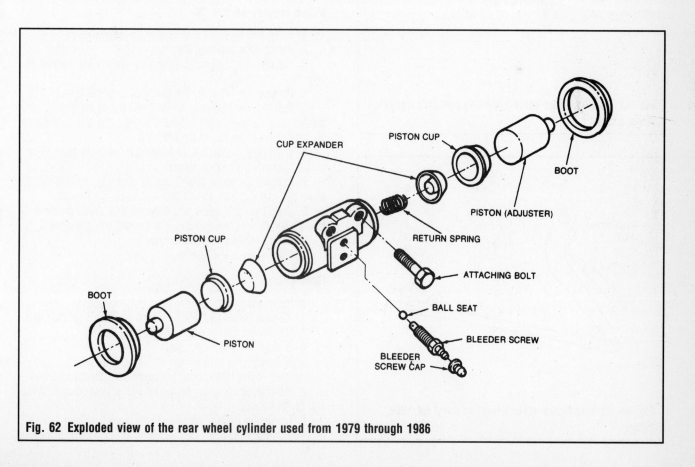

Fig. 62 Exploded view of the rear wheel cylinder used from 1979 through 1986

PARKING BRAKE

Cables

ADJUSTMENT

◆ **See Figures 63 and 64**

1. Adjust the service brakes before attempting to adjust the parking brake.

2. Use the adjusting nut to adjust the length of the front cable so that the rear brakes are locked when the parking brake lever is pulled out:
- 1971–84: 5–10 notches
- 1986: 11–13 notches

3. After adjustment, apply the parking brake several times. Release the parking brake and make sure that the rear wheels rotate without dragging. If they drag, repeat the adjustment.

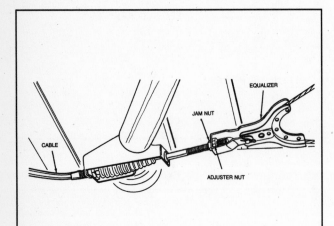

Fig. 63 Parking brake cable adjusting point for trucks through 1984

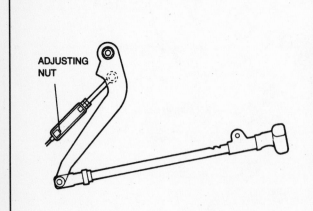

Fig. 64 Parking brake cable adjusting point for 1986 trucks

Turn the adjuster nut to loosen or tighten the parking brake cable—1986 model shown

➡ If the parking brake cable is replaced, prestretch it by applying the parking brake hard three or four times before attempting adjustment.

REMOVAL & INSTALLATION

Front Cable

◆ **See Figures 65 and 66**

1. Raise and support the front end on jackstands.

2. Remove the adjusting nut.

3. Separate the front cable from the equalizer and remove the jam nut.

4. Remove the return spring and boot from the housing.

5. Pull the lower housing forward and out of the slotted frame bracket. Slip the cable shaft sideways through the slot until the cable and housing are free of the bracket.

6. Disengage the cable connector from the brake lever by removing the clevis pin and retainer.

7. Remove the upper cable housing retaining clip and pull the cable and housing from the slotted bracket on the firewall.

8. Push the cable, cable housing and dust shield grommet through the firewall opening and into the engine compartment.

9. Remove the cable and housing.

10. Installation is the reverse of removal.

Rear Cables

1. Raise and support the rear end on jackstands.

2. Remove the pin and disconnect the equalizer from the clevis.

3. Disconnect the right-hand cable from the left.

4. Remove the rear brake shoes.

5. Disengage the cables from the brake shoe levers.

6. Remove the cable housing retainer from the backing plate.

7. Pull the return spring to release the retainer plate from the end of the housing.

8. Loosen the cable housing-to-frame bracket locknut and remove the forward end of the cable housing from the frame bracket.

9. Remove the cable housing retaining clip bolts.

10. Disengage the cable housing-to-frame tension springs and pull the cable out of the backing plate.

11. Installation is the reverse of removal.

Parking Brake Warning Light Switch

REMOVAL & INSTALLATION

1. Apply the parking brake to provide clearance between the switch assembly and the switch stop tab on the parking brake lever shaft.

2. Disconnect the switch wiring connector.

3. Remove the switch from its mounting bracket.

4. Install the attaching screws.

5. Connect the switch wire connector.

6. Turn the ignition switch **ON** and check the operation of the switch. No adjustment to the switch is possible. If it is defective, replace the switch.

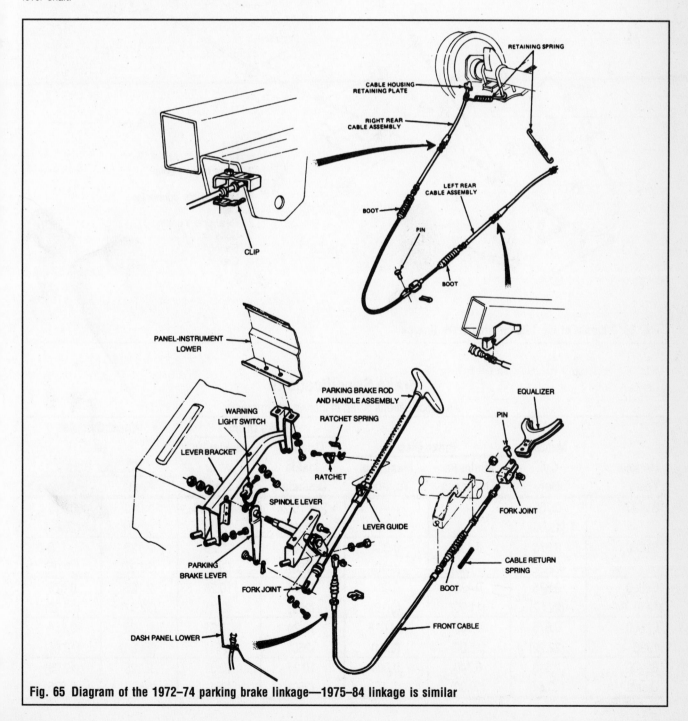

Fig. 65 Diagram of the 1972–74 parking brake linkage—1975–84 linkage is similar

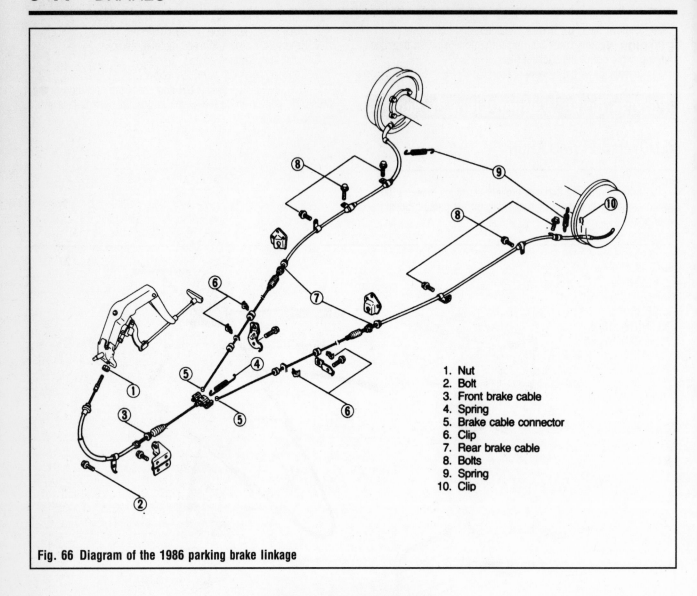

1. Nut
2. Bolt
3. Front brake cable
4. Spring
5. Brake cable connector
6. Clip
7. Rear brake cable
8. Bolts
9. Spring
10. Clip

Fig. 66 Diagram of the 1986 parking brake linkage

Brake Specifications

All specifications given in inches (millimeters)

Models/ Years	Master Cyl. Bore	Brake Disc		Brake Drum		Wheel Cylinder or Caliper Bore	
		Minimum Thickness	Maximum Run-out	Original Inside Diameter	Maximum Wear Limit	Front	Rear
B1600	0.750 (19.05)	—	—	F/R 10.24 (260)	F/R 10.28 (261)	1.000 (25.4)	0.813 (20.64)
B1800	0.875 (22.22)	0.433 (11.00)	0.004 (0.10)	10.24 (260)	10.28 (261)	2.125 (53.97)	0.750 (19.05)
B2000 1979–84	0.875 (22.22)	0.433 (11.00)	0.004 (0.10)	10.24 (260)	10.28 (261)	2.125 (53.97)	0.875 (22.22)
B2000 1986	0.875 (22.22)	0.709 (18.00)	0.0016 (0.04)	10.24 (260)	10.31 (261)	2.126 (54.00)	0.750 (19.05)
B2200 Diesel	0.813 (20.64)	0.748 (19.00)	0.004 (0.10)	10.24 (260)	10.31 (261)	2.125 (53.97)	(19.05) 0.875

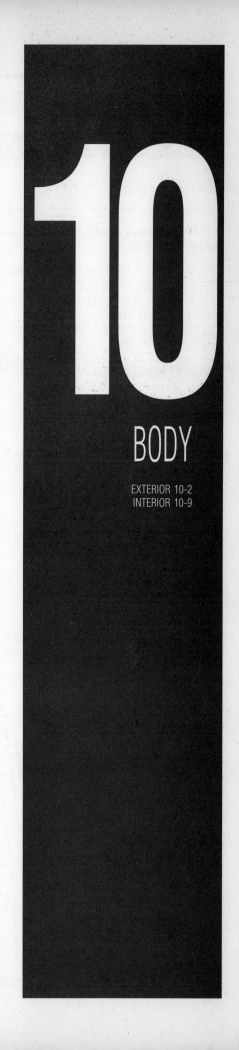

10

BODY

EXTERIOR

Doors

REMOVAL & INSTALLATION

→**If the door being removed is to be reinstalled, matchmark the hinge position.**

1. If the door is to be replaced with a new one, remove the trim panels, weathersheets and all molding.
2. If the door is to be replaced with a new one, remove the glass, locks and latches.
3. Support the door and remove the hinge-to-body attaching bolts. Lift the door from the truck.
4. Installation is the reverse of removal. Perform the alignment procedures indicated below.

ALIGNMENT

→**The holes for the hinges are oversized to provide for latitude in alignment. Align the door hinges first, then the striker.**

Hinges
♦ **See Figures 1 and 2**

1. If a new door is being installed, first mount the door and tighten the hinge bolts lightly. If the door has not been removed, determine which hinge bolts must be loosed to effect alignment.
2. Loosen the necessary bolts just enough to allow the door to be moved with a padded prybar.
3. Move the door in small movements and check the fit after each movement. Be sure that there is no binding or interference with adjacent panels. Keep repeating this procedure until the door

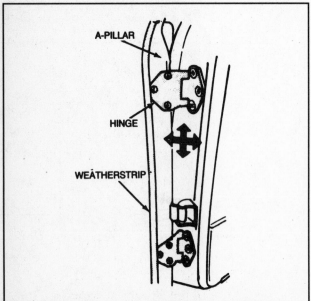

Fig. 1 Door hinge adjustments for 1972–84 trucks

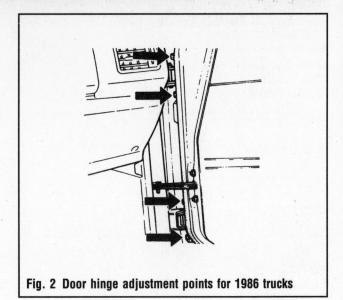

Fig. 2 Door hinge adjustment points for 1986 trucks

is properly aligned. Tighten all the bolts. Shims may be either fabricated or purchased to install behind the hinges as an aid in alignment.

Striker Plate
♦ **See Figure 3**

→**The striker is attached to the pillar using oversized holes, providing latitude in movement.**

Striker adjustment is made by loosening the bolts and moving the striker plate in the desired direction or adding or deleting shims behind the plate, or both. The striker is properly adjusted when the locking latch enters the striker without rubbing and the door closes fully and solidly, with no play when closed.

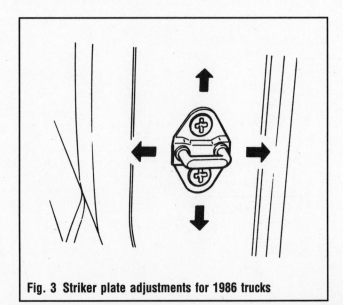

Fig. 3 Striker plate adjustments for 1986 trucks

Hood

REMOVAL & INSTALLATION

→**You are going to need an assistant for this job.**

Models With Self-Supporting Hood

1. Open the hood and trace the outline of the hinges on the body.
2. While an assistant holds the hood, remove the cotter pin from the right side hood stop retaining pin.
3. Remove the retaining pin and the hood stop.
4. Tilt the hood forward and move the torsion bar to one side.
5. Remove the hinge-to-body bolts and lift the hood off.
6. Installation is the reverse of removal. Align the outlines previously made. Check that the hood closes properly. Adjust hood alignment, if necessary.

Mark the hood hinge location on the hood . . .

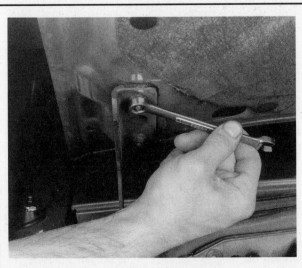

. . . then remove the hood attaching nuts

Models With Hood Prop
▶ **See Figures 4 and 5**

1. Outline the hinge position on the hood.
2. Support the hood and remove the hinge-to-hood bolts. Lift off the hood.
3. Installation of the hood is the reverse of removal. Check the hood for fit and closure. Adjust the hood alignment, if necessary.

ALIGNMENT

▶ **See Figure 6**

On self-supporting hoods, alignment can be adjusted front-to-rear or side-to-side by loosening the hood-to-hinge or hinge-to-body bolts. The front edge of the hood can be adjusted for closing height by adding or deleting shims under the hinges. The rear edge of the hood can be adjusted for closing height by raising or lowering the rear hood bumpers.

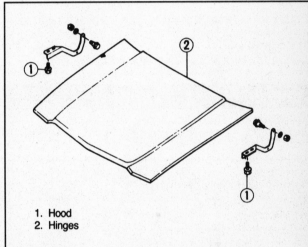

1. Hood
2. Hinges

Fig. 4 Exploded view of the prop rod style hood components

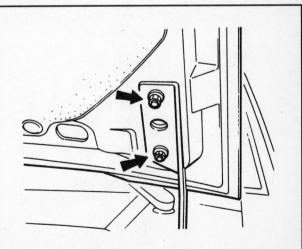

Fig. 5 Hood-to-hinge attachment nuts for prop rod style hoods

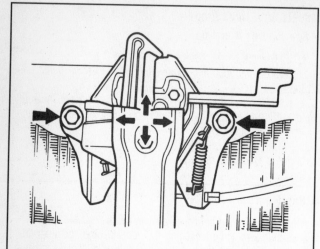

Fig. 6 Hood latch adjustment points for prop rod style hoods—other style similar

. . . then invert the hinged side support and lift up on the tailgate . . .

On hoods supported with a prop, alignment is accomplished by loosening the lockplate bolts and moving the lockplate up or down; side-to-side.

Tailgate

REMOVAL & INSTALLATION

1. Open and support the tailgate.
2. Remove the hinge pins by removing the cotter pins and washers, then driving the hinge pins out.
3. Lift off the tailgate.
4. Installation is the reverse of removal.

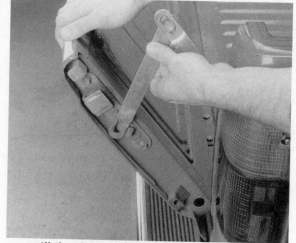

. . . until the slot in the side support aligns with the rectangular post, and pull the support free

Make alignment marks on the tailgate hinges, . . .

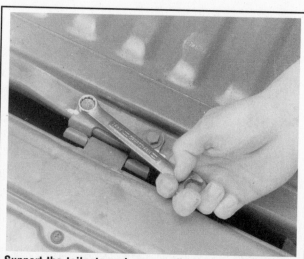

Support the tailgate and remove the tailgate hinge-to-body bolts

Windshield

REMOVAL & INSTALLATION

➡**You'll need an assistant for this job.**

1972–84 Vehicles

▶ **See Figures 7 thru 12**

1. Remove the wiper arms.
2. Carefully snap the windshield molding from the weather-stripping.
3. Using a wood spatula, break the adhesive bond between the weatherstripping and the body flange.
4. Push out the inner lip of the weatherstripping, from inside the truck, while pushing out on the glass.
5. With the aid of an assistant, remove the glass and weather-stripping.

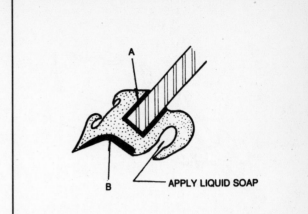

Fig. 9 Apply bonding agent at points A and B—liquid soap in the inside channel will ease installation

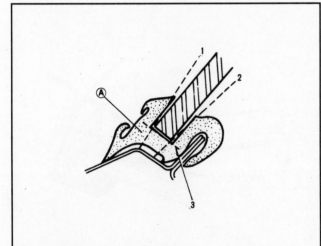

Fig. 7 Cutting the sealer at points 1, 2 and 3 from molding A

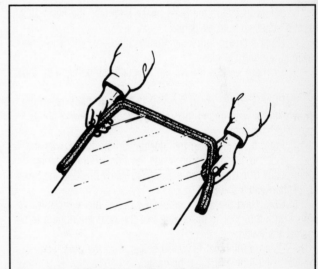

Fig. 10 Installing the weatherstripping

Fig. 8 Apply primer in the area shown

Fig. 11 Fitting the string into the inside channel

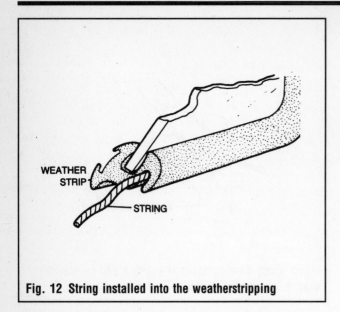

Fig. 12 String installed into the weatherstripping

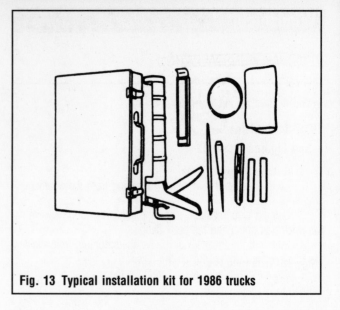

Fig. 13 Typical installation kit for 1986 trucks

6. Before installing the glass, make sure that you clean all of the old adhesive from all parts.

7. Place a coat of primer in the molding. Install the weatherstripping around the glass.

8. Liberally wet the groove in the weatherstripping with liquid soap.

9. Place a string, about 4mm (0.157 in.) in diameter, in the groove all the way around the weatherstripping. Allow a good length to hang free.

10. Place the windshield into position in the frame, with the free end of the string hanging inside the truck. Pull the string while pushing inward on the glass, to properly position the inner lip of the weatherstripping.

11. Go around the inner and outer sides of the weatherstripping with a thin tool to make sure that the weatherstripping is flat against the frame.

12. Using a thin coat of rubber sealer, seal the outer edge of the weatherstripping against the frame.

13. Snap the molding into place.

1986 Vehicles

♦ **See Figures 13 thru 20**

➡A special kit, Mazda #49 0305 870A, is available for replacing glass. The references to adhesives and bonding agents contained in this procedure are taking for granted that this kit is being used. Aftermarket kits are also available which contain all the necessary equipment.

1. Remove the wiper arms.

2. Remove the rear view mirror and front pillar trim molding.

3. Cover the sheet metal around the windshield with masking tape to protect it from scratches.

4. Remove the windshield trim molding. It's best to use a tool made for that purpose, although it can be pried off. If a special tool is not used, it's very easy to damage the molding, so be careful!

5. Drill a small hole through the rubber weatherstripping at its base. Pass a length of piano wire through the hole. Wrap each

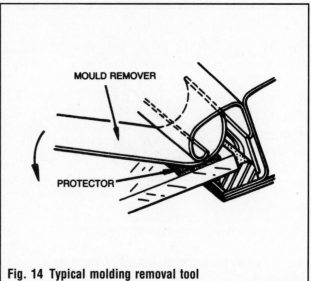

Fig. 14 Typical molding removal tool

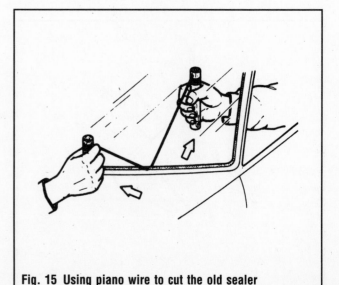

Fig. 15 Using piano wire to cut the old sealer

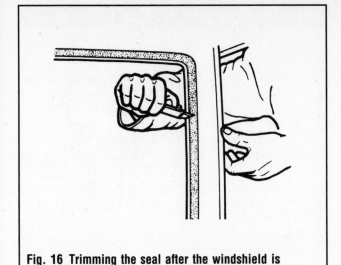

Fig. 16 Trimming the seal after the windshield is removed

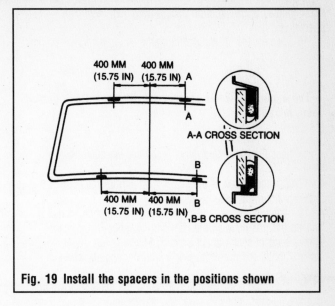

A-A CROSS SECTION

B-B CROSS SECTION

Fig. 19 Install the spacers in the positions shown

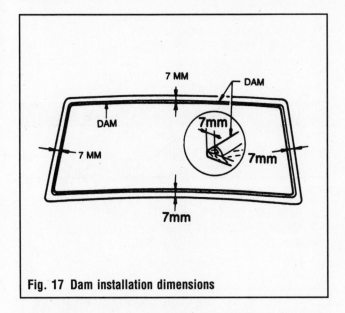

Fig. 17 Dam installation dimensions

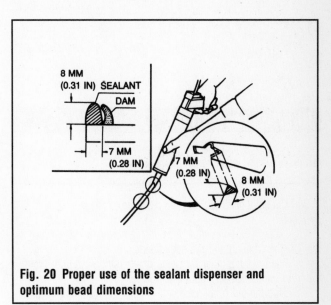

Fig. 20 Proper use of the sealant dispenser and optimum bead dimensions

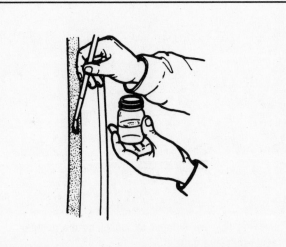

Fig. 18 Apply primer to the bonding areas of the frame and glass

end of the wire around a wood dowel. Grip one dowel in each hand, or have your assistant take one dowel, and, using a sawing motion, pass the wire all the way around the perimeter of the weatherstripping to cut through the sealer.

6. Remove the glass.

7. Using a sharp knife, cut away the old sealer so that a 1–2mm (0.039–0.079 in.) thickness of old sealer remains around the circumference of the frame. If the old sealer comes completely off in any spot, rebuild that spot to the 1–2mm (0.039–0.079 in.) thickness with new sealer.

8. Secure a new windshield trim dam to the glass with a glass cement. The new dam should be positioned so that its outer edge is 7mm (0.276 in.) from the edge of the glass, with the lip facing outward.

9. Apply a thin coat of primer to the bonding areas of the frame and glass. Allow the primer to dry for 30 minutes. Do not allow any dirt or dust to contact the primer while

it's drying. If primer gets on your hands, wash it off immediately.

10. Cement the spacers to the frame as shown in the accompanying illustration.

➡**The upper and lower spacers are different. Don't get them mixed up.**

11. Install the molding clips. If any are defective, replace them.

12. Cut the nozzle of the sealer tube as illustrated, so that it will run along the edge of the glass.

13. Apply sealer around the whole circumference so that it will fill the gap between the dam and the edge of the glass, with a bead of sealer about 8mm (0.315 in.) high. Keep the bead smooth and even, shaping it with the spatula where necessary.

14. Open the door windows. Position the glass in the frame, pushing inward lightly to compress the sealer.

15. Trim away excess sealer and fill any gaps which may have appeared. Give the sealer at least 5 hours to dry at 68°F (20°C); 24 hours at 41°F (5°C).

16. Leak test the glass.

Rear Window Glass

REMOVAL & INSTALLATION

1. Carefully snap the molding from the weatherstripping.

2. Using a wood spatula, break the adhesive bond between the weatherstripping and the body flange.

3. Push out the inner lip of the weatherstripping, from inside the truck, while pushing out on the glass.

4. With the aid of an assistant, remove the glass and weatherstripping.

5. Before installing the glass, make sure that you clean all of the old adhesive from all parts.

6. Place a coat of primer in the molding. Install the weatherstripping around the glass.

7. Liberally wet the groove in the weatherstripping with liquid soap.

8. Place a string, about 4mm (0.157 in.) in diameter, in the groove all the way around the weatherstripping. Allow a good length to hang free.

9. Place the glass into position in the frame, with the free end of the string hanging inside the truck. Pull the string while pushing inward on the glass, to properly position the inner lip of the weatherstripping.

10. Go around the inner and outer sides of the weatherstripping with a thin tool to make sure that the weatherstripping is flat against the frame.

11. Using a thin coat of rubber sealer, seal the outer edge of the weatherstripping against the frame.

12. Snap the molding into place.

Front Bumper

REMOVAL & INSTALLATION

1971–84 Vehicles

1. Support the bumper.
2. Remove the bumper bracket-to-frame bolts.
3. Remove the bumper-to-bracket bolts.
4. Installation is the reverse of removal.

1986 Vehicles

1. Remove the combination lamps from the grille.
2. Remove the grille.
3. Unplug the wiring from the lamps on the bumper skirt.
4. Remove the bumper skirt and end pieces.
5. Support the bumper.
6. Remove the bumper bracket-to-frame bolts.
7. Remove the bumper-to-bracket bolts.
8. Installation is the reverse of removal.

Rear Bumper

REMOVAL & INSTALLATION

1. Support the bumper.
2. Remove the bumper bracket-to-frame bolts.
3. Remove the bumper-to-bracket bolts.
4. Installation is the reverse of removal.

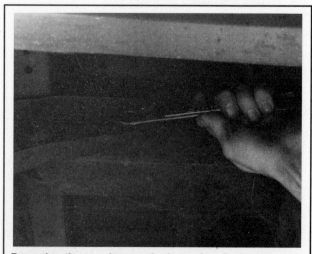

Removing the rear bumper by loosening the bumper bracket-to-frame bolts

Grille

REMOVAL & INSTALLATION

1971–84 Vehicles

1. Open the hood.
2. Remove the grille retaining screws and lift off the grille.
3. Installation is the reverse of removal.

INTERIOR

Door Panels

REMOVAL & INSTALLATION

1972–84 VEHICLES
▶ **See Figures 21 and 22**

1. Invert the door and window handles for easy access to the retaining pins.
2. Push in slightly on the door panel to expose the retaining pin, and drive out the pin from the window regulator handle, from the bottom side, using a small punch.
3. Drive the tapered pin from the door handle in the same manner.
4. Remove the plastic molding from the arm rest, revealing the arm rest attaching screws.
5. Remove the arm rest.
6. Carefully slip a thin prying instrument behind the door panel and slide it along until you hit one of the eight retaining clips. Pry as close as possible to the clip to snap the clip from

1986 Vehicles

1. Open the hood.
2. Remove the combination lamps from the grille.
3. Remove the grille retaining screws and lift off the grille.
4. Installation is the reverse of removal.

the door. Be very careful to avoid tearing the clip from the panel.
7. Once all eight clips have been pried loose, lift the door panel from the bottom channel.
8. Installation is the reverse of removal. When snapping the clips into place, make sure that they are squarely over the holes to avoid bending them.

1986 Vehicles
▶ **See Figure 23**

1. Remove the attaching screw and door handle.
2. Remove the armrest.
3. Push in on the door panel, slightly, at the window handle and pry off the snapring retaining the handle to the regulator stem. Remove the handle.
4. Carefully slip a thin prying instrument behind the door panel and slide it along until you hit one of the retaining clips. Pry as close as possible to the clip to snap the clip from the door. Be very careful to avoid tearing the clip from the panel.
5. Pry out each clip, in turn, and lift off the door panel.
6. Installation is the reverse of removal. When snapping the clips into place, make sure that they are squarely over the holes to avoid bending them.

An inexpensive tool designed for window crank removal eases the process—slip the tool between the door panel and the window crank . . .

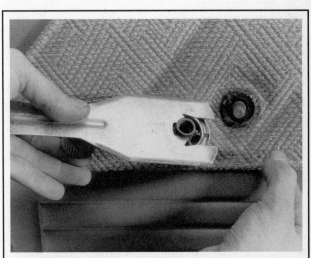

. . . catch the clip as it is pushed out and remove the crank handle

1. Striker seat
2. Door lock striker
3. Door lock rack
4. Door lock
5. Seat No. 1
6. Outer handle
7. Seat No. 2
8. Door hinge
9. Bush
10. Hinge pin
11. Spacer
12. Door checker set plate
13. Check sub spring
14. Check spring
15. Checker washer
16. Checker pin
17. Checker roller
18. Window regulator
19. Escutcheon crown
20. Handle escutcheon
21. Regulator handle
22. Tapered pin
23. Inner handle
24. Anti-burst block
25. Anti-burst block shim
26. Arm rest
27. Garnish

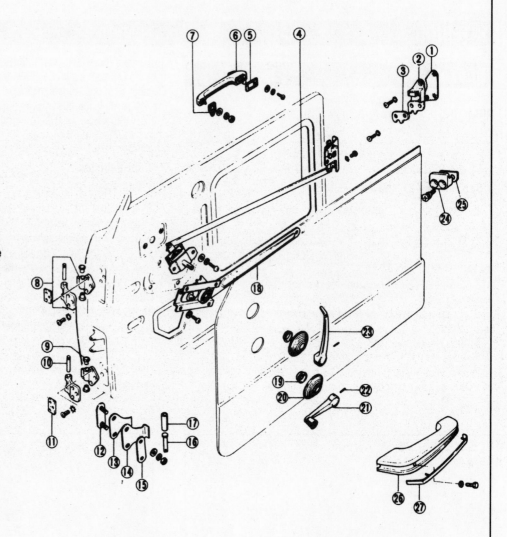

Fig. 21 Exploded view of the door for 1972–76 trucks

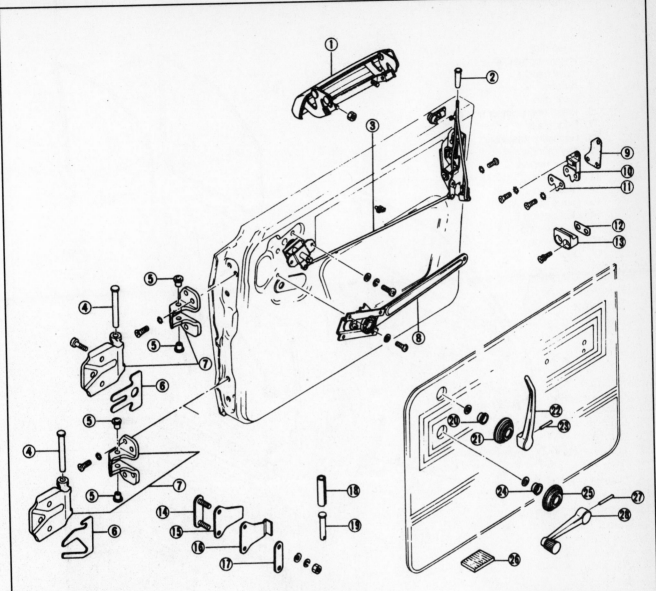

1. Outer handle
2. Door lock knob
3. Door lock
4. Hinge pin
5. Bush
6. Hinge spacer
7. Door hinge
8. Window regulator
9. Striker seat
10. Door lock striker
11. Door lock
12. Anti-burst block shim
13. Anti-burst block
14. Door checker set plate
15. Check sub spring
16. Check spring
17. Checker washer
18. Checker roller
19. Checker pin
20. Escutcheon crown
21. Handle escutcheon
22. Inner handle
23. Tapered pin
24. Escutcheon crown
25. Handle escutcheon
26. Cushion
27. Tapered pin
28. Regulator handle

Fig. 22 Exploded view of the door for 1977–84 trucks

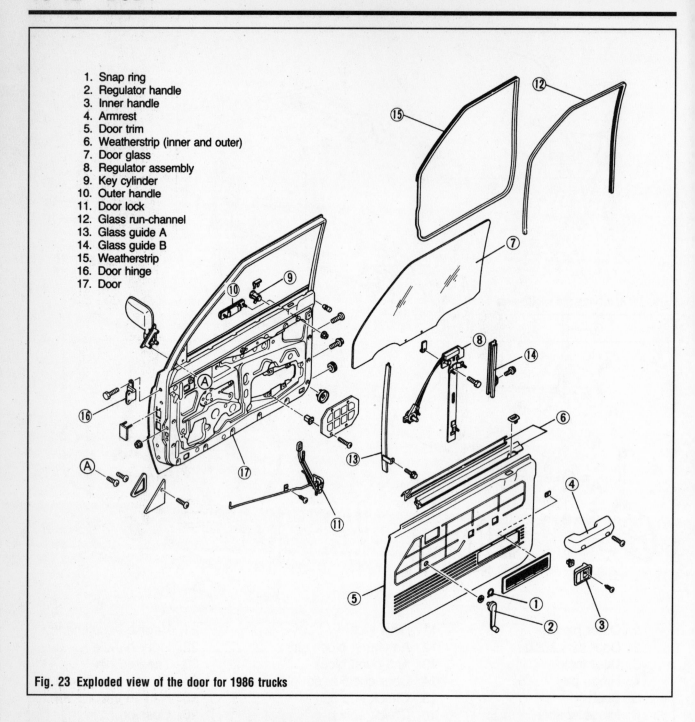

1. Snap ring
2. Regulator handle
3. Inner handle
4. Armrest
5. Door trim
6. Weatherstrip (inner and outer)
7. Door glass
8. Regulator assembly
9. Key cylinder
10. Outer handle
11. Door lock
12. Glass run-channel
13. Glass guide A
14. Glass guide B
15. Weatherstrip
16. Door hinge
17. Door

Fig. 23 Exploded view of the door for 1986 trucks

Door Glass and Regulator

REMOVAL & INSTALLATION

1972–84 Vehicles

◆ **See Figures 24 and 25**

1. Remove the trim panel from the door.
2. Remove the window frame assembly from the door by removing the seven attaching screws.
3. Lower the door glass.
4. Disengage the regulator roller and arm from the glass.

5. Tilt the glass slightly and slide it up and out of the door.
6. Remove and discard the tape from the door glass channel.
7. Unbolt and remove the regulator.
8. Installation is the reverse of removal. Use new tape in the channel. Use waterproof sealer on the window frame screws.

1986 Vehicles

◆ **See Figures 26, 27, 28 and 29**

1. Remove the door panel.
2. Remove the weatherscreening carefully, so that it can be reused.

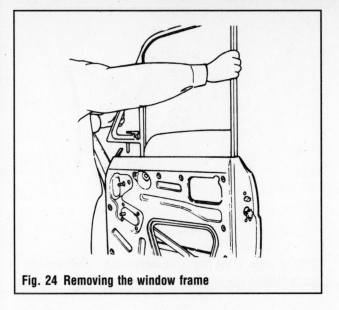

Fig. 24 Removing the window frame

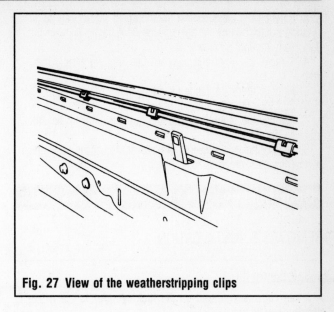

Fig. 27 View of the weatherstripping clips

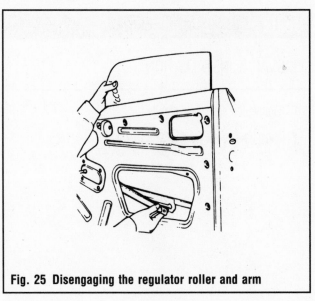

Fig. 25 Disengaging the regulator roller and arm

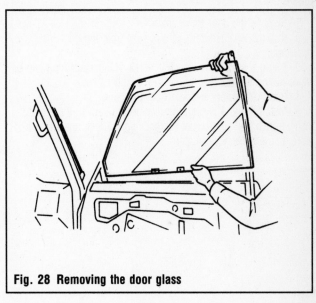

Fig. 28 Removing the door glass

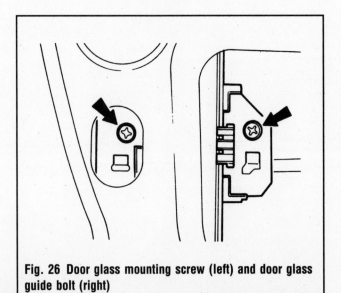

Fig. 26 Door glass mounting screw (left) and door glass guide bolt (right)

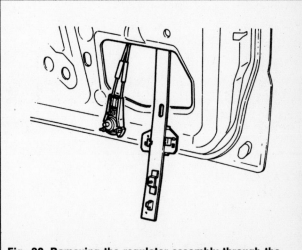

Fig. 29 Removing the regulator assembly through the access hole

3. Position the glass so that the mounting screws can be accessed through one of the holes in the door frame. Remove the door glass mounting screws.

4. Remove the inner and outer weatherstripping around the frame.

5. Remove the glass guide mounting bolt.

6. Pull the glass up and out of the door.

7. Remove the mounting bolts and pull the regulator assembly from the access hole.

8. Installation is the reverse of removal. Adjust the door glass so that it closes properly.

Door Locks

REMOVAL & INSTALLATION

▶ **See Figure 30**

➡**A key code is stamped on the lock cylinder to aid in replacing lost keys.**

1. Remove the door trim panel.

2. Pull the weathersheet, gently, away from the door lock access holes.

3. Using a screwdriver, push the lock cylinder retaining clip upward, noting the position of the lock cylinder.

4. Remove the lock cylinder from the door.

5. Install the lock cylinder in reverse of removal. It's a good idea to open the window before checking the lock operation, just in case it doesn't work properly.

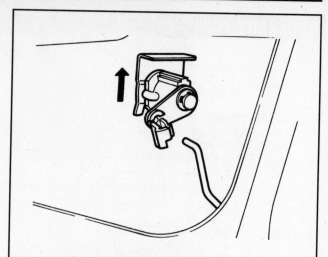

Fig. 30 View of the door lock mechanism—slide the clip up to release the lock from the door

Seats

REMOVAL & INSTALLATION

1. Remove the seat anchor bolts.
2. Lift out the seat.
3. Installation is the reverse of removal.

GLOSSARY

AIR/FUEL RATIO: The ratio of air-to-gasoline by weight in the fuel mixture drawn into the engine.

AIR INJECTION: One method of reducing harmful exhaust emissions by injecting air into each of the exhaust ports of an engine. The fresh air entering the hot exhaust manifold causes any remaining fuel to be burned before it can exit the tailpipe.

ALTERNATOR: A device used for converting mechanical energy into electrical energy.

AMMETER: An instrument, calibrated in amperes, used to measure the flow of an electrical current in a circuit. Ammeters are always connected in series with the circuit being tested.

AMPERE: The rate of flow of electrical current present when one volt of electrical pressure is applied against one ohm of electrical resistance.

ANALOG COMPUTER: Any microprocessor that uses similar (analogous) electrical signals to make its calculations.

ARMATURE: A laminated, soft iron core wrapped by a wire that converts electrical energy to mechanical energy as in a motor or relay. When rotated in a magnetic field, it changes mechanical energy into electrical energy as in a generator.

ATMOSPHERIC PRESSURE: The pressure on the Earth's surface caused by the weight of the air in the atmosphere. At sea level, this pressure is 14.7 psi at 32°F (101 kPa at 0°C).

ATOMIZATION: The breaking down of a liquid into a fine mist that can be suspended in air.

AXIAL PLAY: Movement parallel to a shaft or bearing bore.

BACKFIRE: The sudden combustion of gases in the intake or exhaust system that results in a loud explosion.

BACKLASH: The clearance or play between two parts, such as meshed gears.

BACKPRESSURE: Restrictions in the exhaust system that slow the exit of exhaust gases from the combustion chamber.

BAKELITE: A heat resistant, plastic insulator material commonly used in printed circuit boards and transistorized components.

BALL BEARING: A bearing made up of hardened inner and outer races between which hardened steel balls roll.

BALLAST RESISTOR: A resistor in the primary ignition circuit that lowers voltage after the engine is started to reduce wear on ignition components.

BEARING: A friction reducing, supportive device usually located between a stationary part and a moving part.

BIMETAL TEMPERATURE SENSOR: Any sensor or switch made of two dissimilar types of metal that bend when heated or cooled due to the different expansion rates of the alloys. These types of sensors usually function as an on/off switch.

BLOWBY: Combustion gases, composed of water vapor and unburned fuel, that leak past the piston rings into the crankcase during normal engine operation. These gases are removed by the PCV system to prevent the buildup of harmful acids in the crankcase.

BRAKE PAD: A brake shoe and lining assembly used with disc brakes.

BRAKE SHOE: The backing for the brake lining. The term is, however, usually applied to the assembly of the brake backing and lining.

BUSHING: A liner, usually removable, for a bearing; an anti-friction liner used in place of a bearing.

CALIPER: A hydraulically activated device in a disc brake system, which is mounted straddling the brake rotor (disc). The caliper contains at least one piston and two brake pads. Hydraulic pressure on the piston(s) forces the pads against the rotor.

CAMSHAFT: A shaft in the engine on which are the lobes (cams) which operate the valves. The camshaft is driven by the crankshaft, via a belt, chain or gears, at one half the crankshaft speed.

CAPACITOR: A device which stores an electrical charge.

CARBON MONOXIDE (CO): A colorless, odorless gas given off as a normal byproduct of combustion. It is poisonous and extremely dangerous in confined areas, building up slowly to toxic levels without warning if adequate ventilation is not available.

CARBURETOR: A device, usually mounted on the intake manifold of an engine, which mixes the air and fuel in the proper proportion to allow even combustion.

CATALYTIC CONVERTER: A device installed in the exhaust system, like a muffler, that converts harmful byproducts of combustion into carbon dioxide and water vapor by means of a heat-producing chemical reaction.

CENTRIFUGAL ADVANCE: A mechanical method of advancing the spark timing by using flyweights in the distributor that react to centrifugal force generated by the distributor shaft rotation.

CHECK VALVE: Any one-way valve installed to permit the flow of air, fuel or vacuum in one direction only.

CHOKE: A device, usually a moveable valve, placed in the intake path of a carburetor to restrict the flow of air.

CIRCUIT: Any unbroken path through which an electrical current can flow. Also used to describe fuel flow in some instances.

CIRCUIT BREAKER: A switch which protects an electrical circuit from overload by opening the circuit when the current flow exceeds a predetermined level. Some circuit breakers must be reset manually, while most reset automatically.

COIL (IGNITION): A transformer in the ignition circuit which steps up the voltage provided to the spark plugs.

COMBINATION MANIFOLD: An assembly which includes both the intake and exhaust manifolds in one casting.

COMBINATION VALVE: A device used in some fuel systems that routes fuel vapors to a charcoal storage canister instead of venting them into the atmosphere. The valve relieves fuel tank pressure and allows fresh air into the tank as the fuel level drops to prevent a vapor lock situation.

COMPRESSION RATIO: The comparison of the total volume of the cylinder and combustion chamber with the piston at BDC and the piston at TDC.

CONDENSER: 1. An electrical device which acts to store an electrical charge, preventing voltage surges. 2. A radiator-like device in the air conditioning system in which refrigerant gas condenses into a liquid, giving off heat.

CONDUCTOR: Any material through which an electrical current can be transmitted easily.

CONTINUITY: Continuous or complete circuit. Can be checked with an ohmmeter.

COUNTERSHAFT: An intermediate shaft which is rotated by a mainshaft and transmits, in turn, that rotation to a working part.

CRANKCASE: The lower part of an engine in which the crankshaft and related parts operate.

CRANKSHAFT: The main driving shaft of an engine which receives reciprocating motion from the pistons and converts it to rotary motion.

CYLINDER: In an engine, the round hole in the engine block in which the piston(s) ride.

CYLINDER BLOCK: The main structural member of an engine in which is found the cylinders, crankshaft and other principal parts.

CYLINDER HEAD: The detachable portion of the engine, usually fastened to the top of the cylinder block and containing all or most of the combustion chambers. On overhead valve engines, it contains the valves and their operating parts. On overhead cam engines, it contains the camshaft as well.

DEAD CENTER: The extreme top or bottom of the piston stroke.

DETONATION: An unwanted explosion of the air/fuel mixture in the combustion chamber caused by excess heat and compression, advanced timing, or an overly lean mixture. Also referred to as "ping".

DIAPHRAGM: A thin, flexible wall separating two cavities, such as in a vacuum advance unit.

DIESELING: A condition in which hot spots in the combustion chamber cause the engine to run on after the key is turned off.

DIFFERENTIAL: A geared assembly which allows the transmission of motion between drive axles, giving one axle the ability to turn faster than the other.

DIODE: An electrical device that will allow current to flow in one direction only.

DISC BRAKE: A hydraulic braking assembly consisting of a brake disc, or rotor, mounted on an axle, and a caliper assembly containing, usually two brake pads which are activated by hydraulic pressure. The pads are forced against the sides of the disc, creating friction which slows the vehicle.

DISTRIBUTOR: A mechanically driven device on an engine which is responsible for electrically firing the spark plug at a predetermined point of the piston stroke.

DOWEL PIN: A pin, inserted in mating holes in two different parts allowing those parts to maintain a fixed relationship.

DRUM BRAKE: A braking system which consists of two brake shoes and one or two wheel cylinders, mounted on a fixed backing plate, and a brake drum, mounted on an axle, which revolves around the assembly.

DWELL: The rate, measured in degrees of shaft rotation, at which an electrical circuit cycles on and off.

ELECTRONIC CONTROL UNIT (ECU): Ignition module, module, amplifier or igniter. See Module for definition.

ELECTRONIC IGNITION: A system in which the timing and firing of the spark plugs is controlled by an electronic control unit, usually called a module. These systems have no points or condenser.

END-PLAY: The measured amount of axial movement in a shaft.

ENGINE: A device that converts heat into mechanical energy.

EXHAUST MANIFOLD: A set of cast passages or pipes which conduct exhaust gases from the engine.

FEELER GAUGE: A blade, usually metal, of precisely predetermined thickness, used to measure the clearance between two parts.

FIRING ORDER: The order in which combustion occurs in the cylinders of an engine. Also the order in which spark is distributed to the plugs by the distributor.

FLOODING: The presence of too much fuel in the intake manifold and combustion chamber which prevents the air/fuel mixture from firing, thereby causing a no-start situation.

FLYWHEEL: A disc shaped part bolted to the rear end of the crankshaft. Around the outer perimeter is affixed the ring gear. The starter drive engages the ring gear, turning the flywheel, which rotates the crankshaft, imparting the initial starting motion to the engine.

FOOT POUND (ft. lbs. or sometimes, ft.lb.): The amount of energy or work needed to raise an item weighing one pound, a distance of one foot.

FUSE: A protective device in a circuit which prevents circuit overload by breaking the circuit when a specific amperage is present. The device is constructed around a strip or wire of a lower amperage rating than the circuit it is designed to protect. When an amperage higher than that stamped on the fuse is present in the circuit, the strip or wire melts, opening the circuit.

GEAR RATIO: The ratio between the number of teeth on meshing gears.

GENERATOR: A device which converts mechanical energy into electrical energy.

HEAT RANGE: The measure of a spark plug's ability to dissipate heat from its firing end. The higher the heat range, the hotter the plug fires.

HUB: The center part of a wheel or gear.

HYDROCARBON (HC): Any chemical compound made up of hydrogen and carbon. A major pollutant formed by the engine as a byproduct of combustion.

HYDROMETER: An instrument used to measure the specific gravity of a solution.

INCH POUND (inch lbs.; sometimes in.lb. or in. lbs.): One twelfth of a foot pound.

INDUCTION: A means of transferring electrical energy in the form of a magnetic field. Principle used in the ignition coil to increase voltage.

INJECTOR: A device which receives metered fuel under relatively low pressure and is activated to inject the fuel into the engine under relatively high pressure at a predetermined time.

INPUT SHAFT: The shaft to which torque is applied, usually carrying the driving gear or gears.

INTAKE MANIFOLD: A casting of passages or pipes used to conduct air or a fuel/air mixture to the cylinders.

JOURNAL: The bearing surface within which a shaft operates.

KEY: A small block usually fitted in a notch between a shaft and a hub to prevent slippage of the two parts.

MANIFOLD: A casting of passages or set of pipes which connect the cylinders to an inlet or outlet source.

MANIFOLD VACUUM: Low pressure in an engine intake manifold formed just below the throttle plates. Manifold vacuum is highest at idle and drops under acceleration.

MASTER CYLINDER: The primary fluid pressurizing device in a hydraulic system. In automotive use, it is found in brake and hydraulic clutch systems and is pedal activated, either directly or, in a power brake system, through the power booster.

MODULE: Electronic control unit, amplifier or igniter of solid state or integrated design which controls the current flow in the ignition primary circuit based on input from the pick-up coil. When the module opens the primary circuit, high secondary voltage is induced in the coil.

NEEDLE BEARING: A bearing which consists of a number (usually a large number) of long, thin rollers.

OHM: (Ω) The unit used to measure the resistance of conductor-to-electrical flow. One ohm is the amount of resistance that limits current flow to one ampere in a circuit with one volt of pressure.

OHMMETER: An instrument used for measuring the resistance, in ohms, in an electrical circuit.

OUTPUT SHAFT: The shaft which transmits torque from a device, such as a transmission.

OVERDRIVE: A gear assembly which produces more shaft revolutions than that transmitted to it.

OVERHEAD CAMSHAFT (OHC): An engine configuration in which the camshaft is mounted on top of the cylinder head and operates the valve either directly or by means of rocker arms.

OVERHEAD VALVE (OHV): An engine configuration in which all of the valves are located in the cylinder head and the camshaft is located in the cylinder block. The camshaft operates the valves via lifters and pushrods.

OXIDES OF NITROGEN (NOx): Chemical compounds of nitrogen produced as a byproduct of combustion. They combine with hydrocarbons to produce smog.

OXYGEN SENSOR: Used with the feedback system to sense the presence of oxygen in the exhaust gas and signal the computer which can reference the voltage signal to an air/fuel ratio.

PINION: The smaller of two meshing gears.

PISTON RING: An open-ended ring which fits into a groove on the outer diameter of the piston. Its chief function is to form a seal between the piston and cylinder wall. Most automotive pistons have three rings: two for compression sealing; one for oil sealing.

PRELOAD: A predetermined load placed on a bearing during assembly or by adjustment.

PRIMARY CIRCUIT: The low voltage side of the ignition system which consists of the ignition switch, ballast resistor or resistance wire, bypass, coil, electronic control unit and pick-up coil as well as the connecting wires and harnesses.

PRESS FIT: The mating of two parts under pressure, due to the inner diameter of one being smaller than the outer diameter of the other, or vice versa; an interference fit.

RACE: The surface on the inner or outer ring of a bearing on which the balls, needles or rollers move.

REGULATOR: A device which maintains the amperage and/or voltage levels of a circuit at predetermined values.

RELAY: A switch which automatically opens and/or closes a circuit.

RESISTANCE: The opposition to the flow of current through a circuit or electrical device, and is measured in ohms. Resistance is equal to the voltage divided by the amperage.

RESISTOR: A device, usually made of wire, which offers a preset amount of resistance in an electrical circuit.

RING GEAR: The name given to a ring-shaped gear attached to a differential case, or affixed to a flywheel or as part of a planetary gear set.

ROLLER BEARING: A bearing made up of hardened inner and outer races between which hardened steel rollers move.

ROTOR: 1. The disc-shaped part of a disc brake assembly, upon which the brake pads bear; also called, brake disc. 2. The device mounted atop the distributor shaft, which passes current to the distributor cap tower contacts.

SECONDARY CIRCUIT: The high voltage side of the ignition system, usually above 20,000 volts. The secondary includes the ignition coil, coil wire, distributor cap and rotor, spark plug wires and spark plugs.

SENDING UNIT: A mechanical, electrical, hydraulic or electromagnetic device which transmits information to a gauge.

SENSOR: Any device designed to measure engine operating conditions or ambient pressures and temperatures. Usually electronic in nature and designed to send a voltage signal to an on-board computer, some sensors may operate as a simple on/off switch or they may provide a variable voltage signal (like a potentiometer) as conditions or measured parameters change.

SHIM: Spacers of precise, predetermined thickness used between parts to establish a proper working relationship.

SLAVE CYLINDER: In automotive use, a device in the hydraulic clutch system which is activated by hydraulic force, disengaging the clutch.

SOLENOID: A coil used to produce a magnetic field, the effect of which is to produce work.

SPARK PLUG: A device screwed into the combustion chamber of a spark ignition engine. The basic construction is a conductive core inside of a ceramic insulator, mounted in an outer conductive base. An electrical charge from the spark plug wire travels along the conductive core and jumps a preset air gap to a grounding point or points at the end of the conductive base. The resultant spark ignites the fuel/air mixture in the combustion chamber.

SPLINES: Ridges machined or cast onto the outer diameter of a shaft or inner diameter of a bore to enable parts to mate without rotation.

TACHOMETER: A device used to measure the rotary speed of an engine, shaft, gear, etc., usually in rotations per minute.

THERMOSTAT: A valve, located in the cooling system of an engine, which is closed when cold and opens gradually in response to engine heating, controlling the temperature of the coolant and rate of coolant flow.

TOP DEAD CENTER (TDC): The point at which the piston reaches the top of its travel on the compression stroke.

TORQUE: The twisting force applied to an object.

TORQUE CONVERTER: A turbine used to transmit power from a driving member to a driven member via hydraulic action, providing changes in drive ratio and torque. In automotive use, it links the driveplate at the rear of the engine to the automatic transmission.

TRANSDUCER: A device used to change a force into an electrical signal.

TRANSISTOR: A semi-conductor component which can be actuated by a small voltage to perform an electrical switching function.

TUNE-UP: A regular maintenance function, usually associated with the replacement and adjustment of parts and components in the electrical and fuel systems of a vehicle for the purpose of attaining optimum performance.

TURBOCHARGER: An exhaust driven pump which compresses intake air and forces it into the combustion chambers at higher than atmospheric pressures. The increased air pressure allows more fuel to be burned and results in increased horsepower being produced.

VACUUM ADVANCE: A device which advances the ignition timing in response to increased engine vacuum.

VACUUM GAUGE: An instrument used to measure the presence of vacuum in a chamber.

VALVE: A device which control the pressure, direction of flow or rate of flow of a liquid or gas.

VALVE CLEARANCE: The measured gap between the end of the valve stem and the rocker arm, cam lobe or follower that activates the valve.

VISCOSITY: The rating of a liquid's internal resistance to flow.

VOLTMETER: An instrument used for measuring electrical force in units called volts. Voltmeters are always connected parallel with the circuit being tested.

WHEEL CYLINDER: Found in the automotive drum brake assembly, it is a device, actuated by hydraulic pressure, which, through internal pistons, pushes the brake shoes outward against the drums.

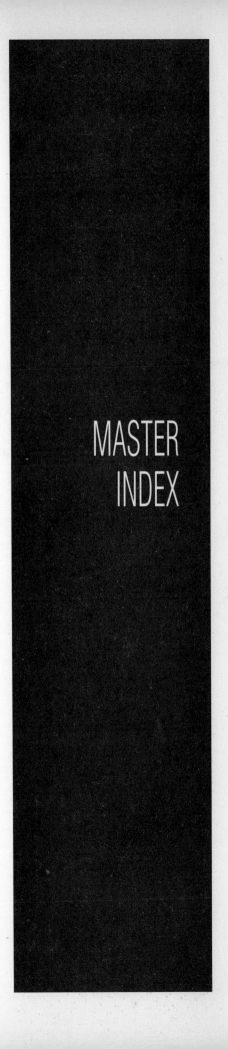

MASTER

INDEX